LYLE

OFFICIAL

ANTIQUES

REVIEW 2003

LYLE

OFFICIAL

ANTIQUES
REVIEW 2003

A PERIGEE BOOK

A Perigee Book
Published by The Berkley Publishing Group
A division of Penguin Putnam Inc.
375 Hudson Street
New York, New York 10014

First edition: December 2002

ISBN: 0-399-52824-5
ISSN: 1089-1544

Visit our website at
www.penguinputnam.com

Printed in the United States of America

10 9 8 7 6 5 4 3 2 1

INTRODUCTION

This year over 100,000 Antique Dealers and Collectors will make full and profitable use of their Lyle Antiques Price Guide. They know that only in this one volume will they find the widest possible variety of goods – illustrated, described and given a current market value to assist them to BUY RIGHT AND SELL RIGHT throughout the year of issue.

They know, too, that by building a collection of these immensely valuable volumes year by year, they will equip themselves with an unparalleled reference library of facts, figures and illustrations which, properly used, cannot fail to help them keep one step ahead of the market.

In its thirty-three years of publication, Lyle has gone from strength to strength and has become without doubt the pre-eminent book of reference for the antique trade throughout the world. Each of its fact filled pages is packed with precisely the kind of profitable information the professional Dealer needs – including descriptions, illustrations and values of thousands and thousands of individual items carefully selected to give a representative picture of the current market in antiques and collectibles – and remember all values are prices actually paid, based on accurate sales records in the twelve months prior to publication from the best established and most highly respected auction houses and retail outlets in Europe and America.

This is THE book for the Professional Antiques Dealer. 'The Lyle Book' - we've even heard it called 'The Dealer's Bible'.

Compiled and published afresh each year, the Lyle Antiques Price Guide is the most comprehensive up-to-date antiques price guide available. THIS COULD BE YOUR WISEST INVESTMENT OF THE YEAR!

Anthony Curtis

All prices quoted in this book are obtained from a variety of auctions in various countries and are converted to dollars at the rate of exchange prevalent at the time of sale. The images and the accompanying text remain the copyright of the contributing auction houses.

The publishers wish to express their sincere thanks to the following for their involvement and assistance in the production of this volume.

ANTHONY CURTIS (Editor)

EELIN McIVOR (Sub Editor)

ANNETTE CURTIS (Editorial)

CATRIONA McKINVEN (Art Production)

ANGIE DEMARCO (Art Production)

NICKY FAIRBURN (Art Production)

PHILIP SPRINGTHORPE (Photography)

CONTENTS

ACKNOWLEDGEMENTS

AB Stockholms Auktionsverk, Box 16256, 103 25 Stockholm, Sweden
Abbotts Auction Rooms, The Auction Rooms, Campsea Ash, Suffolk IP13 OPS
James Adam, 26, St Stephens Green, Dublin 2
Afonwen Antiques, Arts & Crafts Centre, Afonwen, Mold, Flintshire
Henry Aldridge & Son, Devizes Auction Rooms, Wine Street, Devizes
Ambrose, Ambrose House, Old Station Road, Loughton, Essex IG10 4PE
Amersham Auction Rooms, 125 Station Road, Amersham, Bucks.
Jean Claude Anaf, Lyon Brotteaux, 13 bis place Jules Ferry, 69456, Lyon, France
Anderson & Garland, Marlborough Crescent, Newcastle upon Tyne
Antiques on High, 85 High Street, Oxford
The Antiques Warehouse, Badshot Farm, Runfold, Surrey GU9 9HR
Atlantic Antiques, Chenil House, 181–183 Kings Road, London
The Auction Galleries, Mount Rd., Tweedmouth, Berwick on Tweed
Auction Team Köln, Postfach 50 11 19, D-50971 Köln, Germany
Auktionshaus Arnold, Bleichstr. 42, 6000 Frankfurt a/M, Germany
Baddow Antiques Centre, Church Street, Great Baddow, Chelmsford
Banners Collectables & Antiques, Banners Buildings, 620-636 Attercliffe Rd, Sheffield S9 3QS
Barkham Antiques Centre, Barkham Street, Barkham, Berkshire
Barmouth Court Antiques Centre, Barmouth Road, Sheffield S7 2DH
Bartlett St. Antiques Centre, 5/10 Bartlett Street, Bath BA11 3BN
Bearne's, St Edmunds Court, Okehampton Street, Exeter EX4 1DU
Biddle & Webb, Ladywood Middleway, Birmingham B16 0PP
Boardman Fine Art Auctioneers, Station Road Corner, Haverhill, Suffolk
Bonhams & Brooks, Montpelier Street, Knightsbridge, London
Bonhams & Brooks Chelsea, 65–69 Lots Road, London SW10 0RN
Bonhams & Brooks West Country, Dowell Street, Honiton, Devon
Bosleys, The White House, Marlow, Bucks SL7 1AH
Michael J. Bowman, 6 Haccombe House, Newton Abbot, Devon, TQ12 4SJ
Brightwells, Antiques & Fine Art Saleroom, Ryelands Road, Leominster
Bristol Auction Rooms, St John Place, Apsley Road, Clifton, Bristol
British Antique Replicas, School Close, Queen Elizabeth Avenue, Burgess Hill RH15 9RX
Butterfield & Butterfield, 220 San Bruno Av., San Francisco CA 94103, USA
Butterfield & Butterfield, 7601 Sunset Boulevard, Los Angeles CA 90046, USA
Canterbury Auction Galleries, 40 Station Road West, Canterbury
Cavern Antiques & Collectors Centre, Failsworth Mill, Ashton Rd. West, Failsworth, Manchester M35 OED
Central Motor Auctions, Barfield House, Britannia Road, Morley, Leeds
Chapel Antiques Centre, High Street, Barmouth, Gwynedd LL42 1DS
H.C. Chapman & Son, The Auction Mart, North Street, Scarborough.
Chapman Moore & Mugford, 8 High Street, Shaftesbury SP7 8JB
Chappells & The Antiques Centre, King Street, Bakewell, Derbyshire
Cheffins Grain & Comins, 2 Clifton Road, Cambridge
Chipping Norton Antiques Centre, Ivy House, 1 Market Square, Chipping Norton, Oxon.
Christie's (In'tional) SA, 8 place de la Taconnerie, 1204 Genève, Switzerland
Christie's France, 9 avenue Matignon, 75008 Paris
Christie's Monaco, S.A.M, Park Palace 98000 Monte Carlo, Monaco
Christie's South Kensington Ltd., 85 Old Brompton Road, London SW7 3LD
Christie's, 8 King Street, London SW1Y 6QT
Christie's East, 219 East 67th Street, New York, NY 10021, USA
Christie's, Cornelis Schuytstraat 57, 1071 JG Amsterdam, Netherlands
Christie's SA Roma, 114 Piazza Navona, 00186 Rome, Italy
Christie's Swire, 2804–6 Alexandra House, 16–20 Chater Road, Hong Kong
Christie's Australia Pty Ltd.,1 Darling Street, South Yarra, Victoria 3141, Australia
Clarke Gammon, The Guildford Auction Rooms, Bedford Road, Guildford,
Cleethorpes Collectables, 34 Alexandra Road, Cleethorpes, DN35 8LF
Bryan Clisby, Andwells Antiques, Hartley Wintney, North Hants.
The Clock House, 75 Pound Street, Carshalton, Surrey SM5 3PG
Collectors Corner, PO Box 8, Congleton, Cheshire CW12 4GD
Collins Antiques, Wheathampstead, St Albans AL4 8AP
Cooper Hirst Auctions, The Granary Saleroom, Victoria Rd, Chelmsford,
Coppelia Antiques, Holford Lodge, Plumley, Cheshire, WA16 9RS
The Cotswold Auction Co., Chapel Walk Saleroom, Chapel Walk, Cheltenham
Court House Antiques Centre, Town End Road, Ecclesfield, Sheffield
The Crested China Co., Station House, Driffield, E. Yorks YO25 7PY
Cumbrian Antique Centre, St. Martin Hall, Front Street, Brampton, Cumbria CA8 1NT
Dandelion Clock Antiques Centre, Lewes Road, Forest Row, East Sussex
Dargate Auction Galleries, 5607 Baum Blvd., Pittsburgh PA 15206

Dee & Atkinson & Harrison, The Exchange Saleroom, Driffield, Nth Humberside
Diamond Mills & Co., 117 Hamilton Road, Felixstowe, Suffolk
Dorking Desk Shop, 41 West Street, Dorking, Surrey, RH4 1BU
William Doyle Galleries, 175 East 87th Street, New York, NY 10128, USA
Douglas Ross, Charter House, 42 Avebury Boulevard, Central Milton Keynes
Dreweatt Neate, Donnington Priory, Newbury, Berks.
Hy. Duke & Son, 40 South Street, Dorchester, Dorset
Du Mouchelles Art Galleries, 409 E. Jefferson Avenue, Detroit, Michigan 48226, USA
Sala de Artes y Subastas Durán, Serrano 12, 28001 Madrid, Spain
Eldred's, Box 796, E. Dennis, MA 02641, USA
R H Ellis & Sons, 44/46 High Street, Worthing, BN11 1LL
The Emporium, 908 Christchurch Road, Boscombe, Bournemouth BH7 6DL
Ewbanks, Burnt Common Auction Rooms, London Road, Send, Woking
Fellows & Son, Augusta House, 19 Augusta Street, Hockley, Birmingham
Fidler Taylor & Co., Crown Square, Matlock, Derbyshire DE4 3AT
Finan & Co., The Square, Mere, Wiltshire BA12 6DJ
Finarte, 20121 Milano, Piazzetta Bossi 4, Italy
Peter Francis,19 King Street, Carmarthen, Dyfed
Fraser Pinney's, 8290 Devonshire, Montreal, Quebec, Canada H4P 2PZ
Freeman Fine Arts, 1808 Chestnut Street, Philadelphia PA19103, USA
Galerie Koller, Rämistr. 8, CH 8024 Zürich, Switzerland
Galerie Moderne, 3 rue du Parnasse, 1040 Bruxelles, Belgium
GB Antiques Centre, Lancaster Leisure Park, Wynesdale Rd, Lancaster
Gloucester Antiques Centre, 1 Severn Road, Gloucester GL1 2LE
The Goss and Crested China Co., 62 Murray Road, Horndean, Hants
The Grandfather Clock Shop, Little House, Sheep Street, Stow on the Wold GL54 1JS
Graves Son & Pilcher, Hove Auction Rooms, Hove Street, Hove, East Sussex
Green Dragon Antiques Centre, 24 High Street, Wincanton, Somerset BA9 9FJ
Greenslade Hunt, Magdalene House, Church Square, Taunton, Somerset,
Hampton's Fine Art, 93 High Street, Godalming, Surrey
Hanseatisches Auktionshaus für Historica, Neuer Wall 57, 2000 Hamburg 36
William Hardie Ltd., 141 West Regent Street, Glasgow G2 2SG
Andrew Hartley Fine Arts, Victoria Hall, Little Lane, Ilkley
Hastings Antiques Centre, 59–61 Norman Road, St Leonards on Sea
Hauswedell & Nolte, D-2000 Hamburg 13, Pöseldorfer Weg 1, Germany
Halifax Antiques Centre, Queens Road/Gibbet Street, Halifax HX1 4LR
Hobbs Parker, New Ashford Market, Monument Way, Orbital Park, Ashford
Honiton Antiques Centre, Abingdon House, 136 High Street, Honiton
Paul Hopwell Antiques, 30 High Street, West Haddon, Northants NN6 7AP
Ironchurch Antiques Centre, The Ironchurch, Blackburn Road, Bolton BL1 8DR
Hotel de Ventes Horta, 390 Chaussée de Waterloo ,1060 Bruxelles
Jackson's, 2229 Lincoln Street, Cedar Falls, Iowa 50613, USA.
Jacobs & Hunt, Lavant Street, Petersfield, Hants. GU33 3EF
P Herholdt Jensens Auktioner, Rundforbivej 188, 2850 Nerum, Denmark
G A Key, Aylsham Saleroom, Palmers Lane, Aylsham, Norfolk, NR11 6EH
George Kidner, The Old School, The Square, Pennington, Lymington, Hants
Kunsthaus am Museum, Drususgasse 1–5, 5000 Köln 1, Germany
Kunsthaus Lempertz, Neumarkt 3, 5000 Köln 1, Germany
Lambert & Foster, The Auction Sales Room, 102 High Street, Tenterden, Kent
Lawrence Butler Fine Art Salerooms, Marine Walk, Hythe, Kent, CT21 5AJ
Lawrence Fine Art, South Street, Crewkerne, Somerset TA18 8AB
Lawrence's Fine Art Auctioneers, Norfolk House, 80 High Street, Bletchingley
David Lay, The Penzance Auction House, Alverton, Penzance, Cornwall
Lloyd International Auctions, 118 Putney Bridge Road, London SW15 2NQ
Locke & England, 18 Guy Street, Leamington Spa, Warwicks. CV32 4RT
Long Sutton Antiques Centre, 72-74 London Rd., Long Sutton, Spalding, Lincs. PE12 9ED
Longmynd Antiques, Crossways, Church Stretton, Shropshire SY6 6NX
Brian Loomes, Calf Haugh Farm, Pateley Bridge, North Yorkshire
Lots Road Chelsea Auction Galleries, 71 Lots Road, Chelsea, London
Duncan McAlpine, Stateside Comics plc, 125 East Barnet Road, London
Mainstreet Trading, Main Street, St. Boswells TD6 0AT
John Mann, The Clock Showrooms, Canonbie, Dumfries DG14 0RY
Christopher Matthews, 23 Mount Street, Harrogate HG2 8DG
John Maxwell, 133a Woodford Road, Wilmslow, Cheshire, SK7 1QD
May & Son, 18 Bridge Street, Andover, Hants
Morphets, 4–6 Albert Street, Harrogate, North Yorks HG1 1JL

Louis C Morton, Monte Athos 179, Lomas de Chapultepec, CP11000 Mexico
The Mount Antique & Gift Centre, 1 & 2 The Mount, Castle Hill, Carmarthen SA31 1JW
D M Nesbit & Co, 7 Clarendon Road, Southsea, Hants PO5 2ED
Newark Antiques Centre, Regent House, Lombard Street, Newark NG24 1XP
Newark Antiques Warehouse, Old Kelham Rd, Newark, Notts., NG24 1BX
John Nicholson, Longfield, Midhurst Road, Fernhurst GU27 3HA
Norwich Tombland Antique Centre, Augustine Steward House, 14 Tombland, Norwich NR3 1HF
The Old Brigade, 10a Harborough Rd, Kingsthorpe, Northampton NN1 7AZ
Old Mill Antiques Centre, Mill Street, Low Town, Bridgnorth, Shropshire
Onslow's, The Depot, 2 Michael Road, London, SW6 2AD
Outhwaite & Litherland, Kingsley Galleries, Fontenoy Street, Liverpool
Oxford Street Antiques Centre, 16-26 Oxford Street, Leicester LE1 5XU
Packhouse Antique Centre, Hewitts Kiln, Tongham Road, Runford, Farnham, Surrey GU10 1PQ
W & H Peacock, 26 Newnham Street Bedford MK40 3JR
Pendulum of Mayfair, 51 Maddox Street, London W1
Pieces of Time, 26 South Molton Lane, London W1Y 2LP
Pooley & Rogers, Regent Auction Rooms, Abbey Street, Penzance
Preston Antiques Centre, The Mill, Newhall Lane Preston, Lancashire PR1 5UH
The Quay Centre, Topsham Quay, nr Exeter, Devon, EX3 0JA
Peter M Raw, Thornfield, Hurdle Way, Compton Down, Winchester, Hants
Remmey Galleries, 30 Maple Street, Summit, NJ 07901
Ritchie's, 429 Richmond Street East, Toronto, Canada M5A 1R1
Derek Roberts Antiques, 24–25 Shipbourne Road, Tonbridge, Kent
Saltire Antiques, Fenton Barn Leisure & Retail Village, Drem, North Berwick EH39 5BW
Schrager Auction Galleries, PO Box 10390, Milwaukee WI 53210, USA
Scottish Antique & Arts Centre, Abernyte, Perthshire
Scottish Antique & Arts Centre, Doune, Stirlingshire
Selkirk's, 4166 Olive Street, St Louis, Missouri 63108, USA
Sidmouth Antiques Centre, All Saints Road, Sidmouth, Devon EX10 8ES
Skinner Inc., Bolton Gallery, Route 117, Bolton MA, USA
Allan Smith, Amity Cottage, 162 Beechcroft Rd. Upper Stratton, Swindon
Soccer Nostalgia, Albion Chambers, Birchington, Kent CT7 9DN
Sotheby's, 34–35 New Bond Street, London W1A 2AA
Sotheby's, 1334 York Avenue, New York NY 10021
Sotheby's, 112 George Street, Edinburgh EH2 2LH
Sotheby's, Summers Place, Billingshurst, West Sussex RH14 9AD
Sotheby's, Monaco, BP 45, 98001 Monte Carlo
David South, Kings House, 15 High Street, Pateley Bridge HG3 5AP
Don Spencer Antiques, 36a Market Place, Warwick CV34 4SH
Spink & Son Ltd., 5–7 King Street, St James's, London SW1Y 6QS
Michael Stainer Ltd., St Andrews Auction Rooms, Wolverton Rd, Boscombe
David Stanley Auctions, Stordon Grange, Osgathorpe, Leics. LE12 9SR
Michael Stanton, 7 Rowood Drive, Solihull, West Midlands B92 9LT
Station Mill Antiques Centre, Station Road, Chipping Norton, Oxon OX7 5HX
Street Jewellery, 5 Runnymede Road, Ponteland, Northumbria NE20 9HE
G E Sworder & Son, 14 Cambridge Road, Stansted Mountfitchet, Essex
Tennants, Harmby Road, Leyburn, Yorkshire
Thomson Roddick & Medcalf, Coleridge House, Shaddongate, Carlisle
Thomson Roddick & Medcalf, 60 Whitesands, Dumfries
Thomson Roddick & Medcalf, 42 Moray Place, Edinburgh, EH3 6BT
Tool Shop Auctions, 78 High Street, Needham Market, Suffolk IP6 8AW
Venator & Hanstein, Cäcilienstr. 48, 5000 Köln 1, Germany
T Vennett Smith, 11 Nottingham Road, Gotham, Nottingham NG11 0HE
Victorian Village, 93 West Regent Street, Glasgow G2 2BA
Garth Vincent, The Old Manor House, Allington, nr. Grantham, Lincs.
Wallis & Wallis, West Street Auction Galleries, West Street, Lewes, E. Sussex
Wentworth Arts Crafts & Antique Centre, Cortworth Lane, Wentworth, Rotherham S62 7SB
West Street Antiques, 63 West Street, Dorking, Surrey
Whitworths, 32–34 Wood Street, Huddersfield HD1 1DX
A J Williams, 607 Sixth Avenue, Central Business Park, Hengrove, Bristol
Peter Wilson, Victoria Gallery, Market Street, Nantwich, Cheshire CW5 5DG
Wintertons Ltd., Lichfield Auction Centre, Fradley Park, Lichfield, Staffs
Woodbridge Gallery, 23 Market Hill, Woodbridge, Suffolk IP12 4LX
Woolley & Wallis, The Castle Auction Mart, Salisbury, Wilts SP1 3SU
Worthing Auction Galleries, 31 Chatsworth Road, Worthing, W. Sussex
Robert Young Antiques, 68 Battersea Bridge Road, London SW11 3AG

ANTIQUES
REVIEW
2003

The Lyle Antiques Price Guide is compiled and published with completely fresh information annually, enabling you to begin each new year with an up-to-date knowledge of the current trends, together with the verified values of antiques of all descriptions.

We have endeavored to obtain a balance between the more expensive collector's items and those which, although not in their true sense antiques, are handled daily by the antiques trade.

The illustrations and prices in the following sections have been arranged to make it easy for the reader to assess the period and value of all items with speed.

You will find illustrations for almost every category of antique and curio, together with a corresponding price collated during the last twelve months, from the auction rooms and retail outlets of the major trading countries.

When dealing with the more popular trade pieces, in some instances, a calculation of an average price has been estimated from the varying accounts researched.

As regards prices, when 'one of a pair' is given in the description the price quoted is for a pair and so that we can make maximum use of the available space it is generally considered that one illustration is sufficient.

It will be noted that in some descriptions taken directly from sales catalogs originating from many different countries, terms such as bureau, secretary and davenport are used in a broader sense than is customary, but in all cases the term used is self explanatory.

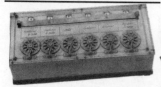

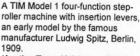

A fine reproduction of Blaise Pascal's first mechanical calculator of 1652, designed principally for currency calculation.
(Auction Team Köln) $11,500

A rare Kuli four-function latch-drive calculator with two-row 1-10 keys and 12 place result, 1909.
(Auction Team Köln) $2,299

A TIM Model 1 four-function step-roller machine with insertion levers, an early model by the famous manufacturer Ludwig Spitz, Berlin, 1909.
(Auction Team Köln) $1,509

A Saxonia roll-top desk-form manual four-function step-drum calculator by Schumann & Co., Glashütte, Saxony, 1910.
(Auction Team Köln) $3,920

A brass sliding cylinder Arithmometer in wooden case, with 8-place insertion and 16 place result, possibly a Burkhardt machine retailed by H. Bunzel, Prague, circa 1908.
(Auction Team Köln) $1,320

A Double Brunsviga Model D 13 R-2 compound machine for special calculations such as land-registry work, each with 10, 8 or 13 place working, circa 1960.
(Auction Team Köln) $289

A Curta Type I four-function step-roller miniature calculating machine by Curt Herzstark, Vienna/Liechtenstein, with metal box.
(Auction Team Köln) $590

A rare Merry One-Times-One toy calculating game, in the form of a puzzle with questions and answers by the Luxus Papier Fabrik, Berlin, circa 1885.
(Auction Team Köln) $303

A Scribola ten-place German adding machine with chain drive and print-out, 1922.
(Auction Team Köln) $1,181

A Burkhardt Arithmometer, the first mass-produced German calculator, with de Colmar's four-function step-drum system, in original wooden case, 1878. (Auction Team Köln) $3,397

A Double Brunsviga adding machine for special calculations, such as land registry work, circa 1958.
(Auction Team Köln) $229

An important Swiss Millionaire calculating machine by Otto Steiger, St. Gallen, for all four functions, with tin cover, 1895.
(Auction Team Köln) $1,724

An Austrian Arithmometer four-function step-drum calculating machine by Hugo Bunzel, Vienna, with 9-place conversion, with slide result.
(Auction Team Köln) $574

An American Calcumeter 7-disk lineal adding machine for British currency, with carry-ten facility, 1901.
(Auction Team Köln) $418

A Double Brunsviga Model D 18 R adding machine for special calculations such as land registry, circa 1962.
(Auction Team Köln) $259

A Mercedes Euklid Model 1 four-function calculator with proportional levers, by Christel Hamann, Berlin, 1905. (Auction Team Köln)
                          $627

An Adix three-place adding machine with latch drive and 9 keys, by Pallweber & Bordt, Mannheim, 1903.
(Auction Team Köln) $564

A British Laytons Improved Arithmometer, with 6 insertion levers and 7 or 12 place result, in mahogany case, lacking cover, 1912. (Auction Team Köln)
                        $1,985

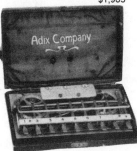

A rare undocumented St Gotthard NS type Swiss adding machine by Rud. Schweizer & Cie., Neuallschwil/Basle, with bakelite cover and nine insertion levers.
(Auction Team Köln) $836

A working replica of the famous four-function step-drum calculator of 1774 by Philipp Matthäus Hahn.
(Auction Team Köln) $25,091

An Adix three place adding machine by Pallweber & Bordt, Mannheim, with latch drive, without on/off switch, 1903.
(Auction Team Köln) $340

A Burkhardt Arithmometer, the first mass-produced German four-function, step-drum calculating machine on the Thomas Colmar principle, 1878.
(Auction Team Köln) $2,763

An Austria Badenia nine-row brass step-drum calculating machine by Math. Bäuerle, St. Georgen, Black Forest.
(Auction Team Köln) $365

An Olympia RAE 4-30/1 German electronic desk calculating machine, German, with LED, 1964.
(Auction Team Köln) $120

Bronze cotton belt route plaque, logo form with raised letters on black ground, 12in. diameter. (Jacksons) $977

A very rare painted sign for the Steamship Portland, probably Boston, circa 1890, the shaped planked sign painted with a pair of American banners with a Canadian emblem at the center, 52¾in. long. (Sotheby's) $26,450

Ice cream advertising sign, porcelain on metal 'Special Ice Cream, McBride Bros & Knobbe' in yellow on blue, minor losses, 30 x 14in. (Jacksons) $258

A Majestic Coca Cola refrigerator with lift-up lid and bottle opener, German wording, 1950, 73 x 100 x 58cm. (Auction Team Köln) $282

A molded and painted cast iron and zinc trade sign, American, late 19th-early 20th century, in the form of a large pocket watch, the dial face painted J.A. Nadeau/Jeweler, 35in. diameter. (Onslows) $4,000

A painted cast-iron bull butcher's trade sign, American, late 19th-early 20th century, the full-bodied form depicting a standing bull, the whole yellow-painted, 11½in. high. (Christie's) $4,830

Civil War broadside 'Shall the Union Be Preserved? Ho! For the South! $100 Bounty $25 Advance A Few More able-bodied, brave, patriotic men wanted for the 81st Regiment, N.Y.S. volunteers, now in active service, under Gen. McClellan…,' 18 x 12in. (Skinner) $1,725

Civil War broadside 'Now is the Time to Serve Your Country. Volunteers Wanted for the 2nd Massachusetts Heavy Artillery!…,'(Salem) printed Gloucester, Massachusetts circa 1861-62, 18½ x 23¼in. (Skinner) $747

Broadside 'Marshal's Sale! on Thursday Oct 10, 1861 at 12 o'clock M., the one-sixteenth part of the Schooner Burrowes, C…', 10½ x 8¼in. (Skinner) $431

'N.E. Rum Chrystal Spring Distillery Felton + Son Distillers Office 17 Broad St. Boston, Mass…,' chromolithograph, Kellogg and Bulkely Co., Hartford, Connecticut, circa 1880, old, possibly original frame, 18 x 24in. (Skinner) $2,875

Carved wooden sign in the form of a double-sided fish, length 80in. height 31in.
(Eldred's) $1,430

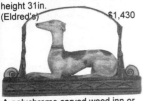

A polychrome carved wood inn or shop display sign, 19th century, modelled as a recumbent hound, above a pierced frieze and iron overframe with chain to his collar, 65in. wide.
(Christie's) $9,936

Carved oak polychrome and gilt tobacconist figure, America or British Isles, 19th century, depicting a Scotsman wearing a plumed headdress and costume, 34½in. high. (Skinner) $6,325

Trade sign, American 19th century, a white-painted pine panel inscribed *Dreibelbis Post Office* in red and black lettering, 23¼in. long.
(Sotheby's) $345

DREIBELBIS POST OFFICE

Polychrome decorated cast-iron and zinc double-sided Optometrist's sign, America, late 19th century, 11½in. high, 26¼in. long.
(Skinner) $4,312

A lithographed tin Shadow-play chocolate dispensing machine, rare model with decorative shadow-play figures on all sides, French version, 1890.
(Auction Team Köln) $353

A Coca Cola display in the form of a filling station, made in molded polystyrene with built-in quartz clock, by Burwood Products Co., USA, 55cm. wide.
(Auction Team Köln) $267

A fine Missouri Pacific Lines calendar, 'Route of the Eagles' with engine #7003 in color litho on tin, removable date cards, 19 x 13in.
(Jacksons) $172

Broadside 'Eastern and Western Mail Stages. Direct Line From Concord, N.H. to Troy, Albany and Saratoga Springs...,' July, 1835, the coach and four horses are depicted, 19¾ x 13¼in.
(Skinner) $1,380

A pair of Ashtead pottery advertising figures designed by Percy Metcalfe for Genozo toothpaste, modelled as a lion on angled plinth in the mottle blue glaze, 9in. wide.
(Andrew Hartley) $308

A fine Indian Princess cigar store figure, attributed to Samuel Robb, New York, third quarter 19th century, on a pine base, together with a second, newer base labelled *Fine Cigars/5 c*, overall height 64in.
(Sotheby's) $26,050

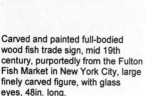

Carved and painted full-bodied wood fish trade sign, mid 19th century, purportedly from the Fulton Fish Market in New York City, large finely carved figure, with glass eyes, 48in. long.
(Skinner) $26,450

A metal Coca Cola icebox, with original Coca Cola wooden crate, top lid and bottle opener on side, circa 1950.
(Auction Team Köln) $276

Riggs Coaches, original advertising poster 'Royal Mail and Other', circa 1885, full color lithograph on paper printed by A. W. Johnson & Sons, Printer, Windermere, 50 x 75cm.
(Bonhams & Brooks) $690

Gilt-metal figural apothecary trade sign, America, late 19th century, in the form of a mortar and pestle, 35in. high, 22in. diameter.
(Skinner) $1,610

Polychrome *C.Marr 1827* tavern sign, Maine, two-sided sign with patriotic eagle and shield within a black frame, 25½ x 26in.
(Skinner) $19,550

British handpainted pub trade sign, 20th century, painted on tin, in an ebonized wood frame with bevelled gold-painted surround, painted to both sides, frame height 48in.
(Skinner) $575

American School, late 19th century, a tailor's advertising poster, depicting a gentleman in top hat, overcoat, and cane in a central cartouche and inscribed *H. Schulte Merchant Tailor*, oil on canvas, 82¼ x 47in. (Christie's) $15,275

Painted two-sided sign board, Massachusetts, late 19th century, *DON'T SPIT ON THE FLOOR*, white lettering on black ground, reverse with black lettering on white ground, 12 x 12¾in.
(Skinner) $2,415

A Suchard advertising clock, white painted soft wood case, the pendulum with Art Nouveau decoration.
(Auction Team Köln) $254

'Anthinea' a patinated copper and alabaster figure, cast and carved from a model by G. Gambogi, 1920s, of naked female wearing a tiara and snake bracelets laying on bear rugged loveseat, 25in. long. (Christie's) $7,560

A 19th century Italian carved alabaster group of two fighting cupids, one attempting to stamp on a fallen heart, 45cm., on serpentine fluted pedestal, 109cm. (Bearne's) $1,541

An alabaster carving of a maiden, the head and shoulders draped, on a canted marble base, 10in. (Woolley & Wallis) $312

Italian carved alabaster figure of a female water bearer, late 19th century with incised signature to base *P. Ruggeri*, the semi-nude kneeling figure stooping to gather water, 16½in. high. (Skinner) $1,092

An Italian alabaster bust of Hermes, late 19th or early 20th century, after the Antique, set on a waisted, splaying socle, 44.8cm. high overall. (Christie's) $1,496

An alabaster bust carved from a model by Cipriani, on striated marble base, incised signature, 38cm. high.(Christie's) $493

An alabaster bust carved from a model by Jef Lambeaux, of a smiling girl, incised signature, 49.5cm. high. (Christie's) $1,788

After the Antique. A 19th century Italian carved alabaster group of The Wrestlers, 49.5cm., on green serpentine plinth. (Bearne's) $2,595

A sculpted alabaster and bronze figure of a snake charmer, late 19th or early 20th century, the plinth inscribed *RVD Franke-Nautschietz*, 11¼in. high. (Christie's) $1,810

A French Roulette Visible three barrel gaming machine with token payout, by Bussoz, Paris, walnut casing with decorative top, 1920.
(Auction Team Köln) $1,411

A mechanical dice game, the basket on revolving axis with three dice, 46 x 45 x 28cm.
(Auction Team Köln) $328

A Globus Test-Your-Strength machine by Jentzsch & Meerz, Leipzig, brass mounted wooden casing, in working order.
(Auction Team Köln) $1,411

A Bajazzo wall-mounted German gaming machine by Jentzsch & Meerz for the British market, for old pence with token payout, in oak case, circa 1915.
(Auction Team Köln) $1,105

An electric Test Your Strength machine in oak case, parts lacking but mechanism in working order, by Jentzsch & Meerz, Leipzig, circa 1925.
(Auction Team Köln) $259

An Allwin de Luxe mechanical pinball machine by Jentzsch & Meerz, Leipzig, for the British market, token payout, unrestored and in working order, circa 1920.
(Auction Team Köln) $1,160

A Roulomint roulette machine by Löwenautomaten, Brunswick, with number and color choice buttons, 1955, 71cm. high.
(Auction Team Köln) $147

A French Jockey gaming machine by Bussoz, Paris, brass mounted oak case, with token payout.
(Auction Team Köln) $663

An Imo-Looping electro-mechanical entertainment machine by Jentzsch & Meerz, Leipzig, oak casing, lacking coin slot and lever, 1935.
(Auction Team Köln) $522

A Bajazzo gaming machine, ball chute with movable pockets, possibly by Jentzsch & Meerz, Leipzig, oak casing, post 1906.
(Auction Team Köln) $679

A Fortuna gaming machine, brass mounted walnut casing, for 5-pfennig pieces, winners receive 'cigars', 1904.
(Auction Team Köln) $679

A Novomat three drum games machine by Günther Wolff, Berlin, walnut veneered wooden casing and side handle, 1958.
(Auction Team Köln) $261

A Bajazzo catch-ball machine with prize dispenser by Jentzsch & Meerz, Leipzig, brown brass-mounted wooden case with red playing surface, 46 x 63 x 17cm., post 1904.
(Auction Team Köln) $2,755

A Lucky Dice or Domino gaming machine by Jentzsch & Meerz for the British market, oak cased, with moving handle and unusual lithography, in working order, 1928.
(Auction Team Köln) $3,040

An Ultra electro-mechanical gaming machine by Bergmann, Hamburg, in wooden case with mirrored glass front, 1955, 80cm. high.
(Auction Team Köln) $124

A Glückspinne gaming machine by Th. Bergmann, Hamburg, a coin balancing machine for 10pfg. pieces, wooden case with mirrored and pressed glass panel, 1953.
(Auction Team Köln) $1,180

A Mills Front OK Vendor one-arm bandit, American three drum slot machine for the German market, wooden casing with metal cover, 1930.
(Auction Team Köln) $182

A Tura Ball machine by C.M. Schwarz, Leipzig, a wooden pinball machine with 5 and 10pfg coin slots, after the Ballyhoo machine by Bally, Chicago, 1933.
(Auction Team Köln) $721

A Phoenician brown stone figure of Bes, circa 6th-4th centuries B.C., seated on a stool, his hands resting on his lap, his mouth open and eyes recessed for inlay, 3¼in.
(Bonhams & Brooks) $420

A sizeable Etruscan hollow terracotta head, circa 3rd-2nd century B.C., of a smiling youthful ?satyr with full cheeks and incised almond eyes, the thick hair brushed up, 9¼in.
(Bonhams & Brooks) $1,190

An Egyptian gesso painted wooden sarcophagus mask, late Period, circa 400 B.C., polychrome painted, shown wearing a lotus petalled banded wig, 9½in. high.
(Bonhams & Brooks) $1,540

A Roman marble portrait of a man, circa 1st century A.D., with an oval, fleshy face, dimpled chin, full lips, and lidded, unarticulated eyes, 9½in. high.(Christie's) $3,220

A hollow glazed pottery vessel fragment, Parthian / Sasanian or later, modelled in the form of a female head, in cream glaze with added details in dark brown, her face framed by neatly layered hair, with two extensions either side of her head, 2¾in.
(Bonhams & Brooks) $1,120

A Roman marble herm head, circa 2nd century A.D., depicting a maenad, wearing a fillet of ivy leaves and berries, the eyes recessed for inlay, 7in. high.
(Christie's) $2,760

A sizeable Roman green glass dish, circa 3rd-4th century A.D., of shallow form, set on a raised foot with a tooled lip below the rim, 14in. diameter.
(Bonhams & Brooks) $4,900

An Etruscan terracotta votive head, circa 3rd century B.C., modelled in the form of a young man with prominent ears, dimpled chin, small lips and slender nose, 11¾in. high.
(Christie's) $5,520

A Hellenistic bronze amphora, circa 3rd-1st centuries B.C., both elements of the chain linked together by a large central hoop, a third element of the chain joined to the circular lid, 12.4cm. high.
(Bonhams & Brooks) $1,190

A Persian bronze mountain goat, circa late 2nd-early 1st Millennium B.C., shown standing in a static pose, with high arching notched horns and deeply recessed eyes, once inlaid, 5in. high.
(Bonhams & Brooks) $18,200

A Palmyran limestone head of a youth, circa 2nd-3rd century A.D., with thick wavy hair, the facial features partially worn, 9½in. high.
(Bonhams & Brooks) $1,050

An Egyptian bronze figure of Selket, late Period, after 700 B.C., the scorpion goddess shown couchant, the tail curled over her ridged back, wearing a tripartite wig, 2¾in.
(Bonhams & Brooks) $3,360

An Egyptian wooden cosmetic spoon, New Kingdom, 18th Dynasty, circa 14th century B.C., the central element of the openwork handle in the form of Bes, his arms held out to support lotus plants and buds, 4in. (Bonhams & Brooks) $17,500

Two Roman bronze appliqués, 2nd-4th century A.D., in the form of actor's masks, one wearing the winged head-dress of Mercury with centrally parted hair beneath, 4in.
(Bonhams & Brooks) $2,240

A hollow Roman terracotta figure of Aphrodite, circa 2nd-3rd century A.D., shown naked within a naos, holding her drapery behind her, her hair held beneath a diadem, 8in. high.
(Bonhams & Brooks) $980

A South Arabian alabaster head, circa 2nd-1st century B.C., with a flat squared head, the eyes deeply recessed to have taken inlays with arching eyebrows, 6cm. high.
(Bonhams & Brooks) $910

A substantial mottled gray stone lion's head, Roman Empire, the crested mane detailed with striations and hatching, with large slanting eyes, 17in.
(Bonhams & Brooks) $2,240

An Attic Red-Figure bell krater, circa 380-360 B.C., enlivened with added cream slip to show on side (a): a central maenad dancing with two satyrs, 11¾in. high.
(Bonhams & Brooks) $1,680

23

A reproduction English pikeman's armor in mid 17th century style, of heavy gauge pressed steel, comprising two-piece wide-brimmed pot, breast plate, back-plate, steel tassets. (Bonhams) $1,380

A composite German black and white half-armor partly second half of the 16th century, comprising an almain-collar, breast-plate, back-plate, and rectangular tassets. (Bonhams) $6,210

A good 19th century Indian kulah khud and dhal, the former with one piece fluted skull finely damascened overall, together with associated shield 14in. diameter. (Wallis & Wallis) $2,448

A mail shirt, 16th/17th century, probably Eastern, entirely of riveted iron rings of varying degrees of thickness, knee length, the skirt split front and rear, elbow-length sleeves, 117cm. long. (Bonhams & Brooks) $759

A fine tosei gusoku, Edo Period (circa 1800), the sixty-two plate helmet with standing flanges, russet iron signed Yoshiyuki, the peak leather covered. (Christie's) $16,767

An English Civil War breast-plate, and associated back-plate circa 1650, breast-plate of heavy steel with low medial ridge, the first 42cm. high. (Bonhams & Brooks) $1,833

A fine Gomai okegawa tosei gusoku, Edo Period (19th century), thirty-two-plate suji bachi, the fine tengu mask russet lacquered with additonal wrinkles in lacquer.
(Christie's) $10,315

A fluted armor in early 16th century German 'Maximilian' style, 19th century, close helmet with one-piece fluted skull rising to a low boldly roped comb and a halberd, Italian late 16th/ early 17th century, on later wooden haft.
(Sotheby's) $10,120

An Okegawa Do Tosei Gusoku (an armor with solid plate cuirass), Edo Period (19th century), the thirty-two plate russet iron helmet of good form with a tosei mabisashi.
(Christie's) $5,249

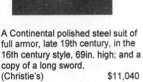

A Continental polished steel suit of full armor, late 19th century, in the 16th century style, 69in. high; and a copy of a long sword.
(Christie's) $11,040

A composite half-armor, partly 17th century, comprising a gorget, breast- and back-plate, arm-defences from a cuirassier armor, and two gauntlets.
(Bonhams) $4,416

A silvered electrotype copy of the parade full armor of Henri II of France, in 16th century style, second half of the 19th century.
(Bonhams & Brooks) $17,940

Imperial German Ersatz conversion bayonet, Great War period example, triangular blade is fitted into an all steel Ersatz pattern hilt with simulated ribbed grip and three-quarter muzzle ring, 17in. long (Bosleys) $312

Police bayonet by ACS of Solingen, short pattern, the grip of two piece stag's horn with silvered police device the cross guard with oak leaf motif. (Bosleys) $256

Belgium M1888 Sawback bayonet, the blade with maker's stamps, the hilt with brass ribbed grip, the crossguard stamped *V 5643*, complete with brass mounted black leather scabbard. (Bosleys) $452

An unusual late 18th century triangular socket bayonet from an officer's fusil or sporting gun, blade 11 in. deeply stamped *A* at forte, conventional socket.   In its leather scabbard with steel chape. (Wallis & Wallis) $359

German Model 1871 sword bayonet, by Gebr. Weyersberg of Solingen, blade with date code 1878, hilt with "S" shaped quillon and a brass grip with pronounced pommel. (Bosleys) $132

A Third Reich police bayonet, the blade by the same maker, the quillon and locket stamped *S.K.g.301*, complete with its leather frog suspension mount, and in fine condition overall, 49cm. (Bonhams) $248

A WWI period brass hilted German Ersatz bayonet, scarce example of a M88/98 bayonet, single edged unfullered blade, with brass hilt and three quarter muzzle ring. (Bosleys) $220

Imperial German Ersatz conversion bayonet, scarce Great War period example, the cruciform blade fitted into an all steel Ersatz pattern hilt with ribbed sides and ¾ muzzle ring. (Bosleys) $540

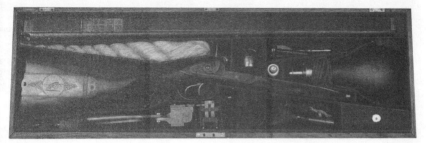

A fine cased combined double barrelled percussion 40 bore rifle and 14 bore shotgun, by Joseph Bourne, circa 1865, with etched twist damscus barrels, the right barrel smooth bore and the left barrel rifled for a winged bullet, six blued folding back-sights each with central platinum sighting line, in original lined and fitted oak case, 76.5cm. barrels. (Bonhams & Brooks) $6,900

A cased 12-bore double barrelled percussion sporting gun, by C. Moore, 77 St. James's Street, London, Maker To The King, No. 2076, circa 1840, with rebrowned twist sighted barrels signed in full on the rib, breeches each with pierced platinum plug and engraved with foliage between, scroll engraved tang, foliate scroll engraved locks engraved *C. Moore's Patent*, figured walnut half-stock, 80cm. barrels. (Bonhams) $2,240

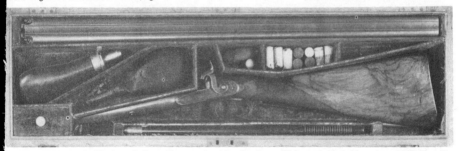

A cased 14 bore double barrelled sporting gun by John Beetham, Richmond, Yorkshire, circa 1840-42, with rebrowned twist sighted barrels signed on the grooved rib, engraved breeches with platinum plugs, scroll engraved tang, scroll engraved locks, figured walnut half-stock, 76cm. barrels. (Bonhams) $1,380

A cased 14 bore double barrelled percussion sporting gun, by Thomas Cartwell, High Street, Doncaster, circa 1820, with rebrowned twist sighted replacement barrels of circa 1860 signed on the rib by the maker *W.R. Pape, Newcastle.on.Tyne*, engraved breeches, foliate engraved tang, figured walnut half-stock.
(Bonhams & Brooks) $1,587

A cased 120 bore five-shot double-action percussion revolver of Webley type, circa 1860, with blued octagonal sighted barrel engraved at the muzzle, case-hardened cylinder numbered from 1 to 5, checkered walnut grip, 23cm.
(Bosleys) $1,035

A fine cased 60-bore self-cocking hammerless six-shot percussion pepperbox revolver by Henry 2 Tatham, circa 1850, with case-hardened fluted barrels engraved with a band of foliage around the muzzles and numbered from 1 to 6 at the breeches, 24cm.
(Bonhams) $5,520

A cased 54-bore Beaumont-Adams Patent five-shot double-action percussion revolver, circa 1860, with blued octagonal sighted barrel, blued cylinder, blued safety-stop and arbor-pin catch, blued rammer and trigger-guard, and checkered walnut butt, 30cm.
(Bosleys) $1,035

A cased pair of 28 bore flintlock duelling pistols by Wogdon & Barton, London, circa 1795, with rebrowned twist octagonal barrels each slightly swamped at the muzzle, silver fore-sights, gold-lined touch holes, figured walnut full stocks, 39cm.
(Bonhams) $3,79

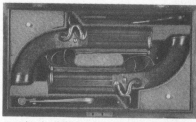

A cased pair of 16 bore over-and-under percussion box-lock pistols, by R.B. Rodda & Co., second half of the 19th century, with browned twist sighted barrels border engraved case-hardened breeches and actions decorated with scrolling foliage, 29cm.
(Bonhams) $3,588

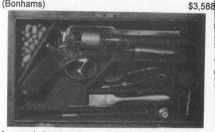

A cased 54-bore Tranter Patent five-shot double-action percussion revolver, by J. Blanch & Son, circa 1860, with blued octagonal sighted barrel engraved at the muzzle, cylinder with roped forward edge, blued border engraved frame, 30.5cm.
(Bosleys) $2,070

A cased pair of 40 bore flintlock duelling pistols, by Staudenmayer, London, circa 1820, with browned twist octagonal sighted barrels, case-hardened patent recessed breeches, foliate engraved case-hardened tangs each incorporating a blued back-sight, 39.5cm.
(Bonhams) $10,350

A rare cased 54 bore Deane-Adams 1854 Model five-shot self-cocking percussion revolver retailed by J. Purdey, circa 1855, with blued octagonal sighted barrel, checkered walnut butt, 33cm.
(Bosleys) $4,416

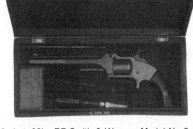

A 6 shot .32in. RF Smith & Wesson Model No 2 Old Issue 'Army' revolver No 10882, 10¾in., octagonal barrel 6in. stamped *Smith & Wesson Springfield Mass*. Sheathed trigger, two piece polished rosewood grips. Retains some original blued finish overall.
(Wallis & Wallis) $1,080

A cased 54 bore Tranter Patent five-shot double-action percussion revolver by Wilkinson & Son, with octagonal sighted barrel engraved at the muzzle and with foliage on each side of the breech, signed engraved top strap, 30.5cm. (Bonhams) $1,104

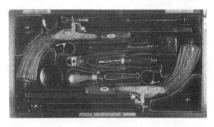

A fine cased pair of French 40 bore percussion target pistols, signed *Fni Par Gastinne-Renette A Paris*, circa 1850-60, with rebrowned rifled octagonal sighted barrels, case-hardened breeches and tangs numbered *1* and *2* in gold respectively and engraved with scrolling foliage, the mounts comprising spur trigger-guards and shaped pommels en suite, 41cm.
(Bonhams) $6,210

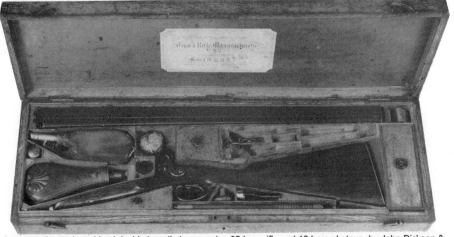

An unusual cased combined double barrelled percussion 32 bore rifle and 16 bore shotgun, by John Dickson & Son, Edinburgh, circa 1852, with browned twist leaf-sighted barrels, border engraved case-hardened breeches, engraved platinum plugs, border engraved case-hardened tang and signed locks, figured walnut half-stock, 71cm. barrels. (Bonhams) $3,036

An unusual 19th century dagger, probably Philippines, wavy shallow diamond section blade 20½in., integral crosspiece with swollen quillon terminals. One piece ivory hilt with filigree silver ferrule, carved pommel of bobbin form. (Wallis & Wallis) $267

An aichuchi, 19th century, with shagreen hilt iron mounts decorated in silver and gilt with seashells and reeds, replacement menuki modelled as a monkey holding a peach kozuka decorated with a bee and kozun modelled as a flowerhead, 18in. long. (Christie's) $790

A fine early 19th century Moro kris, wavy blade 18½in. with wavy central raised rib, fluted and incised tip. Ivory pommel of good color, foliate engraved silver covered grip. (Wallis & Wallis) $847

An aichuchi, 19th century, with shagreen hilt, iron mounts decorated with flowerheads, bronze menuki modelled as monkeyheads, lacquer scabbard decorated in aogai, the blade unsigned, 19¼in. long. (Christie's) $575

A late 19th century Indian pesh kabz, 'T' section blade 11¾in. Four piece jade grips with steel gripstrap and curved pommel, hinged ring to top. (Wallis & Wallis) $256

A tanto, 19th century, of very curved form, with copper simulated ropework decorated hilt, brown lacquer ribbed wooden scabbard, with bronze mounts, the blade untempered, 17½in. long. (Christie's) $822

Ceremonial Japanese carved bone wakizashi, bone hilt tsuba and scabbard heavily carved with Japanese figures and flowers. Simple blade of typical form. Blade length 11in. overall length 23.5in. (Bosleys) $176

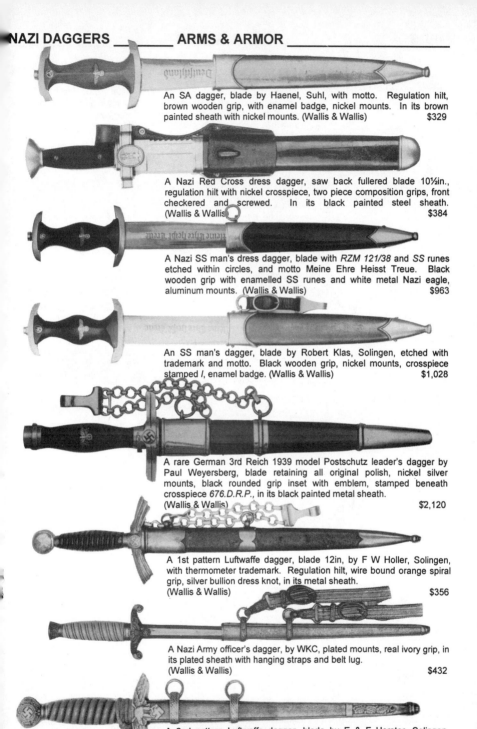

An SA dagger, blade by Haenel, Suhl, with motto. Regulation hilt, brown wooden grip, with enamel badge, nickel mounts. In its brown painted sheath with nickel mounts. (Wallis & Wallis) $329

A Nazi Red Cross dress dagger, saw back fullered blade 10½in., regulation hilt with nickel crosspiece, two piece composition grips, front checkered and screwed. In its black painted steel sheath. (Wallis & Wallis) $384

A Nazi SS man's dress dagger, blade with *RZM 121/38* and *SS* runes etched within circles, and motto Meine Ehre Heisst Treue. Black wooden grip with enamelled SS runes and white metal Nazi eagle, aluminum mounts. (Wallis & Wallis) $963

An SS man's dagger, blade by Robert Klas, Solingen, etched with trademark and motto. Black wooden grip, nickel mounts, crosspiece stamped *I*, enamel badge. (Wallis & Wallis) $1,028

A rare German 3rd Reich 1939 model Postschutz leader's dagger by Paul Weyersberg, blade retaining all original polish, nickel silver mounts, black rounded grip inset with emblem, stamped beneath crosspiece *676.D.R.P.*, in its black painted metal sheath. (Wallis & Wallis) $2,120

A 1st pattern Luftwaffe dagger, blade 12in, by F W Holler, Solingen, with thermometer trademark. Regulation hilt, wire bound orange spiral grip, silver bullion dress knot, in its metal sheath. (Wallis & Wallis) $356

A Nazi Army officer's dagger, by WKC, plated mounts, real ivory grip, in its plated sheath with hanging straps and belt lug. (Wallis & Wallis) $432

A 2nd pattern Luftwaffe dagger, blade by E & F Horster, Solingen. Regulation hilt, wire bound orange spiral grip, silver bullion dress knot, in its metal sheath. (Wallis & Wallis) $219

An unusual early 19th century naval officer's dirk, possibly French, straight double edged blade 11½in., copper gilt hilt and sheath, lion's head pommel with contoured button screw, ivory grip spiral carved with alternate silver tape and copper wire banding. (Wallis & Wallis) $385

A Third Reich Stormtroop dirk, with bright double edged Eickhorn, Solingen blade of flattened diamond section dated *1938* on one side and etched *Alles Für Deutschland* on the other, hilt of Holbein type with wooden grip, 37cm. (Bonhams) $221

A Georgian midshipman's dirk, shallow diamond section double edged blade 10in. Brass crosspiece chiselled with acanthus foliage, baluster turned ivory grip, with bulbous pommel. In its brass mounted leather sheath. (Wallis & Wallis) $431

A Third Reich Second Pattern Luftwaffe dirk, with Eickhorn, Solingen double-edged blade of flattened hexagonal section, quillons formed as an eagle and swastika, globular pommel cast with branches of oak framing a swastika on each side, spirally twist ivorine grip, 42.5cm. (Bonhams) $207

A Nazi naval officer's dirk, bi-fullered blade by Puma, Solingen, etched with fouled anchors, dolphins and foliage. Regulation hilt, white plastic grip, silver bullion dress knot. (Wallis & Wallis) $315

A Third Reich 1936 model army officer's dirk, with Eickhorn, Solingen double-edged blade of flattened hexagonal section, scrolled silvered quillons with eagle and swastika on one side, silvered pommel cast with oak leaves, spirally twist ivorine grip, and silvered bullion dagger-knot, 40cm. (Bonhams) $262

A Georgian naval officer's dirk, circa 1805, straight tapering blade 12in. with central fuller, copper gilt propeller shaped crosspiece, base mount stamped *FT*, copper gilt domed pommel cap, diced tapering square section ivory grip. (Wallis & Wallis) $471

An unusually long Georgian hallmarked silver mounted Scottish dirk set circa 1800, plain single edged blade 14½in. single back fuller pierced with small holes, corded wood hilt, plain silver circular pommel, plain silver base band. (Wallis & Wallis) $2,919

A Victorian Scottish officer's dirk set of the 71st Highland Light Infantry, blade 11¼, retaining most original polish, etched with crown, regimental device, 71st Highland Light Infantry, thistles, drum, St Andrew's cross and flags, battle honors up-to Sebastopol. (Bonhams) $3,197

A Victorian officer's dirk set of the Argyll & Sutherland Highlanders, blade 11½in. by S J Pillin, 31 Gerrard St, etched with regimental devices, thistles and foliage, corded wood hilt, mounted with silver studs, plated mounts with Celtic patterns, imitation Cairngorm pommel. (Wallis & Wallis) $3,197

An Edwardian silver Scottish dress dirk, fullered blade 11in. with scalloped back edge, basket weave carved bog oak grip, silver mounts engraved with Celtic strapwork. (Wallis & Wallis) $1,390

A late Victorian silver mounted Scottish dirk, blade 12in. with single fuller and scalloped back edge, by J Castle, Edinburgh, the ebony hilt carved with strapwork, inset with silver studs, and with thistle embossed mounts and faceted paste pommel. (Wallis & Wallis) $1,130

A Scottish officer's dirk set of the Highland Light Infantry, scallop back blade 11in. by Henry Wilkinson, Pall Mall, retaining all original polish, etched with crown, bugle, *Highland Light Infantry*, elephant and battle honors within scrolls to Egypt 1882. (Wallis & Wallis) $3,475

A Victorian Scottish officer's hallmarked silver dirk set of the Gordon Highlanders, blade 12in. with single fuller and scalloped back edge, corded wood hilt set with silver studs, silver base mount decorated with thistles, elaborate openwork pommel mount with faceted colored glass pommel supported on acanthus fronds. (Wallis & Wallis) $2,641

A Scottish dirk circa 1800, (of the type carried by the Reay Fencibles), plain, tapering clipped back blade 13in., single back fuller, corded wood hilt mounted with silver studs, silver mounts with floral and foliate decoration, roped pommel. (Wallis & Wallis) $1,413

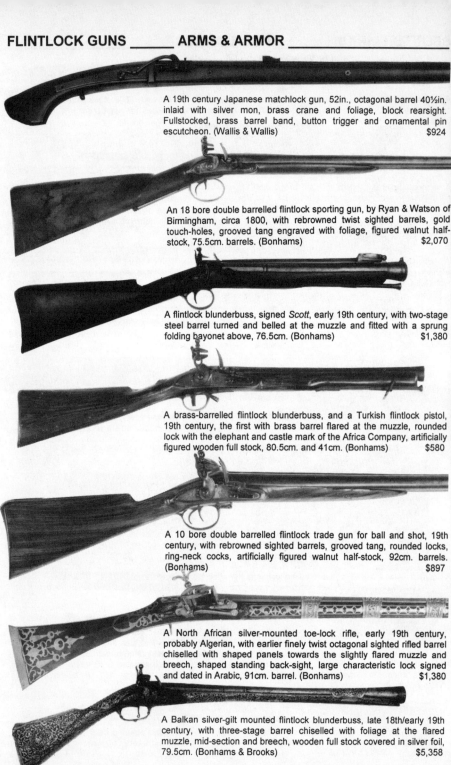

A 19th century Japanese matchlock gun, 52in., octagonal barrel 40½in. inlaid with silver mon, brass crane and foliage, block rearsight. Fullstocked, brass barrel band, button trigger and ornamental pin escutcheon. (Wallis & Wallis) $924

An 18 bore double barrelled flintlock sporting gun, by Ryan & Watson of Birmingham, circa 1800, with rebrowned twist sighted barrels, gold touch-holes, grooved tang engraved with foliage, figured walnut half-stock, 75.5cm. barrels. (Bonhams) $2,070

A flintlock blunderbuss, signed *Scott*, early 19th century, with two-stage steel barrel turned and belled at the muzzle and fitted with a sprung folding bayonet above, 76.5cm. (Bonhams) $1,380

A brass-barrelled flintlock blunderbuss, and a Turkish flintlock pistol, 19th century, the first with brass barrel flared at the muzzle, rounded lock with the elephant and castle mark of the Africa Company, artificially figured wooden full stock, 80.5cm. and 41cm. (Bonhams) $580

A 10 bore double barrelled flintlock trade gun for ball and shot, 19th century, with rebrowned sighted barrels, grooved tang, rounded locks, ring-neck cocks, artificially figured walnut half-stock, 92cm. barrels. (Bonhams) $897

A North African silver-mounted toe-lock rifle, early 19th century, probably Algerian, with earlier finely twist octagonal sighted rifled barrel chiselled with shaped panels towards the slightly flared muzzle and breech, shaped standing back-sight, large characteristic lock signed and dated in Arabic, 91cm. barrel. (Bonhams) $1,380

A Balkan silver-gilt mounted flintlock blunderbuss, late 18th/early 19th century, with three-stage barrel chiselled with foliage at the flared muzzle, mid-section and breech, wooden full stock covered in silver foil, 79.5cm. (Bonhams & Brooks) $5,358

An early Turkish miquelet flintlock gun, 45½in., fine damascus twist barrel 32¾in. with raised breech plate pierced for sighting, chiselled top rib, aprons and swollen muzzle with chiselled tear drops. Fullstocked, lock inlaid with silver foliate designs overall.
(Wallis & Wallis) $500

A scarce mid 17th century 120 bore German flintlock rifle, 50in. overall, deeply rifled heavy octagonal barrel 37in. with standing rearsight, flat lock with unbridled pan, squared frizzen and flat cock, the entire tail of the lock plate chiselled in the form of a stylized elephant's head.
(Wallis & Wallis) $7,224

A 10 bore India Pattern Brown Bess military flintlock musket, 55in. overall, barrel 39in. with traces of Tower Proofs; walnut fullstock with regulation brass mounts, single sling swivel.
(Wallis & Wallis) $1,400

A scarce ·62in. early type Baker military flintlock rifle, 46¼in. overall, twist barrel 30½in. officially adapted to take a socket bayonet, and with Tower proofs at breech, fullstocked without ramrod slit, regulation brass mounts including large squared patch box in butt.
(Wallis & Wallis) $3,892

A good Japanese matchlock gun Tanegashima, 42½in., heavy barrel 31in, signed *Makibari Kawakami Zinaoli Masahara*, decorated with silver nunome foliage and insects, block rearsight, swollen octagonal muzzle. Fullstocked in finely grained Japanese oak.
(Wallis & Wallis) $1,001

A 10 bore India pattern volunteer Brown Bess flintlock musket circa 1800, 55in. overall, barrel 39in., the lock engraved with crowned *GR* and *Tower*, walnut fullstock, steel ramrod, with its original triangular socket bayonet by Woolley & Deakin, dated *1803*.
(Wallis & Wallis) $1,156

An elegant single barrelled 14 bore flintlock sporting gun, by Wogdon, circa 1775, 52in. overall, half octagonal twist barrel 36in. with gold touch hole; plain stepped lock with raised pan and roller on frizzen, the plate with oval gold plaque, lock bolted directly to breech; walnut halfstock with checkered wrist. (Wallis & Wallis) $1,890

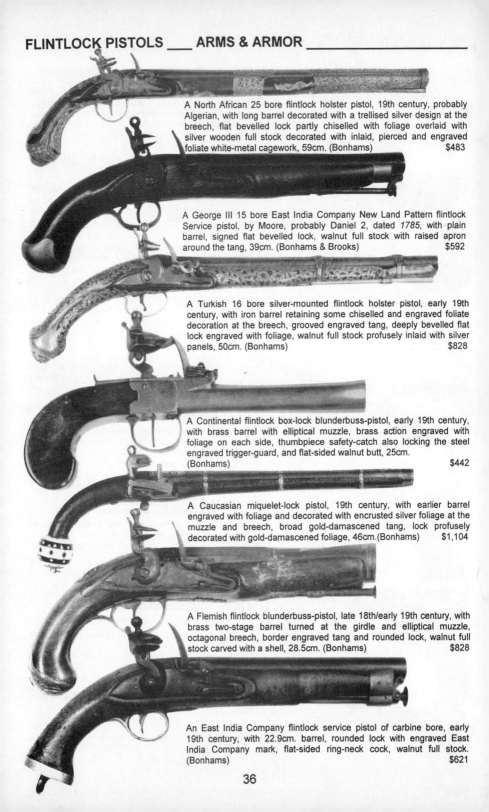

A North African 25 bore flintlock holster pistol, 19th century, probably Algerian, with long barrel decorated with a trellised silver design at the breech, flat bevelled lock partly chiselled with foliage overlaid with silver wooden full stock decorated with inlaid, pierced and engraved foliate white-metal cagework, 59cm. (Bonhams) $483

A George III 15 bore East India Company New Land Pattern flintlock Service pistol, by Moore, probably Daniel 2, dated *1785*, with plain barrel, signed flat bevelled lock, walnut full stock with raised apron around the tang, 39cm. (Bonhams & Brooks) $592

A Turkish 16 bore silver-mounted flintlock holster pistol, early 19th century, with iron barrel retaining some chiselled and engraved foliate decoration at the breech, grooved engraved tang, deeply bevelled flat lock engraved with foliage, walnut full stock profusely inlaid with silver panels, 50cm. (Bonhams) $828

A Continental flintlock box-lock blunderbuss-pistol, early 19th century, with brass barrel with elliptical muzzle, brass action engraved with foliage on each side, thumbpiece safety-catch also locking the steel engraved trigger-guard, and flat-sided walnut butt, 25cm. (Bonhams) $442

A Caucasian miquelet-lock pistol, 19th century, with earlier barrel engraved with foliage and decorated with encrusted silver foliage at the muzzle and breech, broad gold-damascened tang, lock profusely decorated with gold-damascened foliage, 46cm.(Bonhams) $1,104

A Flemish flintlock blunderbuss-pistol, late 18th/early 19th century, with brass two-stage barrel turned at the girdle and elliptical muzzle, octagonal breech, border engraved tang and rounded lock, walnut full stock carved with a shell, 28.5cm. (Bonhams) $828

An East India Company flintlock service pistol of carbine bore, early 19th century, with 22.9cm. barrel, rounded lock with engraved East India Company mark, flat-sided ring-neck cock, walnut full stock. (Bonhams) $621

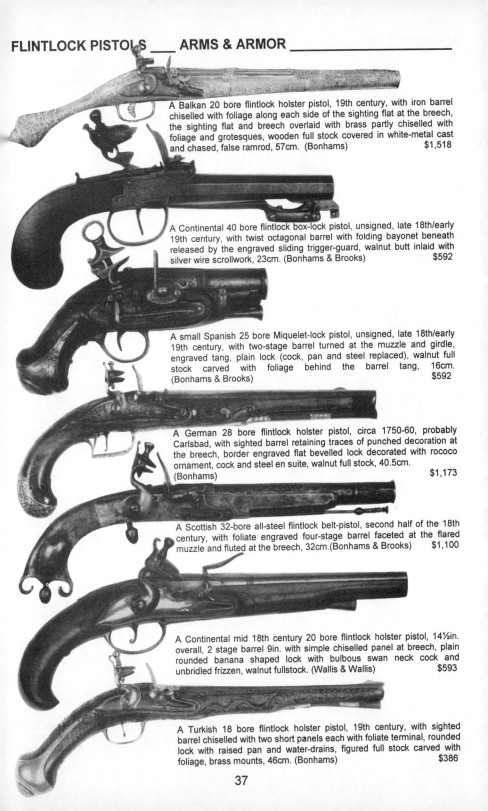

A Balkan 20 bore flintlock holster pistol, 19th century, with iron barrel chiselled with foliage along each side of the sighting flat at the breech, the sighting flat and breech overlaid with brass partly chiselled with foliage and grotesques, wooden full stock covered in white-metal cast and chased, false ramrod, 57cm. (Bonhams) $1,518

A Continental 40 bore flintlock box-lock pistol, unsigned, late 18th/early 19th century, with twist octagonal barrel with folding bayonet beneath released by the engraved sliding trigger-guard, walnut butt inlaid with silver wire scrollwork, 23cm. (Bonhams & Brooks) $592

A small Spanish 25 bore Miquelet-lock pistol, unsigned, late 18th/early 19th century, with two-stage barrel turned at the muzzle and girdle, engraved tang, plain lock (cock, pan and steel replaced), walnut full stock carved with foliage behind the barrel tang, 16cm. (Bonhams & Brooks) $592

A German 28 bore flintlock holster pistol, circa 1750-60, probably Carlsbad, with sighted barrel retaining traces of punched decoration at the breech, border engraved flat bevelled lock decorated with rococo ornament, cock and steel en suite, walnut full stock, 40.5cm. (Bonhams) $1,173

A Scottish 32-bore all-steel flintlock belt-pistol, second half of the 18th century, with foliate engraved four-stage barrel faceted at the flared muzzle and fluted at the breech, 32cm.(Bonhams & Brooks) $1,100

A Continental mid 18th century 20 bore flintlock holster pistol, 14½in. overall, 2 stage barrel 9in. with simple chiselled panel at breech, plain rounded banana shaped lock with bulbous swan neck cock and unbridled frizzen, walnut fullstock. (Wallis & Wallis) $593

A Turkish 18 bore flintlock holster pistol, 19th century, with sighted barrel chiselled with two short panels each with foliate terminal, rounded lock with raised pan and water-drains, figured full stock carved with foliage, brass mounts, 46cm. (Bonhams) $386

1st Lancashire Light Horse Vols 1861-73 helmet, OR's example of the 1847 (Albert) pattern worn by the regiment from 1861 until disbanded in 1873.
(Bosleys) $805

A lobster-tailed pot, first half of the 17th century, with one piece skull adapted from an earlier helmet, pointed integral peak pierced for a nasal with turned and crudely roped border, 26cm. high.
(Bonhams & Brooks) $1,199

1871 Royal Dragoons Trooper's helmet, the silvered skull surmounted by a gilt metal crosspiece and plume socket supporting a black horsehair plume with gilt rose boss.
(Bosleys) $1,099

A good officer's bearskin of the Coldstream Guards, leather backed graduated link chinchain, scarlet feather plume on right.
(Wallis & Wallis) $834

An other ranks shako, circa 1825, of the Yorkshire Hussar Regt. of Yeomanry Cavalry, black beaver body, patent leather peak and top, black patent rosette and ball button.
(Wallis & Wallis) $580

A good Victorian officer's silver plated helmet of the Royal Horse Guards (The Blues), with gilt peak binding, ear to ear laurel wreath, top mount, with silver plated spike, scarlet hair plume.
(Wallis & Wallis) $3,680

Hampshire Carabiniers Officer's 1871 pattern helmet, post 1902 example, the silvered skull mounted with acanthus leaf decoration, crown is with gilt metal spike supporting a white horsehair plume.
(Bosleys) $956

A Georgian officer's Tarleton helmet of the Staffordshire Yeomanry, black leather skull and peak with silver plated binding, red velvet turban with silver plated chains.
(Wallis & Wallis) $5,168

Royal Dragoons 1871 pattern Trooper's helmet, the silvered skull surmounted by a gilt metal crosspiece and plume socket supporting a black horsehair plume with gilt rose boss.
(Bosleys) $973

Montgomery Yeomanry Cavalry 1856-66 Officer's helmet, black burnished skull with applied silver laurel leaves ornamenting the reverse, fluted spike with black black horse hair plume.
(Bosleys) $4,557

A lobster-tailed pot, second quarter of the 17th century, with two-piece skull with low turned comb, pivoted pointed fall with turned edge and three-bar face-guard joined at the bottom to form a point, 28cm. high.
(Bonhams & Brooks) $1,974

North Somerset Yeomanry Cavalry Victorian officer's helmet, 1847 Albert Pattern worn by the Regiment 1854-1901, silvered skull decorated with gilt metal floral leaf design.
(Bosleys) $1,781

Victorian Royal Midlothian Yeomanry Cavalry helmet, officer's helmet adopted by the Regiment circa 1860. Patent leather skull, peak and neck peak, original black feather plume.
(Bosleys) $1,743

A post-1902 other ranks fur cap of The Royal Fusiliers, brass grenade badge, white hair plume on right, correct leather backed brass chin chain. (Wallis & Wallis) $469

4th Durham Rifle Volunteer Corps, 1878 Officer's Home Service Pattern black cloth helmet, complete with blackened metal cross piece, spike and rose head bosses. (Bosleys) $1,176

A Kawabachi kabuto, Edo Period (late 18th century), the solid pressed leather bowl black lacquered with standing ridges imitating multi-plate construction.
(Christie's) $3,015

Imperial German Great War period child's Garde du Corps helmet, of light weight brass, mounted to the front with a helmet plate of white brass depicting a Star, with Prussian Eagle to the center.
(Bosleys) $361

A Sujibachi kabuto, Edo Period (18th century), the thirty-two plate heavy iron bowl black lacquered, the peak later covered with an unusual printed leather.
(Christie's) $3,450

A good French officer's black cloth shako, black patent leather top, peak with brass binding to edge, and headband, gilt lace top band incorporating red stripe.
(Wallis & Wallis) $626

A cabasset circa 1600, formed in two pieces, brass rosettes around base, pear stalk finial to crown.
(Wallis & Wallis) $377

A Persian gold-damascened and etched steel kulah khud, Qajar, 19th century, the skull etched with panels of Arabic script within gold-damascened lines, the front embossed with a devil's face.
(Bonhams) $451

An other ranks white metal helmet of the 5th Inniskilling Dragoon Guards, brass peak binding, ear to ear wreath, top mount, leather backed chinchain and ear rosettes.
(Wallis & Wallis) $663

A post-1902 other ranks lance cap of the 16th (The Queen's) Lancers, black patent leather skull, peak and top, black cloth sides, yellow and scarlet band and woollen rosette.
(Wallis & Wallis) $724

A fireman's brass helmet, of regulation pattern with National Fire Brigades Association badge, comb with dragon sides, leather lining and leather lined chin chains.
(Wallis & Wallis) $800

19th County of London (St. Pancras) officer's Home Service Pattern blue cloth helmet, complete with giltmetal cross piece, spike and rose head bosses.
(Bosleys) $1,370

German Prussian other rank's felt Pickelhaube, first pattern Ersatz issue, with gilt brass metal fittings, complete with Prussian helmet plate. (Bosleys) $274

A good Victorian officer's blue cloth spiked helmet of The Royal Scots (Lothian Regiment), with gilt top mount and spike and ear rosettes.
(Wallis & Wallis) $862

A Victorian officer's blue cloth spiked helmet of The Bedfordshire Regiment, gilt top mount and spike, velvet backed chinchain and ear rosettes.
(Wallis & Wallis) $1,251

A fine Victorian officer's lance cap of the 5th (Royal Irish) Lancers, black patent leather skull, scarlet cloth sides and top, gilt lace and cord trim.
(Wallis & Wallis) $4,170

Scottish Rifles Officer's Wolseley foreign service helmet, of Regimental pattern, seven fold pagri, with 'V' to front, back and sides. (Bosleys) $1,029

A good French mounted Gendarmerie trooper's helmet, brass skull with white metal comb embossed with foliage, with Medusa head crest, black horsehair stand up comb.
(Wallis & Wallis) $740

Imperial German Great War Period child's Garde du Corps helmet, the skull of light weight steel, is mounted to the front with helmet plate of gilt brass depicting a Star, with Prussian Eagle to the center.
(Bosleys) $329

An officer's 1845 pattern Albert shako of the 57th West Middlesex Regiment, of cylindrical form with polished leather top, as with rear and front peaks, fine gilt badge bearing six Peninsula battle honors on rays.
(Wallis & Wallis) $1,355

Imperial German Prussian officer's Pickelhaube, late Great War example with rounded front peak and flash gilt metal fittings. The Prussian eagle with large *FR* to center. (Bosleys) $1,165

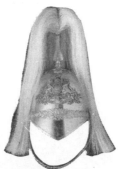

An Important Imperial Yeomanry trial pattern officer's helmet, one of only two examples believed to have been made modelled on the 1871 pattern, gilt metal skull.
(Bosleys) $5,206

A Victorian officer's blue cloth spiked helmet of the 3rd Vol Bn The Royal Scots, silver plated mounts, velvet backed chinchain and ear rosettes, helmet plate with green cloth center backing.
(Wallis & Wallis) $600

Royal Artillery 4 Corps bush hat, Second World War example retaining regimental and Corps badges, to the left flap a Royal Artillery diamond.
(Bosleys) $216

A scarce WWI OR's khaki Tam-o-Shanter of The Seaforth Highlanders, white metal badge, tartan headband stated to be for a 4th Bn, maker's label inside dated 1917. (Wallis & Wallis) $377

East Yorkshire Regiment bush hat, khaki felt with six fold pagri, the top fold being black, the turned up flap bearing regimental flash.
(Bosleys) $156

WW2 Army Engineer officer's cap, with red piping and silver bullion insignia, complete with cap cords.
(Bosleys) $374

Royal Scots Fusiliers Victorian officer's brown fur cap, to the front a Regimental device of a fire gilt grenade. (Bosleys) $932

Luftwaffe steel helmet, a good example of the 1943 pattern with blue paint finish and Luftwaffe eagle to left side. Eagle 98% present.
(Bosleys) $294

A scarce Victorian other ranks busby of the Midlothian Coast Artillery Volunteers, scarlet bag, pewter plume holder badge with primrose hair plume.
(Wallis & Wallis) $449

City of Norwich Volunteers other ranks shako of dark blue material, with a later mohair band to the body, fitted with a scare 1861-69 shako plate. (Bosleys) $334

A Japanese momonari kabuto, unsigned, 17th century or earlier, the hachi decorated in nikubori and katakiribori with two three-clawed dragons surrounding a gilt floral mon, 19cm. high.
(Bonhams) $1,656

A scarce officer's blue peaked cap of the Scinde Horse, white cloth headband and piping, gilt embroidered peak.
(Wallis & Wallis) $373

A Nazi M40 double decal organisation Todt helmet, green finish, leather liner and chinstrap.
(Wallis & Wallis) $432

WW2 Cavalry NCO's cap, pre-war style example, gray felt material, with light green cap band and yellow piping.
(Bosleys) $306

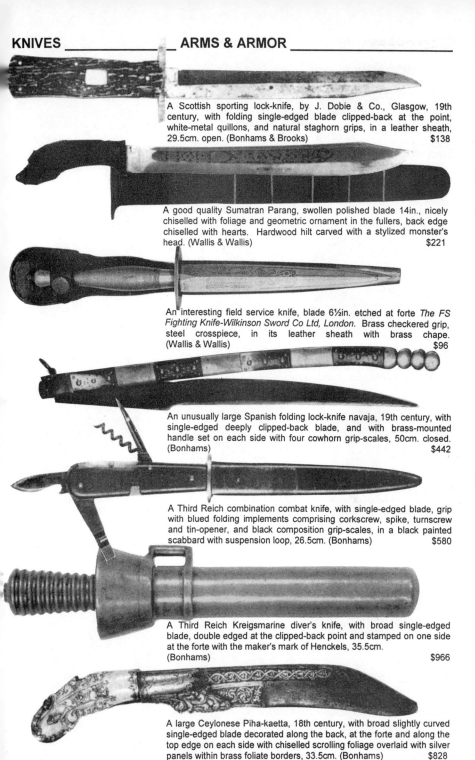

A Scottish sporting lock-knife, by J. Dobie & Co., Glasgow, 19th century, with folding single-edged blade clipped-back at the point, white-metal quillons, and natural staghorn grips, in a leather sheath, 29.5cm. open. (Bonhams & Brooks) $138

A good quality Sumatran Parang, swollen polished blade 14in., nicely chiselled with foliage and geometric ornament in the fullers, back edge chiselled with hearts. Hardwood hilt carved with a stylized monster's head. (Wallis & Wallis) $221

An interesting field service knife, blade 6½in. etched at forte *The FS Fighting Knife-Wilkinson Sword Co Ltd, London*. Brass checkered grip, steel crosspiece, in its leather sheath with brass chape. (Wallis & Wallis) $96

An unusually large Spanish folding lock-knife navaja, 19th century, with single-edged deeply clipped-back blade, and with brass-mounted handle set on each side with four cowhorn grip-scales, 50cm. closed. (Bonhams) $442

A Third Reich combination combat knife, with single-edged blade, grip with blued folding implements comprising corkscrew, spike, turnscrew and tin-opener, and black composition grip-scales, in a black painted scabbard with suspension loop, 26.5cm. (Bonhams) $580

A Third Reich Kreigsmarine diver's knife, with broad single-edged blade, double edged at the clipped-back point and stamped on one side at the forte with the maker's mark of Henckels, 35.5cm. (Bonhams) $966

A large Ceylonese Piha-kaetta, 18th century, with broad slightly curved single-edged blade decorated along the back, at the forte and along the top edge on each side with chiselled scrolling foliage overlaid with silver panels within brass foliate borders, 33.5cm. (Bonhams) $828

A W.W. Greener advertising board, of pressed card depicting the St. George Model box-lock shotgun and cartridges, 43.5 x 28cm. (Bonhams) $386

British Great War gas goggles, of the pattern worn prior to the PH gas hood and small box respirator. Square clear lenses, tailored into a khaki cotton cloth face mask. (Bosleys) $312

A leather cartridge bag for 100 cartridges, and a 12 bore cartridge belt.(Bonhams) $152

An iron strong-box, 17th century, probably German, the flat recessed hinged lid carrying a large and elaborate internal lock mechanism working eight independent bolts, 76.5 x 44cm. (Bonhams) $2,346

A leather roll of tools for a percussion rifle, mid 19th century, comprising turnscrew with swelling figured walnut handle incorporating a threaded pricker, brass cleaning tool, steel powder charge, steel nipple key. (Bonhams & Brooks) $262

A fine framed cartridge display mirror, by Kynoch Ltd, circa 1920, with the central trade mark motif surrounded by examples of cartridges, 30¾ x 26¾in. (Bonhams) $1,173

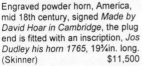

Engraved powder horn, America, mid 18th century, signed *Made by David Hoar in Cambridge*, the plug end is fitted with an inscription, *Jos Dudley his horn 1765*, 19¾in. long. (Skinner) $11,500

79th (Q.O.Cameron Highlanders) officer's sporran, pre 1881 example. The fire gilt cantel is embossed to the center with *79*. (Bosleys) $2,233

A rare J. Astbury Patent breech-loading brass cannon, patent no. 670 for 1877, with three-stage sighted barrel, and fitted with folding calibrated back-sight. (Bonhams & Brooks) $8,970

A rare piper's cast white metal badge of the Canadian Forestry Corps.
(Wallis & Wallis) $1,104

An enamelled Eley and Kynoch shop sign, with yellow back and navy blue writing *Eley And Kynoch Cartridges Sold Here*, 36.8 x 48.3cm. (Bonhams) $304

Great War Pattern aviator's face mask, as worn by British aviators, soft brown leather, with clear glass lenses, open press studs indicating pre 1920s.
(Wallis & Wallis) $207

A very rare framed and glazed cartridge board, by G. Kynoch & Co. Ltd., Birmingham, late 19th century, with metallic and paper military and sporting pin-fire and center-fire ammunition, three railway alarms, wads, 26½ x 38½in.
(Bonhams & Brooks) $9,384

WW2 soldier's wallet containing marksman's lanyard and War Merit Cross (2nd Class with swords) in packet of issue. Also houses a torn photograph of a soldier wearing similar lanyard.
(Wallis & Wallis) $69

East Somerset Yeomanry Cavalry Georgian guidon, presented to the 4th Yeovil Troop in 1794, of crimson silk ground, to the center, painted decoration of the Arms of the Poulett family.
(Wallis & Wallis) $5,848

Imperial German Great War gas hood, heavy weight cotton hood, with a charcoal type coating to the interior, with circular eye pieces and metal filter. (Bosleys) $417

A rare and large framed and glazed Kynoch cartridge display board, whole on a dark velvet back with a simple wooden frame.
(Bonhams) $6,210

First World War PHG gas hood, blue flannel layered cloth, retaining mouth piece and rubber exhaler, with integral tear gas goggles.
(Bosleys) $904

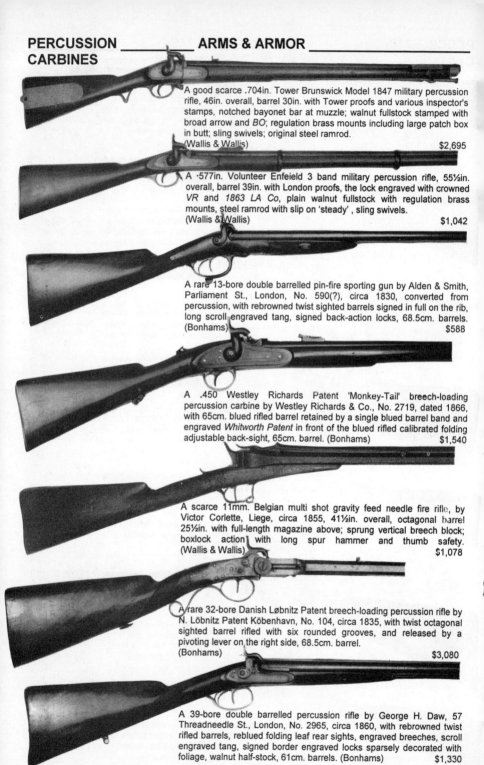

A good scarce .704in. Tower Brunswick Model 1847 military percussion rifle, 46in. overall, barrel 30in. with Tower proofs and various inspector's stamps, notched bayonet bar at muzzle; walnut fullstock stamped with broad arrow and *BO*; regulation brass mounts including large patch box in butt; sling swivels; original steel ramrod.
(Wallis & Wallis) $2,695

A ·577in. Volunteer Enfeield 3 band military percussion rifle, 55½in. overall, barrel 39in. with London proofs, the lock engraved with crowned *VR* and *1863 LA Co*, plain walnut fullstock with regulation brass mounts, steel ramrod with slip on 'steady' , sling swivels.
(Wallis & Wallis) $1,042

A rare 13-bore double barrelled pin-fire sporting gun by Alden & Smith, Parliament St., London, No. 590(?), circa 1830, converted from percussion, with rebrowned twist sighted barrels signed in full on the rib, long scroll engraved tang, signed back-action locks, 68.5cm. barrels.
(Bonhams) $588

A .450 Westley Richards Patent 'Monkey-Tail' breech-loading percussion carbine by Westley Richards & Co., No. 2719, dated 1866, with 65cm. blued rifled barrel retained by a single blued barrel band and engraved *Whitworth Patent* in front of the blued rifled calibrated folding adjustable back-sight, 65cm. barrel. (Bonhams) $1,540

A scarce 11mm. Belgian multi shot gravity feed needle fire rifle, by Victor Corlette, Liege, circa 1855, 41½in. overall, octagonal barrel 25½in. with full-length magazine above; sprung vertical breech block; boxlock action with long spur hammer and thumb safety.
(Wallis & Wallis) $1,078

A rare 32-bore Danish Løbnitz Patent breech-loading percussion rifle by N. Löbnitz Patent Köbenhavn, No. 104, circa 1835, with twist octagonal sighted barrel rifled with six rounded grooves, and released by a pivoting lever on the right side, 68.5cm. barrel.
(Bonhams) $3,080

A 39-bore double barrelled percussion rifle by George H. Daw, 57 Threadneedle St., London, No. 2965, circa 1860, with rebrowned twist rifled barrels, reblued folding leaf rear sights, engraved breeches, scroll engraved tang, signed border engraved locks sparsely decorated with foliage, walnut half-stock, 61cm. barrels. (Bonhams) $1,330

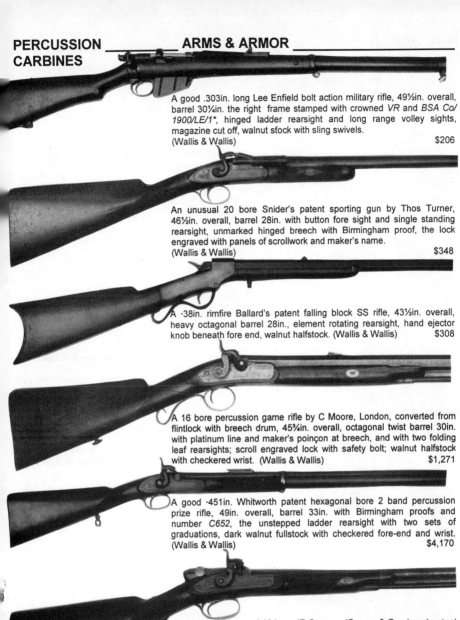

A good .303in. long Lee Enfield bolt action military rifle, 49½in. overall, barrel 30¼in. the right frame stamped with crowned *VR* and *BSA Co/ 1900/LE/1**, hinged ladder rearsight and long range volley sights, magazine cut off, walnut stock with sling swivels.
(Wallis & Wallis) $206

An unusual 20 bore Snider's patent sporting gun by Thos Turner, 46½in. overall, barrel 28in. with button fore sight and single standing rearsight, unmarked hinged breech with Birmingham proof, the lock engraved with panels of scrollwork and maker's name.
(Wallis & Wallis) $348

A ·38in. rimfire Ballard's patent falling block SS rifle, 43½in. overall, heavy octagonal barrel 28in., element rotating rearsight, hand ejector knob beneath fore end, walnut halfstock. (Wallis & Wallis) $308

A 16 bore percussion game rifle by C Moore, London, converted from flintlock with breech drum, 45¾in. overall, octagonal twist barrel 30in. with platinum line and maker's poinçon at breech, and with two folding leaf rearsights; scroll engraved lock with safety bolt; walnut halfstock with checkered wrist. (Wallis & Wallis) $1,271

A good ·451in. Whitworth patent hexagonal bore 2 band percussion prize rifle, 49in. overall, barrel 33in. with Birmingham proofs and number *C652*, the unstepped ladder rearsight with two sets of graduations, dark walnut fullstock with checkered fore-end and wrist.
(Wallis & Wallis) $4,170

A scarce and unusual 16 bore JR Coopers (Cooper & Goodman) patent breech loading percussion short sporting gun, 41in. overall, browned twist barrel 25½in., colour hardened hinge up breech with sliding plug, plain color hardened lock, dark walnut halfstock.
(Wallis & Wallis) $973

A .50in. Sharps Patent New Model breech loading percussion carbine, 39in. overall, barrel 22in. with Lawrence's patent rearsight, the lock with Lawrence's patent pellet primer; walnut halfstock with steel mounts.
(Wallis & Wallis) $1,617

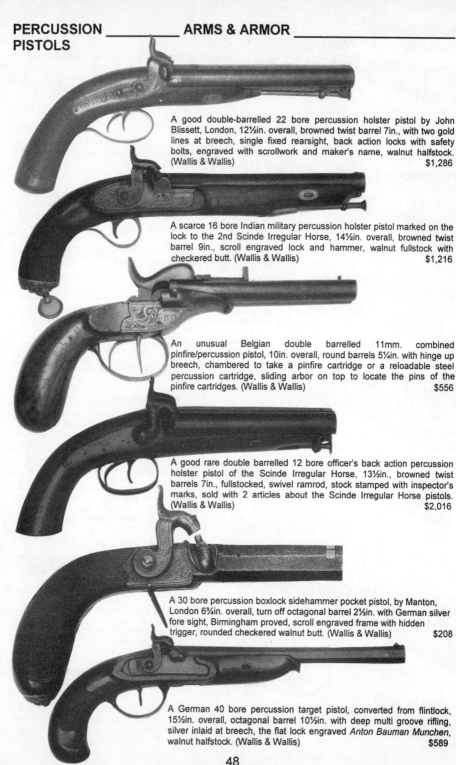

A good double-barrelled 22 bore percussion holster pistol by John Blissett, London, 12½in. overall, browned twist barrel 7in., with two gold lines at breech, single fixed rearsight, back action locks with safety bolts, engraved with scrollwork and maker's name, walnut halfstock. (Wallis & Wallis) $1,286

A scarce 16 bore Indian military percussion holster pistol marked on the lock to the 2nd Scinde Irregular Horse, 14½in. overall, browned twist barrel 9in., scroll engraved lock and hammer, walnut fullstock with checkered butt. (Wallis & Wallis) $1,216

An unusual Belgian double barrelled 11mm. combined pinfire/percussion pistol, 10in. overall, round barrels 5¼in. with hinge up breech, chambered to take a pinfire cartridge or a reloadable steel percussion cartridge, sliding arbor on top to locate the pins of the pinfire cartridges. (Wallis & Wallis) $556

A good rare double barrelled 12 bore officer's back action percussion holster pistol of the Scinde Irregular Horse, 13½in., browned twist barrels 7in., fullstocked, swivel ramrod, stock stamped with inspector's marks, sold with 2 articles about the Scinde Irregular Horse pistols. (Wallis & Wallis) $2,016

A 30 bore percussion boxlock sidehammer pocket pistol, by Manton, London 6¾in. overall, turn off octagonal barrel 2½in. with German silver fore sight, Birmingham proved, scroll engraved frame with hidden trigger, rounded checkered walnut butt. (Wallis & Wallis) $208

A German 40 bore percussion target pistol, converted from flintlock, 15½in. overall, octagonal barrel 10½in. with deep multi groove rifling, silver inlaid at breech, the flat lock engraved *Anton Bauman Munchen*, walnut halfstock. (Wallis & Wallis) $589

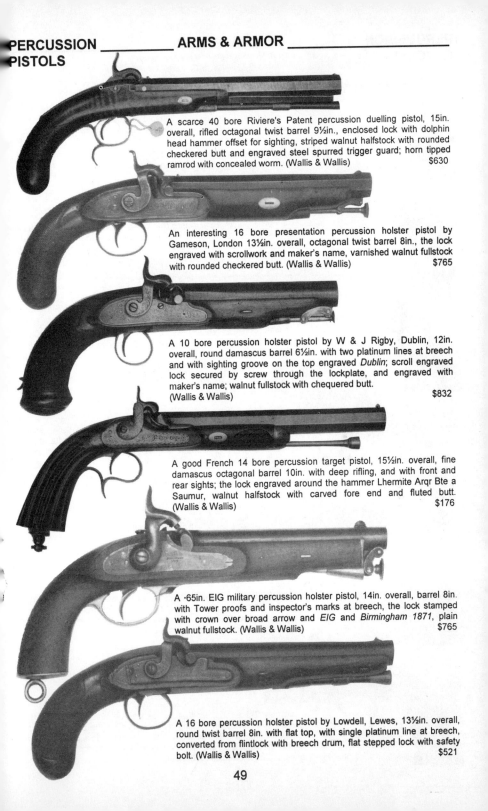

A scarce 40 bore Riviere's Patent percussion duelling pistol, 15in. overall, rifled octagonal twist barrel 9½in., enclosed lock with dolphin head hammer offset for sighting, striped walnut halfstock with rounded checkered butt and engraved steel spurred trigger guard; horn tipped ramrod with concealed worm. (Wallis & Wallis) $630

An interesting 16 bore presentation percussion holster pistol by Gameson, London 13½in. overall, octagonal twist barrel 8in., the lock engraved with scrollwork and maker's name, varnished walnut fullstock with rounded checkered butt. (Wallis & Wallis) $765

A 10 bore percussion holster pistol by W & J Rigby, Dublin, 12in. overall, round damascus barrel 6½in. with two platinum lines at breech and with sighting groove on the top engraved *Dublin*; scroll engraved lock secured by screw through the lockplate, and engraved with maker's name; walnut fullstock with chequered butt. (Wallis & Wallis) $832

A good French 14 bore percussion target pistol, 15½in. overall, fine damascus octagonal barrel 10in. with deep rifling, and with front and rear sights; the lock engraved around the hammer Lhermite Arqr Bte a Saumur, walnut halfstock with carved fore end and fluted butt. (Wallis & Wallis) $176

A ·65in. EIG military percussion holster pistol, 14in. overall, barrel 8in. with Tower proofs and inspector's marks at breech, the lock stamped with crown over broad arrow and *EIG* and *Birmingham 1871*, plain walnut fullstock. (Wallis & Wallis) $765

A 16 bore percussion holster pistol by Lowdell, Lewes, 13½in. overall, round twist barrel 8in. with flat top, with single platinum line at breech, converted from flintlock with breech drum, flat stepped lock with safety bolt. (Wallis & Wallis) $521

49

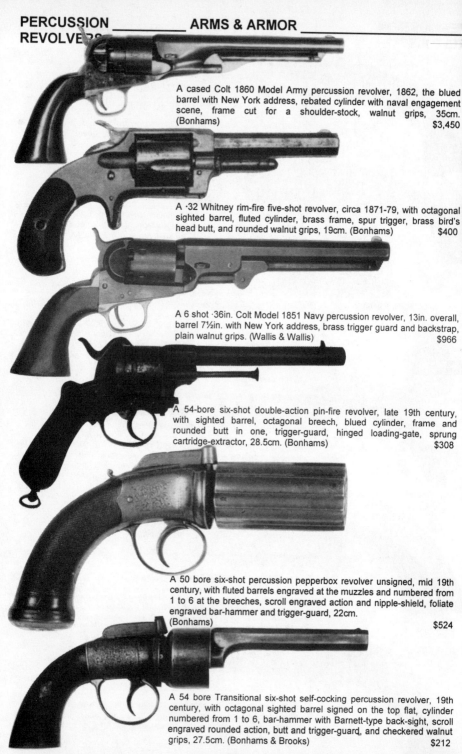

A cased Colt 1860 Model Army percussion revolver, 1862, the blued barrel with New York address, rebated cylinder with naval engagement scene, frame cut for a shoulder-stock, walnut grips, 35cm. (Bonhams)
$3,450

A ·32 Whitney rim-fire five-shot revolver, circa 1871-79, with octagonal sighted barrel, fluted cylinder, brass frame, spur trigger, brass bird's head butt, and rounded walnut grips, 19cm. (Bonhams)
$400

A 6 shot ·36in. Colt Model 1851 Navy percussion revolver, 13in. overall, barrel 7½in. with New York address, brass trigger guard and backstrap, plain walnut grips. (Wallis & Wallis)
$966

A 54-bore six-shot double-action pin-fire revolver, late 19th century, with sighted barrel, octagonal breech, blued cylinder, frame and rounded butt in one, trigger-guard, hinged loading-gate, sprung cartridge-extractor, 28.5cm. (Bonhams)
$308

A 50 bore six-shot percussion pepperbox revolver unsigned, mid 19th century, with fluted barrels engraved at the muzzles and numbered from 1 to 6 at the breeches, scroll engraved action and nipple-shield, foliate engraved bar-hammer and trigger-guard, 22cm. (Bonhams)
$524

A 54 bore Transitional six-shot self-cocking percussion revolver, 19th century, with octagonal sighted barrel signed on the top flat, cylinder numbered from 1 to 6, bar-hammer with Barnett-type back-sight, scroll engraved rounded action, butt and trigger-guard, and checkered walnut grips, 27.5cm. (Bonhams & Brooks)
$212

A Colt 1860 Model Army percussion revolver, 1863, the sighted barrel with New York address, rebated cylinder with naval engagement scene, frame cut for a shoulder-stock, brass trigger-guard, rammer, walnut grips, 35cm. (Bonhams) $1,242

A 54 bore Transitional six-shot percussion revolver retailed by Gibbs, Bristol, mid 19th century, with blued octagonal sighted barrel, case-hardened cylinder, butt with hinged butt-trap cover, and trigger-guard, checkered walnut grip-scales, 31.5cm. (Bonhams & Brooks) $917

A 6 shot ·44in. Remington Army single action percussion revolver No 54757, 14in. octagonal barrel 8in. stamped with traces of *E Remington New York USA*, underlever rammer, brass trigger guard, 2 piece walnut grips with US government inspector's initials. (Wallis & Wallis) $970

An unusual 12 shot 7mm. double action open frame pin fire revolver, 9in. overall, round barrel, 4¾in. with Birmingham proofs, fluted cylinder, loading gate and ejector rod on right, checkered walnut grips, lanyard ring on butt. (Wallis & Wallis) $487

A 120 bore six-shot percussion pepperbox revolver unsigned, mid 19th century, with fluted barrels engraved at the muzzles, foliate engraved rounded white-metal action, engraved bar-hammer, checkered walnut grips, 20cm. (Bonhams) $373

A Colt 1851 Model Navy percussion revolver, 1863, with blued octagonal barrel, blued cylinder with naval engagement scene, case-hardened action and loading-lever, brass trigger-guard and back-strap, walnut grips, 33cm. (Bonhams) $968

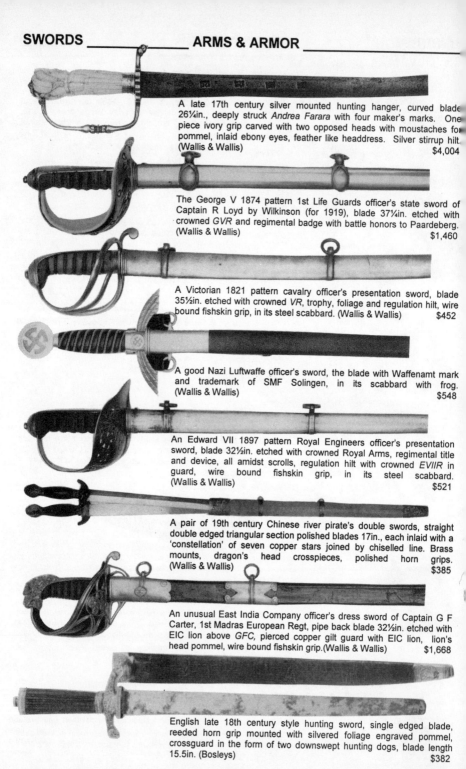

A late 17th century silver mounted hunting hanger, curved blade 26¼in., deeply struck *Andrea Farara* with four maker's marks. One piece ivory grip carved with two opposed heads with moustaches for pommel, inlaid ebony eyes, feather like headdress. Silver stirrup hilt. (Wallis & Wallis) $4,004

The George V 1874 pattern 1st Life Guards officer's state sword of Captain R Loyd by Wilkinson (for 1919), blade 37¼in. etched with crowned *GVR* and regimental badge with battle honors to Paardeberg. (Wallis & Wallis) $1,460

A Victorian 1821 pattern cavalry officer's presentation sword, blade 35½in. etched with crowned *VR*, trophy, foliage and regulation hilt, wire bound fishskin grip, in its steel scabbard. (Wallis & Wallis) $452

A good Nazi Luftwaffe officer's sword, the blade with Waffenamt mark and trademark of SMF Solingen, in its scabbard with frog. (Wallis & Wallis) $548

An Edward VII 1897 pattern Royal Engineers officer's presentation sword, blade 32½in. etched with crowned Royal Arms, regimental title and device, all amidst scrolls, regulation hilt with crowned *EVIIR* in guard, wire bound fishskin grip, in its steel scabbard. (Wallis & Wallis) $521

A pair of 19th century Chinese river pirate's double swords, straight double edged triangular section polished blades 17in., each inlaid with a 'constellation' of seven copper stars joined by chiselled line. Brass mounts, dragon's head crosspieces, polished horn grips. (Wallis & Wallis) $385

An unusual East India Company officer's dress sword of Captain G F Carter, 1st Madras European Regt, pipe back blade 32½in. etched with EIC lion above *GFC*, pierced copper gilt guard with EIC lion, lion's head pommel, wire bound fishskin grip. (Wallis & Wallis) $1,668

English late 18th century style hunting sword, single edged blade, reeded horn grip mounted with silvered foliage engraved pommel, crossguard in the form of two downswept hunting dogs, blade length 15.5in. (Bosleys) $382

A 19th century silver mounted Mexican sword, slightly curved fullered single edged blade 25in., silver hilt with shaped finger grips, pommel and gripstrap, four piece tortoiseshell grips. (Wallis & Wallis) $185

A fine Georgian light Cavalry Officer's sword, curved single edged blade with three-quarter length blue and gilt decoration, depicting, Royal Arms, Royal Cypher, trophies of war and Britannia standing with shield, white ivorine grip. (Bosleys) $1,176

A good Indian sword sossun patta circa 1800, shaped blade 17½in. with T shaped back. Tulwar hilt with knucklebow silver damascened overall with repeated geometric designs. (Wallis & Wallis) $685

A hallmarked silver mounted Turkish shamshir of Mahmud II (1808-1839), curved single edged blade 31½in., silver hilt and scabbard mounts, engraved crosspiece, gripstrap, pommel and grip sides, two piece horn grips with pewter and brass inlay.
(Wallis & Wallis) $1,001

A good late 19th century Ethiopian chieftain's sword shotel, broad curved fullered single edged blade 29in. etched with Amharic inscription with foliage, and at the forte King Rastus with lion of Judah. Large one piece rhino hilt. (Wallis & Wallis) $845

An 18th century Persian sword shamshir, blade 31in. of mechanically watered damascus steel. Two piece ivory grips, steel mounts with gold damascened borders, finely watered steel crosspiece. In Its leather covered scabbard with decorated scrolled border and foliate ornaments. (Wallis & Wallis) $1,008

An unusual early 19th century Indian tulwar with English Georgian military blade, 32in. etched with 1801-16 crowned Royal Arms, figure of Liberty, rearing cavalryman, trophies of arms, union flowers, and *Osborn & Gunby's*, iron hilt gold damascened.
(Wallis & Wallis) $539

A Nepalese sacrificial sword Ram Dao, 23¼in. polished heavy blade 16in., brass inlaid and stamped with 2 peacocks, 2 eyes, floral foliate and geometric decoration, and stamped, brass chevrons inlaid along back edge, wooden grip. (Wallis & Wallis) $462

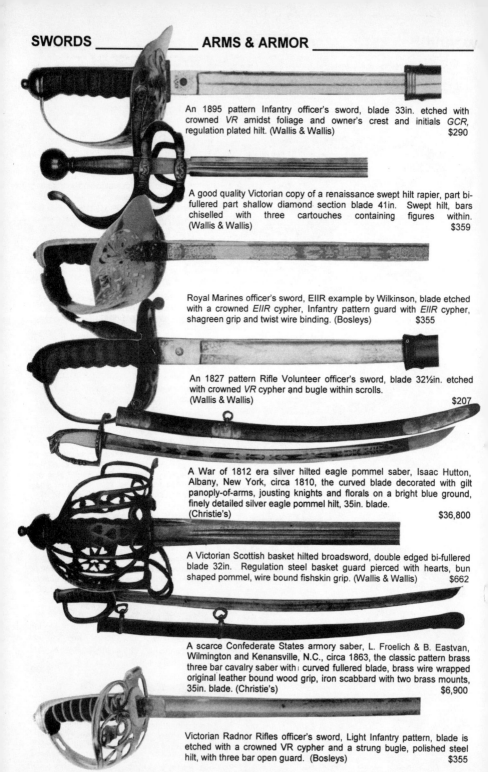

An 1895 pattern Infantry officer's sword, blade 33in. etched with crowned *VR* amidst foliage and owner's crest and initials *GCR*, regulation plated hilt. (Wallis & Wallis) $290

A good quality Victorian copy of a renaissance swept hilt rapier, part bi-fullered part shallow diamond section blade 41in. Swept hilt, bars chiselled with three cartouches containing figures within. (Wallis & Wallis) $359

Royal Marines officer's sword, EIIR example by Wilkinson, blade etched with a crowned *EIIR* cypher, Infantry pattern guard with *EIIR* cypher, shagreen grip and twist wire binding. (Bosleys) $355

An 1827 pattern Rifle Volunteer officer's sword, blade 32½in. etched with crowned *VR* cypher and bugle within scrolls. (Wallis & Wallis) $207

A War of 1812 era silver hilted eagle pommel saber, Isaac Hutton, Albany, New York, circa 1810, the curved blade decorated with gilt panoply-of-arms, jousting knights and florals on a bright blue ground, finely detailed silver eagle pommel hilt, 35in. blade. (Christie's) $36,800

A Victorian Scottish basket hilted broadsword, double edged bi-fullered blade 32in. Regulation steel basket guard pierced with hearts, bun shaped pommel, wire bound fishskin grip. (Wallis & Wallis) $662

A scarce Confederate States armory saber, L. Froelich & B. Eastvan, Wilmington and Kenansville, N.C., circa 1863, the classic pattern brass three bar cavalry saber with curved fullered blade, brass wire wrapped original leather bound wood grip, iron scabbard with two brass mounts, 35in. blade. (Christie's) $6,900

Victorian Radnor Rifles officer's sword, Light Infantry pattern, blade is etched with a crowned VR cypher and a strung bugle, polished steel hilt, with three bar open guard. (Bosleys) $355

A most unusual Chinese sword Jian, circa 1800, 33in. overall, straight diamond section blade 22½in. Brass mounts of square shape,, hardwood hilt and scabbard decorated overall with panels of geometric inlay. (Wallis & Wallis) $690

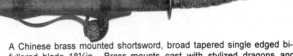

A Chinese brass mounted shortsword, broad tapered single edged bi-fullered blade 18½in. Brass mounts cast with stylized dragons and scrolls in low relief, swollen pommel, round "tsuba" like guard, sharkskin grip. (Wallis & Wallis) $266

A late 18th century Nepalese sword kora, broad polished 'elephant's ear' blade 19½in. chiselled with red filled 'seeing eye' on both sides. Steel hilt, double disc guards, swollen steel grip, pommel with curved shaped finial. (Wallis & Wallis) $414

A 19th century Malayan lacquered parang, 22½in., broad swollen blade 16¼in. with bold pattern welded designs, shaped forte. Black lacquered wooden hilt, in its red lacquered scabbard with gold lacquered flower heads. (Wallis & Wallis) $385

A silver mounted Burmese sword dha, swollen single edged blade 22½in., rattan bound grip, octagonal silver ferrule with large swollen lotus bud shaped pommel. In its silver covered scabbard. (Wallis & Wallis) $447

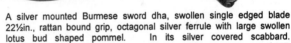

An 18th century Persian sword shamshir, watered steel blade 30½in. with wavy watered pattern showing in silver colored metal. Steel crosspiece with pierced decoration, two piece horn grips inlaid with silver stars. (Wallis & Wallis) $538

A Javanese kris, with double-edged pattern-welded blade, lightly colored wooden hilt, of slightly curved circular section widening towards the top and carved overall with raised ovals against a ground of waved lines, 53.5cm. (Bonhams) $173

A Syrian sword shamshir, broad curved single edged blade 26in., cast brass hilt with trophy in relief to crosspiece, geometric studded grips. In its scabbard with large brass mounts cast with elaborate Koranic inscriptions. (Wallis & Wallis) $385

A Japanese sword katana, blade 62.7cm., mumei, suriage, 2 mekugi ana. Gunome hamon, light cleaning has accentuated the grain but obscured the hamon. Tape bound same tsuka, shakudo gilt menuki as flowers, iron fuchi kashira with gilt dragons. (Wallis & Wallis) $1,599

A fine Japanese 16th century wakizashi, the 18.5in. blade bears a faint signature indicating Musashi Provenance, iron tsuba with pierced floral decoration and to the hilt gilt menuki depicting figures, lacquered simulated shark skin scabbard. (Bosleys) $685

A Japanese sword katana, blade 69cm. signed *Sagami No Kami Fujiwara No Morinaga*, and *Noshu Seki No Ju*. Gunome hamon. Tape bound same tsuka, shakudo menuki, nanako fuchi (kashira) missing). In its black lacquered saya inlaid with silver cherry blossom floating on a lacquered stream. (Wallis & Wallis) $1,529

A Japanese WWII army Officer's sword katana, blade 67.8cm., signed *Showa* to with Seki arsenal stamp, gunome hamon, probably unforged, fairpolish. (Wallis & Wallis) $566

A Japanese courtsword Itomaki-no-Tachi, blade 69.6cm. mumei, suriage, 3 mekugi ana, ito chu-suguha hamon, itame hada, chiselled with a single Bonji character, tape bound same tsuka, menuki as gilt mons, gilt tachi mounts each with mon in relief, Aoi tsuba. In its gold nashiji lacquered saya with gilt mons, tape bound top. (Wallis & Wallis) $3,753

A tanto with archaic style mounts, the blade 16th century, signed *Kane Nori Saku,* with unusual gnarled form iron fittings, shagreen hilt, red and black lacquer scabbard with scattered cell formation, the blade with choji hamon, 22½in. long. (Christie's) $1,809

A fine Japanese 18th century wakizashi, an unsigned 19in. blade, fitted with an iron tsuba, the hilt with black and gilt menukis in the form of a cat with a ball, complete with a lacquered scabbard. (Bosleys) $617

A wakizashi, 18th century, the blade signed *Kanefusa*, with silkbound shagreen hilt, iron tsuba of mokko form decorated in silver and gilt with an equestrian figure and attendant beside a waterfall, gilt bronze menuki modelled as oni, 27½in. long. (Christie's) $1,151

speculative and unusual Japanese sword wakizashi, 31¼in. overall, blade 52.7cm. (details of nakago not available), copper tsuba engraved with dragon amidst waves. Tape bound tsuka and saya extensively decorated with inscriptions and flowering cherry tree. (Wallis & Wallis) $329

wakizashi, 17th century, the blade signed *Kunishige*, with silk bound shagreen hilt, pierced oval iron tsuba, on mounts, bronze menuki modelled as dragons, gilt eyes, black lacquer scabbard, the blade with suga amon, 74.6cm. long. (Christie's) $1,480

World War Two Japanese army officer's sword katana, blade 63.2cm. signed *Katsushima*, ubu nakago, robably Shin Shinto. Gunome hamon, itame hada. In shin gunto mounts with owner's silver mon on kashira, its brown painted steel saya. (Wallis & Wallis) $1,146

A wakizashi, 18th century, the blade signed *Katsumitsu*, with silk bound shagreen hilt, rectangular iron tsuba ncised with monkeys among branches, gilt bronze menuki modelled as cranes on leafy branches and Higo style ron mounts, 26¾in. long. (Christie's) $1,068

A Japanese Shin Shinto sword katana, blade 75.2cm., signed and dated *Genji* (1864). Ayasugi hada, gunome hamon with much nie. Tape bound same tsuka, iron fuchi kashira, spiral shaped red lacquered saya. (Wallis & Wallis) $2,002

A katana in military mounts 16th century, the blade signed *Bizen Kuni Zu Sukemitsu*, with silkbound shagreen hilt, floral molded bronze tsuba and mounts, leather scabbard, the blade with choji hamon, 40in. (Christie's) $2,796

A katana in military mounts, the blade 17th century, with silk bound shagreen hilt, iron Namban tsuba modelled with a writhing dragon above waves, applied in gilt, stippled metal mounts, brown leather scabbard, 39¼in. long. (Christie's) $1,316

An attractive 19th century Japanese shortsword wakizashi, blade 46.3cm., numei, 2 mekugi ana, gunome hamon with well defined nie line. Tape bound black same tsuka, shakudo nanako fuchi kashira inlaid in relief, gold foil floral menuki. Iron kiku tsuba inlaid with gold. (Wallis & Wallis) $1,694

A William IV special constable painted truncheon. (Woolley & Wallis) $14

Salford Special Constabulary truncheon, by Hiatts of Birmingham bearing transfer of Crown with *GR* below, the Arms of Salford, over *Special Constable 1914-1919*. (Bosleys) $246

A Victorian black painted wooden truncheon, painted in gold and colors with crown, *VIR* Red Rose and LC, 15½in. (Wallis & Wallis) $128

A Victorian constabulary truncheon, mid 19th century, of hardwood and painted in polychrome against a black ground with *VR* crowned and *Sergt., H.1* within a red circular band painted *Hove.Police.Force* in gilt letters. (Bonhams & Brooks) $310

A Constabulary tipstaff, first half of the 19th century, with threaded brass head cast and chased as a leaf calyx, on tubular brass socket engraved *John Richmond, Police Officer* and with three raised and knurled bands, and swelling ribbed hardwood grip pierced for a thong, 29.5cm. (Bonhams & Brooks) $565

1937 Coronation gold staff officer's baton. A rare example carried at the 12th May 1937 Coronation of His Majesty King George VI at Westminster Abbey. The gold painted baton has scarlet ends, the top one decorated with a transfer GVIR's Crowned Cypher and *Coronation 1937*. (Wallis & Wallis) $299

An iron tsuba, decorated in ko-sukashi with sakura, ichimagiri, and a broken raft, unsigned.
(Bonhams) $262

An iron tsuba by Masachika, signed *Masachika* and *A Kao*, Edo Period (19th century), oval iron plate with the broad rim formed as a bundle of fern roots from which gilt shoots are springing, 8.2cm.
(Christie's) $4,935

A large tsuba, with two hitsu-ana, decorated with a pair of crabs, among aquatic foliage, unsigned.
(Bonhams) $308

A sentoku Otsuki Mitsuhiro tsuba, signed, 19th century, the broad oval sentoku plate chiselled in katakiri and with cranes and lutus in silver, shibuichi and gilt, 7.3cm.
(Christie's) $12,690

An oval tsuba, decorated in yo-sukashi with lotus leaves, signed Chosu no (ju) Tomotsugu.
(Bonhams) $293

A daisho pair of shakudo tsuba, with signature, 19th century, depicting in iroe takazogan the Three Heroes of Han and Choryo and Kosekiko 7.5cm. and 7.1cm. respectively.
(Christie's) $11,985

A mokko-gata tsuba, decorated with a stylized design of Hikiryo, unsigned.(Bonhams) $115

A large early pierced iron tsuba of rounded form 8.4cm., inlaid with 5 brass Abumi amidst grass and raindrops, 3 shaped openings.
(Wallis & Wallis) $152

An oval tsuba, possibly Higo or Hayashi, decorated in ko & yo-sukashi, with flowers, unsigned.
(Bonhams) $308

Bedfordshire Regiment Great War officer's tunic, of Bedford cord material, each cuff with lace and crown indicating Major. (Bosleys) $348

Regular Line Regiment coatee, scarlet melton cloth with white facing to the collar, cuffs and turn backs of the tails. (Bosleys) $1,084

Honourable Artillery Company Colour Sgt's uniform, post 1902 dress tunic, comprising: peak forage cap, tunic of scarlet woollen cloth. (Bosleys) $611

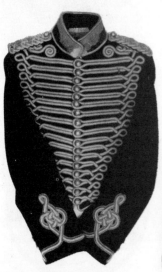

A post-1902 Lieutenant's full dress blue jacket of The Royal Horse Artillery, scarlet collar, gilt lace and cord trim, including 17 loops with ball buttons to chest. (Wallis & Wallis) $445

Child's blue velvet court dress, tail coat of dark blue velvet, matching waistcoat, velvet breeches, cocked hat of black beaver skin, black patent leather shoes, with court sword. (Bosleys) $222

Deputy Lord Lieutenant of Essex uniform, comprising: peaked forage cap, dark blue four pocket tunic, overalls with scarlet line, crimson waist sash with tassels, Wellington boots. (Bosleys) $551

German WWII period Army combat tunic, Model 1936 pattern tunic, green wool material, with pleats to the pocket and green collar. (Bosleys) $695

41st Bengal Infantry officer's coatee, rare Indian Army example, scarlet cloth, with dark blue facings to the collar and cuffs. (Bosleys) $473

Great War period United States Aviation Service pilot's tunic, light colored brown material, tailored with breast and waist pockets and stand collar. (Bosleys) $973

6th Punjab Rifles Victorian officer's tunic and mess jacket, Field Officer's Rifle pattern, tunic of beige melton cloth with scarlet facings to collar and cuffs. (Bosleys) $973

An assembled Victorian trooper's full dress uniform of The 12th (Prince of Wales's Royal) Lancers, including black patent leather lance cap, blue tunic with scarlet facings, yellow and scarlet girdle, webbing waistbelt, gauntlet gloves, overalls. (Wallis & Wallis) $1,248

Indian Army Major General's uniform, 1930 dated scarlet tunic, General officer's frock coat, dark blue material, with blue velvet facings to the cuff and collar. (Bosleys) $500

A Victorian 2nd Lieutenant's full dress scarlet tunic of The East Surrey Regiment, white facings, gilt lace and braid trim, the lace incorporating twin black lines. (Wallis & Wallis) $695

A Nazi army officer's tunic and equipment, comprising four pocket tunic, Iron Cross 1st class and peaked cap with goggles, dress dagger, half length leather boots, leather belt with metal buckle. (Wallis & Wallis) $957

A good post-1902 Major's full dress scarlet doublet of The Royal Scots (Lothian Regiment), blue facings, white edging, gilt lace and braid trim. (Wallis & Wallis) $361

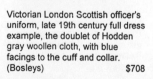

Victorian London Scottish officer's uniform, late 19th century full dress example, the doublet of Hodden gray woollen cloth, with blue facings to the cuff and collar. (Bosleys) $708

South Wales Borderers Great War other rank's tunic. 1902 pattern service dress tunic, sergeant's chevrons and five overseas inverted chevrons. (Bosleys) $630

A Georgian officer's full dress scarlet coatee of the Light Company, 2nd Royal Regiment of Militia (Tower Hamlets), blue facings, 2 gilt lace loops with buttons to collar. (Wallis & Wallis) $612

A post-1902 Lieutenant's full dress scarlet tunic of the 1st (Royal) Dragoons, blue facings, gilt lace, cord and braid trim.
(Wallis & Wallis) $514

Important General's scarlet full dress tunic of Sir Ian (Standish Monteith) Hamilton. Commander of Gallipoli Expedition of 1915.
(Bosleys) $2,740

A scarce other ranks full dress scarlet tunic of the 3rd Lanarkshire Rifle Volunteers, blue facings and shoulder straps, with embroidered 3. (Wallis & Wallis) $370

A Victorian Lt. Colonel's full dress blue tunic of The Royal Regiment of Artillery, scarlet collar, gilt lace and braid trim including braided cuff ornaments for field officer, shoulder cords. (Wallis & Wallis) $417

Royal Dublin Fusiliers Victorian officer's forage cap and uniform, cap of dark blue melton cloth, scarlet tunic, with dark blue facing, overalls and waist belt.
(Bosleys) $2,192

A good full dress scarlet tunic of Major General A.L. Ransome, DSO, MC, blue facings, gilt lace trim, special pattern shoulder cords, 3 buttons to slashed cuffs.
(Wallis & Wallis) $375

A good Chinese Boxer Rebellion period polearm, broad heavy swollen single edged blade 25in. pattern welded, with twin fullers, issuing from a brass dragon's head chiselled in relief. Down turned brass guard of squared form. (Wallis & Wallis) $626

A German mace, 16th century, steel, the head with six shaped flanges and short pointed finial, tubular haft with molding towards the grip and piercing for a thong, spirally fluted grip, and rounded pommel, 55cm. (Bonhams & Brooks) $2,070

A late 16th century Halberd, square section tapered top spike 22½in., bi-fullered blade with 3 acorn shaped openings, back spike pierced en-suite and deeply struck with maker's initials *WW* within lozenge. (Wallis & Wallis) $847

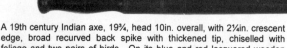

A 12th Lancers cavalry lance, 108in., fluted head 12½in. with open socket, with government inspector's stamps to head, shoe and bamboo haft, white buckskin wrist band and leather grip. (Wallis & Wallis) $517

A 19th century Indian axe, 19¾, head 10in. overall, with 2¼in. crescent edge, broad recurved back spike with thickened tip, chiselled with foliage and two pairs of birds. On its blue and red lacquered wooden haft. (Wallis & Wallis) $381

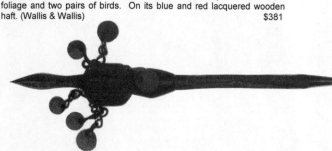

A scarce 19th century Sudanese Dervish mace, 28in. overall, swollen hardwood head with seven vanes, each with iron chain ending in a Turkish copper coin (most dated AH 1277=AD1860). Steel spearhead finials, haft covered with crocodile skin. (Wallis & Wallis) $408

A massive Chinese Boxer Rebellion period two handed executioner's sword, 56½in. overall, broad slightly curved single edged Japanese style blade, 37¾in. deeply chiselled with three Chinese characters. Iron guard, long handle with red leather incorporating raised knobs, iron ferrules. (Wallis & Wallis) $408

Winston S. Churchill, typed signed letter, Whitehall, 23rd May 1927, to W.E. Thompson, President of the Chamber of Commerce Manchester.
(Vennett-Smith) $1,280

Prince Charles & Princess Diana, signed Christmas greetings card, featuring a color photo of the Royal couple, full-length seated in a relaxed pose with the two young Princes William and Harry.
(Vennett Smith) $1,450

Marc Chagall, signed 7.5 x 10.5 bookweight photo in white crayon, overmounted, 11 x 14 overall.
(Vennett Smith) $138

Princess Diana, typed signed letter, in the unusual form 'Lady Diana', one page, Buckingham Palace, 24th March 1981, to Mrs. May Marks, thanking her for her "extremely kind letter of congratulations on my engagement".
(Vennett Smith) $1,692

Queen Elizabeth II, autograph signed letter, two pages, Sandringham, 27th Dec. 1962, to Dear Major David, stating that she was most delighted and surprised to receive 'the lovely earrings' for Christmas.
(Vennett Smith) $1,128

George Bernard Shaw, a souvenir programme for the Malvern Festival, 1935, signed to inside page by George Bernard Shaw, beneath photo.
(Vennett Smith) $254

Winston S. Churchill, signed album page, full signature.
(Vennett-Smith) $651

Edwin Aldrin, signed and inscribed color 8 x 10, half-length in Apollo 11 spacesuit, official NASA photograph.
(Vennett Smith) $160

Florence Nightingale autograph signed letter, one page, 13th Nov 1903, to George Winch, thanking him for his gift of two guineas.
(Vennett Smith) $638

Yuri Gagarin, signed postcard, head and shoulders in uniform. (Vennett Smith) $508

Joe Di Maggio, signed sepia 10 x 8, half-length wearing checked jacket standing at microphone with another gentleman, original still, signed in later years. (Vennett Smith) $96

Jacques Cousteau, signed 4 x 5.75, half-length on bridge of boat. (Vennett Smith) $43

Ferruccio Busoni, signed sepia postcard, head and shoulders with one side of his head resting on his hand, in pensive manner, Montreal, 1910. (Vennett Smith) $178

Russian Cosmonauts, signed 9.5 x 7.25 by Kubasov, Gorbatko, Filipchenko, Shatalov, Volkov (rare) and Yeliseyev, half-length standing and seated in two rows in relaxed mood. (Vennett Smith) $282

Rudolf Nureyev, signed ballet program to front cover, featuring portrait, Nureyev Festival at the London Coliseum, 5th-30th June 1979, three tickets affixed to inside page. (Vennett Smith) $73

John Glenn, signed and inscribed color 8 x 10, head and shoulders in NASA spacesuit and helmet (mercury).(Vennett Smith) $96

Haile Selassie, small piece cut from diary, 2.5 x 1.5, laid down to album page, with attached newspaper photo. (Vennett Smith) $109

Nicolae Ceaucescu, signed color 5.5 x 8.5, to lower white border, head and shoulders smiling. (Vennett Smith) $110

Yasser Arafat, signed 4 x 6.
(Vennett Smith) $92

Bill Clinton, signed color 8.5 x 6,
three quarter length waving at the
1999 Cologne economic summit.
(Vennett Smith) $212

James Hunt, signed 4 x 6 postcard,
half-length.(Vennett Smith) $87

Lillie Langtry, a good sepia cabinet
photo, three quarter length seated
in costume as Cleopatra, presented
by Langtry to her stage manager,
Mr. E.B. Norman.
(Vennett Smith) $493

John Chard, VC, Officer
Commanding Rorke's Drift,
autograph signed letter, one page,
17th Feb. 1880, to George R.
Brown thanking him for his kind
letter and good wishes, written the
month he returned to England from
Zululand..
(Vennett Smith) $1,885

Harry Houdini, signed sepia 4.5 x 7,
with first name only, in green ink,
head and shoulders wearing suit,
smiling, together with a hard-back
edition of Magical Rope Ties &
Escapes by Houdini.
(Vennett Smith) $1,813

Conchita Supervia, signed and
inscribed postcard, head and
shoulders smiling, 1934.
(Vennett Smith) $247

Glamour, signed color 10 x 8 by
both Cindy Crawford and Claudia
Schiffer, head and shoulders back
to back. (Vennett Smith) $101

Anna Pavlova, signed postcard,
full-length wearing white dress, in
ballet dance pose.
(Vennett Smith) $203

Dalai Lama, signed color 5 x 3.5, head and shoulders. (Vennett Smith) $56

Muhammad Ali, signed color 8 x 10, half-length wearing white gown and resting his chin on his hands. (Vennett Smith) $155

Pele, signed 4 x 5.25, half-length heading ball in New York Cosmos jersey. (Vennett Smith) $109

Joe Di Maggio, signed and inscribed 4 x 5, full-length in NY Yankees Sportswear, in dugout, with baseball bat, modern reproduction signed in later years. (Vennett Smith) $85

Napoleon I, documented signed, *Nap*, one page, Paris, 2nd March 1806, in French, to Monsieur Alerini, untranslated although mentioning Italy. (Vennett Smith) $1,301

Benito Mussolini, a good signed 7 x 9, with surname only, half-length reading some papers, dated in his hand *1934*, together with a contemporary piece of sheet music for Al Duce Giovinezza!, (Vennett Smith) $457

Margaret Thatcher, signed 7 x 10, photo as Minister of Education 1970, though signature later. (Vennett Smith) $80

Queen Elizabeth II & Prince Philip, signed Christmas greetings card by both Queen Elizabeth II and Prince Philip. (Vennett Smith) $592

J.K. Rowling, signed and inscribed color 5 x 7, half-length gently resting her head on one hand. (Vennett Smith) $592

J.M. Fangio, signed 4 x 6, half-length in coat and cap.
(Vennett Smith) $85

Jack Swigert, signed first day cover, America's Third Lunar Landing, rare, slight creasing.
(Vennett Smith) $239

Barry Fitzgerald, signed 3 x 4.5, candid pose, half-length standing wearing overcoat and hat, smoking cigarette. (Vennett Smith) $55

Pope John Paul II, signed color 4 x 6, half-length in semi-profile wearing white robes, with one hand slightly raised.
(Vennett Smith) $274

Princess Diana, autograph signed letter, three pages, 26th Jan 1997, to Dearest Margaret (Mrs M.A. Spratt), on her personally monogrammed stationery from Kensington Palace, stating that she was touched to receive her letter.
(Vennett Smith) $2,603

Prince Philip, a signed 16 x 22 photo, to lower photographer's mount, three quarter length standing in RAF uniform, 1953, photo by Baron.
(Vennett Smith) $247

Michael Schumacher, signed color 8 x 12, in red racing kit, speaking on mobile phone.
(Vennett Smith) $92

Gagarin & Titov, signed color 6 x 4 by both Yuri Gagarin and Gherman Titov, half-length seated together reading a newspaper.
(Vennett Smith) $329

Nellie Melba, signed postcard, full-length seated at small table with clasped hands raised to her chin.
(Vennett Smith) $109

Max Baer, signed and inscribed
sepia 7 x 9, head and shoulders
wearing suit and polkadot tie, dated
15th Dec 1933.
(Vennett Smith) $75

A Victorian Invitation to
Westminster Abbey to view the
Coronation of Queen Victoria 1838,
the card by Dobbs.
(Brightwells) $493

Thomas Beecham, signed 8 x 10,
to lower white border, head and
shoulders wearing suit and tie.
(Vennett Smith) $116

Sarah Duchess of York, signed
color 7.5 x 9.5, to lower
photographer's mount, head and
shoulders wearing light brown
leather flying jacket and with a pair
of flying goggles in her hands.
(Vennett Smith) $134

Queen Elizabeth II, autograph
signed letter, two pages,
Sandringham, 7th Jan 1972, to
Dear Archie (Major A. David, the
Queen's Polo Manager), thanking
him for a generous Christmas
present. (Vennett Smith) $592

John F. Kennedy, small, slightly
irregularly clipped signed piece,
hurried example, attractively
overmounted beneath a 4.5 x 6.5
photo, together with a signed color
7 x 9.5 by Ted Kennedy.
(Vennett Smith) $733

Princess Diana, a fine large signed
color 11.5 x 14.5, three quarter
length seated in a formal pose
wearing a plain black dress, dated
in her hand *1986.*
(Vennett Smith) $3,596

Hoagy Carmichael, signed 8 x 10
head and shoulders with inscription
added later in different color ink,
slight wrinkling.
(Vennett Smith) $116

King Edward VII, a rare early
signed sepia 10 x 12.5 photo,
Albert Edward, as Prince.
(Vennett Smith) $575

Rudolf Nureyev, two signed and inscribed 8 x 10s, different ballet poses, some surface creasing.
(Vennett Smith) $130

Muhammad Ali, signed color 8 x 10, half-length in bare-chested pose hitting punch ball.
(Vennett Smith) $103

Wallis Windsor, signed 4 x 5, full-length probably in the Bahamas, creasing and edge knocks.
(Vennett Smith) $218

Princess Diana, a good autograph signed letter, three pages, Kensington Palace, 24th Feb 1991, to Dearest Ivy (Mrs. J. Woodward), on her personal monogrammed stationery.
(Vennett Smith) $3,480

Jawaharlal Nehru, a fine signed 9.5 x 12, to lower white border, head and shoulders in profile, in pensive mood, dated in his hand *1958*, framed glazed, 10.5 x 12.5 overall.
(Vennett Smith) $319

J.K. Rowling, autograph signed letter, one page, no date, to 'Dear Freddie (one of my favourite names)', stating that Donald had written to her saying that her correspondent had enjoyed the Harry Potter books.
(Vennett Smith) $712

Wernher von Braun, signed 8 x 10, head and shoulders wearing suit, with two models of space rockets alongside, original packet. (NASA).
(Vennett Smith) $409

Winston S. Churchill, a 3.5 x 4.5 photo, laid down and signed to mount, 5 x 7 overall, water staining affecting signature.
(Vennett Smith) $987

Buzz Aldrin, signed and inscribed color 8 x 10 photo, half-length wearing white spacesuit, with an image of the moon in background.
(Vennett Smith) $144

1961 Maserati Type 63 V12, engine No. 63010, engine V12, 2989cc, 320bhp at 8,500rpm, the successor to the Tipo 61 Birdcage of 1960 combined the Formula 1 V12 engine in an intricate tubular chassis.(Christie's) $59,454

Original veteran car horn, with double coiled silvered trumpet, 33cm. long. (Auction Team Köln) $401

Major H.O.D. Segrave, The Irving Napier Golden Arrow, steering wheel from the 1929 World Landspeed Record Winning vehicle.
(Bonhams) $6,210

Bugatti tool kit, tan leather zip up case embossed *Bugatti* to the front, opening to interior housing ten tools, case 25 x 19cm.
(Bonhams & Brooks) $3,834

Jo Siffert – Cooper Maserati Monaco 1968; an original pair of wheels from the Rob Walker entered Cooper Maserati, as used in practice by Siffert.
(Christie's) $586

S.C.H. Davis, the 120mph Brooklands Badge, by Spencer of London with its correct '120 M.P.H.' attached black enamel plaque, replacing the B.A.R.C. motif.
(Bonhams) $5,244

A Servizio Assistenza Ferrari sign, printed and embossed plastic in aluminum frame, 91cm. high.
(Bonhams) $1,794

1954 Belgian Grand Prix, original race advertising poster, after an original design by E.A. Hermans, colored screen print on paper by Rapid Press, colored screen print on paper by Rapid Press, Liége, unframed, 55 x 73cm.
(Bonhams & Brooks) $398

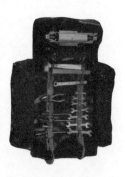

Ferrari 275 – tool kit roll, dark brown vinyl with leather handle and straps, fitted with fifteen tools, jack, and (modern) warning triangle.
(Bonhams & Brooks) $1,988

A radiator for a British Humber car. (Auction Team Köln) $401

G.W. Scott and Sons, a wicker suitcase style, four-person picnic set, fine raffia covered drinks bottle, central food box, sandwich boxes, four serving plates and china cups with saucers. (Bonhams) $1,104

12 Hours of Sebring, 1963, an original poster with artwork by John Zito, mounted on linen, 28 x 20in. (Christie's) $940

Ferrari prancing horse, in bronze on marble base, a token of respect to Luigi Villoresi from an Italian Car Club, 10½ x 5in. (Christie's) $3,450

1930 Bentley 'The Four Models,' a rare brochure for the world exporters, Rootes Ltd, 16pp with grey cover and black and gold tooling, features the 4.5 liter and Blower, Speed Six and Standard Six. (Bonhams) $1,932

A Dependence oil powered rear lamp, by J & R Oldfield of Birmingham, unusual brass-construction version, 1910, oil reservoir missing, 10in. high. (Bonhams) $345

Stephen Grebel electric spotlamp, late 1920s, straw colored nickel plating, correct single arm swivel mounting and correct Grebel etched front glass. (Bonhams) $1,104

A 'fat' Shell glass petrol pump globe by Webb's Crystal, re-lettered in red, some chipping around base rim, 50cm. high. (Bonhams) $524

An Alfa Romeo illuminated sign, circular double sided printed and embossed plastic panels within wall mounting metal frame, 90cm. diameter. (Bonhams) $442

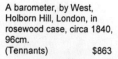

A Queen Anne walnut
column barometer, Daniel

A barometer, by West,
Holborn Hill, London, in
rosewood case, circa 1840,
96cm.
(Tennants) $863

A mahogany stick
barometer, W & S Jones,
London, circa 1800, 37in.
(Christie's) $2,940

Quare, London, early 18th
century, 39½in. high.
(Christie's)
                    $37,720

A wheel barometer, by G.
Groce, York, in mahogany
case, circa 1830, 98cm.
(Tennants) $1,334

An Edwardian inlaid
mahogany wall barometer
by J. Hicks, London, in a
banjo case, 98cm.
(Bearne's) $643

A Victorian walnut cased
stick barometer and
thermometer by J. Hicks of
London, 40in. high.
(Canterbury) $1,320

A large mahogany wheel
barometer with inset
timepiece, George Bianchi,
Ipswich, circa 1810, 50in.
(Christie's) $3,822

A 19th century stick
barometer, the ivory
register inscribed *George
Wâdham, Bath*, with
thermometer, in rosewood
case, 37½in. high.
(Andrew Hartley) $862

A rosewood wheel barometer, English, mid 19th century, unsigned, 98cm.
(Bonhams) $264

An early Victorian oak stick barometer by Negretti and Zambra, London, circa 1850, 120cm. high.
(Wintertons) $1,485

A French giltwood wall barometer, 18th century, the trunk with thermometer and circular card dial, 42½in. high.
(Christie's) $2,180

A carved oak wall barometer, Admiral Fitzroy, mid 19th century, 48in.(Christie's) $809

A rosewood bow fronted stick barometer by Gardner & Co., Glasgow, circa 1840, 98cm.
(Tennants) $5,495

A wheel barometer by G Volanterio, Doncaster with thermometer, in mahogany case with stringing and marquetry, 38¾in. high.
(Andrew Hartley) $875

An early oak stick barometer, John Coggs, London, early 18th century, 43½in.
(Christie's) $2,058

English Georgian mahogany wheel barometer, early 19th century, the dial signed *Dolland, London*, 36½in. long.
(Skinner) $1,840

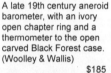

A late 19th century aneroid barometer, with an ivory open chapter ring and a thermometer to the open carved Black Forest case. (Woolley & Wallis) $185

A mahogany angle barometer, John Stenson, Derby, circa 1780, 38in. (Bonhams) $2,760

A mahogany wheel barometer, P Introssi, London, 19th century, 38in. (Bonhams) $690

A George III mahogany stick barometer, George Adams, No. 60, London, 43¼in. high.(Christie's) $16,697

A mahogany wheel barometer, T Ronchetti, London, circa 1810, 39½in. (Bonhams) $994

An aneroid barometer, with thermometer, having silvered dials to the walnut banjo shape case. (Woolley & Wallis) $393

A rosewood wheel barometer, G Arzoni, Canterbury, late 19th century, 39in. (Bonhams) $442

A gilt-metal, walnut and mahogany siphon tube barometer, in the style of Daniel Quare; probably by Garner & Marney; circa 1960, 39½in. high. (Christie's) $10,563

Chemehuevi Indian basketry jar with geometric design, 7in. diameter.
(Sotheby's) $1,840

Fishing creel, shows good age. Latch broken, 12in. by 7in.
(Sotheby's) $517

Zia Pueblo Indian jar with bird motif, signed *Seferina P Bell*, 7½in x 6½in.
(Sotheby's) $1,955

Nantucket light ship purse basket, America, 20th century, oval form with lid, swing handle, carved ivory whale mounted on walnut oval lid medallion, base incised *Made in Nantucket, Jose Formoso Reyes*, with a rendering of the island, 7in. high. (Skinner) $3,105

Yokut-Tulare Indian basketry bowl with geometric design, 12½in. diameter.
(Sotheby's) $3,162

Nantucket light ship basket, America, round form with swing handle, inscribed note on base states *Light Boat Baskets made by Joseph G. Fisher, Nantucket, 1893*, 7½in. high.
(Skinner) $1,840

Covered Nantucket basket, 1973, carved swing handle on round basket, the lid with turned checkerboard inlaid finial and peg, 6in. high. (Skinner) $690

Swing handled Nantucket basket, good patina, 8¾in. diameter.
(Sotheby's) $1,265

Handled Clamath Indian basket with geometric design, 13in. diameter.(Sotheby's) $1,092

A Harding Double Front Steering tricycle, with a 22in. straight tube open frame, 18 x 1³/₈in. steering and 26in. driving wheels, Westwood rims, Sturmey Archer combination 3 speed and brake dated 1956, cable center pull calipers to both front wheels, turned back front bars and Middlemore B2 saddle.
(Bonhams) $221

A Moulton Stowaway bicycle, No 150196, 1960s, apparently unused, complete with a toolbag, pump and other accessories. (Bonhams) $552

A 51in. Ordinary Bicycle, a circa 1882 machine having radial spokes, crescent rims, 18in. rear wheel, Bown bearings, hollow forks, tapered round backbone, cranked down bars, rat-trap pedals and brake lever. Repainted matt black.
(Bonhams) $2,346

A Singer cycle Co. Gentleman's Roadster, No. 153721, circa 1900, the restored machine features a 25in. frame, 28in. wheels, brown enamel with gold lining, Singer 'inflator' bars, steering lock, combination rear contracting band brake and free-wheel or fixed-wheel lock, mudguards, patented front block brake, frame and saddle bag and leather saddle.
(Bonhams) $1,932

A Starley & Sutton 'Meteor' rear steering tricycle, circa 1882, with 42in. driving wheels, a 17in. steerer, 30in. track, radial spokes, crescent rim, chain drive to the left, rear spoon brakes operated from the left handle, rack and pinion steering to the right handle.
(Bonhams) $8,280

Manufacture Francaise d'Armes et Cycles (Manufrance) 'Hirondelle Superbe' Safety Bicyclette, circa 1890, patented sprung frame and handlebars, original horn grips, restored, 26in. front wheel and the 30in. driving wheel have been rebuilt.
(Bonhams) $13,800

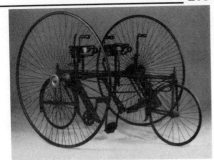

A Coventry Sociable Convertible Quadcycle, circa 1882 with 42in. driving wheels, 22in. rear and forward steering wheels, 52in. track as a sociable, 26in. track as a solo. Radial spokes, crescent rims, rack and pinion steering operated by the left hand rider, each wheel independently driven from cranks and chains. (Bonhams) $41,400

An Itera plastic bicycle, dating circa 1985, this buff colored machine appears to be ready to ride either on VCC club runs or as a means of exercise to the local shops. (Bonhams) $152

A 56in. Ordinary Bicycle, circa 1884 machine with radial spokes, crescent rims, 18in. rear wheel, Bown bearings, hollow forks, tapered round backbone, cow-horn bars, Brooks International saddle, rebuilt rat-trap pedals and brake. (Bonhams) $2,484

A Co 'Parisienne' Velocipede Bicycle, No. 2259, circa 1869, with 34in. front and 27in. rear wheels, original brown enamel with yellow lining, three-bar pedals, front fork oilers (to be fitted), interesting brass clips to leg rests. (Bonhams) $3,588

A Dursley Pedersen bicycle, circa 1914 gentleman's machine having Westwood steel 28 x 1½in. rims, Sturmey Tricoaster hub, number C29631 with control. All the equipment appears to be original and in sound order, machine refinished but fitted with original tool bag and a Lucas No. 65 bell dated January 1923. (Bonhams) $1,656

Coventry Machinist Company 50in. 'Special Club' Ordinary, 1882, nipple adjusted radial spokes, straight handle bars, brake to the driving wheel, CMC patented rubber seat suspension, rat trap pedals, oval backbone, semi-double hollow forks back and front, leg guard and leather covered saddle. (Bonhams) $4,416

A gilt bronze and ivory figure, cast and carved from a model by Lugh Salero, engraved signature to base, 36cm. high.
(Christie's) $3,290

'The Archer' a cold painted bronze and ivory figure, cast and carved from a model by F. Preiss, incised signature to onyx base, 23cm. high.
(Christie's) $16,450

A cold painted bronze and ivory figure, cast and carved from a model by F. Preiss, incised signature to base, 24cm. high.
(Christie's) $24,675

A silvered and patinated bronze figure group, cast from a model by Bouraine, signed in the bronze and engraved *Etling Paris*, 29cm. high.
(Christie's) $3,125

A bronze model of a soldier on horseback, late 19th century, the figure with backpacks shown astride the horse, the naturalistic plinth inscribed *SLD.COLOMA 1882*, 23in. high.
(Christie's) $3,619

A gilt and patinated bronze figure, cast from a model by Bruno Zach, signed in the bornze, stamped *Made in Austria*, 25cm. high.
(Christie's) $3,948

Ferdinand Preiss, 'Flame Leaper', 1930s, cold painted bronze and ivory, modelled as a scantily clad female figure leaping over rising flames, 34cm.
(Sotheby's) $32,408

Demêtre H. Chiparus, fan dancer, 1920s, silvered and cold-painted bronze and ivory, modelled as a kneeling female dancer in a catsuit, 15in. (Sotheby's) $25,738

A French bronze figure of a gladiator 'Corybante', late 19th century, after Louis Leon Cugnot, the figure shown standing with shield and short sword, with a cherub at his feet, 37in. high.
(Christie's) $2,715

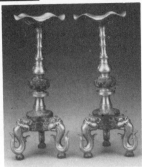

An Art Deco gilt bronze figure, of a snake dancer, 34.5cm. high.
(Christie's) $4,935

A pair of Chinese parcel gilt bronze candlesticks, 19th century, the leafy drip pans above knopped baluster stems and triform bases, 13½in. high. (Christie's) $1,629

A Continental gilt and patinated bronze model of a cherub, late 19th or early 20th century, modelled in relief, the base inscribed
L. Madrassi, 11¾in. high.
(Christie's) $2,353

A French bronze group 'Ravageole and Ravageot', late 19th century, after Emmanuel Frémiet, modelled as two hounds standing, the oval base inscribed E.Fremiet, 5½in. high. (Christie's) $2,715

A French bronze group of two dancing maidens, late 19th century, the partly draped figures shown dancing standing on a simulated checkered floor, inscribed E.Satoris, 23in. high.
(Christie's) $2,715

Prof. Otto Poertzel, 'The Aristocrats', 1930s, cold-painted bronze and ivory, modelled as a woman in a long fur-lined dress, accompanied by her two borzois on leashes, 15¾in.
(Sotheby's) $13,050

'Flute Player' a cold painted bronze and ivory figure, cast and carved from a model by F. Preiss, modelled as a striding flute player, 46cm. high.
(Christie's) $10,199

Prof. Otto Poertzel, minstrel and maiden group, 1920s, modelled as a couple in medieval costume, the woman seated side-saddle on a horse looking down at the young minstrel, 22in.
(Sotheby's) $20,735

A cold painted bronze and ivory figure, cast and carved from a model by Philippe, signed in the bronze, 30.5cm. high.
(Christie's) $15,627

A bronze bust of a Lady, late 19th century, after Georges van der Straeten, the laughing figure shown with hat and loose drapery about her shoulders, 21in. high.
(Christie's) $1,719

A patinated bronze figural group, cast from a model by Branli, 1920s, modelled as female figure in elegant dress standing with attendant dog either side, 29in. diameter. (Christie's) $1,175

A French bronze model of a boy, late 19th century, shown standing with arms clasped behind his back, the base marked, 7in. high.
(Christie's) $1,538

A patinated bronze figure, cast from a model by Lorenzl, 1920s, of naked young female standing holding a bow, on rectangular bronze, green onyx and striated black marble base, 17in. high.
(Christie's) $5,880

Pierre Le Faguays, 'Dancer with Thyrsus', 1920s, gilt and cold-painted bronze, modelled as a semi-nude dancer wearing a skirt, holding a pole draped with fruiting vine behind her shoulders, 55cm.
(Sotheby's) $6,090

An English bronze figure of a female nude, second half 20th century, modelled sitting with naturalistically cast tousled hair, her left knee drawn up, 33in. high.
(Christie's) $995

Gerdago, exotic dancer, 1920s, cold-painted bronze and ivory figure of a female dancer in mid step, wearing a tight fitting catsuit with flared sleeves and legs, 31.5cm.
(Sotheby's) $6,960

'The Hunter' a gilt bronze and marble figural clock, cast from a model by Georges Lavroff, 1920s, the geometric dial flanked by panels cast with leaping gazelles, 20in. diameter.
(Christie's) $2,520

'Bat-Wing Girl' a patinated and cold-painted bronze figure, cast from a model by Otto Poertzel, circa 1920, the young woman in bat-wing dress, cold-painted with metallic pink and with pink paste roundels, 24½in. high.
(Christie's) $7,560

A silvered and cold-painted bronze and ivory figure, cast and carved from a model by Gerdago, 1920s, of an exotic dancer poised on one leg, 12½in. high.
(Christie's) $4,369

Gilt bronze neo-classical-style figural wall plaque of an Autumn Beauty, early 20th century, the reclining figure holding a garland of acorns and oak leaves, 26in. long.
(Skinner) $2,300

'Fan Dancer' a silvered and patinated bronze figure, cast from a model by M. Bouraine, circa 1920s, of naked female standing on tiptoe, holding aloft a large fan, 36.5cm. high. (Christie's) $3,697

A pair of ormolu figures of maidens, late 19th century / 20th century, each in classical dress, one playing the flute, the other a lyre, on a circular rouge griotte base, 11½in. high. (Christie's) $8,009

A black patinated bronze figure, cast from a model by Christa-Winsloe Hatvany, 1920s, modelled as a stylized faun, on a rectangular base, signed in the bronze, 38cm. high. (Christie's) $5,377

A pair of ormolu-mounted marble and bronze seven-light torchères, late 19th century, cast after a model by Mathurin Moreau, each modelled as a scantily clad maiden holding a branch aloft issuing seven foliate scrolling arms, 58in. high.
(Christie's) $32,200

A patinated bronze tray, by Edgar Brandt, 1920s, the rim modelled as snake body, the handles as a pair of facing snake heads biting a ball, the well with scrolling pattern, 13¾in. diameter.
(Christie's) $3,024

An Art Nouveau patinated bronze plate, 32cm. diameter.
(Christie's) $279

A large English bronze figure of a nude girl, last quarter 20th century, modelled seated reading a newspaper inscribed *News Flash*. to the reverse, 50in. high.
(Christie's) $1,266

A bronze figure of Venus drying herself, 20th century, on a rectangular plinth, 28½in. high. (Christie's) $3,739

Isidore Jules Bonheur (French, 1827-1901), large bronze figure of an angry bull, the figure with head lowered, pawing ground with foreleg, 13¾in. high, 24in. long, (Skinner) $5,463

A Neopolitan bronze bust of Seneca, late 19th century, after the Antique, later mounted on an onyx socle, the bronze 13in. high. (Christie's) $5,983

A Rischmann figure of a bird, 1930s, silvered bronze, modelled as the figure of a bird of prey clawing a rock, 26½in. (Sotheby's) $1,083

Austrian cold painted bronze owl figure enclosing a female nude, late 19th/early 20th century, the realistically modelled owl set with glass eyes, standing on stack of small books with trailing ties, 7¾in. (Skinner) $3,450

A patinated bronze model of a crane, 19th century, striding forwards with its head lowered to preen its feathers, set on a quartz base, 11½in. high. (Christie's) $1,974

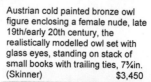

Henri Godet (French, fl. late 19th/ early 20th century), bronze bust of a water nymph, the beauty with long hair and ivy coronet, emerging from frame of bulrushes, 16in. high. (Skinner) $2,645

Antoine-Louis Barye (French 1796-1875), bronze figure of a rearing bull attacked by a jaguar, F. Barbedienne foundry mark, 11in. long. (Skinner) $4,025

A large Neapolitan bronze figure of the seated Mercury, late 19th century, after the Antique, formerly on a marble base, 37in. high. (Christie's) $13,088

A bronze equestrian group of Joan of Arc, late 19th or early 20th century, after Prosper d'Epinay, the figure shown with full suit of armor, 17¼in. high.
(Christie's) $1,522

A pair of French bronze models of sphinxes, late 19th century, each seated on its haunches, 8½in. high.
(Christie's) $2,244

An Italian bronze bust of Nero, possibly 17th century, the emperor portrayed in togate military dress with a brooch to his right shoulder, above a cartouche plaque, 30.8cm. high. (Christie's) $2,362

A Continental bronze group of Hercules and the Lernaean Hydra, indistinctly stamped to the base, second half 19th century, after the Antique, 30.2cm. high.
(Christie's) $2,805

A Continental bronze group of the Wrestlers, early 20th century, after the Antique, 18in. wide.
(Christie's) $2,991

A French bronze bust of a helmeted warrior, possibly Ajax, marked *Richard*, late 19th century, the head facing slightly to dexter, the helmet with lion's mask, 19in. high.
(Christie's) $1,588

An Italian bronze group of the Colleoni monument, after Verrocchio, second half 19th century, on stepped plinth cast with a relief frieze, 22¾in. high.
(Christie's) $2,991

A pair of Continental bronze models of the Furietti Centaurs, possibly late 19th century, after the Antique, 35.8cm. high.
(Christie's) $8,974

Jules Moigniez (French, 1835-1894), bronze figure of a stag, the figure modelled walking down a slope, with dark greenish brown patination, 7⅝in.
(Skinner) $1,380

Mignon, a brown and green patinated bronze bust by E. Villanis, 1896. (Galerie Moderne) $2,102

A large bronze model of a horse, 20th century, shown standing, 45in. high, 69in. long. (Christie's) $2,895

A bronze bust of a lady, early 20th century, after a model by Jules Desbois (b.1851), mounted on a variegated marble plinth, the bust 15in. high. (Christie's) $4,229

A bronze figure Pax et Labor by Emile Louis Picault, modelled as a standing young laborer holding a hammer, 29in. high. (Andrew Hartley) $2,695

An early 19th century bronze figure of Chronos depicted seated on an orb wearing flowing robes, 11¼in. high. (Andrew Hartley) $644

A 19th century Continental cold painted bronze figure of a grouse, depicted standing, impressed mark, 6½in. high. (Andrew Hartley) $1,078

A 19th century Continental cold painted bronze figure of a partridge, lot, 9¼in. high. (Andrew Hartley) $3,080

A Neapolitan bronze portrait roundel, dated 1859, after a model by Charles Henri Joseph Cordier, depicting the bust of a woman in profile, her plaited hair tied up behind her, 17in. diameter. (Christie's) $493

An oriental bronze figure of a seated Buddha, signed, mid brown patination, 6in. high. (Andrew Hartley) $616

An early 19th century leather fire bucket with copper rim and studded welts and leather strap handle. (Dee Atkinson & Harrison)

$231

A pair of George III mahogany and brass bound peat buckets, of tapering form with loop handles, 15½in. high. (Andrew Hartley)

$2,016

A George mahogany navette shaped bucket with brass banding liner and swing handle. (Dee Atkinson & Harrison)

$1,815

Pair of painted leather fire baskets, America, 19th century, both inscribed *Semper Paratus L.T. Jackson*, in gilt in a leafy scroll decorated black cartouche on a red ground, 15½in. high. (Skinner)

$7,475

A pair of George III brass bound mahogany peat buckets, early 19th century, of ribbed tapering form, with reeded bands and loop handles, 16in. high. (Christie's)

$15,228

A pair of paint-decorated leather fire buckets, American, dated *1801*, each with a black leather strap above a black-painted tapering cylindrical body embellished with two gold bands, 12¼in. high. (Christie's)

$2,233

Paint decorated leather fire bucket, *Mechanic Fire Society Marcellus Bufford*, probably Portsmouth, New Hampshire, 12¼in. high. (Skinner)

$13,800

A pair of Irish George III large brass-bound mahogany buckets, each of circular and tapering form with shell-enriched carrying handles and spirally-reeded sides, 18¾in. diameter. (Christie's)

$66,740

An Irish George III mahogany plate bucket, the swing handle with scrolling attachments to brass banding, 15in. high, 14¼in. diameter. (Woolley & Wallis)

$2,644

A Regency tortoiseshell tea-caddy, the rectangular casket with rounded corners inlaid along the edges with silvered-banding, 7½in. wide. (Christie's) $3,337

A Victorian mahogany portable partner's stationery rack, second half 19th century, each breakarch end with a molded panel, a set of letter racks, calendar holder and pen trough to each side, 24¾in. wide. (Christie's) $2,533

A George II brass-inlaid and mounted amboyna casket, inlaid overall to each corner with a foliage scroll, the hinged rectangular top with carrying-handle, 10½in. wide. (Christie's) $13,348

A polychrome oak wall-hanging rush-light or candle-box, North European, possibly Icelandic, 18th century, the sliding cover to the front carved in relief with a bird perched on a leafy bough, 15½in. high. (Christie's) $7,130

A pair of late Victorian 'Regency Revival' mahogany knife-boxes, each with pierced brass gallery on a molded, stepped fiddle-back mahogany domed top, above a panelled swivelling door with fitted reverse, 19in. high. (Christie's) $2,362

Burlwood and brass inlay boxed cordial set, late 19th/ early 20th century, opening to interior fitted for two decanters and ten cordial glasses, together with decanters and thirteen miscellaneous cordials, 10¼in. wide. (Skinner) $115

An early 19th century tortoiseshell tea caddy of rounded oblong form, the domed lid with pewter stringing, raised on four ivory bun feet, 4¾in. wide. (Andrew Hartley) $989

An unusual late Regency rosewood and brass inlaid tea caddy, some damage, 17cm. wide. (Bonhams & Brooks) $600

A Shaker bentwood box, second half 19th century, the oval with a fitted lid, fastened with three tapered swallow-tail fingers, inscribed *J.W. Adams 1862*, 6in. long. (Sotheby's) $920

A Napoleon III ormolu-mounted turquoise ground porcelain-inset tulipwood casket, third quarter 19th century, domed rectangular hinged top inset centrally with a scene of lovers in a landscape, 23¼in. wide.
(Christie's) $5,750

Regency period coromandel writing slope, inlaid with brass foliate designs with mother of pearl detail, the lid enclosing fitted interior, applied throughout with brass strap work, late 18th/early 19th century, 15in. (G.A. Key) $890

Academy polychrome painted and ink decorated pine box, the lid interior inscribed *Nancy B. Green Hartford VT. June 7th 1827*, with an inspirational verse contained in a floral wreath, 3 x 8 x 5in.
(Skinner) $5,750

An early 19th century French flame mahogany musical sewing box, modelled as a grand piano, with boxwood and ebony inlay, the interior set with a mirror, with mother of pearl sewing set, 31cm. long.
(Bonhams & Brooks) $1,540

Alessandro Mendini, made by Bracciodiferro for Cassina, 'Valigia per Ultimo Viaggio', unique piece, 1979, aluminum and concrete, 17in. (Sotheby's) $5,520

Green-painted pine sewing box, America, 19th century, turned finial on round revolving thread holder over a square box with drawer, 6½in. high.(Skinner) $690

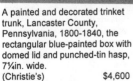

A painted and decorated trinket trunk, Lancaster County, Pennsylvania, 1800-1840, the rectangular blue-painted box with domed lid and punched-tin hasp, 7¼in. wide.
(Christie's) $4,600

A Continental fruitwood tea caddy in the form of an apple, mid 19th century, with iron escutcheon and steel lock, 4¾in. high.
(Christie's) $3,634

A Federal inlaid and veneered tea caddy, American, 1790-1810, the rectangular hinged top with cross-banded edge opening to a conforming case with similarly cross-banded edges, 10in. wide.
(Christie's) $1,380

A late Regency tortoiseshell veneered tea caddy, second quarter 19th century, with pagoda style cover, raised on ivory bun feet, the interior with ivory banding and twin subsidiary covers, 7½in. wide. (Christie's) $3,384

A George III satinwood tea caddy, late 18th century, of rectangular outline with canted blind fluted angles, with oval shell paterae to the top and front, 7½in. wide. (Christie's) $2,907

A Victorian tortoiseshell and mother of pearl veneered tea caddy, mid 19th century, with part-fluted sides and flared foot, raised on bun feet, 8in. wide.(Christie's) $2,199

A Northern European tortoiseshell veneered table casket, probably Dutch, 18th century, with domed cover, the panels with ivory banding, with foliate cast silvered metal mounts, 9½in. wide. (Christie's) $7,106

A Victorian tortoiseshell veneered and ivory banded jewelry box, second quarter, 19th century, the hinged cover with pyramid finial above ogee molded and waisted edges, 23.1cm. wide. (Christie's) $8,554

A late Regency tortoiseshell veneered tea caddy, second quarter 19th century, of pagoda form, with pewter inlay, the interior with twin subsidiary covers and ivory banding, 8in. wide. (Christie's) $4,061

A William IV rosewood letterbox, circa 1830, the rectangular box with pierced sides, the cover with mother of pearl inlaid plaques, *Unanswered* and *Answered*, 8½in. wide. (Christie's) $1,272

A Black Forest carved pine table casket, late 19th or early 20th century, of stepped oval outline raised on scroll feet, the cover surmounted with a group of birds amidst foliage, 13½in. high. (Christie's) $1,184

A George III mahogany and satinwood banded tea caddy, last quarter 18th century, of sarcophagus form, the canted cover rising to a rectangular plateau, with fruitwood stringing overall, 7½in. wide. (Christie's)· $526

A tortoiseshell and mother of pearl veneered table casket, probably Portuguese, early 19th century, the rectangular ebonized case decorated overall with geometric and stylized foliate banding, 18¼in. wide.(Christie's) $6,091

A Victorian oak pillar-type postbox, circa 1875, with hinged door to the front, below the hexagonal domed and molded top, 15¼in. high. (Christie's) $7,896

A large and impressive late Victorian brass mounted oak coal bin, late 19th century, with angled double hinged covers, with brass banding to the borders and pierced decorative scrolls to the panels, 32in. wide.(Christie's) $8,177

A tortoiseshell veneered teacaddy, second quarter 19th century, with ivory stringing and escutcheon, the interior fitted with two canisters with tortoiseshell veneered lids, 10¾in. wide. (Christie's) $3,997

A late Victorian or Edwardian pine post box, late 19th or early 20th century, the rectangular box with molded side panels, the door with letter aperture, 44in. high. (Christie's) $2,876

A Regency tortoiseshell veneered tea caddy, early 19th century, with silver stringing to the borders, the domed cover with engraved cartouche, 7in. wide. (Christie's) $3,997

A late Victorian burr walnut veneered table cabinet, late 19th century, the brass bound rectangular case with twin doors inlaid with silver script *Harry Heney*, 28in. wide.(Christie's) $2,362

A pear shaped fruitwood caddy, with an applied shield shape escutcheon, the stalk missing, 5.25in. high. (Woolley & Wallis) $1,136

A tortoiseshell veneered table casket, probably Dutch, 18th century, of rectangular form with domed cover, with pierced brass escutcheon and mounts to the angles, the interior later fabric lined, 11¼in. wide. (Christie's) $2,369

Painted pine storage box, New England, circa 1830, intricate foliate and scrollwork decoration, the sides with a central rectangle and linear banding at the edges, 11¹/₈in. long. (Skinner) $4,600

An early 19th century satinwood writing slope, of oblong form with ivory banding chased with scrolling foliage, hinged top revealing fitted interior, 15in. wide. (Andrew Hartley) $1,155

A chestnut bible box, possibly American, circa 1780, with iron lockplate, the front panel with stylized foliate designs, 25in. wide. (Christie's) $458

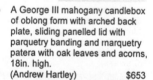

A George III satinwood and polychrome-decorated tea caddy, crossbanded overall in rosewood and decorated with ribbon-tied flowers, 7in. wide. (Christie's) $7,776

A Victorian burr walnut desk set by Hall, Belgravia, with gilt metal strap hinges and inset porcelain roundels, domed letter box, similar stationery box, note pad and miniature bookcase containing five volumes. (Andrew Hartley) $2,780

A George III mahogany candlebox of oblong form with arched back plate, sliding panelled lid with parquetry banding and marquetry patera with oak leaves and acorns, 18in. high. (Andrew Hartley) $653

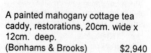

A painted mahogany cottage tea caddy, restorations, 20cm. wide x 12cm. deep. (Bonhams & Brooks) $2,940

A clockmaker's cabinet with six drawers filled with over 100 original glasses of various sizes, circa 1900. (Auction Team Köln) $414

A late Regency tortoiseshell tea caddy with fitted interior, 20cm. wide. (Bonhams & Brooks) $560

Featherweight camera, Shew & Co., London; half-plate, polished mahogany body, aluminum fittings, red leather bellows, alloy barrel Ross/Goerz 7in. lens, Dallmeyer 4in. Tele-Photo attachment.
(Christie's) $1,173

A Rolleiflex 3.5F, German, circa 1980, No. 2817053, with Planer f.3.5 75mm. lens and leather ever ready case.
(Bonhams) $470

Special B no. SB1521, Newman & Guardia, London; 5 x 4in. red-leather covered body, polished-wood interior, red-leather internal bellows, silvered fittings, in maker's case. (Christie's) $603

Super Technika III no. 46685, Linhof, Germany; 6 x 9cm. with 3 Schneider lenses, handgrip, film pack adapter, two rollfilm backs and six Linhof double darkslides, in maker's fitted leather outfit case.
(Christie's) $1,083

A Zeiss Ikon Super Contarex outfit, German, circa 1970-72, with Distagon f4.35mm. lens, Sonnar f2 85mm. lens and covers, Sonnar f4 135mm. lens and covers, two film backs, two film canisters, right angle viewfinder, etc.
(Bonhams) $1,176

Mamiya 645 Super no. 201708, Mamiya Camera Co., Japan; 120-rollfilm, with a Mamiya-Sekor f/2.8 80mm. lens no. 129807 and instruction booklet.
(Christie's) $506

Super Ikonta 532/16 no. T89231, rollfilm, with a Zeiss-Opton Tessar f/2.8 80mm. lens no. 652722, in maker's ever ready case.
(Christie's) $108

A Zeiss Ikon Contaflex (860/24) TLR, German, early 1950s, No.A 46012 with 5cm. Sonnar f1.5 lens and 8cm. viewing lens in leather ever ready case.
(Bonhams) $735

Bronica S2 no. CB71582, Zenza Bronica, Japan; 120-rollfilm, with magazine back, and a Nippon Kogaku Nikkor-P f/2.8 75mm. lens no. 118161, in maker's box.
(Christie's) $686

Alfa-2 camera, WZFO., Poland; blue painted, with a WZFO Euktar f/4.5 45mm. lens no. 18513, in maker's case.
(Christie's) $234

Lighter camera, the chrome-plated lighter casing decoratively engraved on one side, the top hinged marked *Thorens Switzerland*.
(Christie's) $1,497

Stereo SS camera no. 5041, Kern, Switzerland, 35mm., with a pair of Kern, Aarau Kernon f/3.5 35mm lenses, in maker's case.
(Christie's) $3,250

Heidoscop no. 11985, Franke & Heidecke, Germany; 6 x 13cm. with Velleaus rollfilm back, a Carl Zeiss, Jena Triplet f/4.2 7.5cm. viewing lens and a pair of Zeiss Jena Tessar f/4.5 7.5cm. taking lenses.
(Christie's) $1,111

Street camera, with viewing and taking lenses.(Christie's) $246

Prominent no. B6879, chrome, with a Voigtländer Ultron f/2 50mm. lens no. 3265403.
(Christie's) $351

Reflex camera obscura, wood-body, sliding-box, hinged top, 9 x 13cm. screen and lens.
(Christie's) $1,444

Ring camera, brass body decorated with scrolls, with a sprung lion mask lens cover with cut glass eyes, single speed shutter.
(Christie's) $1,467

Royalty stereo field camera, English; half-plate, mahogany and brass, leather square-cut bellows, with a pair of brass bound lenses.
(Christie's) $867

Detective hand camera, Hüttig, Germany; 9 x 12cm., polished wood body, changing bag, lens and shutter: (Christie's) $812

Echo 8 camera lighter, Suzuki Optical Works, Japan; 6 x 6mm., chrome, with an Echor f/3.5 15mm. lens in a B & I shutter with aperture marked *3.5 5.6 8*.
(Christie's) $1,036

Tailboard camera, Ross, London; half-plate, mahogany and brass, lens and accessories.
(Christie's) $1,553

Binoca binocular camera, Binoca Co., Japan, 16mm, white-plastic body, with a Bicon f/4.5 40mm. lens, with instruction leaflet. (Christie's) $787

A KGB buttonhole camera by KMZ, Russia, F-21 miniature camera with special lens holder and adjustable button fastening; post 1951. (Auction Team Köln) $2,350

John Player Special camera, Russian; with certificate dated 1991, in maker's box. (Christie's) $882

Leica M6 Platinum Sultan of Brunei, No. 2177142, commemorative no. HB-142, the top-plate engraved with insignia and legend, with matching Leica Summilux-M f/1.4 50mm. lens. (Christie's) $10,057

Linhof Wide-Angle Technika no. 100509, Linhof, Germany; with a Super Rollex back, Sportsfinder, grip and a Schneider Super-Angulon f/8 65mm. lens (Christie's) $1,534

Challenge Dayspool Tropical camera, J. Lizars, Glasgow; rollfilm, Spanish mahogany body, red-leather bellows, with a Beck Symmetrical lens. (Christie's) $484

Box-form camera, [?]English; 5 x 6in. polished mahogany body, and brass bound lens with rack and pinion focusing engraved Lerebours et Secretan Paris no. 7527. (Christie's) $1,553

Ticka watchface camera, Houghtons Ltd., London; rollfilm, polished chrome body, enamel watchface with Roman numerals, Time and Instantaneous shutter. (Christie's) $1,553

Super Nettel no. Y.30232, black, with a Carl Zeiss, Jena Tessar f/3.5 5cm. lens no. 1399941. (Christie's) $234

Leica M4 no. 1208050, chrome, with a Leica-meter MR and a Leitz black Summicron f/2 35mm. lens no. 2316992, in maker's ever ready case. (Christie's) $3,430

Reflex camera obscura, dovetail constructed wood body, 6 x 7½cm. glass screen, leather-hinged top, internal mirror and 3cm. diameter lens, 17cm. long. (Christie's) $2,115

Sliding box camera, Replica; brass fittings, with removable focusing screen, plate holder and a brass bound lens. (Christie's) $603

René Lalique, 'Saint Christopher' clear glass mascot, with well defined molded *R. Lalique France* on the base.
(Bonhams) $1,656

P. Dreux 'Le Lievre et l'Escargot', a hare and snail mascot, nickel plated on brass, signed and mounted on a radiator cap.
(Bonhams) $1,242

A Mickey Mouse mascot, dating from the late 1930s, with a discolored patina, nickel-plated finish, mounted on a radiator cap, 4in. high. (Bonhams) $552

An elephant with a toothache mascot, small and well defined bronze, elephant with his head bandaged, good patina and mounted on a radiator cap.
(Bonhams) $414

'Tête D'Aigle No. 1138, a clear and frosted car mascot, intaglio-molded *R. Lalique France*, 11.2cm. high.
(Christie's) $2,632

Bourcart, a Centurion's head mascot, Art Deco styling, with strong features, nickel on brass finish, 4in. high.
(Bonhams) $966

Devenet, an Alsatian head mascot, with mouth open, nickel silver finish on bronze, 1920s.
(Bonhams) $414

Sertorio, a sphinx mascot, combination ivory face, nickel plated head dress with wings, one of 3 versions, circa 1923.
(Bonhams) $1,656

'Sanglier' No. 1157, a clear and frosted car mascot, stencil mark, *R.Lalique* France, 6.8cm. high.
(Christie's) $1,068

Darby, Mephisto, a 'Devil Cocking-a-Snook' mascot, original nickel plate finish, 1923, offered by Auto Omnia, 5½in. high.
(Bonhams) $1,035

Antoine Bofill, 'Char Assyrien' a warrior and horse mascot, dating from 1915, finished in nickel silver on bronze with Art Deco styling.
(Bonhams) $1,380

Georges Delperier, 'Petite Poule' mascot, a girl rides the waves mascot, sound nickel plating on bronze, vintage period.
(Bonhams) $1,242

Augustine and Emile Lejeune – a leaping dog mascot, darting from the undergrowth, circa 1930, 3½in. high, unmounted.
(Bonhams) $110

Mr Bibendum, a kneeling Michelin man mascot, supported by a wheel and tire, from hollow cast, nickel silver bronze, circa 1916.
(Bonhams) $1,794

Bentley 3.5 / 4.25 liter mascot, mid 1930s leaning forward, 'flying B' mascot retaining its original chromium plating and mounted on a correct steam valve radiator cap, 3½in. high. (Bonhams) $621

'Archer' No. 1126, a clear and frosted car mascot, wheel-engraved *R.Lalique France*, total height 16.5cm. (Christie's) $987

'Libellule' No. 1145, a clear and frosted car mascot, molded mark *R.Lalique*, 21cm. high.
(Christie's) $4,277

René Lalique, 'Grenouille', a sitting frog glass mascot, 1929, amethyst-tinted, etched signature.
(Bonhams) $15,870

'Coq Nain', a post-war clear and frosted car mascot, modelled as a cockerel, stencil mark *Lalique France,* 20.5cm. high. (Christie's) $459

'Nageuse Egyptienne' mascot, depicting a reclining nude, sold by The Motor Store in France, 180mm. (Bonhams) $1,380

Bruce Bairnsfather, 'Old Bill' a jovial moustachioed Great War veteran wearing a scarf and helmet, in brass. (Bonhams) $207

Felix the Cat mascot, cast in bronze with cold painted black and white enamels, on a brass base inscribed *Felix.* (Bonhams) $897

Frederick Bazin, an Hispano-Suiza flying Stork mascot, nickel silver finish on bronze, 1919. (Bonhams) $1,518

Bourcart, 'Perroquet' parrot mascot, nickel plated on brass, the stylized animal is typical of mid 1920s French angular design. (Bonhams) $1,242

'Faucon' No.1124 a clear and frosted car mascot, molded mark *R.Lalique,* 15.5cm. high. (Christie's) $1,083

Antoine Bofill, a bat mascot, leaning on his wings with his wings outstretched and a grin on his face. (Bonhams) $2,208

Crouching male nude mascot, wearing helmet and goggles, nickel plating on brass finish. (Bonhams) $690

René Lalique, 'Tête d'Aigle' eagle's head, satin and frosted glass mascot, clear *R. Lalique* molded signature.(Bonhams)　　$2,484

Casimir Brau, a leaping horse mascot, mid 1920s, retailed by Hermes in Paris, larger size. (Bonhams)　　$1,518

René Lalique, 'Perch' glass mascot, an amber version, unsigned. (Bonhams)　　$331

'Sangliers' No.1157 a clear and frosted glass car mascot, molded mark *R. Lalique*, 7cm. high. (Christie's)　　$722

A Lalique 'St Christopher' clear, frosted and siena stained car mascot, after 1928, of circular form, intaglio molded with the Saint carrying the Christ child, with metal mount, 19cm. overall. (Bonhams)　　$1,088

'Tête d'Aigle' No. 1138 a clear and frosted car mascot, stencil mark *R.Lalique France*, 11.2cm. high. (Christie's)　　$987

René Lalique, 'Longchamps' horse's head glass mascot, June 1929, 1152A, satin and frosted glass mascot, R. Lalique signature. (Bonhams)　　$8,280

Maxime Le Verrier, a squirrel mascot, in the Art Deco style, in heavy nickel plating on brass, 1920s. (Bonhams)　　$304

'Perche' No.1158 a clear and frosted car mascot, moulded mark *R.Lalique*, 16cm. diameter. (Christie's)　　$686

Circa 1978 Mini 850 Saloon, finished in pristine russet brown with excellent beige vinyl interior, with its original sales invoice and service documents, MoT to October 2001 and Swansea V5 document. (Bonhams & Brooks) $2,208

1913 S.C.A.T. 15hp Five Seat Tourer, original English coachwork by Newton & Bennett of Manchester. British Racing Green livery, full tonneau cover, radiator re-cored, brass fittings, S.C.A.T. detachable wire wheels. (Bonhams & Brooks) $27,600

1931 Aston Martin International Tourer, coachwork by E Bertelli, restored, 1.5 liter engine rebuilt by Elwell Smith, Le Mans rear axle and original, correct upward-opening windscreen and 21in. diameter wheels. (Bonhams) $42,780

1925 Morris Cowley Two seater and Dickey, rebuilt during the period 1990 to 1999, engine rebuilt in 1996, runs on lead free petrol, traditional Morris gray livery with black wings, the interior is reupholstered in green leatherette. (Bonhams & Brooks) $9,384

1943 Humber 4x4 Heavy Utility, 85bhp, six cylinder, side valve engine of 4,086cc , drive to rear wheels only or to all four wheels via a four speed gearbox and two speed transfer box, in remarkably original condition. (Bonhams & Brooks) $10,488

1936 Austin 10hp Sherborne Saloon, this car was the subject of a comprehensive engine rebuild some 5,000 miles ago and the clutch has been relined. The interior has also been professionally retrimmed in red leather. (Bonhams & Brooks) $4,416

1948 Standard 14hp, 1.8 litre, Drophead Coupé, 1,776cc side valve engine, stylish hood pram irons, enclosed rear mounted spare wheel, blade bumpers front and rear and the distinctive Standard 'waterfall' radiator grill. (Bonhams & Brooks) $6,900

1927 Darracq DTS 15/40hp 2.3 Liter Tourer, four cylinder, overhead valve engine of 2.294 cc, with a four speed gearbox, ultra-lightweight coachwork by E.C. Gordon England of Putney, aluminum clad. (Bonhams & Brooks) $31,500

1953 Mercedes-Benz 300s Roadster, engine with triple Solex carburettors and a raised compression ratio. Maximum power output 150bhp and top speed to 110mph. (Bonhams) $117,300

1923 Renault 8.3hp Type KJ 1 Tourer, four cylinder side valve engine with three speed gearbox, Michelin disk wheels, coachwork liveried in mushroom with red coachlining and black wings.
(Bonhams & Brooks) $7,176

1914 Alldays Midget 8.9hp Two Seater, vertical, twin cylinder, water-cooled, monobloc engine with a bore and stroke of 59 x 160mm., giving it a capacity of 875cc. The light two-seater coachwork suspended on quarter elliptic springs, drive through a three speed gear box. (Bonhams) $9,660

The Sam S. Kaye Trophy winning 1913 Sunbeam 12/16hp Four Seat Tourer, comprehensively equipped with wire detachable wheels, hood and full tonneau, Auster screen and all nickel fittings.
(Bonhams) $52,440

1945 Willys Jeep, described as 'one of the lowest-mileage, un-damaged Jeeps in existence', the vehicle comes complete with hood, sidescreens, shovel and ax, and is offered with current MoT and Swansea V5. (Bonhams & Brooks) $7,866

1934 Hillman 9.8hp Aero Minx Streamline Saloon, finished in coffee and cream livery with beige interior and sunburst pattern door panels, with a Swansea V5 registration document, MoT valid to May 2002.
(Bonhams) $12,420

1952 Chevrolet Styleline Deluxe Series Convertible, this restored American classic is finished in maroon with maroon gray interior and has three-speed manual transmission. The car is offered with current MoT and Swansea V5.
(Bonhams & Brooks) $11,040

1941 Daimler Mark II 'Dingo' 4 x 4 Scout Car, rear mounted, six cylinder, 55bhp engine, five speed pre-selector gearbox, independent coil spring suspension and hydraulic brakes.
(Bonhams & Brooks) $5,244

1966 Ford Mustang Convertible, white with black interior and black hood, engine: 90 degree V8, 4728cc, 203bhp at 4400rpm; gearbox: three-speed automatic; brakes: hydraulic drum all round. Left hand drive. (Christie's) $13,041

1959 Ford Fairlane 500 Skyliner Convertible, classic white with tri-tone bronze interior, fully rebuilt 332cid (5.4-litre) V8 engine, all new seats, new chrome, complete new twin exhaust system and new tires. (Bonhams & Brooks) $22,294

1903 Darracq 8hp Model G Four Seat Rear Entrance Tonneau, presented in green livery with yellow wheels and chassis detail and equipped with oil sidelamps and a magnificent center mounted Salisbury Bleriot headlamp, coachwork re-upholstered in green buttoned Connolly hide in 1976.
(Bonhams) $44,160

1973 Lotus Elan S4 Sprint Coupé, red over white/gold with black interior, engine: four cylinders, twin overhead camshaft, 1558cc, twin Weber carburettors, 126bhp at 6,500rpm; Gearbox: manual four speed; brakes: hydraulic four wheel disk with servo. Right hand drive. (Christie's) $12,668

1930 Lincoln Model L Berline Limousine, coachwork by J.B. Judkins Company, black with black leather chauffeur's compartment and rose gray fabric in rear compartment, engine: V8 side valves, 384ci., 95bhp; gearbox: three-speed manual with reverse, brakes: four wheel mechanical drums. Left hand drive. (Christie's) $44,650

1930 Packard Deluxe Eight Model 745 Club Sedan, blue with black fenders, roof and gold pinstriping with blue/gray cloth interior, engine: L-head, straight eight, 384.8ci., 106bhp at 3,200rpm; gearbox: four-speed manual with reverse, brakes: four wheel mechanical drums. Left hand drive.
(Christie's) $56,400

1937 Packard 120 Coupé, baby blue with red pinstriping and gray leather interior, engine: L-head, straight eight, 282ci., 120hp at 3,800rpm; gearbox: three-speed selective synchromesh manual, brakes: four wheel hydraulic drums, left hand drive. (Christie's) $15,275

Circa 1965 Godon-Keeble Coupé, with independent front suspension, De Dion rear axle and four-wheel disk brakes. Styled by Giugiaro at Bertone, elegant glassfiber bodywork by Williams & Pritchard, A 327cid (5.4 liter) Chevrolet V8 engine.
(Bonhams & Brooks) $22,010

1992 Lotus Excel Coupé, British Racing Green with light tan leather interior, engine: four cylinders twin overhead camshaft, 2714cc, 180bhp at 6500rpm; gearbox: manual five-speed with synchromesh; brakes: servo-assisted ventilated disk. Right hand drive. (Christie's) $13,041

1956 Cadillac Series 60 Special Fleetwood, Dusty Rose with a cream top and two-tone blue cloth and leather interior, Engine: V8 331ci., 250bhp at 4,600rpm, gearbox: three-speed column shift automatic, brakes: four wheel drums. Left hand drive. (Christie's) $12,925

1941 Packard 180 Custom Super 8 Seven Passenger Limousine, coachwork by LeBaron, two-tone gray and blue with gray broadcloth passenger's compartment and black leather driver's compartment, engine: straight eight, L-head, 356ci., 160bhp at 3,500rpm, gearbox: three-speed column shift manual, brakes: four wheel hydraulic drums.   Left hand drive. (Christie's) $42,300

1930 Packard Model 733 Standard Eight Dual Cowl Phaeton, battleship gray with black fenders, black leather interior and a black canvas top, engine: L-head, in-line, eight cylinders, 319.2ci., 90bhp at 3,200rpm; gearbox: four-speed manual with reverse, brakes: four wheel mechanical drums, left hand drive. (Christie's) $94,000

1931 Marmon V16 Model 149 Five Passenger Closed Coupled Sedan, coachwork by LeBaron, pine green with tan cloth interior, engine: V16, 491ci., 192bhp at 3,600rpm, torque 407lbs at 1,600rpm; gearbox: three-speed manual, brakes: four wheel mechanical drums. Left hand drive. (Christie's) $82,250

1930 Ford Model A Coupé with rumble seat, black with cream coachline and black leather interior, engine: four cylinders, in-line, 200.5ci, 40bhp at 2,200rpm, gearbox: three-speed manual with overdrive, brakes: mechanical four wheel drum.   Left hand drive. (Christie's) $9,400

1932 Cadillac V-12 model 370B Seven Passenger Limousine, coachwork by Fisher, black with beige broadcloth interior in the rear and black leather in the driver's compartment, engine: twelve cylinder, V-configuration, overhead valves, 368ci, 135bhp, gearbox: three-speed manual, brakes: four wheel hydraulic internal expanding.   Left hand drive. (Christie's) $49,350

1972 Lotus Elan S4 Sprint Drophead Coupé, blue over white/gold with black interior, engine: four cylinders, twin overhead camshaft, twin Weber carburettors, 1558cc 126 bhp at 6,500rpm; gearbox: four speed manual; brakes: hydraulic four wheel disk with servo. Right hand drive. (Christie's) $19,562

1904 Cadillac Model B Surrey, single-cylinder engine mounted horizontally on the left beneath the front seat, conventional two-speeds-plus-reverse planetary transmission and center chain drive to the rear axle. (Bonhams) $33,120

1979 Chevrolet Corvette 'Targa' Coupé, 235.5cid (3.8 litre) overhead-valve straight six is powered by a tuned 7.4litre V8 engine featuring 4-barrel carburettor, Edelbrock inlet manifold, fabricated exhaust manifolds and numerous internal improvements and driving competition clutch to a five-speed manual gearbox. (Bonhams & Brooks) $9,660

1951 Chevrolet Styleline deluxe station wagon, red with woodgrain panelling and tan interior, Engine: modified V8, overhead valve, circa 235ci. 105bhp; Gearbox: Powerglide automatic; Brakes: four wheel hydraulic drum; Left hand drive. (Christie's) $9,200

1924 Alvis 12/50 Ducksback 2/3 Seater, overhead valve, 1,500cc engine, in polished aluminum finish with red wings, with pleated red upholstery and equipped with Brolt electrics and Carl Zeiss windscreen mounted spotlamp. (Bonhams & Brooks) $24,840

1933 6th Series Alfa Romeo 6C-1750 Gran Sport Spider, coachwork by Carrozzeria Touring, the car is from the final 6th series of 6C-1750 Gran Sport models, its original engine nominally as new being of 65mm. bore x 88mm. stroke displacing 1,752cc. Twin-overhead camshaft design. (Bonhams) $345,000

1923 Hillman 11hp Speed Model Two Seater, finished in Ayres red and black livery. The interior trimmed in antiques black hide and a fawn duck hood fitted, equipped with CAV headlamps, Toby side lamps, a one piece folding windscreen, four branch outside exhaust. (Bonhams & Brooks) $9,384

1950 Jowett Javelin Saloon, all-steel, four-door, saloon body; independent front suspension; torsion bar springing; and rack-and-pinion steering, horizontally-opposed four-cylinder engine, 50bhp, four-speed gearbox with column change. (Bonhams & Brooks) $4,278

1932 Morris Family 8 Saloon LG 8575, very nicely presented in British racing green with black mudguards. Ready to use. (Tennants) $6,080

104

A 4-seater Model T Ford Open Tourer, 9200cc., 20hp, 'Z' high compression head and electric starter, folding top and four disk brakes, wheels with wooden spokes and 2 spare tires, 1917.
(Auction Team Köln) $21,653

1941 Cadillac Series 62 convertible coupé, black with tan corduroy interior and black canvas top, Engine: 90 degree V8, L head, 346ci, 150bhp; Gearbox: three speed manual; Brakes: four wheel hydraulic drums. Left hand drive. (Christie's) $56,350

1928 Lancia Lambda 8th Series Coupé, the engine an overhead-valve unit, 2,570cc, 68bhp., original Weymann fabric saloon body was replaced by the present aluminum-panelled, ash-framed coupé coachwork by Airflow Streamline, of Northampton.
(Bonhams) $28,980

1929 Packard 645 Dual Cowl Phaeton, coachwork by Dietrich, two shades of red with dark red fenders and red leather interior, Engine: straight eight, 384.8ci., 120bhp at 3,200rpm.; Gearbox: three-speed manual; Brakes: four wheel drum. Left hand drive. (Christie's) $156,500

1933 Austin Seven Tourer, registration no. YD 6477, chassis no. 169801, engine no. B73306, finished in dark green with black wings, the car comes complete with sidescreens, old-style logbook, MoT to October 2002 and Swansea V5.
(Bonhams & Brooks) $4,968

Morris Minor De Luxe Series II Saloon, finished in sandy beige with original maroon interior, in 'exceptional' condition in all respects, with Heritage Certificate confirming matching chassis/engine numbers, MoT to September 2002 and Swansea V5.
(Bonhams) $6,624

1930 Triumph Super 7 Two Seater with Dickey, part restored, offered with numerous spares including gearbox, brake parts, head gasket, spring bushes, etc, with a Swan V5 registration document and old style log book, blue and black livery with yellow wheels.(Bonhams & Brooks) $2,484

1923 Ford Model T Roadster 'Snow Machine' with skis, 20hp four-cylinder sidevalve displacing 2,896cc, transmission two-speed planetary unit, with the factory option of interchangeable front axle mounted skis for use in snow, left hand-drive.
(Bonhams) $11,040

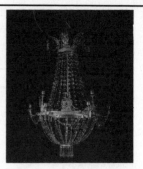

A French gilt-bronze and glass seven-light ceiling light, early 20th century, of coronet form and mounted with strings of faceted glass beads, 25¼in. high. (Christie's) $687

One of a pair of decorative Italian ten branch electroliers, 90cm. wide x 100cm. high.(Bonhams & Brooks) (Two) $1,661

An Empire style gilt bronze twelve branch chandelier, early 20th century, the branches in two registers, raised on openwork lyres, 42in. high.(Christie's) $3,437

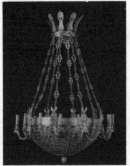

One of a pair of ormolu sixteen-light chandeliers, 20th century, each with a foliate corona surmounted by palm leaves, supporting the bowl with pierced foliage, the frieze headed by eight Minerva's masks, 57in. high.
(Christie's) (Two) $37,720

A Louis XV style ormolu fifteen-light chandelier, late 19th century, in the manner of Jacques Caffiéri, with a pierced foliate scrolling frame issuing three sets of five foliate scrolling arms, 51½in. high.
(Christie's) $81,700

A Louis XVI style gilt-bronze and glass twenty-four light chandelier, late 19th/early 20th century, with acanthus-cast corona hung with beaded chains above twenty-four candleholders on foliate-cast arms, 41½in. high.
(Christie's) $8,050

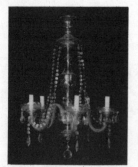

A Continental molded glass five light chandelier, first half 20th century, the lobed drip pans issuing from serpentine scaled branches, emanating from the star-cut baluster stem, 33in. high.
(Christie's) $813

An Italian silvered carved wood eighteen branch chandelier, early 20th century, the foliate capped scroll branches in three graduated registers about the conforming knopped baluster stem, 50in. high.
(Christie's) $14,476

A French Art Deco silvered bronze six light chandelier, early 20th century, the petal glass shades on branches issuing from the hexagonal frame with a frosted foliate dish to the underside, 52¼in. high. (Christie's) $2,715

A glass chandelier, in the style of Barovier, the six scrolling arms of stylized foliate form surmounted by six fluted shades, pendant from central column, 30.5in. high. (Christie's) $4,200

A Louis XV style gilt metal and cut glass bag electrolier, early 20th century, 66cm. high. (Bonhams & Brooks) $980

A gilt sheet-iron six-light chandelier, 20th century, modelled as an openwork balloon, with scroll branches radiating from the basket, 34½in. high.(Christie's) $1,357

A Continental neo-classic style gilt-metal and cut-glass eight-light chandelier, the leaf-tip cast corona above an acanthus cast tier hung with plumes issuing tassels and beaded chains, 34¾in. high. (Christie's) $7,475

A Continental rococo style six-light gilt-metal and glass chandelier, late 19th century, formed as a beaded openwork crown, the foliate-scroll arms hung with spear prisms, 34½in. high. (Christie's) $5,175

A brass and molded glass eighteen light chandelier, first half 20th century, the nozzles and lobed drip pans issuing from scrolling foliate branches, emanating from the central spherical body, 44in. high. (Christie's) $2,081

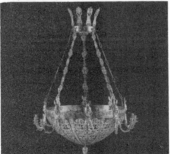

A French gilt bronze twenty-four light chandelier, parts late 19th century, the bifurcating foliate cast scroll branches issuing from a circular well with bacchic masks to the underside, 47in. high. (Christie's) $6,332

A pair of Empire style gilt bronze sixteen light chandeliers, of recent manufacture, the inverted domed wells pierced and cast with panels of rosettes and leafy ornament, 43in. diameter. (Christie's) $13,572

A French Art Deco silvered bronze three light chandelier, early 20th century, the branches with flared shades with molded signature *Deguré* issuing from the triform frame with stylized frosted panels, 35in. high.(Christie's) $2,533

A gilt metal and molded glass chandelier, first half 20th century, with acanthus cast ceiling boss above the conforming corona, graduating faceted beads descending to the circlet, 24¼in. high. (Christie's) $619

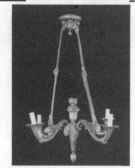

A Continental gilt bronze eight light chandelier, early 20th century, the writhen cornucopia branches with overlaid acanthus leaves, emanating from the central column, 34½in. high. (Christie's) $619

A French ten branch gilt bronze chandelier, late 19th century, the foliate capped scroll branches in two registers about a knopped waisted stem, cast with male and female busts and trailing foliage, 35in. high.(Christie's) $2,895

A Spanish brass votive hanging lamp in the 17th century style, the molded domed corona surmounted by a hanging-loop and flanked by pierced ornaments, hung with pierced lozenge-shaped chains, 67in. high. (Christie's) $1,079

A Dutch style brass six light chandelier, second half 20th century, with molded nozzles and drip pans issuing from scrolling branches, 17½in. high. (Christie's) $390

A French gilt bronze eight light chandelier, early 20th century, in the Régence style, the down turned foliate capped scroll branches with dolphins surmounts and bearded mask terminals, 39in. high. (Christie's) $2,199

Louis XVI style brass and cut glass ten-light chandelier, 20th century, acanthus top suspending continuous glass bead strands, enclosing sixteen further accent lights, approximately 40in. long. (Skinner) $2,300

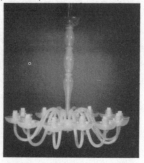

Czechoslovakian glass chandelier, circa 1930, painted metal ceiling mount suspending a yellow-green glass standard with alabaster bulbed segments, drop 23in. (Skinner) $747

A French gilt metal and painted four light electrolier, first quarter 20th century, in the Empire style, with lobed drip pans supported on the beaks of swans issuing from the dished, circular body, 38½in. high. (Christie's) $757

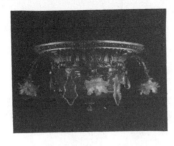

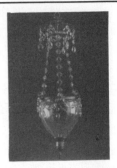

A late 18th century part colored Venetian glass chandelier, decorated with various colored flowers.
(Galerie Moderne) $5,600

A gilt-bronze and glass ceiling light, early 20th century, the domed star-cut shade with cone terminal, the fluted and gadrooned circlet with four branches 14in. high.
(Christie's) $4,686

An early 19th century glass and ormolu mounted chandelier, the corona hung with lusters, 86cm. high.
(Stockholms AV) $4,589

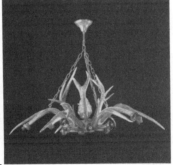

An enamelled and gilt bronze ten light electrolier, 20th century, the lobed serpentine circlet with arabic script on a blue ground with registers of stylized geometric decoration above and below, 22½in. high.(Christie's) $1,397

An antler chandelier, late 20th century, the entwined branches with twelve sockets in two registers, 48in. wide. (Christie's) $531

Bronze neo-classical-style eight-light chandelier, late 19th century, the trumpet-form fluted standard topped by flat leaves, flaring outward to the eight fluted cornucopia-shaped candlearms, approximately 28in. high.
(Skinner) $3,450

A French cut-glass six light chandelier, early 19th century, the central baluster shaft surmounted by a circular faceted dish and hung with a trellis cascade of faceted drops and beads, 40in. high.
(Christie's) $2,657

A pair of large central European bronze three branch chandeliers, mid 19th century, the drip pans with acanthus cast borders on openwork scroll branches, 51in. high.
(Christie's) $20,304

A cut glass eight light chandelier, early 20th century, the scrolling branches radiating in tiers, interlinked by chains of faceted beads, 39in. high.
(Christie's) $3,992

Hampshire Pottery vase, design by Cadmon Robertson, circa 1910, raised rim on a ovoid vessel, water lily and leaf decoration in relief about the sides, matte green glaze, 7in. high. (Skinner) $632

Pair of Handel one-light lily sconces, Meriden, Connecticut, circa 1903, each with naturalistic-style stems supporting a floriform shade of overlapped green and white slag glass petals and two green slag glass buds, 10in. high. (Skinner) $1,380

Saturday Evening Girls Art Pottery vase, early 20th century, Boston, small flared rim on bulbous body, matte drip glaze in shades of blue and green, 6in. high. (Skinner) $259

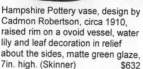

Handel reverse-painted tapestry border lamp, Meriden, Connecticut, early 20th century, interior painted with a floral tapestry border in shades of green, amber, blue, and red on a burnt orange ground, 24in. high. (Skinner) $6,900

Two Grueby Faience Company architectural tiles, designed by Addison B. Le Boutillier, Boston, circa 1909, each depicting a knight on horseback, matte yellow glazed on terracotta, approximately 6in. square. (Skinner) $402

Cobalt decorated stoneware crock, late 19th century, inscribed *T.F. Reppert Eagle Pottery Co., Greensboro*, PA, decorated on one side with an eagle and six stars, a blue band and foliate scrolls, 21in. high. (Skinner) $2,875

Fulper Art Pottery vase, Flemington, New Jersey, circa 1916, hand-thrown vessel with impressed lines encircling the body, heavy mottled black glaze over mottled green and ocher glaze, 6^1/8in. (Skinner) $400

Grueby Pottery vase, Boston, early 20th century, flared rim tapering to bulbous base decorated with repeating raised bud on long flower stem and leaves, 8in. high. (Skinner) $3,163

Saturday Evening Girls vase, Boston, early 20th century, decorated about the rim with stylized petal forms in shades of matte gray-blue outlined in black, 8½in. (Skinner) $920

Two-handled grotesque pottery face jug, Burlon Craig, Vale, North Carolina, ovoid form jug with protruding facial features, 16in. high. (Skinner) $431

Owens Pottery Utopian ware cider set, Zanesville, Ohio, late 19th century, tall cylindrical jug and seven matching mugs, each decorated with cherries on a leafy branch, 12.5 in. high. (Skinner) $1,000

Grotesque pottery face jug, Lanier Meaders, Cleaveland, Georgia, 20th century, ovoid jug with handle, two pebbles used as teeth, incised signature, 10½in. high. (Skinner) $805

Clewell Art Pottery vase, Canton, Ohio, inverted rim on a broad shouldered vessel tapering to base, copper with verdigris finish, 11¼in. (Skinner) $2,760

Marblehead Pottery two-color vase, decorated by Hannah Tutt, Marblehead, Massachusetts, circa 1912, incised stylized floral and geometric decoration in dark olive green on a lighter green ground, 8in. high. (Skinner) $13,800

An 'Order of the Cincinnati' cider jug and cover, circa 1790, finely painted with the medal of the Order of the Cincinnati, the obverse with Cincinnatus receiving his sword from three Roman senators, 10¼in. high. (Christie's) $90,500

Sara Sax decorated ceramic vase, late 19th century, decorated with rose blossoms in peach, yellow, green, and brown on cream colored ground with gilt highlights, 8½in. high. (Skinner) $287

Lonhuda Art Pottery jug, 19th century, in standard two-tone dark brown glaze with raised floral decoration, artist's signature *EA*, possibly Edward Abel, 7¼in. high. (Eldred's) $100

Boston three-gallon stoneware crock, early 19th century, with irregular brown and beige banding, handles at neck, chips at lip. 15in. high. (Eldred's) $200

111

A large Amphora model of a girl in a cart drawn by a billy goat, impressed and painted marks, 43cm. long.
(Woolley & Wallis) $206

Amphora Egyptian vase of tapering cylindrical form decorated with incised panel of an Egyptian theme, 13in. high. (Skinner) $385

Amphora Pottery Judaica Vessel, Austria, early 20th century, double cylindrical mouths on tubular oval body, raised on shaped oblong base, decorated about the body with raised 'Star-of-David' motifs, impressed maker's mark, 16in. high. (Skinner) $690

ARITA

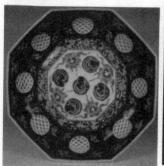

A Japanese Arita Imari octagonal dish, the borders with reticulated panels, the center with five phoenix between jui scrolls, 1st half 18th. century, 22cm.
(Woolley & Wallis) $508

An Arita model of a cockerel, 18th century, the cockerel with its head turned behind, painted in underglaze blue, iron red, green, black enamels and gilt, 10¼in. high. (Christie's) $3,948

A Japanese Arita blue and white molded teapot, decorated with flowers and foliage, 18th century, 18cm., the cover matched.
(Woolley & Wallis) $226

BELLEEK

A Belleek parian bust of a Classical maiden, taken from a figure known as the Prisoner of Love, after a model by Giovanni Fontana, circa 1875, 26cm. high.
(Christie's) $461

A large Belleek 'Panel Jardinière', second period, 1891-1926, the shoulders encrusted with a continuous floral meander and with two birds perched on branches, 30cm. (Bonhams) $575

An unusual Belleek Parian 'Boy Candelabra', first period, 1863-1890, modelled nude seated on a rocky outcrop, issuing forth coral stems rising to form a shaft supporting three bowls, 35cm.
(Bonhams) $2,329

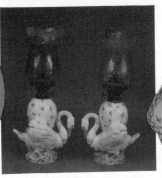

A KPM Berlin plate 'Christmas 1917', with a soldier astride a field gun, clutching a sausage and a bottle of champagne, 19.5cm. diameter. (Arnold) $185

A pair of KLM Berlin Lamps, 16in. high. (G. E. Sworder) $1,280

Berlin porcelain triangular dish, molded with a link border and the center well painted in colors with motif of a bantam, insects and sprigs of flowers, 19th century, 11in. (G.A. Key) $291

A KPM Berlin bellarmine jug with blue and relief decoration, 1849-1870, 44cm. high. (Arnold) $372

Berlin porcelain topographical cup and saucer, Germany, 19th century, gilt banded borders and foliate trim with handpainted center panel, saucer 6in. diameter. (Skinner) $402

A Berlin porcelain goblet, the ovoid gilt bowl painted with cherubs, supported by three figures with spinning wheel, on molded circular base, 5¼in. high. (Andrew Hartley) $440

A KPM Berlin plaque, signed *J. Volk*, 19th/20th century, painted with a semi-clad maiden holding two roses in her hand, 39.5 x 24.5cm. (Christie's) $6,586

A Berlin porcelain plate painted with a mythical figure scene depicting St. Michael destroying Lucifer, within a gilded gothic border, early 19th century, 8in. wide. (Andrew Hartley) $917

A Berlin (K.P.M.) rectangular plaque of Psyche, late 19th/early 20th century, signed *Lauterbach*, finely painted after Kray with the winged nymph in diaphanous drape seated on a grassy knoll beside a pond, 24.4 x 16.5cm. (Christie's) $7,050

A large Bernard Moore flambé vase, decorated with a red flambé glaze with green mottling, height 19¼in. (Sotheby's) $7,200

Bernard Moore flambé mythical animal figure, 15cm. painted *BM*. (Bonhams) $220

A Moore Brothers white porcelain figural comport, the leaf molded circular bowl, issuing from a circular rustic stem flanked by three music making putti, 12½in. high. (Andrew Hartley) $924

BESWICK

A Beswick Beatrix Potter Tom Kitten figural wall plaque, no.2085, modelled by Graham Tongue, dressed in pale blue with mustard buttons, 14cm. high, black and gold backstamp. (Bonhams) $942

Snow White, style one, first version, (hair in flounces), 1954-1955, a rare Beswick Walt Disney character figure, 13cm., gilt marks. (Bonhams) $1,109

A Beswick Beatrix Potter Peter Rabbit figural wall plaque, no. 2083, modelled by Graham Tongue, dressed in blue jacket, 15cm. high. (Bonhams) $1,099

BÖTTGER

A Böttger cream-pot, circa 1720-25, with gilt scroll handle, on three gilt paw feet, gilded at Augsburg with Orientals at various pursuits on terraces with trees, 4½in. high. (Christie's) $851

A Böttger Hausmalerei silver-gilt mounted coffee-pot and cover, circa 1725, the mounts Augsburg by Elias Adam, painted with fantastic insects and botanical specimens between gilt borders, 9¾in. high. (Christie's) $28,964

A Böttger two-handled baluster vase, circa 1725, modelled by J.J. Irminger, molded and enriched with enamels and gilding, each handle with a scrolling leaf above a C-scroll and husk terminal, 9¾in. high. (Christie's) $8,519

A Bow plate, painted in polychrome with two black and yellow birds beside blue rocks, flowers and leaves, no marks, circa 1755-60, 23cm.(Woolley & Wallis) $429

A Bow coffee cup, circa 1755, painted in the manner of James Welsh with a bouquet of flowers including a rose, a tulip and forget-me-nots. (Christie's) $1,363

A Bow circular box and a cover modelled as a rose, circa 1756, the full-blown rose with overlapping petals edged in deep pink, the underside of the base molded with the flower sepals in green, 3¼in. diameter. (Christie's) $2,726

BRANNAM

A C. H. Brannam grotesque puffin jug, incised marks, 1898, 20cm. high. (Christie's) $575

A C. H. Brannam dragon and bird vase, incised marks, 1899, 26cm. high. (Christie's) $395

A C. H. Brannam twin-handled dragon and fish vase, incised mark, 1899, 22cm. high. (Christie's) $410

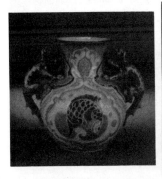

A C. H. Brannam fish jardinière, incised marks, 1901, 21cm. high. (Christie's) $410

A C. H. Brannam Art Nouveau twin-handled vase, incised mark, 1903, 16cm. high. (Christie's) $526

A C. H. Brannam fish jug, incised mark, 1893, 23cm. high. (Christie's) $295

A Herculaneum pottery meat plate, of canted oblong form, with gravy gunnel, blue printed with the 'Etruscan' pattern depicting chariots and classical figure scenes, early 19th century, 18in. wide. (Andrew Hartley) $612

An English yellow-ground topographical inkstand and letter rack, circa 1825, possibly Rockingham, formed as a square with cut corners, flanked by quivers of arrows; the center painted with Barnard Castle Durham, 5¾in. wide. (Christie's) $748

A Roger's pearlware chamfered rectangular blue and white meat plate, printed with a vase issuing large flowers and fruit, circa 1820, 53.7cm. (Woolley & Wallis) $629

A Bursley Ware ginger jar and cover, by Charlotte Rhead, pattern TL85, painted and incised marks, 23.5cm. high. (Christie's) $361

A pair of Longton Hall horses and grooms, circa 1755, after the Meissen models by J.J. Kändler, modelled as two rearing white and pale gray and brown dappled stallions restrained by a black and a white groom in Turkish dress, 8½in. high. (Christie's) $17,038

A Samuel Alcock pottery reproduction Portland vase, the figures in gray and white transfer on a black ground with brown line edging, 19th century, 10½in. high. (Andrew Hartley) $278

A miniature Aller Vale two handled mug, inscribed *May they ever be united* with Union Jack and American flag 4.5cm. high. (Bonhams) $188

A Shelley figure of a gnome by Mabel Lucy Attwell, printed marks, 7cm. high. (Christie's) $1,068

A large Shelley banded jardinière, printed mark, 20cm. high. (Christie's) $624

A Royal Winton Hazel coffee pot and cover, 16.6cm. (Bonhams) $412

'Old Cottage Chintz' a Royal Winton teapot and cover, printed marks, 16cm. high. (Christie's) $245

'Dick Turpin' a Burleigh Ware jug, printed marks, 20.5cm. high. (Bonhams) $441

A Parian ware group 'Prince Arthur and Hubert' from Shakespeare's King John, after Beattie, modelled as a kneeling Prince embracing a seated Hubert, 19th century, 17in. high. (Andrew Hartley) $417

A pair of Caughley porcelain sauce boats, with loop handles, the lobed sides blue printed with chinoiserie river scenes, 18th century, 8½in. wide. (Andrew Hartley) $487

An unusual Watcombe gray stoneware vase, incised and painted in muted enamels, on one side a girl, a goat and goose in a country landscape, 20.7cm. (Bearne's) $627

A Burleigh china jug, painted in color, the handle in the form of a batsman, 8in. high. (Bonhams & Brooks) $454

Mocha Ware pottery pitcher, England, 19th century, upper band of ocher, brown, and white cat's eyes on gray ground with narrow dark brown stripes, 6½in. high. (Skinner) $3,565

A Plymouth polychrome dry-mustard pot, circa 1770, iron-red 24 mark, painted in the Kakiemon palette with insects in flight over flowers and foliage, 3in. high. (Christie's) $1,192

A Burmantofts faience vase, circa 1890, oviform, decorated in low relief with three panels of irises in tones of blue, green and yellow, bordered in green, 35.5cm. (Bonhams) $435

Burmantofts, a pair of faience pottery toads, overall turquoise glaze, impressed marks, 16cm. (Bonhams & Brooks) $356

A Burmantofts faience pottery vase of ovoid form with flared rim, molded in parti-color with flowers in pale blue, yellow and brown on deep blue panels, 13¼in. high. (Andrew Hartley) $728

CANTON

Two Chinese Canton famille rose baluster vases, each decorated with panels of figures in various pursuits, 19th century, 34cm. (Woolley & Wallis) $197

A French gilt bronze mounted Cantonese bowl, late 19th century, the porcelain painted with entwined foliage with reserves of figures and birds on a white ground, 12in. high. (Christie's) $2,544

A pair of ormolu mounted Cantonese vases, late 19th century, the bodies decorated overall with flowers and foliage and reserves with dignitaries and warriors, 28in. high. (Christie's) $6,440

Rose medallion vase, China, 19th century, 12¾in. high. (Skinner) $518

Drum-form rose medallion Canton teapot, 19th century with two cups, fitted wicker case. (Eldred's) $192

A Chinese Canton famille rose large baluster vase and cover, decorated with panels and figures in landscapes and auspicious objects, mid 19th century, 64cm. (Woolley & Wallis) $846

A Capodimonte (Carlo III) double spice-dish or salt, circa 1752, modelled by Giuseppe Gricci, the handle formed as three elaborate rococo C-scrolls terminating at each side of the spice-dish, 14.3cm. high.
(Christie's) $15,334

Two Capodimonte style octagonal plaques, late 19th/early 20th century, blue crowned N marks, one with printed green mark, one molded with Adam and Eve, the other with Poseidon a chariot, $8^5/_8$ in. x 7in. (Christie's) $1,293

A very rare Capodimonte figure of a young man with a dog, 1748-55, modelled by Giuseppe Gricci, standing with his left foot resting on a tree stump, cradling a dog, 6¼in.
(Sotheby's) $27,800

CARLTON WARE

'Devil's Copse' a large circular Carlton Ware wall charger, printed and painted in colors and gilt on a dark blue ground, decorated with stylized tree and foliage, 39.2cm. diameter.
(Christie's) $3,680

'Heron and Magical Tree' a Carlton Ware coffee set for six, pattern 4159, printed and painted in colors and gilt on a maroon ground, decorated with stylized trees and flying heron, coffee pot 19cm.
(Christie's) $2,024

Carlton Ware 'Blackberry' a molded breakfast set, printed script mark (very minor restoration), height of teapot 11cm.
(Christie's) $560

A Carlton Ware *My Goodness-My Guinness* ostrich model.
(Academy) $176

Carlton Ware teapot of slightly tapering cylindrical form, decorated in colors with sprays of spring flowers with deep blue and gilded detail on a blush ground, circa early 20th century.(G.A. Key) $189

A Carlton Ware *Guinness for Strength* horse & cart model.
(Academy) $672

A painted chalkware figure of a standing fireman, probably Pennsylvania, circa 1850, 14in. high.
(Sotheby's) $4,000

Chalkware seated whippet, America, circa 1850, black-spotted white dog on gray base, with Livingstone, New York, tag, 18in. high. (Skinner) $1,840

Chalkware seated cat, America, 19th century, yellow and black striped cat with touches of red on ears, nose, and mouth on a yellow painted oval base, 10in.
(Skinner) $4,600

CHARLOTTE RHEAD

'Manchu' a Charlotte Rhead jug, pattern 4511, printed marks, 20.5cm. high.(Bonhams) $662

A Charlotte Rhead portrait tile, framed, impressed marks, 15.5cm. high. (Bonhams) $1,029

A Charlotte Rhead vase, stamped 212, 7¾in. high.
(Sworders) $203

CHELSEA KERAMIC

Chelsea Keramic Art vase, applied white flowers on crimped squat-form with butterscotch glaze, 5in. wide. (Skinner) $750

Chelsea Keramic Art Pottery pitcher, Chelsea, Massachusetts, circa 1885, angular four sided pitcher with incised Greek key border and geometric linear border decoration around rim, 7¾in. high. (Skinner) $862

Chelsea Keramic Art Works vase, Massachusetts, late 19th century, with relief decoration of squirrels and oak branches, 12in. wide. (Skinner) $1,350

A Chelsea oval two-handled tureen and cover, circa 1755, of silver-shape, painted allover with scattered butterflies, bouquets, sprays, vegetables and fruits, 13½in. wide.
(Christie's) $3,408

A 'Girl in a Swing' gilt-metal-mounted bodkin-case, circa 1750, attributed to the St. James's factory of Charles Gouyn, naturalistically modelled as an asparagus spear and colored in shades of green and pink, 5¼in. long.
(Christie's) $9,370

A pair of Chelsea Derby porcelain figural candlesticks, depicting seated musicians, he playing the bagpipes, she playing the mandolin, 7½in. high.
(Andrew Hartley) $801

A rare Chelsea crinoline figure of Isabella, standing with her head turned to the left, her arm raised and wearing a voluminous skirt, circa 1756, 15.5cm.
(Woolley & Wallis) $2,538

A pair of Chelsea Arbour groups, circa 1762-69, both the lady and the man seated on balustrades in front of flower-encrusted bocage, with a basket of flowers at their side, 25cm. (Bonhams) $2,940

A Harry Parr, Chelsea pottery figure of a satyr riding a cockerel dated 1929, (crack, and restoration) 11¾in. high.
(Sotheby's) $4,800

A Chelsea Triangle Period beaker, circa 1745-49, molded in high relief and polychrome enamelled with the 'Tea Plant' pattern, 7.5cm.
(Bonhams) $3,836

A pair of Chelsea figures of masqueraders, circa 1760, gold anchor marks, modelled as a lady and gentleman in fanciful Turkish dress, both standing before flowering tree-stumps, 13½in. high max.
(Christie's) $15,334

A Chelsea blue-ground dessert-plate, circa 1765, painted with three swags of flowers divided by underglaze blue vase-shaped panels richly gilt with exotic birds, 8½in. wide. (Christie's) $1,176

A Chinese blue and white teapot and cover, decorated with figures in a pagoda landscape, Qianlong, 1736-95.
(Woolley & Wallis) $109

A Chinese blue and white potiche and cover, painted with triangular panels of scrolling lotus and scattered flower sprays, 5in. diameter, Kangxi.
(Christie's) $265

A mid 18th century Chinese famille rose spittoon of waisted heart shape painted in enamels with birds and foliage, 8cm. high.
(Cheffins) $644

A pair of Chinese blue and white octagonal baluster vases painted with alternating sprays of finger citrons, prunus, pomegranates, peaches and further flowers, 19¼in. high, 19th century.
(Christie's) $6,139

A pair of famille rose wall sconces, circa 1780, painted with garden scenes showing ladies holding vases of flowers, with protruding monster masks issuing the curving turquoise candlearms, 19cm. high.
(Christie's) $11,500

A large pair of Chinese blue and white baluster jars and domed covers painted with dragons among blossoming prunus sprays within borders of floral cartouches, 24in. high, 19th century.
(Christie's) $2,527

One of a pair of Chinese famille rose plates, and a matching pair of soup plates, each decorated with two cockerels in a garden, 18th century, 23cm.
(Woolley & Wallis)
(Four) $775

A Chinese blue and white vase, decorated with figures carrying banners in a rocky landscape, Transitional, circa 1650, 25cm.
(Woolley & Wallis) $1,496

A Chinese polychrome monogrammed plate, painted with the initials *JEP* beneath a coronet, 18th century, 24cm.
(Woolley & Wallis) $197

A Chinese celadon glazed ribbed meiping, with short slightly everted neck and slender tapering body, 7in. high, Yuan Dynasty.
(Christie's) $1,189

A large pair of blue and white Guangdong ware elephants, 18th/19th century, modelled in mirror image standing foursquare on rectangular slab bases, their large heads turned slightly back, 49.8cm. wide.
(Christie's) $27,600

A gilt bronze mounted famille rose bowl, 19th century, decorated with figures on terraces within panels, bordered by butterflies amidst dense flowering foliage, 14½in. diameter. (Christie's) $3,271

A pair of famille rose urns with covers, 19th century, with molded lion mask handles and Buddhistic lion finial to the domed cover, 25½in. high.
(Christie's) $4,543

A pair of Chinese blue and white lidded floor vases with all-over floral and bird design.
(Brightwells) $3,915

A pair of 19th century Chinese pottery vases of shouldered oblong form painted with famille verte panels, depicting warriors and landscapes, on a blue foliate ground, 18in. high.
(Andrew Hartley) $980

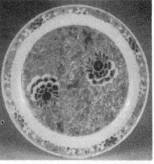

A Chinese blue and white large dish, decorated on the interior with a watery landscape of islands, mountains and pagodas, Wanli, 1573-1619, 17in.
(Woolley & Wallis) $3,520

A matched pair of German polychrome-decorated, gilt-japanned and lacquered Chinese porcelain guéridons, the guéridons second half 19th century, the porcelain Wanli, Kangxi and Qianlong, 36½in. and 38½in.
(Christie's) $56,729

A large Chinese famille rose dish, boldly decorated with peony and lotus flowers and foliage, 18th century, 36.5cm.
(Woolley & Wallis) $149

A Chinese Export Imari armorial oval two-handled basin, 1720-25, the interior painted with the arms and crest of the first Duke of Chandos, 11½in. long. (Sotheby's) $13,200

A Chinese Export lotus-form teapot and cover, 1730-45, the petal-molded body with a bud-form and stem-form handle, height 5in. (Sotheby's) $7,800

A chinese Export armorial barber's bowl, circa 1772, painted in the center with the arms of William Pitt, Viscount Pitt and Earl of Chatham, impaling those of his wife Hester Grenville.(Sotheby's) $10,800

A Chinese Export glazed biscuit figure of a quail, 19th century, modelled standing on a pierced rocky base, the plumage picked out in aubergine, green, yellow and black, 7½in. high. (Sotheby's) $2,400

A pair of ormolu mounted Chinese Export porcelain ducks, the porcelain 19th century, the ormolu late 20th century, each with a pale green duck seated on a polychrome base, 14½in. high. (Christie's) $9,052

A biscuit-glazed wine pot and cover, 19th century, in the form of a shou character, each side with a shaped black-ground panel showing a deity on a rocky point, 9in. high. (Christie's) $920

A Chinese Export blue and white American-market saucer dish, circa 1915 or later, probably commemorating the admission of the State of New Mexico, painted with a large displayed eagle clasping in his right talons three arrows, diameter 27.9cm. (Sotheby's) $9,000

A Chinese Export blue and white European-subject charger 1700-10, after a drawing by Robert Bonnart, engraved by his brother Nicholas, originally titled 'Symphonie du Tympanum, du Luth et de Flute d'Allemagne', 13¼in. diameter. (Sotheby's) $35,250

A blue and white 'arbor' plate, circa 1738, painted in inky tones of cobalt blue with the well-known scene designed by Cornelis Pronk showing a group of ladies and children amusing themselves by a topiary arbor, 10¼in. diameter. (Christie's) $4,830

A tobacco leaf platter, circa 1775, painted in the classic pattern, with scalloped rim and underglaze blue and iron-red peony sprays to the reverse, 15in. long.
(Christie's) $9,200

A Chinese Export trembleuse stand, 1770-80, of shell shape, the central pierced gallery with an iron-red and gilt spearhead border, diameter 8¾in.
(Sotheby's) $2,700

A Chinese Export 'faux marbre' pomegranate tureen, cover and stand, 1750-65, the ends affixed with stalk and twig handles, stand 9¾in.(Sotheby's) $16,800

A Chinese Export blanc-de-Chine equestrian group, 1700-20, modelled as a Dutchman seated on a horse and holding a sword in his right hand, 12in.
(Sotheby's) $19,150

A Chinese Export European-subject coffee cup and saucer circa 1735, finely painted in famille rose enamels with three European gentlemen beneath trees, one riding an elephant, 6cm. diameter.
(Sotheby's) $4,200

A Chinese Export blue and white European-subject coffee pot and cover, 1700-20, after a Dutch Delft original inspired by a European silver shape, of tapering octagonal form on three ball feet, 11½in. high.
(Sotheby's) $10,800

A large Don Quixote plate, circa 1740, richly enamelled with the knight on horseback wearing armor and a deep rose cape, the barber's basin on his head, 12in. diameter.
(Christie's) $25,300

A Chinese Export 'Declaration of Independance' coffee cup circa 1875/76, commemorating the centenary of the signing of the Declaration of Independence, 7.3cm. (Sotheby's) $13,200

A Chinese Export 'Duke of Marlborough' portrait bowl, circa 1735, painted en grisaille with a portrait of John Churchill, 1st Duke of Marlborough, 11½in. diameter.
(Sotheby's) $11,400

'Marilyn' a 'Bizarre' wall mask, in colors, printed marks, 22cm. high. (Christie's) $1,187

'Lido Lady' a rare 'Bizarre' figure, in colors, printed marks, 17cm. high. (Christie's) $11,885

'Crocus' a 'Bizarre' miniature vase in colors, printed marks, 6cm. high. (Christie's) $585

'Latona Bouquet' a 'Bizarre' Athens jug, in colors, printed marks, 19cm. high. (Christie's) $1,188

'Delecia Pansies' a 'Bizarre' Bon Jour coffee set for six, in colors, printed marks, pot 20cm. high. (Christie's) $3,291

'Age of Jazz shape no. 432' a 'Bizarre' centerpiece, in colors, printed marks, 19cm. high. (Christie's) $24,684

'Café Au Lait Red Tulip' a 'Bizarre' single-handled Lotus, in colors, printed marks, 30cm. high. (Christie's) $4,388

'Farmhouse' a 'Fantasque Bizarre' plate in colors, printed marks, 22.5cm. diameter. (Christie's) $1,463

'Delecia Citrus' a 'Bizarre' biscuit barrel with plated cover and handle, in colors, 15cm. high. (Christie's) $639

'Solitude' a 'Fantasque Bizarre' Dragon jug, in colors, printed marks, 16cm. high.
(Christie's) $1,096

'Chahar' a 'Bizarre' mask, in colors, printed marks, 28cm. high.
(Christie's) $2,377

'Red Broth' a 'Fantasque Bizarre' ginger jar, in colors, printed marks (light star-crack), 19cm. high.
(Christie's) $1,463

'Mondrian' a rare double decker Conical rose bowl, in colors, with flower rose printed marks (restored base), 18cm. high.
(Christie's) $4,388

'Latona Red Roses' a Conical coffee set for six, in colors, printed factory marks, 20cm. high.
(Christie's) $4,571

'Grotesque Mask' a 'Bizarre' mask, designed by Ron Birks, in colors, printed marks, (restored), 27cm. high. (Christie's) $5,485

'Orange Roof Cottage', a 'Fantasque Bizarre' single handled Lotus jug, in colors, printed marks, 29cm. high.
(Christie's) $13,714

'Bazique' a 'Bizarre' plate, in colors, printed marks, 23cm. diameter.
(Christie's) $2,926

'Crocus' a 335 biscuit barrel and cover, in colors, printed marks, 16cm. high.
(Christie's) $822

A George III jardinière, John Rose, Coalport, circa 1805-10, of tapering two handled form, painted with a silhouette of the King, inside an oval frame inscribed *A Token From Cheltenham,* 19cm.
(Bonhams) $924

A pair of Coalport globular vases, with short gilt cylindrical necks, each decorated in polychrome enamels with formal stylized flowers and leaves in the Islamic taste, circa 1880, 14.5cm.
(Woolley & Wallis) $628

A Coalport porcelain trophy for Pains Lane races, 1842, in the form of a two-handled cup and cover, royal blue ground with extensive grape and vine and oak leaf and acorn gilding, 13in.
(Sotheby's) $10,764

COPELAND

Copeland circular bowl, printed in blue with the 'Spodes Tower' pattern, 8½in.
(G.A. Key) $184

A Copeland Parian bust of 'Ophelia' by W C Marshall, for Crystal Palace Art Union, 27.5cm.
(Bristol) $330

Clytie, a Copeland parian bust, late 19th century, the maiden looking sorrowful, raised on a socle base, 34cm.
(Bonhams & Brooks) $385

CREAMWARE

A William Greatbatch creamware tortoiseshell-glazed 'fruit basket' teapot and cover, circa 1770-82, the ovoid body molded on each side with clusters of fruit and foliage heightened in manganese-brown, yellow, gray and green, 4½.
(Sotheby's) $2,470

A creamware commemorative cylindrical mug, possibly Liverpool, printed in black with a half-length portrait of Admiral Lord Nelson below the inscription *England Expects every Man to do his Duty,* circa1805, 9cm. high.
(Christie's) $829

A rare Herculaneum creamware George IV coronation plaque, dated 1821, printed in puce with *God Save The King,* 7.8cm. diameter.
(Bonhams) $1,028

Goss wall vase with wreath surround. (Crested China Company) $224

Goss Parian cow and sheep group. (Crested China Company) $1,750

Bird's Nest in a napkin covered in forget-me-nots, 185mm. Goss. (Crested China Company) $630

CROWN DEVON

'John Peel', Crown Devon musical jug, printed marks, 20cm. high. (Christie's) $420

A pair of Crown Devon vases, the blue luster decorated with fairies in gilt. (Bonhams) $294

A Crown Devon Sarrie Marais musical jug, molded in relief with lion handle, painted in colors, 21cm. (Bonhams) $1,102

DAVENPORT

A 19th century Davenport pottery meat plate, with gravy gunnel, gadrooned and leaf molded rim, the center blue printed with a chinoiserie river scene, 20½in. wide. (Andrew Hartley) $218

A pair of Davenport ironstone pot pourri vases, liners and pierced covers, printed and painted with vignettes of Oriental figures and devices between vertical panels of insects among flowers, circa 1830, 22cm. high. (Christie's) $1,845

A Davenport D-shaped bough pot, the sides painted in pink with three landscape panels, circa 1820, 22cm. (Woolley & Wallis) $592

William De Morgan, a ruby luster bowl, exterior decorated with a frieze of stylized rampant lions, the interior with serpent and triangle motifs, artist's monogram, 32.5cm. (Christie's) $1,120

A William De Morgan charger, circa 1890, painted with a scaly fish amongst waterweed, in ruby luster on a white ground, 14in. diameter. (Christie's) $4,606

A William De Morgan pottery tazza, painted by Halsey Ricardo, the well painted with a young deer amongst stylized foliage, 24in, diameter. (Christie's) $4,600

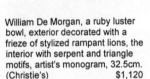

A William De Morgan twin-handled luster vase, decorated with foliate design, 20.6cm. high. (Christie's) $987

A William De Morgan faience vase 1888-1897, decorated in Persian style with three angles in a frieze between foliate bands, height 15¼in. (Sotheby's) $9,600

A William De Morgan Persian vase, circa 1890, painted with large stylized flowers bordered with daisies, in shades of blue, green and purple, 29cm. high. (Christie's) $1,151

DEDHAM

Dedham Pottery Grape Pattern charger, blue stamp, one impressed rabbit, 12in. diameter. (Skinner) $575

Dedham Pottery breakfast plate, in the 'Poppy' pattern with allover decoration and blue background to centre, square blue Dedham stamp, 8½in. diameter. (Eldred's) $500

Dedham Pottery Wolves and Owls Pattern plate, blue stamp, (three tight hairlines, peppering), 12in. diameter. (Skinner) $2,300

A London Delft white fuddling-cup, 17th century, the three globular vases with short cylinder necks each joined with entwined handles, 6¾in. wide.
(Christie's) $3,067

A pair of Dutch Delft blue and white fluted baluster vases, circa 1740, with flared garlic necks painted with scrolling foliage between stiff leaves, the bodies with panels of flowering shrubs, 12¾in. high.
(Christie's) $1,447

A Dutch delft green-ground saucer-dish, circa 1720, painted with four radiating panels of flowering shrubs and grasses within blue and red surrounds, flanked by four stylized iron-red cones, 8½in. diameter.
(Christie's) $1,022

An English Delft blue-dash Adam and Eve charger, circa 1720, probably Bristol, the center painted in blue and manganese with the ill-fated couple flanked by blue-sponged trees, each holding a green leaf in one hand, 13¼in. diameter. (Christie's) $9,370

A Dutch Delft polychrome figure of a toper, circa 1780, seated astride a brown barrel holding a flask and glass and wearing a manganese tricorn hat, breeches and shoes, 12¾in. high.
(Christie's) $6,134

A Dutch Delft ('Greek A Factory') blue and white two-handled jardinière, circa 1690, blue A K monogram for Adrianus Kocks, painted with continuous landscape with deer, peacocks and exotic birds, 43.5cm. high.
(Christie's) $15,334

A Dutch Delft blue and white tulipière, circa 1715-20, of flattened heart-shaped form, the upper edge with five pierced spouts above two winged bird handles at the sides, 8½in. high.
(Christie's) $2,045

A Dutch Delft polychrome figure of a bagpiper, circa 1770, seated on a pale-manganese barrel playing the bagpipes, in manganese hat, green jacket, yellow breeches and manganese shoes, 10½in. high.
(Christie's) $3,748

A Dutch Delft blue and white dish, in the kraak porcelain style, boldly painted with two birds, rockwork and flowers in a central octagonal panel, late 17th century, 39.5cm.
(Woolley & Wallis) $286

A terracotta Della Robbia vase, by Liza Wilkins, incised marks, 10cm. high. (Bonhams) **$441**

A Della Robbia griffin bowl, incised and painted marks, 36cm. diameter. (Christie's) **$575**

A Della Robbia earthenware twin handled vase, dated *1903*, decorated by Cassandra Annie Walker, painted with a maiden and flora, 33.5cm.
(Bonhams) **$3,528**

DERBY

An 18th century Derby porcelain figure of Minerva wearing a helmet and dressed in pink and navy blue floral robes, an owl at her feet, 15½in. high.
(Andrew Hartley) **$672**

A pair of Derby porcelain Mansion House dwarf figures, each in brightly colored dress, one inscribed *Theatre Royal Haymarket* and the other *Auction of Elegant Household Furniture*, late 19th century, 6½in. high.
(Andrew Hartley) **$1,216**

A Derby three-tiered sweetmeat-stand, circa 1760, modelled as seven scallop-shells upheld on branches of coral applied with trailing waterweeds and a variety of shells, 11in. high.
(Christie's) **$3,748**

A Derby figure of Dr. Syntax on horseback, he holds his black tricorn hat as the horse jumps a fence, painted with colored enamels, 2nd half 19th century, 7½in. (Woolley & Wallis) **$572**

A Derby heart shaped dish, brightly decorated with panels of animals and flowers, the reverse with jui panels and leaf scrolls, a blue seal mark, early 19th century, 26cm. (Woolley & Wallis) **$368**

A Derby figure of General Conway, modelled standing with his arm resting on a canon, a putto seated beside him holding a shield with the family crest, circa 1773, 31.5cm. high. (Christie's) **$2,688**

A Derby bough pot and cover, circa 1810, possibly by Robert Brewer or George Robertson, well painted with Cupid Disarmed, in the manner of Angelica Kauffmann, 10in. wide, red. (Bonhams) $3,773

A 19th century Derby porcelain three piece tea set, the teapot of oval form with turned finial on flat lid and with Imari floral pattern No 383, 9½in. wide.
(Andrew Hartley) $677

Derby (Stevenson & Hancock) porcelain dish, decorated in colors with bright Japan pattern, marked in iron red with cross batons, coronet and *D* and the letters *S. H.*, 19th century, 11in. (G.A. Key) $246

A pair of Royal Crown Derby candlesticks, decorated with an Imari pattern No. 1128, circa 1917, 16cm.(Woolley & Wallis) $485

DERUTA

A pair of Derby yellow-ground câche-pots, circa 1790, of flared cylindrical form with shell-molded handles, painted with colorful flower sprays reserved against a yellow ground, 5½in.
(Sotheby's) $5,468

A Derby figure of a lady, sitting playing a mandolin and raised on a scrolling base, no mark, circa 1780, 16cm.(Woolley & Wallis) $338

A Deruta basin, late 17th century, of silver shape, molded in relief with gadrooned panels radiating from the center, painted with a figural scene, 17¼in.
(Sotheby's) $4,335

A Deruta rectangular votive plaque, late 16th/early 17th century, brightly painted with the Madonna and child seated on a throne, accompanied by two female saints, 7 x 8¼in.
(Skinner) $4,669

A Deruta maiolica crespina, early 17th century, painted with a circular panel of flowering plants, grotesques and scrolling foliage, 11in. (Sotheby's) $747

'The Menagerie', a Doulton Lambeth stoneware clockcase circa 1885, by George Tinworth, assisted by Emily Partington, impressed oval factory marks, 9½in. high. (Sotheby's) $16,800

A Doulton Lambeth white stoneware wall plaque, early 20th century, by Harry Simeon, decorated with a peacock, painted *Doulton Lambeth*, 20¼in. diameter. (Sotheby's) $3,300

'The Waits', a Doulton Lambeth stoneware mouse group spill vase circa 1885, by George Tinworth, impressed oval factory mark, 14.3cm. (Sotheby's) $1,800

A Royal Doulton stoneware vase, 1907, by Mark V. Marshall, glazed with foliage and fleur-de-lis motifs, impressed lion, crown and circle mark, 13¼in. high. (Sotheby's) $1,560

A Doulton Lambeth stoneware silver-mounted tyg, 1875, by Hannah B. Barlow, boldly incised with three groups of donkeys and pigs, the silver hallmarked London 1875, 7¼in. high. (Sotheby's) $2,040

A large Douton Lambeth Impasto vase, 1884, by Florence C. Roberts and Rosa Keen, decorated with three roundels of large peony flowers and blossoming branches, (crack to rim), 51.1cm. high. (Sotheby's) $1,080

A Doulton Lambeth stoneware large vase, 1890s, by Frank A. Butler, boldly modelled, tube-lined and incised with stylized leaves, 16in. high. (Sotheby's) $3,000

A Royal Doulton flambé large shallow bowl, 1920s, decorated inside with a woodland landscape, black printed lion, crown and circle mark and *Flambé*, 15¼in. diameter. (Sotheby's) $1,080

A Doulton Lambeth stoneware two-handled vase, 1875, by George Tinworth, with molded cherub handles, incised *GT* monogram, 8in. high. (Sotheby's) $1,200

A Doulton Lambeth faience pilgrim flask, 1880s, painted on one side with irises and on the other with daisies, 11¼in. high. (Sotheby's) $600

A Doulton Lambeth stoneware jardinière, 1890s, by Mark V. Marshall, carved and slip-trailed with seaweed scrolls, 20.6cm. high. (Sotheby's) $2,160

A massive Doulton Lambeth stoneware vase, 1880s, by Hannah B. Barlow, the borders by Frank A. Butler, incised with sheep, 21¼in. high. (Sotheby's) $1,800

A Doulton Lambeth stoneware jardinière, 1890s, by Mark V. Marshall, tube-lined with four owl masks with pierced eyes, 20cm. high. (Sotheby's) $1,680

A Doulton Lambeth green-tinted stoneware wall plaque, early 20th century, by Harry Simeon, decorated with a bird perched on a flowering branch, impressed *Pinder Bourne & Co.,* 17¼in. diameter. (Sotheby's) $3,300

A Doulton Lambeth stoneware two-handled jardinière, 1882, by Hannah B. Barlow, assisted by Lucy A. Barlow, incised with ponies and lions, 16.8cm. high. (Sotheby's) $3,600

A Doulton Lambeth stoneware two-handled urn, 1877, by Frank A. Butler, molded in low relief with a panel of Neptune and attendants above a frieze of grotesque heads, 13in. high. (Sotheby's) $840

'Scandal', a Doulton Lambeth stoneware figural group 1880s, by George Tinworth, impressed circular factory mark, incised artist's monogram, 14.3cm. high. (Sotheby's) $4,800

A Hannah Barlow Doulton Lambeth stoneware tapering cylindrical jug, incised with a frieze depicting cattle in a landscape, signed with monogram, silver plated rim, 9½in. high. (Wintertons) $840

Granny (toothless) D5521, a Royal Doulton large character jug, 17cm. (Bonhams) $462

Royal Doulton large character jug 'Mephistopheles', plain back stamp without verse, circa 1937/48, 5½in. (G.A. Key) $942

Florence Nightingale, HN 3144, number 2724 of an edition of 5000, a Royal Doulton figure, 21cm., printed marks. (Bonhams) $647

A Doulton Lambeth stoneware jug, the neck molded with a band of winged bull, the ovoid body applied with Persian warriors in white bas reliefs, late 19th century, 20cm. (Woolley & Wallis) $114

A pair of Doulton Lambeth stoneware and brass mounted candlesticks bearing monograms for Eliza Simmance etc, incised stylized foliate decoration, 20cm. high. (Wintertons) $219

A Hannah Barlow Doulton Lambeth jug, impasto decorated with birds amongst daisies on a cross hatch ground, set with twin panels of cattle, 9in. (Academy) $960

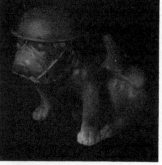

A Royal Doulton 'Sung' Buddha, signed *Noke*, the figure modelled seated in flowering robes in a rich red and mottled purple glaze, 18.5cm. (Bonhams) $3,696

A Royal Doulton 'Tommy' Bulldog figure, modelled in a seated pose wearing a helmet, Sam Brown and ammunition bag, all over khaki glaze, 15.5cm. (Tennants) $730

Royal Doulton loudspeaker cover, (made for Artandia Limited), in the form of a feathered cockatoo perched on a rock, 15½in. high. (G.A. Key) $276

Queen Victoria and Prince Albert, HN 3256, number 105 of an edition 2500, a Royal Doulton group, 20.3cm, printed marks (with Certificate).
(Bonhams) $345

Leopard on a Rock, HN 2638, a Royal Doulton animal figure, naturalistically colored, 20.2cm.
(Bonhams) $585

A Doulton Lambeth stoneware jug, of bellied form, applied with a continuous frieze of fish amidst scrolling foliage on a brown ground, circa 1895, 25cm.
(Tennants) $628

Royal Doulton jardinière by Frank Butler, molded with rosettes and bosses throughout and also with cream pelleted scrolled detail, dated *1876*, 7in.
(G.A. Key) $261

A Royal Doulton 'Reynard the Fox' coffee service, comprising coffee pot and cover, hot water jug and cover, cream jug, sugar bowl and six cups and saucers.
(Bonhams) $770

A large Doulton Lambeth faience pilgrim flask, 1890s, by Mary Butterton, assisted by Alice Campbell, painted with a bluetit and insects in flight above purple irises and foliage, height 14¼in.
(Sotheby's) $960

A Royal Doulton pottery vase by Frank Butler, incised with Art Nouveau style flowers and trailing foliage in shades of brown, blue and green, 13¾in. high.
(Andrew Hartley) $672

A pair of Royal Doulton stoneware flasks, circa 1880, the square body decorated in muted turquoise and blue, decorated by Elizabeth J Adams and Pd, 20.5cm. high.
(Bonhams) $431

A Royal Doulton group, entitled 'The Perfect Pair', H.N.581, withdrawn 1938.
(Bearne's) $308

A 19th century porcelain urn, the domed lid and circular bowl encrusted and painted with flowers and butterflies amongst gilt banding, 4¾in. wide. (Andrew Hartley) $200

A pair of late 19th century vases of ovoid form with painted mythological figures, 19½in. high. (Lloyds International) $309

A Continental two-handled urn and cover on majolica lavishly decorated with colored glazes on classical moldings of scrolls, fruit festoons, ram's and maiden heads, etc, 21in. (Brightwells) $537

Continental porcelain cabinet plate, possibly Hutschenreuther, Bavaria, late 19th /early 20th century, with central printed portrait of Empress Louise, 9¼in. diameter. (Skinner) $115

A large Austrian pottery model of an owl, circa 1900, naturalistically modelled perched on two books, the uppermost open, on which rests an inkpot and quill, 22in. (Sotheby's) $3,881

Austrian porcelain oyster plate, 19th century, with shell-shaped wells to center, the scalloped rim with blue and gilt enamel decoration of flowers, fish, and birds, 9⅞in. (Skinner) $173

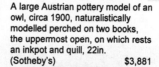

An Austrian porcelain chocolate cup, cover and saucer, painted with a scene from classical mythology reserved on a gilt embellished navy blue ground, bud finial on domed lid, 5in. high. (Andrew Hartley) $722

One of a pair of Austrian decorated vases, 12in. tall. (Whitworths) $264

A large porcelain bust of a young lady wearing a bonnet, stamped *ESC*, Stellmacher Teplitz, 17½in. high.(Lloyds International) $323

Pair of Robj Classical figures
porcelain standing figures of a man
and woman in Classical Greek
garb, 11in. (Skinner) $460

Continental porcelain model of
standing pug dog with rattles on its
collar, naturalistically painted in
shades of brown and with orange
eyes, blue and gilded detail, circa
late 19th century, 5in.
(G.A. Key) $223

Pair of Continental bisque nodding
figures, modelled as a young man
and his female companion, both
with naturalistic faces and gilded
and blue/green detail throughout,
11in. (G A Key) $188

Gouda Art Pottery handled vase,
Holland, raised rim on a double
bulbed vessel, the two sides raised
to form a continuous handle, glossy
glaze with stylized iris blossoms in
purple, blue, green, and taupe,
13in. high. (Skinner) $920

Large pair of enamel decorated
earthenware putti figures, Austria,
early 20th century, possibly
depicting two of the four seasons,
designed by M. Powolny, 35¾in.
high. (Skinner) $4,600

A Continental porcelain plaque of
Napoleon Bonaparte, late 19th
century, oval, nearly half-length and
three quarters to dexter, as
Emperor, wearing green jacket with
red collar, 13cm.
(Bonhams) $647

A pair of porcelain figures of a
Finnish man and woman by the
Imperial Porcelain Factory, St.
Petersburg, period of Nicholas II,
1912, 39cm. high and slightly
smaller. (Christie's) $3,649

Two Gustavsberg majolica cat jugs,
each tabby cat naturalistically
modelled seated on its haunches,
with a dead mouse under its right
paw, on shaped oval green mound
bases, late 19th century, 23.5cm.
high. (Christie's) $2,208

A De Porceleyne fles blue and
white faience jar and cover, the
baluster body boldly painted with
panels of flowers, 58cm. high,
painted marks, circa 1900.
(Bearne's) $503

Fairing, late 19th century 'How Happy I Could Be With Either', 3½in.
(G A Key) $338

Fairing, late 19th/early 20th century, 'Returning From The Ball', 4in.
(G A Key) $419

Fairing, late 19th/early 20th century, 'Please Sir What Would You Charge To Christen My Doll', 4in.
(G A Key) $338

FAMILLE ROSE

A Chinese famille rose ewer, the conical body decorated with peony and phoenix, 18/19th century, 27cm. (Woolley & Wallis) $394

A pair of famille rose shaped octagonal jardinières, each painted with shaped panels of vases, censers, precious objects, peonies, prunus and chrysanthemums, 7½in. wide, Qianlong.
(Christie's) $2,656

Famille rose porcelain jar and cover, China, 19th century, baluster form, decorated with a female sprite figure emerging from flower blossom, 18in. high.
(Skinner) $747

FAMILLE VERTE

A Chinese famille verte brush pot, decorated with a prancing kylin in a rocky landscape, Kangxi, 1662-1722, 19cm. diameter.
(Woolley & Wallis) $2,176

A famille verte biscuit lobed brushwasher, Kangxi six-character mark and of the period (1662 - 1722), enamelled in the center with crickets, a butterfly and chrysanthemums, 5½in. diameter.
(Christie's) $46,288

A Chinese famille verte circular dish, painted with warriors on horseback, Kangxi 1662-1722, 37cm. cracked in half and riveted.
(Woolley & Wallis) $338

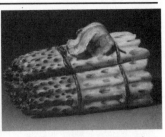

A French Nevers faience blue and white cistern, circa 1710, each end moulded with a satyr's mask, the footrim molded with gadroons divided by two leopard's heads, 34¼in. wide.
(Christie's) $14,904

A faience and glass cat in the style of Gallé, 34cm. high.
(Christie's) $312

A Sceaux asparagus-tureen and cover, circa 1750, naturally modelled as a tightly stacked bundle of asparagus spears bound with trailing vine, the finial formed as a vine leaf, 17.5cm. wide.
(Christie's) $6,134

A French ormolu mounted blanc de Chine porcelain centerpiece, 19th century, modelled with two figures supporting a basketwork urn fitted with a gilt brass floral spray with porcelain flowerheads, 15½in. high.
(Christie's) $4,738

A pottery charger, by Longwy, for Primavera, 1920s, the shallow circular dish incised and glazed in shades of green, gray-blue, black and gilt with stylized female and birds, signed *Claude Levy*, $16^2/3$in. diameter.(Christie's) $2,520

A Chantilly quatrefoil Kakiemon sugar-bowl, a cover and a stand, painted with insects among sprigs of flowers, the finial of the cover formed as three flowers, circa 1745, the sugar-bowl, 15.5cm. wide.
(Christie's) $2,245

A pair of 19th century French porcelain pot pourri vases, urn shaped with flower finial on domed lid, painted with marine scenes on a navy blue ground, 12in. high.
(Andrew Hartley) $2,940

A French porcelain group of Diana bathing, the goddess semi-naked, with three nymphs and two hounds in attendance, on a high rocky mound above a stream, circa 1880, 41cm. high. (Christie's) $1,200

A pair of French silvered-bronze and gilt-metal mounted san-de-boeuf-ground baluster vases and two covers, late 19th/20th century, gilt with opposing rampant lions before an angled scrollwork band, 25½in. high.
(Christie's) $19,975

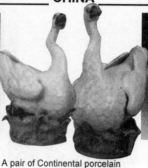

A Strasbourg bullet-shaped teapot and cover, circa 1765, the handle and short curved spout formed and painted to simulate branches, the handle's upper terminal issuing trailing branches, 4¼in. high. (Christie's) $2,214

A pair of Continental porcelain models of swans, perhaps Samson, modelled after Meissen originals by J.J. Kaendler, on mound bases issuing aquatic plants, late 19th century, 28cm. high. (Christie's) $2,352

A Strasbourg cabbage-tureen and cover, circa 1745-50, naturally modelled and painted in grand feu colors, the tureen with three concentric layers of large green leaves with pale-yellow veins, 15¾in. wide. (Christie's) $37,483

A pair of Paris scroll-molded two-handled green-ground vases each painted with a cartouche of amorous figures in a landscape, within gilt-scroll border, 22cm. high. (Christie's) $614

A pair of French porcelain flower-encrusted pot-pourri baskets and covers, modelled as fluted baskets with handles, the pierced covers issuing three extensive bouquets of flowers, mid 18th century, 11cm. high. (Christie's) $2,245

A pair of Paris (Boyer) pale-blue-ground baluster vases with flared necks, painted with a shepherd and companion in a wooded landscape, circa 1860, 38cm. high. (Christie's) $2,479

A Lunéville two handled gadrooned jardinière, probably circa 1770, molded with puce feuilles-de choux above gadroons and below a molded hexafoil lobed rim, 7½in. high. (Christie's) $170

A Limoges (Giraud Brousseau) rectangular plaque of Henry VIII, 20th century, green printed mark, incised numerals, inscribed *Leighton Maybury*, 11¾ x 7¾in. within amber velvet and gilt-gesso frame. (Christie's) $1,410

A French white porcelain figural group depicting putti playing with a goat, raised on gilt embellished oval base with bracket feet, 10¾in. wide. (Andrew Hartley) $471

Gardner biscuit figure of a man, Russia, mid 19th century, the seated figure modelled with legs crossed and playing an accordion, printed mark, 6½in. high.
(Skinner) $863

Gardner biscuit figure group, Russia, circa 1870, depicting two children, one standing in a pose, the other seated on a broken cartwheel, 5½in. high.
(Skinner) $805

Gardner biscuit figure group of two boys playing with eggs, Russia, mid 19th century, a standing and seated figure mounted on a rectangular base, 5½in. high.
(Skinner) $1,035

Gardner porcelain figure group, Russia, circa 1840, modelled as a small boy holding a crab and about to awaken his sleeping companion with it, 5½in. high.
(Skinner) $978

Gardner biscuit figure of a mother and child, Russia, mid 19th century, the seated female figure modelled feeding an infant seated on her lap, red printed mark, 6½in. high.
(Skinner) $863

Gardner biscuit figure group of three tipsy men, Russia, circa 1860, one figure modelled holding up a bottle, another playing an accordion, 10in high.
(Skinner) $2,415

Gardner porcelain figure of peasant with wheelbarrow, Russia, circa 1820, modelled pushing a wheelbarrow supporting a box and cover molded as a bundle of logs, 5¾in. high. (Skinner) $546

Gardner biscuit figure of two men conversing, Russia, mid-19th century, modelled as two male figures standing on a rectangular base, 8¼in. high.
(Skinner) $1,035

Gardner biscuit figure group, Russia, mid 19th century, depicting two children, one seated on a trestle, another standing and playing a horn, 4¾in. high.
(Skinner) $748

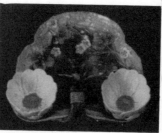

George Jones majolica sardine box, the lid molded with three sardines, painted in colors, trug shaped base, decorated in treacle and mottled green, impressed marks and date cypher for 1882, 9in. (G.A. Key) $911

A George Jones majolica strawberry dish, modelled as a rectangular trough with D-shaped ends, the handle formed as a trestle overgrown with fruiting strawberry plants, S for 1875, the sugar and cream bowls lacking, 38cm. (Woolley & Wallis) $4,312

A George Jones majolica dessert dish molded in relief with three green vine leaves, reserved on a pale-pink ground, modelled with the head of a fox and forepaws leaning over the side of the dish, 1870, 28.5cm. wide. (Christie's) $1,771

A George Jones majolica tapering square-section jardinière molded in relief with lily-of-the-valley and Canterbury bells, reserved on a pale-blue ground, circa 1870, 23cm. high. (Christie's) $673

A George Jones trefoil strawberry dish, with cable handle, the dish molded as a lilypad with strawberry leaves and blossom, 1876, 27cm. wide. (Christie's) $1,640

A large George Jones majolica jardinière, molded with birds perching on rushes among dragonflies above flowering lily pads beneath a yellow rim, circa 1870, 39.5cm. high. (Christie's) $4,145

A George Jones majolica cheese dish and cover, molded in relief with nasturtiums, painted in yellow and green on a blue basket weave ground, 7½in. high. (Andrew Hartley) $5,236

A George Jones majolica tureen, liner and cover, circa 1875, of tapering oval shape molded with trophies of dead game, instruments and weapons between swag-shaped nets. (Sotheby's) $5,376

A George Jones majolica cockerel teapot and cover, circa 1870, naturalistically modelled and colored, his tail forming the handle, 11in. (Sotheby's) $6,582

A Sitzendorf figure of a spaniel, molded and naturalistically painted, 25cm. wide.
(Thomson Roddick & Medcalf) $203

Two similar German porcelain articulated pagoda figures after a Meissen original, typically modelled seated cross-legged with nodding hands, heads and tongues, painted and gilt with deutsche Blumen, late 19th century, 12cm. high.
(Christie's) $1,594

German stoneware bellarmine of baluster form, the spout and body below molded with a grotesque mask and wheel motif respectively, 18th century, 9in.
(G A Key) $320

A pair of Mettlach cylindrical vases, each with four raised panels incised and painted with maidens emblematic of the seasons with the signature *C. Warth*, 33.5cm.
(Tennants) $1,256

A set of five German porcelain game plates, of divided form, decorated by C. M. Hutschenreuther with named American game birds after Pope, late 19th century, 24cm.
(Tennants) $1,148

A pair of German porcelain figures of a lute and tambourine player, modelled standing, the man holding a cat and his companion a dog, on shaped bases, late 19th century, 41cm. high.
(Christie's) $1,175

A Kiel or Stockelsdorf shaped botanical dish, circa 1765-75, painted with a loose bouquet including a pink rose and blue bell flowers surrounded by specimen flower-sprays, 11¼in. wide.
(Christie's) $682

A pair of German majolica nautilus vases, the shell-shaped bowls molded with bearded masks and lions, supported by fauns, late 19th century, 40cm. high.
(Christie's) $920

A gray stoneware tankard, painted in green, blue, red, yellow, white black and manganese with bear hunting scenes between borders, pewter cover with monogram and dated *1683*, Creussen, last quarter 17th century, 15.7cm. high.
(Lempertz) $9,943

A German fayence duck-tureen and cover, circa 1755, naturally modelled and painted in grand feu colors enriched with petit feu manganese enamel, with an ochre and brown beak with manganese markings, 9¼in. high.
(Christie's) $64,743

A Hannoversch-Munden two-handled pierced basket and stand, circa 1760, exterior with manganese and green flowerheads at the intersections, the pierced border of the circular stand similarly decorated, the basket 9¼in. wide.
(Christie's) $1,704

An asparagus dish in shades of green in the form of a bunch of 19 pieces of asparagus, the top four detachable as the lid, South West Germany, 18th century, 17cm. long.
(Lempertz) $6,803

A Frankfurt faience pewter-mounted lobed Enghalskrug painted in blue with a peacock, other birds and insects among flowering shrubs, the neck with stylized foliage, circa 1700, 26cm. high. (Christie's) $361

Two Glienitz parrot-jugs and covers, circa 1765, modelled as parrots perched on curved branches issuing from short tree-stumps, their necks forming spouts and the covers formed as the upper part of their heads, 26cm. high.
(Christie's) $7,666

An 18th century Bellarmine jug medallion mask spout and loop handle with orange peel glaze, 9in. high. (Brightwells) $764

A Northern European fayence watch-stand, circa 1765, probably Eckernförde, blue cross mark, the Swiss or French watch last quarter of the 18th century, painted in petit feu colors, 5½in. high.
(Christie's) $1,363

A German fayence turkey-tureen and cover, circa 1750, painted in petit feu colors with cream colored plumage with brown tips and dark-brown markings, 9¼in. high.
(Christie's) $8,519

A pair of German porcelain winged mythical figures, wearing flowing robes, with entwined fish tails, on Nymphenburg square waisted plinths painted with sprays of flowers, 18th century, 15.5cm. high. (Christie's) $410

Goldscheider, peacock dancer, circa 1930, creamware, glazed in shades of green, blue, brown, black and cream, 19in.
(Sotheby's) $14,790

A Goldscheider polychrome pottery mask, impressed *K6774 12*, 20cm. long. (Christie's) $461

A Goldscheider polychrome pottery figure, printed factory marks, impressed numerals *7581 33431 G*, 36cm. high.
(Christie's) $1,068

A polychrome pottery figure, by Goldscheider, from a model by Dakon, 1920s, of young female in pantaloons and multi-colored waistcoat and angular hat, 13¾in. high. (Christie's) $2,520

A polychrome pottery figure group by Goldscheider, from a model by Dakon, 1920s, modelled as two stylized dancers, wearing patterned peaked hats and matching batwing capes and pink dresses, 15in. high.
(Christie's) $8,737

A polychrome pottery figure, by Goldscheider, from a model by Dakon, 1920s, modelled as three stylized female dancers, wearing lilac backless frilly dresses, poised standing in a line, 14in. high.
(Christie's) $12,601

A Goldscheider polychrome pottery figure from a model by Lorenzl, printed factory marks, *Lorenzl* and impressed numerals, 32cm. high.
(Christie's) $822

A Goldscheider ceramic vase with faces molded in relief, after design by A. Larroux, 46cm. high.
(Christie's) $2,138

A Goldscheider polychrome pottery figure from a model by Dakon, printed factory marks and Dakon signature, 34cm. high.
(Christie's) $1,316

A polychrome pottery figure by Goldscheider, 1920s, of an elegant young woman wearing long blue fur trimmed coat and hat, standing with one arm raised, 15in. high.
(Christie's) $2,347

Goldscheider, a figural ashtray, the quatrefoil section dish, applied with cigarette rests and a stylized female bust, in polychrome, printed marks, 19cm.
(Bonhams & Brooks) $329

'The Captured Bird', a polychrome pottery figure, by Goldscheider, from a model by Lorenzl, 1920s, modelled as a female dancer poised on tiptoes with arms outspread, 19½in. diameter.
(Christie's) $3,520

HAN

A painted gray pottery chimera-form stand, Han dynasty, the recumbent beast molded with an elongated body coiled around a central socket and a pair of small wings sprouting from the shoulders, 9in. long.
(Sotheby's) $540

A Han painted pottery model of a horse and rider, the rider wearing a red and black surcoat, his hands held out, the saddle cloth painted in red, black and green pigments, 36.5cm.
(David Stanley) $1,739

A large Chinese gray pottery model of a hound seated on its haunches wearing a studded collar, 28¾in. high, Han Dynasty.
(Christie's) $4,153

HANS COPER

Hans Coper, a stoneware black spade-shaped vase, covered in a burnished black manganese glaze, the body with lateral incised lines, circa 1970, 20.6cm. high.
(Christie's) $4,606

Hans Coper, a stoneware bulbous bottle with wide disk rim set on short cylindrical neck, covered in a biscuit buff glaze with dense areas of manganese, circa 1965, 17.2cm. high. (Christie's) $7,402

Hans Coper, a stoneware spade form vase, the gently swollen upper section tapering towards the rim, covered in a bluish buff slip, circa 1970, 17.5cm high.
(Christie's) $13,160

A Höchst tortoise tureen and cover, circa 1750, naturally modelled and painted in grand feu manganese and yellow, with a molded yellow band about its neck, manganese scales to its neck and shoulders, 25.7cm. long.
(Christie's) $23,853

A 19th century Höchst Damm white faience figure of Venus with a putto and doves, 37cm. high.
(Arnold) $798

A large Höchst rococo oval two-handled tureen and cover, circa 1750, iron-red wheel mark, painted in petit feu colors with large specimen flower-sprays, 22½in. wide. (Christie's) $28,964

A Höchst model of a parrot, circa 1750, painted by Johannes Zechinger, with red patches about its eyes, its neck, shoulders and tail with pale-blue plumage with dark-blue markings, 38.5cm. high.
(Christie's) $125,063

A Höchst chocolate-pot and cover, circa 1752, painted in grand feu colors with scattered bouquets and flower-sprays, 20cm. high.
(Christie's) $6,815

A Höchst group of musicians, circa 1775, blue wheel mark, modelled by J. P. Melchior, as a man in a black hat and pale-blue cloak playing the fiddle before a tree-stump, 9in. high.
(Christie's) $2,764

A Höchst group of 'Der Lauscher am Brunnen', circa 1760, modelled by Laurentius Russinger, as a gentleman wearing a puce jacket and iron-red breeches and holding a posy, 22cm.
(Sotheby's) $9,730

A Höchst figure of a youth, circa 1775, modelled by J.P.Melchior, standing holding a strawberry in each hand and a hat filled with the fruit, 5½in.(Sotheby's) $1,008

A Höchst model of 'Die Verschuttete Milch', modelled by J.P. Melchior, standing crying over a bowl of spilt milk, circa 1775, 12cm.
(Woolley & Wallis) $1,132

A large Imari baluster jar, 19th century, painted and gilt with numerous carp above a profusion of irises on riverbanks, 19in. high.
(Christie's) $3,619

An Imari model of a standing bijin, the lady wearing long flowing robes decorated with swirling waters and scattered flowers,13¼ in. high, circa 1700.
(Christie's) $1,771

A Japanese Imari small globular teapot, decorated with two shaped panels of birds in flight over blossom, 18th century, 13cm.
(Woolley & Wallis) $300

A 19th century Imari porcelain charger, with all over floral and geometric panels in iron red, blue and green with gilt embellishment, 22in. wide.
(Andrew Hartley) $739

A pair of 19th century Japanese Imari jardinières of circular honeycomb form, the hexagonal panels painted with figures playing games, birds and deer, 12in. wide.
(Andrew Hartley) $3,031

A 19th century Japanese Imari porcelain charger, painted with a Geisha girl on a garden terrace surrounded by panels of flowers, signed, 17½in. wide.
(Andrew Hartley) $1,330

A large Imari dish, 17th century, the center with tsuru-kame and sho-chiku-bai by a river, 18¹/₈in. diam.
(Christie's) $6,561

A large Imari circular jardinière, 19th century, painted and gilt with panels of exotic birds in flowering gardens, 20in. diameter.
(Christie's) $2,467

One of a pair of 19th century Imari porcelain chargers, with blue and white floral center, on a green, blue and red diaper ground, 18¼in. wide. (Andrew Hartley) $957

An Urbino Istoriato dish, circa 1540, painted with Europa riding Jupiter in the form of a white bull by a shore with a fortified city and mountains in the distance, 10¾in. diameter. (Christie's) $9,370

Faience Urbino or Deruta globular baluster vase, painted in colors with head and shoulders portraits of Roman officer and legionary, on a typically foliate scrolled ground with deep blue detail, 18th/19th century, 6in. (G A Key) $1,042

A Montelupo dish, second quarter of the 17th century, boldly painted in blue, yellow, turquoise, ocher and manganese with a man on horseback in a stylized landscape, 12¼in. diameter. (Christie's) $1,873

A blue glazed maiolica dish, decorated in ocher, blue, manganese and green with a striding soldier with a sword in each hand, Montelupo, 17th century, 31.5cm. diameter. (Lempertz) $1,989

A Faenza globular wet-drug jar, circa 1520, with slender waisted neck, the centre named for ·AQ·ACETOSA· on a long stylized scroll against a ground of richly scrolling blue, ocher, brown and turquoise foliage, 10in. (Christie's) $6,474

A Nove large shaped dish, circa 1770, the center painted with fruit supported by yellow and blue foliage scrolls, the border molded with gadroons and painted with trailing flowering branches, 38.5cm. wide. (Christie's) $1,704

A late 19th century Cantagalli majolica vase, the sides painted with two Renaissance style panels on a ground decorated with figures and arabesques, 31cm. high. (Cheffins) $412

A Venice Istoriato dish, circa 1560, painted with four figures at discussion before an apparition of Jupiter on a cloud above a rocky wooded shore, Europa riding the bull in the distant sea, 9½in. diameter. (Christie's) $7,156

Castelli pilgrim's flask, circa 1760, of flattened circular form with short neck, each side painted with figures by buildings in wooded landscapes with distant mountains, approximately 17cm. high. (Christie's) $1,447

A Japanese blue and white
reticulated vase, decorated with
flowers and foliage, 20th century,
22cm.(Woolley & Wallis) $190

A rare Japanese Kakiemon
tankard, of European form,
moulded with panels of dragons
and chrysanthemum on an
unglazed 'fish roe' ground, circa
1670, 14cm.
(Woolley & Wallis) $28,560

A Japanese Hirado model of a
tiger, standing four square, 19th
century, 21.5cm.
(Woolley & Wallis) $1,035

A Japanese blue and white dish,
the border molded with panels of
mon, the center painted with a long
tailed bird perched on a branch,
Fuku mark, circa 1700, 21.5cm.
(Woolley & Wallis) $1,170

Pair of 19th century Japanese wall
plaques decorated in underglazed
blue with figures of irises in the
water with carp swimming, shaped
edge, 37cm. (Thomson Roddick &
Medcalf) $585

A Japanese blue and white U-
shaped jardinière, decorated with
four panels of birds on a floral
ground, circa 1900, 41.5cm.
diameter.
(Woolley & Wallis) $212

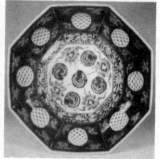

A large Japanese polychrome dish,
painted with a butterfly, a large
poppy and other flowers on a coral
ground, late 19th century, 47cm.
(Woolley & Wallis) $367

A large Fukugawa baluster vase,
19th century, panted in pastel
shades with clusters of variously
colored irises on a gilt geometric
pattern ground, 17¾in. high.
(Christie's) $822

A Japanese Arita Imari octagonal
dish, the border with reticulated
panels, the center with five phoenix
between jui scrolls, 1st half 18th
century, 22cm.
(Woolley & Wallis) $816

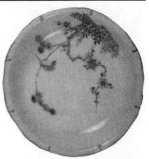

A Japanese blue and white shaped dish, decorated with ho-ho birds, flowers, foliage and rockwork, early 18th century, 12in.
(Woolley & Wallis) $477

Unusual Japanese Satsuma teapot, the handle and spout modelled as a dragon and elaborately painted in colors with humorous scenes of tribal robber bands, 19th century, 9½in. (G A Key) $528

A Japanese Kakiemon circular dish, decorated in iron red, yellow, green, blue and black with a bird perched on bamboo, 18th century, 14cm.
(Woolley & Wallis) $1,787

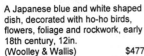

An enormous Japanese Imari vase, gilt and painted with oval panels of figures in landscape and on verandah divided by pavilions, 83cm. (Bristol) $879

Three of a set of nine Japanese plates painted in colored enamels and gilt with baskets containing vases of flowers and leaves, 7¾in. diameter, 19th century.
(Christie's) (Nine) $812

A Japanese porcelain vase of flattened ovoid form with molded dragon handles, painted with figure scenes on a gilded turquoise ground, 19th century. 12¼in. high.
(Andrew Hartley) $125

A porcelain footed dish, Okawachi, Nabeshima Ware, Edo Period (18th century), decorated with ribbonate flower-heads in reserve against a pale under-glaze-blue ground and in red, yellow and green enamels, 7¾in. diameter.
(Christie's) $40,250

A Japanese polychrome incense burner, modelled as a seated shi shi, with a removable and rotating head, his mane and tail picked out in brown and gilt, 18th / early 19th century, 16cm.
(Woolley & Wallis) $502

A pottery wickerwork baluster vase with applied crabs, 19th century, stamped seal to base, the vase of compressed form with two crabs applied to the side, and further applied shells to the neck, 10in. high. (Christie's) $3,125

A Kakiemon vase, late 17th century, decorated in iron red, green, yellow, blue and black enamels depicting boats in a lakeside landscape, 9¹³/₁₆in. high.
(Christie's) $19,682

A large and rare Japanese Kakiemon blue and white molded dish, the center painted with figures in a boat beneath flowering prunus, Fuku mark, circa 1690, 31.5cm.
(Woolley & Wallis) $5,168

A French porcelain pot-pourri, probably Chantilly, of baluster form, painted in the Kakiemon palette with Oriental birds between flowering branches, circa 1750, 16.5cm. high.
(Christie's) $1,316

KANGXI

A biscuit-glazed model of a Dutch ship, Kangxi period, with small black-hatted figures on deck, working with ropes or at the small foremast, 9½in. long.
(Christie's) $21,850

A pair of biscuit-glazed hen ewers and covers, Kangxi Period, each bird seated with small green chicks at her side, a splash-glazed chick on her back serving as the cover, tail feathers extending as a handle, 6¹/₈in. long.
(Christie's) $12,650

A pair of Chinese famille verte spiral molded small baluster vases, decorated with flowers and foliage, Kangxi, 1662-1722, 15cm.
(Woolley & Wallis) $925

KLOSTER VIELSDORF

A Kloster Veilsdorf miniature figure of Pantaloon, modelled by Wenzel Neu after an engraving by J.B. Probst, in a black snood and cape and iron-red suit, holding a candle, 1765, 7.5cm. high.
(Bonhams) $3,140

A pair of Kloster Veilsdorf figures of Harlequin and Columbine from the Commedia dell'Arte Series, circa 1767, modelled by Wenzel Neu, 15 and 16.9cm., respectively.
(Christie's) $22,149

A Kloster Veilsdorf group emblematic of Summer, circa 1775, modelled as a young man and companion, standing and seated before sheaves of corn, decorated in a pale palette, 12.5cm. high.
(Christie's) $1,363

A Japanese Kutani plate, decorated with a square panel and a set of six Kutani cups painted with figures, late 19th/early 20th century.
(Woolley & Wallis) $105

A Kutani bowl, Edo Period (late 17th century) decorated in iron-red, green, yellow, aubergine and black enamels with a central pomegranate branch bordered by a wide continuous band, 17.8cm. diameter. (Christie's) $903

A Kutani porcelain charger painted with figures and flowers on a river bank, in orange, pale green, pink, blue and brown, signed 14in. wide.
(Andrew Hartley) $208

LEACH, BERNARD

Bernard Leach, a stoneware bowl, tan glaze with gray and brown concentric circles to the interior interspersed with Oriental type motifs and undulating lines, 28cm. diameter. (Christie's) $532

An outstanding tall stoneware vase by Bernard Leach, white with combed decoration and vertical indents, circa 1965, 16¾in. high.
(Bonhams) $12,583

A stoneware dish by Bernard Leach, speckled green and brown, with five distinctive unglazed areas in the well, circa 1932, 10¼in. diameter.
(Bonhams) $1,022

LEEDS

A Leeds creamware two handled cup, inscribed *I. Barns* and painted with flower sprays beneath a pink border decorated with pink and blue dots, circa 1800, 16cm.
(Woolley & Wallis) $500

A Leeds creamware plate, the center painted with the portraits of the Prince and Princess William V of Orange, 24.7cm.
(Bearne's) $325

A Leeds creamware sauceboat, of shell shape with an entwined handle, and crayfish terminals, circa 1770.
(Sworders) $217

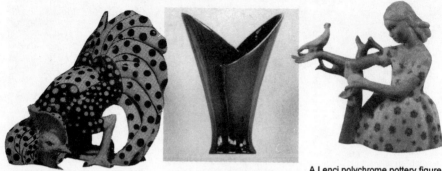

A Lenci figure of a rooster, painted marks *Lenci 1936 S.P.*, 29cm. high. (Christie's) $3,260

A 1950s vase with twin bodies intertwined, green with gold lines, 1950s, marked *Lenci Made in Italy*, 31.5cm. high. (Finarte) $915

A Lenci polychrome pottery figure, by Adele Jacopi, modelled as a young girl with blond hair, wearing floral sprig dress, painted factory marks, impressed signature, 23cm. high. (Christie's) $870

'La Studentessa' a polychrome pottery figure, modelled by Helen Konig Scavini for Lenci, 1930s, modelled as a young woman wearing tartan cap and scarf, black dress, 15in. high. (Christie's) $2,860

A Lenci pottery mask vase, painted marks, 15cm. high. (Christie's) $9,047

A Bambi polychrome ceramic figure, 1950s, marked *Lenci Italy*, 25.5cm high. (Finarte) $686

African Motherhood, a 1930s plaque in high relief in polychrome opaque ceramic, marked *Lenci Made in Italy*, 25 x 13.5cm. (Finarte) $640

'Nella' a Lenci polychrome pottery figure, from a model by Helen Konig Scavini, painted marks, 23.5cm. high. (Christie's) $2,796

A Lenci pottery figure of a young girl with cropped blonde hair, wearing a black and white polka dot dress, with applied song bird, 15¾in. (Wintertons) $6,486

Liverpool creamware jug, England, early 19th century, black transfer decorated with the Farmers Arms *In God is Our Trust*, 9in. high. (Skinner) $805

Liverpool black and white transfer decorated pitcher, England, early 19th century, obverse depicting a portrait of Commodore Stephen Decator (sic) ; the reverse with Major General Jacob Brown, 5½in. (Skinner) $2,070

Liverpool creamware jug, England, early 19th century, black transfer decoration, obverse, *Washington in Glory-American in Tears*, portrait facing left, 9¼in. high. (Skinner) $1,725

Liverpool creamware jug, England, early 19th century, black transfer decoration with black-painted striping and decoration, depicting The Farmers Arms with banner *IN GOD IS OUR TRUST*, 9¼in. high. (Skinner) $748

Transfer decorated Liverpool pitcher, England, early 19th century, obverse with an oval reserve depicting a military scene, reverse with American warship 'John', 10in. high. (Skinner) $690

Liverpool creamware jug, England, early 19th century, black transfer decoration with black-painted striping, obverse, depicting the Cooper's Arms with a ribbon inscribed, *Prosperity attend the integrity of our cause*, 9in. high. (Skinner) $547

Transfer decorated Liverpool pitcher, England, early 19th century, black transfer decoration depicting a spread eagle with flag, shield, and *E Pluribus Unum* banner. (Skinner) $2,070

Liverpool pitcher, England, early 19th century, black transfer decoration, obverse *Massacre of the French King, La Guillotine*, 7¾in. high. (Skinner) $3,220

Herculaneum transfer decorated Liverpool pitcher, Liverpool, 1796-1840, depicting *Washington in Glory America in Tears*, 9in. high. (Skinner) $2,070

Dame Lucie Rie, a shallow stoneware dish with curved sides, the top covered in a matt manganese glaze with sgraffito decoration, circa 1958, 35.1cm. wide. (Christie's) $1,771

Dame Lucie Rie, a stoneware jug of rounded body, pulled lip and strap handle, covered in a thick, pitted greyish white glaze with iron-brown specks, 18cm. high. (Christie's) $822

Dame Lucie Rie, a porcelain footed bowl, covered in pale pink and turquoise-blue banding with manganese run rim and well, the body decorated with sgraffito, circa 1980, 18.5cm. diameter. (Christie's) $12,337

LUDWIGSBURG

A rare Ludwigsburg figure of a female coffee drinker from the series of 'Große Musiksoli', circa 1770-75, modelled by Johann Christian Wilhelm Beyer, painted by J.J. Grooth, 7½in. (Sotheby's) $19,460

A Ludwigsburg group of harvesters, emblematic of Autumn from a set of the Seasons, probably modelled by J. Göz, seated, he wearing a black hat with a white coat and green waistcoat and breeches, 1760-62, 16cm. high. (Christie's) $1,809

A Ludwigsburg figure of a lady spinet player, circa 1770, from the series of the 'Kleine Musiksoli' modelled by Josef Nees, 4¾in. (Sotheby's) $2,449

LUSTER

A lusterware ovoid jug, each side printed in black with a man, woman and a shepherd with sheep before a country house, 19th century, 13.5cm. (Woolley & Wallis) $114

A 19th century silver luster jug with leafage design on a canary yellow ground, 5¹/₈in. (Brightwells) $462

Liverpool pitcher, England, 19th century, decorated with a bust of Captain Jacob Jones of the Macedonian, in black transfer in an oval reserve against a yellow ground with pink luster collar, 6¾in. high. (Skinner) $1,725

A majolica cheese dish and cover, of cylindrical form with rustic loop handle, modelled as a tree trunk with trailing bramble, 10in. high.
(Andrew Hartley) $1,320

A Brownfield's majolica model of a kitten, lying on its back holding a ball of wool which forms a box, all raised on a turquoise rectangular cushion, 2nd half 19th century, 29cm. across.
(Woolley & Wallis) $293

A Southern Italian maiolica wine pitcher, 18th/19th century, the cylindrical spout applied with a rope twist extending to the rim, painted *VINO* beneath, 34cm.
(Bonhams) $471

MALING

Maling circular bowl, border decorated with bunches of grapes on a blue luster ground, printed black castle mark and pattern number 917, 8½in.
(G.A. Key) $102

Maling Lustre circular bowl, the border decorated in colors with grapes and foliage, the center decorated with a motif of a butterfly, 9in. (G A Key) $163

Maling decorative toilet set comprising: jug and bowl, decorated in colors with botanical design within a blue geometric border. (G.A. Key) $508

MARTINWARE

A Martin Brothers stoneware face jug, incised marks, *5/1910*, 14cm. high. (Christie's) $1,233

A good large Martin Brothers stoneware vase, dated 1894, finely incised with a wide variety of stylised sea life, heightened in various oxides, height 16¾in.
(Sotheby's) $7,200

A Martin Brothers stoneware mask jar and cover, dated *1901*, each side modelled with a different grinning face, 7¼in.
(Sotheby's) $13,160

159

A Martin Brothers stoneware incised dragon ewer dated *1890,* inscribed *Martin Brothers/London & Southall,* 4-1890, 9¼in. high. (Sotheby's) $4,500

A Martin Brothers stoneware grotesque figural spoon warmer dated *1880,* inscribed *R.W. Martin/London & Southall,* 6¼in. high.(Sotheby's) $12,000

A Martin Brothers stoneware double-sided face jug, dated *1902,* inscribed *Martin Bros./London & Southall,* 5-1902, 6¾in. high. (Sotheby's) $16,800

A Martin Brothers stoneware bird jar, dated *1902,* black-painted wood socle, flange and base inscribed *Martin Bros London & Southall,* 4-1902, 10¼in. high. (Sotheby's) $9,000

A pair of R.W. Martin stoneware figures of lions, dated *1877,* each impressed *R.W. Martin/Pottery/Southall* 36.5cm. (Sotheby's) $9,600

A Martin Brothers stoneware bird jar, dated *1899,* black-painted wood socle, flange and base inscribed *Martin Bros./London & Southall/1-1899,* 27.6cm. (Sotheby's) $24,900

A Martin Brothers incised stoneware aquatic vase circa 1890, inscribed *R.W. Martin/& Bros./London &/Southall,* 21.3cm. high. (Sotheby's) $3,300

A Martin Brothers incised stoneware two-handled vase and pitcher, both circa 1882, both inscribed *Martin Brothers/London & Southall,* 6 and 9in. high. (Sotheby's) $2,700

A Martin Brothers stoneware grotesque figural ewer dated *1881,* inscribed *R.W. Martin/London & Southall/28-8-81,* 11¾in. long. (Sotheby's) $3,900

A Martin Brothers stoneware grotesque figural jar, circa 1890, flange and base *inscribed Martin Bros./London & Southall*. 20cm. high. (Sotheby's) $7,800

A Martin Brothers stoneware grotesque figural sculpture circa 1880, *inscribed Martin Bros./London & Southall*, 9in. wide. (Sotheby's) $12,000

A Martin Brothers stoneware incised dragon ewer dated *1893*, inscribed *Martin Bros./London & Southall, 11-1893*, 9½in. high. (Sotheby's) $4,500

A Martin Brothers stoneware double-sided face jug, dated *1911*, inscribed *R.W. Martin & Bros./London & Southall/22-1-1911*, 8¾in. high. (Sotheby's) $5,100

A Martin Brothers stoneware covered bird jar, dated *1880*, base inscribed *R.W. Martin/Southall/20-3-1880*, repair to back, 18.7cm. high. (Sotheby's) $13,200

An early Martin Brothers stoneware vase, dated *1874*, inscribed *R. W. Martin/London/12-74*, also *F-1*, 21.3cm. high. (Sotheby's) $4,200

A Martin Brothers stoneware figural grotesque spoon warmer dated *1882*, inscribed *Martin/London/ & Southall, 5-9-1882*, 16.8cm. high. (Sotheby's) $11,400

A fine Martin Brothers carved and incised dragon jardinière, dated *1887, inscribed R.W. Martin & Bros./London & Southall, 1-1887*, 21.9cm. high. (Sotheby's) $1,800

A Martin Brothers stoneware molded and incised reptillian vase, dated *1889*, inscribed *Martin Brothers/London & Southall, 12-1889*, 9in. high. (Sotheby's) $2,700

A Masons Ironstone drainer, circa 1813-1820, brightly enamelled and gilt with a central lotus bordered by Oriental flowers, 35.5cm. length. (Bonhams) $630

A Masons's Ironstone oval footbath, with panel molded sides and scroll handles, decorated with flowers and leaves, no mark, circa 1820-30, 48.5cm.
(Woolley & Wallis) $3,381

An Ironstone octagonal section jug, with a serpent handle, decorated with a Japan pattern, no marks, early 19th century, 24cm.
(Woolley & Wallis) $191

A set of ten small Mason's Ironstone plates, decorated in iron red, blue and orange with vases, flowers and foliage, factory marks impressed in a line, early 19th century, 15.5cm.
(Woolley & Wallis) $564

A pair of Mason's Ironstone tapered hexagonal section two handled vases and covers, the pierced covers with coiled dragon finials, the vases with dragon handles, circa 1825, 54cm. high.
(Christie's) $2,245

A large Mason's type rectangular meat plate, boldly decorated in blue, red, green and brown with a scaly dragon amidst flower heads, a pseudo Chinese mark, circa 1820, 53.5cm.
(Woolley & Wallis) $685

A Mason's Ironstone octagonal section jug, with a dragon handle decorated with vases of flowers and leaves in the Imari palette, 1st half 19th century, 20cm.
(Woolley & Wallis) $301

A Mason's Ironstone scrolling dish, decorated with flower sprigs, impressed mark, 27cm. and a Copeland and Garrett two handled cup, cover and stand, all 19th century.
(Woolley & Wallis) $192

A Mason's Ironstone hexagonal jug, with a dragon handle, decorated with flowers and foliage, *Ironstone China* impressed, early 19th century, 17cm.
(Woolley & Wallis) $191

A Meissen pagoda figure, 20th century, after a model by J.J. Kaendler, with nodding head, tongue and hands, attired in indianische Blumen robe, 16cm.
(Bonhams) $2,192

A pair of Meissen outside-decorated 'Kinderbusts' emblematic of Autumn and Winter, 19th century, each ruddy cheeked child with his attribute above rocaille scrolls, 11¾in. high.
(Christie's) $2,070

A Meissen figure group of Europa and the bull, late 19th century, she modelled astride the beast's back decking floral garlands from his horns and neck, passed to her by attendants, 22cm.
(Bonhams) $1,165

A Meissen Commedia dell'Arte figure of Captain Spavento, circa 1745, modelled by Reinicke, from the Duke of Weissenfels series, standing in a bold, defiant attitude, his left hand on his hip, 14cm.
(Bonhams) $3,836

Two rare Meissen chamber candlesticks, mid 18th century, both with floral nozzles and leaf-molded drip-guards picked out in green and puce, 15.5cm.
(Bonhams) $6,850

A Meissen style floral encrusted vase and cover, circa 1880, of inverted pear form, modelled either side with two putti, between polychrome summer flowers, 25cm.
(Bonhams) $206

A Meissen figural group of Terpsichore, 18th century, possibly modelled by Meyer, the Muse of Dancing, seated wearing a decolleté white robe and draped in a yellow cloak, her lute missing, 22cm. (Bonhams) $1,781

A Meissen figural group of a shepherd and shepherdess, circa 1745, modelled by J.J. Kaendler, she seated playing the lute, attired in pink hat, he stylishly dressed in white coat, 14cm. high.
(Bonhams) $2,466

A 19th century Meissen porcelain allegorical group 'Evening', modelled as a seated bearded god in crimson robes and holding a gold cup, flanked by young maidens, 13¾in. high.
(Andrew Hartley) $2,233

A Meissen figure group of Diana in her chariot, circa 1880, seated in a stag-drawn chariot attended by a putto within molded clouds, 17½in. wide, overall.
(Christie's) $4,700

Meissen figural group of vintners, late 19th century, 8¼in. high.
(Skinner) $2,645

A Meissen model of lovers, after Kändler, he wearing a gray jacket, she with a wide crinoline dress, 2nd half 19th century, 8¼in.
(Woolley & Wallis) $800

A Meissen figure of a dancer, second half 18th century, modelled standing in dancing pose lifting her overskirts above her ankles, wearing a gilt-edged red hat, 7¼in.
(Sotheby's) $4,763

A pair of Meissen ewers, emblematic of Earth and Water, after models by Johann Joachim Kaendler, circa 1880, each with raised decoration and applied figures, on an oval spreading foot, Earth: 26½in. high, Water 25½in. high. (Christie's) $11,040

A 19th century Meissen figure, Chocolate Girl, modelled as a standing maid servant in mustard and pale green dress with a bonnet and holding a tray, raised on gilded square rustic base, 15¼in. high.
(Andrew Hartley) $1,200

Meissen porcelain gardener group, Germany, late 19th century, modelled as five figures in various acts of gardening, set on a freeform circular base, 11½in. high.
(Skinner) $1,840

A Meissen armorial saucer from the Diedo Service, 1735-40, painted with the Arms above figures in a river landscape, gilt scrollwork border to rim, the reverse with indianische Blumen, 4¾in.
(Sotheby's) $1,316

A Meissen figure of a boy, circa 1956, after the model by Konrad Hentschel, seated on a hobby horse, wearing a newspaper hat, a white smock and slippers, 6¾in.
(Sotheby's) $2,194

Two Meissen models of crocodiles devouring infants modelled by J.J. Kaendler, the reptiles naturalistically modelled with their tails raised and each with a baby in its jaws, circa 1745, 28cm. long.
(Christie's) $2,392

A large Meissen figure of Count Bruhl's tailor, circa 1880, after a model by J.J. Kändler, the bewigged and spectacled gentleman wearing a pink floral coat, boots and tricorn hat, 17in.
(Skinner) $9,171

A large Meissen figure of Galatea, wearing loose drapes, modelled seated in a shell-molded throne borne by nymphs and tritons, circa 1875, 57cm. wide.
(Christie's) $9,870

A Meissen enamelled metallic-ground baluster vase, circa 1865, probably by Leuteritz, finely enamelled in the Rococo taste, a scantily clad nymph rests below in a rocaille scroll teasing a child with a wreath of flowers, 29cm. high.
(Christie's) $7,050

A large pair of Meissen groups of 'The Decisive Choice' and 'The Noble Decision', circa 1880, after models by J. C. Schönheit, one group depicting a man touching the chin of his chosen lover.
(Sotheby's) $7,056

A Meissen porcelain group, depicting Cupid standing by a pillar, firing an arrow, love birds and roses at his feet, 18.5cm. high, incised G30. (Bearne's) $682

A 19th century Meissen porcelain figure of a seated lady, her arm resting on a table, in pink, lemon, lilac and blue floral dress, raised on bow fronted base, 7¼in. high.
(Andrew Hartley) $862

An unusual Meissen teabowl and saucer, circa 1740, each painted in underglaze-blue, puce enamel and gilding with pagodas flanked by flowering plants.
(Sotheby's) $1,848

19th century Meissen center piece depicting a central therm surrounded by a couple of lovers with attendant dog and sheep, 32cm. (Thomson Roddick & Medcalf) $2,002

Two Meissen silver-mounted Kakiemon cutlery-handles, circa 1730, contemporary mounts, of pistol-grip form, painted with an iron-red dragon flying over a stylized pine trees and flowering branches of peony and plum. (Christie's) $682

A Meissen Kakiemon flared beaker, circa 1728, blue crossed swords mark, painted with the Flying Fox pattern, with a yellow squirrel among vine and stylized bound hedges, 2½in. high. (Christie's) $1,618

A Meissen (Marcolini) lobster-tureen and three covers, circa 1790, with a red shell, its mouth-parts, legs and tip of its tail with black markings, its tail curled beneath its body, 8½in. long. (Christie's) $5,962

A Meissen pot-pourri vase, circa 1750, modelled by J.J. Kändler as a basket-work molded baluster vase, on a four-footed scroll-molded base lightly applied with a lady and putto seated beside a basket of flowers, 10¾in. high. (Christie's) $3,408

A pair of Meissen busts of Prince Louis Charles de Bourbon and Princess Marie Zéphérine de Bourbon, circa 1753, circa 1753, modelled by J.J. Kändler, 16.2cm. and 15.3cm. high. (Christie's) $12,777

A Meissen armorial baluster hot-milk jug and cover, circa 1723, each side painted with oval shields and arms surrounded by gilt strapwork, scrolling foliage and scale-pattern panels, 6¾in. high overall. (Christie's) $11,926

A Meissen outside-decorated figure group emblematic of 'The Sacrifice of Love', 19th century, after a model by M.V. Acier, modelled as a Classical couple before an altar attended by a putto, 8in. high. (Christie's) $1,610

A pair of Meissen porcelain vases, in the Rococo style, circa 1875, each with a pierced scroll and foliate lid surmounted by spring flowers, 34½in. high. (Christie's) $33,120

A Meissen silver-gilt mounted cartouche-shaped purple-ground snuff-box, circa 1740, the contemporary mounts with later control mark, probably French, 3in. wide. (Christie's) $16,185

A Meissen group of dancing figures, late 19th/20th century, blue crossed swords mark, modelled in the round as five dancing figures with musical instruments at their feet, 9in. high.
(Christie's) $4,025

A Meissen outside-decorated figure group, 19th century, after a model by M.V. Acier, modelled in the round, as a bagpiper and hurdy-gurdy player beneath a tree, 46.7cm. high.
(Christie's) $2,070

A Meissen cane-handle, circa 1738, modelled as the head and neck of a horse, incised and with dark-brown markings, the lower part painted with a continuous scene with four Orientals on a terrace, 3in. high.
(Christie's) $5,452

A Meissen ewer, circa 1755, after a Vincennes model with helmet-shaped lip and baluster lower part, the green branch loop handle with applied flower and foliage terminals, 21.3cm. high.
(Christie's) $2,726

A pair of Meissen two-handled baluster pot-pourri vases and covers, circa 1900, after a model by J.J. Kändler, each finial formed as a bouquet of flowers above pierced turquoise and gilt-enriched domed covers, 24in. high.
(Christie's) $18,400

A Meissen figure group emblematic of Spring, late 19th/20th century, blue crossed swords mark, modelled in the round with six figures of gardeners, 28.9cm. high.
(Christie's) $2,300

A Meissen porcelain group of Count Bruhl's tailor, circa 1880, shown seated on a goat, with tailor's accoutrements, underglaze blue crossed swords mark, 17in. high.
(Christie's) $12,880

Pair of Meissen blue-ground dragon-handled pâte-sur-pâte vases and covers, late 19th century, with female figures of Ceres and Aphrodite on a light-blue ground, 15¾in. high.
(Christie's) $36,800

A Meissen figure group of Cybele, circa 1880, the scantily draped goddess seated on a lion, holding a cornucopia and a key, attended by four putti, 9½in. high.
(Christie's) $5,750

A Ming blue and white dish, Wanli six character mark and of the Period (1573-1619), painted with two seated scholars and boy attendants among rockwork, 11½in. diameter. (Christie's) $4,410

A Provincial Ming Chinese blue and white guan of baluster shape painted with ducks and trailing floral frieze, 12in. high, lacks cover. (Brightwells) $4,620

A Ming Imperial yellow saucer dish, Jiajing six character mark and of the Period (1522-66), the rounded sides rising to a flaring rim, covered overall in a pale yellow-glaze, 7in. diameter. (Christie's) $1,613

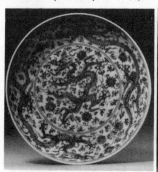

A Ming blue and white 'Dragon' dish, four-character mark and of the Period (1506-1521), vividly painted in dark lines, and lighter washes of underglazed blue with a striding five-clawed dragon among scrolling lotus , 8¼in. diameter. (Christie's) $55,272

A blue and white jar, Guan, Ming Dynasty, 16th century, molded with four ingot-shaped handles, boldly painted with a continuous band of peonies above bamboo and rockwork, 11¾in. high. (Christie's) $4,317

A very large Ming blue and white 'Dragon' dish, Jiajing six-character mark and of the period (1522 – 1566), vividly painted to the center with two five-clawed dragons chasing the flaming pearl, 22½in. diameter. (Christie's) $25,921

A Ming blue and white baluster jar, with short slightly everted neck, painted with a broad band of peony flowers, 11¾in. high. (Christie's) $768

A large Sancai-glazed seated dignitary, Ming Dynasty 16th/17th century, the bearded and stern faced figure modelled seated on a rectangular plinth, dressed in an official's robe, 31in. high. (Christie's) $4,410

A large glazed Tileworks Buddhistic lion stand, Ming Dynasty, the striding figure with mouth open in a roar showing the tongue and teeth, 29in. high. (Christie's) $19,550

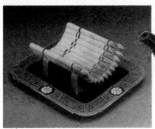

A Minton majolica asparagus server, the C-section dish molded as a bundle of asparagus tied with pink bands, the legs molded with key pattern bands, cypher for 1873, 25cm. wide. (Christie's) $1,397

A Minton majolica 'Chinaman' teapot and cover, circa 1874, impressed *Mintons,* year cypher and shape number, 5¾in. high. (Sotheby's) $1,440

A Minton's majolica teapot, 1878, modelled in the form of a fish amongst waves, 18.1cm. (Sotheby's) $35,250

One of a pair of Minton Hollins & Co 8in. tiles in the manner of John Moyr Smith, each printed and painted with a classical lady figure and titled 'Mechanics' and 'Botany', 8in. high.
(Wintertons)   (Two) $764

A pair of Mintons Paris Exhibition turquoise-ground four-light candelabra, dated *1878,* each with a circular reticulated basket above an angular urn painted with a classical medallion, 26½in. high. (Christie's) $18,400

A Minton Parian figure Dorothea by John Bell, modelled as a maiden seated on a rock and dressed as a youth, 14in. high. (Andrew Hartley) $832

A Minton majolica jardinière with three cherub supports, 16.2in. (Brightwells) $2,942

A pair of Minton painted Parian figures of dancing maidens, date cypher for 1870, after A. Canova, each modelled as a young girl dancing before a tree-stump, the taller 37.8cm. high. (Christie's) $1,610

Minton, a majolica centerpiece, a merman supporting a shell above his head, raised on an oval section base, impressed marks, 38.5cm. (Christie's) $3,220

A William Moorcroft Hazledene landscape bowl, circa 1915, impressed *Moorcroft, Burslem England*, 10¼in. diameter. (Sotheby's) $1,800

William Moorcroft Florian Ware two handled small globular vase, decorated with the 'Poppy' design, made for Liberty & Co., registration No. circa 1900, 3in. (G A Key) $944

A Moorcroft Macintyre Claremont vase, circa 1905, (firing crack to underside of base), painted script signature, 15.6cm. high. (Sotheby's) $1,680

A large Moorcroft 'landscape' vase, circa 1928, tube-lined with trees in a rolling landscape, in vivid shades of russet, orange, lime-green, pink and purple, drilled as a lampbase, 12in. (Sotheby's) $6,500

Moorcroft 'Peacock Feathers' an incense burner green signature, 27.5cm. high. (Christie's) $6,198

A Moorcroft 'Fish' vase, circa 1930-35, with spherical body and cylindrical neck, tube-lined with fish and sea-plants in tones of yellow, blue and sage-green, 12in. (Sotheby's) $3,611

Walter Moorcroft balustered circular jardinière decorated with the Four Seasons Winter pattern, circa 1992, 7in. (G A Key) $240

Moorcroft 'Eventide' a tobacco jar and cover, paper labels, 18cm. high. (Christie's) $4,428

A William Moorcroft flambé Orchid vase, (minor firing chip to foot), impressed facsimile signature, 12½in. high. (Sotheby's) $1,680

Moorcroft Pottery 'Sunflower' a vase, green monogram, silver dash, 19cm. high.
(Christie's) $389

A Moorcroft MacIntyre 'Florian Ware' vase, circa 1898, of inverted baluster form, tube-lined in white with stylized tulips and forget-me-nots in shades of blue, 9¼in.
(Sotheby's) $1,986

William Moorcroft Florian Ware small baluster vase, decorated in blue and green with the 'Cornflower' design, on mottled blue ground, circa 1900, 3in.
(G A Key) $1,258

A Moorcroft MacIntyre 'Florian Ware' two-handled vase, circa 1908-1909, tube lined with cartouches of forget-me-not sprays and pink tulips on a white ground, 10¼in.
(Sotheby's) $3,250

A Moorcroft orchid vase, of ovoid form with short collar neck, decorated in colors on a woodsmoke ground, 27cm.
(Bonhams) $1,134

A Moorcroft ovoid vase, with a waisted neck and flared rim, decorated with the leaf and berry pattern under a flambé glaze, impressed, 23.5cm.
(Woolley & Wallis) $829

A Moorcroft graduated set of three pink magnolia jardinières, 22cm. and smaller, painted and impressed marks. (Bonhams) $648

Moorcroft Pottery fish vase, England, circa 1930, decorated about the body with fish and seaweed, glossy glaze in shades of yellow, orange, and green, 7¼in.
(Skinner) $3,680

Moorcroft 'Sunflower' a charger, green monogram, silver dash, 35cm. diameter.
(Christie's) $354

NAPLES

CHINA

A pair of late 18th century Naples (Real Fabbrica Ferdinandea) ice pails, painted with birds and with gilt floral and foliate bands and borders, 37.5cm. high.
(Finarte) $12,138

A Naples style shaped rectangular gilt-metal-mounted box and hinged cover molded, painted and gilt with a classical female figure and attendants, 19th century, 24cm. wide. (Christie's) $708

A pair of Naples style shouldered urn-shaped vases and covers with key handles, molded, painted and gilt with a continuous frieze of classical figures, late 19th century, 50cm. high.
(Christie's) $2,656

PARIS

A pair of Paris blue-ground pierced gilt-bronze-mounted vases and covers, circa 1790, the mounts later, each side reserved with gilt-edged circular panel finely painted with merry figures drinking, eating and dancing, 43cm.
(Sotheby's) $8,400

One of two Paris cabinet plates, early 19th century, one painted with four ducks, the other with a hawk-type bird holding its prey in its talons, 23.8cm.
(Bonhams) (Two) $329

A Paris blue-ground part dessert service, gilt with a stylized flowerhead and foliate sprigs, comprising: nine plates and three shallow dishes, early 19th century.
(Christie's) $1,397

PEARLWARE

A blue and white pearlware jug, circa 1780-1800, with large loop handle, amusingly painted in an intense blue with a man ploughing with three diminutive horses, 22cm.
(Bonhams) $1,058

A Staffordshire pearlware bull baiting group, typically modelled with a man standing with his arms raised beside a bull, the bull being attacked by two terriers, circa 1830, 37cm. wide.
(Christie's) $5,165

A Pearlware puzzle jug, of baluster form with loop handle, molded spout and neck and inscribed *H.J.*, the body molded in relief and painted with a fox hunting scene, early 19th century, 8¼in. high.
(Andrew Hartley) $584

A Pilkington's Royal Lancastrian luster bowl, circa 1914, designed by Walter Crane, decorated by William S. Mycock with a frieze of lions above roses and heart shapes, 8½in. diameter.
(Sotheby's) $780

A Pilkington's Royal Lancastrian luster double-gourd vase, 1935, by William S. Mycock, decorated with flying birds amongst foliage, 23.8cm. (Sotheby's) $2,700

A Pilkington's Royal Lancastrian luster ewer, 1914, by William S. Mycock, decorated on each side with a lion, 20cm. high.
(Sotheby's) $2,400

An impressive Pilkington's Lancastrian luster plaque, circa 1906-1913, decorated by Charles Cundall after a design by Walter Crane, lavishly painted with a peacock in full display in copper luster and red on a mauve ground, diameter 48.6cm.
(Sotheby's) $16,800

A Pilkington's Royal Lancastrian luster globular vase, 1924, by William S. Mycock, decorated with blue flowers on a pale blue ground, 7¾in. high. (Sotheby's) $1,320

A Pilkington's Lancastrian luster vase, 1910, by Charles Cundall, decorated with a frieze of mythical beasts running amongst trees, 7¾in. high.
(Sotheby's) $3,000

A Pilkington's Royal Lancastrian luster large vase, 1924, by Richard Joyce, decorated with fruiting vine, 15¾in. high.
(Sotheby's) $1,680

A Pilkington's Royal Lancastrian luster charger, circa 1920, by Richard Joyce, molded and decorated in luster with a King on horseback, 11¾in. diameter.
(Sotheby's) $1,920

A Pilkington's Lancastrian luster vase, circa 1908, by Richard Joyce, decorated with three prowling panthers, height 20.6cm.
(Sotheby's) $1,200

A twin-handled Poole Pottery octagonal tray, shape no. 486, the well pierced with swooping bluebird and flower design, painted in shades of pink, blue, green and yellow, 32cm. wide.
(Christie's) $349

'Springbok' a pair of Poole Pottery bookends designed by John Adams, 1926, shape no. 831, slip cast, glazed in an ice green glaze, on rectangular base, impressed marks, 8¼in. high.
(Christie's) $2,856

A large CSA Poole Pottery vase, pattern ZW, shape no. 684, impressed mark (minor glaze nick to base rim), 35cm. high.
(Bonhams) $441

QIANLONG

A pair of gilt bronze mounted famille rose biscuit figures, the bearded squatting men in theatrical costume, holding lozenge-shaped dishes upon their heads, Qianlong, 9¼in. high. (Bonhams) $847

A famille rose kingfisher, Qianlong period, perched on a blue-green tree stump base, his breast enamelled in a vivid rose enamel and his pointed beak and claws iron-red, 8in. high.
(Christie's) $3,680

Two similar Chinese blue ground rectangular section baluster vases, decorated in gilt with landscapes and extensive calligraphy, Qianlong, 1736-95, 40.5cm. and 38.5cm.
(Woolley & Wallis) $1,199

REDWARE

Redware deep dish, 18th century, 8½in. diameter together with matching side-spouted handled cup, 5½in. diameter.
(Eldred's) $302

A near pair of brown glazed redware campana vases, each decorated in gilt with one panel of a chariot and horses and another of scrolling acanthus, 1st half 19th century, 20cm.
(Woolley & Wallis) $693

A sgraffito- and polychrome-decorated oval redware platter, Pennsylvania, 1790-1820, some chips to glaze and exfoliation to underside, 15¾in. long.
(Sotheby's) $5,000

A porcelain decanter and stopper, by Robj, 1930s, modelled as three stylized sailors wearing blue and white uniforms, standing back to back, 10¾in. high.
(Christie's) $789

Two Robj brule parfum, late 1920s, each with a lightbulb fitment, black printed marks, tallest 8¾in. high.
(Sotheby's) $987

A porcelain box and cover, by Robj, 1930s, humorously modelled as a large French policeman, printed marks, numbered *132*, 9in. high.
(Christie's) $1,625

ROOKWOOD

Rookwood, a pottery shape 2720 vase, designed by Vera Tischler, dated *1925*, decorated with a flowering branch in green, yellow and red, on a mottled matt blue ground, 16.5cm.
(Bonhams & Brooks) $438

Rookwood pottery jardinière, Cincinnati, Ohio, 1886, wide mouth on bulbous body, golden brown **stylized chrysanthemums with dark** brownish-green stems on shaded gold and amber ground, 8½in. diameter. (Skinner) $920

Rookwood Pottery sailing scene vellum vase, decorated by Fred Rothenbusch, Cincinnati, Ohio, 1908, inverted rim on an elongated ovoid vessel, 9in. high.
(Skinner) $4,025

ROYAL COPENHAGEN

A 'Flora Danica' plate with pierced gilt border and serrated rim, painted with a specimen spray of a cornflower, 22.5cm. diameter, circa 1925. (Christie's) $616

A Copenhagen cabinet cup and saucer, circa 1830, in the Empire style, well painted with a stylized border of classical motifs including swags and pendants, between molded rims of acanthus.
(Sotheby's) $1,097

Royal Copenhagen figure of a nymph with a satyr, Denmark, timid satyr kneeling at the feet of a nude female nymph, on naturalistic ovoid base, 20th century, 15¼in. high. (Skinner) $1,093

A Royal Dux porcelain figure 'Bather Surprised' depicting a nude maiden seated on a rock, in ivory, green and pink palette, 16in. high. (Andrew Hartley) $1,529

A pair of Royal Dux porcelain figures of male and female watercarriers in pink classical dress, each holding a jar and carrying another on the shoulder, 11½in. (Andrew Hartley) $647

A Royal Dux porcelain group of a young peasant woman and a girl depicted standing, each holding a hod of grapes on the shoulder, 19¼in. high. (Andrew Hartley) $616

A Royal Dux Art Nouveau porcelain figure of a young maiden in green and pink flowing robes, leaning against a column on the edge of a pool, 14½in. high. (Andrew Hartley) $834

A pair of Royal Dux figural lampbases modelled as Art Nouveau maidens, one with cornucopia, the other with floral bouquet, applied pink triangle factory mark, 85cm. and 80cm. high. (Christie's) $5,254

A Royal Dux porcelain group of a boy on a mule in ivory and green palette with gilt embellishment, on rustic oblong base, 10½in. wide. (Andrew Hartley) $1,251

A Royal Dux pair of figures, of male and female water carriers, applied pink triangle and impressed marks, 50.5cm. (Bristol) $867

A Royal Dux camel group of a sheikh in flowing robes on a camel, an Arab boy below carrying baskets, in tones of ivory, pink and green, 49cm. high (Bearne's) $1,520

A pair of Royal Dux porcelain figures, depicting shepherd and shepherdess, both in green, pink and gold dress, she feeding a goat, 21in. high. (Andrew Hartley) $1,386

A Ruskin high-fired vase dated *1908*, the trumpet neck rising from a shouldered onion base covered in a mottled green glaze, speckled with black and purple, 5¾in.
(Sotheby's) $2,347

A pair of Ruskin stoneware vases shouldered form, shape no.282, covered in a running royal blue soufflé glaze, impressed Howson Taylor monogram, 31cm. high.
(Christie's) $2,585

A Ruskin vase, decorated with a vine around the shoulder on an iridescent orange glaze, scissor mark and *Ruskin 1911* impressed, 21cm.(Woolley & Wallis) $245

RUSSIAN

Imperial porcelain Catherine II service platter, Russia, circa 1765, basket weave molded border, enamel painted floral decoration, 18½in. long.
(Skinner) $1,840

Nikolai Michailovitch Suetin, a Constructivist inkwell and cover, designed 1922-23, executed late 1920s by Alex Lutkin at the Leningrad porcelain factory, 5¾in. widest. (Christie's) $12,639

A porcelain easter egg by the Imperial Porcelain Factory, St. Petersburg, period of Nicholas I, painted with St. Helena, half-length, 3¾in. high.
(Christie's) $4,801

A porcelain plate from the St. Andrew service by the Gardner Factory, Moscow, circa 1780, the center painted with the star of the order, 24.5cm. diameter.
(Christie's) $10,563

A topographical cabinet cup and a saucer, possibly Moscow, Gardener's factory, circa 1830, depicting Unter den Linden, titled in French in red and on the underside.
(Sotheby's) $475

A Russian porcelain teapot and cover, with a circular body and an acanthus capped handle, brightly painted with a yellow Sirin, Imperial porcelain factory, the porcelain factory, the porcelain 2nd half 19th century, the decoration, 1921.
(Woolley & Wallis) $616

A Samson vase, decorated in the Kakiemon style with flowers and leaves beneath a blue border, late 19th century, 19.5cm. (Woolley & Wallis) $49

A pair of century Samson porcelain cornucopia wall vases with waved rim, painted and transfer printed with birds on fruiting branches over a pink swag, Derby mark, 8¼in. high. (Andrew Hartley) $308

A Samson group of Cupid in disguise, the young god sits advising three maidens in the art of love, 2nd half 19th century, 23cm. (Woolley & Wallis) $476

A Samson porcelain figure of Falstaff, in the Derby style, modelled standing with sword and shield, wearing floral dress in pink, deep blue and yellow, and raised on scrolled base, 16½in. high. (Andrew Hartley) $500

A pair of Samson porcelain bocage figures of a shepherd and shepherdess, each in polychrome floral dress, he with a dog at his feet, 11in. high. (Andrew Hartley) $648

A Samson arbor group, with two figures reading from a book, the trellis work arbor applied with flowers, 2nd half 19th century, 21.5cm. (Woolley & Wallis) $571

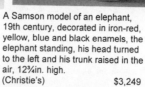

A very large pair of Samson biscuit-glazed figures, 19th century, a court lady and a warrior, she with her hair in a high topknot, he wearing elaborate armor and head-dress, 27½in. high. (Christie's) $3,680

A Samson model of an elephant, 19th century, decorated in iron-red, yellow, blue and black enamels, the elephant standing, his head turned to the left and his trunk raised in the air, 12¾in. high. (Christie's) $3,249

A pair of Samson porcelain vases and covers, late 19th century, in the Chinese famille verte style, painted with writhing green dragons on a ground of prunus and peony vines, 14¾in. high. (Christie's) $2,070

A fine Satsuma koro, signed *Kinkozan zo*, late 19th century, gilt with three panels on a floral and geometric ground, 6¾in. high. (Christie's) $6,580

A Satsuma botanical bowl, signed *Dainihon Kyoto-Fu Ryuzan Tsukuru,* Meiji Period (late 19th century), decorated in brightly colored enamels and gilt, with numerous insects, beneath a dense band of flowers, 9in. diameter. (Christie's) $10,716

A Satsuma teapot and cover, with domed body, painted and gilt with ladies, boys and gentlemen in a blossoming garden, 11cm. diameter, signed. (Christie's) $1,645

A Satsuma pottery vase, with two fan shaped panels, each painted with women and children in landscapes, 16cm. high. (Bearne's) $4,293

A large pair of Satsuma baluster vases and covers, with gambolling karashishi finials, painted and gilt with panels of warriors in a mountainous landscape, 30in. high. (Christie's) $2,303

A Satsuma squat baluster jar and cover, decorated with shaped panels of ladies in a garden playing musical instruments and seated with children, 6¾in. high. (Christie's) $5,922

A Satsuma ovoid vase, with short neck and everted rim, painted and gilt with a profusion of flowering chrysanthemum on a riverbank, 11¾in. high. (Christie's) $2,961

A Japanese Satsuma rectangular box and cover, with a chrysanthemum knop, two sides decorated with figures and two with butterflies, signed *Kyozan,* 8.5cm. (Woolley & Wallis) $3,696

A large Satsuma baluster vase, molded to the shoulder with a band of foliage above trailing blossoming branches and molded swirling waters to the foot, 16¾in. high. (Christie's) $1,151

A Sèvres bleu-celeste gold-mounted oviform vinaigrette, circa 1785, the bleu-céleste lobed borders edged in gilding suspending swags of pink roses, red and blue flowers, 2¼in. long. (Christie's) $10, 018

A Sèvres teapot and cover, circa 1775, finely painted with two reserves of loosely arranged summer flowers on a cobalt blue ground, 4¾in. high. (Bonhams) $847

A Sèvres, two-handled ecuelle, cover and stand, late 19th century, each piece painted with titled battle scenes within white jewelled reserves, 9½in. (Sotheby's) $2,166

A Sèvres style blue-ground shaped rectangular cache-pot with leaf-molded handles, painted with a loose spray of flowers within a shaped circular cartouche gilt with scrolls, late 19th century, 17cm. high. (Christie's) $885

Sèvres earthenware figure of a polar bear, first half 20th century, the seated bear with granulated slip finish, and enamel detailing, 11in. high. (Skinner) $863

A Sèvres coffee can, date code *CC* for 1780, painted *S…*, a painted bust portrait of a young man looking sideways, in an oval tooled gilt frame titled *Raphael*, on a bleu Nouveau ground, 6cm. (Bonhams) $539

Important pair of Sèvres porcelain vases and covers, France, 19th century, gilt-metal mounted, cobalt ground with scrolled gilt foliage and enamelled jewelled borders. (Skinner) $32,200

A pair of Sèvres white biscuit portrait busts of King Louis XVIII and the Duchesse de Berri, circa 1820, he turned slightly to the left, his hair en queue, in military uniform, 11in. and 12in. high. (Christie's) $17,273

A magnificent pair of gilt-bronze and 'Sèvres' vases, Paris, circa 1880, ovoid body painted with scenes of lovers in idyllic landscapes in the manner of Fragonard, signed *Maxant*, 132cm. high. (Sotheby's) $83,130

A Sèvres style cobalt-blue ground jewel box and cover, late 19th century, signed *Aubé*, the hinged cover painted after Boucher with a fishing scene within elaborate gilt rocaille and trellis border, 29.5cm. (Christie's) $3,290

A Sèvres stoneware model of a squirrel, the rectangular base with factory stamp, 23.2cm. (Bristol) $102

A 'Sèvres' porcelain and gilt-bronze jardinière, Paris, circa 1860, the shaped sides centered by a cartouche of a lady, signed *Seiffert*, 42cm. wide. (Sotheby's) $12,334

A Sèvres style dark-blue-ground oval gilt-metal-mounted box cover, painted with a church and houses beside a river, circa 1880, 8cm. wide. (Christie's) $619

A pair of French ormolu-mounted parcel gilt blue-ground jewelled Sèvres porcelain pots-pourri, in the Louis XVI style, circa 1875, 11¼in. high. (Christie's) $10,120

A 'Sèvres' turquoise-ground coffee cup and saucer, late 19th century, the cup painted with a circular portrait panel of the young Dauphin, the saucer with emblems of the French Royal court. (Sotheby's) $1,264

A 'Sèvres-style' blue-ground gilt-metal-mounted garniture, late 19th century, each painted by Lepage, signed, painted with scenes of lovers in pastoral landscapes, 32in. high. (Sotheby's) $18,410

Sèvres porcelain figurine, a lady in a voluminous ballgown, clutching a fan in her right hand, her skirt with rosette decoration in puce and green, 7½in. (G A Key) $272

A pair of ormolu-mounted Sèvres style cobalt-blue ground drum-shaped vases and covers, late 19th century, painted with figures by the sea and in gardens within beaded and gilt surrounds, 27½in. high. (Christie's) $16,450

A Staffordshire blue and white earthenware dish, second quarter 19th century, the oval plate with raised border inscribed with fifteen American states, the center decorated with figures of Justice and Liberty, 16¾in. wide. (Christie's) $6,948

19th century Staffordshire jug, baluster form, luster decorated with sporting scene of a figure by his mount and hounds, green and puce detail on a cream ground, 7½in. (G.A. Key) $131

A Staffordshire creamware equestrian figure of Hudibras, of Wood type, wearing black hat, green coat and breeches and black boots, modelled seated holding the hilt of his sword, circa 1790, 29cm. high. (Christie's) $920

A 19th century Staffordshire pottery pastille burner, in the form of a pagoda encrusted with flowers, with gilt embellishment, 6½in. high. (Andrew Hartley) $203

A pair of 19th century Staffordshire pottery spaniels depicted seated with black and white coloring, yellow eyes, orange muzzle and gilt chains, 12½in. high. (Andrew Hartley) $416

A figure of General Sir James Simpson wearing cocked hat and military uniform, modelled standing holding a manuscript in his right hand, circa 1854, 45.5cm. high. (Christie's) $619

A pair of children and St. Bernard groups, possibly the Royal children, modelled standing facing left and right, the children lying on their backs, mid 19th century, 23cm. high. (Christie's) $2,708

A Staffordshire silver luster pearlware jug, molded with Pan's head, early 19th century, 16cm. (Woolley & Wallis) $74

Two groups of spaniels seated with their pups, modelled facing left and right, the adults painted with iron-red patches, the pups with black patches, mid 19th century, 20cm. & 20.5cm. high. (Christie's) $992

A pair of models of rabbits, modelled seated on all fours facing left and right, each nibbling a lettuce leaf, circa 1850, 25cm. wide. (Christie's) $4,694

A Staffordshire Toby jug, brightly decorated with colored enamels, 2nd half 19th century, 15cm. (Woolley & Wallis) $162

A pair of 19th century Staffordshire figures of seated poodles having gravelware bodies and lightly painted details, 10½in. (Brightwells) $588

Good 19th century Staffordshire Biblical spill vase group, modelled as Joseph and Mary and the infant Christ with a donkey, painted in colors, 7½in. (G.A. Key) $102

Pair of 19th century Staffordshire seated spaniels, both with naturalistic faces, black body markings, gilded collars and leads, 10in. (G.A. Key) $942

A Walton 'Flight to Egypt' group, typically modelled, before a flowering bocage, on a titled mound base applied with leaves and flowers, circa 1825, 20cm. (Christie's) $1,083

Two groups of children and hounds, one modelled standing over a naked child, 16.5cm. high; the other modelled seated on its back with a decapitated serpent at their feet, mid 19th century, 17cm. high. (Christie's) $1,083

A Staffordshire model of a cow, standing before a tree stump which forms a vase, painted with colored enamels, circa 1900, 27cm. (Woolley & Wallis) $279

A pair of spaniel jugs, the spaniels modelled facing left and right, painted with iron-red patches, late 19th century, 19.5cm. high. (Christie's) $631

183

Janet Leach, a twin-handled stoneware vase, the exterior covered in a matt dark brown glaze with off-white poured decoration, 35.6cm. high.
(Christie's) $653

A large 'Fountain' bowl by Michael Cardew, stoneware, red rust and brown with an incised design, 12½in. diameter.
(Bonhams) $1,887

Michael Cardew, an earthenware vase of bulbous body and collar rim, covered in an olive-brown glaze with areas of ocher-brown, 10.4cm. high.
(Christie's) $243

Cobalt decorated ovoid stoneware jug, attributed to Jonathan Fenton, Boston, circa 1800, incised codfish decoration, 15½in. high.
(Skinner) $1,495

A very rare large Burmese glazed storage jar, post Pagan dynasty, probably 14-15th century, the heavily potted jar with a repeating impressed design at the sloping shoulder, 16in. diameter.
(Christie's) $6,373

Elizabeth Fritsch, a stoneware 'Piano Pot', the front decorated with step-shaped pale blue, black, lavender and orange geometric design, circa 1978, 26.6cm. high.
(Christie's) $7,452

A glazed stoneware face jug, probably Southern, early 20th century, the jug with flattened pulled ears and grimacing stylized face covered in streaky, gray-green glaze, 10¾in. high.
(Sotheby's) $8,625

Decorated stoneware jug, *Boston 1804*, ovoid handled jug with impressed cobalt blue swag and tassel decoration, 14¼in. high.
(Skinner) $2,530

Cobalt decorated double-handled stoneware jug or cooler, America, signed *John B. Wilson* and dated *1839*, 16in. high.
(Skinner) $18,400

Katherine Pleydell-Bouverie, a stoneware footed bowl with everted rim, covered in a bluish-green translucent glaze with incised stylised leaf decoration, 18.4cm. diam. (Bonhams) $335

A large cylindrical stoneware loving cup, applied with a hunting scene and other reliefs, 19th century, 28.5cm. wide. (Woolley & Wallis) $29

A rounded stoneware vase, by Katherine Pleydell-Bouverie, squat spherical form with a short neck, incised diagonal fluting, blue-green, 5¾in. (Bonhams) $315

Brown salt glazed stoneware sculptured jug, probably Missouri or Ohio, circa 1860-70, the jug with a lizard or salamander applied handle above the sculptured face of a man, 9¾in. high. (Skinner) $26,450

Stoneware tree trunk planter, 19th century, brown glazed planter decorated with vines in relief around the trunk, impressed *S.L. PEWTRESS & CO. NEWHAVEN CONN* on base, 12³/₈in high. (Skinner) $373

A Habaner baluster jug, Western Slovakia, dated *1674*, the lobed baluster body painted with stylized flowers and foliage in white and yellow enamel against a blue ground, 6¼in. (Sotheby's) $1,828

A large stoneware vase on stand, by Ernest Chaplet, circa 1883-85, of banded cylindrical form, decorated with a frieze of harvesting peasants, the vase 23in. high. (Christie's) $12,109

A glazed cobalt-decorated stoneware crock, stamped *Thomas Harrington* (Active 1840-1872), Lyons, New York, third quarter 19th century, 12¼in. high. (Christie's) $4,025

A German red stoneware jug with finely molded bacchus mask spout, 8in., possibly by Böttger. (Brightwells) $792

A sancai glazed pottery amphora, with guei dragon handles, cup shaped mouth and slender tapering body, ocher and green, glaze, 15in. high, Tang Dynasty.
(Christie's) $4,571

A pair of sancai-glazed earth spirits and a large sancai-glazed figure of a lokapala guardian, Tang Dynasty (618 – 907), each seated recumbent with cloven feet and small flame-shaped wings, the lokapala modelled standing on a recumbent bullock, 33¾in. high.
(Christie's) $6,665

A rare blue and sancai-glazed pottery figure of a Bactrian camel, Tang Dynasty, covered in a deep amber glaze with the areas of heavier hair on the head, upper front legs, tail and humps left unglazed, 20in. high.
(Christie's) $32,200

VIENNA

A Vienna style charger painted with three classical maidens and Cupid tied to a tree, titled to the reverse *Gracien Rache*, late 19th century, 37.5cm. diameter.
(Christie's) $673

A Vienna cup and saucer, circa 1775, each finely painted with a vignette depicting natives in lush landscape settings.
(Sotheby's) $1,097

A Vienna animal group, circa 1760, modelled as a lion attacking a black and white hound at the neck, on a grassy scroll-molded shaped base, 8¼in. long.
(Sotheby's) $1,272

A Vienna circular dish, the center well painted with a young wood nymph sitting on rocks beside a lake with a butterfly on her hand, signed *Dittrich,* circa 1870, 24cm.
(Woolley & Wallis) $1,694

A Vienna coffee-cup and saucer, circa 1750, the cup painted with wooded landscape vignettes, the saucer with a man seated on a barrel. (Christie's) $509

A Vienna porcelain plate painted with The Death of Wallenstein, after von Piloty within blue rim with floral and scrolling foliate gilding, late 19th century, 9in. wide.
(Andrew Hartley) $403

A rare Volkstedt gilt-metal-mounted snuff box, circa 1770, the inside cover with a puce topographical view of the princely Residence of Heidecksburg above the town of Volkstedt, 2¾in. long.
(Sotheby's) $7,722

A Volkstedt figure group of a shepherd and his companion, cancelled blue monogram mark, he seated on rockwork embracing his companion, 9¾in. high.
(Christie's) $1,160

A Volkstedt conversation group, modelled with a gentleman wearing 18th century dress, standing by his seated female companion, a couple curtsying and bowing to them, 20th century, 60cm. wide.
(Christie's) $1,562

A Volkstedt fluted pear-shaped coffee-pot and cover, painted with trailing garden flowers from the shaped purple-scale borders, circa 1770, 26cm. high.
(Christie's) $1,450

A Volkstedt mantel clock, with a couple sitting beneath the dial and applied with cherubs, 37cm. and a pair of Continental porcelain baluster vases and covers painted and applied with flowers, all circa 1900.
(Woolley & Wallis) $497

A pair of Volkstedt models of parrots, blue monogram marks, one perched on a high leafy trunk, the second eating a cherry, 15½in. high. (Christie's) $3,625

WADE

Donald Duck, a Wadeheath hand-painted pottery teapot modelled as Donald Duck, the handle formed from Donald's wings, the spout from his beak, 6½in. high.
(Christie's) $532

Wade porcelain Disney model of 'Lady' (Blow up Series), Wade black transfer printed mark, 4½in.
(G.A Key) $125

A Wade cellulose glazed figure, 'Sadie', no.5, 33.2cm.
(Bristol) $303

A Wedgwood figure designed by Arnold Machin of a sea nymph on a sea horse, covered in a gray and brown glaze, 23cm. high. (Christie's) $640

A set of five Wedgwood plates, printed in blue with flowers and leaves within floral diaper borders, 21cm. (Woolley & Wallis) $212

A Wedgwood majolica oyster plate circa 1865, modelled with twelve oyster-form wells, impressed *Wedgwood*, 11½in. wide. (Sotheby's) $1,320

Wedgwood black basalt 'Portland' vase, circa 1900, impressed *WEDGWOOD* and *ENGLAND*, 10¼in. high. (Freeman) $1,400

'Bubbles II' a Wedgwood Fairyland luster malfrey pot and cover, Z5257, printed marks, 18.5cm. high. (Christie's) $19,740

A Wedgwood vase, by Keith Murray, KM monogram, 15.5cm. high. (Christie's) $395

'Nizami' a Wedgwood Fairyland luster Melba footed bowl, printed factory marks, Z5485, 8cm. high. (Christie's) $1,645

A Wedgwood Parian group 'Pharoah's Daughters Discovering Moses in the Bulrushes' after Beattie, and modelled as two female figures, one standing beside a sphinx, 20¼in. high. (Andrew Hartley) $723

'Fairy Gondola' a Wedgwood lily plate, printed marks, 33cm. diameter. (Christie's) $7,896

A large Wemyss seated pig painted with clover-leaf, in shades of green, pink, yellow and black on a white ground, painted marks, 41cm. wide.
(Christie's) $1,120

A Wemyss pottery pig painted green shamrocks, 6in. green painted mark.
(Brightwells) $528

Wemyss style container, modelled as a pig, decorated in dark green with foliage, on a paler green ground, one leg with indistinct impressed marks, 3½in.
(G A Key) $94

A Wemyss spiral molded jardiniere, painted with roses impressed mark, 22cm. diameter.
(Woolley & Wallis) $127

A large Wemyss tyg, with pink tulips and green foliage, impressed marks, 19cm. high.
(Sworders) $816

A Wemyss square section honey box, cover and stand, with a thistle knop, painted with bees buzzing about hives, 18.5cm.
(Woolley & Wallis) $504

WIENER WERKSTÄTTE

Wiener Werkstätte type, an earthenware figural group, of a man riding a horse, supporting a scantily clad maiden, glazed in colors, 21cm.
(Bonhams & Brooks) $1,096

Wiener Werkstätte, an earthenware figure, of a man standing, his dog beside, holding flowers behind his back, glazed in colors.
(Bonhams & Brooks) $2,055

Wiener Werkstätte, an earthenware candleholder, designed by Vally Wieselthier, of compressed conical form pierced and molded with organic and geometric motifs, surmounted with three sconces, 22cm.
(Bonhams & Brooks) $548

A rare Worcester octagonal 'famille verte' bowl, circa 1753-58, the interior with a central flower spray in iron-red, within a green cell and diaper border set with four floral vignettes, 4½in.
(Sotheby's) $7,314

A Royal Worcester vase by C Baldwyn, of ovoid form with flared rim and leaf capped scrolled lug handles, the body painted with swans in flight amongst foliage, 13in. high.
(Andrew Hartley) $4,774

An impressive 'Royal Monogram' teapot and cover from the Royal Service, Flight, Barr and Barr, Worcester, circa 1807-13, each side with a gilt scrolling *GR* beneath a crown in a circular reserve framed with gilt oak leaves and acorns, 24.5cm.(Bonhams) $13,090

A Worcester Barr, Flight and Barr pastille burner, pierced cover and liner, circa 1804-13, of urn shape raised on three sphinxes with claw feet on a triangular base, painted with baskets of summer flowers, 7½in. (Sotheby's) $1,176

A Barr Worcester coffee can and saucer, circa 1792-1807, painted in the manner of Thomas Baxter, with specimen feathers in shades of yellow, ocher, iron-red, gray and black, the saucer 5⅛in. diameter.
(Sotheby's) $2,293

A Royal Worcester reticulated miniature 'Chelsea-style' ewer, date cypher for 1908, signed *H.Chair*, reticulated by George Owen, of 'Hebe' form, with frilly mouth and loop handle, 16.8cm. high.
(Christie's) $4,700

A large Worcester blue printed cabbage jug, circa 1770 printed with 'The Pine Cone Group' pattern flanked by 'Wispy Chrysanthemum' pattern and 'The Natural Sprays Group' pattern, 30cm.
(Bonhams) $1,727

A rare Worcester teapot and cover, with a globular body and loop handle, transfer printed in brick red with *The Fishing Party* to one side, and *The Singing Lesson* to the reverse, both designs by Boitard and Hancock, circa 1755-60, 14.5cm. long.
(Woolley & Wallis) $9,240

A rare Worcester cylindrical mug, printed in black with a three quarter portrait of Admiral Boscawen holding a map titled *Louisbourg*, the reverse with two men o' war and Boscawen's coat of arms, circa 1760, 8.5cm.
(Woolley & Wallis) $5,544

A Barr, Flight and Barr Worcester plate, richly decorated in iron red, blue, gold and pink with flowers and foliage, printed and impressed marks, 1807-13, 24cm.
(Woolley & Wallis) $277

A Flight Barr and Barr Worcester porcelain tureen and stand, painted with blue floral sprays with gilt embellishment, 12in. wide.
(Andrew Hartley) $689

Late 18th century Worcester leaf molded plate, also painted in colors with sprigs of flowers within a gilded border, circa 1770, 7in.
(G.A. Key) $863

A Dr Wall Worcester cabbage leaf mask jug decorated with three puce prints of rural scenes on a yellow ground, 9in. high.
(Brightwells) $1,645

An impressive Royal Worcester circular plaque, circa 1902, painted by C.H.C. Baldwyn, signed, with six swans in flight amongst foliage on a pale blue ground, 23in. overall.
(Sotheby's) $5,055

A Royal Worcester two-handled urn shaped vase and cover painted with still life of fruit including peas and cherries, signed *Chivers*, blue and gilt surround, 10½in.
(Brightwells) $2,573

A Chamberlains Worcester porcelain armorial plate, the shaped gadrooned rim painted with flowers on a green ground with gilt embellishment, 10¼in. wide.
(Andrew Hartley) $290

A Royal Worcester jug, with a cleft top, gilt handle and compressed circular body, decorated with carnations, poppies and other flowers on an ivory ground, a puce mark, circa 1891, 13.5cm.
(Woolley & Wallis) $292

A Worcester blue-scale cabbage-leaf-molded mask-jug, circa 1770, blue square seal mark, painted with birds perched on branches and in flight on shrubby river islands with trees in the distance, 11½in. high.
(Christie's) $4,506

A pair of Royal Worcester gilt-metal-mounted circular turquoise-glazed terracotta plaques, molded in high relief with Bacchus and Ariadne with Pan and Faun in attendance, circa 1865, 25.5cm. diameter. (Christie's) $624

A Worcester (Flight, Barr & Barr) plate from the Stowe service, circa 1813, the center painted with the arms of the Marquess of Buckingham and his wife Lady Anne Brydges, 24cm. diameter. (Christie's) $12,777

A pair of Royal Worcester porcelain vases and covers by Harry Davis, the body painted with sheep beside a river, signed, within molded stiff leaf banding, 10in. high. (Andrew Hartley) $7,784

A Chamberlain's Worcester bright-green-ground two-handled ice-pail, cover and liner, signed and dated E.A. Woosnam. / Dec.' 1832., with two rectangular pale-yellow-ground panels of garden flowers, 12¾in. high. (Christie's) $3,748

A pair of Royal Worcester porcelain figural flower holders, depicting male and female figures in green and gold dress, both holding baskets, 10½in. high (Andrew Hartley) $1,540

A Flight period porcelain cabbage leaf jug with mask-head spout, brightly painted with the 'Queen Charlotte' pattern, 20cm. high, blue crescent mark, circa 1790. (Bearne's) $739

A Royal Worcester porcelain figure of a red devil Toby jug, no. 2850, 8.5cm. high.(Thomson Roddick & Medcalf) $189

A Hadley's Worcester faience jardinière, brown painted with flowers on a cream/peach ground within blue strapwork, applied with dragon masks, 11¾in. wide. (Andrew Hartley) $896

A Royal Worcester porcelain vase, the body painted with terrapins on rocks, in blue, green, brown and purple on cream ground, 13¼in. high. (Andrew Hartley) $4,620

Bolex H16 no. 113341, Paillard-Bolex, Switzerland; 16mm. with a three-lens turret holding various lenses, extension tubes, pistol grip, instruction booklet, in maker's fitted case. (Christie's) $306

Bolex H8 Reflex no. 198695, Paillard-Bolex, Switzerland; 8mm., with a three-lens turret mount holding a Kern Macro-Yvar f/3.3 150mm. lens, a Kern Macro-Switar f/1.3 12.5mm., a Kern Macro-Switar f/1.4 36mm. lens. (Christie's) $361

Beaulieu R16 Automatic camera, Beaulieu, France; 16mm. with an Angénieux zoom 17-68mm. f/2.2 lens no. 1103126 and instruction booklet, in a case. (Christie's) $506

Professional-16AT BTL ciné camera no. 27440, Pathé, France; 16mm., with two external 400ft. magazines, a Berthiot Macro-zoom lens, a Pathé electric film winder, a Berthiot Pan-Cinor f/2 17-85mm. lens. (Christie's) $867

Pathé cinematographic camera no. 1047, 28mm., black leather covered body, hand-crank, parallel-mounted internal film magazines and a Berthiot Stellor f/4.5 45mm. lens no. 80831. (Christie's) $5,417

Williamson ciné camera, 35mm. polished mahogany body, hand-cranked (crank lacking), two film magazines and an Aldis Bros. 7.5in. lens. (Christie's) $2,708

Beaulieu R16 camera, 16mm. with 200ft magazine, an Angenieux Zoom Type 4 x 17B f/2.2 17-68mm. lens no. 1211842, with battery and adapter. (Christie's) $686

Cinematographic camera, 35mm. wood body, hand-cranked, internal film magazine with engraved brass plaque for Debenham & Co. Kinomatographers. York. (Christie's) $2,708

Arriflex 35 no. 2002, Arnold & Richter, Germany; 35mm., with three-lens turret holding three lenses and a film magazine, in a case. (Christie's) $1,534

A blue lacquer and japanned musical bracket clock, Thomas Prior, London, circa 1760, the triple fusee 6 pillar movement with verge escapement with bob pendulum, 23in. (Christie's) $9,555

A green Vernis Martin bracket clock, Boucheret et Paris, circa 1770, the round flat bottomed movement with count wheel striking on a bell, the case decorated in dark green lacquer, 19½in. (Christie's) $1,103

A black lacquer bracket clock, Thomas Gardner, London, circa 1750, the twin fusee 5 pillar movement with a verge escapement and bob pendulum, striking on a bell, 20½in. (Christie's) $5,880

A small mahogany bracket timepiece with alarm, Samuel Dalton, Rugby, late 18th/ 19th century, 5½in. restored painted dial with a central alarm setting concentric disk, 15in. (Christie's) $2,499

An ebony cased bracket timepiece former quarter repeating with alarm, Thomas Darlon, circa 1700, the single fusee movement with 4 vase shaped pillars, (lacking repeating and alarm work), with a converted anchor escapement, 18½in. (Christie's) $2,205

An ebonized and brass chamfered top bracket clock, English, circa 1820, 8in. painted dial with a faded signature, the triple fusee movement striking on a bell in a case with a chamfered and reeded top, 19¼in.(Christie's) $2,352

A mahogany single pad top bracket clock, James Day, London, circa 1790, the twin fusee 5 pillar movement with an anchor escapement, engraved back plate and striking on a bell, 17in. (Christie's) $4,410

A large oak chiming bracket clock with matching bracket, Penlington & Hutton, Liverpool, circa 1870, the triple fusee movement chiming on 8 bells and a single wire hour gong, 29in., bracket, 11in. (Christie's) $1,470

A walnut 17th century style bracket clock, English, late 19th /20th century, 7in. dial with a silvered chapter ring, matted center with a mock pendulum aperture marked *Issac Lowndes*, 16in. (Christie's) $1,764

An ebonised George III bracket clock, the 8 day verge movement striking on a bell, with an engraved back plate, dial inscribed *Thos Field, Bath*, 19in.
(Woolley & Wallis) $3,836

An ebonized quarter chiming bracket clock, Coates, Wakefield, circa 1810, with a concealed rise/fall regulation subsidiary behind the doors, 25in.
(Bonhams) $4,140

An ebonised bracket clock, John Roberts, London, circa 1780, the twin fusee and line movement with a verge escapement with disc pendulum bob, 21½in.
(Bonhams) $4,830

A Queen Anne ebony miniature bracket clock with pull quarter repeat, Thomas Tompion & Edward Banger, London No. 414, restored verge escapement with blued steel pendulum rod suspended from the brass rise-and-fall arm, 10in. high.
(Christie's) $515,838

A Queen Anne walnut bracket timepiece with pull quarter repeat, John Knibb, Oxford, the case with gilt-metal repoussée double basket top with four foliate urn finials flanking the handle formed as two addorsed caryatides, 17in. high.
(Christie's) $23,853

A George III mahogany striking bracket clock with calendar, Thomas Willmore, London, five pillar twin wire fusee movement with verge escapement and strike on a bell, 23½in. high.
(Christie's) $8,178

A good mahogany bracket clock, E Dent & Co, London, circa 1880, 5½in. convex dial, the twin fusee movement with a dead beat escapement and maintaining power, 18½in.
(Bonhams) $3,588

A George III ormolu musical and automaton bracket clock, Francis Perigal, London, the arch with a painted scene in the foreground with ships passing in the background against a glass- rod automaton waterfall, 24in. high.
(Christie's) $54,520

A mahogany single pad top bracket clock, unsigned, late 18th century, the twin fusee movement with a verge escapement and bob pendulum, 19in.
(Bonhams) $3,450

A mahogany bracket clock with engine turned gilt dial, pierced front frets and standing on brass feet, in a later case, Gilliot, Paris, 19th century, 38cm.
(Bonhams) $548

A Victorian ebonized bracket clock, last quarter 19th century, the 12cm. arched brass dial with silver chapter ring, slow fast dial to arch, movement stamped *WH & Son*, 43cm. high. (Bonhams) $596

A mahogany cased bracket clock with round dial and carved grape moldings and shaped top, French, 19th century, 33cm.
(Bonhams) $339

An Irish George III mahogany striking bracket clock, by Charles Craig, Dublin, the case with unusual gilt-brass handle to the shallow molded inverted bell top, glazed sides, the molded base on bracket feet, 16½in. high.
(Christie's) $10,363

A walnut cased bracket clock, English, third quarter 19th century, the painted 19cm. dial with Roman numerals, with a bell striking single fusée movement, with wall bracket, 36cm. wide.(Bonhams) $1,221

An ebonized cased triple fusée chiming bracket clock, Howell & James, London, with 20cm. arched dial, sounding on eight bells and a gong, with pendulum and keys, 64cm. high.
(Bonhams) $2,059

A walnut cased bracket clock with carved top and brass side frets silvered dial signed *R.H. Halford & Sons*, German, 1890s, 32cm.
(Bonhams) $1,771

A Gothic Revival oak cased twin fusee bracket clock, last quarter 19th century, 15cm. silvered arched dial, a chime/ not chime dial to the arch, with pendulum, key and two winding keys, 59cm. high.
(Bonhams) $1,420

A walnut veneer bracket clock with silvered brass arched dial, pierced side frets and scroll feet, Winterhalder & Hoffmeier, Germany, 1890s, 37cm.
(Bonhams) $370

A Victorian gilt-metal giant carriage clock with twin up-and-down dials, Charles Frodsham, London, the early Gorge-style case with heavy bevelled glasses, with the original mahogany travelling box, 8¼in. high. (Christie's) $46,943

A 19th century French brass cased repeating carriage clock with alarm, signed *H.P. Turner, Belfast Chambers 156 Regent St. London*, 17cm. high. (Bonhams) $680

A Victorian gilt-metal quarter striking giant carriage clock, Payne & Co., London, third quarter 19th century, the case with bevelled glasses throughout, 8¼in. high. (Christie's) $21,689

A small silver and yellow guilloche enamel desk timepiece, Austrian 1920s, enamel dial, the short duration cylinder watch movement in a rectangular yellow guilloche enamel case, 2¾in. (Bonhams) $345

A Swiss brass chronometer carriage clock with Neuchâtel grande sonnerie, alarm and date, C.F. Klentschi, circa 1830, the case with stepped top and dentil cornices, reeded fluting to the angles, 6'/₃in. high. (Christie's) $16,185

An early Victorian gilt-metal striking carriage clock with alarm, Barraud & Lund, London, second quarter 19th century, the case with foliage engraving to the base on bracket feet and to the top with faceted handle, 7½in. high. (Christie's) $4,514

A French brass cased carriage clock, the 8 day lever repeating movement striking on a gong, impressed *R & Co,* Made in Paris, to a white enamel dial, 6'/₈in. high. (Woolley & Wallis) $832

A 19th century French brass repeater carriage clock, fitted with a gong striking movement and enamel dial, set in a plain corniche case, 17cm. high. (Bonhams) $680

A French brass carriage timepiece, mid 19th century, the one-piece with white enamel Roman dial, moon hands, silvered lever platform to bimetallic balance, 4½in. high. (Christie's) $405

A gilt brass repeating carriage clock with alarm, French, circa 1880, the movement with a gilt lever escapement and striking on a gong in a polished case, 8in.
(Bonhams) $1,104

An unusual French gilt-brass striking and repeating carriage clock with alarm and date, Berrolla à Paris, mid 19th century, 6in. high.
(Christie's) $2,896

A French brass striking and repeating carriage clock with alarm, Bolviller à Paris, no.76, second quarter 19th century, the cariatides case mounted with figures in niches to the angles, 7¼in. high.
(Christie's) $1,533

A brass repeating carriage clock, French, circa 1880, enamel dial signed *Charles Frodsham Clockmakers To Queen*, with a gilt foliage engraved mask, the gong striking movement in a rectangular case, 7½in.
(Bonhams) $1,449

A French brass R.E.D. carriage timepiece, last quarter 19th century, the circular case with typical glazed mid section and loop handle, solid rear door with shuttered winding hole, 4¾in. high.
(Christie's) $987

A fine bronzed twin fusee repeating carriage clock, John Moore & Sons London, circa 1840, 4in. one piece silvered dial, the substantial twin fusee and chain movement with turned baluster pillars, 10in.
(Bonhams) $11,040

An unusual electro-typed cased carriage timepiece, English, second half 19th century, the French movement finished in the English style with a going barrel and platform escapement, signed *Rofs Exeter*, 7in. (Bonhams) $552

An engraved gilt oval cased repeating carriage clock with alarm, French, circa 1870, the bell striking movement with a lever escapement in an oval foliage engraved case, 7¼in. (Bonhams) $3,588

A French gilt-brass and Limoges enamel mounted striking and repeating carriage clock, No. 1986; retailed by Le Boutillier & Co. Paris, fourth quarter 19th century.
10¹/₃in. (Christie's) $4,259

A champlevé enamel panelled carriage timepiece, French, 1900s, the movement with a silvered lever escapement in a polished corniche case, 7in. (Bonhams) $304

A small silver cased carriage timepiece, Swiss, 1920, enamel dial signed *Barraclough Leeds*, the frosted gilt movement with a lever escapement, 2¾in. (Bonhams) $580

A polished brass oval repeating carriage clock, French, circa 1880, enamel dial signed *Martin & Co Paris & Cheltenham,* the movement with a silvered lever escapement, 7½in. (Bonhams) $1,173

A brass cased carriage clock with a decorative surround, French, 1900s, enamel dial, the movement with a silvered lever escapement and striking on a gong, stamped on back plate with Richard & Co trade mark, 7in. (Bonhams) $386

A small French gilt-brass grande sonnerie carriage clock with alarm, late 19th century, the cariatides case with openwork floral masks overlaid on plain gilt-brass panels to the sides, travel case, 5in. high. (Christie's) $5,962

A brass cased repeating carriage clock, French, 1885 enamel dial signed *Bristol Goldsmiths Alliance*, the gong striking movement with a silvered lever escapement, 7½in. (Bonhams) $1,242

A silver cased carriage timepiece, English case, French movement, 1905, late enamel dial signed *Dubois Genève*, the movement with a lever escapement in polished case, 4¼in. (Bonhams) $442

A French brass striking and repeating novelty carriage clock in the form of a sedan chair, late 19th century, the twin barrel movement with platform lever escapement, 9¾in. high.(Christie's) $4,089

A Swiss gilt-brass grande sonnerie carriage clock with date and alarm, J.F. Bautte & Cie, Genève, third quarter 19th century, the cariatides case with Renaissance figures of a huntsman and a lady, 15.5cm. high. (Christie's) $4,259

A French gilt brass striking carriage clock, late 19th century, the rococo case cast overall with trailing foliage and floral swags, the twin barrel movement with strike on bell, 7in. high, over handle.
(Christie's) $4,399

A tortoiseshell and silver carriage timepiece, French/English, 1911, the movement with a lever escapement in a domed top case with inlaid decoration, 6¾in.
(Christie's) $1,029

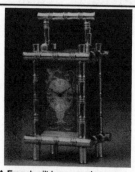

A French gilt brass carriage timepiece, late 19th century, the bamboo case with silvered and gilt heightened dial with satyr mask, dragon and snake, inscribed *Le Roy & Fils*, 4¼in. high, over handle.
(Christie's) $2,537

An ornate cast brass repeating carriage clock, French, Bolviller, circa 1870, enamel dial signed *Lowe Paris*, the bell striking movement with an engraved lever escapement, in an ornate cast case, 8½in.(Christie's) $1,250

A white onyx and brass carriage timepiece, French, 1900, enamel dial with a frosted gilt mask, the movement with a cylinder escapement in a case with a sloping pediment and carrying handle, 4½in.(Christie's) $110

A gilt brass repeating carriage clock, French, circa 1880, enamel dial signed for J W Benson 25 Old Bond St London, the gong striking movement with a silvered lever escapement, in a molded cannelée case, 6¼in.
(Christie's) $1,323

A small silver carriage timepiece, English/French, 1904, 1¼in. enamel dial, the movement with a lever escapement in a spot hammered case with carrying handle, 3½in.
(Christie's) $662

A gilt brass and silvered carrriage clock, Le Roy ET Fils, Nos 3498 circa 1840, shuttered back engraved *This Clock formerley belonged to Thomas Carlyle 1795-1881*, 6¼in.
(Christie's) $8,526

A large gilt brass carriage style clock, French, 1900s, 3in. enamel dial with regulation at 12' O'clock, the drum gong striking movement with a replaced lever escapement, 9¾in. (Christie's) $588

A Louis XVI ormolu cartel clock, after a design by Jean-Charles Delafosse, the circular enamelled dial with Roman and Arabic chapters, inscribed *Gide / A Paris*, 32in. high.(Christie's) $4,904

Good Scandinavian gilt wood wall clock, elaborately crested with ribbons and foliage, circular Arabic chapter ring and 8 day movement, 23in. (G.A. Key) $580

A carved gilt wood Swedish cartel wall clock, German, 1900s, 9in. painted dial, the bell striking movement marked *Lenzkirch* in an ornate carved case decorated with flower heads and berried hanging garlands, 28in.
(Bonhams) $690

A Louis XV style ormolu cartel d'appliqué, circa 1880, the rocaille shaped case surmounted by a spray of flowers above a pair of flowers above a pair of birds and hung with a floral pendant to each side, 19in. high.
(Christie's) $2,500

A Louis XVI-style ormolu cartel clock and barometer en suite, after a model by Jean-Charles Delafosse, circa 1890, each with urn finial and shaped case with dial flanked by scrolled handles draped with a lion-pelt, each: 31in. high. (Christie's) $8,625

A Louis XVI ormolu cartel clock, the circular enamel dial inscribed *Hubert / A Paris*, with pierced scrolling hands, flanked by laurel swags and surmounted by a double-headed eagle on a fluted plinth, with pendulum, 17in. high. (Christie's) $2,900

A Louis XVI style ormolu cartel d'appliqué, circa 1890, the enamelled dial with Roman and Arabic chapters and twin-train movement, flanked by ram's head masks, over a lion's head mask, 77.2 high.(Christie's) $3,290

A French ormolu cartel clock, in the Louis XV style, by Henry Dasson, Paris, dated *1889*, surmounted by a fluted vase neck filled with flowers, 12½in. high.
(Christie's) $4,048

A French gilt-bronze cartel clock, in the Louis XV style, circa 1880, surmounted by a sunburst, with Cupid in a chariot with doves, 40½in. high.
(Christie's) $11,762

A French gilt bronze mantel clock and garniture, circa 1880, the cylindrical case with architectural pediment and acorn leaf swagged urn surmount, the twin barrel movement with strike on bell, 21in. high, and a pair of five light candelabra en suite.
(Christie's) $3,214

A French ormolu and white marble clock garniture, in the Louis XVI style, circa 1875, comprising a mantel clock and a pair of six-light candelabra, the clock surmounted by a putto, above the sphere shaped case, the clock 22½in. high.
(Christie's) $11,762

A gilt-bronze and malachite clock garniture, the movement by Tiffany & Co. France, comprising a mantel clock and a pair of six-light candelabra, the timepiece surmounted by two doves on a nest, the timepiece 18½in. high. (Christie's) $10,418

A Napoleon III ormolu-mounted and paste-set white marble clock garniture in the Louis XVI style, circa 1870, the clock shaped as a lyre, surmounted by a sunburst mask with swags, above a white enamel dial signed *F...Le jeune, Paris*, clock 25¾in. high.
(Christie's) $9,200

A French gilt bronze mantel clock and garniture, circa 1860, the drum case on a waisted pedestal flanked by three cavorting cherubs entwined, inscribed *Charpentier & Cie. Bronziers Paris, Rue Charlot 8*, 26in. high, and a pair of conforming gilt bronze side urns en suite, 23in. high.(Christie's) $16,073

A Black Forest carved and stained wood mantel clock and garniture, late 19th or early 20th century, the shaped case surmounted by the figure of a stag and another deer, 31¼in. high, and a pair of conforming tazza stands en suite, each modelled with a pheasant amidst foliage, 10in. high. (Christie's) $6,768

A patinated figural spelter, marble and onyx clock garniture, comprising central clock and two vases, 41.5cm. high. (Christie's) $493

A French gilt-bronze and blue-ground porcelain clock garniture, circa 1875, the mantel clock as two putti on a chariot drawn by two goats, the wheel as a dial, signed *Lahoche a Paris*, candelabra 22¼in. high. (Christie's) $12,512

A Restauration ormolu and yellow marble striking mantel clock, first quarter 19th century, the drum case held under the arm of a figure of Chronos, with strike on bell and with later vertically positioned lever escapement, 18½in. high. (Christie's) $3,452

A Napoleon III ormolu-mounted parcel-gilt turquoise-ground jewelled porcelain clock garniture, by Pannier-Lahoche, Paris, circa 1867, the timepiece surmounted by two putti holding a finial, the timepiece 19¼in. high. (Christie's) $10,921

A French gilt-and patinated-bronze clock garniture, in the Louis XV style, circa 1890, comprising a mantel clock and a pair of ten-light candelabra; the clock centered by a white enamel dial, the twin-train movement striking on a bell, the movement signed *JLES DUCHÉ A PARIS / 551*, the garniture: 37in. high. (Christie's) $36,800

A silvered and parcel-gilt bronze clock garniture, late 19th century, by Mathurin Moreau, modelled as a Classical nymph standing beside an urn on a flower-draped column above the rectangular marble clock case, the candelabra with nymphs holding aloft candleholders, the candelabra 29¾in. high. (Christie's) $6,900

A French gilt-spelter and porcelain mounted striking mantel clock and garniture, last quarter 19th century, the case with urn surmount and scroll side supports terminating in oval porcelain panels decorated with flowers, 17in. high. (Christie's) $1,463

A three-piece Art Deco clock garniture by Lateulere Marseille and further inscribed *Just*, eight-day movement, red variegated marble and black slate case, the garnitures in the form of rectangular tazzas, the clock 50cm. wide. (T.R. & M) $551

A French gilt bronze and porcelain mantel clock and garniture, last quarter 19th century, the Sèvres style urn surmount with white panels on a blue ground heightened with gilt, above a waisted spreading square section case with lion mask ring handles, 17in. high. and a pair of conforming five light candelabra en suite, 19¾in. high.
(Christie's) $7,728

A gilt metal and porcelain mounted clock garniture, French, circa 1890, 3in. chapter on a painted porcelain dial decorated with birds around a nest and foliage, 13in., garnitures 9in.
(Bonhams) $1,727

A French bronze clock garniture, late 19th century, the drum case with stylized lion masks on foliate capped volute scrolls above a raised plinth, the twin barrel movement with countwheel strike on bell stamped *Vincent & Cie*, 16in. high. (Christie's) $2,180

A Louis XVI style gilt bronze and white marble mantel clock, late 19th century, the square case flanked and surmounted by Cupid and a partially clad maiden amidst stylized clouds, 14⅝in. high.
(Christie's) $5,152

Three-piece champlevé clock garniture, France, 19th century, consisting of a rococo style clock with cherub finial, 19½in. high, together with a pair of five-light candelabra, 20³/₈in. high. (Skinner) $7,475

A French gilt bronze mantel clock and garniture, circa 1860, the drum case on a waisted pedestal flanked by three cavorting cherubs, inscribed *Charpentier & Cie. Bronziers Paris, Rue Charlot 8*, 26in. high, and a pair of conforming gilt bronze side urns en suite. (Christie's) $13,572

A gilt metal four glass clock garniture, French, 1900s, 3½in. enamel dial with floral decorated center, the gong striking movement with a mercury pendulum, together with a pair of matching vases, 10½in. (Bonhams) $560

A French ormolu clock garniture, late 19th century, the case of architectural outline, surmounted by the figure of a robed maiden carrying an amphora over her right shoulder above the circular Roman dial, 26in. high. (Christie's) $2,726

A French silvered bronze chinoiserie design mantel clock and garniture, late 19th century, the case with pierced foliate cresting and stylized beasts to the angles, 15in. high, and a pair of twin branch candelabra en suite, 36cm. high. (Christie's) $1,991

A three-piece Egyptian Revival marble mantel clock set, signed by Tiffany & Company, New York City, circa 1890, comprising a clock and two obelisks: the clock with bronze figure of a sphinx resting on a rectangular outset shelf, obelisks; 17in. high. (Christie's) $3,680

A small early 18th century West Country lantern clock, the 8 day movement with a verge escapement, striking on a bell to the dome with pierced frets, 10in. (Woolley & Wallis) $2,130

A brass 30 hour lantern clock, late 17th century, the posted movement with baluster turned corner columns, front fret marked *George Boyce fecit 1698*, lacking corner finials and side doors, 13¾in. (Christie's) $5,586

A Japanese double foliot gilt-brass floor-standing lantern clock, unsigned; first half 19th century, the padouk pedestal plinth case decorated with gilt scrolling karakusa on the legs and hood, 34½in. high. (Christie's) $16,185

A Continental gilt-brass miniature lantern clock with alarm, unsigned; possibly Italian, second half 17th century, the two train movement with verge and balance wheel escapement, 7½in. high. (Christie's) $14,481

A French brass striking capucine clock with alarm, A.ne Nosada neveu à Marselles, first quarter 19th century, the twin barrel movement with plain steel three arm balance with lever escapement, 10in. high. (Christie's) $1,533

A George II brass striking lantern clock, signed *Thomas Moore, Ipswich*, later hour hand, foliate pierced and engraved gallery frets above enclosing a large bell, 14¼in. (Christie's) $2,045

A brass lantern style clock with single fusee movement, passing strike and large chapter ring, English, 20th century, 27cm. (Bonhams) $462

A Charles II brass striking lantern clock, Nicholas Coxeter, London, two-train movement with anchor escapement, countwheel strike on the large bell above, 14½in. high. (Christie's) $8,178

A late 18th century oak longcase clock, eight day movement, by G. Hewitt & Marlboro, 92½in. (Wintertons) $3,010

An oak longcase clock, P Carless, Tewkesbury, 19th century, 7ft.5in. (Christie's) $1,029

A late Victorian oak longcase clock, stamped *Arnold & Lewis, Manchester*, 82½in. high. (Wintertons) $4,200

A George III mahogany longcase clock, the eight day movement by Fielders of Atherstone, 7ft. 1¾in. (Wintertons) $1,470

A George III oak longcase clock, eight day movement, signed *Blinman & Co. of Bristol*, 197cm. high. (Wintertons) $1,771

A mahogany longcase clock, eight day movement, signed *Riley Causeway*, 83in. high. (Andrew Hartley) $5,112

A 19th century oak and mahogany crossbanded longcase clock, eight day movement, Bell of Uttoxeter, 219cm. high. (Wintertons) $2,132

A 19th century oak and mahogany crossbanded longcase clock, movement by W. Noon of Ashby, 222cm. high. (Wintertons) $2,541

A mahogany longcase clock, Henry Loat, Nantwich, circa 1800, 8ft. (Bonhams) $8,164

A 30 hour longcase clock, English, Thomas Pinfold Middleton, 1770s, 213cm. (Bonhams) $906

A mahogany cased eight day longcase clock, W Potts, Pudsey, circa 1840, 253cm. high. (Bonhams) $4,932

A mahogany cased tubular chiming longcase clock, English, circa 1880, 7ft.10in. (Bonhams) $10,780

Walnut and tiger maple inlaid tall case clock, possibly Pennsylvania, circa 1828, eight-day brass weight-driven movement, 92½in. (Skinner) $2,185

The David Harris Chippendale mahogany block-and-shell tall case clock, dial signed by Samuel Rockwell, Providence, RI, case, Townsend-Goddard School, 95½in. high.(Christie's) $611,000

Chippendale birch tall case clock, with dial signed *L. Bailey N Yarmouth*, Maine, late 18th century, the arch molded crest with pierced fretwork and three plinths surmounted by wood finials, 88in. high. (Skinner) $17,250

Queen Anne mahogany block and shell carved tall case clock, with dial engraved *Caleb Wheaton Providence*, Rhode Island, 1785-1810, 96¼in. high. (Skinner) $266,500

A Queen Anne gilt lacquer longcase clock, 8 day 5 pillar movement Samuel Stevens, London, 8ft.3½in. (Woolley & Wallis) $5,760

A Federal inlaid and figured mahogany tall case clock, Isaac Brokaw, Bridge Town, New Jersey, circa 1800, height 8ft. 3in. (Sotheby's) $11,400

A late 18th century oak Salisbury longcase clock, 8 day movement, James Crabb, Salisbury, 6ft. 8in. high. (Woolley & Wallis) $2,720

A mahogany cased eight day longcase regulator, R & A Allan Cumnock, 193cm. high. (Bonhams) $2,192

A teak wall mounted twin dialled railway station platform longcase timepiece, English, 19th century, repainted 17in. dials now signed for Eaton Elliot Alderley Edge, 7ft.9in. (Bonhams) $1,540

A black and gold lacquer longcase clock, 8 day movement, William Underwood, London,6ft.11in. high. (Woolley & Wallis) $2,400

Grain-painted pine tall case clock, Connecticut, early 19th century, the shaped scrolling crest over glazed tombstone door enclosing a painted wooden dial with Arabic and Roman numeral chapter ring, 84in. high. (Skinner) $2,990

A Federal grain-painted tall-case clock, Pennsylvania, 1800-1820, grain-painted in shades of salmon, 98in. high. (Christie's) $9,200

A French ormolu-mounted onyx longcase clock, in the Louis XVI style, circa 1880, 112½in. high.
(Christie's) $46,000

A walnut veneered longcase clock, Samuel Townson, circa 1720, 7ft.6in.
(Christie's) $5,880

A Chippendale walnut tall case clock, dial by Nathan Howell, New Haven, Connecticut, 1765-1784, 91in. high.
(Christie's) $3,525

A mahogany longcase clock, James Tregent, Leicester Square London, circa 1770, 8ft.3in.
(Christie's) $6,468

A Chippendale carved mahogany tall case clock, dial signed by John Barnes, Philadelphia, 1750-1760, 96in. high.
(Christie's) $28,200

A Federal inlaid figured-maple tall case clock, dial by David Gobrecht, Hanover, Pennsylvania, 1800-1810, 93¼in. high.
(Christie's) $25,850

A German giltwood and porcelain-mounted longcase clock, the porcelain panels painted by J.Hoss, circa 1880, 77in. high.
(Christie's) $69,280

A Chippendale pine tall-case clock, George Solliday, Bucks County, Pennsylvania, circa 1810, 92¾in. high.
(Christie's) $16,100

A walnut veneered longcase clock, John Hall, early 18th century, 7ft. 4in. (Bonhams) $5,244

A George III mahogany longcase clock, John Ellicott, London, 8ft.7in. high. (Christie's) $16,185

A mahogany railway weight driven wall regulator, Muirhead & Son, Glasgow, 19th century, 4ft.10in. (Bonhams) $1,311

A William and Mary walnut month-going longcase clock, Thomas Tompion, No. 333, 7ft.6in. high. (Christie's) $452,038

A late Victorian carved mahogany quarter chiming longcase clock, R. Comber, Lewes, 8ft. high. (Christie's) $10,223

A mahogany longcase clock, Joseph Lawley, Bath, early 19th century, 6ft. 9in. (Bonhams) $2,070

An early George III walnut longcase clock, Jasper Taylor, London, 7ft.10½in. high. (Christie's) $11,586

An oak cased hour longcase clock, E Sagar, K Stephen, 18th century, 6ft. 11in. (Bonhams) $2,070

A George III oak cased thirty hour longcase clock, Peter Upjohn, Biddeford, 189cm. high. (Bonhams) **$994**

A 19th century oak and mahogany longcase clock, eight day movement, dial inscribed *Wells,* 6ft. 11in. high. (Woolley & Wallis) **$1,595**

A mahogany cased thirty hour longcase clock, John Farr, Bristol, 205cm. high. (Bonhams) **$1,022**

A chinoiserie longcase clock, Henry Wood, London, first quarter 18th century and later, 224cm. high. (Bonhams) **$2,982**

An early Victorian oak Scottish longcase clock, 8 day striking movement signed *Andr. Spmington, Kettle,* 7ft. (Woolley & Wallis) **$1,633**

A Sheraton Revival satinwood longcase clock, 19th century, the 32cm. arched brass dial with silvered chapter ring, 228cm. high. (Bonhams) **$12,070**

An oak longcase clock, Thmas Partington, Manchester, the 32cm. arched brass dial with silvered chapter ring, 225cm. high. (Bonhams) **$1,022**

An early 19th century East Coast oak and mahogany clock, the eight day striking movement, dial inscribed *Hall, Grimsby,* 7ft.2in. (Woolley & Wallis) **$2,175**

A Napoleon III gilt-bronze and Sèvres-pattern porcelain mantel clock, in the Louis XVI style, circa 1885, white enamel dial signed *SF14 J. Howell & Co / Paris*, 9¾in. wide. (Christie's) $2,392

A small Turkish market mounted and red tortoiseshell musical table clock, Markwick, Markham, Borrell London, circa 1800, the break arch case veneered in stained red shell, 16½in. (Christie's) $32,340

A gilt ormolu and bronzed mantel clock, French, circa 1840, the movement with a silk suspension and striking on a bell, contained in a rectangular bronzed case, 13in. (Christie's) $3,822

A Napoleon III gilt-and-patinated bronze mantel clock, in the Louis XV style, circa 1870, twin-train movement striking on a bell, stamped *Von Dewint Her/185 A. Paris*, 20½in. high. (Christie's) $6,992

'Ronde des Heures' a clear and frosted glass table clock, by Sabino, circa 1930, the central circular metallic dial surrounded by two bare-breasted female figures, marked *Sabino*, 6½in. high. (Christie's) $2,016

A late Louis XVI ormolu, black and white marble mantel clock, the circular white-enamelled Roman dial surmounted by an eagle seated on a sphere and flanked by lions, 28in. high. (Christie's) $20,022

A gilt ormolu and porcelain mounted mantel clock, French, circa 1880, 3½in. painted porcelain dial with central winged putti, the bell striking movement in a case with a pine finial, 15in. (Christie's) $1,617

A rosewood four glass mantel timepiece, James Whitelaw, Edinburgh, circa 1840, the single fusee movement with an anchor escapement in a rectangular glazed case, 8¼in. (Christie's) $2,940

A Napoleon III gilt-bronze and parcel gilt blue-ground jewelled porcelain timepiece, circa 1870, twin-train movement with countwheel strike, inscribed *S. Marti*, 26in. high. (Christie's) $10,921

An Art Deco 'Sun Flower' table clock, with spring driven eight day movement having engine turned dial in a gilt metal petal surround, 14¼in. high. (Andrew Hartley) $1,108

A Louis Philippe bronze and ormolu mantel clock, circa 1840, the case surmounted by a lion suppressing a serpent below its front right paw, lacking key and pendulum, 19in. high. (Christie's) $3,634

A French ormolu mantel clock in Louis XV style, the eight day movement stamped *Raingo, Paris*, having pierced and embossed brass dial, in waisted rococo case, 19th century, 22in. high. (Andrew Hartley) $1,946

A Louis XVI gilt bronze and white marble portico mantel clock, late 18th century, the cylindrical case with draped canopy above, supported on four columns above a demi-lune base, stamped *LE ROY & FILS*, 18¼in. high. (Christie's) $2,030

A late Regency white marble mantel clock, first quarter 19th century, modelled as a cinerarium, the rectangular case carved in high relief with birds and a floral swag below a volute scrolled top, 14in. wide. (Christie's) $1,496

A Restauration bronze and Siena marble mantel clock, first quarter 19th century, modelled with the figure of a classically robed and garlanded man, with scroll inscribed *Oui l'âme est Immortelle*, 23¾in. high. (Christie's) $1,496

A Napoleon III gilt and patinated bronze mantel clock, circa 1870, the cylindrical case with urn surmount, on an openwork base with outset scrolls, stamped to the backplate *Japy Freres & Cie, 227*, 20in. high.(Christie's) $2,537

A Louis XVI ormolu mounted white and gray marble portico mantel clock, last quarter 18th century, the drum case with urn finial raised on a portico, 23in. high. (Christie's) $3,816

An ormolu and green porcelain mounted mantel clock, French, circa 1875, 3½in. porcelain dial decorated with a putti, the bell striking movement in a case surmounted by an urn, 14in. high. (Christie's) $1,470

A Restauration gilt bronze mantel clock, second quarter 19th century, the portico case with fruiting swags to the frieze, indistinctly signed *Tarault a Paris*, 21½in. high.
(Christie's) $1,447

Carved walnut mantel clock, America, circa 1900, the carved case of oak trees flanking the bezel and dial above two elk with eight-day spring-driven movement, 22in. high. (Skinner) $1,265

A French mantel clock, the eight day striking movement having chased brass dial, in waisted boulle case surmounted by a figure of an angel, 24in. high.
(Andrew Hartley) $1,668

A Restauration bronze and Siena marble mantel clock, first quarter 19th century, the case modelled with the semi-naked figure of a Greek warrior, wearing a plumed helmet, flanked by trophies about a tree stump, 24in. high.
(Christie's) $1,775

A Louis XVI gilt bronze mantel clock, circa 1880, the base with twin seated putti above a fluted white marble plinth, inscribed *Julien Leroy A Paris*.
(Christie's) $2,907

A French silvered and gilt bronze mantel clock, late 19th century, the case within a cylindrical pedestal, with a muse figure, in the manner of Pradier, seated on drapery above, on a rouge marble square section plinth, 23in. high.
(Christie's) $3,046

A gilt ormolu and jewelled porcelain mounted mantel clock, French, 1870s, 4¼in. green and gilt decorated porcelain dial signed for Hurt & Son Birmingham, with a bell striking movement, 17¼in.
(Christie's) $1,911

A brass combination timepiece, French, 1900s, round enamel dials with frosted gilt marks, the movement with a silvered lever escapement in an oval sided case with top carrying handle, 5½in.
(Christie's) $441

Classical carved mahogany and mahogany veneer 'Hollow Column' mantel clock, George Marsh & Co., Farmington, Connecticut, circa 1825-30, with eight day brass weight-driven movement, 37½in. high. (Skinner) $7,475

A red horn and gilt metal mounted mantel clock, French, 1900s, the gong striking movement in a waisted case veneered with red horn surmounted by a dragon, 12in. (Bonhams) $442

A gilt ormolu and porcelain mounted clock, French, 1880s, 3½in. enamel dial signed *Hry Marc A Paris*, the drum bell striking movement contained in a case surmounted by two putti at play, 17in. (Bonhams) $1,656

A carved mahogany mantel clock, Simmons, London, circa 1820, 8in. painted dial, the twin fusee bell striking movement in a scrolled top case surmounted by a carved finial, 19in.(Bonhams) $1,518

A walnut cased drum head mantel timepiece, circa 1880, 8in. painted dial signed *Samuel Dixon Cornhill London*, the associated single fusee movement with turned pillars, standing on a convex sided stepped base, 16in. (Bonhams) $662

A gilt ormolu and porcelain mounted mantel clock, French, circa 1880, 3in. enamel dial signed *Howell & Cie A Paris*, the bell striking movement in a drum case surmounted by a blue enamel globe with gold stars with astronomy instruments below, 11in. (Bonhams) $1,518

An oak cased ting tang quarter striking mantel clock, Winterhalder & Hoffmeier, 1880s, the movement striking the quarters on twin gongs in a break arch case surmounted by gilt cone finials, 15¾in. (Bonhams) $966

A mahogany mantel clock with applied carvings, Horatio Finer, London, circa 1870, gong striking and repeating movement in a case with a concave sided pediment with applied carved foliage moldings, 18in. (Bonhams) $994

A carved beech mantel clock, Black Forest, 19th century, the French drum movement contained in a well carved case surmounted by a pair of pheasants, 23in. (Bonhams) $856

A white and black marble clock with ormolu mounts, Jacques Le Roy, late 18th century, pierced gilt hands lacking ends, the bell striking movement with a silk suspension in a gilt drum case, 17in. (Bonhams) $2,691

A gilt ormolu and porcelain mantel clock, French, late 19th century, 3¼in. porcelain dial with a center decorated with portraits, the bell striking movement in an ornate gothic case, 12½in. (Bonhams) $552

A French ormolu grande sonnerie pendule d'officier with alarm, Le Roi & Fils, early 19th century, the twin barrel movement with vertically positioned plain three arm balance, 7in. high.(Christie's) $9,370

Gilt metal mantel clock, French, circa 1880, 3½in. restored enamel dial signed *Charles Frodsham & Co to the Queen Paris 18918*, the drum bell striking movement in an arched top case, 11in.(Bonhams) $828

A gilt ormolu and jewelled procelain mounted mantel clock, French, circa 1880, blue porcelain dial with numeral reserves and decorated with a romantic scene, the bell striking movement in a cast case, 13in. (Bonhams) $828

A late 19th French gilt metal 'Chariot of Diomedes' mantel clock French, circa 1880, the bell striking movement with a silk suspension mounted within the body of the chariot shaped case, with dome 25in. (Bonhams) $3,312

A white marble and gilt ormolu mantel clock, French, circa 1790, 3½in. enamel dial signed *Folin L'ainé A Paris*, the bell striking movement with a silk suspension in a gilt drum case, 16½in. (Bonhams) $2,015

An English rosewood eight-day four-glass mantel chronometer, Thomas Mercer, St. Albans, third quarter 20th century, the case with brass handle to the stepped top with escapement viewing glass, 9½in. high.(Christie's) $6,815

A late 19th century French mantel clock, the movement striking on a bell, the circular dial painted moonphase aperture and subsidiary calendar dials, 10¼in. high. (Woolley & Wallis) $630

A rosewood and brass inlaid mantel clock, James McCabe, Royal Exchange, London, 19th century, the twin fusee bell striking movement with a decorated back plate, the case with a curved top, 17¾in. (Bonhams) $1,794

Federal pillar and scroll mahogany shelf clock, Seth Thomas, Plymouth, Connecticut, circa 1825, the scrolled crest joining three plinths with urn brass finials, 17½in. wide. (Skinner) $3,738

A gilt ormolu and porcelain mounted mantel clock, French, circa 1880, 3¾in. painted porcelain dial decorated with a winged putti in the center, the bell striking movement in a drum case, 11in. (Christie's) $956

An inlaid rosewood Ting Tang quarter striking mantel clock, Winterhalder & Hofmeier, 1900s, 7in. dial with a silvered chapter ring signed for Z Barraclough & Son, 15½in. (Christie's) $470

An inlaid brass and ormolu mounted boulle clock, French, 1880s, gong striking movement in a waisted sided case decorated with brass foliage inlay, 17½in. (Christie's) $412

A gilt ormolu mantel clock, French, circa 1880, 3in. enamel dial, the bell striking movement set in a cast case flanked by two winged putti standing on a pierced base, 11in. (Christie's) $515

A gilt brass four glass mantel clock, French, 1880s, 3¼ two piece enamel dial with central visible Brocourt escapement, signed for J. W. Benson Ludgate Hill London, 10½in. (Christie's) $470

A red and brass inlaid boulle clock, French, 1880s, 3¼in. twelve piece enamel dial with decorated center, the gong striking movement in a waisted sided case, 12in. (Bonhams & Brooks) $341

A green onyx and ormolu four glass mantel clock, French, 1880s, with drum gong striking movement in a flat top case with lower tapered columns, 15½in. (Christie's) $809

Carved wooden gilt and painted gesso figural mantel timepiece, mid 19th century, surmounted by an eagle suspending a blue and flower-decorated drapery, 15½in. high. (Skinner) $1,265

A light blue porcelain and gilt mantel clock, Austria, 1900s, standing on a square base decorated with classical ladies within blue and gold painted panels, 15in. (Christie's) $1,029

A Napoleon III ormolu mantel clock, in the Louis XV style, by Charpentier & Cie, Paris circa 1870, surmounted by a figure of a cherub holding roses, 19in. high. (Christie's) $9,200

A Japanese Meiji mantel clock, the striking movement to an open dial, of a brass foliage engraved plate with dragon hands, 18½in. high. (Woolley & Wallis) $960

An oak cased temple style mantel clock, Winterhalder & Hofmeier, 1900s, 6in. silvered dial, gong striking movement in a case with Corinthian columns and patterned stepped base, 16in. (Christie's) $221

An engraved gilt brass four glass mantel clock, French, circa 1880, 3¼in. enamel dial, the drum bell striking movement with a mock mercury pendulum in a glazed case, 10in. (Christie's) $809

An onyx and champlevé decorated four glass mantel clock, French, circa 1900, 4in. gilt dial with an enamelled center, the gong striking movement with a mercury compensated pendulum in a glazed sided case, 13½in. (Christie's) $662

A George IV ormolu and jewelled-paste mantel clock, the Victorian movement by Joseph & Alfred Jump, supported on a scaled serpent dragon, on a D-ended rectangular molded plinth. (Christie's) $14,200

An oak cased ting tang quarter striking mantel clock, Winterhalder & Hofmeier, 1900s, 6in. dial with a silvered chapter ring and matted center, gong striking movement in a chamfered top case, 16in. (Christie's) $279

A green boulle mantel clock, French, 1880s, 5in. twenty five piece enamel dial, the square plated gong striking movement in an arched top case decorated with green shell with inlaid brass foliage, 16¼in. (Christie's) $706

A mid 19th century brass skeleton timepiece, the 8 day fusee movement with a pierced silvered chapter ring and a plush covered rosewood oval base, 14in. high. (Woolley & Wallis) $966

A 19th century brass framed skeleton clock with fretted silvered dial and nameplate applied to the front *E. Bragg, Windsor* ,15¾in. high, under glass dome. (Canterbury) $1,023

A mid 19th century brass skeleton timepiece, with painted chapter rings, the rosewood veneered base with a glass dome, 17¾in. (Woolley & Wallis) $1,015

A brass skeleton timepiece with a passing strike, English, mid 19th century, 4¾in. silvered dial signed *W & F Terry Manchester*, polished double screwed pierced frame, with six spoke wheel crossings, 18in. (Bonhams) $1,656

A brass escapement model of a Peto cross-detent, Sinclair Harding, modern, the movement resting on a mahogany base and covered by a rectangular glass dome, 18½in. high. (Christie's) $6,035

A brass skeleton timepiece with a passing strike, English, 19th century, 6in. pierced silvered chapter ring, the polished ivy leaf frame with 5 double screwed pillars, with a single fusee and chain movement, 19in. (Bonhams) $1,242

19th century brass and silvered skeleton clock on marble plinth with single fusee movement and strike, under associated glass dome. (Bonhams) $754

Late 19th century brass skeleton clock with engraved scroll and foliage decoration, the eight day striking movement by Henry Marc, Paris, overall height 22in. (Ewbank) $749

A brass skeleton timepiece with passing strike, English, mid 19th century, the single fusee movement with pierced brass gothic style frame, 16in.(Christie's) $1,323

An early ebonized and gilt basket top table clock, Samuel Watson, Coventry circa 1680 and later, the 5 ringed pillar movement with later twin fusee and chain, restored trains, 13in.
(Bonhams) $4,830

An Italian rosewood and ormolu mounted quarter striking table clock with alarm, unsigned; possibly Italian, mid 18th century, 21¾in. high. (Christie's) $3,408

A Continental brass and enamel musical singing bird clock, the musical movement by Nicole Frères, circa 1900, 33¾in. high. (Christie's) $46,001

A Swiss ormolu quarter striking singing birdcage clock, FR (Frères Rochat) No. 586; circa 1825, the filigree case formed as a birdcage with rope twist loop handle to the domed top, 11in. high.
(Christie's) $356,338

A German gilt-metal striking table clock, signed *Wilhülm Köberle, in Eichstädt;* first quarter 18th century, the hours struck via a blued steel and gilt hammer, in the form of a mask, 4½in. diameter.
(Christie's) $8,178

A fine small-size burr walnut chiming library clock, Thomas Simpson, Oxford Street London, circa 1840, strike silent lever in the arch, the 6 ringed and tapered pillar movement with triple fusee and chain, 10in.
(Bonhams) $7,590

A late George III ormolu and paste-set musical automaton table clock, unsigned, re-painted farmyard scene with animals and farm laborers moving in the background against a glass-rod simulated waterfall backdrop, 26¼in. high.
(Christie's) $81,780

A Continental gilt-metal and silver-mounted tortoiseshell striking hexagonal table clock, Fridelinus Scalor; possibly German, circa 1690, original calibrated countwheel with rosette-engraved center, later Continental foliate pierced bridgecock, 7in. diameter.
(Christie's) $15,334

A late George III ormolu, colored glass and silver-mounted musical automaton table clock, Francis Perigal, London, with automaton parade of various court figures, attendants and laborers, 23¾in. high. (Christie's) $88,378

An imposing tortoiseshell and ormolu musical and quarter striking table clock made for the Turkish market, unsigned, 34½in. high. (Christie's) $109,113

A German gilt-metal striking table clock, unsigned; case late 16th century, chapter ring and movement 19th century, the case on hairy paw feet to each angle, 4¼in. sq. (Christie's) $2,555

A magnificent walnut and brass-inlaid musical and quarter chiming table clock with full calendar and moonphase, signed *John Ellicott, London.*
(Christie's) $117,088

A brass inlaid rosewood table clock, G Searle 15 Wellington Street, Goswell St. London, circa 1840, the twin fusee movement striking bell in an arched top case with side ring handled and brass fish scale frets, 15in. (Bonhams) $2,484

A German brass hexagonal table, clock, Hans John, Königs Berth; first half 18th century, the partially re-trained movement with fusee and chain to the spring barrel, 5¾in. diameter.
(Christie's) $7,666

An Austrian burr birch quarter striking table clock with pull quarter repeat and alarm, Christian Wagner, Bresslau, circa 1700, the case with foliate cast gilt-metal handle to the cushion-molded top, 14¾in. high.
(Christie's) $12,777

An Austrian quarter striking silver-mounted table clock movement with calendar, Francois Schmidt, à Graüz; third quarter 18th century, the dial 21 x 30cm.
(Christie's) $1,533

A Polish gilt-brass hexagonal quarter striking small table clock, FR:Heckel, Warschau, first half 18th century, on six turned brass feet, the case sides set with glazed D-ended windows, 3¾in. wide.
(Christie's) $8,178

A late George III ebonized and ormolu mounted quarter striking automaton table clock, unsigned, the strike operated by levers atop the plates with indirect wires leading to the jacquemart above, 28in. high.(Christie's) $5,962

A late 19th century oak cased fusee wall timepiece, 8 day movement, 12in. painted dial inscribed *W. Carter, Salisbury.*
(Woolley & Wallis) $312

A mahogany cased drop dial wall timepiece, early 19th century, 30cm. painted convex dial, fitted with a single fusee movement, with brass inlay, 45cm. high.
(Bonhams) $1,165

A Mercer bulkhead timepiece, having a circular painted 5in. dial, inscribed *Mercer ...S Wood Road, St. Albans,* having a sweep seconds hand.
(Woolley & Wallis) $199

A Victorian circular wall timepiece, the single fusee movement to a painted dial inscribed *Alfd. Porter, Hartley Wintney,* in a mahogany case, 15in. diameter.
(Woolley & Wallis) $667

A mahogany octagonal dial timepiece, English, 20th century, 12in. painted dial marked GPO, the single fusee movement in an 8 sided case, 15in.
(Bonhams) $828

A mahogany dial timepiece, the 33cm. painted dial signed *Stevens & Son, Collumpton*, the single fusée movement in a turned case, cast bezel and pegged back, 45cm. diameter. (Bonhams) $966

A rosewood and mother of pearl inlaid wall timepiece, C. Maggs, Axbridge, 19th century, later single fusee movement in a case with a wide bezel inlaid with mother of pearl foliage, 12¾in.
(Bonhams) $621

A mahogany cased single fusée double sided GPO timepiece, the 30½in. circular dials, set with Roman numerals, surrounded with brass bezel, one glass cracked and one missing, 38cm. diameter.
(Bonhams) $511

A twenty four-hour chronometer wall clock, the circular off white enamel painted 12in. dial inscribed *Dent, London,* in an oak case, 20th century.
(Woolley & Wallis) $329

An oak drop dial wall timepiece, English, late 19th century, dial marked *Kingston College*, 30in. (Bonhams) $386

A mahogany cased wall timepiece, John Brydnt, London, 19th century, 12½in. (Bonhams) $1,932

A mahogany drop dial wall timepiece, English, 19th century, 12in. discolored painted dial, the single fusee movement with shaped plates, 20in. (Bonhams) $759

A mahogany drop dial wall timepiece, English, 19th century, 12in. restored painted dial signed *Tree GT Dover, London*, the single fusee movement in a case with a turned surround, 17in. (Bonhams) $414

A burr maple veneered drum wall timepiece, 19th century, 6¾in. repainted dial marked *James Mc Cabe London*, round plated single fusee movement in a drum case, 9½in. (Bonhams) $828

A small size mahogany wall timepiece, C. Lupton, Cornhill, London, 19th century, the single fusee movement in a case with a turned surround and pegged back, 11in. (Bonhams) $1,932

A mahogany drop dial wall timpiece, A Grant & Co, 19th century, the single fusee movement with shaped plates, the case with a turned surround, 17in. (Bonhams) $621

A mahogany drop dial wall timepiece, English, 19th century, the single fusee movement in a case with a turned surround and pegged back, 21in. (Bonhams) $690

A mahogany wall timepiece, case, movement, dial associated, 19th/20th century, 12in. restored convex dial signed *W N Last Bury St Edmunds*. (Bonhams) $662

An early 19th century mahogany drop trunk wall clock, the 8 day fusee movement with a convex 12in. convex enamel painted dial. (Woolley & Wallis) $164

A mahogany and brass inlaid octagonal wall timepiece, Thwaites & Reed, circa 1840, the single fusee movement with shaped plates in an 8 sided case, 17in. (Bonhams) $552

A Victorian drop trunk wall clock, the 8 day fusee movement with a 12in. circular painted dial to the mahogany case. (Woolley & Wallis) $795

A brass cased bulk head wall timepiece, English, mid 19th century, 8in. painted dial with a subsidiary seconds signed *Hallett Brighton,* the round single fusee movement with a lever escapement, 10in. (Bonhams) $580

A mahogany and brass inlaid octagonal wall timepiece, Hanson & Son, Windsor, 10in. painted convex dial, the single fusee movement with shaped plates in an 8 sided case, 15in. (Bonhams) $897

A brass inlaid rosewood wall timepiece, English, 19th century, the single fusee movement in a case with a pegged back and the bezel decorated with inlaid brass foliage, 15in. (Bonhams) $414

A mahogany cased wall timepiece, English, 19th century, the single fusee movement in a case with a turned surround and pegged back, 17in. (Bonhams) $690

An ebonized oval cased vineyard wall timepiece, French, late 19th century, 9in. glass dial with a white ground signed for *Barthe Baty Reims*, with a colorful inlaid surround, 23in. (Bonhams) $207

A mahogany dial timepiece, English, 20th century 12in. painted dial, the single fusee movement in a case with a turned surround and pegged back, 15in. (Bonhams) $414

An early 20th century Swiss lever with rare patriotic polychrome enamel dial in a silver open face case, nickelled split three quarter plate keyless movement with going barrel, circa 1915, 48mm. diameter. (Pieces of Time) $794

An unusual enamelled triangular Masonic desk clock, small circular gilt split three quarter plate keyless movement with going barrel, metal easel stand, Swiss, circa 1900, 107 x 112mm. (Pieces of Time) $1,518

A late 18th century Swiss verge in a silver and gilt case with a polychrome enamel portrait of Napoleon. Full plate gilt fusee movement, restored enamel dial, signed *Coladon a Geneve* circa 1800, diameter 56mm. (Pieces of Time) $4,692

A large late 18th century Swiss verge with a fine polychrome enamel dial in a gold open face case, full plate gilt fusee movement, finely and engraved bridge cock with steel coqueret, anonymous Swiss, circa 1790, 51mm. diameter. (Pieces of Time) $4,002

A rare late 17th century English verge with glazed sided and silver cock in silver pair cases, deep full plate fire gilt movement, the gilt pillars with engraved faces depicting a vase, signed *Markwich London 3789*, circa 1700, 57mm. diameter. (Pieces of Time) $6,555

An early 20th century Swiss lever in a silver and niello full hunter case with shooting scenes, gilt three quarter plate keyless movement with going barrel, signed *Moeris – Non Magnetic*, circa 1910, 49mm. diameter. (Pieces of Time) $1,311

A rare 19th century English lever with unusual six-hour and minute dials in a silver case, gilt three quarter plate keywind movement with fusee and chain, signed *Clerke 1 Royal Exchange London*, circa 1860, 48mm. diameter. (Pieces of Time) $5,451

A late 18th century French verge in a gold and enamel case, full plate gilt fusee movement, finely pierced and engraved bridge cock with steel coqueret, signed *Breguet a Paris*, circa 1790, 51mm. diameter. (Pieces of Time) $4,278

A late 18th century French verge in a fine pearl set gold and enamel consular case, depicting a couple in a formal garden, dark translucent bleu background, signed *Chevalier & Comp.*, 51mm. diameter. (Pieces of Time) $4,968

An early 19th century French verge in a gold open face case with portrait miniature, full plate gilt fusee movement, circa 1810, 42mm. diameter.
(Pieces of Time) $3,795

A 20th century triangular Swiss lever Masonic watch with mother of pearl dial in a silver triangular case, circular keyless nickelled bar movement with going barrel, circa 1930, 50mm.
(Pieces of Time) $1,759

An early 18th century English verge with an unusual rotating disk of polychrome enamel portraits in a silver consular case, deep full plate fire gilt movement with Egyptian pillars, signed _Gedeon Rigaud 695_, circa 1710, 55mm. diameter.
(Pieces of Time) $4,761

A rare early 19th century German watch with automated dial in a nickel open face case, enclosed movement with large central mainspring, signed _Thiers Watch Fearless Germany_, circa 1910, 52mm. diameter.
(Pieces of Time) $897

A small early 20th century Swiss lever by Vacheron and Constantin in a gold and enamel open face case, keyless nickelled bar movement with going barrel, 30mm. diameter, circa 1925.
(Pieces of Time) $3,450

A 19th century Swiss duplex for the Chinese market in a fine gold and enamel case, set with split pearls, unusual keywind bar movement and suspended going barrel, circa 1830, 57mm. diameter.
(Pieces of Time) $11,040

A rare late 18th century Swiss bras en l'air verge in a gold open face case, full plate gilt fusee movement of unusual layout, the polished steel top of the fusee visible under a small engraved bridge, circa 1790, 54mm. diameter.
(Pieces of Time) $16,284

An unusual late 19th century Swiss lever with flyback chronograph in a gunmetal open face case, gilt three quarter plate keyless movement with going barrel, grained steel chronograph work above the plates, Swiss, circa 1890, 52mm. diameter.
(Pieces of Time) $794

A late 18th century Swiss cylinder in a gold and enamel case, slim full plate movement with engraved resting barrel, polychrome scene of a couple in a formal garden, signed _Fres & Ge Achard a Geneve_, circa 1780, 51mm. diameter.
(Pieces of Time) $4,554

A silver and shell mounted triple cased verge watch, windmills, 1789, the gilt movement with Egyptian pillars and pierced balance cock, 58mm.
(Bonhams & Brooks) $853

A 9ct. gold and tortoiseshell repeating keyless lever timepiece, Swiss, retailed and mounted by Albert Barker Ltd., London, 1903, dark red guilloche enamel dial, square tortoiseshell case, 59mm.
(Christie's) $1,151

A gold pair cased verge clockwatch for the Turkish market, signed *Dan.L De St. Leu*, 2nd half 18th century, outer case with pierced and chased flower and scroll decoration, diameter 68mm.
(Christie's) $7,100

A gold and enamel hunting cased pocket watch for the Turkish market, Auguste Courvoisier & Co., Chaux de Fonds, circa 1845, the case finely enamelled with a portrait of the young Queen Victoria, diameter 48mm.
(Christie's) $4,733

An 18ct. gold hunting cased keyless lever pocket watch, Longines/E. Francillon, 1992, Roman numerals, subsidiary seconds, blued steel hands, frosted gilt half plate movement, diameter 55mm, with a gold Longines chain.
(Christie's) $1,554

A large and unusual silver open faced clockwatch with calendar and alarm, signed *A.D. Bornand, London, 1827*, the backplate mounted with a simple weekday calendar, plain polished case, diameter 80mm.
(Christie's) $3,043

A gold and enamel hunting cased pocket watch for the Russian market, signed *Tobias, London*, Swiss, circa 1850, the front cover enamelled with a portrait of a Russian officer, the back cover with a spray of flowers, diameter 48mm.
(Christie's) $3,212

A gold quarter repeating hunting cased keyless lever pocket watch with concealed erotic automata, Swiss, circa 1910, gold cuvette with further cover opening to reveal the enamelled erotic scene, chased and engraved case, diameter 50mm. (Christie's) $8,453

An enamel and pearl set open faced duplex pocket watch, signed *Ilbery*, London, circa 1830, the back cover with an enamelled rustic scene of two young girls feeding chicks, diameter 51mm.
(Christie's) $16,905

An 18ct. gold and enamel hunting cased keyless lever pocket watch, Tavannes Watch Co., circa 1920, the back painted with the heads of three wild horses, diameter 46mm. (Christie's) $2,796

A gold quarter repeating chronograph keyless hunter pocketwatch, signed *Tavannes Watch Co.*, 1910, the frosted gilt, half plate movement, jewelled to the center with bimetallic balance, 57mm. diameter. (Christie's) $1,183

A silver verge oignon pocket watch with alarm, Continental, circa 1700, chased and pierced case decorated with a scene of Leda and the Swan, diameter 58mm. (Christie's) $2,961

A silver repolussé striking and pull trip quarter repeating alarm clockwatch, signed *Jean Francois Poncet A Dresden*, mid 18th century, in heavy pierced repoussé case, the back with classical scene, diameter 105mm. (Christie's) $10,988

A gold, turquoise and pearl set open faced verge pocket watch, circa 1820, of turquoises, diameter 40mm. (Christie's) $9,298

Bovet Fleurier, a gold, enamel and pearl set duplex pocket watch for the Chinese market, signed *Bovet Fleurier*, circa 1830, the back finely painted and enamelled with a spray of flowers against a pale blue ground, diameter 56mm. (Christie's) $8,453

A silver open faced verge calendar moonphase pocket watch with day and night aperture, anonymous, circa 1820, white enamel dial decorated with cherubs holding the attributes of science, diameter 55mm. (Christie's) $1,974

A gilt verge oignon pocket watch, Bizot a Paris, circa 1710, later white enamel dial with Roman numerals, eccentric winding hole, cast and chased case, diameter 54mm. (Christie's) $1,233

A silver and gold open faced keyless lever six time zone pocket watch, Fritz Piguet & Bachmann Genève, circa 1890, case chased and engraved with foliage and scrolls, diameter 52mm. (Christie's) $2,235

A 20th century Swiss dress watch in a silver and enamel case with gold inlay, silver rectangular case covered with black enamel, the doors with applied gold decoration, signed *Dunhill La Captive, Tavannes Watch Co.*, 46 x 33mm. (Pieces of Time) $586

A 20th century Swiss lever deck watch by Rolex in a nickel open face case, nickelled split three quarter plate keyless movement with going barrel, circa 1930, 49mm. diameter. (Pieces of Time) $932

A small 19th century Swiss cylinder in a gold half hunter case mounted in a pearl set gold and enamel bangle, keyless gilt bar movement, with frosted steel wolf's teeth winding, signed *Berguer & Fils Geneve*, circa 1860, 36mm. diameter. (Pieces of Time) $1,621

A 20th century Swiss lever with patent winding system in an enamelled purse watch, keyless circular nickelled bar movement with going barrel, nickel hunter purse case, plain black enamel , signed *Eterna*, circa 1930, 38 x 40mm. (Pieces of Time) $725

A 20th century digital Swiss lever in a nickel purse watch, the hours, minutes and seconds indicated by three circular disks visible through apertures in the front of the case, Swiss, circa 1930, 34, x 40mm. (Pieces of Time) $538

A chrome pocket cigarette case combined with a lighter and watch, Swiss rectangular wrist watch movement, dial visible in the lid of the cigarette case, signed *Evans*, circa 1950, 115 x 62mm. (Pieces of Time) $297

A mid 19th century crab tooth duplex with mock pendulum dial in gilt metal full hunter case, richly engraved keywind gilt bar movement, large symmetrical pierced central bridge, Swiss, circa 1860, 56mm. diameter. (Pieces of Time) $1,966

A 19th century German lever by Assman in a decorative gold full hunter case made for South American market, circa 1870, diameter 51mm. (Pieces of Time) $5,382

An early 20th century Swiss lever in an open face case containing a polychrome enamel nude, keyless bar movement with going barrel, signed *Juvenia Casa Michel*, circa 1910, 47mm. diameter. (Pieces of Time) $2,553

A 19th century Swiss lever in silver case, gilt three quarter plate keywind movement with going barrel, silver cuvette with large oval opening to allow the movement to be rotated in the case, signed *Courvoisier Freres,* circa 1880, 45mm. diameter.
(Pieces of Time) $552

A slim late 19th century Swiss lever in a gold and enamel full hunter case, the front cover depicting two horses, keyless nickelled bar movement with going barrel, signed *Quartier Girard,* circa 1900, 50mm. diameter.
(Pieces of Time) $2,898

A pink gold Swiss double dialled calendar and moonphase keyless hunter pocketwatch, unsigned, early 20th century, the white enamel dial with numerals replaced by Greek letters spelling *Leora Patsis,* 52mm. diameter.
(Christie's) $1,625

A 20th century Swiss lever in a chromed open face case, nickelled split three quarter plate keyless movement with going barrel, plain open face chromed case, signed *Longines,* circa 1920, 46mm. diameter.(Pieces of Time) $276

A 20th century Swiss and enamel lever purse watch, keyless circular nickelled bar movement with going barrel, unusual case of silver covered in plain black enamel, marked *Juvenia,* circa 1920, 41 x 32mm. (Pieces of Time) $725

A late 18th century French pearl set gold and enamel consular cased watch, full plate gilt fusee movement, the back of fully restored polychrome enamel depicting a couple meeting in a garden, signed *Gregson a Paris,* circa 1790, 49mm. diameter.
(Pieces of Time) $4,416

A late 19th century English lever in a gold full hunter case with gold chain, gilt three quarter plate keyless going barrel movement, signed *Read & Son 2 Gresham Buildings Guildhall London 8/8349,* 54mm. diameter.
(Pieces of Time) $1,449

An early 20th century Swiss quarter repeating lever in a folding silver travelling case, gilt split quarter plate keyless movement with going barrel, maker's mark *C&C* in a rectangle, 80 x 87mm.
(Pieces of Time) $1,311

An early 20th century Swiss lever tourbillion in a gunmetal open face case, full plate gilt keyless movement with steel winding work on the back plate, signed *Mobilis,* circa 1920, 52mm. diameter.
(Pieces of Time) $2,415

An 18ct. rose gold wristwatch, Longines, 1970s, silvered dial, shaped 17 jewel nickel movement in a polished signed two piece case, 34mm.
(Bonhams & Brooks) $308

A 9ct. gold wristwatch, Longines, 1960s, restored black dial with gilt Arabic numerals and subsidiary seconds, the frosted gilt movement in a polished case, 30mm.
(Bonhams & Brooks) $420

Vacheron & Constantin. An 18ct. gold single button center seconds chronograph wristwatch, circa 1930s, the gilt movement jewelled to the center, 32mm. diameter.
(Bonhams) $4,968

A chrome plated cushion case wristwatch, Rolex, Oyster, 1930s, quartered silvered dial with Arabic numerals, subsidiary seconds, 16 jewel manual-wind movement, 31mm.
(Bonhams & Brooks) $1,120

A stainless steel center seconds chronograph wristwatch, Breitling, Top-Time, 1950s, silvered dial, baton hour markers, sweep center seconds, blue outer scale, subsidiaries for running seconds, 38mm.
(Bonhams & Brooks) $1,050

A stainless steel automatic twin-time zone center seconds calendar bracelet watch, Rolex, Oyster Perpetual, GMT Master, 1990s, nickel 27-jewel chronometer movement with hack seconds, 40mm. (Bonhams) $1,794

A bi-metal automatic calendar wristwatch, Omega, recent, white dial with applied Roman numerals, sweep seconds, date aperture at 3, gilt self-winding movement in a polished case, 36mm.
(Bonhams & Brooks) $364

Breguet, a fine 18ct. pink gold automatic wristwatch with calendar, phases of the moon and power reserve, circa 1996, the caliber 502 striped nickel 37 jewel movement adjusted to five positions, 36mm. diameter.(Bonhams) $13,110

A gold shell center seconds calendar watch, Omega, Constellation, 1950s, two tone silvered dial with center seconds and calendar aperture, gilt Cal.550 self-winding movement, 32mm.
(Bonhams & Brooks) $280

Omega, a stainless steel wristwatch with enamel dial, circa 1939, the nickel 15 jewel movement with compensated monometallic balance, 34mm. diameter.
(Bonhams) $552

An 18ct. gold quartz wristwatch, Cartier, Ceinture, 1980s, the enamel dial with Roman numerals and secret signature at 7, in a three color gold step sided case, 26mm.
(Bonhams) $966

An 18ct. gold wristwatch, Tissot, circa 1948, silvered dial with Arabic and dot hour markers, subsidiary seconds, 15 jewel nickel movement in a polished case, 34mm.
(Bonhams & Brooks) $364

An 18ct gold lady's calendar bracelet watch, Omega, Constellation, 1970s, gilt dial with sweep center seconds, calendar aperture at 3, jewelled nickel movement, 24mm.
(Bonhams & Brooks) $392

A gold shell center seconds alarm watch, Vulcain, Cricket, 1950s, two-tone silvered dial with Arabic numerals, outer alarm and seconds graduation, 17 jewel nickel movement, 32mm.
(Bonhams & Brooks) $560

Patek Philippe, a fine and rare 18ct. gold wristwatch with perpetual calendar, moon phase and split-second chronograph, recent, rhodium finished 28-jewel lever movement with Gyromax balance, 36mm.(Bonhams) $52,440

A stainless steel chronograph wristwatch, Breitling, Long Playing, 1970s, silvered dial with subsidiaries for running seconds, 30 minute and 12 hour recording with an outer timing scale, 38mm.
(Bonhams & Brooks) $252

A 9ct. gold lady's bracelet watch, Rolex, ref. 4216, 1926, white enamel dial with Arabic hour markets, subsidiary seconds, nickel manual wind movement in a polished case, 24mm.
(Bonhams & Brooks) $490

A stainless steel automatic calendar watch, Breitling, J-Class, 1980s, white dial, baton hour markers, date aperture at 3, sweep center seconds hand, jewelled automatic movement, 43mm.
(Bonhams & Brooks) $504

A gents Rolex Oyster Perpetual date watch, with gilt dial in 14ct gold case upon a strap, with holder. (Tennants) $1,360

An 18ct. gold 'Tank' style wristwatch, Chopard, 1960s cream dial, Roman numerals, gilt 17 jewel movement, in a polished rectangular case, 33 x 25mm. (Bonhams & Brooks) $1,232

A lady's gold oval wristwatch, signed *Cartier, Model Baignoire*, the nickel plated movement signed *Jaeger-LeCoultre*, 1960s, 25 x 19mm. (Christie's) $1,414

A bi-color automatic center second calendar bracelet watch, Cartier, Santos, white dial, Swiss made nickel movement, sapphire set button, and fitted on a matching bracelet with screw heads on each link, 28mm.
(Bonhams & Brooks) $770

A stainless steel calendar chronograph wristwatch, Heuer, Monaco, recent, black dial with baton hour markers with luminous tips, sweep center seconds hand, subsidiaries for running seconds, 37mm.
(Bonhams & Brooks) $1,120

An early 18ct. gold wristwatch, English hallmark for 1919, white enamel dial with luminous coated Arabic numerals, subsidiary seconds, 17 jewel nickel manual-wind movement in a heavy gold polished case, 36mm.
(Bonhams & Brooks) $308

An 18ct. gold rectangular wristwatch, Cartier, Tank, movement signed for Jaeger Le Coultre, circa 1980s, the (refinished) white dial with Roman numerals, in a rectangular polished case, 22 x 30mm.
(Bonhams) $2,070

A stainless steel center seconds bracelet watch, Rolex, Oyster Perpetual Air King, ref 1002, 1970s, silvered finished dial with slim baton hour markers, 26 jewel nickel self-winding movement, 33mm.
(Bonhams & Brooks) $868

An 18ct. gold rectangular wristwatch, Cartier, Tank, circa 1980s, striped nickel 17 jewel movement, in a polished case with cabochon sapphire set winding button, 29 x 23mm.
(Bonhams) $2,135

A gold and enamel rectangular wristwatch, Cartier, model: Tank, 1960s, 18-jewel Cartier movement adjusted to three positions, monometallic balance, 30 x 22cm. (Christie's) $3,455

Breitling, an 18ct. gold waterproof chronograph, Premier, the nickel 17 jewel movement with compensated monometallic balance and blued steel overcoil hairspring, 34mm. diameter.(Bonhams) $1,794

A gold shell center seconds automatic wristwatch, Rolex, Oyster Perpetual 'Bubbleback', 1940s, silvered dial with center seconds, Arabic numerals with outer seconds track, 32mm. (Bonhams & Brooks) $1,147

A stainless steel center seconds calendar watch, Longines, Conquest Calendar, 1960s, two-tone silvered dial with gold hour markers, date aperture and center seconds, 19 jewel nickel self-winding movement, 35mm. (Bonhams & Brooks) $210

An unusual 18ct. gold, enamel and diamond set quartz dual timezone bracelet watch, Edward Evans, London, Swiss movements, 1985, twin plain black dial marked *E E* with diamonds above and below the dials, 35mm. (Bonhams & Brooks) $3,500

A stainless steel and gold calendar wristwatch, Cartier, Santos, 1980s, white dial with Roman numerals, secret signature at 7, date aperture, sweep center seconds, the self-winding movement in a polished steel case, 29mm. (Bonhams & Brooks) $1,190-

An 18ct. gold tonneau shaped wristwatch, Swiss, 1920s, silvered dial with large Roman numerals, jewelled manual wind movement in a polished curved case, 35 x 25mm. (Bonhams & Brooks) $392

An 18ct. gold midsize automatic center seconds calendar wristwatch, Rolex Datejust Chronometer, 1959, gilt dial, the nickel 26 jewel movement with 5 adjustments in a case with a replaced milled bezel, 30mm. (Bonhams & Brooks) $1,260

An 18ct. gold 'Tank' style wristwatch, Jaeger LeCoultre, nos 4421, 1950s, silvered dial with slim baton hour markers, the nickel manual wind movement in a slim rectangular case, 24 x 30mm. (Bonhams & Brooks) $504

A Chinese cloisonné small jardinière, decorated with roundels of dragons, 19th century, 20cm. wide. (Woolley & Wallis) $137

A tapered olive green cloisonné vase, signed Kin'unken zo, late 19th century, decorated in various colored enamels, gold and silver wire with sprays of irises, 18cm. high. (Christie's) $2,708

Two cloisonné enamel tea-glass holders, one marked with the cyrillic initials of Gustav Klingert, both Moscow, 1896-1908, 4in. high. (Christie's) $1,921

A pair of Japanese cloisonné waisted cylindrical vases, each decorated with song birds amidst wisteria, the foot and neck mounted in silver, marks of Ando Jubei, Meiji, wood stands. (Woolley & Wallis) $3,808

A pair of Japanese cloisonné baluster vases decorated with birds in flight amongst blossoming prunus in a landscape scene, 13½in. high, 19th century. (Christie's) $999

A pair of Chinese cloisonne gu vases with dental rimmed side flanges and key-fret borders, decorated with stylized taotie masks within borders of scrolling lotus flowers, 13¼in. high, 19th century. (Christie's) $646

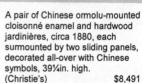

A pair of Japanese cloisonné plaques, each decorated with birds and chrysanthemums, 19th century, 30.5cm. (Woolley & Wallis) $204

A pair of Chinese gilt bronze and cloisonné models of Buddhistic lions, seated with a brocade ball and cub at their feet, set on raised rectangular bases, 4¼in. high, 19th century. (Christie's) $2,180

A pair of Chinese ormolu-mounted cloisonné enamel and hardwood jardinières, circa 1880, each surmounted by two sliding panels, decorated all-over with Chinese symbols, 39¼in. high. (Christie's) $8,491

Elaborate Continental gilt-metal birdcage, late 19th century, formed as a palazzo-style house with gothic-arch windows and arcade, 19in. high.(Skinner) $1,092

19th century copper jelly mold, molded as a turret, 5in. (G.A. Key) $207

A pair of 19th century cast brass dwarf candlesticks, in the Puginesque Gothic style, with drip pans to the hollow candleholders, 7in. (Woolley & Wallis) $548

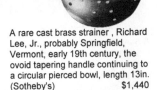

Patinated copper vase by Marie Zimmermann, 1915, ribbed flaring oval form with scalloped rim, raised on oblong footed base, 6$^7/_8$in. high. (Skinner) $4,312

A Victorian copper large saucepan and cover, both with iron handles, marked *TW 1860 11*, 28.5cm. diameter. (Bristol) $90

A brass dog collar, 18th century, engraved *John Hawk (Park)*, lacking clasp, 6in. diameter. (Christie's) $956

A rare Guild of Handicraft brass charger, designed by John Pearson, made by John Pearson and John Williams, dated *1889*, circular form, hammered in relief, the well with tree of life and Greek inscription *eat*, 24½in. diameter. (Christie's) $8,225

A rare cast brass strainer , Richard Lee, Jr., probably Springfield, Vermont, early 19th century, the ovoid tapering handle continuing to a circular pierced bowl, length 13in. (Sotheby's) $1,440

A late Victorian mahogany and brass-mounted stick-stand, the galleried top above a panelled back with pierced slats and flanked by finials, with central brass rail above a molded dished plinth base, 23in. wide. (Christie's) $4,491

A copper coal scuttle, circa 1895, flaring form, hammered in relief with panels of honesty seedheads, the foot with a band of heart motif, 14in. high. (Christie's) $1,316

A pair of French gilt brass twin light candelabra, the circular laurel molded and fluted bases to torch stems with entwined branches, 8in. (drilled for electricity). (Woolley & Wallis) $123

Margaret Gilmour, Scotland, a brass tray, executed by Margaret Gilmour, circa 1901, brass oval crescent form decorated in repoussé with Celtic entrelac designs, 520mm. wide.
(Bonhams) $1,887

A good copper kettle, David Price, Philadelphia or North Carolina, (w.1793-1820) the mushroom-shaped handle stamped on both sides *D: Price*, height 11in.
(Sotheby's) $3,600

Gilt copper eagle, America, 20th century, full-eagle with outstretched wings perched on a sphere, mounted on a blue felt covered board, 31½in. long.
(Skinner) $1,380

A Newlyn copper mirror, circular, hammered with fish swimming amongst stylized waves, stamped *Newlyn*, 39cm.
(Bonhams) $870

An early 19th century copper samovar, the bulbous body with chased bell metal leaf and cable borders and two leaf scroll handles, 13in. (Woolley & Wallis) $160

A Keswick School of Industrial Arts copper wall mirror, by W.H. Mawson, impressed mark, 30cm. diameter. (Christie's) $739

A pair of brass cache pots, late 19th or early 20th century, the spherical repoussé bodies with flared necks and lion mask ring handles, on paw feet, 8¼in. high.
(Christie's) $1,522

A Regency copper water urn, early 19th century, the crescent moon finial to the cover repeated below, supported on Egyptian style caryatid figures, 13½in. high.
(Christie's) $635

A German hammered brass box and cover with part-ivory lid handle, stamped *Munich Bavaria 35*, 22cm. high. (Christie's) $241

A John Pearson copper casket, dated *1900*, rectangular, the lid cast with a bird of prey with outstretched wings, blue velvet lining, inscribed *JP 1900*, 24cm. length.
(Bonhams) $798

A rare copper sauce pan, Jonathan Witman, Pennsylvania, circa 1805, the mushroom-shaped handle stamped *I. Witman* above a flaring body, height 11in.
(Sotheby's) $9,600

Polychrome molded copper-over-wood trotting horse, attributed to Louis Jobin (active 1870-90), Quebec City area, with twilled mane and tail, 19¾in.
(Skinner) $4,887

A copper bowl, cast from a model by Gurschner, stamped in the metal, 7.7cm. high.
(Christie's) $490

A fine copper kettle, Israel Roberts, Philadelphia, Pennsylvania, (w.1800-1837), the hinged mushroom handle stamped *I Roberts Phila.* above an ovoid body fitted with a circular lid, turned finial and a gooseneck spout.
(Sotheby's) $1,800

A brass warming pan, English, dated 1600, the cover punch and repoussé decorated, the center depicting a dragon and dated *1600*, within multiple foliate and geometric borders, 12¼in. diameter.
(Christie's) $327

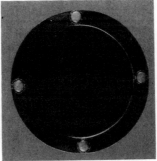

A large circular brass log bin with lion head handles, on paw feet.
(Lloyds International) $397

A Liberty copper mirror, of circular form with Ruskin Pottery turquoise glazed cabochons, retailer's plaque printed *Liberty London*, 56cm.
(Bonhams) $899

An Arts and Crafts copper fire screen, with wrought iron frame, 77cm. high. (Christie's) $461

A copper wall charger, circa 1895, circular form, hammered in relief, the well with thistle motif, the rim a band of grape and vine, 20in. diameter. (Christie's) $1,068

A Benham and Froud copper and brass ewer, circa 1880, flat disk form with cylindrical neck and foot, curved ebonized wood handle, with waisted cylindrical spout, stamped mark, 10in. high. (Christie's) $1,974

A Benham and Froud brass charger, circa 1880, punched with a panel of sunflowers, inside geometric border, 22½in. diameter. (Christie's) $2,632

A Dutch brass cache pot, on three scroll legs with paw feet, the circular body repoussé decorated with an armorial and a rural landscape, 6¾in. diameter. (Woolley & Wallis) $99

A pair of Gothic brass candlesticks, circa 1850, tapering conical base with knopped twist stem and flaring crenellated sconce, the knop and base set with hardstone cabochon, 18in. high.(Christie's) $2,303

A large set of brass, copper and steel weighing-scales, late 19th/early 20th century, of pyramidal form, with four turned supports with frame upper stretcher, suspending a balance, 79in. wide. (Christie's) $25,909

A copper vessel, with repoussé and chased foliage, fruit and an armorial, with two handles, used as a stick stand, 15in. high. (Woolley & Wallis) $207

A mid 19th century copper coffee pot, of tapering form, with a swan neck spout and a turned ebony handle, the hinged domed cover with a bell metal acorn finial, 12¾in. (Woolley & Wallis) $125

A Russian brass kedgeree dish, stamped with Imperial duty marks for 1889 and 1896, with a deep flared border, a later wall fixing, 17in. diameter. (Woolley & Wallis) $185

English gentleman's embroidered waistcoat, late 18th/early 19th century, cream faille ground embroidered with mauve toned floral border down front and at sides. (Skinner) $230

A Surrey Wanderers cricket blazer, 1920s, believed to have belonged to Frank Schibald. (Bonhams) $270

A silk stocking belonging to Queen Victoria, English, 19th century, the white stocking embroidered crown and *V.R.* near the top, with further embroidery above the ankle, 83in. x 41cm. (Bonhams) $428

A short sleeved day dress of black silk printed in greens, purple, pinks, ivory and yellows, probably circa 1915-20. (Christie's) $3,452

Bes Ben, banana and leaf hat, 1940s, close fitting velvet and net headpiece adorned with papier-mâché yellow bananas and green leaves with gold leaf embellishment. (Skinner) $546

A sleeveless cocktail dress of black tulle, embroidered in self-colored bugle beads, mid 1920s. (Christie's) $508

Brian Lara. A yellow and blue Warwickshire replica cricket shirt, signed in ink *Best Wishes Brian Lara*, mounted in a display frame. (Bonhams) $330

A pair of ladies' shoes of pale blue kid, with pointed toe and 1in. wedged heel, lined in ivory linen, straights, circa 1795. (Christie's) $1,553

Nimbus: The 1949 Derby and 2,000 Guineas winning silks worn by Charlie Elliot by D. Gilbert & Son, Racing Saddlers, Newmarket, a cerise and white hooped 'silk' jacket with blue sleeves. (Sotheby's) $1,408

A sleeveless cocktail dress overlaid with pale blue chiffon around the bodice, mid 1920s, in the manner of Callot Soeurs.
(Christie's) $1,264

Bergdorf Goodman, scarlet cocktail dress, 1958, scarlet cut-velvet below-the-knee length dress with fitted short sleeved bodice with square neckline and bow at right side. (Skinner) $258

Bob Mackie, beaded evening gown, late 1970s, black, sequin, and bugle bead floor-length gown with purple, fuchsia, red, gold, blue and aqua stripes. (Skinner) $920

An Edwardian lady's plain olive silk satin outfit, the jacket with stand-up collar, R.D. Franks, London.
(Woolley & Wallis) $70

Christian Dior, lace cocktail dress, 1950s, bodice of black chantilly lace over ivory satin with sweetheart neckline, black silk taffeta cummerbund wraps around to tie at front waist.
(Skinner) $201

A dress of black crepe, the skirts with deep horizontal bands of yellow and red, unlabelled, Ossie Clark, early 1970s.
(Christie's) $368

Balenciaga, red wool coat, 1950s, three-quarter length, cocoon silhouette with center front three-button closure, roll collar. (Skinner) $287

Chanel, a black lace 1930s evening dress, the petticoat style top with flared skirt of tapering lace and net panel design. (Woolley & Wallis) $126

Jean-Louis Scherrer, gold crochet cocktail suit, mid-1970s, A-line mid-calf length skirt lined with textured lamé. (Skinner) $431

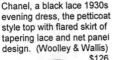

Paul Balmain, coral evening ensemble, 1960s, ankle-length cheongsam tunic with long sleeves, bold coiled metallic gold cuffs, matching slim pants. (Skinner) $460

A Pierre Balmain gold and silver Indian inspired embroidered robe French, 1990s, the pale truquoise ground densely embroidered with a lattice pattern enclosing three dimensional flowerheads, minute glass beads and sequins, fastened by faux pearls and diamanté, 34in. (Sotheby's) $1,008

Geoffrey Beene, forest green knit dress, 1970s, wool tweed below-the-knee length dress with matching jacket, with ruffled hem. (Skinner) $287

A pair of Aubusson tapestry cushions, late 18th century, each with a flower-spray issuing from a ribbon-tie, on an ivory ground, 21 x 14in. (Christie's) $2,670

Three Aubusson tapestry cushions, late 18th or early 19th century, each with tapestry fragments to one side, with animals within floral borders with tasselled edges. (Christie's) $1,607

A pair of Beauvais tapestry cushions, late 18th century, each with an armorial trophy within foliage and strapwork, on a light brown ground, 22 x 24in. (Christie's) $4,338

A pair of Aubusson tapestry cushions, the tapestry circa 1890, each woven in wools and silks, depicting a vase of flowers on a cream ground, 20in. square. (Christie's) $1,680

A Louis XVI Aubusson tapestry cushion, depicting a boy watering flowers with a girl lying on the grass, watching him, probably a tapestry fragment, 22 x 18in. (Christie's) $4,715

A pair of French Aubusson tapestry cushions, the tapestry circa 1880, each woven in wools and silks, depicting spring flowers on a cream ground, 18in. wide. (Christie's) $2,856

A pair of Flemish tapestry cushions, second half 17th century, each with a bird among foliage and berries, with a beige and pink fringe, 20½ x 15in. (Christie's) $1,501

Three Beauvais tapestry cushions, mid 18th century, each with a fox in a landscape, one also with a cockerel in a tree, 21-29in. high. (Christie's) $9,776

A pair of Flemish tapestry cushions, late 16th century, each with a figure beneath a canopy, flanked by a flower vase, one 18 x 26in. and 18 x 19in. (Christie's) $2,670

Spear fishing decoy in the likeness of a brown trout, attributed to Harry A. Seymour, Bemus, Lake Chautauqua, New York, last quarter 19th century, carved wooden fish, copper fins and leather tail, 7¼in. long.(Sotheby's) $6,325

Spear fishing decoy in the likeness of a trout, Harry A. Seymour, Bemus, New York, last quarter 19th century, carved wooden fish with copper fins and inserted leather tail, 7½in. long. (Sotheby's) $8,050

Spear fishing decoy in the likeness of a northern pike, Otto Faue, 1920-1954, carved wooden decoy with painted eyes and metal fins. 10¼in. long. (Sotheby's) $4,312

Spear fishing decoy in the likeness of a crappie, William Faue, Wright County, Minnesota, circa 1930 to 1950, carved wooden fish with metal fins and tail, 7¼in. long. (Sotheby's) $5,462

Spear fishing decoy, trout, with metal fins and leather tail, maker unknown, Lake Chautauqua, last quarter 19th century, wonderful original painted surface, 7¼in. long.(Sotheby's) $7,475

Spear fishing decoy, perch, with metal fins and leather tail maker unknown, Lake Chautaugua, last quarter 19th century, fine original condition with great patination, 7½in. long.(Sotheby's) $10,925

Spear fishing decoy, William Faue, Wright County, Minnesota, circa 1930-1950, excellent original paint with minor wear. (Sotheby's) $7,475

Spear fishing decoy with metal fins and tail, William Faue, Wright County, Minnesota, circa 1930 to 1950, 6½in.long. (Sotheby's) $2,587

Spear fishing decoy, maker unknown, Lake Chautauqua, last quarter 19th century, the species is a sucker with metal fins and leather tail. (Sotheby's) $32,200

Spear fishing decoy, William Faue, Wright County, Minnesota, circa 1930 to 1950, original painted surface. (Sotheby's) $2,185

A carved and black-painted wood crow decoy, attributed to Charles H. Perdew (1874-1963), Henry, Illinois, circa 1930, the black-painted body with glass eyes and wire legs, mounted on a block base, 34¾in. high. (Christie's) $823

Ruddy turnstone, Lothrop Holmes, Kingston, Massachusetts, mid-to-last quarter 19th century, retains superb original paint in the spring or breeding plumage. (Sotheby's) $470,000

Standing pintail drake, Charles Schoenheider Sr., Peoria, Illinois, first quarter 20th century, on cast iron leg, made for winter ice and field shooting, hollow carved approximately 18in. long. (Sotheby's) $85,000

Black-bellied plover in a feeding pose, Obediah Verity, Seaford, Long Island, New York, last quarter 19th century, of solid construction with carved eyes and wings characteristic of the 'Seaford' school of carving. (Sotheby's) $156,500

Hudsonian curlew or 'whimbrel', Luther Lee Nottingham, Chesapeake, and Cobb's Station, Virginia, last quarter 19th century, of solid construction with painted eyes, inserted and splined hardwood bill. (Sotheby's) $98,750

A carved and painted plover, probably New England, early 20th century, abstracted in the form of a black and white-painted bird with elongated beak and single tail, 8½in. high with base. (Christie's) $470

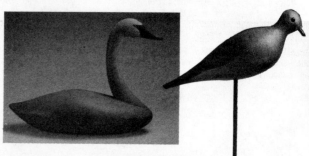

A carved and painted yellowlegs, probably New England, early 20th century, the abstracted carved bird with metal bill and white-painted breast, 10½in. high. (Christie's) $353

Whistling swan, Charles Bergman, Astoria, Oregon circa 1905, hollow carved with glass eyes, old repaint by Bergman, professional repair to the bill.(Sotheby's) $35,650

Passenger pigeon, glasseye model, Mason Decoy Factory, Detroit, Michigan, circa 1900, retains the original paint. (Sotheby's) $10,637

Presentation Canada Goose, George Boyd, Seabrook, New Hampshire, circa 1902, canvas over wooden frame, construction with carved tail, breast, neck and head.(Sotheby's) $36,800

Eider drake with mussel in mouth, Gus Wilson, Monhegan Island and South Portland, Maine, his earlier 'Monhegan Island style' second quarter 20th century, inlet head, carved eyes and bill, and relief wing carving.
(Sotheby's) $82,250

Important mallard drake attributed to 'Hucks' Caines, Georgetown, South Carolina circa 1910, a large decoy, (approximately 16in. long body) with relief wing carving and swanlike neck.
(Sotheby's) $189,500

'Stick up' Canada goose, Charles Hart, Gloucester, Massachusetts, circa 1900, hollow carved with good feather paint detail.
(Sotheby's) $17,250

Hollow black-bellied plover, maker unknown, believed to be Cape Cod, Massachusetts, last quarter 19th century, of very thin-shelled, hollow, two-piece construction with inset glass eyes.
(Sotheby's) $5,750

Exceptional Canada goose from Massachusetts or lower Susquehanna River, last quarter 19th century, a large hollow carved decoy, approximately 31in. long, with removable head that is dovetailed into the body.
(Sotheby's) $233,500

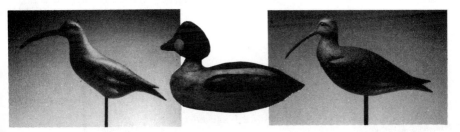

Hudsonian curlew, William Bowman, Lawrence, Long Island, New York, last quarter 19th century, is written under the tail, 15½in. long bill to tail.
(Sotheby's) $87,750

Goldeneye drake, attributed to Charles McCoy, Tuckerton, New Jersey, first quarter 20th century, hollow carved with traditional Delaware River weight.
(Sotheby's) $5,462

Long-billed curlew, William Bowman, Lawrence, Long Island, New York, last quarter 19th century, of hollow, pegged construction with inset eyes, carved shoulders and wing tips, 16½in. long.(Sotheby's) $464,500

Golden plover, John Dilley, Quogue, Long Island, New York, probably last quarter 19th century, of solid construction with inset glass eyes and carved wings.
(Sotheby's) $27,600

Very rare redbreasted merganser drake, Captain Preston Wright, Osterville, Massachusetts, first quarter 20th century, relief wing carving, glass eyes and horse hair crest.(Sotheby's) $52,900

Dowitcher, John Dilley, Quogue, Long Island, New York, probably last quarter 19th century, of solid construction with glass inset eyes, raised wing carving.
(Sotheby's) $37,950

Rare feeding pintail drake, John Tornberg, Mill Valley, California, second quarter 20th century, hollow carved with layered carved wing tips and detailed bill carving.
(Sotheby's) $19,556

Brant decoy, Nathan Cobb Jr., Cobb Island, Virginia, circa 1870, rare belligerent pose, hollow carved with shoe button eyes and typical Cobb V wing carving.
(Sotheby's) $101,500

A painted cast-iron sink duck, probably Susquehanna Flats, early 20th century, the brown and black-painted flat-bottomed bird form depicting a high-necked canvasback drake, 14in. wide.
(Christie's) $588

Large curlew, Alfred Chopin, Sete, France, circa 1950, of solid construction with inset glass eyes, carved wings and detachable bill.
(Sotheby's) $4,600

Pintail drake, Charles Walker, Princeton, Illinois, second quarter 20th century, flat bottom style with slightly turned head and relief wing tip carving, highly detailed feather painting.
(Sotheby's) $63,000

Ruddy duck drake, Alvirah Wright, Duck, North Carolina, circa 1910, finely sculpted, slightly lifted head.
(Sotheby's) $29, 900

Black-bellied plover, Harry V. Shourds, Tuckerton, New Jersey, last quarter 19th century, of solid construction with painted eyes and inserted hardwood bill.
(Sotheby's) $10,350

Important wood duck drake, Mason Decoy Factory, premier grade, first quarter 20th century, Mackey collection stamp on the underside, hollow carved with slightly turned head, only known hollow example.
(Sotheby's) $354,500

Yellowlegs, Ira Hudson, Chincoteague, Virginia, first quarter 20th century, of solid construction with inserted hardwood bill. *Ira Hudson* written on the bottom.
(Sotheby's) $48,875

Red breasted Merganser drake decoy, A. Elmer Crowell, East Harwich, Massachusetts, bears the oval *CROWELL* brand on the underside, original paint, 19½in. long. (Skinner) $8,625

Mallard hen, Mason Decoy Factory, Detroit, Michigan, premier grade, circa 1895, rare hollow 'slope breasted' model with head turned approximately 20 degrees. (Sotheby's) $28,750

Merganser drake, George Boyd, Seabrook, New Hampshire, first quarter 20th century, a rare 'paddle tail' model with slightly turned head and inserted wooden bill. (Sotheby's) $87,750

Long-billed dowitcher, maker unknown, Massachusetts, last quarter 19th century, of solid construction with sealing wax eyes, carved, split-tail with raised and separated wings. (Sotheby's) $112, 500

Rare Canada goose, Enoch Reindahl, Stoughton, Wisconsin, circa 1940, very rare hollow carved decoy with highly detailed feather carving and crossed wing tips. (Sotheby's) $65,750

Hudsonian curlew, Nathan Cobb, Jr., Cobb Island, Virginia, last quarter 19th century, of solid construction with inset glass eyes. (Sotheby's) $27,600

Hudsonian curlew, Nathan Cobb, Jr., Cobb Island, Virginia, last quarter 19th century, of solid construction with inset glass eyes, bears Nathan Cobb's serified N carved on the underside. (Sotheby's) $31,625

Outstanding sleeping Canada goose, Elmer Crowell, East Harwich, Massachusetts, circa 1917, the exceptionally fine paint detail with wet on wet blending, layered carved wing tips, fluted tail, finely sculpted head and neck. (Sotheby's) $684,500

Exceptional redhead drake, Elmer Crowell, East Harwich, Massachusetts, first quarter 20th century, bears the oval Crowell brand in the underside, slightly turned and slightly lifted head. (Sotheby's) $40,250

Yellowlegs, maker unknown, Accord area of Massachusetts probably first quarter 20th century, of solid construction with tack eyes. (Sotheby's) $5,462

Wood duck drake, Elmer Crowell, East Harwich, Massachusetts, first quarter 20th century, oval Crowell brand in underside, head turned approximately 45 degrees and slightly lifted, carved crest. (Sotheby's) $211,500

Canada goose decoy, A. Elmer Crowell (1862-1952), East Harwich, Massachusetts, bears the rectangular *CROWELL* stamp on the underside, original paint, 23½in. long. (Skinner) $3,450

A Kämmer & Reinhardt character doll, German, circa 1912, with weighted blue eyes, closed mouth, original long blonde mohair wig, on floating ball wood and composition body. 19½in.
(Sotheby's) $4,410

A Kämmer & Reinhardt all-bisque character baby doll, German, circa 1925, with weighted brown flirty eyes, open mouth with two teeth and quivering tongue, 15¾in.
(Sotheby's) $847

A Bru Jne 7 Bébé, with fixed brown eyes, closed mouth, pierced ears, bisque shoulder plate and arms, the jointed kid body with carved and painted wooden legs, 20in. high.
(Christie's) $18,095

A Bähr & Pröschild Googlie Eye 608 child doll, with blue side-glancing sleeping eyes, closed smiling mouth and rigid-limb composition body wearing original white frock and bonnet with red embroidery, 9in. high.
(Christie's) $1,809

A rare Gebrüder Heubach character 8548, the bad-tempered boy with strongly molded curls, closed pouting mouth, frowning brows and blue sleeping eyes, the jointed toddler body with diagonal hip joints, 20in. high.
(Christie's) $14,805

A rare Kammer & Reinhardt for Kathe Kruse cloth doll, with painted hair and features, raised seams on the crown and cloth body with ball joints at knees, also jointed at thigh and shoulder, wearing original provincial costume and underclothes, 17½in. tall, 1911.
(Christie's) $3,619

A fine Bébé by A. Thuillier, in pressed bisque, with closed mouth, brown yeux fibres, shaded brows, pierced ears, remains of fair mohair wig over cork pate and gusseted kid body, 21in., circa 1880.
(Christie's) $39,480

A poured wax lady doll, English, circa 1830, with elongated face and sloping shoulders, having blue glass eyes and painted lips, long and intricately plaited brown wig, a cloth body with wax lower arms, wearing original clothes, 17in. tall.
(Bonhams & Brooks) $278

An Armand Marseille Fany 230, with molded and painted short blonde curls, closed mouth, fixed pale blue eyes and jointed toddler body, 19in. high.
(Christie's) $4,277

A fine Bébé Schmitt, with closed mouth, blue yeux fibres, shaded brows, pierced ears and blonde mohair wig over fixed wrist body with ball joints at elbows, 15½in. circa 1880.
(Christie's) $4,277

A rare fully jointed all-bisque googly doll and another googly doll, German, circa 1915, probably by Kestner, both 5in.
(Sotheby's) $2,205

A circle Dot Bru Jne, with fixed pale blue eyes, open/closed mouth with molded teeth and original blonde mohair wig, on an early Steiner papier mâché jointed body, 17in. high. (Christie's) $8,225

A Jumeau child doll, with fixed blue eyes, open mouth, pierced ears, blonde mohair wig and jointed wood and composition body wearing blue velvet frock with lace trim, 25in. high.
(Christie's) $2,961

A Montanari type poured wax doll, with fixed sky blue eyes, inset reddish-gold hair, down-turned mouth, cloth body and wax limbs wearing original cream satin wedding dress, 17in. high, circa 1860. (Christie's) $1,151

A pressed bisque swivel-headed fashionable doll, with fixed deep blue eyes, closed mouth, blonde mohair wig with cork pate, ears pierced into the head and gusseted kid body, 11in. high, circa 1870. (Christie's) $1,233

A Simon & Halbig all-bisque child doll, with fixed blue eyes, fair mohair wig, molded two-bar shoes, blue socks, kid washers at shoulders, neck and hips, blue frock, 8¾in.
(Christie's) $3,619

A J.D. Kestner character baby, with blue sleeping eyes, open mouth with two upper teeth, blonde painted hair and jointed composition body wearing white cotton dress and under-garments, 17in. high.(Christie's) $822

A Tête Jumeau Bébé, with fixed brown eyes, closed mouth, pierced ears and jointed composition body with fixed wrists wearing pink and muslin frock, 12in. high.
(Christie's) $3,125

A Kammer & Reinhardt 122 character baby, with brown sleeping eyes, short brown mohair wig, open mouth with trembling tongue and jointed composition baby's body, 17in. high.
(Christie's) $790

An Armand Marseille bisque head doll, impressed *A 4 M 390n Germany* with open mouth, four top teeth, sleeping brown eyes, circa 1915-20. 20in., tall.
(Woolley & Wallis) $138

A Simon and Halbig 1129 Oriental bisque head doll, German, circa 1910, with slanted and weighted brown glass eyes, black mohair wig, on a fully jointed composition body, 13½in. tall.
(Bonhams & Brooks) $486

A Tête Jumeau 1907, with fixed blue eyes, open mouth, pierced ears, brown hair wig, jointed wood and papier mâché body wearing white frock, underwear and corset, 26in. high, impressed *1907*.
(Christie's) $987

A Heubach Koppelsdorf 321 bisque head doll, German, circa 1910, with weighted blue glass eyes, open mouth and short blonde wig, on a composition baby body, wearing a white dress and pink knitted jacket and bonnet, 15in. tall.
(Bonhams & Brooks) $167

A pair of Bambola Artistica composition shoulder-headed child dolls, modelled as a boy and a girl with molded hair, painted features and hard stuffed jointed cloth bodies in original embroidered romper, 15in. high.
(Christie's) $904

A composition Shirley Temple by Ideal, American, 1930s, with weighted green eyes, open smiling mouth and dimples, short curly brown hair and on a five piece composition body, 19in. tall.
(Bonhams & Brooks) $556

A pair of Sonneberg papier mâché-headed dolls, with painted features, green and blue eyes, painted black hair, dressed in shells, probably French, circa 1830, 13in. high.
(Christie's) $690

An S.F.B.J. 236 child doll, with blue lashed sleeping eyes, open/closed mouth with two upper teeth, short blonde mohair wig and jointed composition body, 28in. tall, wig replaced.
(Christie's) $1,068

A Victorian composite model of a butcher's shop, late 19th century and later, arranged inside with simulated marble counters, an iron rail with meat hooks and hanging meat, cleavers and knives, a mincer, and various other elements, 20in. wide. (Christie's) $263

A Silber and Fleming box type dolls' house, of five bays and two storeys painted and transfer printed to represent stone and brickwork with wood balcony, opening to reveal four rooms with staircase, 30in., wide, mid 19th century. (Christie's) $2,796

The Windermere 'Dolls' House', English, 1919-28, a unique model built in the Elizabethan half timbered style, with 'slate' roof tiles and satin walnut chimneys, the front entrance with projecting porch and oriel window above. (Bonhams & Brooks) $2,363

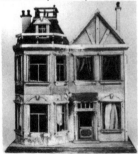

A Moritz Gottschalk dolls house, German, circa 1900, the paper brick effect lithographed house with green tiled roof and carved wooden balustrading, front opening in two wings to reveal four rooms, with a good selection of furniture, 30in. wide.
(Bonhams & Brooks) $1,668

A fine No: 3 Lines Bros. dolls house with gardens and side motor garage English, circa 1905, the façade painted in cream, and with paper brick effect to sides, furnished, 40in. high, 40in. wide. (Bonhams) $1,896

A large painted wooden dolls house, English, 1920s, painted grey double pitched roof with hinged sides for access to attic rooms, opening to reveal four rooms, with a good quantity of furniture and furnishings, house 39½in. wide. (Bonhams & Brooks) $1,251

School House, a painted wooden dolls' house, made from a Maxown margarine box, simulating brickwork and slate with steeply pitched roof and two tall chimney stacks, opening at the back to reveal two rooms, 12½in. wide, late 19th century. (Christie's) $319

'The Toll House', English, early 19th century, on two levels with a painted red brick effect façade, house: 18½in. high. (Bonhams) $2,209

Unusual dolls' town houses, of painted brickwork, two houses with central green painted front doors flanked by windows on each floor, opening to reveal three rooms in each house, 59in. high, late 19th century. (Christie's) $987

253

A Georgian enamelled snuff box with gilt metal mount, the domed cover painted with two men on horseback, the sides painted with flowers, 1¾in. wide.
(Andrew Hartley) **$156**

A Viennese silver-gilt and enamel urn, by Hermann Ratzersdorfer, circa 1880, flanked to each side by a female handle, above a bulbous bowl painted with figures in a landscape, 11¾in. high.
(Christie's) **$20,240**

A Viennese silver and enamel casket, by Hermann Boehm, circa 1880, the spreading lid with strapwork frieze, the sides with conforming friezes, each centered by a mask, 4in. high.
(Christie's) **$3,496**

An enamel desk-form desk stand with silver-gilt mounts, maker's mark of Rudolf Linke, Vienna, circa 1895, the desk surmounted by a small circular watch-shaped timepiece below openwork scrolling and supported by two chased putti, 8¾in. (Sotheby's) **$3,528**

A Viennese silver and enamel wedding cup and saucer, circa 1880, the cup modelled as a woman in costume, holding the upper bowl between her arms, 4¾in. high.
(Christie's) **$1,656**

An enamel plaque, Birmingham or Bilston, circa 1770, oval, painted vividly with Abraham dismissing Hagar and Ishmael, after Wagner, after Giuseppe Zocchi (1711-1767), 6in. (Sotheby's) **$1,499**

A Viennese silver and gem-set timepiece modelled as a cockerel, circa 1880, the fusée movement inscribed *Chevalier et Coche N. 3177* with verge escapement, within a gem-set silver border, 6½in. high.
(Christie's) **$4,784**

Pair of Aesthetic Movement enamel ormolu mounted urns, late 19th century, the enamel baluster bodies decorated with a single carp amidst water grasses on faux bronze ground, 11in. high.
(Skinner) **$1,610**

A Viennese silver and enamel ewer and charger, circa 1880, shaped spreading rim above a slender waisted neck, oval stepped tapering body, the charger with serpentine edge, and oval plate, the ewer 7in. high, the charger 5½in. wide. (Christie's) **$1,656**

A 19th century enamelled and gilt metal pill box form, the cover painted with flowers and jewelling within gilding the base and sides gilded with stars, 1½in. wide. (Andrew Hartley) **$85**

An enamel dog bonbonnière, Bilston, circa 1775, the top molded and painted with an appealing black and white King Charles spaniel, 1½in. diameter. (Sotheby's) **$1,470**

A Georgian enamelled patch box with gilt metal mounts, the domed cover painted with a figure in a landscape with mirrored interior, late 18th/early 19th century, 1¾in. wide. (Andrew Hartley) **$185**

An enamel cup, the base signed and dated: *Durand 1861, Paris*, painted en plein with polychrome birds and flowers on white, reserved on a translucent blue ground, 4½in. high. (Sotheby's) **$4,649**

A Viennese gem-set and silver-mounted enamel figure of a sea-horse, circa 1880, the horse's back surmounted by a figure of Atlas, opening as a box, on an oval spreading gadrooned base, 13½in. wide. (Christie's) **$14,720**

A Viennese silver-gilt and enamel oval cup and cover, by Karl Rössler, circa 1880, the lid surmounted by a full-length bust of a man holding a jug and pipe, 13in. high. (Christie's) **$8,280**

C. Fauré enamel vase, Limoges, France, foil under opalescent white, blue, teal, and black, gilt signature, 7in. high. (Skinner) **$3,335**

A pair of late 19th century Viennese silver mounted enamel vases, Hermann Boehm, two caryatid mounted scroll handles, the body with two classical scenes in oval cartouches, 31.5cm. high. (Bonhams & Brooks) **$6,720**

A Viennese silver-gilt and enamel vase, circa 1880, with a gadrooned spreading circular rim above an ovoid stem, 20.5cm. high. (Christie's) **$2,944**

A volcanic fan, a rare printed fan, the leaf a hand-colored aquatint of a volcano erupting by night, decorated with a border of sequins, the horn sticks gilt, 9in., Iberian, circa 1810.
(Christie's) $1,272

The Hunt, signed *Auguste Delierre*, a fine fan, the leaf painted with a gentleman and five hunt servants, with hounds in the foreground, the verso of canepin with monogram *W.* and doves, signed with initials *A.D.*, with mother of pearl sticks, 11½in., circa 1865.
(Christie's) $11,771

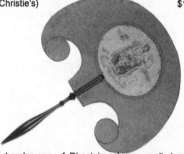

Le Jugement de Midas, a handscreen, the mount a hand-colored etching of a scene from the Comedy, with five figures in a hall, with wooden handle, 14in. French, circa 1775. (Christie's) $1,635

A handscreen of Directoire shape, applied with an oval stipple engraving of a goddess? accompanied by a sheep sitting in a chariot drawn by six butterflies driven by Cupid, turned wooden handle, 13in., French, circa 1800. (Christie's) $182

The Marriage of the Dauphin, a fan, the leaf painted with portraits of Marie Antoinette and the Dauphin and their coats of arms against a blue ground, the ivory sticks carved, pierced and gilt, 9½in., French, 1771.
(Christie's) $4,543

A Gunsen or war fan, the stiff paper leaf painted recto with a red sun on gold and verso with a silver moon on black, with black lacquered wooden sticks and iron guardsticks inlaid with silver geese and corn, 12in., Japanese, late 19th century.
(Christie's) $2,725

View from Mount Righi, Switzerland, a rare fan, the leaf and hand-colored engraving, inscribed *R. Leuzinger gest,*. with a bird's eye view of the mountains, recto with Sargans to Newchâtel, verso Besançon to Graz, with pierced bone sticks, 12in. circa 1860. (Christie's) $4,361

Venus, after Albani, with dark kid leaf, the verso painted with three sprays of tulips, honeysuckle and carnations, with ivory sticks, 10in., Italian, circa 1720.
(Christie's) $1,362

A fan, the leaf painted with a cockerel and other birds pecking by a well with a farmhouse beyond, the ivory sticks lacquered with birds and flowers in Imari style, 10in., circa 1730, in 18th century fan box. (Christie's) $727

A fan signed *Micahels*, the canepin leaf painted with three ladies watching lovers in a garden whilst a gentleman picks flowers in the foreground, ivory sticks painted with the continuation of the scene and carved, 14in., circa 1890. (Christie's) $909

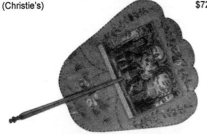

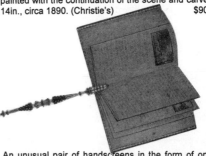

Map of Italy by Robert [de Vaugondy], a handscreen, the recto with garlands of flowers and trophies, the verso applied with a hand-colored map L'Italie et ses Isles circonvoisines, with wooden handle, 15in., French, circa 1770. (Christie's) $908

An unusual pair of handscreens in the form of open books, the rectos with the text of the Lady of the Lake, Canto I and Ellen Fitzarthur, Canto II, both with applied hand-colored engravings, turned parcel gilt wooden handles, 15in., South Netherlands, 1826. (Christie's) $4,724

A fan, the green paper leaf painted with a shepherd and shepherdess, the ivory sticks carved with a staghunt, and pique with silver, 10in., probably Italian, circa 1740, in early 19th century box. (Christie's) $1,090

South East view of Cheltenham Well by Thomas Robins the Elder, unsigned, a rare topographic fan painted with the artist himself sketching the view to the left, 11in., English, circa 1742. (Christie's) $21,804

Musique Champêtre, a fan signed *Tony Faivre* and dated *1876*, the leaf painted in smoky tones on a yellow ground, heightened in gold and white, inscribed *Duvelleroy London 1877*, the ivory sticks finely carved, 12in., French for the English market, 1877. (Christie's) $7,268

The Hongs of Canton, a fan, the leaf painted with a view of the Hongs, with the English church in the foreground and figures and junks, the sticks lacquered in black, gold, pink and blue with butterflies and dragons, 11in. circa 1850. (Christie's) $5,814

Traci Lords' Dress 'Cry-Baby', American, 1989, the cream sleeveless, button-through dress with red patterned inserts at the pockets.
(Bonhams & Brooks) $173

A wicker basket from the MGM Studios, formerly the property of Stanley Kubrick, with canvas top, two handles, metal bolt and fastener, 78cm. long.
(Bonhams) $417

Gloria Swanson golden globe award for "Sunset Boulevard", 1950, 8½in.
(Christie's) $25,850

Independence Day Alien, a grotesque, detailed, full-scale model, molded latex foam, with winged head and skeletal arms, hands and legs, 106in. high, with eight additional tentacles, each, 107in. long.
(Christie's) $1,353

Gene Kelly Argyle sweater from "Singin' In The Rain", MGM, 1952, a tan, red and navy blue wool argyle sweater with a v-neck and long sleeves.
(Christie's) $18,800

Aliens, a grotesque detailed full-scale replica alien creature made of molded rubber in one piece, with outstretched arms and long ridged tail of foam, approximately 89in.;and a similar alien creature costume.
(Christie's) $1,083

A life size model of Darth Vadar, Licensed Limited Edition No. 390/500, manufactured by Pop Replica, black ribbed latex body with cloak, helmet, accessories and flashing lights, on plinth base, 6ft. 10in. high.(Bonhams) $2,250

Audrey Hepburn, a brass compact, owned by Audrey Hepburn, containing mirror, powder puff and traces of face powder, with ornate clasp of costume diamonds and rubies, with certificate of authenticity.
(Vennett Smith) $609

Gone With The Wind, a brass key and fob for Clark Gable's personal dressing room on set,1939, fob inscribed *Dressing Room 24 CLARK GABLE* with MGM insignia engraved on reverse, mounted with white image of Gable and Leigh, 21 x 29in. (Bonhams) $863

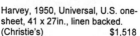

Harvey, 1950, Universal, U.S. one-sheet, 41 x 27in., linen backed.
(Christie's) $1,518

La Grande Illusion, 1937, R.A.C., French, 63 x 94in. Art by Brodsky.
(Christie's) $3,415

Dracula, 1931, Universal, U.S. window card, 22 x 14in.
(Christie's) $16,128

Greed/Den Giriga, 1925, M.G.M., Swedish, 47 x 34½in., art by Eric Rohman (1891-1949).
(Christie's) $4,542

You Only Live Twice, United Artists, 1967, UK 30 x 40in. poster, style C, featuring Bath House Girls artwork by Robert McGinnis, 76 x 102cm. (Bonhams) $304

Chain Lightning/Pilote Du Diable, Warner Brothers, 1949, France, Grande, 47 x 63in., linen backed. Artist: René Peron.
(Christie's) $705

Man Hunt/Duello Mortale, 1941, Twentieth Century Fox, Italian two-foglio, 55 x 39in., linen-backed, art by Alfredo Capitani (1895-1985).
(Christie's) $542

United Artists, 1962, UK 30 x 40in. poster, a rare two-color version, 76 x 102cm.
(Bonhams) $248

Romola, 1925, M.G.M., Swedish, 39 x 28in., art by Eric Rohman (1891-1949)
(Christie's) $4,361

Rear Window, Paramount, 1954, one sheet, linen backed, 41 x 27. (Christie's) $5,640

Citizen Kane, 1941, R.K.O., U.S. title card, 11 x 14in., framed. (Christie's) $1,948

Bus Stop, 1956, T.C.F., U.S. one sheet, 41 x 27in. (Christie's) $531

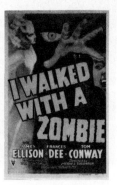

The Other Man, Triangle Keystone, 1916, 1 sheet, 28 x 41in. folded. (Christie's) $1,645

Marnie, 1964, Universal, British quad, 30 x 40in. (Christie's) $531

I Walked With A Zombie, RKO, 1943, one sheet, linen backed, 41 x 27in. (Christie's) $1,763

The Greatest Thing In Life, 1918, Artcraft Pictures, U.S. one sheet, 41 x 27in., linen backed. (Christie's) $2,834

Dr. No, 1962, United Artists, British quad, 30 x 40in., linen backed. (Christie's) $1,771

Moulin Rouge, 1957, Poland, 23 x 32in., linen backed. Artist: Lucjan Jagodzinski. (Christie's) $2,350

Cat On A Hot Tin Roof, 1958, M.G.M., U.S. one sheet, 41 x 27in., linen backed.(Christie's) $1,417

The Birds, 1963, Universal, British quad, 30 x 40in. (Christie's) $886

On The Waterfront, Columbia, 1954,1 sheet, 27 x 41in., folded. (Christie's) $1,763

Taxi Driver, Columbia, 1976, American poster, 60 x 40in. Spectacular art from the creator of David Bowie's Diamond Dogs album cover art. (Christie's) $2,115

La Bête Humaine, 1938, Paris Film, French double panel, 63 x 94in., linen backed. (Christie's) $1,771

You Were Never Lovelier/Non Sei Mai Stata Cosi Bella, 1942, Columbia, Italian four-foglio, 79 x 55in., linen backed, art by Anselmo Ballester (1897-1974). (Christie's) $6,730

To Catch A Thief, Paramount, 1955, 1 sheet, 27 x 41in., linen backed. (Christie's) $1,998

The Bride of Frankenstein, 1935, Universal, U.S. jumbo lobby card, 14 x 17in. (Christie's) $27,146

La Dolce Vita, 1960, Cineriz, style A Italian four foglio, 79 x 55in. (Christie's) $7,600

The Mummy, Universal, 1959, one-sheet, linen backed, 41 x 27in. (Christie's) $1,116

The Jazz Singer, Warner Bros., 1927, half-sheet, paper-backed. This is the only half-sheet from this film ever to be offered at auction, 22 x 28in. (Christie's) $30,550

Hot Water, Pathé, 1924, one sheet, linen backed, 41 x 27in. (Christie's) $5,875

Hell's Angels, United Artists, 1930, window card, 22 x 14in. (Christie's) $1,293

Thunderball, 1965, United Artists, British quad, 30 x 40in. (Christie's) $973

Prison Bars, Barnsdale, 1901, poster, 42 x 28in. (Christie's) $588

Fifth Avenue Girl, 1939, R.K.O., U.S., one sheet, 41 x 27in., linen backed, art by H.M. Froehlich. (Christie's) $229

Help! United Artists, six sheet, linen backed, 1965, 81 x 81in. (Christie's) $999

All Quiet On The Western Front, 1930, Universal, U.S., one sheet, 41 x 27in., linen backed. (Christie's) $30,762

Peeping Tom, 1959, Anglo Amalgamated, British one sheet, 40 x 27in. linen backed.
(Christie's) $673

La Dame aux Camélias, 1910, Delac & Co., French, 63 x 47in., linen backed.
(Christie's) $708

Forbidden Planet, 1956, M.G.M., U.S., one sheet, 41 x 27in., linen backed. (Christie's) $12,666

Snow White And The Seven Dwarfs/Blanche Neige et les Sept Nains, 1937, Walt Disney, French 31 x 23in., linen backed, framed.
(Christie's) $5,428

Grand Hotel, MGM, 1932, 1 sheet, 27 x 41in., linen backed. Tooker Litho, NY. The only known U.S. poster for this title to have appeared at auction.
(Christie's) $49,350

Blow Up, MGM, 1967, Italy, Quattro, 55 x 79in., linen backed. Artist: Ercole Brini.
(Christie's) $646

The General Died At Dawn/L'Oro Della Cina, Paramount, 1936, Italy, 28 x 39in., paper backed.
(Christie's) $1,880

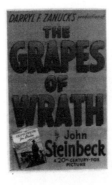

The Grapes Of Wrath, Style B. 20th Century Fox, 1939, 1 sheet, 27 x 41in., folded.
(Christie's) $705

Sold Out Appetite, Goskino, 1928, Russian, 41 x 28in.
(Christie's) $11,750

Harrison Ford, signed 8 x 10, half-length as Indiana Jones.
(Vennett Smith) $70

Cameron Diaz, signed color 8 x 10, full-length in mini dress.
(Vennett Smith) $42

Roy Rogers, signed 8 x 10, half-length in cowboy hat.
(Vennett Smith) $109

Kelly & Charisse, signed 8 x 10 by both Gene Kelly and Cyd Charisse, full-length embracing each other in dance pose.
(Vennett Smith) $110

Titanic, signed 8 x 10 by both Leonardo Di Caprio and Kate Winslet, full-length standing together embracing, on board ship in a scene from Titanic.
(Vennett Smith) $137

Phil Silvers, signed and inscribed 7 x 9, half-length in costume as Sergeant Bilko, shouting a command.
(Vennett Smith) $226

Elizabeth Taylor, signed and inscribed 4 x 6, head and shoulders.
(Vennett Smith) $203

Alan Ladd, signed and inscribed 5 x 7, half-length standing by wall.
(Vennett Smith) $58

Ursula Andress, signed color 8 x 10, three quarter length in black mini dress with machine gun, in silver. (Vennett Smith) $42

Robert Donat, signed sepia 6 x 8.5, head and shoulders. (Vennett Smith) $78

Julie Andrews, signed color 8 x 10, half-length in silver. (Vennett Smith) $106

Gene Kelly, signed and inscribed 8 x 10, head and shoulders. (Vennett Smith) $56

Russell Crowe, signed and inscribed color 8 x 10, with first name only, full-length in costume in a scene from Gladiators. (Vennett Smith) $110

The Glen Miller Story, signed 4 x 6, by both James Stewart and June Allyson, to lower white border, head and shoulders together cheek-to-cheek in a scene from The Glenn Miller Story.(Vennett Smith) $75

Ronald Reagan, signed and inscribed color 8 x 10, to lower white border, three quarter length standing. (Vennett Smith) $252

Fred Astaire, signed sepia 5 x 7, full-length in dance pose wearing top hat and white bowtie, holding cane. (Vennett Smith) $153

Carrie Fisher, signed color 8 x 10, from Star Wars, in thick blue ink, EX. (Vennett Smith) $64

James Stewart, signed 8 x 10 half-length from How The West Was Won, later signature. (Vennett Smith) $160

Basil Rathbone, signed sepia 3.5 x 5, half-length wearing suit. (Vennett Smith) $212

James Stewart, signed 10 x 8, head and shoulders as Glenn Miller with trombone. (Vennett Smith) $113

Gary Cooper, signed postcard, portrait. (Vennett-Smith) $170

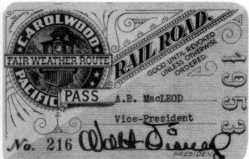

Alec Guinness, signed and inscribed 5 x 8, to lower white border, with Christmas greetings, head and shoulders in costume, annotated in his hand 'Star Wars' and dated 1979. (Vennett Smith) $48

Walt Disney, a good signed admittance pass ticket for the Carolwood Pacific Rail Road, 1953, The Carolwood Pacific Rail Road was Disney's miniature railway constructed at his home. (Vennett Smith) $1,668

Marty Feldman, signed postcard, with first name only, to lower white border, head and shoulders with one hand raised to face. (Vennett Smith) $77

Clark Gable, a good signed 4.5 x 7.5, to lower white border, three quarter length seated with script (?) in his hands. (Vennett Smith) $395

Montgomery Clift, bold pencil signature, on the reverse of a restaurant guest check, dated in another hand beneath, 15th July 1948. (Vennett Smith) $103

Ernest Thesiger, signed postcard, to lower white border, head and shoulders in profile. (Vennett Smith) $100

Paul Newman, signed postcard, head and shoulders, Picturegoer D881. (Vennett Smith) $160

Easy Rider, signed color 10 x 8, by Dennis Hopper, Peter Fonda and Jack Nicholson, three quarter length on bikes from Easy Rider. (Vennett Smith) $174

Ingrid Bergman, signed sepia postcard. (Vennett Smith) $120

Laurel and Hardy, signed postcard by both Stan Laurel and Oliver Hardy, half-length in characteristic pose with bowler hats. (Vennett Smith) $522

Laurel and Hardy, signed sepia 7 x 5 by both Stan Laurel and Oliver Hardy, to lower white border, head and shoulders smiling, original packet (with Laurel and Hardy vignette). (Vennett Smith) $537

Johnny Weissmuller, signed album page, over-mounted in green and ivory beneath 8 x 10 reproduction photo of Weissmuller as Tarzan. (Vennett Smith) $96

Boris Karloff, signed sepia 5 x 7, wearing suit. (Vennett Smith) $212

Psycho, a pair of 7 x 8.5 photos, signed by Janet Leigh and Anthony Perkins (darker portion), overmounted in gray and cream above name plaque. (Vennett Smith) $106

Noel Coward, signed postcard, three quarter length seated, wearing suit, with a lit cigarette in one hand, Picturegoer 354, photo by Dorothy Wilding. (Vennett Smith) $73

Norma Shearer, signed real photograph Picturegoer, 206. (Vennett Smith) $68

Roscoe Arbuckle, signed and inscribed album page, 5.5 x 3.75, in full *Roscoe 'Fatty' Arbuckle*, extremely rare. (Vennett Smith) $290

Alastair Sim, signed sepia postcard, head and shoulders wearing suit. (Vennett Smith) $99

Jean Harlow, a pair of screw type rhinestone earrings, laid down to red velvet, overmounted in cream and red beneath a 8 x 10 photo, with certificate of authenticity. (Vennett Smith) $155

Stan Laurel, an unusual signed and inscribed 8.5 x 6.5 by Stan Laurel, showing him in later years alongside Oliver Hardy and with a young Norman Wisdom, also signed and inscribed by Wisdom. (Vennett Smith) $353

Princess Grace of Monaco, signed color 5.5 x 8.25 magazine photo head and shoulders in profile. (Vennett Smith) $130

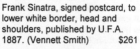

Frank Sinatra, signed postcard, to lower white border, head and shoulders, published by U.F.A. 1887. (Vennett Smith) $261

Audrey Hepburn, signed 5.5 x 4, being a reproduction from one of her films with Gregory Peck, signed in later years. (Vennett Smith) $141

Harpo Marx, signed sepia postcard, half-length in costume, playing harp, slightly weaker contrast to surname.(Vennett Smith) $254

Ronald Colman, signed postcard, head and shoulders in profile, early April 1918.(Vennett Smith) $116

Slim Pickens, signed and inscribed 9 x 8, full-length riding on bucking horse, (Vennett Smith) $96

Rock Hudson, signed postcard, half-length in tank top. (Vennett Smith) $137

Rita Hayworth, signed piece, 4 x 3, overmounted in pink and white beneath 7 x 9 photograph, full-length in gown holding cigarette and fur coat, framed and glazed. (Vennett Smith) $123

Charles Chaplin, signed 11.5 x 9.5, three quarter length standing wearing hat and jacket alongside his daughters Vicky and Josephine, in tennis dresses. (Vennett Smith) $494

Roy Rogers, signed and inscribed 6 x 4 postcard, by both Roy Rogers and Dale Evans, full-length standing together in Western outfits alongside Trigger. (Vennett Smith) $36

Yul Brynner, a signed early postcard, full name, showing him half-length in evening suit. (Vennett Smith) $85

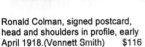

Groucho Marx, signed 10 x 8, with first name only, head and shoulders in character alongside, but not signed by, Chico and Harpo Marx, promoting An Evening With Groucho.(Vennett Smith) $141

Charles Chaplin, signed postcard, full-length standing in costume as the tramp, photo by Essanay Films. (Vennett Smith) $756

Cary Grant, an excellent signed and inscribed 8 x 10, half-length seated. (Vennett Smith) $381

Harrison Ford, signed 8 x 10, early portrait, laughing. (Vennett Smith) $89

Tyrone Power, signed 6.5 x 8.5, half-length wearing light gray suit, smiling. (Vennett Smith) $75

Betty Grable, signed and inscribed 8 x 10, half-length seated wearing an off the shoulder gown and pearl choker, slight surface and corner creasing.
(Vennett Smith) $99

Barbara Streisand, signed and inscribed 7.5 x 9.5, full length in costume seated on stage alongside Michael Craig, also signed and inscribed by Craig.
(Vennett Smith) $319

Ginger Rogers, signed and inscribed sepia 8 x 10, half length leaning slightly backward, together with signed and inscribed sepia 5 x 7s of Alexis Smith and Ann Blyth.
(Vennett Smith) $85

Phil Silvers, signed 8 x 10, half-length in suit, wearing spectacles, leaning against rail.
(Vennett Smith) $148

Sonja Henie, signed and inscribed 8 x 10, full-length seated in dressing gown, Hollywood 1937.
(Vennett Smith) $70

Mae West, signed sepia 5 x 7, vintage, in red, head and shoulders in ornate hat.
(Vennett Smith) $189

A sepia headshot of Norma Shearer wonderfully hand-tinted in vibrant hues with her blue fountain-pen ink signature in the lower margin, (Christie's) $176

Joseph Cotton, inscribed and signed, circa 1940s, 8 x 10in. (Christie's) $230

A sepia photograph depicting Joan Crawford standing against a wall with her black fountain-pen ink signature on the lower right-side margin, 10 x 8in. (Christie's) $306

An autographed photograph of Jayne Mansfield, dated *July 16 1958*, signed *To Ann, I'll Always Remember Your Sweet Smile And Charming Ways- Till Next Time Jane Mansfield*, 21 x 17cm. (Bonhams & Brooks) $345

Baywatch, signed color 8 x 10 by both Pamela Anderson and Yasmin Bleeth, three quarter length standing together wearing red swimsuits in a scene from Baywatch. (Vennett Smith) $39

Sean Connery, signed and inscribed 8 x 10 head and shoulders, in costume from The Hunt For Red October. (Vennett Smith) $51

Ramon Navarro, signed and inscribed sepia 8 x 10, half-length wearing suit, with arms folded. (Vennett Smith) $78

Fairbanks & Pickford, signed 6.5 8.5, full-length with Chaplin (but not signed by), full-length. (Vennett Smith) $212

Michael Landon, signed and inscribed 8 x 10, head and shoulders smiling. (Vennett Smith) $89

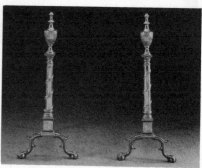

A pair of blackened iron firedogs, attributed to Eugène Printz, 1920s, of stylized geometric form, 8½in. high. (Christie's) $2,016

A pair of Chippendale brass andirons, Philadelphia, 1770-1790, each with reeded urn-form top with lobed finial above a meandering-vine tapered columnar support, 28½in. high. (Christie's) $70,500

A pair of French gilt-bronze chenets, last quarter 19th century, modelled as dragons resting on scroll bases cast with classical profile portraits, 14½in. high. (Christie's) $2,362

A pair of Empire style gilt and patinated bronze sphinx chenets, 20th century, the recumbent sphinx on raised stepped rectangular plinths with winged torchère and eagle mounts to the frieze, 23.2cm. high. (Christie's) $1,991

A pair of cast brass hound andirons, American, late 19th-early 20th century, each molded in the half-round depicting a profile hound seated at attention with rear legs and tail tucked underneath hind quarters, 13¼in. high. (Christie's) $3,220

Pair of Louis XVI style gilt and patinated bronze and jasperware chenets, circa 1860, each with cherub finial in animal pelts and instruments, inset with a Wedgwood medallion, 14in. high. (Skinner) $3,335

A polished cast iron and brass mounted fire grate, late 19th or early 20th century, the serpentine railed front above a foliate pierced fret, 31in. wide.
(Christie's) $4,360

A 19th century cast iron fire back, the arched plate cast with a figure of Flora, converted to a fire grate, 33 x 24½in.(Bonhams) $585

An Adam style white metal and iron serpentine firebasket, a pair of andirons and three fire irons, 55cm. wide x 53cm. high.
(Bonhams & Brooks) $420

A polished steel and brass firegrate, early 20th century, the railed basket with beaded flanges above a pierced frieze, 27in. wide.
(Christie's) $3,629

An Aesthetic Movement brass and cast iron hob grate, circa 1870, the rectangular backplate above the serpentine railed basket, flanked by repoussé foliate panels, 32¼in. wide. (Bonhams) $1,001

A late Victorian cast iron and steel firegrate, circa 1890, in the Neoclassical taste with serpentine railed front, the fret applied with concentric ring moldings flanked by tapering standards, 28in. wide.
(Christie's) $2,725

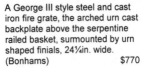

A George III style steel and cast iron fire grate, the arched urn cast backplate above the serpentine railed basket, surmounted by urn shaped finials, 24¼in. wide.
(Bonhams) $770

An early George III style white metal fire grate, 2nd half of the 20th century, 80cm. wide x 94cm. high.
(Bonhams & Brooks) $14

A late Victorian style brass and cast iron fire grate, the shaped railed basket with scrolling front supports surmounted by flaming urn finials, 24in. wide.(Bonhams) $678

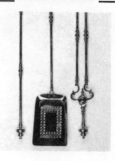

Various brass fire tools, some
engraved flowers, comprising: a
hearth brush, a shovel, a poker and
two pairs of fire tongs.
(Woolley & Wallis)　　　　$96

A set of three Edwardian brass fire
irons, with a knopped and waisted
pommels on shafts with turned
intersections, 31in.
(Christie's)　　　　$1,677

A set of three brass fire irons, in
Arts and Crafts style, consisting of
poker, tongs and hearth brush.
(Woolley & Wallis)　　　　$96

A set of three polished steel
fireirons, mid 19th century, with
faceted tapering pommels, cast
with stiff-leaf ornament on writhen
shafts, the flared shovel with a
pierced oval, 32in.
(Christie's)　　　　$1,454

A set of early Victorian steel fire
irons, mid 19th century, the brass
grips with star-cast tops to
lanceolate leaf cast pommels, the
pierced shovel, 29¼in. high.
(Christie's)　　　　$767

A pair of polished steel fireirons,
mid 19th century, the brass grips
cast with gargoyle masks, the plain
shafts with knopped intersections,
the flared shovel with a pierced
oval, 32⅜in. long.
(Christie's)　　　　$1,269

A set of three steel fireirons,
second quarter 19th century, with
faceted cone pommels on
cylindrical shafts with baluster
intersections, 29½in.
(Christie's)　　　　$1,999

A set of three polished steel fire
irons, 19th century, the foliate cast
pommels and grips on knopped
cylindrical shafts, the shovel, 30in.
long.
(Christie's)　　　　$2,180

A set of three steel fireirons, mid
19th century, the foliate cast
baluster grips with gadrooned
pommels, on faceted shafts, with
shaped pierced shovel, 29¼in.
(Christie's)　　　　$1,090

A carved and painted mantel, possibly American, 19th century, the rectangular molded cornice above an incised decorated frieze over a tripartite panelled backboard centered by an applied circular fan enclosed by similar quarter fans, 69¾in. wide.
(Christie's) $4,000

A variegated white and red marble chimneypiece, late 19th century, the jambs with tapering column uprights above square section block feet supporting the rectangular shelf with molded border above the conforming frieze, overall 42in. high.
(Christie's) $1,354

A Jacobean style carved oak fire surround, late 19th/early 20th century, 166cm. wide x 138cm. high, the aperture 88cm. square.
(Bonhams & Brooks) $420

A French iron and brass fireplace with stripped pine surround, in the early 19th century style, late 19th century, the arched hearth with foliate rocaille cresting above the lobed cowl, the pine chimneypiece and overmantel with plain jambs, 79in. high.
(Christie's) $1,417

A Napoleon III ormolu-mounted white marble chimney-piece, in the Louis XVI style, circa 1870, the breakfront platform above a scrolling foliate frieze, supported by two fluted volute uprights, 65in. wide.
(Christie's) $15,545

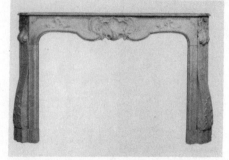

A large Louis XV style white marble chimneypiece, 19th century, the jambs with leaf capped volute scroll panels and conforming side returns supporting the shallow serpentine shelf with molded border, overall 56in. high, 88in. wide. (Christie's) $2,537

A Victorian orange and beige marble chimneypiece, 19th century, the part fluted jambs supporting a conforming frieze within panelled tablets below a rectangular shelf, 71¼in. wide, overall. (Christie's) $9,048

Colonial Revival carved and painted pine mantel and fireplace surround, New England, late 19th century, with beaded and egg-carved outer edge and projecting bowed and dentil molded mantel on demi-lune turned bracket, 65in. wide. (Skinner) $4,600

A Egyptian Revival ebonized and parcel-gilt mantel, New York City, 1860-1890, the molded shelf with outset front corners above a moulded and gilt-incised frieze centering an outset panel carved with a cherub driving a chariot with winged horse, 75in. wide. (Christie's) $8,050

A Louis XV style variegated gray and black marble chimneypiece, circa 1870, the jambs with shell crestings and molded volute scroll panels supporting the shelf, overall 42¾in. high, 56½in. wide. (Christie's) $2,707

A Louis XV Brocatello marble chimneypiece, the jambs with molded panels supporting the serpentine shelf with molded frieze centered by a heart shaped cartouche, overall, 45¾in. high, 63in. wide. (Christie's) $2,537

A French bronze fender, late 19th century, the ewer standards suspended with floral swags, flanking a pierced and gadrooned rail with female mask, re-patinated and re-gilt, 52in. wide.
(Christie's) $3,214

A Regency brass and wirework fender, 97cm. wide.
(Bonhams & Brooks) $140

A Louis Philippe bronze and gilt metal adjustable fender, mid 19th century, with sphinx and foliate cast mounts, 150cm. wide x 39cm. high.
(Bonhams & Brooks) $1,680

A Louis XVI style gilt metal and gray marble adjustable fender, with urn finials and guilloche frame, 136cm. wide.
(Bonhams & Brooks) $1,050

A French gilt bronze fender, late 19th century, of naturalistic form, the openwork standards with cherubs flanking the conforming rail with stepped plinth, 58in. wide. (Christie's) $2,537

A French gilt and patinated bronze fender, late 19th century, the standards with loosely draped cherubs, the bases with pierced foliate panels, with conforming adjustable rail and side returns, 50in. wide at smallest.
(Christie's) $2,876

A French gilt and patinated bronze fender, second quarter 19th century, the stepped plinths with lion surmounts flanking the polished steel rail 12¼in. high, 50½in. long. (Christie's) $2,876

A polished cast iron club fender, 20th century, Carron foundry, the padded seat with central U-section and part-writhen supports above the plinth, stamped to the underside, 62½in. wide. (Christie's) $1,544

A Restauration gilt and patinated bronze fender, circa 1820, the standards with cone finials flanking a polished steel rail with acanthus clasped supports, 41¾in. wide. (Christie's) $2,907

A French gilt bronze adjustable fender, late 19th century, the standards with openwork spiral twist urns with ring handles, over canopies with recumbent lions below, 58in. extended. (Christie's) $1,448

An early George III brass fender, circa 1770, of serpentine form, the upper edge with stylized openwork decoration above beading, the main gallery with foliate and geometric designs, 45in. wide. (Christie's) $658

A brass club fender, 20th century, the padded leather seat above cylindrical uprights and a stepped plinth, 47½in. wide. (Christie's) $2,722

A William IV polished steel fender, second quarter 19th century, the curved frieze with pierced conjoined circular pattern and beaded borders with urn finials, the moulded plinth on raised bun feet, 53in. wide and a pair of steel andirons, 14¾in. high. (Christie's) $1,463

A polished brass club fender, 20th century, the padded buttoned leather seat on plain cylindrical shafts with reeded intersections above a stepped molded plinth, 70in. wide. (Christie's) $3,128

A Regency pierced brass fender, early 19th century, of D section, with acorn finials above the tubular upper rail, the two pierced galleries with scrolling foliage within interlinked circlets, 38¾in. wide. (Christie's) $581

A late Regency brass fender, 120cm. wide. (Bonhams & Brooks) $70

An Empire gilt and patinated bronze fender, early 19th century, the rectangular plinths with recumbent lion surmounts flanking the adjustable pierced arcaded rail, 62in. extended. (Christie's) $3,271

A William IV steel and brass fender, second quarter 19th century, the serpentine pierced rail with a band of stylized foliage on a molded plinth, 49½in. wide. (Christie's) $1,996

An early Victorian brass fender, 122cm. long. (Bonhams & Brooks) $168

A Victorian brass and leather upholstered club fender, late 19th century, the cushioned seat above column supports with a 'U' shaped stretcher to their center, on a plinth base, 59in. wide. (Bonhams) $2,800

A Louis Philippe bronze and ormolu fender, circa 1840, the twin standards mounted with recumbent lions, the plinths and rail with pierced gilt foliate mounts, 53in. wide. (Christie's) $5,814

A Victorian brass fender, the railed front inset with oval and scrolled panels, with upholstered seats to either end, on a molded plinth, 67in. wide.
(Christie's) $1,899

A Victorian copper coal scuttle, helmet shaped, with a swing handle.
(Woolley & Wallis) $92

A brass fan fire screen, 68cm. high x 100cm. wide.
(Bonhams & Brooks) $210

Pair of bell metal andirons, America, early 19th century, belted ball-top finials, short tapering shafts on square plinths, 18in. high.
(Skinner) $1,610

A 19th century brass coal scuttle, helmet shaped with embossed flower and foliate panels, foliate loop handle with turned ebony grip, shovel to match, 22in. high.
(Andrew Hartley) $616

A 19th century brass footman, with pierced decoration, shaped fret edge frieze, on front angular legs with pad feet, iron back legs, 16½in.
(Woolley & Wallis) $213

A copper coal scuttle, helmet shaped, with curving handle and side grip handles, on a molded pedestal foot.
(Woolley & Wallis) $110

A Victorian japanned iron purdonium, mid 19th century, painted green overall, the sloping serpentine front with raised reserve with a painted scene of swans in a river (possibly later), 22in. high overall. (Christie's) $493

A polished brass club fender, early 20th century, the padded seat on a tubular frame with stepped plinth with mesh guard to the lower section, 58in. wide.
(Christie's) $7,360

A fine Hardy 1891 pattern brass 'Perfect' fly reel, the winding plate with ivory handle, with a nickel silver Bickerdyke style wire line guide attached to three raised brass supports.
(Bonhams) $5,796

A rare Hardy brass 'Silex' 4¾in. reel with twin ivorine bulbous handles on nickel silver elliptical mount, nickel silver foot and quarter star back. (Bonhams) $1,260

An ABU Ambassadeur 30 big game multiplying reel, the largest production Ambassadeur reel, 3.4:1 ratio, brushed stainless steel frame with twin harness lugs, non-reversing handle.
(Bonhams) $414

Hardy Brothers: A 4¼in. wide drum 'Perfect' alloy reel with ventilated drum, bridged tension screw, ivorine handle, and smooth brass foot. (Bearne's) $690

A scarce unnamed 4½in. "Wheelback" Nottingham centerpin reel, walnut drum with brass flange and twin pear shape wood handles. (Bonhams) $377

A 5½in. Nottingham frogback reel, walnut with twin bulbous ebony handles, pierced faceplate, brass line guard. (Christie's) $469

Hardy Brothers: A 3½in. 'Perfect' alloy trout reel, with ventilated drum, bridged tension screw, ivorine handle and smooth brass foot. (Bearne's) $207

A Hardy 'Perfect' alloy and brass wide drum salmon fly reel, with smooth brass foot, brass strapped rim tension, ivory handle, stamped with maker's oval and straight line logos and Rod and Hand trademark, 1896 check, 4¼in.
(Bonhams) $635

A fine 1896 Hardy brass "Perfect" 4¼in. wide drum fly reel, all brass construction with scarce ivory handle, brass bearings, early caliper check.
(Bonhams) $2,041

A stuffed pike in bow front case inscribed *Pike. 19lbs. Caught in River Wye near Ross. 20th Nov. 1930.* (Bearne's) $1,336

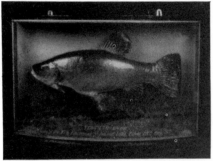

A tench mounted in bow front case against reeds and grasses, bears Cooper label, case inscribed in gilt Tench 4lb 8½oz *caught by Ken Eastmead at Bowood Lake Caln 23rd August 1951*, 25½in. (Bonhams) $1,320

A roach by F.W. Anstiss mounted in a setting of reeds and grasses against a light blue background, set in a gilt lined bow front case with gilt inscription *Roach 1lb, caught by W. Naire at Harefield, January 24th 1915.* (Bonhams) $1,173

An Edwardian glazed wood case containing a stuffed pike, dated *1907*, the fish naturalistically arranged with river weeds, the bow fronted case with *Pike caught by M.Sherlock on Lough Erne. March. 1907. Weight 30lbs.5oz Length 46ins. Girth 24ins.* in gilt lettering, 53¼in. wide. (Christie's) $4,935

A stuffed pike mounted in a river bed setting, in a glazed and ebonized bow fronted case, with the label for J Cooper & Sons, St Luke's, London, 28in. wide. (Andrew Hartley) $580

A roach attributed to J. Cooper & Sons mounted in a setting of reeds and grasses against a green background, set in a gilt lined bow front case with gilt inscription *Roach, 2lbs 1oz, taken by W.F. Grimmett, September 1912*, case 21¾ x 13¼in. (Bonhams) $635

A late Victorian presentation half block salmon, (chipped) inscribed on the verso *Salmon caught at The Vanstone by Major Trafford with a small Jack Scoll fly, July 13 1894*, 3ft.9½in. long, 34½lbs. (Woolley & Wallis) $6,028

A pike in reeds and grasses, set in gilt lined bow front case (glass loose, split in backboard), case 46in. long. (Bonhams) $660

A Dutch style carved and ebonized reverse profile frame, first quarter 20th century, the eared corners with ripple molding, 23¾ x 18¾in. x 7in. (Christie's) $822

An Italian 18th century style carved and gilded frame, with cavetto sight, bound and centered leaf and fruit D-section top edge, 12¾ x 10 x 3¾in.(Bonhams) $1,260

A Northern European bird's eye maple veneered molding frame, late 19th century, with wide ovolo descending to a later giltwood slip, 19¾ x 16½ x 4¾in. (Christie's) $739

An Italian parcel-gilt and ebonized cassetta frame, 17th century, with astragal at the outer edge, the centers and corners of the fascia with cherubs and other figures amongst cauliculi, 39¾ x 27 x 4½in. (Christie's) $4,935

An Italian carved and gilded reverse profile frame, 17th century, the reverse ogee with acanthus to the corners, the sides with further acanthus alternating with bell-flowers, 17 x 14⅛ x 2¾in. (Christie's) $3,619

A French Louis XV carved and gilded oak frame, mid 18th century, with chain-link to the outer edge, the raised and pierced centers and corners of the cavetto with rocaille motifs, 12 x 7 x 3in. (Christie's) $2,961

A Louis XIV carved and gilded frame, with leaf ogee sight, sanded frieze, and leaf and strapwork to the cross-hatched ogee, 39¼ x 31 x 5in. (Bonhams) $5,586

A Dutch carved and ebonized molding frame, early 19th century, with various ripple and wave moldings around an ovolo at the outer edge, 27¼ x 20½ x 10¼in. (Christie's) $1,645

A North Italian 18th century carved and gilded frame of reverse profile, with foliage ogee sight, incised panels to the cushion-molded top edge, 89.2 x 68.7 x 12.7cm. (Bonhams) $3,528

An Italian carved and ebonized frame, 18th century, with gilt imbricated husk course to the outer edge, reverse ogee, 63.8 x 47.6 x 10.2cm.(Christie's) $1,810

Carved redwood picture frame, California, 1900-10, bas relief of draped window and wide staircase, 24in. high. (Skinner) $1,840

A French early 19th century gilded composition Empire frame, with plain sight, pearl, scotia, pin and ribbon-twist, fluted hollow with acanthus corners, 134 x 96.9 x 14cm. (Bonhams) $2,205

An Italian 19th century carved and gilded frame, with cavetto tondo sight, leaf and shield ogee, scrolling leaf and cherub heads to the punched spandrels, 28 diameter x 10½in. (Bonhams) $2,590

A French Louis XV carved and gilded frame, with composite waterleaf to the outer edge, cavetto with raised and pierced top edge, 26¼ x 22 x 5½in. (Christie's) $1,086

A 19th century carved, pierced and gilded Florentine style frame, with ogee sight, and boldly scrolling acanthus running between grotesque mask centers, 32 x 26⅝ x 7½in. (Bonhams) $1,400

A French Louis XIV carved and gilded frame, with dentilled outer edge, the raised corners of the torus with acanthus flanked by leaves and flower heads in high relief, 29 x 24 x 3½in. (Christie's) $1,537

An Italian parcel-gilt and ebonized cassetta frame, early 17th century, with raised moldings to the outer edge, the fascia with cauliculi to the centers and corners, 64.8 x 53.4 x 9.8cm. (Christie's) $2,303

An English carved and silvered frame, 18th century, with schematic foliate outer edge, the ovolo with acanthus to the corners and entwining foliage flanking twin swelling reposes, 29 x 24¼ x 4½in. (Christie's) $1,719

A George I walnut-veneered armoire with cavetto cornice, two feather-banded doors, 149cm. wide. (Bearne's) $6,400

A French Provincial chestnut armoire, later brass fittings, the arched doors with brass fret escutcheons and hinges, 5ft. 4in., (Woolley & Wallis) $959

An 18th century French Provincial chestnut armoire, the cornice later, the pair of panelled doors with foliage carving, 33½in. wide. (Woolley & Wallis) $1,136

A light oak 18th century Liège armoire, with molded cornice and canted corners, the panelled doors decorated with finely carved volutes, on bun feet. (Galerie Moderne) $3,710

An oak wardrobe, with carved frieze and panelling, basically 17th century, 4ft.3in. (Woolley & Wallis) $1,044

A Biedermeier satinbirch armoire, 19th century, the stepped pediment with a concealed drawer above a twin panelled door with a further drawer below, on block feet, 47in. wide. (Christie's) $1,240

Continental mahogany Empire-style two-door armoire, early 19th century, with shaped cornice above two panelled doors opening to shelves, 42in. wide. (Skinner) $1,610

A German ivory, brass and pewter-inlaid walnut and fruitwood armoire, Brunswick, 18th century, two panelled doors with shaped rectangular reserves depicting costumed soldiers, 70½in. wide. (Christie's) $9,053

A French walnut armoire, late 18th/early 19th century, the molded cornice above a pair of triple shaped panelled doors carved with lattice decoration, 60in. wide. (Christie's) $1,806

A North European painted armoire, 19th century and later decorated, with a molded arched cornice above a pair of panelled doors enclosing a shelf and rail, 58in. wide. (Christie's) $822

Art Deco mahogany veneer armoire, France, circa 1930, three-section curvilinear piece comprising a center section with two short open shelves about a cupboard with hinged drop door, 71in. long. (Skinner) $1,955

A French sang-de-boeuf painted armoire, early 19th century, with a molded overhanging cornice above a shell-carved frieze and a pair of panelled doors, 60in. wide. (Christie's) $1,512

Grain painted and decorated pine armoire, Scandinavia, circa 1815, the cornice molding with saw tooth patterning, two panelled doors opening to four shelves above two drawers, molded base and square feet, 72½in. high. (Skinner) $2,300

A South German walnut and inlaid armoire, 19th century, with a concave fronted cornice, above a pair of crossbanded and inlaid panel doors flanked by similar side sections, 77in. wide. (Christie's) $2,184

A North European walnut and marquetry armoire, early 19th century, decorated throughout with flowering vines, dated 1822 and with a monogram cartouche, with fielded panels inlaid with vases of flowers, 71in. wide. (Christie's) $1,899

French Provincial oak armoire, 19th century, the cased doors covered allover with foliage, fruit and birds, on scrolled feet, fitted with an apron drawer, 88in. high. (Skinner) $2,415

A polychrome painted pine armoire, Swiss, late 18th/early 19th century, boldly decorated overall with floral sprays, rocaille and scrolls, with a molded arched cornice inscribed *Johan Gryorg Arldo 1791*, 58in. wide. (Christie's) $1,848

A French mahogany and gilt-metal mounted breakfront armoire, late 19th/early 20th century, with an egg-and-dart, foliate molded cornice centered by a cartouche with musical trophy, 57in. wide. (Christie's) $1,554

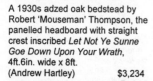

A 1930s adzed oak bedstead by Robert 'Mouseman' Thompson, the panelled headboard with straight crest inscribed *Let Not Ye Sunne Goe Down Upon Your Wrath*, 4ft.6in. wide x 8ft.
(Andrew Hartley) $3,234

Luigi Massoni, a large circular bed, designed 1969, for Poltrona Frau, the circular white vinyl covered frame with central sprung frame, with brown leather and chromed steel padded headboard, diameter 84in. (Christie's) $1,676

A good Empire highly figured mahogany sleigh bed, Boston circa 1840, each concave end with a reverse-scrolling crest joined by shaped rails, 6ft. 8in. long.
(Sotheby's) $9,600

An oak half tester bedstead, European, probably Northern France, late 17th/early 18th century, the canopy with a panelled roof with stylized floral carved decoration around a recessed central panel, 74in. wide.
(Bonhams) $6,900

A satinwood four-post bed, early 20th century, of George III style, inlaid overall with ebonized lines, the Gothic cornice with pale blue sunburst canopy, above a panelled headboard, supported by a pair of leaf-wrapped fluted columns, 72in. wide. (Christie's) $25,909

A mahogany and inlaid four poster bed, 19th century, in the Hepplewhite style, with molded cornice on ring turned and reeded knopped urn shaped columns with wheatear and foliate ornament, the canopy 61in. wide.
(Christie's) $5,790

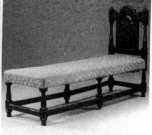

A child's late 19th century white painted iron folding cot, the brass headboard rails with finials to the painted openwork, 24in. wide.
(Woolley & Wallis) $355

One of a pair of late Victorian satinwood single beds, by Holland and Sons, each with a solid panelled head and footboard inlaid with geometric lines, each end with a Greek-key inlaid frieze with marquetry flowerheads, 44in. wide.
(Christie's) (Two) $10,363

A joined oak day bed, English, late 17th/early 18th century, the back with an arcaded panel flanked by turned baluster uprights, 66in. long.
(Bonhams) $2,070

An Anglo-Indian parcel-gilt silvered-metal day bed, probably circa 1880, the serpentine headboard surmounted by an urn finial, centered by a deity's mask above peacocks, 55in. wide.
(Christie's) $7,057

Full-size four-post bed, in curly maple. (Eldred's) $1,870

The Luman Reed fine and rare Federal brass-mounted, part-ebonized and highly figured mahogany bedstead, Duncan Phyfe, New York, circa 1820, 5ft. wide. (Sotheby's) $14,400

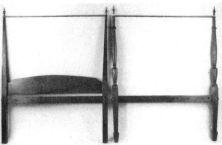

Antique American Sheraton bed, early 19th century, in mahogany with ornately carved acanthus head and foot posts, scrolled headboard, and pineapple carved post ends, 52in. across bolt holes.
(Eldred's) $4,290

Federal maple tester bed, New England, circa 1810, the vase and ring-turned foot posts continuing to tapering square legs and molded spade feet, 51in. wide.
(Skinner) $805

An oak tester bed, with carved panels, the headboard with applied figures, the free standing posts carved and fluted, altered to take a 4ft. 6in. mattress.
(Woolley & Wallis) $2,201

A carved hardwood and stained beechwood four poster bed, 19th century, composed of William IV carved hardwood posts, possibly Colonial, 19th century Italian, the canopy in two parts, 72in. wide.
(Christie's) $13,198

A Federal turned maple bedstead, 1810-1830, Virginia, the headposts and footposts with tapered tops above ball and reel-turned shafts with reeded balusters, 57in. wide.
(Christie's) $5,288

A walnut and stained beech four poster bed, 19th century, possibly Spanish, the canopy on four ring-turned uprights with finials, with pierced, scrolled and spindle ends and waved side rails, 64½in. wide.
(Christie's) $4,277

Red painted low post press bed, New England, early 19th century, the shaped headboard with original rails hinged for folding attached to the footposts, 49¾in. wide. (Skinner) $805

An oak cradle, early 20th century, carved with foliate scrolls and stylized leaves, with an arched hood, on rockers, 36in. long. (Christie's) $575

A green-painted maple and poplar folding bedstead, Pennsylvania, the shaped rectangular headboard flanked by turned reel-form finials, 4ft. 9in. wide. (Sotheby's) $920

Federal maple and birch tall post bed, New England, 19th century, the tapering pencil headposts flanking an arched headboard and joined by rails to reeded vase, 53½in. wide. (Skinner) $1,380

An oak bureau-bed, North Country, early 19th century, the front with faux mahogany-banded fall and four long drawers, the reverse with twin panelled doors enclosing an elm framed bed, 45in. wide. (Christie's) $3,680

A Regency mahogany child's bed, attributed to Butler, each corner with a turned column surmounted by brass finials, further surmounted by two collapsible arched canopy supports, joined by three metal struts, 26¼in. wide. (Christie's) $13,348

A Regency mahogany and caned cradle, the hooded cradle hung between turned and square section standard end supports joined by similar stretchers. (Christie's) $1,272

Jacobean carved oak tester bed, with molded cornice carved with elongated cabochons and leaf tips supported on a fluted column (one lacking). (Skinner) $2,760

An Anglo-Indian parcel-gilt metal-mounted four-poster bed, Western India, the head and footboard of serpentine shape, the headboard centered by an oval mirror, 90in. wide. (Christie's) $6,909

A Victorian mahogany library bookcase cabinet, the ogee cornice above two glazed doors enclosing four adjustable shelves, 121.5cm. wide. (Bristol) $2,254

A pair of mahogany book troughs, 20th century, in the George III style, each with a gadrooned shelf above a trough with Chinese fret-carved divisions, 37in. wide. (Christie's) $1,725

A Regency mahogany 'waterfall' open bookcase, the three shelves above a frieze with two drawers, on turned rope twist legs, 33½in. wide. (Woolley & Wallis) $5,410

Italian rococo style chinoiserie decorated open bookcase, late 19th century, of serpentine form with three shelves and cabriole legs, decorated with Chinese scenes on a green ground, 38in. wide. (Skinner) $690

A pair of mahogany open bookcases, 20th century, each with an open section flanked to either side by projecting fluted columns with later oak foliate-carved and mask capitals, 41in. wide. (Christie's) $1,809

A circular mahogany and checker line-inlaid revolving bookcase, 20th century, the radially veneered top above two tiers and vertical slats to the sides, on an X-frame support with castors, 22½in. wide. (Christie's) $575

Late Regency mahogany breakfront bookcase, early 19th century, with concave fronted cornice, the frieze carved with anthemion, 84in. wide. (Skinner) $7,475

A Victorian mahogany bookcase, the cushion molded frieze drawer with a hinged fall front and fitted interior with a leather-lined writing surface, 47in. wide. (Christie's) $904

George III style mahogany breakfronted secrétaire bookcase, the upper section fitted with four glazed doors, the lower section fitted with a sliding secrétaire drawer, 85in. wide. (Skinner) $8,050

A mid Victorian mahogany bookcase, 131cm. wide.
(Bonhams & Brooks) $1,694

A George III mahogany breakfront bookcase, circa 1770, the molded cornice above a pair of astragal glazed doors, flanked by a further pair, 90¾in. wide.
(Bonhams) $12,636

An oak three-tier Globe Wernike bookcase 87cm. wide.
(Bonhams & Brooks) $462

A Napoleon III ormolu-mounted boulle and ebonized glazed bibliothèque, circa 1855, surmounted by a serpentine pediment centered by a foliate cartouche, flanked to each side by a finial, 51in. wide.
(Christie's) $5,041

Charlotte Perriand, a painted aluminum, pine and mahogany room divider, designed 1953, chromatic scheme designed by Sonia Delaunay, executed by Ateliers Jean Prouve, for use in the Maison du Mexique dormitory of Cité Universitaire, 72in. wide.
(Christie's) $31,671

A classical mahogany bookcase, possibly Portsmouth, New Hampshire, 1825-1845, in three sections: the upper with rectangular carved crest above a plain frieze centered and flanked by inlaid rectangular reserves, 63in. wide.
(Christie's) $6,900

A Victorian mahogany breakfront library bookcase, the upper part with a molded overhanging recessed and stepped ogee cushion cornice, 108in. wide.
(Christie's) $9,953

A green painted and decorated four tier revolving bookcase, with circular graduated revolving open shelves divided by simulated books with leather spines, the base 22½in. diameter.
(Christie's) $7,238

A Victorian mahogany bookcase, of broken and bowed outline, with a molded cornice enclosed by three arched glazed panelled doors, 117in. wide.
(Christie's) $19,905

An oak revolving bookcase, early 20th century, of three quartered open tiers with slatted sides, on a cruciform base with castors, 23½in. square. (Christie's) $937

A Regency mahogany and fiddleback-mahogany bookcase, the rectangular top above three graduated tiers united by reeded S-scrolls with conforming central partition, 49¼in. wide. (Christie's) $7,631

An Edwardian walnut bookcase, 124cm. wide. (Bonhams & Brooks) $770

A Victorian oak and inlaid triple arched library bookcase, with foliate and paterae cresting surmounted by an urn finial and enclosed by glazed astragal panelled doors, 112in. wide. (Christie's) $18,999

A mahogany and boxwood-strung breakfront bookcase, late 19th century, the upper part with a molded cornice and trellis strung frieze fitted with adjustable shelves and enclosed by glazed astragal doors, 88in. wide. (Christie's) $7,238

A George IV rosewood dwarf open bookcase, the waved back gallery with patera to each end, above a rectangular top with beaded rim, above two adjustable shelves flanked by gadrooned sunken panels, 49¾in. wide. (Christie's) $8,177

A Continental walnut and brass mounted bibliothèque or side cabinet, 19th century, probably German, Biedermeier, in the Empire taste, 38¾in. wide. (Christie's) $4,343

A Victorian breakfront bookcase, the upper part with a molded cornice and fitted with adjustable shelves with projecting brackets, 81in. wide. (Christie's) $9,953

An Aesthetic Movement carved and inlaid walnut bookcase, New York, 1870-1880, the upper section with a central finial above a carved broken pitch pediment with gilt incised lines flanked by a spindle arcade, 75½in. wide. (Christie's) $14,100

An early Victorian mahogany bookcase with molded cornice, two glazed doors enclosing adjustable shelving, 50in. wide. (Andrew Hartley) $2,933

A companion pair of early 19th century mahogany and satinwood banded bookcases, part Regency and adapted, the upper parts with molded cornice and frieze, 41in. wide. (Christie's) $11,218

A Victorian figured mahogany chiffionier bookcase, the upper part with molded cornice fitted with four adjustable shelves enclosed by a pair of arched glazed doors, 45in. wide. (Canterbury) $3,564

A French pale green painted bookcase, early 20th century, with a rosette and guilloche carved frieze above a pair of wire grille doors flanked by fluted stiles with foliate corbels, 42in. wide. (Christie's) $658

An Italian walnut bookcase, 19th century, the upper section with an arched deep molded cornice, above a central open shelf section flanked by twin cartouche panelled doors with chicken wire, 68in. wide. (Christie's) $1,316

An early Victorian birch bookcase with a boldly beaded cornice above a pair of glazed doors and a scrolled foliate cresting above a pair of similar doors, 42¾in. wide. (Christie's) $2,184

A small 19th century French rosewood and kingwood open bookcase, with gilt metal mounts, the shaped top with leather covering over an open leather lined interior, 24½in. wide. (Andrew Hartley) $943

A Regency carved mahogany dwarf open bookcase, possibly Scottish, with rectangular overhanging top with a beaded edge and similar panelled frieze, 42¾in. wide. (Christie's) $4,705

Arts & Crafts oak bookcase, early 20th century, rectangular top on four-shelf bookcase, four D-shaped cutouts on canted side boards, 16¾in. long.(Skinner) $1,495

A mahogany bookcase-on-stand, George III and later, with a Chinese fretwork and rosette decorated swan neck pediment, dentil molded cornice and astragal glazed doors, 54½in. wide.
(Christie's) $1,427

A mahogany breakfront bookcase, 20th century, with a cushion molded cornice above four astragal glazed doors enclosing shelves, 96in. wide.
(Christie's) $1,974

Biedermeier maple and part-ebonized bookcase, circa 1820, the later arched cresting with open shelf and frieze drawer, 81in. high.
(Skinner) $4,600

A mahogany open bookcase, parts 19th century, with a molded and beaded cornice, the open section flanked by turned, tapering, foliate-headed columns, 60in. wide.
(Christie's) $2,856

A mahogany bookcase, early 20th century, the upper part with a molded cornice and fitted with adjustable shelves enclosed by four glazed astragal panelled doors, 84in. wide.(Christie's) $5,757

A good George III style satinwood, rosewood and harewood marquetry low bookcase, the arched back above three graduated open shelves and a panelled door inlaid with a vacant floral cartouche on a trellis ground, 67cm. wide.
(Bonhams) $3,388

A mahogany crossbanded and line-inlaid bookcase, 20th century, the molded arched cornice with large fan motif above two astragal glazed doors, 48½in. wide.
(Christie's) $1,645

An Empire mahogany brass inlaid bookcase, with an inlaid white marble top above a pair of glazed doors, between canted angles with brass mask headed tapered stiles, 60in. wide. (Christie's) $1,068

A mahogany library bookcase, late 19th/early 20th century, the upper section with a molded cornice and blind fret frieze, above a pair of geometrically astragal glazed doors, 56in. wide.
(Christie's) $1,809

A Victorian carved oak three tier buffet with two central drawers. (Academy) $352

An early 19th century Dutch mahogany bow-front klap buffet with boxwood stringing throughout, the double folding top opening to provide a splashback with shelves, 105cm. wide. (Bearne's) $1,287

A Victorian mahogany buffet, the mirrored gallery back with an arched pediment and fluted split column pilasters, 78in. wide. (Christie's) $1,191

A late Regency mahogany and ebony strung two tier buffet, the top tier with raised back and sides, rounded molded edge front on turned uptapering column supports, 45½in. wide. (Dreweatt Neate) $7,473

A French pine buffet à deux corps, early 19th century, the upper section with glazed scroll-carved doors and with panelled doors below, 54in. wide. (Christie's) $1,480

A William IV mahogany buffet, now with fixed top, the molded frieze on standard lotus carved and dual scroll end supports, 36in. wide. (Christie's) $1,990

Arts and Crafts oak server, circa 1915, in the style of the Shop of the Crafters, the whole rectangular canted form having a long mirror with arch on rectangular top, over two short drawers, 42in. wide. (Skinner) $1,265

A sycamore and marble buffet, designed by Franz Messner, circa 1900, marble top and back panel with single shelf above four shallow frieze drawers and two panelled doors, 45¼in. wide. (Christie's) $5,796

A French Provincial elm buffet, late 18th/early 19th century, the upper part with a molded arched cornice and frieze with stylized foliate stems with a central roundel, possibly Provençal, 60in. wide. (Christie's) $5,520

Queen Anne walnut bureau bookcase, early 18th century, molded cornice above mirrored door and slide, 31in. wide. (Skinner) $6,325

A 19th century mahogany and satinwood inlaid bureau bookcase, associated, 101cm. wide. (Bonhams) $2,910

A small yew wood bureau bookcase, late 20th century, with astragal glazed door enclosing shelves, 25¼in. wide. (Christie's) $263

A George III mahogany bureau bookcase, alterations and associated, 103cm. wide. (Bonhams) $1,701

A George III style mahogany bureau bookcase with dentil cornice, two astragal-glazed doors, 94cm. wide. (Bearne's) $3,146

Dutch Queen Anne style oak double-dome bookcase, composed of 18th century elements, 38in. wide. (Skinner) $5,750

A mid 18th century oak and mahogany cross-banded bureau bookcase with a flared cornice above a pair of panel doors, 37½in. (Anderson & Garland) $4,063

A good late George II mahogany bureau bookcase, circa 1750, minor losses, 113cm. wide. (Bonhams) $26,730

Centennial carved mahogany desk/bookcase, third quarter 19th century, swan's neck cresting over a pair of glazed mullioned doors, 29in. wide. (Skinner) $4,313

A George III mahogany bureau bookcase, the molded and dentil cornice with flower carved swan neck pediment, 51in. wide. (Andrew Hartley) $4,867

A George III mahogany bureau cabinet, of narrow proportions, with a molded dentil cornice and blind fret frieze, 34¼in. wide. (Christie's) $4,343

A Queen Anne walnut bureau cabinet, circa 1710, the scrolled pediment above a pair of fielded panelled doors, 96cm. wide.(Bonhams) $14,000

An Anglo Dutch walnut, checker-banded and marquetry double dome bureau cabinet, the upper part with a molded cornice and simulated dentil frieze, 46½in. wide. (Christie's) $12,719

A small George II Cuban mahogany bureau cabinet, the top with a cavetto molded cornice above a divided interior, enclosed by a rectangular door with a mirror panel, 31½in. wide.
(Woolley & Wallis) $6,160

A late 19th century lady's French rosewood bureau bookcase, the whole inlaid with marquetry of floral and leaf scroll form and with gilt brass moldings, 35in. wide. (Canterbury) $3,078

A Chinese-export black and two-tone gilt-lacquer bureau-cabinet, late 18th century, decorated overall with zig-zag patterns filled with scrolling foliage and vines, 31in. wide.
(Christie's) $145,905

A French ebonized and giltmetal mounted cylinder bureau, 20th century, with a glazed cabinet superstructure, the fall front with a tortoiseshell and brass-inlaid panel, 30in. wide.(Christie's) $1,554

A Dutch mahogany bureau bookcase, late 18th/early 19th century, the molded cornice above a pair of glazed doors enclosing two shelves and two drawers between stop-fluted quarter column angles, 45½in. wide.
(Christie's) $1,809

Late Victorian 'Sheraton Revival' mahogany and marquetry bureau-bookcase the carcase 18th century, crossbanded overall with tulipwood, the dentilled cornice above a pair of geometrically-glazed doors.
(Christie's) $12,110

A mahogany bureau bookcase, late 18th/19th century, the upper part with an angled molded cornice, fitted with adjustable shelves and enclosed by a pair of glazed arched astragal panel doors, 47in. wide. (Christie's) $3,454

The Thomas Powars Chippendale mahogany block-front desk-and-bookcase, signed *John Diamond, Boston*, circa 1782, in two sections, the upper with molded and dentil-carved broken pediment, 44¾in. wide. (Christie's) $101,500

A mahogany bureau bookcase, 19th century, crossbanded overall, the upper section with a molded cornice and a pair of astragal glazed doors, 42½in. wide. (Christie's) $3,192

A George III mahogany bureau bookcase, the upper section fitted with shelves enclosed by a pair of astragal glazed doors, on bureau with fitted interior, 3ft.4in. wide. (Brightwells) $7,200

A South German walnut, crossbanded and inlaid bureau cabinet, 18th century and later, in three sections, with renewal and restoration and re-veneering, 50in. wide. (Christie's) $2,467

A William and Mary walnut bureau-cabinet, featherbanded to the front, the molded cornice above a pair of shaped arched panelled doors with later plates, above a pair of candleslides enclosing a fitted interior, 42½in. wide. (Christie's) $26,696

A rosewood and brass-inlaid piano top bureau bookcase, early 19th century and later, converted from an upright piano, with a foliate-carved cornice and an inlaid frieze above glazed doors enclosing shelves, 51in. wide. (Christie's) $1,233

A Chippendale cherrywood desk-and-bookcase, Hartford or New London County, Connecticut, 1750-1770, upper part with rectangular top and molded broken swan's-neck pediment, 41¼in. wide. (Christie's) $18,800

An oak bureau bookcase, English, late 18th century, the upper section with Greek key molded cornice and a pair of arched panel doors, enclosing adjustable shelves, 42½in. wide. (Christie's) $5,851

An Italian walnut bureau cabinet, 20th century, of undulating outline, the upper part with a broken scroll arched pediment, fitted with shelves and drawers and enclosed by a pair of mirror panel doors, 42in. wide. (Christie's) $6,332

An Italian oak bureau bookcase, 20th century, with an arched molded cornice above a pair of glazed doors enclosing shelves, the lower section with a shaped panelled fall front, 43in. wide. (Christie's) $722

A fine Louis XVI style kingwood, tulipwood and marquetry inlaid bureau à cylindre, French, last quarter 19th century, 140cm. wide x 66cm. deep x 127cm. high.
(Bonhams & Brooks) $7,000

An oak Globe Wernicke bureau, bearing label 90cm. wide.
(Bonhams & Brooks) $231

A George III mahogany and boxwood strung bureau, 107cm. wide.
(Bonhams & Brooks) $3,700

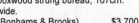

A mahogany and brass mounted cylinder bureau, late 19th/early 20th century, by Tozer, London in the Louis XVI style, the superstructure with pierced brass guilloche gallery and white veined marble top with brass borders, 44½in. wide.
(Christie's) $9,953

Chippendale carved tiger maple slant-lid desk, Massachusetts, 1760-80, the lid on a case of thumb-molded graduated drawers and a molded shaped bracket base with a central fan-carved pendant, 36in. wide.
(Skinner) $76,200

A Dutch mahogany and floral marquetry cylinder bureau, 18th century, in two sections, the top with cornucopiae and sprays flowers and pierced interlaced brass gallery with finials, 48in. wide.
(Christie's) $7,268

A Dutch walnut and floral marquetry bombé fronted bureau, 19th century, in two sections, the upper part with oval floral panels to the top, 53in. wide.
(Christie's) $10,997

A George III mahogany bureau, the rectangular top above a hinged slope, enclosing a fitted interior, 31in. wide.(Christie's) $3,634

A George III mahogany bureau, the sloping fall enclosing an architectural fitted interior, two short and three long drawers, on ogee bracket feet, 43¾in. wide.
(Christie's) $4,399

A Regency mahogany bureau, possibly Scottish, with pierced brass quatrefoil three-quarter gallery and panelled slope enclosing a fitted interior, 32in. wide. (Christie's) $1,990

A North Italian walnut bureau, first half 18th century, the molded rectangular top above a channelled writing-slope, above a serpentine frieze and three long panelled drawers, 51in. wide. (Christie's) $10,939

A German rosewood cylinder bureau, 19th century, with a scrolled shell-carved pediment above a pair of mirrored doors and panelled drawers and a panelled cylinder front, 47in. wide. (Christie's) $2,125

A South German walnut, crossbanded and marquetry bureau, 18th century and later, with a crossbanded top and sloping fall, veneered with trompe l'oeil cube inlay, 50in. wide. (Christie's) $4,399

A walnut bureau-on-stand, basically early 18th century, crossbanded overall, the rectangular fall-front above a drawer flanked by lopers, on a stand with club legs, 31½in. wide. (Christie's) $3,271

A George II walnut and feather banded bureau, circa 1730, the fall enclosing a fitted interior with two short and two long drawers below, on bracket feet, restorations, 36¼in. wide. (Bonhams) $11,057

A walnut veneered bureau, early 18th century, with some later re-veneering, probably Anglo Dutch, in two sections, the upper part with a sloping fall inset with a leather-lined panel to the reverse, on bracket feet, 38½in. wide. (Christie's) $8,686

A walnut bureau-on-stand, early 18th century and later, the feather and crossbanded fall enclosing a fitted interior, with a frieze drawer below, on later cabriole legs, 36½in. wide. (Christie's) $4,073

A North Italian walnut bureau, second quarter 18th century, Lombardy, decorated with shaped panels framed by scrolling channelled moldings, later rounded rectangular top, 46½in. wide. (Christie's) $24,193

Early 18th century walnut herringbone banded bureau, the fall front enclosing a fitted stepped interior of drawers, pigeon holes and well, over two short and two long drawers, with bracket feet, 36½in. (G A Key) $4,876

A rare Queen Anne highly figured maple desk-on-frame, Massachusetts, 1750-1770, in two parts, the upper section with a divided interior above a long drawer, the base with three short drawers, 30in. wide. (Sotheby's) $29,500

Chippendale walnut inlaid slant lid desk, coastal southern Massachusetts, 18th century, the compass inlaid lid, above a case of thumb-molded drawers, 36in. wide. (Skinner) $4,600

A North Italian fruitwood bureau, 19th century, with a panelled fall front (locked) and an arrangement of drawers below, 30¾in. wide. (Christie's) $1,208

Chippendale tiger maple slant-lid desk, New England, late 18th century, the slant lid opens to an interior of a central concave molded compartment with short drawers above and below, 36in. wide. (Skinner) $9,200

Oak drop front desk, attributed to Gustav Stickley, gallery top, veneered drop front, interior fitted with compartments over two half drawers, 32in. wide. (Skinner) $862

A George III mahogany bureau, with four cockbeaded drawers, raised on bracket feet, 41½in. (George Kidner) $2,656

George III mahogany bureau with fall flap revealing a fitted interior, four graduated long drawers under, on bracket feet, 39in. wide. (Ewbank) $2,640

An early George III walnut and feather strung bureau, the sloping fall enclosing a well fitted interior with drawers and pigeon holes, 30¼in. wide. (George Kidner) $2,988

Federal walnut inlaid slant lid desk, Pennsylvania, early 19th century, the lid and cockbeaded drawers outlined in stringing, 40in. wide.
(Skinner) $3,450

A Japanese ebonized and parquetry cylinder bureau, late 19th century, the upper section with a molded cornice and inlaid frieze and arrangement of pigeon holes, drawers, cupboard doors and letter slides, 41½in. wide.
(Christie's) $8,464

A Victorian cylinder top bureau with fitted satinwood interior and leather lined writing surface and two panelled doors under, 42½in. wide.
(Lloyds International) $1,470

A walnut and stained beech bureau-on-stand, 20th century, in the William and Mary style, the stand on turned tapering legs with bun feet, 29in. wide.
(Christie's) $605

Dutch Baroque burl-walnut slant-lid desk, 18th century, rectangular top over a slant-lid enclosing a fitted writing compartment, 45in. wide.
(Skinner) $4,830

A George III satinwood and marquetry cylinder bureau, the marquetry possibly of a later date, in the Sheraton style, crossbanded and inlaid with lines, the top with a laurel leaf border, 34¼in. wide.
(Christie's) $14,476

Federal wavy birch slant-lid desk, New Hampshire, early 19th century, the lid opens to a two-stepped interior above the case of drawers with cockbeaded surround, 37½.
(Skinner) $2,760

An Oriental carved, gilded, red and green-painted bureau, early 20th century, carved throughout with dragons, urns and Buddhist symbols, the fall front revealing an interior with drawers.
(Christie's) $840

A George III oak bureau, the cleated fall front revealing a fitted interior with drawers and pigeon holes around a serpentine panelled cabinet, 34in. wide.
(Christie's) $1,480

A mahogany and line-inlaid bowfronted dentist's cabinet, late 19th/early 20th century, the superstructure with a shaped cornice above three glazed cabinets, 41in. wide.
(Christie's) $4,523

A Victorian mahogany hanging cabinet, 77cm.
(Bonhams & Brooks) $326

A peach mirror-glass cabinet, English, 1930s, the rectangular top above three graduating frieze drawers, above a pair of cupboard doors, on ebonized plinth base, 18in. wide.(Christie's) $1,260

An Italian ebony and ivory cabinet on stand, in the Renaissance style, circa 1880, the cabinet with two cupboard doors, each decorated with a warrior in an arch, surrounded with military and flower trophies, 25in. wide.
(Christie's) $5,520

A Victorian walnut, marquetry and gilt-metal mounted dwarf side cabinet, with cavetto frieze enclosed by a pair of ebonized re-entrant panelled doors inlaid with sprays of marquetry heightened in harewood, 54in. wide.
(Christie's) $3,619

A walnut and crossbanded cabinet-on-chest, early 18th century and later, the upper part with a molded cornice and enclosed by a pair of glazed astragal doors with cushion moldings, 41in. wide.
(Christie's) $6,876

A Spanish gilt-metal mounted, tortoiseshell, horn, ebonized and parquetry table cabinet-on-stand, 19th century, decorated overall with engraved plaques with hunting scenes and animals,45½in. wide.
(Christie's) $9,176

A Victorian plum pudding mahogany side cabinet/press, the molded top above two foliate-carved panelled doors flanked by rosette-mounted fluted stiles, 53¾in. wide.
(Christie's) $1,533

Daniel Cottier, elaborately decorated cabinet, circa 1890, the whole intricately painted and gilded with stylized palmettes, flowers, birds, butterflies, griffins and grotesques, 58¼in. wide.
(Sotheby's) $50,750

A Dutch walnut bombé cabinet, 18th century, the undulating molded arched cornice centered by a cresting with rocaille scrolls around a bird, 80in. wide.
(Christie's) $5,429

A mahogany and ebony inlaid side cabinet, 84cm. wide.
(Bonhams & Brooks) $4,466

A Continental painted and découpage applied cabinet on stand, mid 19th century, 65cm. wide x 122cm. high.
(Bonhams & Brooks) $1,260

A Louis XVI style tulipwood and marquetry side cabinet, by Forest, with a chamfered rectangular ormolu-molded upper case centrally fitted with a circular enamel dial above seven various sized drawers, 41in. wide.
(Christie's) $12,650

A pair of green japanned and simulated bamboo side cabinets, 20th century, each with a concave shaped green variegated marble top with a frieze drawer above a pair of doors, 25½in. wide.
(Christie's) $4,430

An English parcel-gilt, ebonized and porcelain-mounted side cabinet, circa 1860, the upper part with a stepped pediment above a breakfront frieze, carved with egg-and-dart, above a pair of panelled doors, each inset with three porcelain panels, 54in. wide.
(Christie's) $14,352

A Dutch William and Mary olivewood, ebony, marquetry and parquetry cabinet-on-stand, the rectangular molded cornice above a pair of doors, each centered by a flower vase, 70½in. wide.
(Christie's) $16,685

A Napoleon III concave fronted rosewood collector's cabinet, with a stepped top, cushion molded drawer and a pair of molded and panelled cupboards below, 44in. wide. (Christie's) $2,555

A late 19th century North European walnut cabinet, carved with figures and sea monsters in high relief, 210cm. wide.
(Bonhams & Brooks) $1,776

An Italian carved walnut and inlaid cabinet-on-stand, the cabinet late 17th/early 18th century and later, the stand of a later date, the cabinet 26½in. wide.
(Christie's) $4,229

A Napoleon III ormolu-mounted marquetry and kingwood side cabinet, circa 1860, surmounted by a serpentine stepped black marble top, the freize centered by an acanthus leaf, 68½in. wide.
(Christie's) $15,122

A rosewood and ebonised dwarf side cabinet, early 19th century, with a pair of silk lined brass grille doors flanked by turned columns, on turned feet, restorations, 32½in. wide. (Christie's) $3,290

A French Provincial walnut and elm buffet à deux corps, 19th century, the upper part with a molded cornice and enclosed by a pair of panel doors with mulberry like veneers and heart shaped inlay to the frieze, 62½in. wide.
(Christie's) $4,229

A pair of early Victorian rosewood small side cabinets, each with a later rectangular gray-veined white marble top and three-quarter brass gallery and later giltwood molding, above a brass trellis-panelled door, 18in. wide.(Christie's) $6,360

A walnut and burr-walnut cabinet-on-chest, the base basically 18th century, the molded rectangular cornice, above a pair of doors, enclosing a later fitted interior, 37¼in. wide.
(Christie's) $8,722

A late Louis XVI brass-mounted bureau à cylindre, late 18th century, the rectangular cornice above a plain frieze and a pair of glass-panelled doors, 50in. wide.
(Christie's) $14,182

An Edwardian walnut folio cabinet, the panelled front with pierced brass hinges and brass handles to each end, on an A-frame support, 58in. wide.(Christie's) $1,948

A Victorian oak and brass-bound military cabinet-on-chest, with a rosette and guilloche carved frieze concealing two shallow drawers and fielded panelled cupboards below, 40in. wide.
(Christie's) $4,606

A late Victorian walnut and line inlaid pier cabinet, 59cm. wide.
(Bonhams & Brooks) $770

A late Victorian mahogany filing cabinet, in three sections, with an egg-and-dart molded cornice, each section with a tambour front and enclosing eight numbered drawers, 123in. wide.(Christie's) $1,363

A Regency ormolu-mounted mahogany and ebonized side cabinet, the superstructure with three graduated shelves, supported by Egyptian herm pilasters, 32½in. wide. (Christie's) $17,262

A French kingwood, marquetry and ormolu mounted serpentine side cabinet, early 20th century decorated throughout with flowers and foliage within scrolled borders and with a red variegated marble top, 38in. wide.
(Christie's) $1,417

A Japanese lacquer cabinet-on-stand, the cabinet late 18th/19th century, applied with engraved copper angles, hinges and keyplates with panels of prunus blossom and flowers, cabinet 36¾in. wide.
(Christie's) $5,921

A French ormolu-mounted amaranth, burr maple and parquetry bonheur-du-jour, in the Louis XVI style, circa 1890, the upper-structure surmounted by a breakfront brèche rose marble top, 37¼in. wide.
(Christie's) $9,200

A walnut crossbanded and feather-banded cabinet-on-chest, late 17th/early 18th century and later, the upper part with a molded cornice fitted with a cushion frieze map drawer, 49¼in. wide.
(Christie's) $4,229

An oak cabinet, designed by Sir Alfred Waterhouse, late 19th/early 20th century, with rectangular top and molded recessed fronts with rosettes above a pair of panel doors, and two other matching of a later date, 52½in. wide.
(Christie's) $1,522

A French ebonized brass inlaid and scarlet-tortoiseshell veneered side cabinet, 19th century, in the manner of Boulle, with projecting canted corners inset with a white marble top and inlaid frieze, 32in. wide. (Christie's) $1,817

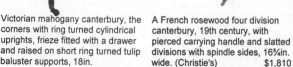

Victorian mahogany canterbury, the corners with ring turned cylindrical uprights, frieze fitted with a drawer and raised on short ring turned tulip baluster supports, 18in.
(G.A. Key) $1,668

A French rosewood four division canterbury, 19th century, with pierced carrying handle and slatted divisions with spindle sides, 16¾in. wide. (Christie's) $1,810

A Victorian ebonized canterbury, late 19th century, the divided superstructure with turned supports and a pierced handhold, 16¾in. wide. (Sotheby's) $805

A Victorian walnut, burr-walnut and thuyawood-banded canterbury whatnot, the upper tier with a fret-carved three-quarter gallery, on slender turned foliate-carved supports, 23½in. wide.
(Christie's) $1,151

A late Regency mahogany four division canterbury, with slatted open compartments with a carrying handle, on ring-turned supports and conforming legs, 17¾in. wide.
(Christie's) $2,280

A small Victorian walnut canterbury whatnot, the upper tier with a low fret-carved gallery supported by spiral carved uprights and with a three division canterbury below, 18in. wide. (Christie's) $1,068

A walnut canterbury, gallery back over top tier supported by pierced supports over magazine rack above single drawer raised on carved supports. (Academy) $1,312

A Victorian ebonized and burr walnut canterbury whatnot, the inlaid rectangular top on turned fluted supports over three divisions and single drawer, 66cm. wide.
(Bristol) $659

A mahogany four division canterbury, 20th century, with a pierced carrying handle and drawer, on square tapering legs, 18in. wide.
(Christie's) $361

An oak corner armchair, English, late 18th century, with flattened horse-shoe shaped armrest and column supports with pierced·vase splats. (Christie's) $2,260

A mid 18th century mahogany corner armchair, with shaped splats, the drop in seat frame to a frieze altered from a night commode fitting, a central cabriole leg.
(Woolley & Wallis) $720

A George III elm and burr elm corner armchair, the outswept scroll arms above two pierced vertical splats. (Cheffins) $380

Queen Anne cherry roundabout chamber chair, southeastern New England, circa 1740-60, the shaped crest rail continuing to scrolled arms on vase and ring-turned supports. (Skinner) $4,312

Painted corner chair, New England, late 18th/early 19th century, the curving arms with scrolled terminals and an attached shaped crest above a rush seat, 32¼in. high. (Skinner) $1,265

Maple and cherry commode corner chair, New England, early 19th century, the curving arm with scrolled handholds and a shaped crest above a molded seat rail and deeply shaped skirt. (Skinner) $2,300

Renaissance Revival carved walnut corner armchair, circa 1880, elaborately carved with seraphs, dolphins, and foliage, on circular legs. (Skinner) $690

Maple corner chair, New England, late 18th/early 19th century, the arms with scrolled terminals and a shaped crest over scrolled horizontal splats, 30½in. high. (Skinner) $1,610

A late Victorian mahogany corner armchair with a shaped, foliate-carved and overscrolled central high-back, rope-twist spindles and square drop-in seat. (Christie's) $1,295

307

A Victorian oak corner chair.
(Bonhams & Brooks) $370

English Provincial elmwood and ash corner chair, with U-shaped arm, open work splats, slip seat, and circular turned legs.
(Skinner) $1,265

A good George III style walnut corner desk chair.
(Bonhams & Brooks) $1,001

A Chippendale mahogany corner armchair, mid-Atlantic States, 1760-1780, the shaped crest above a bowed armrail continuing to outscrolling grips above column-turned supports centering solid vasiform splats.
(Christie's) $4,700

A Queen Anne carved walnut corner chair, Philadelphia, 1740-1760, the bowed crestrail with downward scrolling arms with knuckled grips over molded and shaped supports, 33in. high.
(Christie's) $68,500

A Queen Anne carved cherrywood corner chair, Connecticut, 1750-1770, the shaped crest above a concave armrail continuing to outscrolling grips above column and ring-turned stiles centering solid inverted baluster splats.
(Christie's) $18,400

A George II mahogany corner desk chair, the shaped rounded toprail with outscrolled arms, above three vase-shaped splats and turned arm supports. (Christie's) $8,177

A Chippendale mahogany corner chair, Boston, 1760-1780, the notched crest above shaped armrails continuing to outscrolling grips over column-turned supports centering pierced interlaced splats.
(Christie's) $10,925

American Chippendale mahogany corner chair, late 18th century, with u-shaped cresting, raised on cabriole legs ending in later claw and ball feet.
(Skinner) $1,610

Two of a set of five Victorian balloon back dining chairs, the open channelled frame with pierced and scrolled bar back, cabriole front legs and peg feet. (Andrew Hartley) (Five) $695

Two of a set of eight Regency mahogany dining-chairs, comprising six side chairs and two open armchairs, each with curved tablet toprail between reeded uprights. (Christie's) (Eight) $7,268

Two of a set of eight Regency mahogany dining-chairs, comprising six side chairs and two open armchairs, each with curved and shaped foliate-wreathed tablet top rail. (Christie's) (Eight) $9,085

Two of a set of nine George IV mahogany dining-chairs, by Gillows, the craftsman T.Bradley, each with heavily reeded frame, the serpentine padded back and the seat covered in green leather, on ring-turned tapering legs. (Christie's) (Nine) $30,889

Two of a set of six George III mahogany chairs, including an elbow chair, in the Sheraton style with stringing, curved top rail, reeded bar back. (Andrew Hartley) (Six) $1,251

Two of a set of six George III mahogany chairs, the open bar backs with panelled top rail and similar tapering uprights with pointed finials. (Andrew Hartley) (Six) $778

One of a set of four chairs designed by Harry Bertioa, with bent and welded steel wire mesh seats on steel supports.
(Andrew Hartley) (Four) $571

Two of a set of six Victorian walnut balloon back dining chairs, the waisted backs with shell carved crest above 'C' and 'S' scroll infill.
(Bristol)   (Six) $1,963

One of a set of seven George III mahogany chairs, the arched crest over pierced fan shaped splat, on square tapering legs joined by stretchers, including an elbow chair.
(Andrew Hartley) (Seven)
$3,454

Two of a set of six George IV solid rosewood and caned dining chairs, each curved overscrolled top-rail above a roundel centered foliate-carved horizontal splat.
(Christie's)   (Six) $3,167

Two of a set of four Victorian walnut side chairs, the sloping upholstered backs with a panel outline and floral crests, stamped Gillow, circa 1875.
(Woolley & Wallis)(Four) $941

A Federal carved mahogany side chair stamped by Stephen Badlam (1751-1815), Dorchester Lower Mills, Massachusetts, 1790-1800, the arched molded crestrail with foliate-carved ears above a shield-shaped splat.
(Christie's) $8,625

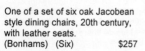

One of a set of six oak Jacobean style dining chairs, 20th century, with leather seats.
(Bonhams)   (Six) $257

Pair of balloon back Windsor side chairs, Pennsylvania, circa 1860, the chair back stencil decorated with basket of fruit on the crest above the vase splat.
(Skinner) $460

One of a set of four Victorian mahogany framed upholstered dining chairs, with turned legs and ceramic castors.
(Bonhams)   (Four) $186

A Regency blue-painted and parcel-gilt Officer's chair, the serpentine toprail above a rectangular padded back with reeded border and a pair of lion masks, above a padded loose seat.
(Christie's) $8,343

Two of a set of six Victorian mahogany balloon back dining chairs with cover over seats on cabriole legs.
(Thomson Roddick & Medcalf)
(Six) $1,305

A Queen Anne carved mahogany side chair, Boston, 1740-1750, the arched crestrail centering a lobed and scalloped shell above a solid vase-shaped splat, 39½in. high.
(Christie's) $27,600

One of a set of six Victorian mahogany dining chairs, with curved crest on bar back, overstuffed seats on turned tapering front legs, stamped *T Wilson*, London.
(Andrew Hartley) (Six) $616

Two fancy painted side chairs, Salem, Massachusetts, circa 1815, the tablet crest paint-decorated with landscapes above a guilloche and band backrails flanked by molded and ring-turned stiles, 34in. high.
(Christie's) $6,325

Joined pine and maple 'Great Chair', Northern Europe, 1681-1730, the rectangular fielded-panel back above the plank seat and rectangular rail over block and baluster-turned front legs.
(Skinner) $1,150

One of a set of four Victorian mahogany dining chairs, curved crest on scroll and leaf carved bar back.
(Andrew Hartley) (Four) $893

Two of a set of six George III mahogany and inlaid chairs with scrolled uprights and curved crest, bar back centered by a roundel.
(Andrew Hartley)(Six) $3,234

One of a set of six Victorian walnut balloon back dining chairs with arched crest, scrolled bar back, overstuffed seat, raised on cabriole front legs with pad feet.
(Andrew Hartley)(Six) $1,040

Chippendale cherry upholstered open armchair, Connecticut, 1765-75, the serpentine crest above upholstered arms joined to curving arm supports flanking a tight seat. (Skinner) $20,700

A pair of Indian parcel-gilt silvered-color metal throne arm-chairs, circa 1880, flanked to each side by a padded arm rest supported by a deer, 31in. wide. (Christie's) $22,080

A good mid Victorian walnut and beadwork nursing chair. (Bonhams & Brooks) $431

A mahogany tub desk chair, late 19th century, with a leather upholstered and deep buttoned top-rail with a spindle back, horse-hair padded seat. (Christie's) $1,363

Two of a set of four central European antler chairs, 19th century, comprising a pair of armchairs and a pair of side chairs, the padded seats covered in deer skin. (Christie's) (Four) $10,845

A Rococo-Revival painted and gilded cast-iron centripedal armchair, patented by Thomas E. Warren, 1849, manufactured by the American Chair Company, Troy, New York, circa 1850, 44in. high. (Christie's) $17,625

A Federal mahogany lolling chair, Massachusetts, 1790-1810, the serpentine crest above a canted rectangular upholstered back over shaped arms, 43¾in. high. (Christie's) $10,575

Maurice Dufrêne, bergére, circa 1913, mahogany, the U-shaped frame with scrolling arm rests, shell shaped back, 86cm. (Sotheby's) $6,960

A William IV mahogany upholstered open armchair, the deep buttoned back with a foliate cresting and with scrolled lotus-carved open padded arms. (Christie's) $1,447

An upholstered bergère designed by Henry van de Velde, 1902, horseshoe form, arched seat rail. (Christie's) $28,964

An early Victorian rosewood armchair. (Bonhams & Brooks) $181

A Louis XV beechwood bergère, adapted, probably from a canapé, cabriole legs and on scrolling feet, one side later. (Christie's) $2,336

A Louis XV pale-green and white painted and parcel-gilt bergère, by Ponce Gérard, with channelled frame, arched back and waved seat-rail, on cabriole legs. (Christie's) $12,513

A pair of fruitwood bergères, designed by Leon Jallot, circa 1920, each with curving padded back above squab cushion within foliate carved frame, on square channelled uprights. (Christie's) $5,880

A Napoleon III walnut child's fauteuil, the toprail centered by a foliate and floral spray to the center with a medallion with coronet, 26½in. high. (Christie's) $943

An Italian giltwood armchair, circa 1740, Venice, the cartouche-shaped frame with central scallop-shaped and scrolling acanthus, rockwork and C-scrolls. (Christie's) $13,348

A Louis XVI cream-painted bergère l'oreille, by Jacques Lechartier, with channelled frame, on a stop-fluted turned tapering legs headed by square patera panels. (Christie's) $2,836

A walnut upholstered cassirer armchair, designed by Henry van de Velde, 1897/98, curved back, shaped arms and seat rail. (Christie's) $13,630

English Provincial rush and oak armchair, 19th century, with tub shaped backrest above a slip seat on square tapered legs.
(Skinner) $1,035

A pair of Tyrolean antler armchairs, circa 1890, each formed from interlocking antlers, with an arched back and a pair of arm supports, with fur-upholstered cushions.
(Christie's) $7,350

A late Victorian prie dieu chair, the mahogany show frame with trellis and floral needlework upholstery, the sprung seat on front turned legs with castors.
(Woolley & Wallis) $287

A William IV walnut framed salon chair in green velvet covering, arched button upholstered back, open padded arms on scroll and flower carved supports.
(Andrew Hartley) $1,223

A lounge chair and ottoman designed by Charles Eames, with bent plywood shells in rosewood veneer, on blackened and polished cast aluminum base.
(Andrew Hartley) $2,536

A Victorian walnut framed nursing chair, arched padded back with pierced and carved scrolling foliate surmount, overstuffed seat.
(Andrew Hartley) $500

An early Victorian mahogany reclining easy armchair, with a shaped button back, part padded arms with lotus scrolled terminals and a padded seat with a hinged footrest.
(Christie's) $822

An Anglo-Indian metal-mounted armchair, in the 17th century style, circa 1920, the rectangular arched back with an oval padded center, flanked to each side by a scrolled arm support.
(Christie's) $5,329

A carved painted chair in the form of a lobster, early 20th century, the hinged back and seat incorporating upholstered padded panels.
(Christie's) $34,960

An Anglo-Indian metal-mounted armchair, circa 1890, the trefoil back centered by two oval medallions, the serpentine shaped padded seat flanked to each side by a lion. (Christie's) $2,590

High-back easy chair, designed by Borge Mogensen, 1956, Denmark, oak frame with cane seat, adjustable. (Skinner) $1,035

A late Victorian ebonized tub chair, together with another late Victorian chair. (Bonhams) $125

A Victorian mahogany framed invalid's chair, the curved caned back with arched crest, scrolled downswept padded arm, upholstered seat and adjustable foot rest.
(Andrew Hartley) $995

One of a pair of late Victorian tub armchairs, each with a square back, out-turned arms and padded seat, on turned tapering legs with castors.
(Christie's) (Two) $1,480

A mahogany caned bergère, 19th century, reeded frame, with caned back, seat and sides, flanked by padded arms on reeded baluster supports.(Christie's) $2,168

A mahogany and leather-upholstered open armchair, 19th century, with a rectangular back, part padded arms, with foliate-carved arm supports and foliate cabriole legs with hairy paw feet.
(Christie's) $3,948

A William IV mahogany and upholstered easy armchair, with a deep buttoned padded back and out-turned arms, with foliate and scroll-carved supports.
(Christie's) $1,480

Oak and cane spindle armchair, America, circa 1925, wide even crest rail and curved arms with woven cane panels over nine vertical back and side spindles.
(Skinner) $1,725

An oak and elm primitive child's chair, possibly Welsh, 18th century, the solid back with pierced motif at the top, the arm rests with twin splats to either side pierced with hearts. (Christie's) $1,948

An oak panel back armchair, Warwickshire, late 17th century, with an arched toprail, carved with the date *1667*, above an arcaded panel filled with stylized flowers. (Christie's) $4,250

An elm child's armchair, North Country, 19th century, with solid arched back, flattened arms, solid angled seat and sides extending to feet. (Christie's) $265

A rosewood chair, circa 1900, in the Arts and Crafts style. (Bonhams & Brooks) $216

A pair of mid Victorian caned open armchairs, by Gillows, each with square caned back and seat on an X-frame centered by a patera and joined by turned baluster stretchers. (Christie's) $3,997

Black-painted comb-back Windsor armchair, New England, circa 1810, with serpentine cresting and bamboo turnings. (Skinner) $4,025

A fruitwood, elm and ash Windsor armchair, Buckinghamshire, mid 19th century, with shaped bar toprail and central vertical splat pierced with a roundel-centered star motif. (Christie's) $1,070

A cedar and oak panel back armchair, English, the inlaid panel 17th century, with a molded toprail and channelled frieze, above a marquetry panel depicting stylized flowers. (Christie's) $2,921

Robin Day, a metal, plywood and leather elbow chair, designed 1951, specifically for use in the Royal Festival Hall, the curving panel back with shallow elbow rests, of rosewood-faced plywood. (Christie's) $4,098

A Queen Anne walnut open armchair, circa 1710, the double scrolled top rail and vase shaped back continuing to shaped downswept "shepherd's crook" arms. (Bonhams) $3,949

An oak panel back armchair, English, late 17th century, the profusely carved back with an arcaded lozenge and roundel filled design centered with a crown and Tudor rose. (Christie's) $5,667

A yew-wood primitive armchair, Welsh or Irish, late 18th / 19th century, the rectangular slatted back with bar toprail, the outswept arms with scroll terminals. (Christie's) $2,496

Painted slat-back armchair, Delaware River Valley, last half 18th century, old black paint, replaced rush seat. (Skinner) $2,990

Ludwig Mies van der rohe, a chromed tubular steel armchair, MR20, designed 1927, manufactured by Berliner Metallgewerbe and Josef Müller and Bamberg Metallwerkstätten prior to 1931. (Christie's) $9,315

An oak high back armchair, English, late 17th century, with a molded toprail and arched cresting surmounted by later finials. (Christie's) $2,657

An early Victorian burr-elm, cedar and burr-yew open armchair, the cartouche shaped solid back above an oval dark green leather covered drop-in seat, flanked by shepherd's crook arms, on cabriole legs. (Christie's) $5,451

An oak open armchair, probably Welsh, early 18th century, with an arched toprail, inset with a beech tablet inscribed *R.I. 1742* above a chamfered panel with line inlaid arch. (Christie's) $19,481

A Regency ormolu-mounted ebonised open armchair, with a reeded and panelled frame, the back with later scrolled foliate handle, with a caned seat, on sabre legs. (Christie's) $3,997

An oak turner's chair, English, 17th century.
(Bonhams & Brooks) $308

One of a set of six late Victorian beech and elm tub chairs.
(Bonhams & Brooks)
(Six) $518

A mid 19th century ash and elm Windsor chair, distressed.
(Bonhams & Brooks) $444

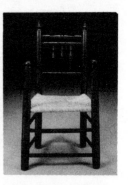

A yew and elm low splat back Windsor armchair, Nottinghamshire, mid 19th century, the pierced splat and turned spindles joining a saddle seat, on ring turned legs.
(Bonham's) $1,540

One of two pairs of Dutch walnut, beechwood and marquetry inlaid armchairs.(Bonhams & Brooks)
(Four) $1,260

An oak turned and joined great chair, Plymouth County, Massachusetts, 1715-1730, the flame and ring finials above turned and incised stiles, rush seat, on cylindrical legs joined by double box stretchers, 38¾in. high.
(Christie's) $8,050

One of a set of four ash and elm low hoop back Windsor chairs, Buckinghamshire, early 19th century, including a pair of armchairs, each with a gothic tracery back and saddle seat.
(Bonham's) (Four) $2,772

A mahogany armchair, designed by Henry van de Velde for the Galerie Arnold, Dresden, circa 1905, open slat back, rectangular carrying handle, upholstered seat, shaped front legs. (Christie's) $6,815

Carved and painted bannister-back armchair, New England, late 18th century, the scrolled, carved, and pierced crest above five split bannisters flanked by bulbous finials. (Skinner) $10,350

318

Painted sack-back Windsor chair,
Massachusetts, late 18th century,
old surface with brown paint and
yellow striping.
(Skinner) $68, 500

A good William IV oak desk chair.
(Bonhams & Brooks) $755

A yew and ash highback Windsor
armchair, Yorkshire, mid 19th
century, the hoop back and pierced
splat flanked by turned spindles.
(Bonham's) $924

The Waln-Large family Queen
Anne carved walnut armchair,
Philadelphia, 1740-1760, the
serpentine crest centring a carved
shell flanked by double volutes
above rounded and shaped stiles,
42in. high.
(Christie's) $1,982,500

A Consulat mahogany fauteuil by
Georges Jacob, with curved tablet
toprail, above a pierced horizontal
splat, with down swept arms.
(Christie's) $4,672

A Federal mahogany armchair,
Massachusetts, 1795-1810, the
molded shield-shaped back above
three banisters, the center with
flared and pierced upper section
over a carved rosette.
(Christie's) $2,530

An Empire mahogany fauteuil de
bureau, the curved and panelled
back with a central patera, flanked
by palmettes.
(Christie's) $2,452

A Régence elm fauteuil, Liège, the
serpentine-shaped pierced back
with four shaped splats, the toprail
with a lappeted foliate and scaled
cartouche, 39in. high.
(Christie's) $7,167

One of a matched pair of elm and
beech open armchairs, East Anglia,
early 19th century, each with a solid
seat and square tapering legs tied
by stretchers.
(Bonham's)   (Two) $431

One of a set of six Regency mahogany chairs including an elbow chair, brass inlaid curved top rail with scrolled surmount and carved with scrolling foliage.
(Andrew Hartley)(Six) $3,190

Federal birch carved armchair, probably New England, circa 1790-1800, the rectangular beaded crest above three shaped incised splats on panelled beaded stiles.
(Skinner) $805

Fine 16th century oak elbow chair, the back and frieze elaborately carved with twining foliage and berries and the two arm rests supported by linen fold panels.
(G.A. Key) $2,433

A 19th century oak and mixed woods cottage armchair with a spindle back, bowed arms, solid seat, turned legs on an H-stretcher.
(Thomson Roddick & Medcalf) $261

Windsor writing armchair, Connecticut, circa 1780, with single drawer under writing surface, old refinish with traces of original colour. (Skinner) $2,070

An unusual mahogany and brass-mounted armchair, 19th century, with curved spindle top-rail and brass splayed uprights, on stylized foliate ring-turned uprights.
(Christie's) $1,288

An Edwardian painted satinwood elbow chair, the shield back and pierced waisted splat painted with flowers, leaves and centered by a miniature portrait of a lady.
(Andrew Hartley) $903

L. & J.G. Stickley oak armchair, Fayetteville, New York, circa 1914, model no. 1352, wide curved horizontal crest rail over two narrow back rails, shaped flat arms with through front leg posts.
(Skinner) $345

A painted Windsor armchair, the raked hoop back with incurving arm supports, saddle seat, on turned front legs joined by H stretcher, late 18th/early 19th century.
(Andrew Hartley) $924

A Victorian mahogany revolving desk chair, with a curved top-rail, scrolled arm terminals and pierced shaped splats, above a circular seat. (Christie's) $1,446

A pair of stained beech and leather upholstered open armchairs, late 19th century, each with foliate swan neck finials and curved bars to the back. (Christie's) $691

A Charles II walnut armchair, the twin panel caned back frame pierced and carved with foliage and rosettes, a carved 'Crown and Boys' crest, on turned feet. (Woolley & Wallis) $941

Painted continuous arm maple and ash brace-back Windsor chair, Rhode Island or Connecticut, late 18th century, the incised bowed crest over thirteen turned spindles and two braces, 35in. high. (Skinner) $3,105

Two George III mahogany Lancashire elbow chairs, the spindle backs with pierced shaped crests. (Woolley & Wallis) $1,360

Painted slat-back armchair, New England, circa 1750-80, the four arched slats joining ring-turned stiles surmounted by ball finial, 46in high. (Skinner) $1,610

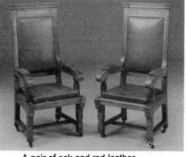

An oak chairman's chair, the back carved with the Royal Coat of Arms, on square tapered legs. (Tennants) $5,445

A pair of oak and red-leather upholstered high-back chairs, early 20th century, each with a molded and panelled top rail, a padded back and padded open arms with scrolled terminals. (Christie's) $167

A Continental carved beechwood and decorated fauteuil de bureau, Italian or French Provincial, with curved bar top-rail and scallop shell splat. (Christie's) $815

One of a set of four Victorian carved oak hall chairs, in the Gothic taste, each rectangular panelled back with pointed arched tracery and cusp and trefoil ornaments.
(Christie's) (Four) $2,353

A pair of Victorian mahogany hall chairs.
(Bonhams & Brooks) $181

A pair of mid Victorian mahogany hall chairs, cartouche shaped carved backs, on carved and turned front legs.(Wintertons) $392

One of a set of eight early Victorian carved mahogany hall chairs, each foliate cartouche shaped back with berries and foliate scrolls centred by shield panels.
(Christie's) (Eight) $8,142

Two of a set of four mid-19th century mahogany hall chairs, the arched waisted solid backs each carved with a crest in a roundel.
(Bearne's) (Four) $2,359

Carlo Bugatti, hall chair, circa 1900, walnut, constructed as a series of circular and geometric forms, the whole inlaid with bone, yellow metal and copper stringing with geometric motifs, 99.5cm.
(Sotheby's) $13,050

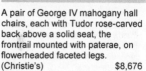

A pair of George IV mahogany hall chairs, each with Tudor rose-carved back above a solid seat, the frontrail mounted with paterae, on flowerheaded faceted legs.
(Christie's) $8,676

Two of a set of six late Victorian oak hall chairs, carved throughout with flowers, oak leaves and ivy, each with an arched panel depicting a saint, and a panelled seat.(Christie's)(Six) $3,896

A pair of mid Victorian oak hall chairs, with shaped carved backs, plank seats and turned legs.
(Bonhams) $277

A George III mahogany open arm library chair, of Gainsborough design, with stuff-over re-entrant cartouche shaped back and padded splayed scroll arm supports.
(Christie's) $4,935

Fine Regency brass-mounted mahogany leather upholstered library chair, circa 1825, with bell-shaped back and enclosed arms, above a tufted loose cushion seat and plain frieze.
(Skinner) $2,645

A Victorian mahogany library armchair, upholstered in button-down leather with scroll back and padded seat, with padded splayed arm supports.
(Christie's) $3,680

A mahogany and caned library bergère, late 19th/early 20th century, inlaid throughout with boxwood and ebonized lines with a rectangular back and caned arms with scrolled terminals and tapering reeded supports.
(Christie's) $2,893

Regency caned mahogany library chair, early 19th century, with tufted leather seat on reeded saber legs, on casters.(Skinner) $2,760

A Regency mahogany library and reading bergère, with reeded and curved caned back and padded arm supports with later solid seat and cushions.
(Christie's) $6,360

A Regency mahogany library bergère, with reeded frame, caned back, sides and seat with button-down leather cushions and padded arm supports.
(Christie's) $2,895

A Regency simulated rosewood and brass embellished library bergère, the curved top-rail with roundel ornament, caned back and sides, with ball finials and caned seat with button-down leather squab. (Christie's) $5,790

A George IV mahogany reclining library armchair, with adjustable slatted back, with radiating turned uprights to the arm supports.
(Christie's) $2,353

A mahogany Yorkshire knitting chair, the winged panel back with arched top rail, scrolled arms on turned supports, solid seat, 19th century.
(Andrew Hartley) $1,668

Inlaid oak rocking chair, America, circa 1910, arched curved crest rail over three back slats, the center slat inlaid with an Art Nouveau style foliate motif. (Skinner) $1,035

An alder child's rocking wing armchair, North Country, 19th century, with shaped high back and pierced arms, solid seat and shaped front apron.
(Christie's) $1,063

Shaker armed rocker, with bar incised *6* Mt. Lebanon, New York, a production chair, 1880-1900, the shawl bar above four arched slats joined to curving arms with mushroom caps.
(Skinner) $460

A bentwood and cane rocking reclining chair, no. 7500, manufactured by Thonet, circa 1880, the adjustable back hinged in the centre.
(Christie's) $7,728

An ash and elm Windsor rocking chair, the high back with shaped and pierced splat, scrolled arms on baluster turned supports, similar legs joined by H stretchers, 19th century.
(Andrew Hartley) $1,216

Victorian platform rocker, turned back and arm rests, mounted on a base with spring action.
(Jackson's) $99

Arts and Crafts oak rocker, circa 1910, curved and shaped crest rail over three horizontal slats, flat arms with cut corners, raised arm posts.
(Skinner) $575

A mid Victorian mahogany rocking chair.
(Bonhams & Brooks) $237

A yew-wood and elm Windsor chair, Thames Valley, early 19th century, in the style of The Prior Workshop, the hoop back with three vertical pierced splats centered with roundels.(Christie's) $623

A Winthrop-Folsom Family Chippendale carved mahogany side chair, School of Job Townsend, Sr., Newport, circa 1750.(Christie's) $138,000

A North Italian silvered wood grotto side chair, late 19th or early 20th century, the back carved as a dolphin with stylized wave, the seat as a shell on encrusted legs, 35½in. high.(Christie's) $1,448

The George Washington Chippendale carved mahogany side chair, Philadelphia, 1760-1780, the serpentine crest above an interlaced-gothic splat flanked by fluted stiles over a trapezoidal slip-seat. (Christie's) $118,000

Gerrit Rietveld, an oak Zig-Zag chair, designed 1934, of circa 1950s production, the geometric form of butt-jointed construction and secured by brass bolts and nuts, stamped *H.G.M. G.A.v.d., Groenikan, De Bilt, Nederland.* (Christie's) $6,334

The John Cadwalader Chippendale carved mahogany side chair, attributed to the shop of Benjamin Randolph, 1721-1791, Philadelphia, circa 1769, the serpentine crest above a pierced splat. (Christie's) $1,432,500

Chippendale carved walnut side chair, Philadelphia, 1740-85, the serpentine crest centering a fluted shell above a vasiform splat. (Skinner) $9,775

A pair of Burmese hardwood chairs, 19th century, each with profusely carved pierced backs, seat rails and short cabriole legs. (Bonhams & Brooks) $910

A Chippendale carved mahogany side chair, New York, 1750-1780, the carved serpentine crestrail with molded ears above a pierced and ruffle-carved splat flanked by molded stiles. (Christie's) $1,763

Queen Anne maple side chair, Massachusetts, mid-18th century, the serpentine crest with raked molded ears above the vasiform splat. (Skinner) $3,105

Pair of Federal mahogany side chairs, attributed to Adams and Kneeland, Hartford, Connecticut area, early 19th century, the shield backs center a carved urn in a pierced splat, 39in. high. (Skinner) $690

Painted and decorated Chippendale side chair, Concord, Massachusetts area, 1780-90, the serpentine crest ending in raked molded terminals above the pierced crest.(Skinner) $345

Decorated and yellow painted fancy chair, New England, circa 1825-30, the crest splat above horizontal and vertical spindles joining raked turned stiles on the shaped seat. (Skinner) $345

Pair of whimsical Continental carved walnut lyre-back side chairs, late 19th century, each carved with cherubs, seraphim, and foliage. (Skinner) $2,070

Arts & Crafts inlaid oak side chair, England, circa 1910, molded straight crest rail surmounting inlaid panel with stylized floral design. (Skinner) $747

Painted banister side chair, possibly Connecticut, last half 18th century, shaped and molded crest above three half balusters, rush seat on turned legs and double-turned stretchers. (Skinner) $1,093

Pair of painted birdcage Windsor side chairs, Jonathan Tyson, Philadelphia, 1808-1818, the curving birdcage crests centring octagonal panels over seven turned spindles flanked by bamboo turned stiles, 34in. high. (Skinner) $862

Queen Anne black walnut side chair, Boston, 1730-60, the yoked crest rail continues to reverse curved tapering stiles, rounded in the back, flanking a similar reverse curved vasiform splat. (Skinner) $9,775

Queen Anne walnut easy chair, Massachusetts, 18th century, the serpentine crest above the wings, outscrolling arms and arris cabriole legs ending in pad feet.
(Skinner) $21,850

A carved stained beechwood bergère à l'oreilles, late 19th/ early 20th century, the foliate scrolled cresting and shaped upholstered back between pierced foliate scrolls and shaped sides.
(Christie's) $1,173

A mahogany wing armchair, parts 18th century, with padded back, arms and squab cushion, on square tapering legs joined by stretchers, inscribed beneath *141/6156/7148*.
(Christie's) $768

Federal upholstered easy chair, New England, circa 1815-20, the serpentine crest above outward flaring arms and straight skirt.
(Skinner) $4,600

Chippendale mahogany easy chair, New England, 1780-1800, the serpentine crest above the curving wings and outwardly scrolling arms on a cushioned seat.
(Skinner) $7,475

Federal mahogany easy chair, New England, early 19th century, the shaped crest above a tight seat with flanking scrolled arms.
(Skinner) $1,725

A George III mahogany wing armchair with a padded back, arms and seat covered in floral material, on square tapering legs joined by stretchers.
(Christie's) $1,641

A fine and very rare Chippendale carved mahogany easy chair, Philadelphia, circa 1770, the arched crest flanked by ogival wings on C-scroll supports.
(Sotheby's) $203,750

William and Mary style walnut and upholstered wing armchair, late 19th century, arched back, ourscrolled arms, on carved cabriole legs.
(Skinner) $1,150

A 17th century and later oak blanket box, hinged lid, the front fitted with three arched panels with leaf, flower head, scroll carved detail, 65in. wide.
(Wintertons) $662

A pine domed trunk, English, late 18th century, with strap bindings and carrying handles to the sides, lacking stand, 30in. wide.
(Bonhams) $301

An 18th century mule chest in oak with mahogany crossbanding, with four arched fielded front panels, 5ft. 4in. (Brightwells) $1,850

Middle Eastern/Damascus pewter and mother of pearl inlaid fall front chest, 19th century, rectangular front with door, chip carved and inlaid with elaborate geometric designs, 51in. wide.
(Skinner) $1,437

A paint-decorated blanket chest, possibly Dauphin County, Pennsylvania, dated 1810, the rectangular molded lid with two painted oval reserves with red-stencilled flowers on a green ground, 51¾in. wide.
(Christie's) $8,625

Syrian pewter and mother of pearl inlaid fall-front druze, 19th century, inlaid with elaborate geometric panels, with shaped returns and projecting foliate carved legs, 58in. wide. (Skinner) $2,875

A polychrome wood chest, central European, 19th century, of rectangular form with domed cover, the panels with trailing foliage and flowers, 24½in. wide.
(Christie's) $1,129

A 19th century mahogany cellaret, sarcophagus shaped, the fascia with applied shield flanked by fluted pilasters, 32in. wide.
(Andrew Hartley) $1,428

A red and black faux-painted six board chest, American, 19th century, the hinged molded rectangular top with red and black grain painting above a conforming case, 36in. wide.
(Christie's) $5,288

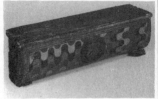

A 15th century Florentine painted wood marriage chest, decorated with geometric motifs in red, ivory, brown and ocher, the bombé front with central painted shield, 151cm. long. (Finarte) $17,659

A large Regency mahogany sarcophagus cellaret, the canted lid with ribbed knop handle and gadrooned edge, 93cm. wide.
(Tennants) $3,200

Shaker maple and cherry oval covered sewing carrier, probably Mount Lebanon, New York, circa 1930, the body with three lapped fingers and swing handle, lined in pink silk, 6in. wide.
(Skinner) $488

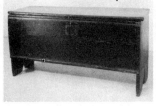

An oak six plank chest with hinged lid, the fascia with molded edging, the sides extending to feet, 17th century, 52in. wide.
(Andrew Hartley) $806

Grain painted pine six-board chest, probably Maine, 1820-30, the hinged lid, with molded edge opens to a well with beaded lidded till, 43¹/₃in. wide.
(Skinner) $2,760

A 17th century oak coffer, the molded edge lid reveals an elm candlebox, the diamond panelled front with carved friezes, 3ft.11in.
(Woolley & Wallis) $442

Middle Eastern brass inlaid blanket chest, late 19th century, of typical form with brass studding, deep well and three base drawers, 54in. wide.
(Skinner) $1,725

Painted and decorated six-board chest, probably New York state, 19th century, the hinged, molded top opens to a cavity above a molded base, old red, white and light blue wavy painting on the top and sides, 37¾in. wide.
(Skinner) $1,725

A Charles II oak coffer, the triple panelled lid above a carved panelled front with ebonized style moldings, 4ft.2in.
(Woolley & Wallis) $712

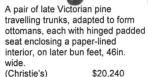

Painted pine six-board chest, southeastern Massachusetts, 1675-1710, the hinged top lifts above a cavity on legs with straight fronts and curving insides, 40in. wide.
(Skinner) $4,600

A pair of late Victorian pine travelling trunks, adapted to form ottomans, each with hinged padded seat enclosing a paper-lined interior, on later bun feet, 46in. wide.
(Christie's) $20,240

A good inlaid and figured walnut blanket chest, Pennsylvania, initialled G.S. and dated 1760, the cleated rectangular top opening to a well fitted with a till and a secret drawer, 4ft.4in. wide.
(Sotheby's) $10,350

A late 17th century oak coffer bach, the hinged lid with iron clasp and iron lock plate to the front, carved with foliage panels above two drawers, 23½in.
(Woolley & Wallis) $607

An 18th century oak coffer bach with three fielded panels over drawer and shaped frieze, 2ft. 1in. wide. (Brightwells) $1,300

A late 17th century oak coffer, the triple panelled lid above a foliage lunette carved frieze, and later carved motifs to the three panels, 3ft.7¾in.
(Woolley & Wallis) $740

An early George III mahogany chest, with a molded edge and baize lined brushing slide containing four long graduated drawers, 38½in. wide. (Christie's) $9,951

A George III mahogany chest of drawers, circa 1810, fitted with two short and three long drawers, raised on ogee bracket feet, 126cm. wide. (Bonhams) $784

An early Georgian walnut chest of five drawers with cross-banding to the top and front, on bracket feet, 3ft.2in. (Brightwells) $2,730

Classical mahogany veneer carved chest, North Shore area Massachusetts, 1820s, the two small drawers over a stepped-out top drawer and three other long drawers, 39in. wide. (Skinner) $1,035

Oak and white pine panelled and joined chest, Salem, Massachusetts, 1660-90, the oak top with molding below, above the case of four drawers with applied moldings in geometric shapes, 42in. wide. (Skinner) $189,500

Federal cherry and bird's-eye maple inlaid chest of drawers, attributed to Spooner and Fitts, Athol, Massachusetts, 1808-13, the rectangular two-board cherry top with inlaid edge above a case of cockbeaded drawers, case 38½in. wide. (Skinner) $17,250

A Victorian flame mahogany chest of drawers, with two short and three long graduated drawers flanked by rounded stiles, on squat turned feet, 43½in. wide. (Christie's) $987

Federal mahogany veneer and cherry inlaid chest, Baltimore, Maryland, circa 1810, the cherry top over oval strung deep drawer above other drawers which are also outlined in stringing, top 40in. wide. (Skinner) $3,450

George III period mahogany bachelor's chest, molded edge, the canted front corners molded with blind fret work decoration, raised on four graduated drawers, 29½in. (G.A. Key) $3,180

An early 19th century faded mahogany chest, a reeded edge veneered top, above a barrel front with four long graduated veneered drawers, 3ft.9in.
(Woolley & Wallis) $2,320

A walnut chest, 19th century and later, with a quarter-veneered top and two graduated drawers, on foliate and scroll-carved cabriole legs with scrolled feet, 44in. wide.
(Christie's) $987

A mahogany and line-inlaid chest, early 19th century, with a molded top, cross grained frieze and two short and three graduated long drawers, 52in. wide.
(Christie's) $493

Federal cherry and mahogany veneer carved bowfront chest of drawers, New Hampshire or Vermont, 1815-25, the swell front top with ovolo corners above a case of cockbeaded mahogany veneer drawers, 40in. wide.
(Skinner) $4,025

Federal mahogany and bird's-eye maple bureau, probably Massachusetts, circa 1825, the rectangular top with two short drawers above the case of four drawers, 38in. wide.
(Skinner) $1,840

A small figured walnut bachelor's chest, with feather banding, the single flap top quarter veneered and crossbanded, the interior veneered in a different walnut, 28½in. wide.
(Woolley & Wallis) $8,000

An oak chest of drawers, English, late 17th century, the rectangular top above three geometric fielded panelled drawers, on later bun feet, 33½in. wide.
(Bonham's) $1,694

A Victorian Irish mahogany military chest, with brass corners, the carcase in two halves, fitted with two short and three long drawers, 3ft.3in. overall.
(Woolley & Wallis) $1,760

A William III oyster olivewood chest, of two short and three long drawers, the top and drawers strung and beaded with holly, 93cm. wide.
(Tennants) $6,280

A George III mahogany serpentine chest, crossbanded with stringing, baize lined slide over two long drawers, deep drawer below as two dummy drawers, 42½in. wide.
(Andrew Hartley) $2,919

A George III mahogany chest of small size, with possible elements of re-construction, having a molded edge, containing four drawers, 24½in. wide.
(Christie's) $7,613

A George IV mahogany serpentine chest of three cockbeaded drawers, canted corners and molded edges, octagonal cast brass ring handles, 47in. wide.
(Wintertons) $4,200

A George III walnut bow fronted chest with crossbanding and stringing, quarter veneered top, two short over three long drawers, 35½in. wide.
(Andrew Hartley) $2,100

A mahogany specimen chest of oblong form, molded edged top over two arched doors with carved leaf capped pilasters, 37in. wide, early to mid 19th century.
(Andrew Hartley) $4,118

A walnut and burr-walnut chest, parts early 18th century, decorated throughout with feather-banding, of two short and three graduated long drawers, 38½in. wide.
(Christie's) $2,834

A George III mahogany serpentine chest, crossbanded with stringing and parquetry banding, three small drawers over three long drawers, 47in. wide.
(Andrew Hartley) $2,572

A George III mahogany chest, with a molded top and plain frieze above five graduated drawers with pressed brass, thistle decorated handles, 39½in. wide.
(Christie's) $4,112

A George III mahogany chest of two short and three long drawers, with molded edged top, brass drop handles and bracket feet, 37½in. wide.
(Andrew Hartley) $2,030

Northern European brass mounted fruitwood chest of drawers, early 19th century, the rectangular case fitted with one projecting drawer over three long drawers, 45in. wide. (Skinner) $3,105

Federal mahogany inlaid chamber chest, attributed to the Seymour Workshop, Boston, circa 1815, the rectangular top with inlaid edge overhangs a case of a single tripart drawer, 44¾in. wide. (Skinner) $42,550

A George II mahogany chest of drawers, two short above three graduated long cock-beaded drawers, brass swan neck handles, 47in. wide. (Wintertons) $2,100

An oak and walnut chest, early 18th century, with a crossbanded top and four long drawers, each inlaid with boxwood lines and with later drop handles, 39in. (Christie's) $2,479

Continental walnut three-drawer chest, second quarter 19th century, with canted top and three drawers, on square tapered legs, 23in. wide. (Skinner) $1,955

A George III mahogany chest of two short and three long drawers with molded edged crossbanded top, 34½in. wide. (Andrew Hartley) $1,946

A George III mahogany chest, the top with a reeded edge above three short and three graduated long drawers, with ivory escutcheons and bracket feet, 46in. wide. (Christie's) $950

A Classical gilt and stencilled mahogany chest, New York, 1820-1830, the horizontal rectangular mahogany-framed mirror with stencilled corners centring a glazed plate, 40in. wide. (Christie's) $6,463

A George III oak chest with two short and three long drawers, on bracket feet, restorations, 38¼in. wide. (Christie's) $739

A George III mahogany chest on chest, 99cm. wide.
(Bonhams) $3,476

An early 19th century mahogany bowfront tallboy chest of eight drawers and fitted brushing slide, with gothic arcade frieze and splay feet, 3ft.10in. wide, 6ft.4in. high.
(G.A. Key) $4,611

A George III mahogany chest on chest, 99cm. wide.
(Bonhams) $2,370

A Chippendale carved cherrywood chest-on-chest, Concord area, Massachusetts, 1760-1790, in two sections, the upper with molded broken swan's-neck pediment, 41½in. wide.
(Christie's) $94,000

A German oak cupboard on chest, 18th century, the lower part of arc en arbelète outline, fitted with a slide containing three long drawers, 45½in. wide.
(Christie's) $3,271

A George I walnut, crossbanded, featherbanded and inlaid chest-on-chest, the upper part with a molded cornice and cavetto frieze containing three short drawers and three long drawers flanked by fluted canted angles, 42in. wide.
(Christie's) $14,476

A walnut chest on chest with feather banding, molded cornice and cushion frieze drawer, three small drawers over three long drawers, 38in. wide, 18th century.
(Andrew Hartley) $4,439

A Green japanned and chinoiserie decorated chest-on-chest, 19th century with later decoration, the upper part with a molded cornice containing two short and three long drawers, 40½in. wide.
(Christie's) $12,719

A George III mahogany chest on chest, with molded dentil cornice over two short and three long drawers with brass drop handles, 43½in. wide.
(Andrew Hartley) $1,546

A George I walnut veneered chest on stand, on cabriole legs with pointed pad feet, 98cm. wide.
(Bearne's) $2,800

A Colonial red-stained hardwood gilt-metal mounted coffer-on-stand, early 20th century, the hinged top above a deep body enclosing a candle box with carrying handles to the sides, 51in. wide.
(Christie's) $987

A Queen Anne mahogany chest-on-frame, in two sections: the upper with molded cornice above a rectangular case, 41¾in. wide.
(Christie's) $9,200

A walnut and crossbanded chest-on-stand, 18th century, with a molded cornice, two short and three long feather-banded drawers, restorations, 39in. wide.
(Christie's) $3,455

An oak, burr walnut and crossbanded chest-on-stand, late 17th/early 18th century and later, the upper part with a molded edge containing two short and three long drawers, 39in. wide.
(Christie's) $5,269

An 18th century walnut chest on stand, the top with molded pediment over two short drawers and three long graduated drawers, 38in. wide. (Dee Atkinson & Harrison) $3,840

Queen Anne cherry high chest, New London or Stonington Counties, Connecticut, 1740-60, the flaring cove-molded cornice over a case of four thumb-molded graduated drawers, 38in. wide.
(Skinner) $29,900

Painted Queen Anne chest on frame, Connecticut, 1740-70, the flaring cornice with cove molding above a case of thumb-molded drawers, 40in. wide.
(Skinner) $9,200

A George II walnut and feather-banded chest-on-stand, on later supports, the upper part with a molded cavetto cornice and frieze fitted with three short and three long drawers, 41½in. wide.
(Christie's) $7,238

A mid Victorian mahogany chiffonier, circa 1860, 108cm. wide. (Bonhams & Brooks) $1,078

An early Victorian rosewood and marble topped chiffonier, circa 1840, 141cm. wide. (Bonhams & Brooks) $2,156

A Regency rosewood veneered chiffonier, outlined with boxwood stringing, 53cm. wide. (Bearne's) $2,359

A rosewood and brass inlaid chiffonier, early 19th century, the shelved superstructure with pierced brass gallery, mirror panel back, on lotus and turned columns, 44½in. wide. (Christie's) $5,414

A Regency gilt-metal-mounted ebonized and amboyna chiffonier, the rectangular mirror-backed top cross-banded in satinwood with ebonized columns and brass X-frame supported two-tier superstructure, 40in. wide. (Christie's) $4,361

An early Victorian mahogany chiffonier, with a flame figured pediment and an open shelf supported by turned uprights above a bolection molded drawer and panelled cupboards, 42in. wide. (Christie's) $1,316

A William IV rosewood chiffonier, the shelved superstructure with foliate and C-scroll arched top-rail, on scroll bracket supports, 48½in. wide. (Christie's) $3,089

An Edwardian walnut and marquetry chiffonier, decorated throughout with ribbon-tied swags and a vase of flowers, the superstructure with a molded cornice, 54in. wide. (Christie's) $1,233

An early Victorian mahogany chiffonier, the raised back with scroll and leaf carved edging, three shelves on scrolled supports, 62 x 67¾in. (Andrew Hartley) $1,750

A Victorian mahogany clothes press, the detachable molded cornice, above sliding trays enclosed by a pair of domed panelled doors, 4ft.8½in.
(Woolley & Wallis) $1,380

A fine George IV mahogany gentleman's press cupboard.
(Bonhams & Brooks) $3,234

A Regency mahogany clothes press, circa 1820, fitted with panelled doors with dummy drawers, a single base drawer, 132cm. wide.
(Bonhams) $1,176

A George III mahogany clothes-press, the rectangular dentilled cornice above a plain frieze and a pair of cedar-backed panelled doors enclosing two slides, 49½in. wide. (Christie's) $10,902

A late 18th century mahogany clothes press, the detachable dentil cornice above sliding trays enclosed by panelled doors, 4ft.4in. wide.
(Woolley & Wallis) $2,329

One of a pair of George III ebony-inlaid mahogany clothes-presses, possibly by John Linnell, each crossbanded overall in satinwood and tulipwood, 56in. wide.
(Christie's) (Two) $31,091

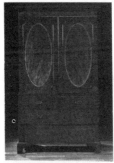

A mahogany gentleman's wardrobe, George III, circa 1790, the cornice with dentil frieze above a pair of panelled doors inlaid with ovals, 4ft.2in. wide.
(Sotheby's) $2,113

A late 18th century mahogany cupboard, later divided and fitted with shelves, formerly for a fold away bed, 4ft.6in.
(Woolley & Wallis) $822

A George III mahogany clothes-press, the rectangular dentilled cornice above a pair of panelled doors incorporating four simulated drawers, 52½in. wide.
(Christie's) $15,445

A Louix XV ormolu-mounted amaranth, tulipwood and parquetry bombé commode, by Jacques Bircklé, the waved breccia marble top above three short and two long drawers, 52¼in. wide.
(Christie's) $14,145

A Maltese walnut, ebonized and marquetry commode, early 18th century, inlaid overall with shaped panels of scrolling foliage, 76in. wide. (Christie's) $19,187

An early Louis XV ormolu-mounted tulipwood, kingwood and parquetry commode, by Jean Mathieu Chevallier, the later molded rectangular serpentine white-veined gray marble top above a central drawer, 51in. wide.
(Christie's) $17,917

A Provincial Louis XV walnut serpentine commode, mid 18th century, the shaped top with molded edge above a pair of deep molded long drawers, the waved apron carved with scrolling designs, 50¼in. wide.
(Bonhams) $11,846

A Continental rosewood and, marquetry commode, late 19th century, of undulating outline, with gilt metal ornament, 34½in. wide. (Christie's) $2,353

A mahogany, satinwood, harewood and amaranth marquetry demi lune commode, 20th century, of George III style, in the manner of William Moore of Dublin, radially veneered with central lunette with engraved pen-work beaded and trellis decoration, 49½in. wide.
(Christie's) $11,763

An Italian rosewood and marquetry, serpentine commode, 18th century, the top quarter veneered with a cartouche of scrolls, within a feather-banded border, 38¾in. wide. (Christie's) $5,067

A South German walnut and inlaid serpentine commode, restorations, 78cm. wide.
(Bonhams & Brooks) $1,680

A French ormolu-mounted boulle and ebony commode à vantaux, by L'Hoste, circa 1875, surmounted by a shaped gray Sarrancolin marble top, above a central door, headed by a medallion profile of King Louis XIV, 61¾ wide.
(Christie's) $53,768

An Italian walnut, crossbanded and inlaid bombé commode, 19th century and later, with serpentine molded, crossbanded top containing two short cavetto frieze drawers and two long drawers, 46in. wide.(Christie's)　　$3,619

A Transitional style walnut and kingwood marquetry petit commode, circa 1900, 52cm. wide. (Bonhams & Brooks)　　$493

A Napoleon III ormolu-mounted marquetry, ivory and mother of pearl commode, after the model by Schlichtig, circa 1855, surmounted by a breakfront gris de Caunes moucheté marble top, 50¾in. wide. (Christie's)　　$10,921

An Italian ormolu-mounted kingwood commode, mid 18th century, possibly Genoa, crossbanded overall, the later waved eared molded rectangular breche violette marble top above two drawers, 37in. wide. (Christie's)　　$15,017

A Louis XV ormolu-mounted amaranth, tulipwood and marquetry commode, by Pierre Roussel, the brèche violette eared molded marble top above two drawers inlaid sans traverse with ribbon-tied floral marquetry, 25¼in. wide. (Christie's)　　$92,660

A Sicilian polychrome-painted and parcel-gilt commode, decorated overall with simulated kingwood and applied gesso decoration, with foliate scrolls and flowers, 42½in. wide. (Christie's)　　$13,202

A Dutch inlaid palisander bombé commode, circa 1790, the shaped crossbanded top inlaid with a central fan patera, above three long drawers, 40¼in. wide. (Bonhams)　　$4,739

A North German brass-mounted mahogany commode, late 18th century, the canted rectangular top above a frieze drawer carved with an interlaced chain motif and mounted with knobs, 24¾in. wide. (Christie's)　　$8,343

A French kingwood, crossbanded and inlaid serpentine commode, with parts Régence with re-construction in the 19th century, surmounted by a later molded serpentine marble top, 51½in. wide. (Christie's)　　$4,523

A mahogany tray top commode, enclosed by a tambour door, above a false drawer front on square legs, 42cm. wide.
(Dreweatt Neate) $1,377

An ash child's commode armchair, probably Scottish, early 19th century, with one-piece arm bow and spindle supports, on whittled splayed legs.
(Christie's) $695

A George III mahogany tray top bedside commode, the borders with pierced carrying handles above a pair of doors and pull-out drawer, 51cm.
(Dreweatt Neate) $1,328

A George III mahogany tray top commode, circa 1780, the galleried top above a pair of cupboard doors and a pot slide faced as two false drawers, 19½in. wide.
(Bonhams) $1,400

A late George III mahogany commode, modelled as a chest of drawers, with molded hinged top enclosing a fitted interior, 25in. wide. (Christie's) $1,379

A 'Chippendale' period night commode, the rectangular top with a shaped gallery, pierced hand grips, the front with a hinged veneered flap, 23.5in.
(Woolley & Wallis) $4,006

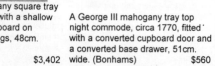

A George III mahogany square tray top night commode with a shallow drawer above a cupboard on square chamfered legs, 48cm. wide.
(Dreweatt Neate) $3,402

A George III mahogany tray top night commode, circa 1770, fitted with a converted cupboard door and a converted base drawer, 51cm. wide. (Bonhams) $560

Late Georgian cross-banded mahogany night table, fitted with lifting handles, a tambour cupboard, and a sliding base drawer, 29in. high, 20in. wide.
(Skinner) $1,035

An ash, elm, beech and mahogany
child's Windsor commode armchair,
Thames Valley, late 19th century.
(Christie's) $194

A Regency mahogany tray-top
commode, 49cm. wide.
(Bonhams & Brooks) $1,386

A mahogany commode chair, 19th
century with high bar back, scrolled
arms and a green leather
upholstered drop in seat.
(Christie's) $363

A George III mahogany and inlaid
tray top commode, with pierced
gallery and carrying handles,
enclosed by a pair of panelled
doors with a sliding compartment,
20½in. wide.(Christie's) $1,544

A George III mahogany tray top
commode, with ogee arched
gallery and pierced carrying
handles fitted with a slide and
enclosed by a pair of panelled
doors, 24in. wide.
(Christie's) $3,271

A George III mahogany tray top
commode, the rectangular top with
a shaped gallery and pierced
carrying handles, with two line-
inlaid cupboard doors above a
sliding drawer with leather lined top
and ceramic bowl, 21in. wide.
(Christie's) $937

Child's painted bow-back Windsor
commode chair, New England,
1790-1815, the arched crest above
the incised spindles, turned arms
and similar splayed legs.
(Skinner) $316

A George III mahogany tray top
bedside commode, with ogee
shaped gallery and open
compartment below, previously with
a tambour shutter, 23¼in. wide.
(Christie's) $1,099

A George III mahogany tray top
commode, the shaped gallery with
pierced handles above a tambour
shutter and with a drawer below, on
chamfered square section legs,
adapted, 20in. wide.
(Christie's) $1,677

A George III mahogany standing corner cupboard, crossbanded with stringing, molded breakfront cornice over two arched doors, 44¼in. wide.
(Andrew Hartley) $4,170

A late 18th century oak corner cupboard, with later carving.
(Bonhams & Brooks) $539

A George II pine corner cupboard, the molded cornice with Greek-key pattern frieze, above a pair of arched and glazed doors, 53¼in. wide. (Christie's) $3,997

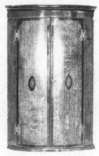

A George III oak bow fronted corner cupboard, with mahogany crossbanding and string inlay, molded cornice, two doors each with a marquetry patera, 27¼in. wide x 40½in. high.
(Andrew Hartley) $1,040

An early Georgian green-painted and gilt-japanned bow front hanging corner cupboard, doors decorated with chinoiserie scenes depicting pagodas and people carrying out various pursuits, 23¼in. wide.
(Christie's) $2,369

A French ebonized and ormolu mounted encoignure, 19th century, of bowfront outline, veneered in scarlet tortoiseshell and inlaid with a marquetry of cut brass in the manner of Boulle, 26in. wide.
(Christie's) $1,272

A George III oak bow fronted corner cupboard, crossbanded with parquetry banding and stringing, molded cornice, two doors each with shell marquetry paterae, 28½in. wide.
(Andrew Hartley) $1,001

An Italian decorated and parcel-gilt upright corner cupboard, 18th century, with alterations to the base, door with twin panels painted with figures in an arcadian landscape en grisaille, 43in. wide.
(Christie's) $18,612

A George III mahogany bow fronted corner cupboard, with stringing, molded cornice over a frieze with three marquetry cameos depicting a bird and two lions, 30in. wide.
(Andrew Hartley) $1,168

A mahogany Biedermeier corner cupboard, with leather lined glazed upper section, 249 x 130 x 80cm. (Arnold) $3,192

An oak hanging corner cupboard, Welsh, mid 18th century, with a single arched panelled door and canted corners, 33in. wide. (Bonham's) $693

A George III mahogany standing corner cupboard, with a dentil molded cornice above a pair of astragal glazed doors enclosing shelves, on bracket feet, 38in. wide. (Christie's) $2,796

Federal cherry, maple and tiger maple glazed corner cupboard, probably New Jersey, circa 1820, the cornice with applied reeding above a glazed door which opens to a three-shelf interior, 52in. wide. (Skinner) $3,220

A pair of German ormolu-mounted and ivory and mother of pearl inlaid kingwood, fruitwood and marquetry encoignures, mid 18th century, of bowed shape, molded griotte marble-top above two quarter-veneered doors, 30¼in. high. (Christie's) $13,202

An Alsace walnut fruitwood and marquetry upright corner cupboard, 18th century, the upper part with a molded cornice enclosed by an arched panelled door flanked by half columns, 36½in. wide. (Christie's) $2,835

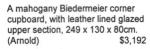

Chippendale pine panelled corner cabinet, Southern States, 1760s, the heavy projecting cornice molding above an arched molded surround, flanking similarly shaped raised panel doors, 64in. wide. (Skinner) $7,475

18th century oak and mahogany crossbanded bow-fronted corner cupboard, two panelled doors inlaid in the center with Sheraton style shell motifs, enclosing fitted shelving, 34½in. (G.A. Key) $1,590

A carved pine corner cupboard, 20th century, of Georgian style, carved throughout with rosettes and foliage, with a swan neck pediment and a glazed arched door, 38in. wide. (Christie's) $4,073

An oak cwpwrdd deuddarn, West Wales, early 19th century, with molded cornice and drop-pendant frieze, above a pair of ogee arched fielded panelled doors, 46½in. wide. (Christie's) $5,348

An oak cupboard by Heal & Co, with panelled door flanked by two small doors over two drawers, on plinth, 38¾in. wide. (Andrew Hartley) $1,120

An oak press cupboard, English, late, 7th century and later, of small size, with molded top and strapwork-carved friezes, above a central door with foliate panel, 44in. wide. (Christie's) $2,227

A Baltic speckled blue, light blue and white-painted pedestal cupboard, late 18th/ early 19th century, the rectangular top above a foliate-carved frieze, above a door centered by a rosette, 23in. wide. (Christie's) $5,006

Vinegar painted pine panelled wall cupboard, New England, early 19th century, the flat molded cornice over nail constructed case containing two cupboard doors, 28in. wide. (Skinner) $12,650

A joined oak tridarn, North Wales, late 18th century, the associated top section with molded edge and turned supports above an overhanging canopy with turned drop pendants and a pair of cupboard doors, 53¾in. wide. (Bonham's) $3,850

An early Victorian gothic oak hanging cupboard, with a molded scroll-carved cornice and a frieze with blind fret-carved quatrefoils above a pair of pointed arched doors, 56in. wide. (Christie's) $1,948

An oak hanging cupboard, English, 17th century and later, with molded cornice and channel moldings throughout, the upper section enclosed by a pair of spindle-framed doors, 33in. wide. (Christie's) $4,991

A fruitwood hanging cupboard, French, late 18th century, with removable molded cornice and fluted frieze enclosed by an astragal-glazed four-pane door, 29in. wide.(Christie's) $1,426

Red painted recessed panel cupboard, New England, 1830s, the rectangular top overhangs a double-panelled door which opens to a three-shelved interior, 37in. wide. (Skinner) $1,610

Painted pine and cherry panelled tall cupboard, probably New England, early 19th century, containing a single door with four recessed panels, 27¾in. wide.(Skinner) $4,370

Painted pine cupboard, New England, early 19th century, flat molded cornice above a cockbeaded case of two shelves, 54¾in. wide. (Skinner) $920

A North European walnut cupboard, late 19th century, in the Biedermeier taste, the angled cornice with applied egg-and-dart molding, above two doors, flanked by mask-headed, projecting, ebonized, tapering columns, 42in. wide. (Christie's) $904

A 17th century style oak press cupboard, of small proportions, the overhanging canopy with a scrolled dragon carved frieze, held by turned supports, 39in. wide. (Bonham's) $3,388

A pine press cupboard, English, late 17th century, with ebonized moldings throughout, with molded cornice and a pair of twin-panelled doors with vertical channel moldings, 51½in. wide. (Christie's) $4,813

Painted cherry glazed panelled step-back cupboard, Pennsylvania or Ohio, 1830-40, the flaring cornice molding above the fluted frieze and glazed doors which open to a two-shelf interior, 50in. wide. (Skinner) $18,400

An oak hanging glass-case, English, mid 17th century, with triangular molded pediment and acorn finials, above a pair of doors enclosing shelves, 41¼in. wide. (Christie's) $17,825

Red stained poplar glazed cupboard, probably Pennsylvania, early 19th century, the top section with flat cove molded cornice above two glazed doors, 48½in. wide. (Skinner) $9,200

A Victorian rosewood Davenport with green leather inset to slope, four real and four dummy drawers with small pull-out ink drawer, turned feet and castors, 22 x 34in. (Canterbury) $1,254

A late Victorian oak davenport, 54cm. wide.
(Bonhams) $790

A Victorian figured walnut piano top davenport, the rectangular top with raising letter-rack and hinged surface revealing a fret-carved gallery, 22½in. wide.
(Christie's) $5,520

A Burmese carved hardwood davenport, pierced and carved throughout with scrolling berried foliage, figures and animals, on carved animal mask supports and naturalistically carved feet, 23¼in. wide.(Christie's) $1,151

A Victorian walnut davenport, circa 1870, the concave superstructure enclosing a compartmented interior above a leather inset fall, 23½in. wide. (Christie's) $2,509

A William IV rosewood davenport with sliding top, inset leather writing slope enclosing small drawers, 21in. wide.
(G.A. Key) $2,544

A Victorian inlaid walnut davenport music cabinet, circa 1880, the concave superstructure with domed lid enclosing a compartmented interior, 22¼in. wide.
(Christie's) $3,136

An Edwardian inlaid walnut davenport, 53cm. wide.
(Bonhams & Brooks) $801

A William IV rosewood davenport, 56cm. wide.
(Bonhams) $1,510

A William IV rosewood davenport, with gallery and hinged leather-lined slope enclosing a fitted interior, with stylized foliate-carved frieze fitted with four drawers, 24in. wide. (Christie's) $2,392

A late Victorian mahogany davenport, 20¼in. wide. (Bonhams) $711

A Victorian walnut and tulipwood banded davenport, the hinged superstructure with a low brass gallery, above a leather-lined writing slope, 21½in. wide. (Christie's) $1,900

A George IV oak davenport, the sliding top with writing slope inlaid in green leather, fitted with two interior drawers and pull-out pen drawer to side, 20in. wide. (Canterbury) $1,420

A Victorian piano top davenport, veneered in burr walnut, the sprung rising top with stationery rack, a hinged cover with pierced fret interior gallery to a molded edge, 23¼in. overall. (Woolley & Wallis) $4,553

A Victorian walnut and burr-walnut davenport, decorated throughout with line-inlaid foliate scrolls, the stationery compartment with a hinged lid above a leather-lined slope, 21in. wide. (Christie's) $1,974

A Victorian figured walnut davenport inlaid with boxwood and ebonized arabesques, boxwood stringings and burr-wood bandings, 22in. wide. (Canterbury) $2,025

A Victorian walnut davenport desk, with pen and stationery compartments under a domed cover, the fall revealing a fitted interior, 56cm. wide. (Wintertons) $1,155

A Victorian walnut harlequin davenport, circa 1870, the hinged retractable top with three quarter gallery and enclosing compartments, 23in. wide. (Christie's) $3,450

A mid Victorian satinwood davenport, 54cm. wide. (Bonhams & Brooks) $2,100

A Victorian burr walnut harlequin davenport with pierced brass gallery on rising stationery rack, piano top enclosing two drawers over a sliding writing surface, 22in. wide. (Andrew Hartley) $3,475

A mid Victorian walnut davenport, 57cm. wide. (Bonhams & Brooks) $3,780

A late Regency mahogany davenport, the sliding superstructure with pierced fret quatrefoil gothic gallery and tooled leather lined crossbanded slope, 22¾in. wide. (Christie's) $2,362

A Regency rosewood davenport, the raised back with turned vertical spindles, the sloped front with tooled leather inset, enclosing two opening drawers, fitted with small side pen drawer with inkwell, 58cm. wide. (Wintertons) $1,764

A Victorian burr walnut and inlaid davenport writing desk, the top with raised compartment fitted for pens and stationery, the rear of the desk fitted with a hinged folio compartment, 24½in. wide. (Wintertons) $3,500

A Victorian walnut davenport, fretwork damaged, 58cm. wide. (Bonhams & Brooks) $1,812

A mid Victorian rosewood davenport, distressed, 56cm. wide. (Bonhams & Brooks) $981

A Victorian rosewood davenport, circa 1850, 52cm. wide. (Bonhams & Brooks) $3,080

A Victorian walnut pier cabinet, 84cm. wide.
(Bonhams & Brooks) $1,001

A Dutch walnut china cabinet, 19th century and later, of small size, with canted sides, the lower part containing two drawers with a shaped apron, 46in. wdie.
(Christie's) $3,271

A Chippendale style mahogany display cabinet 112cm. wide.
(Bonhams & Brooks) $493

A mahogany ormolu-mounted and Vernis Martin vitrine, early 20th century, of serpentine outline, with an arched cornice above a glazed door and painted panels depicting an amorous couple, 28in. wide.
(Christie's) $1,645

An Edwardian mahogany and inlaid display cabinet, inlaid throughout with satinwood-banding and checkered lines, with a shaped gallery above a bowed frieze with central urn inlay and foliate swags, 59in. wide.(Christie's) $3,365

A French ormolu-mounted kingwood bombé-shaped vitrine, by François Linke, Paris, circa 1890, surmounted by a Villefranche de Conflent marble top above a waisted pediment centered by a female mask, 52in. wide.
(Christie's) $47,047

A Regency mahogany china cabinet-on-stand, the upper part with beaded tablet scroll and roundel cresting, possibly Irish, 45in. wide.
(Christie's) $2,907

An Edwardian satinwood and polychrome decorated display cabinet, astragal glazed doors with four oval painted plaques depicting female figures, two cupboard doors below with painted panels, 41in. wide. (Christie's) $3,948

An Edwardian satinwood and marquetry vitrine, decorated throughout with plain and checkered lines and bellflower swags, with a molded cornice and a panelled and glazed door, 51in. wide. (Christie's) $7,402

A Victorian mahogany parlour display cabinet, in the Rococo Revival manner, mirrored back with scrolled surmount, 54½in. wide. (Andrew Hartley) $983

Early 20th century mahogany crossbanded small vitrine, applied with pierced gilt metal gallery surround, glazed door below, 21in. (G A Key) $1,117

A Victorian walnut and marquetry inlaid pier cabinet with ormolu mounts, 84cm. wide. (Bonhams & Brooks) $962

George III painted and parcel-gilt satinwood breakfront vitrine, circa 1800, bow-front outline fitted with three glazed doors in the upper section and three drawers and two doors in the lower section. (Skinner) $19,550

A mahogany, gilt-metal mounted and Vernis Martin decorated vitrine, early 20th century, in the French taste, of breakfront outline, with a variegated marble top and glazed front and sides with painted panelled inlay, 57in. wide. (Christie's) $1,480

A French mahogany, parquetry and ormolu mounted vitrine, late 19th century, in the Louis XVI style, inset with a breccia marble top, the frieze hung with floral garlands and enclosed by a glazed panelled door, 30½in. wide. (Christie's) $3,312

A kingwood and gilt-metal mounted vitrine, 20th century, with a rectangular red mottled marble top, glazed front and sides above floral filled lattice panels, 29½in. wide. (Christie's) $2,303

A French ormolu-mounted kingwood and mahogany vitrine cabinet, in the Régence style, first quarter 20th century, surmounted by a breakfront brocatelle jaune marble top, 63in. wide. (Christie's) $22,080

A late Victorian mahogany and polychrome decorated display cabinet, decorated overall with floral decoration, the arched molded cornice above a glazed door flanked by angled glazed sides, 56in. wide.(Christie's) $2,743

Edwardian inlaid mahogany display cabinet, 30in. wide.
(Jacobs & Hunt) $480

A late Victorian walnut and ebonized pier cabinet, 87.5cm. wide.
(Bonhams & Brooks) $1,001

An Edwardian mahogany break front display cabinet.
(John Maxwell) $1,696

A French kingwood, ormolu mounted and Vernis Martin vitrine, early 20th century, of serpentine outline, with an arched cornice, a glazed front and sides enclosing shelves, 52in. wide.
(Christie's) $2,138

A French ormolu-mounted kingwood bombé-shaped vitrine, in the Louis XV style, by François Linke, Paris, circa 1890, surmounted by a brèche violette marble top above a waisted pediment centered by a female mask, 47¼in. wide.
(Christie's) $69,280

Stickley Brothers oak china closet, Grand Rapids, Michigan, circa 1914, straight crest rail on a rectangular top, mirrored top interior panel.
(Skinner) $2,875

A French mahogany and ormolu mounted vitrine, late 19th century, in the Louis XV/XVI Transitional style surmounted by a molded marble top and frieze with foliate vine leaves, 28½in. wide.
(Christie's) $4,277

A brass and ebonized wood vitrine, late 19th century, with a stepped sectional glazed superstructure on a table top display case with a hinged top, 53½in. wide.
(Christie's) $1,480

An Edwardian mahogany and marquetry display cabinet, with a shaped fret-carved foliate gallery with open shelves and mirrored back, 54in. wide.
(Christie's) $1,022

A Dutch mahogany and parcel-gilt vitrine, the rectangular top above a plain veneered frieze and cupboard door with two horizontal glazing bars enclosing two shelves, 34½in. wide. (Christie's) $1,250

A mid Victorian walnut display cabinet, the breakfront top above a concave frieze with three glazed cupboard doors under, 183cm. wide. (Bonhams) $2,695

A late Victorian satinwood and tulipwood crossbanded vitrine, 48cm. square. (Bonhams & Brooks) $1,400

A Dutch mahogany and floral marquetry miniature display cabinet, 19th century, with molded undulating cornice surmounted by projecting and ribband portrait medallion, the base 30in. wide. (Christie's) $5,921

Dutch fruitwood marquetry inlaid walnut display cabinet, late 19th century, with a pair of glass doors, the case inlaid with scrolling leafy vines, 36in. wide. (Skinner) $1,150

A French mahogany, parquetry and marquetry ormolu-mounted vitrine, late 19th century, in the Louis XV style, of serpentine undulating outline, the upper part with a cavetto frieze and enclosed by glazed panel door, 36in. wide. (Christie's) $4,524

A Dutch walnut and floral marquetry china cabinet, 19th century, with canted sides, having a shaped apron, between canted sides with vases of flowers and birds, on spirally turned feet, 49in. wide. (Christie's) $5,921

An Edwardian mahogany and crossbanded display cabinet, the raised back with cartouche bevelled mirror, astragal glazed door, on square tapering block legs and spade feet, 22½in. wide. (Wintertons) $500

A Dutch mahogany and floral marquetry miniature display cabinet, 19th century, with a molded arched cornice with urn finials enclosed by a glazed arched panel door, 22½in. wide. (Christie's) $3,997

A 19th century pine Welsh dresser, 163cm. wide.
(Bonhams & Brooks) $2,220

An oak dresser, 19th century, the base with three drawers between split moldings, above a pair of foliate-carved panelled doors, 71in. wide. (Christie's) $1,680

An 18th century style oak open dresser, late 19th / 20th century 170cm. wide.
(Bonhams & Brooks) $2,695

An oak and crossbanded open dresser, South Wales, early 19th century, the plate rack with three shelves above a base with three frieze drawers, 74in. wide.
(Bonham's) $5,544

An ash, elm, pine and walnut dresser, Alpine, 18th/19th century, the upper section with molded front, open compartments to the side, 40½in. wide.
(Christie's) $1,217

An oak open dresser, South Wales, probably Glamorganshire, late 18th/early 19th century, the plate rack with molded cornice above three shelves, 69¼in. wide.
(Bonham's) $5,852

An oak dresser, English, mid 18th century and later, the boarded plate rack with ogee and arched frieze above three shelves and wavy sides, the base with later top, 70in. wide. (Christie's) $2,856

An oak dresser, South Wales, late 18th century, the open plate rack with molded cornice and wavy frieze with cup hooks, above three shelves, the middle one with spoon rack, 54½in. wide.
(Christie's) $9,143

An oak open dresser, South Wales, late 18th century, the open plate rack with dentil molded cornice and a waved frieze, above three shelves, 52¼in. wide.
(Bonham's) $2,926

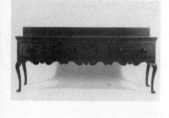

An oak low dresser with mahogany crossbanding, molded edged plank top, three frieze drawers with pierced brass drop handles, basically 18th century, 72in. wide. (Andrew Hartley) $4,726

A painted pine dresser, Swiss, 18th century, with molded cornice and an upper panel door painted with a vase of flowers, over an open shelved section, 30½in. wide. (Christie's) $2,435

An 18th century oak dresser base, raised back, fitted with three frieze drawers, brass escutcheons, turned wooden handles, shaped apron, on cabriole legs, 82½in. wide. (Wintertons) $6,624

An oak dresser, Yorkshire, late 18th century, with a plate rack with dentil molded cornice and three shelves with two small drawers below between fluted pilasters, 69in. wide. (Christie's) $9,043

An oak dresser, South Wales, mid 18th century, the open plate-rack with molded cornice and fret-carved frieze, above three shelves, the base with molded top and two frieze drawers, 61in. wide. (Christie's) $6,239

An oak enclosed dresser, North Wales, late 18th century, the plate rack with molded cornice and two shelves above a base with three frieze drawers and a pair of panelled cupboard doors, 51in. wide. (Bonham's) $8,470

A Georgian oak dresser, with molded edge top, panelled sides, the fascia with three deep frieze drawers over a central recess with ogee panelled door, 18th century. (Andrew Hartley) $834

Pine red painted pewter dresser, possibly North Shore, Massachusetts, late 18th century, the three molded shelves framed by cockbeaded surrounds on a projecting base, 69¾in. long. (Skinner) $13,800

A George III oak and mahogany banded low dresser, with frieze drawers over a central tier of three drawers between panelled cupboards, 164cm. wide. (Tennants) $4,160

A George III mahogany and brass dumb waiter, 64cm. wide.
(Bonhams) $1,896

A late Victorian walnut 3 tier dumb waiter, lacking finials, 120cm. wide, 122cm. high.
(Bonhams & Brooks) $474

A mid Victorian mahogany four tier dumb waiter, fitted with one drawer to lower tier, baluster turned supports, 59cm. wide.
(Wintertons) $1,925

A Victorian mahogany dumb waiter, of elevating metamorphic design, with foliate scroll back ledge and rectangular tiers, 48in. wide.
(Christie's) $1,635

A George III mahogany three tier dumb waiter with triple graduated circular tiers, on turned supports and tripod legs with pad feet, the lower tier, 24½in. diameter.
(Christie's) $2,707

A Victorian mahogany dumb waiter, of three rectangular open tiers, each with a low three-quarter gallery, on bulbous turned and reeded supports, 48in. wide.
(Christie's) $1,948

A George IV mahogany two tier dumb waiter, the circular revolving trays with a molded edge, the top detachable turned stem to a ring turned and partly ribbed tapering main stem, 24in. diameter.
(Woolley & Wallis) $2,720

An early Victorian mahogany metamorphic dumb waiter, of three tiers, on rectangular standard end supports, shaped platform bases and scrolled feet, 43in. wide.
(Christie's) $1,122

A George III mahogany dumb waiter, the molded circular dished top, above a cut-baluster shaft and a further conforming tier, 24¼in. diameter.
(Christie's) $3,271

A Queen Anne figured maple flat-top high chest of drawers, New England probably Connecticut, circa 1760, 39in. wide.
(Sotheby's) $21,850

A Queen Anne figured cherrywood flat-top high chest of drawers, New York, circa 1750, in two parts, width of lower section 39in.
(Sotheby's) $8,625

Antique American William & Mary highboy, in walnut veneers, upper section with two drawers over three drawers, 41½in. wide.
(Eldred's) $3,960

Queen Anne cherry carved high chest, probably Litchfield County, Connecticut area, mid 18th century, the cornice molding above five thumb-molded drawers, a mid molding, and three small drawers, 38¾in. wide.
(Skinner) $19,550

A William and Mary walnut veneered high chest-of-drawers, Massachusetts, 1700-1730, rectangular molded cornice above conforming case with two short over three graduated long drawers, 41¾in.wide.
(Christie's) $11,163

Chippendale cherry high chest of drawers, attributed to Eliakim Smith, Hadley, Massachusetts, circa 1760, the molded bonnet top with three finials above a cockbeaded case, 39in. wide.
(Skinner) $23,000

Baroque poplar high chest of drawers, New England, circa 1680-1720, the flat molded cornice above a blind convex drawer and upper double arch molded case, 39¼in. (Skinner) $37,375

Queen Anne walnut and maple carved high chest, North Shore, Massachusetts, 18th century, with a cove molding above graduated thumb-molded drawers, 37in. wide. (Skinner) $8,050

Antique William and Mary highboy, in maple with figured maple veneered drawer fronts, four drawers above and three drawers below, 41in. wide.
(Eldred's) $2,200

A mid-Victorian oak pedestal desk, the canted rectangular molded leather-lined top above three frieze drawers to the front, 54¼in. wide. (Christie's) $7,728

Post-war walnut and brass desk, design attributed to Gilbert Rhode, manufactured by Herman Miller, Zeeland, Michigan, 45½in. long. (Skinner) $1,150

A Victorian oak partner's pedestal desk, with a green leather lined top, shallow drawers and leather lined slides to each frieze, 66½in. wide. (Christie's) $1,645

A mahogany partner's pedestal desk, 20th century, the top inset with a panel of green tooled leather, fitted with three drawers and an enclosed cupboard to each pedestal, 67in. wide. (Christie's) $1,397

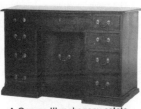

A George III mahogany estate desk, the rectangular top above a frieze drawer enclosing a slide and twelve lidded compartments, 46in. wide. (Bonhams) $8,280

A mahogany and gilt-metal mounted pedestal desk, late 19th/early 20th century, the plum-pudding figured top with an inset gilt and tooled leather cloth, 55in. wide. (Christie's) $3,454

A mahogany pedestal desk, 20th century, of George III style, the red leather lined top with a gadrooned edge, two slides and three frieze drawers, 60in. wide. (Christie's) $4,724

An early Victorian mahogany cylinder front pedestal desk, with three-quarter gallery top above cylinder enclosing five pigeonholes flanked by four drawers, with pull-out adjustable writing surface, 152cm. wide. (Bristol) $2,320

A Victorian satinbirch pedestal desk, by Holland and Sons, circa 1880, the rectangular top with a three quarter baluster gallery above nine drawers to the kneehole, 62¼in. wide. (Bonhams) $4,736

A mahogany pedestal desk, George III and later with a gilt tooled red-leather lined top, three frieze drawers with panelled tablets to either end, 66in. wide. (Christie's) $2,418

An early Victorian mahogany pedestal desk, the rectangular top with damaged leather inset and three frieze drawers, 48in. wide. (Bonhams) $1,109

A walnut serpentine partner's desk, 20th century, the green leather-lined top with canted corners and a gadrooned edge and three frieze drawers to each side, 63in. wide. (Christie's) $2,796

An oak kneehole desk, 18th century, with a molded top and seven drawers surrounding the kneehole, on bracket feet, 37¾in. wide. (Christie's) $1,068

A late Victorian mahogany pedestal desk, decorated with checker-lines, the superstructure fitted with a hinged central compartment enclosing letter divisions, 54in. wide. (Christie's) $4,844

A Victorian birch pedestal desk, with a red leather lined top and an inverted breakfront frieze with three drawers, 48in. wide. (Christie's) $1,974

An oak and parquetry kneehole desk, 19th century, Continental, probably Belgian, in the gothic taste, the superstructure with pierced fleurs de lys and foliate three quarter gallery, 64½in. wide. (Christie's) $5,814

A Victorian mahogany roll top desk, 121cm. wide. (Bonhams) $786

A mahogany pedestal desk, early 19th century, the rectangular top with molded overhanging edge and divided into six panels, the center panel with adjustable ratcheted slope, 45¾in. wide. (Christie's) $5,451

A mahogany kneehole desk, late 19th/early 20th century, the rectangular top with a molded edge above a frieze drawer, 39in. wide. (Christie's) $1,188

An Edwardian satinwood and inlaid kidney-shaped desk, decorated throughout with crossbanding and line-inlay, with a green leather-lined top and nine drawers around the kneehole, 47in. wide. (Christie's) $4,605

An early Georgian walnut kneehole desk, the quarter veneered and feather banded top with molded edging and rounded corners, 30¾in. wide. (Andrew Hartley) $12,760

A George III rosewood crossbanded and walnut veneered kneehole desk, the rectangular crossbanded top inset with a panel of green tooled leather with a molded edge, 49½in. wide.
(Christie's) $5,451

A George III mahogany kneehole desk, the rectangular top inset with a gilt-tooled green leather, above a frieze drawer with a recessed cupboard door, 45in. wide.
(Christie's) $3,353

A Victorian mahogany pedestal partner's desk, the rounded rectangular green and gilt tooled leather lined top with three frieze drawers to either side, 60in. wide.
(Christie's) $5,088

A late Victorian oak roll-top desk, with low scroll-carved three quarter gallery, above a cylinder front, three frieze drawers below and three further graduated drawers to each pedestal, 51½in. wide.
(Christie's) $2,125

Queen Anne walnut inlaid bureau table, Boston, 1735-60, the top, outlined in stringing, has a molded edge above a single drawer and two banks of small drawers flanking the raised panel door, 33¾in. wide.
(Skinner) $25,300

A good mid Victorian oak and burr walnut pedestal desk, circa 1865, the galleried and balustraded rear superstructure with two sets of graduated drawers with Wellington action locks above a leather inset slope, 60in. wide.
(Bonhams) $4,312

A Victorian mahogany pedestal desk, the molded rectangular top with hinged flap to one side and with green leather writing-surface, above two drawers to the front and two to the reverse, 53¾in. wide.
(Christie's) $5,088

A Victorian mahogany kneehole desk, the rectangular lined top above a frieze fitted with a long slide enclosing a ratcheted writing surface, 45in. wide.
(Christie's) $4,605

A Victorian mahogany pedestal desk, of Dickens type, the superstructure with shelved gallery between raised banks of four drawers enclosed by locking stiles, 61¾in. wide.
(Christie's) $3,271

A mahogany linen press, early 19th century, the checker-banded and machicolated cornice above a line-inlaid frieze, 50in. wide.
(Christie's) $3,496

A George III mahogany breakfront clothes-press, the molded rectangular cornice above a pair of geometrically-panelled doors, enclosing a modern lined interior, 110½in. wide.
(Christie's) $20,727

A Regency mahogany clothes press, the detachable cornice with a tablet, above sliding trays enclosed by panelled doors, 4ft.4in.
(Woolley & Wallis) $1,380

A mahogany linen press, the molded cornice over two panelled doors with applied beading, two short over two long drawers below, 19th century, 49½in. wide.
(Andrew Hartley) $1,362

An oak and inlaid linen cupboard, English, circa 1895, pair of cupboard doors enclosing shelves, each door decorated with rectangular panels of dark stained wood inlaid with metal stylized flowers, 56½in. wide.
(Christie's) $2,961

A George III mahogany linen press, the dentil cornice above the panelled and satinwood banded double doors, the lower section fitted with two short above two long drawers, 50½in. wide.
(Wintertons) $2,660

A George III mahogany linen press with molded cavetto cornice, two panelled doors enclosing slides, two short over two long drawers, 49¼in. wide.
(Andrew Hartley) $4,402

A 19th century mahogany dining room linen press, with a molded cornice above sliding trays enclosed by panel doors, 4ft.3in. wide.
(Woolley & Wallis) $1,704

A George III mahogany linen press, molded cornice above panelled double doors, the lower section fitted with two short over two graduated long cock-beaded drawers, 50in. wide.
(Wintertons) $2,310

Early 19th century mahogany
crossbanded lowboy, canted front
corners, molded edge, fitted with
two short frieze drawers over a full
width drawer, 30in.
(G A Key) $3,200

An oak lowboy, 18th century, the
later rectangular top above five
drawers and raised on slender
carved cabriole legs with pad feet,
92cm. wide.(Bonhams) $795

An oak lowboy on ring turned
supports with two frieze drawers,
69cm. wide.
(Bonhams & Brooks) $216

A George I walnut lowboy, the
cross and feather-banded quarter-
veneered top with re-shaped re-
entrant corners, above three
drawers and a shaped apron,
30¼in. wide.
(Christie's) $6,541

A walnut lowboy, early 18th
century, possibly Anglo Dutch, of
unusual design, the overhanging
serpentine top with re-entrant
corners, possibly of a later date,
34½in. wide.
(Christie's) $8,460

A George I walnut lowboy, the
molded rectangular quarter-
veneered and crossbanded top with
re-entrant corners above a small
frieze drawer and a shaped arch
and flanked by a deep drawer to
each side, 29in. wide.
(Christie's) $7,350

A George II oak low boy with yew
wood cross banding to the top and
to three small drawers arranged
about a kneehole.
(David Lay) $2,393

Queen Anne walnut lowboy, with
rectangular top and three frieze
drawers above a scrolled apron on
cabriole legs ending in pad feet.
(Skinner) $1,840

A George I walnut lowboy, inlaid
with boxwood lines, the quarter-
veneered canted rectangular
associated top above three short
drawers around a shaped
kneehole, 32¼in. wide.
(Christie's) $9,994

An Italian walnut and bone-inlaid bedside cupboard, late 19th/early 20th century, in the Renaissance taste, inlaid a la certosina, with broken pediment ledge back with panel inlaid with a putti, 20½in. wide. (Christie's) $1,180

A pair of Edwardian mahogany marble topped pot cupboards. (Bonhams) $729

A Regency mahogany pot cupboard, with a low three-quarter gallery and hinged fall front, on tapering ring-turned legs, 15½in. wide. (Christie's) $246

A Dutch mahogany and marquetry cylinder pot cupboard, 19th century, with an inlaid bird and cherub surrounded by floral and foliate decoration to the top, 15in. diameter.
(Christie's) $1,068

A pair of Regency mahogany bedside tables, each with rounded square three-quarter galleried top above a door, the sides with pierced carrying-handles, on ring-turned and reeded tapering legs and feet, 14in. square.
(Christie's) $10,345

An Italian decorated and parcel-gilt bedside cabinet, 18th century, of tapering form, of serpentine outline, inset with a later marble top containing a drawer enclosed by a shaped panel door, 15¾in. wide.
(Christie's) $5,414

A Federal mahogany marble-top basin stand, New York, 1800-1820, the rectangular dished marble top with cusped corners above a conforming case fitted with a drawer over a cupboard, 19in. wide.
(Christie's) $17,250

Louis XVI style mahogany marble-top table de nuit, late 19th century, with brass three quarter gallery and gray and white marble top above three drawers, 24in. wide.
(Skinner) $460

An Italian walnut, crossbanded and marquetry bedside cabinet, the crossbanded top with roundel inlay, containing a deep drawer and enclosed by a panel door below, 21½in. wide.(Christie's) $1,272

A pair of early 19th century black lacquered wooden face screens of waisted oblong form with scrolled corners, depicting various Egyptian motifs in yellow, 9in. wide.
(Andrew Hartley) $508

A Victorian rosewood pole screen, the oblong Crossley Mosaic panel depicting a mother and children with a barrow, 56½in. high.
(Andrew Hartley) $464

English gros point and petit point five-panel floor screen, 18th/19th century, depicting allegorical scenes of figures with town views in background, scrollwork, drapery, and flowers, each panel 78 x 20¾in. (Skinner) $5,750

A Victorian carved walnut three-fold screen, in the Renaissance taste, with pierced foliate winged beast cresting and armorial shield with initials of Charles Frederick Huth, each panel 27in. wide, 81in. high.
(Christie's) $3,619

Alvar Aalto, a pine screen, Model No. 100, designed 1935-36, manufactured by Oy Huonekalu-ja Rakennustyötehdas AB for Artek, the rolled pine slats strung with wire, 74in. long.
(Christie's) $10,833

An early 19th century giltwood screen, the frame as two cornucopiae centered by a panel embroidered on both sides, on eagle headed column and platform base, 100cm. high.
(Finarte) $32,579

A William IV mahogany and beadwork firescreen, circa 1835, the later beadwork sliding frame set on four carved legs, 55cm. wide.
(Bonhams) $252

A French mahogany, elm and gilt-metal mounted polescreen, 19th century, in the Empire taste, the roundel centered arched cresting depicting a Napoleonic emblem above a shield-shaped upholstered panel, 45½in. high.
(Christie's) $812

A French giltwood and silk four-fold screen, each rectangular panel with a channelled frame and foliate cresting, the silk woven with foliate scrolls, 58¼in. high.
(Christie's) $3,496

A mid Victorian carved rosewood firescreen of large proportions, with original tapestry panel, 83cm. wide. (Bonhams & Brooks) $1,120

A rare Queen Anne carved walnut firescreen, Philadelphia, circa 1750, the urn-form finial above a flaring shaft mounted with a rectangular needlework panel, 4ft.9½in. high. (Sotheby's) $20,700

A French gilt bronze firescreen, late 19th or early 20th century, the cartouche-shaped frame of naturalistic form, with loop handle and on splayed feet, 26½in. wide. (Christie's) $1,086

A Biedermeier mahogany three-leaf screen, first half 19th century, of gothic form, each leaf with gothic cresting above triple gothic-arched panel, each leaf 82 x 24½in. (Christie's) $3,395

A pair of early 19th century black lacquered wooden face screens, depicting Middle Eastern figure scenes in yellow with turned ivory handles, 14½in. long. (Andrew Hartley) $490

An Arts & Crafts oak framed three-leaf draught screen with three Liberty style fruit embossed panels above frieze of inset brass studs, 5ft.8in. high.(Brightwells) $662

A late 18th century painted leather three-fold screen 168cm. long x 199cm. high. (Bonhams & Brooks) $2,960

A good late Victorian three-fold walnut and parcel gilt relief rule screen, 220cm. long x 198cm. high. (Bonhams & Brooks) $981

A Victorian rosewood fire screen with tapestry inset panel, 66cm. wide. (Bonhams & Brooks) $585

A Regency mahogany secrétaire bookcase, with a molded cornice and a pair of astragal glazed doors, the panelled fall front with knob handles, 47in. wide.
(Christie's) $5,428

A Regency mahogany and satinwood secrétaire bookcase with a pair of astragal glazed doors, banded to the sides, the fall front with pierced foliate handles and floral escutcheons.
(Christie's) $25,909

A George III mahogany secrétaire linen press, the upper part with a molded cornice fitted with trays and enclosed by a pair of panelled doors, 49in. wide.
(Christie's) $8,122

A Regency mahogany and brass-inlaid secrétaire bookcase, the molded cornice above a brass inlaid frieze with monogram decoration to the corners above a pair of astragal glazed doors, 45¼in. wide.
(Christie's) $4,343

An early Victorian yew wood secrétaire-cabinet, by T & G Seddon, the pierced cresting with central vase, flanked by a cherub on a horse-drawn chariot, above a canted rectangular cabinet, 52in. wide. (Christie's) $9,994

A mahogany secrétaire bookcase, George III top and lower part associated, the upper part with a molded dentil cornice and crossbanded frieze, 41½in. wide.
(Christie's) $4,543

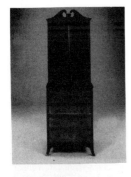

A fine late Victorian inlaid satinwood secrétaire bookcase, restorations, 72cm. wide.
(Bonhams & Brooks) $9,800

A George III mahogany secrétaire bookcase, the upper stage with molded cornice and fitted double astragal glazed doors, the lower stage with fall front, 33in. wide.
(Wintertons) $11,040

A Classical carved mahogany desk-and-bookcase, attributed to Anthony H. Jenkins, Baltimore, circa 1835-1840, in two sections, 41¼in. wide.
(Christie's) $9,200

Federal mahogany and mahogany veneer desk bookcase, probably Massachusetts, circa 1825, the top section with flat molded cornice above two glazed doors, 39in. wide. (Skinner) **$1,610**

A small late 18th century mahogany secrétaire bookcase, the base with a fall front with a molded outline, reveals a fitted interior, later handles, 3ft.½in. wide. (Woolley & Wallis) **$67,200**

Classical rosewood veneer glazed desk and bookcase, New York City, 1840s, the molded cornice above a frieze and glazed doors with applied gothic ornament, 44in. wide. (Skinner) **$5,175**

English Provincial Regency inlaid oak bureau bookcase, the upper section with two panel and glass doors opening to shelves, the lower section fitted with two short over three long drawers, 45in. wide. (Skinner) **$1,725**

A George III mahogany secrétaire bookcase, the upper section with a dentil molded cornice and a pair of astragal glazed doors, 47¾in. wide. (Christie's) **$6,909**

Classical carved mahogany veneer glazed desk and bookcase, Boston, 1830s, the cove-molded cornice above the glazed doors flanked by columns with leaf carved tops and turned bases, 44¾in. wide. (Skinner) **$11,500**

A mahogany and marquetry secrétaire bookcase, with a swan neck pediment, checker-banded, molded cornice above a pair of astragal glazed doors, 44in. wide. (Christie's) **$1,848**

A North European mahogany secrétaire bookcase, 19th century, with two glazed doors to the upper section, enclosing shelves and a drawer below, 41in. wide. (Christie's) **$1,974**

Late Federal mahogany veneer desk/bookcase, North Shore area Massachusetts, 1820s, the scrolled pediment above the recessed panel doors, 42in. wide. (Skinner) **$4,025**

A Victorian rosewood secrétaire/music cabinet with stringing and marquetry, raised mirrored back with shelf on foliate supports, 22½in. wide.
(Andrew Hartley) $1,077

An Edwardian mahogany pedestal desk, with satinwood banding and stringing, the molded edged top with inset green leather, ivory inlaid turned wood handles, 41½in. wide.
(Andrew Hartley) $1,738

A French rosewood, tulipwood crossbanded and marquetry bonheur du jour, 19th century, with ormolu mounts, the upper part with cavetto frieze and pierced S-scroll gallery, 31in. wide.
(Christie's) $9,085

A Queen Anne walnut writing cabinet, with feather banding, the molded cornice over cushion frieze drawer, fall front, the base with two short over two long drawers, 48in. wide.
(Andrew Hartley) $4,620

A Louis XV style ormolu-mounted green-painted and polychromed bureau de dame, late 19th century, attributed to Joseph E. Zwiener or François Linke, the serpentine rectangular top above a bombé case, 29in. wide.
(Christie's) $12,075

An Irish walnut military chest with brass trim by Ross & Co, Dublin, hinged top revealing two folding serpentine shelves, secrétaire drawer with fall front, 19th century, 44in. wide.
(Andrew Hartley) $6,116

A 19th century Biedermeier walnut secrétaire, with molded cornice over frieze drawer, fall front below, three long drawers under, 39½in. wide.
(Andrew Hartley) $1,232

A brass and simulated tortoiseshell inlaid ebonized desk, 20th century, with a central frieze drawer and cupboard below flanked to either side by frieze drawers, 47in. wide.
(Christie's) $987

A bird's eye maple wellington chest with rosewood banding, five graduated drawers with turned wood handles, secrétaire as two dummy drawers with fitted interior, 25in. wide.
(Andrew Hartley) $4,727

A late Federal mahogany veneered desk-and-bookcase, Massachusetts, 1810-1820, the upper part with shaped cornice centering a fluted reserve, 43in. wide. (Christie's) $4,700

An unusual Regency mahogany and ebony inlaid secrétaire serving table, with ebonized moldings, the stepped superstructure, with lead baize lined compartments, 51½in. wide. (Christie's) $3,452

A Charles X burr-elm secrétaire-cabinet, the molded rectangular cornice above a shaped frieze-drawer and a pair of silk-backed glazed doors, 39in. wide. (Christie's) $4,715

A Spanish walnut and gilt-metal mounted vargueño on later stand, late 17th/early 18th century, with restoration, partially fitted interior containing drawers, with engraved ivory panels and scrolls, the cabinet, 41½in. wide. (Christie's) $2,030

A Federal inlaid mahogany secretary desk, North Shore, Massachusetts or Portsmouth, New Hampshire, 1790-1810, the upper part with rectangular top and molded edge, 41in. wide.(Christie's) $9,400

A late Louis XV ormolu-mounted tulipwood, amaranth and parquetry semainier, by Pierre Harry Mewesen, quarter-veneered overall, the shaped molded brèche d'alep marble top above seven drawers, 30in. wide. (Christie's) $7,921

A walnut crossbanded and feather-strung secrétaire on chest, early 18th century, the upper part with a molded cornice and fitted with a cushion frieze drawer, having a fall enclosing a fitted interior, 39in. wide. (Christie's) $7,600

A Scottish mahogany secrétaire cabinet, early 19th century, the door with a fall front revealing ten fruitwood banded drawers on pedestals, each with a molded gadrooned door, 46in. wide. (Christie's) $1,771

A Franco Flemish rosewood and brass-bound travelling writing chest or cabinet, late 17th/early 18th century and later, on later stand, 29in. wide. (Christie's) $4,061

A William and Mary figured walnut and featherbanded fall front secrétaire chest, late 17th century, restorations and later handles 106cm. wide x 168cm. high.
(Bonhams & Brooks) $9,240

An Italian brass-mounted walnut commode, late 17th/early 18th century, decorated overall with scrolling foliage and flowers, the rectangular top above a panelled hinged frieze secrétaire-drawer, 57in. wide.
(Christie's) $8,343

A Federal inlaid mahogany cylinder-top desk-and-bookcase, Baltimore, 1800-1815, on three sections, the rectangular molded and dentilled cornice above a frieze inlaid to simulate fluting, 44½in. wide. (Christie's) $32,900

A Federal inlaid mahogany secretary desk, attributed to the shop of John and Thomas Seymour, Boston, circa 1800, the upper section with a rectangular top with banded and inlaid edges.
(Christie's) $52,875

A Federal inlaid mahogany writing bureau, Mid-Atlantic States, 1790-1810, the rectangular top with string-inlaid edges above a conforming case fitted with a string-inlaid fall-front lid with cockbeaded surround, 43¼in. wide.
(Christie's) $2,820

A Napoleon III ormolu-mounted Japanese lacquer, mother of pearl, ebony, amboyna and mahogany secrétaire à abattant, in the manner of Adam Weisweiler, circa 1855, the Japanese lacquer Edo Period (1615-1868). 29½in. wide.
(Christie's) $36,966

A Regency rosewood and brass mounted lady's secrétaire chiffonier, circa 1815, the raised shelf superstructure with an interlocking arch pierced three quarter brass gallery, 30½in. wide.
(Bonhams) $6,002

A Victorian Irish walnut military chest, of two sections, with an arrangement of long and short drawers including a secrétaire drawer with a fall front, 44in. wide.
(Christie's) $4,277

A Restauration ormolu mounted mahogany secrétaire à abattant, the rectangular later top above a frieze-drawer and a fall-front, 37½in. wide.
(Christie's) $7,166

A Scottish George III mahogany sofa, with waved padded back, outscrolled arms and padded serpentine seat, on square tapering legs and block feet, with later brass and ceramic castors, 89in. wide. (Christie's) $8,722

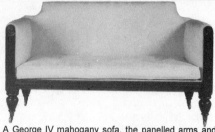

A George IV mahogany sofa, the panelled arms and seat-rail above turned tapering baluster legs, later supports to the underside, reduced in size, 61in. wide. (Christie's) $6,360

A rosewood chaise longue, alterations, lacking castors, 208cm. wide. (Bonhams & Brooks) $693

An early Victorian mahogany chaise longue, 217cm. wide. (Bonhams & Brooks) $847

A French giltwood and Aubusson tapestry upholstered canapé, 19th century, the channelled floral carved frame with overscrolled arms above a serpentine seat-rail, with foliate garland frieze, on short cabriole legs, 71½in. wide. (Christie's) $1,447

A mahogany and inlaid hall bench, parts 19th century and later, the shaped molded back with roundel ornament and oval stringing, 58in. wide. (Christie's) $1,480

A Federal carved and inlaid mahogany sofa, probably Portsmouth, New Hampshire, circa 1810, the arched crest flanked by upholstered arms terminating in reeded hand-rests above reeded baluster arm supports, 78½in. wide. (Christie's) $11,750

A Continental mahogany scroll end sofa, 19th century, in the Biedermeier style, with arched foliate scroll top-rail and upholstered panelled back and sides with bolsters and stuff-over seat, 84¾in. wide. (Christie's) $2,715

A George III mahogany sofa, the arms later embellished and carved with acanthus leaves and quatrefoil panels, on square molded legs headed by pierced fretwork brackets, 78½in. wide.
(Christie's) $6,360

A pair of Louis-Philippe mahogany billiard benches, each with tripartite pierced x-shaped splat back centered by a patera and with a molded tablet toprail, 89¾in. wide. (Woolley & Wallis) $18,860

A George IV mahogany day bed, the serpentine side rest carved with Greek key pattern to the top with panelled sides, shaped back rest with scrolled terminal and paw support, 67in. long.
(Christie's) $6,360

A William IV carved mahogany sofa, with molded rectangular and upholstered panelled back, cushion seat and padded arm supports with foliate scroll terminals, each rail centered by a rosette, 83in. wide.
(Christie's) $4,705

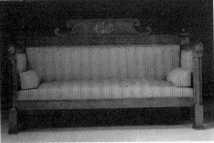

A Swedish Biedermeier giltmetal-mounted and brass-inlaid birch sofa, first half 19th century, banded overall with ropetwist, the C-scrolled tablet cresting centered by a fruited mount, previously with further finial to the top rail, part remounted, 83in. wide.
(Christie's) $2,452

A matched pair of William IV rosewood sofas, after a design by John Taylor, each with panelled toprail with acanthus-carved ends, above a padded back and seat-cushion, 86¾in. wide.(Christie's) $15,445

An oak box seat settle, French, 18th / 19th century, with rectangular back and sides, plank seat and panelled front incorporating two hingeless doors held by swivel catches, 66½in. wide.
(Christie's) $1,604

Edwardian style tufted brown leather chesterfield sofa, of typical form, with brass tacking, 79in. long. (Skinner) $2,185

Windsor ash, pine and maple bamboo turned settee, New England, circa 1810, the straight crest rail with bowed ends above twenty-five spindles and slightly scrolled arms on shaped seat and eight legs joined by stretchers, 75¹/₈in. long. (Skinner) $5,175

An Anglo-Indian metal-mounted sofa, probably circa 1880, the arched convex back surmounted by floral ornament, flanked to each side by peacocks, the frame flanked to each side by a lion armrest, 77in. wide. (Christie's) $9,242

Italian neo-classical fruitwood day bed, early 19th century, with post form supports, the arms and legs carved with lappets, on ball feet, 69½in. long. (Skinner) $460

A Biedermeier satinbirch, ebonized and parcel gilt sofa, 19th century, the curved top-rail and upholstered back with rounded arms and padded seat between stiff-leaf capped detached column supports, raised on block feet, 75in. wide. (Christie's) $1,463

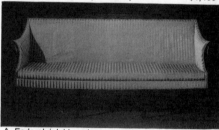

A Federal inlaid mahogany sofa, New York, 1800-1815, the string-inlaid crest centred by a raised tablet with fleur-de-lys, swag and quarter-fan inlay above string-inlaid downswept arms with outscrolling and paterae-inlaid handholds, 80½in. wide. (Christie's) $16,100

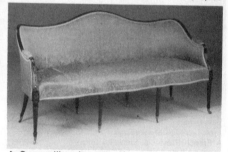

A George III mahogany sofa, with molded arched upholstered back and undulating stuff-over seat, with padded molded arm supports with foliage ornament, 79in. wide. (Christie's) $7,896

A pair of early Victorian upholstered sofas, each with padded back, arms and seat, covered in studded black leather, the shaped carved arms with palmette panels on turned gadrooned legs, the back legs replaced, each 84in. wide. (Christie's) $4,935

American Renaissance Revival carved walnut and parcel-gilt settee, attributed to John Jeliff, circa 1865-70, with low back and raised and tufted ends, carved with foliage, pendants, and with masks on the arms, on turned circular legs on castors, 81in. long. (Skinner) $2,070

A Biedermeier satinbirch sofa with a shaped pedimented top-rail, padded back, overscrolled arms with turned ebonized rails, and a drop-in seat with compartment below, 100in. wide. (Christie's) $863

A French Provincial fruitwood hump-back serpentine canapé, early 19th century, with scroll-carved shaped apron, on cabriole legs terminating in scroll feet, 79in. wide. (Christie's) $2,812

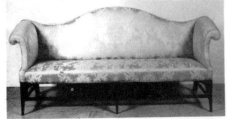

A Georgian mahogany framed settee with shaped back and scrolled arms, upholstered in green damask on six slender square taper supports with understretchers, outswept back supports, 8ft.long. (G.A. Key) $4,293

Federal mahogany and bird's-eye maple veneer sofa, Massachusetts or New Hampshire, circa 1810, the raked veneered crest divided into three panels by cross-banded mahogany inlay and flanked by reeded arms, 75½in. wide. (Skinner) $6,900

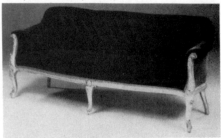

A carved giltwood sofa, late 19th century, with a deep buttoned back and arms, with foliate scroll carved terminals and a serpentine seat, with a guilloche carved front-rail and foliate and shell capped cabriole legs with scrolled feet, 84in. wide. (Christie's) $1,974

L. & J.G. Stickley even-arm settle, Fayetteville, New York, circa 1912, straight-capped horizontal rail over sixteen wide vertical slats, rail continuing to sides over five wide vertical slats, 76in. wide. (Skinner) $4,600

A classical carved mahogany sofa, New York, 1810-1825, the veneered backscrolling tablet crest above an upholstered back flanked by similar outscrolling arms over reeded S-shaped supports, 88¼in. wide. (Christie's) $7,050

A pair of park benches 'Parkbänk nr. 2', Folke Bensow för Näfveqvarns Bruk, the end of black cast iron, green painted wood seats, 1925, 108cm. long. (Stockholms AV) $2,388

Gothic Revival oak hall bench, composed of some antique elements, with tall backrest inset with foliate and figural panels, 34in. wide. (Skinner) $690

Marcel Breuer for Isokon 1935-6. Long chair with dark stained bent laminated frame and bent birch ply seat with original cream tweed cushion, unmarked, 145cm. long. (Bristol) $3,454

Painted pine settle, possibly Long Island, New York, early 19th century, the flat top above a beaded long and grooved back joining shaped sides continuing to arms. (Skinner) $2,415

One of a pair of French Provincial twin chair back straw seat settles, 19th century, each with wavy splats, upswept arms with baluster supports, squab cushions and trailing floral carved front rails, 43½in. wide. (Christie's) (Two) $3,365

A carved-oak 'Gothic' settle, French, the rectangular back with six panels filled with tracery and arches, surmounted by three pierced geometrical tracery panels between uprights, 74½in. wide. (Christie's) $11,586

Gothic style carved walnut two-seat choir bench, late 19th century, with high back pierced with tracery-style carving, over quatrefoil and fleur-de-lis diamond patterned back, 46in. wide. (Skinner) $2,300

A William Morris ebonized settee. (G. E. Sworder) $1,280

Gothic style oak hall bench, late 19th century, with tall backrest fitted with three figural, foliate and seraph carved panels, 60in. wide. (Skinner) $1,955

A pair of Central European polychrome parcel-giltwood architectural wall brackets, 18th century, each modelled with two human heads and stylized foliate scrolls, 38¾in. high,
(Christie's) $3,476

A yew-wood fret-cut hanging corner shelf, possibly 19th century, with three tiered and bowfronted shelves, 38in. high.
(Christie's) $1,070

An adzed oak delft rack by Robert Thompson, Kilburn, with molded cornice, three central small bow fronted shelves flanked on either side by three shelves, 55½in. wide.
(Andrew Hartley) $1,675

An Edwardian mahogany set of folding shelves, possibly for maritime use, early 20th century, the serpentine cresting, apron and sides with inset brass stringing, 10½in. protrusion when opened.
(Christie's) $822

Rosewood grained and painted wall shelf, probably northern New England, 1825-35, the scrolled crest continues to shaped sides which flank three light gray painted shelves, 42in. wide.
(Skinner) $11,500

Mahogany and poplar medicine chest, probably New England, first half 19th century, the scrolled sides flank graduated shelves with round perforations above two small drawers, inscribed *Grandmother Beal's Medicine Chest*, 13in. wide.
(Skinner) $460

Walnut whale-end four-tier shelf, New England, 19th century, 30in. high, 19in. long, 7½in. deep.
(Skinner) $1,725

A pair of early Victorian giltwood corner shelves, each with pierced, scrolling, foliate, beaded and stiff-leaf decoration, with three shaped tiers and mirrored backs, 22in. wide. (Christie's) $3,948

Red-painted pine three-tier hanging wall shelf, New England, 19th century, with canted sides, 28½ x 25¼in. (Skinner) $978

An Edwardian mahogany sideboard of Sheraton design, the whole of bold shaped outline with incurved ends and brass curtain rail to back, 62in. wide.
(Canterbury) $2,682

Aesthetic Movement carved mahogany sideboard, 1870s, by the Cincinnati Women's Wood Carving Movement, the super-structure with mirror frame flanked by shelves, 58in. wide.
(Skinner) $10,925

A George III mahogany bowfront sideboard, decorated with crossbanding, lines and quartered fan medallions, 53in. wide.
(Christie's) $8,384

A mid Victorian walnut mirror back sideboard, the central of the three plates to the back arched and with carved cresting, 182cm. long.
(Dreweatt Neate) $4,050

A George IV mahogany veneered sideboard, the low back with an open shelf on carved brackets and with an anthemion carved crest, 66in. (David Lay) $2,034

An Art Nouveau oak sideboard, the raised mirror with shaped molded cornice and scrolling stylized leaf carved decoration, 60in. wide.
(Dreweatt Neate) $874

An Arts and Crafts oak sideboard, circa 1905, stamped by Shapland and Petter on one lock, with copper panels, 184cm. wide.
(Bonhams) $1,960

A Regency mahogany bowfront sideboard, fitted with a central frieze drawer with a recessed apron drawer below, 48in. wide.
(Christie's) $3,997

Classical mahogany and mahogany veneer server, probably Boston, circa 1825, the gallery with beaded edge joining two end plinths with brass inlay, 42in. wide.
(Skinner) $12,650

A mahogany sideboard, early 20th century, the upper section with a molded cornice and a central arched bevelled plate flanked to either side by a glazed cabinet, 68in. wide. (Christie's) $904

A carved oak sideboard 'Modèle Chicorée', designed by Louis Majorelle, circa 1905, central drawer above open shelf with twin-door cabinet below, width. 63¾in. (Christie's) $18,630

An Arts and Crafts oak sideboard, the arched superstructure with an oval mirror, flanked by astragal glazed cabinets, the lower section with two frieze drawers and two further central drawers, 66in. wide. (Christie's) $164

A William IV flame mahogany sideboard, with a shaped pierced, scrolled and foliate-carved gallery back, above three cushion molded frieze drawers and a pair of pedestals, 76in. wide. (Christie's) $2,467

Arts & Crafts oak sideboard, retailed by Paine Furniture, Boston, no. 5229, circa 1915, shallow shelf above mirrored backsplash, rectangular top over three short center drawers flanked by side cabinets. (Skinner) $1,265

A mid Victorian mahogany mirror-back sideboard, of inverted breakfront outline, the arched rectangular mirror centered with a cabochon cresting with a central frieze drawer and arched panel door below, 62in. wide. (Christie's) $987

A Victorian oak and pollard sideboard, of breakfront D-shaped outline, with channelled line, lozenge and stylized flowerhead decoration, the mirror back with urn finials and roundels, 84in. wide. (Christie's) $1,068

A Victorian walnut Gothic Revival sideboard with ebonized banding and inlaid in various woods, the mirrored back with straight crest flanked by leaf carved columns, 66in. wide. (Andrew Hartley) $3,170

Classical carved mahogany veneer sideboard, New York, 1830s, the splashboard with molded edge and four spiral carved and turned columns topped by urn-shaped finials over a rectangular top, 60½in. wide. (Skinner) $2,760

Federal octagonal mahogany tilt-top stand, New England, late 18th/early 19th century, the top tilts over a vase and ring-turned post on tripod leg base, ending in pad feet, 26½in. high. (Skinner) $1,285

A pair of mahogany magazine stands, late 20th century, each with gilt brass ball finials and downcurved sides, on square legs with castors, 15¼in. wide. (Christie's) $635

Stickley Brothers pedestal, original finish, Quaint Furniture decal, 34in. high, 13 x 13in. (Skinner) $805

British 'Military' painted washtub on stand, 19th century, the tub painted black and with inscription *J.C. Craster, 5th Fusiliers*, the stand with iron banded edge, height of stand 29in. (Skinner) $517

An Edwardian mahogany plate/cutlery stand, the D-end top with spindle gallery and flatware compartment, on turned tapering supports, 25in. wide. (Christie's) $402

Pine and oak stand, New England, 1720-40, the round pine top above the square tapering chamfered oak standard, on cross-based oak feet, 17¼in. diameter. (Skinner) $748

Federal mahogany chamber stand, New England, circa 1815-25, the shaped splash-back with flanking quarter round shelves above a pierced top, 20½in. wide. (Skinner) $2,070

A Coalbrookdale cast iron corner stick stand, third quarter 19th century, third quarter 19th century, of triangular bowed form, the plateau with four circular apertures, 14½in. deep.(Christie's) $1,467

A green onyx and gilt metal mounted stand, the stepped square top raised on four turned and collared columns with Corinthian capitals, 13¼in. wide. (Andrew Hartley) $1,960

A 19th century mahogany urn stand, the square galleried top, over sliding shelf with brass drop handle, raised on four square tapering supports, 12in. wide.
(Andrew Hartley) $1,099

Lifetime Magazine rack, No. 253, three shelves, side slats, paper label, 26in. wide.
(Skinner) $518

A Victorian oak and brass stick stand, the galleried shelf with a drip pan below, on bracket feet, 22½in.
(Christie's) $3,496

Painted pine basin stand, New England, early 19th century, the backsplash with shaped sides over oblong top on conforming base with reeded skirt, 18¾in. wide.
(Skinner) $1,610

An inlaid mahogany lectern, designed by Josef Urban and Heinrich Leffler, 1908, the rectangular angled top above arched apron sides, each inlaid with a frieze of floral motifs in mother-of-pearl, 33¼in. wide.
(Christie's) $14,904

Federal mahogany and bird's eye maple veneer basin stand, attributed to the Seymour Workshop, Boston, circa 1810-15, 28¼in. high.
(Skinner) $36,800

Federal cherry one drawer stand, New England, late 18th/early 19th century, the oblong slightly overhanging top on four square tapering legs, 29½in. high.
(Skinner) $1,380

Cherry and inlaid maple and mahogany stand, probably Massachusetts, early 19th century, the cherry top overhangs a cockbeaded drawer inlaid with bird's eye maple, 26¾in. high.
(Skinner) $2,185

Classical tiger maple chamber stand, probably New York, circa 1825-30, the rectangular top on a conforming case with frieze drawer flanked by blocks, 24in. wide.
(Skinner) $4,600

A late Victorian mahogany and brass-mounted stick-stand, the galleried top above a panelled back with pierced slats and flanked by finials, 23cm. wide.
(Christie's) $7,268

A George III mahogany table lectern, late 18th or early 19th century, the angled support with two stays, on a turned knopped stem with wooden screw for height adjustment, 11in. wide.
(Christie's) $790

Chippendale mahogany tilt-top candlestand, Massachusetts, circa 1790, the molded top with serpentine sides and square corners tilts on a vase and ring turned post, 20in. wide.
(Skinner) $4,313

A George IV mahogany coat and hat hall stand, by Gillows, with two turned and gadrooned baluster uprights, surmounted by ball finials, the uprights lacking all the coat and hat branches, 55in. wide.
(Christie's) $2,180

A Scottish George IV mahogany trunk stand, the slatted rectangular top, above the rail with bronze plaque inscribed Cassillis, on turned baluster legs joined by conforming stretchers, 25in. wide.
(Christie's) $3,089

A William IV rosewood folio-stand, attributed to Smee and Son, the slatted hinged uprights with crossed ratcheted stands joined by baluster stretchers, on panelled trestle ends, 25½in. wide.
(Christie's) $4,724

Federal painted candlestand, probably New Hampshire, circa 1810, the square top with canted corners over an urn-shaped pedestal with chip carving joined to exaggerated cabriole legs, 15¾in.
(Skinner) $10,925

A North European carved burr maple gallery easel, first quarter 20th century, the A-frame uprights with stylized scrolled motifs to the finials and feet, 68in. high when lowered. (Christie's) $1,809

A Federal carved cherrywood candlestand, Norwich area, Connecticut, circa 1800, the circular dished top with scalloped edge above a ring and urn-turned support, 13in. diameter.
(Christie's) $13,800

A Victorian bedsteps night commode, veneered in satinwood with satinwood with carpet treads to the pull out fitting and lidded compartment, 27in. high.
(Woolley & Wallis) $1,378

A set of mahogany commode bed steps, English, late 19th century, with three tiers, the top two hingeing, the center fitted with a ceramic bowl and cover, 16½in. wide.
(Christie's) $1,747

A set of early 19th century bed steps, the treads with stretchers.
(Woolley & Wallis) $667

A set of Regency mahogany metamorphic library steps, in the manner of Morgan and Sanders, circa 1815, the bowed top rail and carved stretcher continuing to reeded over scrolled arms, caned seat, the steps 28¼in. high.
(Bonhams) $8,800

Whimsical mahogany miniature spiral staircase, 19th century, with dark rosewood-grained finish, on rectangular base with demi-lune cut out to center, 22'/8in. high.
(Skinner) $1,495

A set of mid Victorian bedsteps, each with black simulated leather lined step flanked by scrolled handles, the top step hinged and concealing a compartment, 20¼in. wide. (Christie's) $6,360

A set of George III style mahogany library steps 45cm. wide x 52cm. deep x 81cm. high.
(Bonhams & Brooks) $277

A set of mahogany triple tread library steps, 19th century, inset with red tooled leatherette panels, on baluster-turned and saber uprights, 30½in. wide.
(Christie's) $1,809

A late Victorian set of oak library steps, the square canted post with spherical finial, above double-sided steps each with gilt-tooled brown leather tread, 65½in. high.
(Christie's) $7,268

A Continental maple stool, second quarter 19th century, the rectangular upholstered seat on X-form supports.
(Sotheby's) $1,265

A joined oak stool, English part mid 17th century, the later molded seat, above a channelled frieze, on turned baluster legs.
(Bonham's) $539

A 19th century 'Gothic Revival' stool, the rectangular top covered wine patterned material, the grained wood frame with pierced and carved arched legs, 10½in. wide.
(Woolley & Wallis) $616

Arts & Crafts oak window bench, America, circa 1912, four square post legs with through tenon side stretchers on rectangular slat bench, 26¾in. long.
(Skinner) $690

One of a pair of 18th century Italian walnut rococo Inginocchiatoi, the molded shaped tops inset composite marble to a carved frieze, on a leaf carved scroll support, 26in. wide x 5ft.1in. high.
(Woolley & Wallis)
(Two) $3,002

A late Federal mahogany stool, Boston, 1810-1820, the rectangular over-upholstered seat above a conforming frame, on ring-turned, reeded cylindrical legs, 15in. wide.
(Christie's) $4,700

An early Victorian rosewood stool, the rectangular drop in seat to a molded frame, on leaf scroll appliqué molded cabriole legs, 23in.
(Woolley & Wallis) $847

An oak joined stool, English, early 20th century, in the early 17th century style, with molded top and arcaded friezes, 18in. wide.
(Christie's) $3,011

A William IV mahogany long stool, the rectangular top on X-frame scrolling legs, joined by two turned stretchers, 20in. wide.
(Christie's) $3,353

Classical mahogany carved footstool, Boston, 1825-29, the over-upholstered stool with a curule base including leaf carving, C-scrolls, and central concentric circles, 22½in. wide.
(Skinner) $1,265

An Italian carved walnut prie dieu, 18th/early 19th century, carved throughout with rosettes, shells, ribbon-tied floral swags and guilloche, 37in. wide.
(Christie's) $2,302

Good 19th century rosewood rectangular X frame stool, molded with foliage and a central rosette boss, joined by ring turned stretcher, tapestry upholstered seat and scrolled feet, 24in.
(G.A. Key) $1,099

A rosewood stool, 19th century, with padded striped seat, on molded cabriole legs with flowerhead and scroll ornament to the seat-rail terminating in tablet scroll feet and brass castors.(Christie's) $552

A late Victorian brass-mounted oak hall stool, attributed to James Shoolbred & Co., the rectangular seat with rectangular back with pierced baluster gallery, flanked by downswept arms on disk supports, 21½in. wide.
(Christie's) $3,503

A Regency mahogany and part-bronzed stool, the padded rectangular seat covered in associated earlier floral needlework, on an X-frame support with four sheep heads, 26in. wide.
(Christie's) $39,727

A Regency rosewood stool, early 19th century, the buttoned leather seat above the foliate carved X-frame with turned stretcher, 24in. wide. (Christie's) $3,619

Victorian mahogany duet stool of rectangular form, raised on ring turned tapering cylindrical supports with peg feet, 40in.
(G.A. Key) $232

A George I walnut oval stool, inset with a drop-in seat in the arched shaped seat-rail, on cabriole legs with foliate pendant and scallop shell carved knees terminating in pad feet, 20½in. wide.
(Christie's) $6,541

A Victorian cut-velvet upholstered ottoman, with hinged top and tassels to the corners enclosing a silk lined compartmentalized interior, 21in. square.
(Christie's) $724

A small yew-wood and fruitwood stool, English, late 17th century, with rectangular top and molded friezes, on block and bulbous turned legs, 14½in. wide.
(Christie's) $6,774

A mahogany stool, late 19th /early 20th century, the padded rectangular seat, on elaborately carved acanthus cabriole legs and scrolled feet, 26½in. wide.
(Christie's) $6,905

An oak joined stool, English, late 17th century, with molded rectangular top and molded scroll-carved friezes, on ring-turned legs, 18in. wide.
(Christie's) $4,278

A pair of Louis XVI white-painted walnut tabourets, seat-rail carved with Vitruvian scrolls and rosettes.
(Christie's) $10,845

A Regency mahogany chamber horse, with spirally-reeded baluster top-rail, above a pierced trellis horizontal splat, with a retractable step, 26¼in. wide.
(Christie's) $3,452

A Robert 'Mouseman' Thompson burr elm stool, 38cm. high.
(Christie's) $987

A walnut stool, 19th century, of William and Mary style, the molded rectangular frame with a drop-in seat on square cabriole legs, 18¼in. wide.
(Christie's) $2,362

An Edwardian mahogany and marquetry inlaid x-frame stool, 56cm. wide.
(Bonhams & Brooks) $770

A walnut stool, of George II style, 19th / early 20th century, the rectangular padded seat covered in gros and petit point needlework, on cabriole legs headed by shells and scrolled ears, 26in. wide.
(Christie's) $10,539

A Louis XV style gilt and molded stool, mid 19th century, gilding refreshed.
(Bonhams & Brooks) $169

A mahogany stool, of George II style, late 19th / 20th century, the square padded seat on lion monopodia cabriole legs with rosette and scrolled acanthus ears, 23in. square
(Christie's) $6,723

A joined oak backstool, late 17th century.
(Bonhams & Brooks) $154

A pair of North European gray-painted parcel-gilt and lacquered window stools, 19th/20th century, each with channelled armrests with ram's heads and on foliate balusters, 42½in. wide.
(Christie's) $6,601

An oak joined stool, English, mid 17th century, with molded rectangular top and geometrical strapwork friezes, on ring-turned legs, 18in. wide.
(Christie's) $3,387

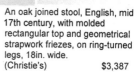

A George III mahogany chamber horse, the sprung seat covered in close-nailed black horse hair flanked by rounded rectangular arms, above a retractable step, 35½in. high.
(Christie's) $2,370

A Regency giltwood X-frame stool, restorations, later strengthening to underframe, 93cm. wide.
(Bonhams & Brooks) $1,050

A late Victorian rosewood adjustable piano stool, 44cm. wide.
(Bonhams & Brooks) $315

A French giltwood salon suite, late 19th century, in the Louis XV style, comprising a canapé, a set of four armchairs and a pair of bergères, each with a scroll-centered channelled rail with padded back and shaped arms with serpentine upholstered seat, the canapé, 78in. wide. (Christie's) $9,047

Two of a set of six Louis XVI giltwood fauteuils, each with arched channelled padded back, arms and seat covered in 18th century Aubusson tapestry, together with a near matching canapé, restorations, canapé 96in. wide. (Christie's)   (Seven Pieces) $11,680

An Anglo-Indian silvered-metal canapé, probably circa 1860, the foliate toprail centered by a monogram *CRM*, the back and seat deeply-buttoned in yellow damask, flanked to each side by an armrest with lion head terminal, the seat with a foliate apron, on four foliate baluster feet, 62½in. wide. (Christie's) $5,377

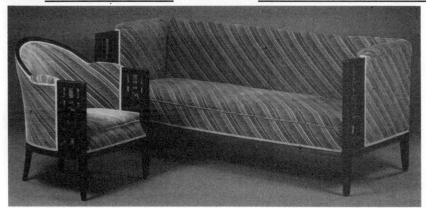

A walnut upholstered lounge suite, designed by Paul Follot, circa 1915, the three-seater settee with rectangular padded back and sides terminating in pierced panels with carved baskets of stylized flowers, with a pair of matching armchairs. (Christie's) $5,880

A Renaissance Revival ormolu-mounted rosewood suite of seating furniture, New York City, 1860-1880, comprising a sofa, armchair and two side chairs, the armchair with carved and gilded crest above an upholstered seat with incised gilt columns headed by turned finials over upholstered arms, 72in. wide. (Christie's) $2,990

'Aubepine', a giltwood salon suite, designed by Louis Majorelle, circa 1905, comprising: two armchairs and one settee. (Christie's) $20,445

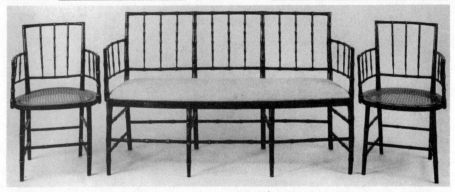

Suite of George III black lacquer and faux bamboo seating furniture, early 19th century, comprising a settee and pair of armchairs. (Skinner) $1,265

Impressive American Rococo Revival rosewood parlor suite, circa 1855, attributed to John Henry Belter, comprising a settee, pair of lady's chairs and a pair of side chairs, each with laminated rose and foliate carved cresting and grapevine openwork sides, settee 65in. long. (Skinner) $14,375

Suite of American Renaissance Revival carved walnut seating furniture, circa 1870, comprising a settee, pair of armchairs and four side chairs, each with foliate carved frame, settee 72in. long. (Skinner) $2,990

Suite of Empire style gilt bronze mounted mahogany seating furniture, comprising a settee, pair of armchairs and pair of side chairs, each with foliate and figural mounts, settee 80in. long. (Skinner) $1,725

A French matched giltwood suite, late 19th century, in the Louis XV style, comprising a pair of armchairs, a sofa and four side chairs, each with cartouche-shaped back and floral cresting. (Christie's) $3,188

A gilt wood and gesso five piece salon suite, French, late 19th century, in early 18th century style, comprising a canapé, a pair of armchairs and a pair of side chairs. (Sotheby's) $6,413

Suite of Louis XVI style giltwood seating furniture, late 19th century, comprising a pair of armchairs and a settee, each with ribband and foliate carving on circular fluted legs, settee 54in. long. (Skinner) $978

George III mahogany architect's table, late 18th century, the top with ratcheted center section, drop leaves and sliding front with fitted interior, 42in. wide.
(Skinner) $4,600

A George III mahogany architect's desk, adjustable rising rectangular top, fitted with two slides to the sides with gilt metal pulls, the front fitted with a dummy drawer.
(Wintertons) $5,586

A Regency mahogany architect's table, in the manner of Gillows, the double-hinged ratcheted top with reeded edge and with removable book rest to each side, 43¼in. wide.
(Christie's) $9,994

A George III mahogany draughtsman's or architect's table, the rectangular hinged double ratcheted adjustable top with push-out book ledge and fitted with swivel candle slides to the sides, 41¾in. wide.
(Christie's) $9,953

A George III mahogany architect's or draughtsman's table, of small size, with double hinged ratcheted top and brass holes for book ledge containing a pull-out frieze with re-entrant baize lined panelled slide, 36in. wide.(Christie's) $6,334

An early 19th century mahogany draughtsman's table, the lift up top on an easel, candlestands and an undertier on trestle ends, with splay legs on brass castors, 3ft.
(Woolley & Wallis) $1,704

An early George III mahogany architect's table, the later carved frieze enclosing a slide and an arrangement of fitted compartments 89cm. wide.
(Bonhams & Brooks) $3,696

A George III mahogany and inlaid architect's table, crossbanded in rosewood, inlaid with lines, the hinged double ratcheted top with molded edge and hinged flap to the back, 29¼in. wide.
(Christie's) $6,514

A George III mahogany architect's table, the sloping ratcheted top with a book rest and slides to either side, 44in. wide.
(Christie's) $9,200

A Regency rosewood and brass inlaid breakfast table, restorations, 120cm. diameter.
(Bonhams & Brooks) $4,340

An early Victorian rosewood breakfast table, the circular tilt top with a molded edge, on a boldly reeded bulbous pedestal, 53in. wide. (Christie's) $2,632

A William IV carved mahogany breakfast table, early 19th century, the circular snap top with reeded frieze divided by acanthus leaf carved panels, 61½in. diameter.
(Christie's) $14,476

A George III mahogany breakfast-table, the oval crossbanded and quarter-veneered tilt-top on a turned baluster column and three reeded cabriole legs, 49¾in. wide.
(Christie's) $3,271

A late George III mahogany and line-inlaid oval breakfast table, the crossbanded top with a molded edge and turned column support and downswept legs with brass caps and castors, 60in. wide.
(Christie's) $6,217

A George IV mahogany breakfast table, the circular tilt top on a tapering stepped square section pedestal and a concave sided platform base, 48in. diameter.
(Christie's) $2,834

An early Victorian mahogany fold over breakfast table, of rectangular form, scrolled and acanthus leaf apron, on an octagonal column with molded edge, 36in. wide.
(Wintertons) $910

A mid Victorian mahogany segmentally veneered breakfast table, 133cm. diameter.
(Bonhams & Brooks) $1,480

A George IV pollard oak breakfast table, circa 1825, the circular top with a shallow band frieze and beaded edge, on a faceted column 53½in. diameter, the top.
(Bonhams) $14,216

A late Regency rosewood and brass inlaid card table, two later Apollo mask mounts, minor losses to inlay, 92cm. wide.
(Bonhams & Brooks) $2,800

A late Regency burr-figured, possibly burr-oak, and marquetry card table, in the manner of George Bullock, the baize-lined top with ebonized border, 36in. wide.
(Christie's) $2,715

An early Victorian rosewood card table, circa 1840, alterations, 91cm. wide.
(Bonhams & Brooks) $770

A Chippendale carved mahogany card table, Philadelphia, 1760-1780, the rectangular hinged top above a conforming case with gadrooned edge fitted with a drawer, 36in. wide.
(Christie's) $49,350

A George III carved mahogany and inlaid serpentine card table, the hinged baize lined top crossbanded in kingwood or possibly tulipwood and inlaid with harewood and boxwood lines, 36¼in. wide.
(Christie's) $5,790

A Chippendale carved walnut card table, Philadelphia, 1760-1780, with outset rounded corners above a conforming frame fitted with a thumbmolded drawer flanked by outset turret corners, 34½in. wide.
(Christie's) $58,750

An unusual Dutch walnut and marquetry inlaid card table, circa 1820, 82cm. wide.
(Bonhams & Brooks) $1,201

A Federal inlaid cherrywood card table, Philadelphia, 1800-1810, the rectangular hinged top with serpentine front and string-inlaid edges above a conforming frame, 40½in. wide.
(Christie's) $5,875

A mid Victorian burr walnut card table, 88cm. wide.
(Bonhams & Brooks) $2,100

A Classical mahogany lyre base card table, New York, 1810-1830, the rotating top with inset corners above a conforming skirt over a carved lyre-form support centering three brass rods, 36in. wide.
(Christie's) $5,875

A George IV mahogany card-table, the rounded rectangular hinged swivel top, cross-banded in rosewood, enclosing a green baize lined interior, 36in. wide.
(Christie's) $1,817

A 19th century mahogany folding card table, with satinwood banding, stringing and marquetry, the serpentine swivel top with foliate paterae, 33in. wide.
(Andrew Hartley) $2,130

A Federal inlaid mahogany card table, North Shore, Massachusetts, 1790-1810, the hinged D-shaped top with inset rounded corners and banded edges above a conforming frame centered by an oval-inlaid reserve, 35¾in. wide.
(Christie's) $15,275

A mahogany, tulipwood crossbanded inlaid and decorated demi lune card table, 19th century, the baize lined hinged top with counter recesses and painted floral border, 49in. wide.
(Christie's) $8,460

A George III mahogany demi lune card table, satinwood crossbanded with ebony stringing, the folded top with marquetry panel depicting shell, birds and trailing branch, 30¼in. wide.
(Andrew Hartley) $1,946

A mid Victorian walnut serpentine card table, 92cm. wide.
(Bonhams & Brooks) $1,386

A kingwood, mahogany and marquetry envelope card table, 20th century, applied with gilt-metal mounts and decorated with flower-filled urns and meandering foliage, 27in. wide.(Christie's) $1,726

A Victorian rosewood folding card table, the D shaped top having panel frieze with beaded edging and flanked by leaf and scroll carved brackets, 36in. wide.
(Andrew Hartley) $1,077

A North European walnut and marquetry center table, 19th century, inlaid throughout with floral and foliate decoration, the rectangular top with a central tavern scene and portrait medallions to each corner, 43½in. wide.
(Christie's) $5,667

A George III mahogany occasional or tea table, the circular snap top on a ring-turned column with writhen spirally turned knop and tripod supports terminating in pointed pad feet, 30in. diameter.
(Christie's) $4,061

A late Victorian inlaid walnut center table, 117cm. wide.
(Bonhams & Brooks) $462

A Victorian ebonized and burr yew center table, with satinwood banding and stringing and gilt embellishment, molded edged octagonal top with radial veneers, 39in. wide.
(Andrew Hartley) $834

An Italian marble table top of circular form inlaid in various colored marbles in a batwing pattern with central rosette, white, 19th century, 26¾in. wide.
(Andrew Hartley) $1,390

A Victorian rosewood center table, crossbanded with stringing, the molded edged circular top with central marquetry and mother of pearl flower and shell roundel, 32½in. wide.
(Andrew Hartley) $2,556

A vellum center table, Italian, 1940s, the circular top above central cylindrical pedestal, on circular plinth base, 50½in. diameter.
(Christie's) $3,192

A Victorian rosewood occasional table, the circular top with scrolled frieze, baluster stem, scrolled and leaf carved tripod base with brass castors, 19¾in. wide.
(Andrew Hartley) $1,190

A rosewood center table, the oblong top and plain frieze raised on pierced trestle end supports joined by a pole stretcher, 19th century, 41¾ x 21½in.
(Andrew Hartley) $612

An Austrian walnut center table, circa 1830, 85cm. diameter.
(Bonhams & Brooks) $604

A Louis XV style kingwood and parquetry inlaid center table, 61cm. diameter x 76cm. high.
(Bonhams & Brooks) $728

A late Victorian walnut center table in the Gothic taste, 76cm. diameter.
(Bonhams & Brooks) $302

A Dutch giltwood and gilt-composition center table, second half 17th century, the rectangular molded Sarrancolin marble top above a garlanded winged putto frieze, 31¼in. wide.
(Christie's) $11,346

A Classical mahogany gilt-stencilled marble-top center table, New York, 1820-1830, the circular marble top above a conforming frame decorated with gilt cornucopiae-stencilling, 33½in. diameter.(Christie's) $10,575

An English gilt and patinated-bronze, blue-john, and mahogany center table, circa 1840, surmounted by a rectangular top, supported by two lyre-shaped uprights, each centered by a female term, 26½in. wide.
(Christie's) $23,524

An American 'Aesthetic Movement' parcel-ebonized walnut and marquetry center table, circa 1865, with a shaped-oval top inset with a conforming panel inlaid with a turned trophy and foliate scrolls, 49in. wide.
(Christie's) $5,520

A Continental mahogany center table, 19th century, in the Empire style, probably French, surmounted by a molded fossilized gray marble top, 32½in. diameter,
(Christie's) $4,342

A Renaissance-Revival marble-top center table, New York, 1860-1880, the rectangular marble top with serpentine ends enclosed by a conforming molded frame with raised rosette-carved corners, 41¾in. wide.
(Christie's) $2,350

Regency mahogany and marble-top center table, early 19th century, circular molded Carrara marble top over a plain frieze, raised on reeded support, 36in. diameter.
(Skinner) $5,750

A Regency brass-inlaid rosewood library center table, the octagonal tilt-top with gadrooned molding and inlaid with stylized foliage, 51in. diameter.
(Christie's) $12,184

A Victorian circular shaped mahogany tip-up-top center table raised on a knopped stem with quatriform base and turned feet, 5ft. diameter.
(Anderson & Garland) $1,593

A George III harewood oval center table, circa 1790, the leather inset oval top above a single frieze drawer, on square section tapered legs, 39¼in. wide.
(Bonhams) $7,700

A late Regency oak circular center table, with an inset variegated marble top, a reeded frieze and a faceted panelled and reeded pedestal, 31in. diameter.
(Christie's) $14,805

A mid Victorian yew wood and rosewood center table, circa 1870, fitted with later mounts, the whole with crossbanding and stringing, restorations, 93cm. wide.
(Bonhams) $2,240

An early Victorian walnut center table, the rectangular top inset with figured marble, the burr veneered frieze with a molded edge, 3ft.
(Woolley & Wallis) $832

A carved and stained beech center table, 20th century, the oval serpentine top with an inset mirrored panel, on a base of four carved dolphins, 35½in. wide.
(Christie's) $1,233

A Victorian mahogany, rosewood and Tunbridge-banded octagonal center table, the top centered by a circular and star motif, on a triangular support and concave tricorn base, 39in. wide.
(Christie's) $588

Louis XVI giltwood marble-top console table, circa 1785-90, with **D-shaped fossilized yellow top** above a fluted and beaded frieze raised on leaf carved circular fluted and tapered legs, 48in. wide.
(Skinner) $9,775

A Regency later painted console table, probably Irish, with a rectangular white marble top, the frieze with later giltmetal neoclassical mounts, the mirrored back between molded stiles, 26½in. wide.
(Christie's) $6,178

Regency style marble top giltwood console table, late 19th century, with inset marble top above a foliate molded frieze, raised on dolphin form supports, 36in. wide.
(Skinner) $1,150

Renaissance Revival carved walnut and onyx-top console table, the inset top above a frame carved with lion masks, foliage, and ending in paw feet, 36in. wide.
(Skinner) $1,955

One of a pair of Continental walnut console tables, early 19th century and later, surmounted by rectangular marble tops with molded edges having cavetto friezes, 20¼in. wide.
(Christie's) (Two) $4,705

French Second Empire marble-top mahogany, painted, and parcel-gilt console table, second quarter 19th century, with rectangular speckled black marble top above a frieze drawer applied with wreaths, 37½in. wide.(Skinner) $2,300

An oak console table, late 19th century, **the molded top with canted corners, with geometric decoration to the frieze centered by a tablet with applied roundels,** 53¾in. wide.
(Christie's) $822

Continental Rococo Revival marble-top rosewood console table and matching mirror, mid 19th century, the table with serpentine top and foliate carved base, 43in. wide. (Skinner) $1,438

A carved, green-painted and parcel gilt console table, 18th century and later, with a red variegated marble top, above a rosette and guilloche frieze, 46in. wide.
(Christie's) $3,125

A Spanish giltwood console table, mid 18th century, the associated serpentine-fronted molded rounded rectangular brocatelle top above a pierced waved rockwork frieze, 45½in. wide.
(Christie's) $8,676

A rosewood and marquetry inlaid two tier console table 67cm. wide.
(Bonhams & Brooks) $431

A satinbirch and mirror-glass console table, English, 1930s, the shaped rectangular with peach colored mirror-glass tiles and upswept edge, on three ribbed columns, on shaped plinth base, 63in. wide. (Christie's) $419

One of a pair of Italian carved giltwood consoles, 19th century, with elements renewed and some of an earlier date, in the baroque style, surmounted by shaped Siena marble tops, 31½in. wide.
(Christie's)   (Two) $2,199

A Louis XVI brass-mounted mahogany console desserte, by Jean Caumont, the pierced three-quarter galleried white-veined gray marble top above a panelled frieze with an acanthus leaf border, 38½in. wide.
(Christie's) $8,487

A Swedish carved giltwood console, mid 18th century, with renewal and restoration, surmounted by a molded mottled marble top of re-entrant outline flecked with iron pyrites, the top 31in. wide.
(Christie's) $3,046

A giltwood console table, of Régence style, 19th century, the gray and pink rectangular marble top above a frieze centered by a faun mask within a scrolling foliate cartouche, 109.5cm. wide.
(Christie's) $10,845

Emile-Jacques Ruhlmann, console, 1920-23, palisander, demi-lune top supported on slender tapering fluted curving stem support, 20in. wide. (Sotheby's) $29,073

An Italian carved giltwood and gesso console table, 19th century, in the rococo taste, with shaped top with incised lozenge decoration, 50in. wide.(Christie's) $3,634

Painted chair table, New England, late 18th century, the pine round scrubbed top tilts above the dark green painted arm supports and legs, 42in. wide.
(Skinner) $4,025

An early 19th century mahogany dining table, circa 1830, without central section, 113cm.
(Bonhams & Brooks) $801

A French walnut, ebonized and oak draw-leaf dining-table, 19th century, of Renaissance style, inlaid overall with white gesso foliage, the rectangular top with two extra pull-out leaves, 96¾in. wide extended.
(Christie's) $8,487

A late Victorian oak, brown oak and ebony dining table, the top divided into crossbanded quarter-veneered panels with two additional leaves, on turned and chamfered square section legs, 63½in. extended.
(Christie's) $1,068

An early Victorian faded rosewood loo table, the circular veneered top with a heavy gadroon edge, the faceted and acanthus carved stem with a large turned pendant finial, 4ft.1in. diameter.
(Woolley & Wallis) $1,312

A Victorian walnut and burr-walnut extending dining table, the oval top with a molded edge and seven additional leaves, on a panelled cruciform base with reeded vase-turned columns, approximately 170in. extended.
(Christie's) $8,855

A Victorian burr-walnut and walnut loo table, with a quarter veneered oval serpentine shaped top, on a turned, faceted, tapering cabochon and lotus-leaf decorated support, 58in. wide.
(Christie's) $1,809

A French burr ash extending dining table, 19th century, the oval top with drop leaves and one additional associated leaf, on six turned tapering supports, 101½in. extended.
(Christie's) $10,626

A mahogany extending dining table, early 20th century, with three additional leaves, the rounded carved and molded edge with a plain frieze, 94½in. fully extended.
(Christie's) $1,240

A Victorian walnut loo table with quarter veneered molded edged top, on quadripartite scrolled supports, 57½ x 42in.
(Andrew Hartley) $3,520

A William IV mahogany twin section dining table, the molded edge rectangular top over eight tapering ring-turned supports, 178cm. wide.
(Bristol) $1,585

A Victorian walnut loo table, the quarter veneered and banded tip up top with parquetry and stringing and central marquetry floral motif.
(Andrew Hartley) $1,599

A George III mahogany D-end dining table, the rectangular top with demi-lune ends in two sections, each with rectangular drop flap, 129.5cm. wide.
(Phillips) $3,840

A Victorian mahogany extending dining table, with a circular molded top and three additional leaves, on bulbous turned tapering legs, 110in. extended.
(Christie's) $4,277

A Victorian mahogany extending dining table, with molded edge to the rounded rectangular top and on cabochon-carved lobed baluster legs, 309cm.
(Bearne's) $2,512

A mahogany, satinwood, burr-yew, rosewood and tulipwood crossbanded dining table, of recent manufacture, the circular top with a reeded edge, 66in. diameter.
(Christie's) $2,555

A fine George IV rectangular mahogany extending dining table with plain frieze, 103in. long complete with three spare leaves.
(Anderson & Garland)
          $10,230

Stickley Brothers oak dining room table, circa 1916, raised on corbelled pedestal base, with five leaves in original box, 54in. diameter, each leaf 11in. wide.
(Skinner) $4,025

A Regency mahogany extending dining table of unusual design, the rectangular snap top with rounded corners and reeded edge opening to accommodate two extra leaves, the top 126¾in. with leaves extended.(Christie's) $7,268

A mahogany radially extending octagonal dining table, 20th century, the top with an additional leaf for each side, on four turned baluster shaped supports and concave sided platform, 85in. extended.(Christie's) $4,935

Classical mahogany carved and mahogany veneer dining table, probably New England, circa 1820, the rectangular overhanging top with rounded leaves on lyre form supports, 50in. wide, open.
          $2,990

An unusual Edwardian mahogany and satinwood crossbanded two tier table vitrine, 61cm. wide.
(Bonhams & Brooks) $570

A mahogany and parcel-gilt vitrine table, 19th century, with a hinged brass-bound top and glazed sides, on tapering square section supports, 44in. wide.
(Christie's) $1,771

Louis XVI style gilt bronze mounted mahogany vitrine table, circa 1880, with bevelled glass panels and turned legs joined by stretchers, 26in. wide.(Skinner) $3,450

A small mahogany bijouterie table, early 20th century, with bevelled glass and waterleaf molding throughout, with a hinged top, 15in.
(Christie's) $1,083

A pair of Napoleon III gilt-bronze vitrines, Paris, circa 1870, each with a hinged glazed top and glazed sides with a beaded border, the corners with ribbon tied floral mounts, 63cm. wide.
(Sotheby's) $25,280

Elegant gilt metal mounted trefoil formed bijouterie table, glazed top and side, raised on slender cabriole supports, circa early 20th century, 18in. (G A Key) $1,256

A French ormolu-mounted kingwood vitrine table, by François Linke, Paris, circa 1900, the hinged rectangular top with a serpentine edge, opening to reveal a velvet-lined base with glazed sides, 25¼in. wide.
(Christie's) $13,800

Dutch Neoclassical-style walnut and floral marquetry kidney-shaped vitrine table, late 19th century, with inset glass top and sides, 33in. wide. (Skinner) $1,725

A North European kingwood, rosewood and line-inlaid vitrine table, late 19th century, the superstructure with a quarter-veneered and brass galleried top glazed throughout.
(Christie's) $1,316

A Directoire style fruitwood kneehole dressing table, 113cm. wide.
(Bonhams & Brooks) $1,386

An Art Nouveau dressing table, late 19th century, the raised back with brass mounted arched pediment, with an arched bevelled swivel mirror between inlaid stiles, raised on square tapering legs with block feet, 45in. wide.
(Christie's) $878

Queen Anne hard pine dressing table, possibly New Jersey, circa 1740-60, the overhanging under-molded rectangular top above a valanced case of three thumb-molded short drawers, 29½in. wide. (Skinner) $4,025

Mid Georgian mahogany kneehole dressing table, circa 1760, the rectangular case fitted with one long drawer, six short drawers and a recessed kneehole, 35in. deep.
(Skinner) $1,093

A Victorian walnut dressing table, 122cm. wide.
(Bonhams & Brooks) $830

A Queen Anne cherrywood dressing table, New London County, Connecticut, 1750-1780, rectangular molded top above conforming case, 33¼in. wide.
(Christie's) $35,250

A George III mahogany gentleman's dressing table, the hinged crossbanded top revealing a fitted interior, front with an arrangement of true and false drawers, one with a cane seat, 31in. wide. (Christie's) $1,233

A mahogany half round toilet table, the top rises to reveal a lift up easel mirror and divisions, a veneered frieze, 3ft.2in.
(Woolley & Wallis) $1,470

A mid Victorian mahogany pedestal dressing table, circa 1880, fitted with fifteen assorted drawers, with restoration, 138cm. wide.
(Bonhams) $784

A George IV bowfront dressing table, mahogany veneered, the top with ebony stringing and crossbanded above two short and one long drawer, 3ft.10in.
(Woolley & Wallis) $1,750

Grain painted and stencil decorated dressing table, New England, circa 1820, the scrolled splashboard above two small convex drawers, and a table top with convex long drawer below, 33in. wide.
(Skinner) $1,840

A Louis XVI ormolu-mounted mahogany dressing-table, by Joseph Feurstein, the hinged and sliding rectangular top with central hinged gilt-tooled leather-lined writing-surface, 46¼in. wide.
(Christie's) $12,513

A Queen Anne cherrywood dressing table, Wethersfield, Connecticut, 1750-1780, a thumbmolded long drawer over three thumbmolded short drawers, the center with carved fan above a scalloped skirt, 36in. wide.
(Christie's) $40,250

A George III mahogany dressing-table, the divided hinged rectangular top enclosing a dished surface with a rising mirror, above one long and two short drawers, 24in. wide.
(Christie's) $3,003

A Chippendale carved walnut dressing table, possibly Winchester area, Virginia, 1770-1800, the rectangular molded top with cusped corners above a conforming case, thumbmoulded short drawers, 41¾in. wide.
(Christie's) $7,475

Queen Anne tiger maple dressing table, Delaware Valley, 1710-20, the top with molded edge and canted front corners, overhanging a case of thumb-molded drawers, case 29¾in. wide.
(Skinner) $20,700

A bird's-eye-maple and walnut dressing table, English, circa 1935, the shaped rectangular mirror-glass with hinged side mirrors above a rectangular back panel, 90½in. extended width.
(Christie's) $503

Queen Anne cherry carved dressing table, Wethersfield County, Connecticut area, 1750-80, the thumb-molded top overhangs a case of four drawers with the central one fan-carved, width at top 33½in. (Skinner) $43,125

Antique American Sheraton drop-leaf table, in maple with turned legs. Old repair to top, 44 x 17in. plus two 16in. drop leaves. (Eldred's) $220

Chippendale mahogany drop-leaf dining table, New England, circa 1780, the rectangular overhanging drop-leaf top on four molded straight legs, 47¼in. wide. (Skinner) $1,150

18th century oak large drop leaf dining table supported on heavy turned ringed legs with bottom refectory stretchers, oval leaf, 4ft. 6in. wide. (G.A. Key) $1,020

Federal mahogany veneer drop-leaf table, Massachusetts or New Hampshire area, 1815-20, the rectangular top with hinged leaves having rounded corners flanking straight recessed panelled veneered skirts, 50¾in. extended. (Skinner) $805

An oak and walnut single drop-leaf gateleg table, English, early 18th century, with a rounded rectangular top and frieze drawer above arcaded freizes, on ring-turned baluster and block legs, 21in. extended.(Christie's) $3,565

A fine and rare Queen Anne carved walnut drop-leaf table, mid Atlantic States, probably New Jersey, 1740-60, the oblong top with bowed ends flanked by D-shaped leaves, 4ft. wide, open. (Sotheby's) $34,500

Federal tiger maple and maple drop-leaf table, New England, circa 1800-15, the rectangular overhanging top with rounded leaves on four square tapering legs, 36in. wide. (Skinner) $1,380

A 19th century mahogany drop leaf dining table 89cm. wide. (Bonhams & Brooks) $724

An early Victorian mahogany extending dining table, the rounded rectangular top including one additional leaf above a frieze with reeded panels, 67in. extended. (Christie's) $5,313

Antique American Sheraton drop-leaf dining table in mahogany, six turned legs on castors, top 48 x 17½in. plus two 17½in. leaves. (Eldred's) $330

A good Federal figured mahogany Cumberland-action drop leaf dining table, Boston, Massachusetts, circa 1815, the rectangular top flanked by D-shaped molded leaves, open 5ft. 4in.(Sotheby's) $16,800

Queen Anne maple drop-leaf table, New England, 18th century, the half round hinged leaves flank scrolled skirts above cabriole legs, 44¾ x 45in. (Skinner) $3,738

Chippendale cherry drop-leaf table, New England, circa 1780, the overhanging serpentine drop-leaf top on a straight beaded skirt joining four square molded Marlborough legs, 35½in. long. (Skinner) $3,105

A fruitwood spider-leg single drop-leaf table, English, early 18th century, with later rounded rectangular mahogany top, arcaded friezes and frieze drawer, 21¼in. extended. (Christie's) $1,783

Diminutive Queen Anne maple, south eastern New England, circa 1740-60, the oval overhanging drop leaf top above a straight skirt and four block-turned tapering legs, 38¼in. wide. (Skinner) $6,325

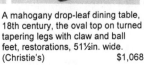

A George II oak drop leaf dining table, 76.5cm. wide. (Bonhams & Brooks) $339

A mahogany drop-leaf dining table, 18th century, the oval top on turned tapering legs with claw and ball feet, restorations, 51½in. wide. (Christie's) $1,068

A small George III mahogany drop leaf table, 102cm. wide flaps up. (Bonhams & Brooks) $262

A mahogany and boxwood strung revolving drum top library table, 19th century, with crossbanded top and a reeded edge, the top 38¾in. diameter. (Christie's) $7,268

A mahogany oval drum-top library table, early 19th century, the top inset with a later tooled red leather panel, fitted with four drawers between dummy panel fronts, reeded splayed legs, brass caps and castors, 48¼in. wide. (Christie's) $7,238

A mahogany and tulipwood crossbanded drum library table, 71cm. wide. (Bonhams & Brooks) $4,620

A mahogany drum top library table, 19th century, top and base associated, the base later than the top, the circular revolving top crossbanded and inset with a panel of red-tooled leather, 48½in. diameter. (Christie's) $8,122

A Maltese fruitwood, possibly olivewood, and inlaid drum top occasional table of small size, 19th century, in the Regency style, 26½in. diameter. (Christie's) $6,876

A mahogany drum table, 20th century, with a green leather lined top, four frieze drawers and four false drawers, on a turned tapering pedestal, 42in. diameter. (Christie's) $1,974

A Regency mahogany drum tale, circa 1810, the revolving top with a later collar and set on a tripod base, 81cm. diameter. (Bonhams) $3,780

A late Georgian circular mahogany drum table with inset tooled gray leather top fitted with four short and four dummy drawers, 41½in. diameter. (Anderson & Garland) $3,250

A mahogany drum table, part 19th century, the circular crossbanded top with central ebonized dot inlay and above a flame veneered frieze, 39in. diameter. (Christie's) $739

An oak gateleg table, 112cm. wide.
(Bonhams & Brooks) $360

A William and Mary style walnut
gateleg table, 135cm. wide.
(Bonhams & Brooks) $616

An oak gateleg table, early 20th
century, 106cm. wide.
(Bonhams & Brooks) $431

Continental rustic painted pine
drop-leaf gate-leg table, 18th
century, with rectangular plank top
above a frieze drawer on bobbin-
turned legs, 48½in. deep.
(Skinner) $2,185

An oak gateleg table, English, mid
17th century, with oval plank top
and plain friezes, on reel turned
legs, 57in. extended.
(Christie's) $5,348

A small 17th century style oak
gateleg table, 90cm. wide.
(Bonhams & Brooks) $59

Tiger maple and maple gate-leg
table, New England, 1730-50, the
oval top with drop leaves flanking a
single drawer above block,
baluster, and ring-turned legs,
45½in. deep.
(Skinner) $14,950

A substantial oak gateleg table,
English, early 18th century, the
thick oval top above a single end
frieze, on elongated compound
baluster legs, 61½in. wide.
(Bonham's) $4,312

A William and Mary maple
diminutive gateleg table, New
England, 1720-40, of rare small
size, the oblong top with D-shaped
leaves above a frieze drawer, width
open 45in.
(Sotheby's) $15,600

A late 19th century walnut extending dining table, the molded top with three leaves, on four ring-turned baluster supports, 254 x 136cm. extended. (Bristol) $1,727

George III mahogany three-pedestal dining table, late 18th/19th century, of typical form, with reeded edge, molded splayed legs ending in brass paw feet, 49in. wide with two leaves.
(Skinner) $2,070

A Victorian mahogany extending dining table, the rounded rectangular top with four additional leaves, on bulbous turned tapering legs with brass capped castors, 124in. extended. (Christie's) $5,264

Pine painted harvest table, New England, early 19th century, the scrubbed top with hinged leaves which flank the painted base with its ring-turned tapering legs, 102¾in. long. (Skinner) $11,500

A Regency mahogany D-end dining table, with a drop-leaf center section with a gate-leg action and ebony strung frieze, on ring-turned tapering legs, 106in. long extended. (Christie's) $3,290

Classical mahogany and mahogany veneer three-part dining table, Burlington, Vermont area, 1840s, the center section with rectangular drop-leaves flanking the convex and concave veneered skirts above ring-turned and blocked legs on castors, 51in. wide. (Skinner) $2,415

An oak extending dining table, 20th century, with four additional leaves, the top with a carved decorated edge, on turned, square section, foliate-carved and molded supports, 130in. extended.
(Christie's) $1,727

A Regency mahogany extending dining-table, the rounded rectangular molded top above a plain frieze, on turned reeded tapering legs, brass caps and castors, with three later leaves, 131in. long, fully extended. (Christie's) $11,680

George III mahogany three-pedestal dining table, late 18th century, rectangular top with rounded corners and reeded edge, 80in. wide.
(Skinner) $10,925

A Victorian mahogany extending dining table, with two additional leaves, the molded top on turned and reeded legs with brass caps and castors, lacking winder, 81in. extended.
(Christie's) $2,245

An Edwardian mahogany extending dining table, with two additional leaves, the molded rounded rectangular top on square tapering fluted legs with molded block feet and inset castors, including a winder, 99in. extended. (Christie's) $2,961

A mahogany four pillar dining table, 20th century, including three extra leaves, the top with a reeded edge, on turned vase columns and reeded splayed supports terminating in brass caps and castors, 235in. long extended.(Christie's) $3,800

A Classical carved mahogany three-pedestal dining table, Philadelphia, circa 1820-1830, in three sections: the two outer sections with D-shaped tops and hinged leaves flanking a central section with a square top, all above three bulbous waterleaf-carved pedestals, 132in. wide. (Christie's) $189,500

An extending dining table, 19th century, possibly teak and walnut, with two additional leaves, the rounded rectangular molded top on five turned stylized foliate-carved and octagonally faceted tapering legs, 95in. fully extended. (Christie's) $1,208

A 19th century mahogany twin pillar dining table with molded edged rounded oblong top, single leaf, turned pillars on four downswept legs, 83½in. long.
(Andrew Hartley) $6,960

An early Victorian mahogany extending dining table, with two additional leaves, the molded rectangular top on turned, and boldly reeded tapering legs, 92in. fully extended. (Christie's) $1,809

A Federal mahogany two-part dining table, New York, 1790-1810, each with D-shaped top and one drop leaf above a conforming crossbanded skirt, with swing-leg and four stationary tapering turned and reeded legs, 93½in. deep, open. (Christie's) $15,275

A Federal mahogany dining table, Philadelphia, 1800-1810, in two sections, each with a D-shaped top and rectangular hinged leaf above a conforming frame, on tapering reeded legs, 51in. wide. (Christie's) $9,988

An oak refectory table, early 20th century, with a rectangular plank top, on chamfered supports joined by H-stretchers, 96in. long. (Christie's) $2,385

A George IV mahogany extending dining-table, comprising two end sections and three leaves, the rounded rectangular molded top above a plain frieze, 123in. long, fully extended. (Christie's) $8,722

A late Victorian walnut extending dining table, including three additional leaves, the rectangular top with a molded edge and canted corners, above a panelled frieze, 118in. extended. (Christie's) $2,467

An early Victorian mahogany extending dining table, the oval top with a molded edge and a conforming frieze, on bulbous turned, lapetted and foliate-carved legs, no additional leaves, 63in. long. (Christie's) $2,834

A late Regency mahogany twin pedestal dining table, with three additional leaves of various sizes, two in rosewood, with a rounded rectangular top, 105in. fully extended. (Christie's) $16,185

A Regency mahogany extending dining-table, possibly Scottish, comprising two ends and three leaves, the rounded rectangular molded top above a plain frieze with telescopic undertier, 104½in. long, fully extended. (Christie's) $25,438

A Victorian mahogany extending dining table, the rounded rectangular top with four additional leaves, on five tapering turned, fluted and foliate-carved legs with porcelain castors, 137in. extended.
(Christie's) $4,935

A Victorian mahogany telescopic extending dining table, with a molded overhanging top and frieze, on polygonal and ring-turned tapering legs with brass cappings and swivel castors, 130in. long including leaves. (Christie's) $7,631

A late Victorian oak library table, with a green, tooled leather inset top with canted corners, three panelled frieze drawers and similarly decorated sides, 89in. wide. (Christie's) $6,909

A Louis XV style ormolu-mounted mahogany and tulipwood extension dining table, with an ormolu-molded oval top above a conforming freize, 93in. extended. (Christie's) $8,050

A Victorian pollard oak extending dining table, the rounded rectangular top with a molded edge and two additional leaves, above a molded frieze, on turned foliate-carved legs, 107in. extended.
(Christie's) $14,168

A Victorian mahogany extending dining table, the rectangular top with a molded edge, raised on five turned and lotus-carved tapering legs with brass caps and carpet castors, stamped *A. Blain, Liverpool*, overall length 147in. (Christie's) $7,238

A good early Victorian mahogany dining table with two extra leaves, restorations 312cm. long, extended.
(Bonhams & Brooks) $7,084

A George IV mahogany extending dining table, comprising two D-end sections and four leaves, the rounded rectangular top with molded edge above a plain frieze, 129½in. long. (Christie's) $14,536

411

A Victorian oak library table, having molded rectangular top fitted with frieze drawer, with baluster and carved end supports, 5ft. wide. (Russell Baldwin & Bright) $2,117

Renaissance style carved oak library table, late 19th century, rectangular top carved at the edge with foliage, 47in. wide. (Skinner) $2,645

An early Victorian rosewood library table fitted with two drawers, on cheval frame with panelled ends and carved paw feet, 5ft. wide. (Russell Baldwin & Bright) $5,598

Edwardian painted satinwood desk-form gaming table, circa 1895, painted with floral swags, the hinged top opening to a felt playing surface above a single drawer with divided interior, 30in. wide. (Skinner) $1,150

A Renaissance Revival rosewood library table, New York City, 1860-1890, the rectangular molded top with rounded corners inset with modern leather writing surface above a frame fitted with two short drawers centering an outset panel, 53¼in. wide. (Christie's) $21,850

An early Victorian oak chamber writing-table, by Gillows of Lancaster, after a design by A.W.N. Pugin, circa 1850, with hinged pen and ink tray to the back edge, 38¾in. wide. (Christie's) $29,072

Limbert oak library table, Grand Rapids and Holland, Michigan, circa 1907, model no. 106, rectangular top over two-tiered open shelves with vertical slats at each end, 48in. wide. (Skinner) $1,380

A Victorian oak octagonal library table, with a red leather lined top and a molded edge above a frieze with four drawers and four false drawers, on turned lapetted and foliate-carved supports, 59in. wide. (Christie's) $8,501

A Victorian mahogany library table, with a molded green leather lined top and two frieze drawers to each side, on tapering turned and faceted legs with brass capped castors, 54in. wide. (Christie's) $1,645

An oval giltwood marble topped occasional table, 20th century, with a black variegated marble top and **molded rope-twist surround**, with a floral and beaded decorated surround, 50in. wide.
(Christie's) $1,645

Classical carved mahogany tilt-top table, New York State, 1820s, the shaped top tilts above a turned and carved pedestal on leaf-carved hairy legs and paw feet, 27½in. wide. (Skinner) $978

Michele de Lucchi for Memphis, 'President' low table, prototype, designed 1983, no longer in production, marble, circular glass top, 100cm. diameter.
(Sotheby's) $1,986

A late 19th century mahogany satinwood and inlaid étagère, with glass tray top above two inlaid tiers linked by scrolled supports, 33½in.
(Wintertons) $1,470

A Classical mahogany gilt-stencilled marble-top pier table, New York, 1815-1825, the rectangular marble top above a conforming frame centering swan and scrolled stencilling flanked by lyre-stencilled reserves, 42in. wide. (Christie's) $6,463

A George IV rosewood nest of quartetto tables, on slender baluster turned legs joined by bowed stretchers, on trestle supports, 21in. wide.
(Andrew Hartley) $3,780

A simulated rosewood and parcel-gilt whatnot, 20th century, of six graduated shaped tiers, each with a reeded edge, a central column and turned supports, 27in. wide.
(Christie's) $2,467

A nest of three reproduction walnut veneered tables of shaped rectangular form, on baluster and block turned legs united by wavy stretchers.(Wintertons) $441

An Edwardian mahogany and marquetry two-tier étagère, each oval tier with a low waved gallery inlaid with ribbon-tied floral swags, shells, paterae and foliate scrolls, 27in. wide.
(Christie's) $2,213

A George III mahogany circular tripod table, with baluster-shaped support, cabriole legs, and pad feet, 34in. wide.(Christie's) $1,068

A George III mahogany occasional table, the galleried square top above a fluted frieze with concealed slide, 12½in. square. (Christie's) $13,628

A mahogany galleried octagonal occasional table, late 19th century, in the Chippendale style, the octagonal snap top with canted pierced fret gallery, 29in. diameter. (Christie's) $4,738

An Irish fruitwood, marquetry and parquetry occasional table, 19th century, Killarney, the circular hinged top with radiating chequer designs and crossbanded with a border of trailing flowers and foliage, 27½in. diameter. (Christie's) $6,091

A Russian fruitwood, amaranth and marquetry kidney-shaped table, last quarter 18th century, the top crossbanded in laburnum and inlaid with an urn flanked by scrolling foliage, 37¾in. wide. (Christie's) $25,028

A mahogany tripod table, the legs George III, the top and column 19th/20th century, the circular top with molded gallery and marquety roundel on a baluster column and cabriole legs, 10½in. diameter. (Christie's) $3,089

A Victorian tulipwood, kingwood, marquetry and parquetry occasional table, in the Louis XV taste, by Collinson & Locke, London, 18½in. wide. (Christie's) $2,907

A Louis XVI ormolu-mounted fruitwood guéridon, in the manner of Canabas, the circular gray and white marble tilt-top with pierced gallery above a ring-turned and fluted shaft, 21½in. diameter. (Christie's) $4,715

An Edwardian mahogany, satinwood and inlaid oval two-tier étagère, with detachable oval glazed tray with brass handles, 25in. wide. (Christie's) $2,707

An Edwardian mahogany bijouterie table, crossbanded and inlaid with lines, the glazed panelled hinged top and frieze drawer fitted with a gilt-lined slide.
(Christie's) $1,817

An oak draw-leaf table, French, early 18th century, with rectangular cleated top and molded friezes, on ring-turned and block legs, 97½in. extended.(Christie's) $4,456

A French tulipwood, possibly kingwood veneered, ormolu and porcelain mounted occasional table or table en ambulant, 19th century, in the Louis XV style, in the manner of Martin Carlin, 16½in. wide. (Christie's) $5,088

A German ormolu-mounted parcel-gilt and polychrome-decorated porcelain and ebonized tripod table, circa 1885, surmounted by a shaped rectangular tray with a baluster rail, surmounted by five urns and six figures, 24in. wide.(Christie's) $7,057

A Russian Alexandre II ormolu-mounted malachite low table, the table top circa 1860, the base late 19th century, the shaped stepped oval top with four scroll and foliage cartouches, 39½in. wide. (Christie's) $42,006

A Brazilian oyster-wood veneered circular occasional table, 20th century, the molded top inset with geometric pattern of butterfly's wings, on a knopped tapering pedestal, the interior wired for electric light, 26½in. high. (Christie's) $2,632

A Victorian walnut occasional table, second half 19th century, the octagonal top inset with specimen marbles, arranged in a radiating pattern, 17in. wide.
(Christie's) $3,552

A mahogany reading table, early 20th century, in the form of a miniature seat, the folding frame with brass fittings, the rectangular tray with reading stand above, 19in. high. (Christie's) $2,369

A mahogany tripod table, 19th century, the circular piecrust top on a pierced tripartite scrolled column, on cabriole legs issuing from a concave-sided platform, 20¾in. diameter. (Christie's) $3,997

A walnut occasional table, early 20th century, the quarter veneered oval undulating hinged top on a molded ribbed baluster column and splayed quadruped supports, 32½in. wide.
(Christie's) $1,363

Louis XV Provincial fruitwood table, 18th century, with rectangular top and frieze drawer on slender cabriole legs, 30in. wide.
(Skinner) $1,150

A walnut tripod table, English, late 19th century, the rectangular tilt-top inset with an early 19th century rosewood and floral marquetry panel inlaid with specimen woods and ivory, 14½in. wide.
(Christie's) $6,199

A Victorian walnut occasional table. the shaped oval top and frieze with drawer, raised on shaped fretwork end supports, 21¼in. wide.
(Andrew Hartley) $785

Pair of Continental inlaid mahogany two-drawer end tables, late 19th century, each with rectangular top and two cross-banded drawers raised on square tapered legs, 18in. wide. (Skinner) $2,645

George III mahogany tilt-top tripod table, third quarter 18th century, with circular top, turned standard and cabriole legs, 29½in. diameter.
(Skinner) $1,092

Cherry table, Connecticut, 1730-50, the rectangular top with molded edge overhangs the base with a single thumb-molded drawer, 15½in. wide.
(Skinner) $19,550

French Aesthetic Movement brass and pottery pedestal table, circa 1875-80, with square top and recessed tile decorated with foliage, the pedestal with pottery cylinder, on four angular legs, 14in. wide.
(Skinner) $8,050

A nest of three rosewood tables, late 19th/early 20th century, each rounded rectangular top on twin turned standard end supports joined by a stretcher, on outswept feet, 28in. wide.
(Christie's) $624

Federal cherry inlaid Pembroke table, probably central Massachusetts, early 19th century, the top with hinged half-round leaves flanking bowed skirts with stringing, 37in. long.
(Skinner) $2,530

A Regency faded mahogany Pembroke table, the reeded edge rectangular top with rounded corners to the side flaps, an end freize drawer and dummy drawer the other end, 3ft. wide.
(Woolley & Wallis) $720

George III sided mahogany Pembroke table, circa 1800, with rounded leaves, the square tapered legs inlaid with pendant bellflowers, 41in. wide. (Skinner) $1,380

A mahogany Pembroke table, the oval boxwood lined top above a frieze drawer and opposing false drawer, on square tapering legs, restorations, 35½in. wide.
(Christie's) $790

A fine George III mahogany Pembroke table, circa 1765, the top with serpentine leaves and a molded edge above a single end frieze drawer backed by a false drawer, 39½in. wide open.
(Bonhams) $14,000

A satinwood veneered oval Pembroke table, of Sheraton design, with ebonized edge moldings to the twin flap top, ebony stringing to square tapering legs, 27in.
(Woolley & Wallis) $2,240

Federal mahogany inlaid Pembroke table, New England, 1795-1810, the oval top with stringing in outline on a conforming base with string inlaid drawer, 32in. wide.
(Skinner) $10,925

An early Victorian mahogany Pembroke table, the rectangular drop leaf top set on turned tapered legs, 90cm wide.
(Bonhams) $372

A Regency mahogany Pembroke table, the rounded rectangular top with a reeded edge, with a frieze drawer opposed by a dummy drawer, 41½in. wide.
(Christie's) $987

A George III mahogany serpentine serving-table, the crossbanded rectangular top above a waved frieze, on square channelled legs, the center of the frieze cracked. 60½in. wide.
(Christie's) $6,564

Antique American two-drawer tavern table, in walnut, probably Pennsylvania, 18th century, removable top probably not original, 34 x 50½in.
(Eldred's) $990

A George III mahogany serving-table, the geometrically-veneered top above a blind Gothic fretwork frieze, on square chamfered channelled legs headed by lappets, 66½in. wide.
(Christie's) $25,909

An early Victorian rosewood coaching-table, the hinged rounded rectangular top above an X-frame support joined by baluster stretchers, 39¾in. wide (open).
(Christie's) $3,972

A small envelope table in Virginian walnut, the veneered and mahogany banded drop leaf top to a frieze on four plain turned legs with lambs tongue capping and pad feet, 24½in.
(Woolley & Wallis) $852

A George III mahogany drop flap side table, second quarter 18th century, the rectangular top with single drop flap to the reverse, above a single long drawer on cabriole legs, 83cm. wide.
(Bonhams) $738

A Regency mahogany serving table, circa 1820, the rectangular top above two panelled drawers to the frieze, on lion's paw and scrolled monopodia end supports, 64½in. wide.
(Bonhams) $8,436

An early 19th century oak farmhouse serving table, the planked top with cleated ends, above a frieze drawer with brass knob handles, 3ft.8½in.
(Woolley & Wallis) $685

A mahogany serving table, in Hepplewhite style, the top with a front molded edge above a fluted and oval paterae carved frieze, 4ft.11¼in.
(Woolley & Wallis) $1,233

An early 19th century oak side table, distressed, 76cm. wide. (Bonhams & Brooks) $622

A Dutch brass-inlaid and mounted mahogany ebonized side table, early 19th century, the associated gray marble top above a frieze drawer, on female herm supports, 37¼in. wide. (Christie's) $5,339

A William and Mary style mahogany side table, 64cm. wide. (Bonhams & Brooks) $414

An oak side table, possibly Welsh Borders, mid 18th century, with molded plank top and two frieze drawers above a triple pointed ogee-arched apron, 28½in. wide. (Christie's) $4,456

A Louis Philippe ormolu and porcelain mounted tulipwood side table, with an eared oval ormolu-molded top centrally inset with a turquoise-ground Sèvres style platter depicting lovers in a landscape, 20¼in. wide. (Christie's) $7,475

An oak side table, English or Dutch, mid 17th century, with rectangular twin-plank top and frieze drawer, on bulbous knop and ring-turned legs, 29in. wide.(Christie's) $7,487

A Regency mahogany side table cross-banded with yew wood having reeded top above frieze drawer, 3ft wide. (Brightwells) $1,064

An Italian giltwood side table, late 18th century, probably Rome, the later rectangular Cipollino Mandolato Verde marble top above the panelled frieze with a central medallion of a Roman emperor, 52¾in. wide. (Christie's) $20,746

Louis XV style Provincial walnut side table, 19th century, with rectangular thumb-molded top above a frieze drawer and shaped skirt on cabriole legs, 27in. wide. (Skinner) $978

A penwork decorated writing table, 19th century and later, with recent decoration, in the Regency Oriental taste, the rectangular top painted with a processional scene beside a lake with palm trees and Oriental buildings, the top 63in. long.
(Christie's) $17,919

A French carved rosewood sofa table, 19th century, the rectangular top with a gadrooned edge applied with foliate scroll decoration with pendant ornament, 59in. wide extended. (Christie's) $3,257

A George IV mahogany sofa table, the faded flame figured rectangular top with 'D' shape end flaps, crossbanded in rosewood, the friezes with alternate drawers, on pierced lyre shape end supports, 3ft.6in. wide.
(Woolley & Wallis) $4,800

A mahogany and satinwood banded sofa table, 20th century, the rounded rectangular top above a frieze with two drawers and opposing false drawers, 57in. wide.
(Christie's) $1,809

A Regency mahogany sofa table with reeded top fitted with two drawers on cheval frame, 5ft. wide.
(Russell Baldwin & Bright)
                                $9,405

A mahogany and ormolu mounted Empire style sofa table, Stockholm, 94cm. wide.
(Stockholms AV) $2,626

A mahogany and boxwood lined sofa table, early 20th century, with a rounded rectangular top, two frieze drawers and opposing false drawers, on standard end supports with saber legs, 64in. wide.
(Christie's) $1,974

A mahogany writing table, 18th century and later, the rectangular gilt tooled leather lined top with drop leaves and opposing frieze drawers, 55in. extended.
(Christie's) $2,303

A Regency burr ash, amboyna and ivory inlaid sofa table, the hinged top with rounded corners crossbanded in amboyna, with ivory lines and partridgewood or snakewood outer border, 58½in. extended.(Christie's) $5,429

A mid Victorian walnut Sutherland table, distressed, 76cm. wide x 100cm. deep x 73cm. high.
(Bonhams & Brooks) $570

A Victorian rosewood Sutherland table, the oval top with molded serpentine edging, raised on scrolled and leaf carved quadripartite base, 44 x 36¼in.
(Andrew Hartley) $1,738

A Victorian walnut Sutherland table, 82cm. wide.
(Bonhams & Brooks) $585

A mid Victorian mahogany Sutherland table, 104cm. wide, 84cm. deep.
(Bonhams & Brooks) $483

An Edwardian mahogany crossbanded Sutherland table, 91cm. wide.
(Bonhams & Brooks) $287

An Edwardian mahogany and satinwood crossbanded Sutherland table, 68cm. wide.
(Bonhams) $389

An Edwardian mahogany and satinwood crossbanded Sutherland table, 78cm. wide.
(Bonhams & Brooks) $539

A Victorian rosewood Sutherland table with butterfly wing top, on reeded baluster end supports, 24¾in. wide.
(Andrew Hartley) $629

An Edwardian walnut Sutherland table, 54cm. wide.
(Bonhams & Brooks) $208

A fine George IV rectangular mahogany tea table, the hinged swivel top and plain frieze decorated with molded bead border, 40in. wide. (Anderson & Garland) $2,557

A George III mahogany demi lune folding tea table, crossbanding with stringing, the top with fan shaped veneers and plain patera, inlaid panelled frieze, 39in. wide. (Andrew Hartley) $3,625

Classical carved mahogany veneer table, 1815–30, Massachusetts, the veneered hinged top above a similar skirt on a leaf carved and ring-turned pedestal, 36in. wide. (Skinner) $978

Chippendale mahogany tilt-top tea table, Massachusetts, circa 1780, the molded top with shaped corners tilts on a vase and ring-turned post and tripod cabriole leg base ending in arris pad feet, 28½in. high. (Skinner) $863

Louis Majorelle, two-tier table, circa 1895, walnut, of shaped rectangular form, both tiers inlaid with fruitwood marquetry depicting stylized flowering stems and scrolling leaves, 77cm. (Sotheby's) $3,828

Federal mahogany tilt-top tea table, North Shore, Massachusetts, late 18th century, the serpentine top with molded edge tilts above the standard with urn shaping, 33in. wide. (Skinner) $2,070

A Regency mahogany tea table, the reeded rectangular top above a small frieze drawer, on turned tapering legs, 36in. wide. (Bonhams) $739

Chippendale carved mahogany tilt-top tea table, Massachusetts, 18th century, with scrolled piecrust top above a pedestal, 29½in. diameter. (Skinner) $2,990

Chippendale cherry molded birdcage tea table, Pennsylvania, 18th century, the dish top tilts on a birdcage support above a turned pedestal, 32¾in. diameter. (Skinner) $2,990

A George III mahogany demi lune tea table, crossbanded with parquetry stringing, the folding top with marquetry batwing panel, 36in. wide. (Andrew Hartley) $1,020

Chippendale mahogany carved tilt-top tea table, Newport, Rhode Island, 18th century, the top with chamfered underside tilts, 32¾in. diameter. (Skinner) $2,760

A Regency brass-mounted mahogany and ebonized tea table, the rounded rectangular twin-flap top above two frieze drawers to one side and two simulated drawers to the other, 64in. wide. (Christie's) $15,640

A George III mahogany concertina action tea table, the folding oblong eared top on plain frieze with drawer, 33¾in. wide. (Andrew Hartley) $1,540

A George II walnut demi-lune tea table with well, restorations, 68cm. wide. (Bonhams & Brooks) $1,850

The Randall family Chippendale mahogany dish-top tea table, Coastal Massachusetts, 1760-1790, the circular dish-turned top tilting and turning above a birdcage support, 37in. diameter. (Christie's) $70,500

A Victorian walnut serpentine top teatable, the molded swivel top on a reeded baluster column and four carved and splayed legs with scrolled toes, 36in. wide. (Thomson Roddick & Medcalf) $870

A George II mahogany occasional or tea table, the circular snap top with bird cage action, on ring-turned baluster column and tripod splayed legs, 32in. diameter. (Christie's) $3,125

A Queen Anne mahogany tilt-top tea table, Rhode Island, 1740-1760, the circular top tilting above a ring-turned and tapering columnar shaft, on a tripartite base, 31in. diameter. (Christie's) $4,700

A birch and rosewood work table, 19th century and later, the hinged rectangular top with canted corners above an arrangement of false and true drawers, 18in. wide.
(Christie's) $904

A William IV mahogany work table, 62cm. wide.
(Bonhams & Brooks) $1,309

A Victorian walnut writing and work table, the burr veneered serpentine top with a hinged lid revealing a leather inset flap on a ratchet, pen wells, a glass inkwell and a divided drawer, 27in.
(Woolley & Wallis) $1,386

Federal mahogany and maple veneer workstand, North Shore, Massachusetts, circa 1800, the mahogany top with ovolo corners above ring-turned and reeded tapering legs, overall width 20½in.
(Skinner) $6,325

A late Victorian walnut, burr-walnut and foliate marquetry work table, the hinged top with a central oval medallion revealing a fitted interior, 24in. wide. (Christie's) $855

Classical two-drawer mahogany and mahogany veneer workstand, New England, 1825-35, the top with two shaped leaves and scratch beading along the edges, 35in. wide extended.
(Skinner) $230

A Regency mahogany work table, the elongated octagonal body with hinged top enclosing a compartmented interior, 51cm. wide. (Bearne's) $1,887

A good Regency figured mahogany and rosewood crossbanded work table, 63cm. wide.
(Bonhams & Brooks) $2,156

A William IV work table, figured rosewood veneered, the rectangular twin flap top with rounded corner side flaps, two frieze drawers at one end, 19in.
(Woolley & Wallis) $1,760

A George IV mahogany work table, with a molded hinged top containing two drawers and sliding frame below (now fixed), 34in. wide extended.(Christie's) $2,011

A late Regency mahogany work table, lacking drawer partitions, 51cm. wide.
(Bonhams & Brooks) $462

A Victorian walnut games and work table, the rounded rectangular hinged and quarter-veneered top with later inlaid chess and backgammon boards, 23in. wide. (Christie's) $2,576

Classical mahogany veneer drop-leaf work table, Boston, 1820, the solid top with hinged rounded drop leaves with beaded edges which flank two convex veneered drawers, 19in. wide.
(Skinner) $977

A Federal inlaid mahogany octagonal-top work table, Boston or Salem, 1790-1810, the octagonal top with oval-and-sunburst veneer and banded edges above a conforming case fitted with a drawer with geometric inlaid surround, 20¼in. wide.
(Christie's) $101,500

A William IV rosewood sewing table, the twin flap veneered top with rounded corners above two graduated frieze drawers, the reverse with dummy drawers, 15½in. wide.
(Woolley & Wallis) $2,079

Federal maple work table, New England, circa 1800-1810, the rectangular top with canted corners and chamfered edge above a compartmented drawer and a bag drawer, 20¾in. wide.
(Skinner) $2,875

A George III mahogany work table, circa 1810, with two drawers, on square tapered legs united by a later X stretcher, 58cm. wide.
(Bonhams) $1,260

A Regency mahogany reception table, the molded rectangular twin-flap top with reeded edge above a fitted drawer and a further drawer to one side, 30½in. wide, open.
(Christie's) $6,992

Victorian mahogany work table, with galleried top, two drawers on S-scrolled legs joined by a shelf stretcher, 19in. wide.
(Skinner) $489

A Victorian octagonal papier mâché and mother of pear inlaid work table, fitted interior, trumpet shaped pedestal to trefoil platform base, 72cm. high.(Wintertons) $862

A Victorian walnut worktable with octagonal top, opening to reveal fitted interior with needlework store, raised on four scroll carved supports, 44cm. wide.
(Wintertons) $1,540

A Federal carved mahogany work table, Salem, Massachusetts, circa 1810, the rectangular top with outset corners carved with concentric circles above a conforming case with three drawers, 25½in. wide.
(Christie's) $6,900

A Victorian walnut and marquetry work table, in the Louis XV style, with gilt-metal mounts, the serpentine top crossbanded in tulipwood and inlaid with central dark ground spray of flowers, 20½in. wide.
(Christie's) $2,907

A Classical mahogany and figured-maple veneered work table, Baltimore, 1815-1830, the rectangular top with outset rounded corners above a conforming case fitted with two stacked short drawers, 22½in. wide.
(Christie's) $7,050

A French tulipwood, parquetry and ormolu mounted lady's work and dressing table, 19th century, in the Louis XV style, the hinged parquetry dished top with foliate border, 25in. wide.
(Christie's) $6,360

A 19th century Continental walnut shaped rectangular work table, fitted interior and two drawers, on melon lobed pedestal and scrolled and pierced cabriole legs, 50cm.wide.(Wintertons) $924

A German silvered-bronze-mounted pale yellow-painted and polychrome-decorated work table, attributed to Johann Fredrich and Heinrich Wilhelm Spindler, circa 1760-1765, 17in. wide.
(Christie's) $8,343

A late Regency mahogany writing table, the leather lined top with a molded edge, on panelled standard end supports joined by a turned stretcher, 39in. wide.
(Christie's) $1,316

An Empire ormolu-mounted mahogany table à écrire, with a rectangular dished top above two frieze drawers, the top drawer fitted with a writing slide, 20¾in. wide.
(Christie's) $16,685

A lady's Art Nouveau mahogany writing table, with raised slatted and stained glass back, inset leather writing surface, bowed center section with frieze drawer, 39in. wide.
(Andrew Hartley) $1,390

Charles & Ray Eames, an early D-10-N First Series Esu desk, designed 1949-50, for Herman Miller, the rectangular birch plywood top on zinc angle-iron uprights with rubber pad feet, the understructure of masonite panels, 44in. wide.(Christie's) $6,520

Edwardian style marquetry inlaid mahogany writing table, 20th century, with U-shaped superstructure fitted with drawers and doors above a serpentine case fitted with drawers, 35in. wide.
(Skinner) $2,645

A French brass-mounted red tortoiseshell boulle marquetry bureau Mazarin, 19th century, inlaid overall in première and contre-partie with bérainesque figures, animals and scrolling foliage, 44in. wide. (Christie's) $10,373

A French kidney-shaped, ormolu-mounted, kingwood writing desk, 20th century, surmounted by a serpentine superstructure centered by a ribbon tied timepiece, above four gilt-tooled green leather doors, 59in. wide.
(Christie's) $4,606

A French kingwood, crossbanded, ormolu and porcelain mounted bonheur du jour, 19th century, of slight serpentine outline, in the Louis XV style, 26½in. wide.
(Christie's) $3,722

An ormolu-mounted tulipwood and marquetry writing table, the shaped eared rectangular top centered by a basket of flowers within a scrolled cartouche and fruitwood floral sprays at the angles, 29½in. wide.
(Christie's) $4,715

An Edwardian satinwood Carlton House desk, with painted decoration, crossbanding and checker stringing, 142cm. wide. (Phillips) $8,000

Blue painted school master's desk, Smithtown, Long Island, 1840-60, the scrolled gallery above the top which is hinged, 27¾in. wide. (Skinner) $1,495

A mahogany leather lined desk, the raised superstructure with a hinged writing slope flanked by a drawer at either side and three frieze drawers below, 59½in. wide. (Christie's) $1,316

A Victorian burr-walnut and marquetry bonheur du jour, in the Louis XV style, crossbanded in tulipwood and applied with gilt-metal ornament with mirrored and galleried superstructure, 34½in. wide. (Christie's) $3,799

A Louis XV style ormolu-mounted tulipwood and marquetry bureau plat and cartonnier, late 19th century, by Emanuel Zwiener, the arched bombé cartonnier fitted with a clock surmounted by two putti and a hound, 58in. wide. (Christie's) $63,000

A North German gilt metal-mounted mahogany writing table, third quarter 18th century, the rectangular three-quarter pierced galleried brocatello di Spagna marble top above a panelled frieze with inset lozenges, 25½in. wide. (Christie's) $5,658

A satinwood Carlton House desk, English, circa 1990, of typical form, the incurved superstructure with two sets of three drawers flanked by two incurved doors and two further sets of three drawers, 155.5cm. wide. (Sotheby's) $21,960

A French ebonized, pietra dura and ormolu mounted writing cabinet or bonheur du jour, 19th century, the lower part fitted with a central slide and containing two drawers in the frieze, 48in. wide. (Christie's) $4,568

A late Victorian mahogany desk, of serpentine outline, blind-fret carved throughout, the superstructure with two pairs of small bowed drawers and a hinged covered stationery compartment, 48½in. wide. (Christie's) $1,480

A good kingwood and gilt-bronze bureau plat by Sormani, Paris, circa 1890, on cabriole legs headed by masks, on hoof feet, 141cm. wide. (Sotheby's) $18,230

A combined walnut and marquetry music stand and desk, which opens further to become a games table, Rome, mid 19th century, 89cm. wide. (Finarte) $10,059

A rare Federal mahogany writing desk, New England, circa 1785, the rectangular top surmounted by shelves and pigeonholes, 4ft. 9½in. wide. (Sotheby's) $24,150

A Regency brass-mounted mahogany and satinwood bonheur du jour, inlaid overall with boxwood, ebonised and satinwood lines, the three-quarter baluster gallery on column supports above a shelf and a cylinder-bureau, 24½in. wide. (Christie's) $8,982

A rare and unusual Victorian mahogany patent enclosed desk, by Urquhart and Adamson, Cabinet Makers, Liverpool, the rectangular adjustable ratcheted top inset with a panel of tooled leather inscribed D.W. 1981, with trailing strawberry plants and foliage, 28¾in. wide. (Christie's) $6,800

A late Louis XV tulipwood and parquetry bonheur du jour, by Guillaume Cordié, inlaid à quatre faces and crossbanded overall with boxwood and amaranth, 26in. wide. (Christie's) $5,281

A Sheraton period mahogany writing table, the quarter segment veneered rectangular top, inlaid with fine checker stringing and crossbanded, the front with two frieze drawers, 27½ x 34in. (Woolley & Wallis) $4,160

Victorian walnut cylinder lady's desk, circa 1860, with frieze drawers, fitted interior, and sliding writing surface, above two drawers on cabriole legs, 46in. high. (Skinner) $575

A George III mahogany tambour writing desk, the fall enclosing a fitted interior, fitted with two frieze drawers, 38¼in. wide. (Christie's) $4,360

A mid 18th century tallboy, the front in Virginian walnut, the ogee molded cornice above four long graduated drawers, oak lined, 3ft.9½in. wide.
(Woolley & Wallis) $9,600

Shaker eleven-drawer tall chest, 19th century, two small drawers above two small drawers above seven graduated drawers, 44in. wide. (Eldred's) $4,950

A Victorian mahogany Wellington chest of six graduated drawers flanked by pilasters, one hinged, on plinth base with bun feet, 61.5cm. wide. (Bristol) $1,812

Red washed carved birch tall chest, New Hampshire, circa 1815, the cove molded flaring cornice above the thumb-molded five drawer case, the top drawer centers a deeply carved pinwheel, 39¼in. wide.
(Skinner) $48,875

A late George III mahogany and marquetry tallboy chest, with checker feather banding, the upper part with a molded cornice and frieze with harewood oval medallions with Prince of Wales feathers, 44½in. wide.
(Christie's) $4,229

Chippendale walnut tall chest, Chester County, Pennsylvania, 1784, the flaring cornice molding above ten thumb-molded drawers flanked by quarter engaged fluted columns, 40¼in. wide.
(Skinner) $13,800

Chippendale tiger maple tall chest, southeastern New England, circa 1780, the flat-molded cornice above a case of seven thumbmolded drawers, 36in. wide.
(Skinner) $3,220

A Dutch mahogany tall chest, 19th century, with a dentil molded cornice above seven drawers with fluted canted angles and fluted square tapering legs, 35½in. wide.
(Christie's) $2,138

Federal walnut tall chest of drawers, circa 1790-1810, molded overhanging cornice over three narrow over five graduated wide drawers, 42¹/₈in. wide.
(Freeman) $6,440

A Victorian walnut teapoy with burr wood interior, 35cm. wide x 30cm. deep x 72cm. high.
(Bonhams & Brooks) $260

A mahogany teapoy, the sarcophagus shape top with fittings and gadrooning, the turned stem on a quadriform base, 16in.
(Woolley & Wallis) $754

An early 19th century black lacquered japanned teapoy with pen work decorated interior, 53cm. wide. (Bonhams) $445

A William IV mahogany teapoy, restorations and lacking interior, 39cm. wide.
(Bonhams & Brooks) $453

A William IV rosewood teapoy, of sarcophagus shape, lid reveals two lidded caddies and spaces for mixing bowls, 19in.
(Woolley & Wallis) $795

A Regency calamander, ebonised and parcel-gilt teapoy, the octagonal hinged top enclosing a fitted interior, on a later base with spirally-fluted and turned baluster column, 14¼in. diameter.
(Christie's) $2,544

A Victorian rosewood teapoy, of sarcophagus form, the hinged top enclosing a fitted interior with glass mixing bowl, 17in. wide.
(Christie's) $1,173

A William IV rosewood teapoy, the lid reveals two lidded caddies and spaces for mixing bowls (missing), scroll and gadroon bun feet on brass castors, 19in.
(Woolley & Wallis) $825

A Regency rosewood teapoy, circular top with molded edge, fitted interior lacking two canisters, 51cm. diameter.
(Wintertons) $1,155

A Victorian mahogany wardrobe, circa 1860, the corbelled cavetto cornice over two arched panel doors, 4ft. 7in. wide.
(Sotheby's) $2,400

A Regency mahogany wardrobe, the central suspended chest with reeded rectangular top above two short drawers and four long drawers, 92in. wide.
(Christie's) $9,085

A polychrome decorated wardrobe, early 20th century, with a molded cornice and beaded frieze above a pair of shaped panelled doors decorated with St George and the Dragon, 41in. wide.
(Christie's) $1,447

A Sheraton Revival mahogany and painted wardrobe by Walker & Edwards, London, central mirrored door, flanked on either side by a panelled door with painted paterae, late 19th century, 74¼in. wide.
(Andrew Hartley) $4,448

An Edwardian mahogany, satinwood crossbanded and marquetry breakfront wardrobe, in the Georgian style, with pierced fret swan neck pediment and dentil cornice and flowerhead inlaid centered frieze, 102in. wide.
(Christie's) $8,144

An Edwardian satinwood wardrobe, crossbanded with stringing, molded and dentil inlaid cornice over inlaid fluted frieze, bow fronted central section, 27in. wide.
(Andrew Hartley) $3,058

A mid Victorian mahogany and inlaid triple section wardrobe, with a molded cornice and three twin panelled doors centered with urn or patera inlay and all with shell inlaid corners, 78in. wide.
(Christie's) $1,562

A Victorian mahogany wardrobe, the molded cornice above two panelled doors enclosing pull-out shelves and hangers, 48in. wide.
(Christie's) $1,480

A Victorian mahogany gentleman's wardrobe, with a molded cornice and three arched panelled doors enclosing hanging space, sliding trays and drawers, on a plinth base, 76in. wide. (Christie's) $851

A Victorian mahogany wardrobe, of inverted breakfront form, the stepped and molded cornice with carved and scrolled surmount, four doors with applied panelling, 92in. wide.
(Andrew Hartley) $2,710

An early Victorian burr walnut wardrobe 194cm. wide.
(Bonhams & Brooks) $693

A 'Regency Revival' brass-inlaid mahogany and padouk gentleman's wardrobe, circa 1880, four folding panelled doors each inlaid with Greek-key borders, 81cm. wide.
(Christie's) $10,902

A birch, rosewood and shagreen wardrobe, French, circa 1930, the stepped rectangular top above a pair of cupboard doors decorated with shagreen and ivory in a diamond pattern, 45¼in. wide.
(Christie's) $7,560

A Victorian walnut breakfront wardrobe, with a molded cornice, central mirrored door enclosing drawers and sliding trays flanked by panelled cupboards, 86½in. wide.
(Christie's) $987

A French grey-painted and gilt heightened wardrobe, late 19th/early 20th century, the shaped arched flowerhead decorated frieze with a pierced cresting of crossed quiver and torch, with flowers, 80in. wide. (Christie's) $1,809

A Victorian mahogany wardrobe with a molded cornice and a pair of panelled doors enclosing hanging space and sliding trays, 52½in. wide.
(Christie's) $164

A classical carved mahogany three-part wardrobe, Baltimore, 1820-1840, in three sections, the center section with a rectangular case fitted two panelled doors flanked and separated by applied reeding, 84in. wide.
(Christie's) $9,988

A mahogany wardrobe, late 19th/early 20th century, with a dentil-molded cornice, a pair of double panelled line-inlaid doors, mirrored to the reverse, 53½in. wide. (Christie's) $2,138

An English ebonized and walnut three-tier what-not, in the manner of Lamb of Manchester, circa 1870, the top shelf with baluster back-rail, the lower shelf with a two-drawer frieze, 49½in. wide.
(Christie's) $10,120

A mid Victorian burr walnut and inlaid whatnot cabinet, the brass gallery above a tier supported on six turned and molded columns, the base fitted with a fall front enclosing a shaped shelf, 25in. wide. (Wintertons) $1,330

A Victorian ebonized burr-wood or possibly amboyna and inlaid three-tier what-not, of bowed outline, with brass berried finials and pierced gallery with mirror backs, 39½in. wide. (Christie's) $1,840

Victorian 'chinoiserie' bamboo and lacquer whatnot corner stand, late 19th century, the frame set with two diamond shaped mirrors, and shelves, 22in. wide.
(Skinner) $230

A lacquered two-tier étagère, early 20th century, decorated with birds amongst foliage and a monkey climbing a flowering branch, 32½in. wide. (Christie's) $1,125

Late Regency walnut whatnot, 19th century, fitted with four tiers with bobbin turned supports, and with apron drawer.
(Skinner) $1,035

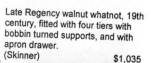

A North European walnut étagère of five rectangular open tiers between turned supports with a deep drawer below, a raised plinth and turned feet, 33in. wide.
(Christie's) $691

A pair of French brass-mounted tulipwood and amaranth parquetry three-tier étagères, second half of the 19th century, on slender toupie feet, 13½in. wide.
(Christie's) $11,551

A mahogany whatnot, early 19th century, of four rectangular open tiers, the upper tier with a low three quarter gallery with turned supports and drawer below, on 26½in. wide. (Christie's) $1,397

A Victorian mahogany marble topped washstand, 108cm. wide. (Bonhams & Brooks) $277

A Regency mahogany and ebony inlaid washstand, 91cm. wide. (Bonhams & Brooks) $770

A Regency mahogany washstand in the manner of Gillow, raised molded edged back and shaped sides, the reeded edged top with bowl aperture, 29½in. wide. (Andrew Hartley) $417

Louis XVI Provincial walnut rafraîchissoir, early 19th century, the top with two wells and frieze drawer, raised on turned legs joined by shelf stretchers, 18in. wide. (Skinner) $805

A German mahogany pedestal washstand, 2nd quarter 19th century, in the form of an Ionic Capital and fluted column, the hinged rectangular top enclosing a mirror and a later fitted interior, 21¾in. wide. (Christie's) $5,451

A Federal walnut washstand, Massachusetts, 1790-1805, the square molded top centering a circular recess backed by two smaller circular recesses above a double ogee-carved apron, 13¼in. wide. (Christie's) $1,840

A Regency mahogany Empire style washstand, the upper stage with arched mirror supported by gilt metal urn mounts, two small side drawers, gray rectangular marble top above three frieze drawers, 83cm. wide. (Wintertons) $1,400

A good George III mahogany enclosed washstand with Wedgwood creamware bidet and associated washbowl and soap dish 62cm. wide. (Bonhams) $1,782

A George II mahogany corner wash stand, inlaid overall with boxwood lines and crossbanded in tulipwood, the arched gallery with small shelf, above a bow-fronted top, 22½in. wide. (Christie's) $1,817

A George III mahogany oval wine cooler with molded hinged lid and plain brass banding, 24¼in. wide. (David Lay) $2,393

A George III mahogany and brass bound octagonal cellaret-on-stand, with hinged molded top and brass ring carrying handles, the top 19½in. wide. (Christie's) $3,214

A Regency brass-mounted mahogany wine cooler, the stepped canted rectangular hinged top enclosing a blue baize lined lid and metal lined interior, 42in. wide. (Christie's) $18,400

A George III mahogany and later brass-bound octagonal cellaret, with a hinged top and brass carrying handles, having a fluted frieze, on molded chamfered splayed legs, 17¼in. wide. (Christie's) $4,343

A late 19th century Georgian style mahogany oval wine cooler on leafage scroll carved cabriole legs and ball and claw feet, 2ft. 2in. wide. (Russell Baldwin & Bright) $724

A George III mahogany and satinwood-banded oval wine cooler, inlaid with crossbanded lines, the hinged top enclosing a divided interior, 21¾in. wide. (Christie's) $3,452

A George III mahogany cellaret, the hinged top revealing an interior divided for eight bottles, with brass swan neck handles to each end, 21in. wide.(Christie's) $1,616

A George II style mahogany wine cooler, late 19th century 72cm. wide. (Bonhams) $3,885

An Edwardian walnut wine cooler, of circular waisted form, with slatted sides and a brass liner, on three splayed legs with brass paw feet, 14in. diameter. (Christie's) $790

A Victorian oak sarcophagus wine cooler, profusely carved with foliage, the hinged top with cartouches carved *A.O.1601*, 33in. wide. (Christie's) $4,124

George III brass bound mahogany tripod wine cooler, circa 1800, with bell-form top and cylindrical body on a tripod base with brass paw casters, 29½in. high. (Skinner) $863

A Regency mahogany wine cooler, the front corners having bold carved scroll trusses with carved paw feet, 75cm. (Tennants) $5,024

A mahogany oval wine cellaret, early 19th century and later, of coopered construction with a galvanized liner, the stand with cabriole legs and pad feet, 25in. wide. (Christie's) $1,022

A George III mahogany wine cooler, the octagonal brass banded body with a hinged lid enclosing a lead lined interior, 50cm. (Tennants) $5,338

A George III mahogany and boxwood strung octagonal cellaret on stand, circa 1770, the hinged top above a tapered body with carrying handles to the sides, 19in. wide. (Bonhams) $5,320

A Georgian style mahogany cellaret, 71.5cm. (Bonhams) $1,896

A George III mahogany and brass-bound hexagonal wine cooler-on-stand, the hinged top enclosing a compartmented interior, 19¼in. wide. (Christie's) $5,814

A Regency style mahogany wine cooler of sarcophagus form, set on a stand with brass castors, the whole with boxwood stringing, 39cm. wide. (Bonhams) $770

Painted wood triple game board, America, late 19th/ early 20th century, applied frame on rectangular board, 17 x 24in. (Skinner) $1,840

Polychrome painted checkerboard, possibly New England, circa 1870, with applied frame, 18½in. square. (Skinner) $1,840

Painted wood gambling wheel America, 19th century, the wheel with red, blue, and yellow-painted pie-shaped sections with black numerals, 16in. diameter. (Skinner) $2,070

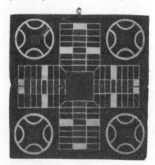

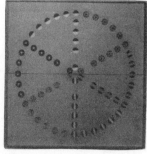

Polychrome painted folding double-sided game board, America, late 19th century, the obverse with checkerboard, interior with parcheesi in green, red, and yellow, breadboard ends, 21in. wide., 21in. long. (Skinner) $1,840

Polychrome painted double-sided lap checkerboard, America, late 19th century, the obverse with canted sides and checkerboard flanked by panels centering the letter B, 15in. wide, 29in. long. (Skinner) $2,990

Polychrome painted folding game board, America, circa 1920, the circular flag motifs including American, British, German, and French forming a circle with six radiating arms enclosed by a larger circle, 25in. square. (Skinner) $2,300

Polychrome painted double-sided game board, America or Canada, circa 1900, the obverse with parcheesi board stencil decorated with star, maple leaves, and cartouches, 18in. wide., 30in. long. (Skinner) $1,380

Polychrome painted double-sided game board, possibly Canada, late 19th century, the obverse with parcheesi board centering interlocking crescent design, 27in. square. (Skinner) $5,463

Polychrome incised and painted game board, possibly Canada, early 20th century, the obverse with parcheesi board flanked by two tin-lined compartments with sliding lids, 19in. wide, 31in. long. (Skinner) $5,750

438

Polychrome painted parcheesi board, America, late 19th century, paper on board, applied frame, 18in. wide, 18in. long. (Skinner) $1,265

Polychrome painted parcheesi board, America, late 19th century, with breadboard ends, reverse with incised fox and geese game 18in. square. (Skinner) $2,300

Polychrome painted parcheesi game board, Midwest, circa 1920, box constructed square game board with pull-out copper fronted game piece drawer, 15½ x16in. (Skinner) $1,725

Painted polychrome parcheesi board, America, circa 1880, with stencilled gilt scroll and floral devices, applied frame, 27in. square. (Skinner) $4,025

Polychrome painted checkerboard, America, circa 1880, the checkerboard and surround with all-over marbleized surface, applied frame, reverse stencilled *Fd. Champagne*, 19in. wide., 31in. long. (Skinner) $3,450

Polychrome painted parcheesi board, American, early 20th century, painted on artist board, 20in. square. (Skinner) $1,150

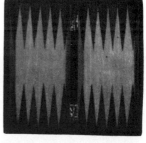

Polychrome painted and gilded roulette wheel 'Ten For One', America, circa 1890, the recessed wheel framed by alternating suits of painted cards interspersed with four racehorses, 24in. square. (Skinner) $3,335

Polychrome painted double-sided game board, America, circa 1900, the obverse stencilled *Railroad Game or Trip Around the World*, the reverse with red and white checkerboard, 22in. diameter. (Skinner) $2,530

Polychrome painted folding double-sided game board, America, circa 1880, the obverse with checkerboard, interior backgammon in red and green on yellow, 17 x 19in. (Skinner) $1,265

Polychrome parcheesi gameboard, late 19th century, red, yellow, orange, and green paint, 20 x 19in. (Skinner) $1,955

Painted folding gameboard, mid 20th century, avocado green with colorful raised segmented tracks, opens for storage, 31 x 12½in. (Skinner) $575

Painted and gilt decorated checkerboard with molded edge, Saco, Maine, 19th century, reverse reading *Saco Lodge No-2*, 18¾ x 20in. (Skinner) $5,175

Painted checkerboard, America, 19th century, red, pink, green, white, yellow, and black paint with rose blossoms and leafy stems, applied border, 15½ x 15¾in. (Skinner) $2,185

Painted checkerboard, America, circa 1849-50, brown and yellow paint, the obverse with checkers, the reverse with a caricature of President Zachary Taylor, 14½ x 14¼in. (Skinner) $3,105

Painted folding parcheesi gameboard, Massachusetts, circa 1870, with American flag and spade, heart, diamond, and club motifs, 18½ x 18½in. (Skinner) $46,000

Painted double-sided gameboard, mid 19th century, the obverse with checkerboard, reverse with snake-motif game, apple green, brown, and black paint, 12 x 12¼in. (Skinner) $36,800

Painted gameboard, New York, circa 1870, the squares are numbered 1 to 32, 16½ x 14½in. (Skinner) $4,312

Painted checkerboard, stamped *CA BROWN 1852* on the reverse, gold, red, crimson, and black paint, 22¹/₈in. x 22¼in. (Skinner) $1,380

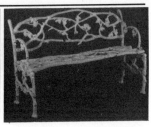

A cast-stone garden bench circa 1910, with a rectangular backrest and seat flanked by intertwined trunk-form supports.
(Sotheby's) $11,500

A 19th century Italian simulated marble balustrade, with turned columns, 195cm. wide, 78cm. high.
(Phillips) $2,132

A Victorian Coalbrookdale cast iron garden seat, white painted, naturalistic fruiting vine design, width 130cm.
(Wintertons) $768

A Coalbrookdale cast iron garden seat, the back cast with oval panels of flowering plants flanked by paterae and with straight crest, stamp for 5 May 1883, 75in. wide.
(Andrew Hartley) $2,511

A Victorian Coalbrookdale lily of the valley cast iron garden seat, having wooden slatted seat, repairs to ironwork, 74in. wide.
(Michael J. Bowman) $2,296

A reconstituted stone bench, late 20th century, the rectangular seat with foliate molded edge, on voluted scroll supports, 60in. wide.
(Christie's) $656

An Italian brêche violette and carrara marble wall fountain, circa 1870, the shaped back with shell crest above scrolled top and sides, centered by triple addorsed upended dolphins with entwined tails, 43in. wide. (Christie's) $25,850

A pair of black-painted cast-iron dog garden ornaments, J.W. Fiske and Company, New York City, each cast in the full round, the hair-molded lying bodies with articulated ears, eyes, snout, mouth, 14½in. wide.
(Christie's) $25,850

An early 20th century lead garden figure of a putto dancing with ribbon, on square base and rectangular concrete plinth, 49in. overall. (Brightwells) $2,103

An Italian marble bench, the rectangular back surmounted by a voluted crest continuing to foliate carved arm supports, 6ft. long.
(Sotheby's) $14,375

A terracotta bas relief copy of the Borghese Dancers, the marble in the Louvre, 18th century, 9 x 38 x 84cm. (Finarte) $1,868

An 18th century marble table top, composed of a fragment of Roman micromosaic with geometric and foliate motifs, with ormolu edging, 130 x 67cm.
(Finarte) $18,526

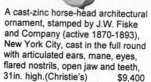

A Coalbrookdale fern and blackberry pattern cast iron seat, circa 1870, the back and sides pierced with ferns and clusters of blackberries above a wooden slatted seat, 60in. wide.
(Christie's) $5,527

A cast-zinc horse-head architectural ornament, stamped by J.W. Fiske and Company (active 1870-1893), New York City, cast in the full round with articulated ears, mane, eyes, flared nostrils, open jaw and teeth, 31in. high.(Christie's) $9,400

A Victorian cast iron seat, Morgan, Macaulay and Wade, circa 1870, the pierced back with four oval panels, each depicting a laborer representing a season with attribute, 72in. wide.
(Christie's) $8,636

A reconstituted stone urn, late 20th century, in the gothic manner, the octagonal sided jardinière with a frieze of quatrefoil tracery, 29¼in. high. overall.
(Christie's) $1,729

A two tiered lead fountain, late 20th century, the fountain spout and upper bowl with scalloped edge supported by putti, the larger bowl above a fluted stem and triform base with swans to the angles 55in. high. (Christie's) $1,295

A Victorian cast iron urn and pedestal, circa 1880, of shallow campana form, with everted egg and dart molded rim above the lobed underside, on a fluted socle, 46in. high, overall.
(Christie's) $3,455

A Victorian cast iron seat, Yates Haywood Foundry, third quarter 19th century, the serpentine scrolling and lattice pierced back rest entwined with trailing blackberry and leaves below the fan shaped cresting, 55in. wide.
(Christie's) $3,947

A lead bird bath, early 20th century, the winged cherub above a scallop shell, a quiver across his shoulder and holding an arrow aloft, the bowl on paw feet, 17in. high.
(Christie's) $2,392

An Italian sculpted limestone seat, late 20th century, the rectangular panelled back with volute scroll cresting carved in relief with trailing foliage, flanked by seated winged lion arm supports, 66in. wide.
(Christie's) $6,564

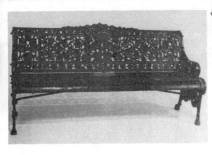

A Coalbrookdale cast iron garden seat in Nasturtium pattern with wooden slatted seat, stamped Coalbrookdale on the seat, 72in. wide.
(Andrew Hartley) $1,649

A red-painted cast-iron rooster mill weight, American, 20th century, cast in the full round with articulated comb, eye, beak and wattle with "rainbow" molded tail, 24¾in. high. (Christie's) $5,640

A cast iron Royal coat of arms, late 19th century, with quartered shield flanked by the unicorn and lion and cast with the motto *Dieu et Mon Droit,* 49in.
(Bonhams) $2,400

A pair of Victorian cast iron urns, circa 1880, of campana form, with gadrooned rims, the upper sections cast in relief with continuous bands of foliate scrolling ornament, 31in. high. (Christie's) $4,491

A carved stone drain terminal, possibly gothic, modelled as a winged mythical beast, 24in. protrudence.
(Christie's) $1,553

Two lead models of cockerels, late 20th century, each shown standing on oval bases cast with scattered fruit and sheaves of corn, 27in. high. (Christie's) $691

A cast iron and marble top table, J.King & Co., Hull, circa 1880, the white marble top with molded border and entrant corners, 48in. long. (Christie's) $1,122

A pair of late Victorian or Edwardian cast iron hopper heads, modelled with mythical winged beasts above concave waisted sections cast in relief with floral motifs, 21in. high. (Christie's) $2,764

A Coalbrookdale cast iron seat, circa 1860, the triple arched pierced back with trailing foliage amidst trefoil designs above an iron slatted seat, 68in. wide.
(Christie's) $5,527

A mid Victorian cast iron armchair, probably cast by Archibald Kenrick & Sons, West Bromwich, the horseshoe shaped back pierced with foliate scrolls and strapwork. (Bonhams) $412

A pair of 19th century stone pedestals, of square waisted form, 24in. high. (Bonhams) $353

A Regency wrought iron garden chair. (Bonhams & Brooks) $588

A pair of French cast iron garden urns, late 19th or early 20th century, the tapering bodies cast with anthemions and with waisted flared necks, with angular outset handles, dated 1926, 25in. high. (Christie's) $1,184

A set of four lead cherubs representing the Seasons, early 20th century, each shown with attributes, damages, 23½in. high, and a lead birdbath, modelled with a cherub supporting a dish, 27in. high. (Christie's) $2,537

A large terracotta campana urn, late 19th or early 20th century, Doulton, Lambeth, the everted rim with egg and dart border, the body with handles issuing from satyr masks beneath a band of trailing vine, 36½in. high. (Christie's) $2,537

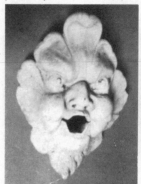

A French white marble fountain mask, 19th century, carved as a grotesque mask in deep relief, 17in. high. (Bonhams) $1,103

A Byzantine style Istrian stone wellhead, late 19th/early 20th century, the rectangular top with a gadrooned rim and female masks to the corners, the body carved with birds and animals, 27 x 33in. (Bonhams) $2,352

A decorative bronze jardinière, modern, cast as a pair of Egyptian female figures supporting an urn, 54in. high. (Bonhams) $2,646

An Italian Carrara marble fountain, circa 1870, the circular pool base surmounted by the figural fountain head carved as a naked putto holding a fish, base restored, 44½ x 46in. (Bonhams) $3,528

A pair of Victorian terrace vases, white painted cast iron, of campana outline, raised on cast iron plinth bases, overall height 44in. (Wintertons) $1,103

A pair of Continental terracotta bench ends, 20th century, each modelled as a winged sphinx, with impressed stamps within a circle, 40½in. high. (Christie's) $1,692

A statuary marble bust of a Lady, mid 19th century, draped 'all' antica', on a turned socle, indistinctly signed, weathered, 24in. high. (Bonhams) $735

A set of four lead figures of the Seasons, circa 1930, each cast as a scantily clad boy holding their respective attributes, 15¾in. to 19¼in. high. (Bonhams) $2,058

An early Victorian English statuary marble bust of Sir Walter Scott, by F Saunders, his face inclined to sinister and with a tartan cloak with a brooch to his left shoulder, 30½in. high. (Bonhams) $2,940

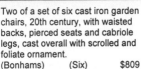

A pair of stone gate pier finials, each carved as a ball on a spreading circular foot and rectangular plinth, one damaged, 20½in. high. (Bonhams) $735

Two of a set of six cast iron garden chairs, 20th century, with waisted backs, pierced seats and cabriole legs, cast overall with scrolled and foliate ornament. (Bonhams) (Six) $809

A pair of terracotta rustic garden urns, probably Scottish, early 20th century, the bowls modelled as sections of tree trunk above conforming plinths, 24½in. high. (Christie's) $1,184

Two of an assembled set of six painted and gilded cast-iron garden chairs, each backrest with drapery and masks above two warriors, all above an openwork frieze. (Skinner)　　　(Six)　　　$4,313

An Italian carved white marble bench, circa 1880, with scrolled acanthus and shell-carved cresting, above the panelled rectangular back centered by a cartouche flanked by scrolling acanthus, mythical beasts and butterflies, 76¾in. wide. (Christie's)　　　$32,900

A set of four lead satyr musician figures, J.P. White Bedford, early 20th century, each shown playing various instruments, on waisted concave-sided square bases, 24in. high four Portland stone tapering square section pedestals, 40in. high.
(Christie's)　　　$17,075

A rustic style cast iron garden seat, the back and seat pierced with truncated branches, 52in. wide. (Andrew Hartley)　　　$1,218

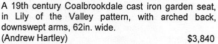

A 19th century Coalbrookdale cast iron garden seat, in Lily of the Valley pattern, with arched back, downswept arms, 62in. wide.
(Andrew Hartley)　　　$3,840

A Victorian rustic style cast iron garden seat, the arched back and seat pierced with truncated branches, similar sides with entwined snakes, 51in. wide. (Andrew Hartley)　　　$955

A balustroid ale glass, circa 1735, the slender funnel bowl with a tear to the solid lower part, 7½in. high.
(Christie's) $1,873

An airtwist ale flute, circa 1750, the pan-topped slender funnel bowl supported on a stem with swelling waist knop, 20cm. high.(Christie's) $596

An engraved airtwist ale glass, circa 1750, the slender ogee bowl engraved with a loose bouquet 19.5cm. high. (Christie's) $1,022

A toasting-glass, mid 18th century, of slender drawn-trumpet shape, on a conical foot, 22cm high. (Christie's) $477

An engraved airtwist ale glass, circa 1750, the slender bell bowl engraved with a hop and two ears of barley, supported on a double-knopped stem, 20cm. high.
(Christie's) $1,192

An engraved airtwist ale glass, circa 1750, the slender funnel bowl engraved with two ears of barley and a hop-spray, supported on a double-knopped stem, 8¼in. high.
(Christie's) $937

An engraved facet-stemmed ale glass, circa 1785, of drawn form, the slender ogee bowl engraved and polished with a hop-spray and two ears of barley, 19.5cm. high.(Christie's) $851

An engraved balustroid ale glass, circa 1740, the slender funnel bowl engraved with an ear of barley entwined with a hop-spray, 7¾in. high. (Christie's) $766

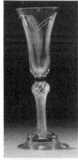

An airtwist ale glass, circa 1750, the slender bell bowl engraved with four ears of barley, supported on a shoulder-knopped stem, 7¾in. high.
(Christie's) $1,363

An incised-twist ale-flute, circa 1750, the slender funnel bowl with everted rim and light honeycomb molding to the lower part, 8¾in. high.
(Christie's) $3,408

An engraved facet-stemmed ale-glass, late 18th century, the slender funnel bowl engraved with an equestrian figure and two hounds, 6¾in. high. (Christie's) $766

A mixed-twist flute, of drawn-trumpet form, the stem with an opaque gauze core enclosed within two spiral air threads, 7½in. high. (Christie's) $1,022

A Bohemian pale-blue and opaque overlay beaker, the ogee bowl cut with a stylized leaf band painted and gilt with leaves, circa 1860, 14cm. high. (Christie's) $581

A rare Medieval 'Nuppenbecher' of Schaffhausen-type, circa 1400, Germany or Switzerland, of densely seeded pale-green metal, the cylindrical body decorated all over with applied prunts beneath an applied trailed thread, 3¾in. high. (Christie's) $22,856

A large German Goldrubinglas beaker, Potsdam or South German, circa 1700, the slightly flared cylindrical form of dark ruby tint, 13cm. (Sotheby's) $8,400

BOTTLES

An early and large sealed wine bottle, dated *1706*, the squat onion form of olive-green tint, with short tapering neck and string-rim, applied with a moulded circular seal inscribed *W.W. 1706*, 20.5cm. (Sotheby's) $8,674

A Hukin & Heath silver mounted novelty oil/vinegar bottle, Birmingham 1931, modelled as a duck in clear and green glass, the hinged head set with glass eyes and the scrolled handles modelled as wings, 9½in. wide. (Bonhams) $1,104

Two Venetian latticinio slender cylindrical bottles and covers, late 17th /early 18th century, in vetro a reticello, the high domed covers with knob finials in vetro a fili, 16cm. high. (Christie's) $4,388

A 'shaft and globe' green tint wine bottle with string rim, tapering neck and kick-in base, circa 1680, 23cm. high. (Christie's) $2,544

An olive green glass wine bottle, the tapering neck with applied ring, 18th century, 18cm. (Woolley & Wallis) $155

A green onion-shaped wine bottle with tapering neck and string rim, with kick-in base (chipped and scratched), 18cm. high. (Christie's) $328

'Poissons No. 1' No.3211 a clear and opalescent bowl, faint molded marks *R. Lalique*, 23.9cm. diameter. (Christie's) $624

A cameo glass bowl, French, 1920s, the pale opalescent glass internally mottled with yellow, overlaid in cherry red, acid-etched and carved with stylized poppies and foliage, 15cm. diameter. (Christie's) $452

'Lys' No.382 a clear and frosted bowl, wheel-engraved *R.Lalique France*, 23.5cm. diameter. (Christie's) $2,303

René Lalique opalescent fishes low bowl, France, model created in 1931, press-molded shallow bowl with intaglio fishes spiralling from the center of 'bubbles', 11½in. diameter. (Skinner) $258

A bowl and dish by Simon Gate for Orrefors, 1927, engraved with a frieze of dancing female figures with veils, deer and birds, the dish also engraved, bowl 23cm. high. (Stockholms AV) $15,161

'Asters No.2' No.10-3039, a clear and opalescent bowl, stencil mark *R. Lalique France*, 25cm. diameter. (Christie's) $505

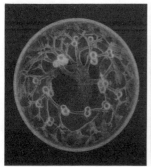

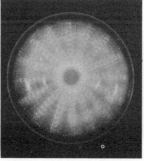

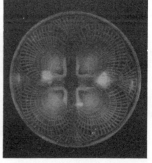

'Gui No.2' No.3224 a clear and frosted bowl, molded mark *R.Lalique*, 23.7cm. high. (Christie's) $578

'Oursins No. 2' No.3310 a clear and opalescent bowl, stencil marks *R.Lalique*, 25.5cm. diameter. (Christie's) $690

'Coquilles No.3202 a clear, frosted and opalescent bowl, engraved *R.Lalique France No.3202*, 18cm. diameter. (Christie's) $342

A fine pair of 19th century 14½in. two-light two-branch candelabra with scrolling arms, center pyramids and cut luster and drop ornamentation, 23in. high. (Anderson & Garland) $910

A pair of George III style glass three light candelabra, late 19th or early 20th century, with nozzles and drip pans on faceted scroll branches about central spike finials, 26in. high.(Christie's) $3,981

A pair of two branch candelabra, ruby and clear glass with white painted floral decoration, with clear glass lustres, 66cm. (Bonhams) $870

CANDLESTICKS

Pair of colorless pressed lacy glass candlesticks, Boston & Sandwich Glass Company, Sandwich, Massachusetts, 1828-35, with socket number one and stepped quatrefoil bases, 5⅝in. high. (Skinner) $558

A pair of façon de Venise candlesticks, 17th century, of a slightly brown tint, the cylindrical nozzles with everted folded rims and swelling low parts, 7in. high. (Christie's) $8,228

A pair of Tiffany gold favrile candlesticks, New York, early 20th century, broad flared cups over spiral ribbed body flaring to base, amber glass with gold iridescent surface, 7in. high. (Skinner) $747

CASKETS

A French cut-glass giltmetal-mounted square casket set with a sulphide, mid 19th century, with allover hobnail cutting, the hinged cover inset with a sulphide medallion depicting Cupid seated on two lions, 6¼in. square. (Christie's) $1,533

Colorless pressed lacy glass salt with cover, Boston & Sandwich Glass Company, Sandwich, Massachusetts, Basket of Flowers and Scroll pattern, 3in. high. (Skinner) $1,763

Colorless pressed lacy glass casket, cover and tray, Boston & Sandwich Glass Company, Sandwich, Massachusetts, 1835-45, with Gothic Arch, hearts, versica-and-dome, 7⅛in. long. (Skinner) $4,994

A Bohemian glass stand, with a decagonal bowl, amber flashed and engraved with deer beneath trees and vines, 18cm. diameter. (Woolley & Wallis) $315

A pair of French ormolu and glass centerpieces, late 19th century with three graduated foliate cut glass dishes to the stems, cast with eagle finials above balusters and figures of the Three Graces, 23¼in. high. (Christie's) $9,953

A glass centerpiece, with a central lift out trumpet engraved with flowers and foliage, the circular bowl similarly decorated, 19th century, 37cm. (Woolley & Wallis) $206

COMPORTS

Colorless pressed lacy glass comport, Gothic Arch pattern with Heart and Leaf border on twisted rib and Diamond pattern circular foot, 10½in. diameter. (Skinner) $4,406

A 19th century Bohemian cranberry glass fruit comport, the circular bowl with shaped rim and floral painted panels alternating with diamond cut panels, 11in. high. (Andrew Harley) $393

A 19th century Daum glass comport, comprising a shallow circular blue glass and gold fleck bowl with molded rim, raised on a WMF metal stand, 14in. wide. (Andrew Hartley) $448

COUPES

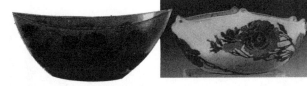  

A Gallé boat-shaped coupe, circa 1900, gray glass overlaid with electric orange/red and etched with flowering stems, 17.5cm. (Sotheby's) $812

A Gallé roses coupe, circa 1900, dichroic slightly opalescent/amber glass, overlaid with pinkish red and etched with flowering and budding stems and leaves, 8in. maximum width. (Sotheby's) $1,986

A Schneider glass coupe, the purple glass dish graduating to yellow towards rim, on an amethyst striped foot, 34.8cm. diameter. (Christie's) $588

An English coromandel and white metal mounted tantalus, first quarter 20th century, the angled cross bar with canted handle above serpentine openwork sides, 15½in. long. (Christie's) $397

Sheffield silver plate tantalus, England, late 19th / early 20th century, the central casket with two engraved hinged lids below the handle, 15in. long, 5¾in. wide. (Skinner) $489

A Betjemann's Patent four-bottle marquetry tantalus with brass fittings, retailed by Clark, Old Bond St. London, 44cm. (Bearne's) $1,962

A Dutch mahogany and gilded glass decanter set, circa 1900, restorations to case, 33cm. wide. (Bonhams & Brooks) $700

A George III mahogany decanter box with rounded lid, four square section gilt decorated decanters and a glass, 20cm. (Bearne's) $1,130

A good late Victorian oak and cut glass tantalus and humidor, 34cm. wide. (Bonhams & Brooks) $326

A magnum engraved decanter for *WILTSHIRE'S BEST* named within a shaped cartouche issuing fruiting hops, late 18th century, 33cm. high. (Christie's) $1,003

A Victorian oak and white metal mounted tantalus, late 19th century, with molded serpentine sides, the base front of the tantalus with a compartmentalized box and a drawer, 14in. wide. (Christie's) $850

A rare engraved 'Jacobite' decanter and a stopper, circa 1750, of Chasleton Manor type, of shaft and globe form engraved on one side with an eight-petalled rose and two buds, 29.4cm. (Sotheby's) $9,438

A cruciform decanter, the shoulder applied with four lions' mask prunts, mid 18th century, 29cm. high. (Christie's) $456

Gothic Revival oak tantalus, early 20th century, case with incised geometric detailing, applied metal strapwork, and lifting handles, enclosing three press molded decanters, 14¹/₈in. wide. (Skinner) $546

An enamelled glass decanter and stopper by Gallé, circa 1880, the topaz glass gently ribbed and enamelled in shades of blue, red, brown and gilt with a grasshopper amongst scrolling foliage, 27cm. high. (Christie's) $3,261

A late 19th century French kingwood marquetry liqueur box, the top and sides opening to reveal four gilt decorated decanters and sixteen glasses, 35cm. wide. (Bearne's) $1,413

A fine Bohemian intaglio-engraved decanter and stopper, circa 1850, the tapering octagonal form with tall neck and everted rim, deeply engraved with a continuous scene of stags and deer in a woodland landscape, 13¾in. (Sotheby's) $3,528

A mid Victorian maple tantalus, set with three cut glass decanters, the silver plated lock and carrying handle stamped *Betjemanns Patent 55756*, 41cm. wide. (Bonhams) $1,478

Silver plated tantalus of trefoil shape with raised beaded edge, central carrying handle and supported on three cast scrolled feet, 13in. tall. (G.A. Key) $272

A Baccarat pale-amber liqueur service enamelled and gilt with berries and foliage, comprising: two decanters and faceted ball stoppers, six liqueur glasses, and a rectangular tray, late 19th century. (Christie's) $1,094

An engraved Royal armorial cut-glass decanter and stopper from the Prince of Wales Service, circa 1800, faceted mushroom stopper, 22cm. (Skinner) $6,337

A Venetian latticinio large serving-dish, early 18th century, in vetro a retorti with radiating bands of gauze and entwined threads, the center rising to a low point, 15¾in. diameter.(Christie's) $5,851

Cobalt blue pressed lacy glass dish, Boston & Sandwich Glass Company, Sandwich, Massachusetts, 1830-45, Daisy and Peacock Eye pattern, 6¼in. diameter. (Skinner) $353

Colorless pressed lacy glass dish, Boston & Sandwich Glass Co. Sandwich, Massachusetts, 1830-40, Hairpin pattern, 8in. diameter. (Skinner) $294

Colorless pressed lacy glass shell-form dish, Boston & Sandwich Glass Company, Sandwich, Massachusetts, 1830-40, the handled dish with Peacock Eye motif, 9½in. long. (Skinner) $5,581

Colorless pressed lacy glass dish on foot, Boston & Sandwich Glass Company, Sandwich, Massachusetts, 1835-40, Eagle pattern dish on scrolling triangular standard, 5½in. high. (Skinner) $7,638

Colorless pressed lacy glass handled dish, Boston & Sandwich Glass Company, Sandwich, Massachusetts, 1830-40, the shaped dish centering a Diamond and Scroll pattern, 12in. long. (Skinner) $1,116

ÉPERGNES

Late 19th century cranberry épergne, the central flute applied with clear glass prunts, flanked on either side by two similar flutes, 23½in. (G A Key) $628

A Victorian cranberry épergne, with central trumpet above two subsidiary trumpets and two baskets, on spreading foot base with wavy edge everted rim, 55cm. (Bristol) $867

A French parcel gilt bronze and glass épergne, late 19th century, the flared vase with reeds to the base above a lobed dish, the base with mermaids on a raised circular foot, 17½in. high. (Christie's) $2,537

Cobalt blue pressed glass toy ewer and basin, Boston & Sandwich Glass Company, 1850-70, panelled, pitcher 2¼in., basin 7¹/₈in. high.
(Skinner) $1,116

A rare Venetian diamond-engraved armorial ewer and basin, late 17th century, the ewer engraved in diamond-point with the arms of Ferretti beneath an archbishop's hat, the ewer 9in. high, the basin 16¾in. diameter.
(Christie's) $40,227

A façon de Venise baluster ewer, first half of the 16th century Venice, with lightly molded vertical ribs, the dark-blue scroll handle with traces of a gilt band and pincered terminal, 18.8cm. high.
(Christie's) $1,829

A façon de Venise 'ice-glass' ewer, 16th/17th century, Barcelona, of brown tint, the tapering oviform body of 'ice-glass', the slender flared neck with a vermicular collar at the base, 28cm. high.
(Christie's) $4,388

A pair of glass and gilt metal ewers, 30cm. high.
(Bonhams & Brooks) $392

A fine engraved claret ewer, Stourbridge or Edinburgh, circa 1870, finely engraved overall with grasses, foliage and insects, 13in.
(Sotheby's) $1,940

FLASKS

Amethyst blown molded glass flattened Pitkin-type pocket flask, double-molded, 5in. long.
(Skinner) $705

Two Continental glass rectangular section flasks, the larger painted with two birds and both with flowers and leaves, 18th century, 20cm. and 17cm.
(Woolley & Wallis) $438

A Venetian polychrome enamelled small metal-mounted flask, second half of the 18th century, Osvaldo Brussa, enamelled in a bright palette with a finch perched on a flowering plant, 3¾in. high overall.
(Christie's) $7,679

A South Bohemian lithyalin goblet, circa 1835-45, Buquoy Glasshouse, of marbled olive-green color, 4¾in. high. (Christie's) $1,277

A baluster goblet, circa, 1715, the tulip-shaped bowl with solid lower part, supported on a drop knop, 20cm. high. (Christie's) $4,259

A large glass hunting goblet, with a U-shaped body with a figure riding a horse and a fox, 19th century, 27.5cm. (Woolley & Wallis) $887

An engraved airtwist goblet, circa 1750, the funnel bowl engraved with a butterfly hovering over a spiralling branch of fruiting-vine, 8in. high. (Christie's) $937

A Dutch-engraved armorial light baluster goblet, circa 1750, the round funnel engraved with the crowned arms of The Hague, flanked by rampant lion supporters, 7½in. high. (Christie's) $2,045

A pedestal-stemmed goblet, circa 1750, the double-ogee bowl lightly molded with vertical ribs, supported on an octagonally molded pedestal stem,17cm. high. (Christie's) $937

A Dutch-engraved Royal armorial light-baluster goblet, mid 18th century, the slightly waisted funnel bowl engraved with the crowned Royal Arms of England, 20.5cm. high. (Christie's) $4,089

A moulded airtwist goblet, circa 1750, the vertically ribbed generous bell bowl supported on a shoulder-knopped stem filled with airtwist spirals, 19.5cm. high. (Christie's) $1,022

A gilt-decorated goblet, third quarter of the 18th century, the ogee bowl gilt probably in the atelier of James Giles, 18.7cm. high. (Christie's) $1,873

A green-tinted goblet, circa 1760, the lightly ribbed cup-shaped bowl supported on a plain stem enclosing an elongated tear, 13cm. high. (Christie's) $1,106

A baluster goblet, circa 1710, the thistle-shaped bowl with straight sides and solid lower part, supported on a mushroom knop, 7¾in. high. (Christie's) $5,111

A heavy baluster goblet, circa 1710, the round bowl supported on a wide angular knop above a base knob enclosing a tear, on a folded conical foot, 17.5cm. high. (Christie's) $1,533

Tiffany blue favrile glass and bronze inkwell, late 19th century, hinged bronze cap with raised scrolled decoration, brown patina, mounted above an eight sided bulbed gourd form of cobalt glass, 5½in. (Skinner) $8,050

A Whitefriars concentric millefiori ink bottle and stopper with predominantly pink, blue, yellow, green and white canes, late 19th century, 14cm. high. (Christie's) $401

A silver mounted inkwell, London 1912, William Comyns, circular form, the hinged cover set with a watch, 8cm. high. (Bonhams) $768

JUGS

A Victorian silver mounted glass claret jug, W & G Sissons, Sheffield, 1872, the glass etched with classical chariots above fruit swags, 10¾in. high. (Sotheby's) $3,864

Pair of Continental silver-mounted and cut glass claret jugs, with Art Nouveau foliate motifs, 11¾in. high. (Eldred's) $2,640

A Stourbridge white-metal-mounted cameo claret jug and hinged cover, the white overlay carved with a flowering shrub, on a pale-blue-ground, late 19th century, 23cm. high. (Christie's) $1,137

Dark olive amber brown glass pitcher with lily pad decoration, New York or New Jersey, early 19th century, wide threaded neck and tooled handle, applied foot, 8⅝in. (Skinner) $8,050

A Cristal Lalique Chene clear and frosted lemonade jug, the exterior and handle moulded in relief with oak leaves, 22cm. (Bonhams) $279

An applied and cameo glass jug, by Le Verre Francais, circa 1923, the yellow glass internally mottled with aqua-blue and overlaid with mottled red and navy, 12in. high. (Christie's) $2,520

A 19th century liqueur set comprising four cut glass and etched decanters with ball stoppers and fourteen glasses, on gilt metal stand with loop handle, in oblong ebonized rosewood case, 13¼in. wide.
(Andrew Hartley) $2,156

A Venetian latticinio 'Maigelein' or feeding vessel, late 16th century, in vetro a retorti with allover gauze cable decoration, 6in. wide.
(Christie's) $3,408

Continental inlaid cordial set, late 19th century, the case lid inlaid to top and front with central brass and mother of pearl cartouche, 10¼in. high, 12¾in. wide, 9¾in. diameter.
(Skinner) $1,380

A Bohemian clear glass drinking glass with white incised decoration and two gold medallions, on faceted baluster stem, second quarter 18th century, 21cm. high.
(Lempertz) $1,884

A pair of Victorian green glass luster vases, the white overlaid turned over rim gilded with acanthus leaves and supporting prismatic lusters, on spreading foot, 10¼in. high.
(Andrew Hartley) $806

Armand-Albert Rateau, pair of towel rails, 1926, crystal rail with elaborate gilt bronze mounts, 18½in. length of each rail.
(Sotheby's) $83,130

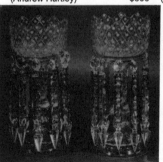

A bobbin-knopped mead-glass, circa 1720, the cup-shaped bowl with gadrooned lower part, supported on four 'bobbin' knops, 5in. high.
(Christie's) $6,815

A pair of 19th century clear Bohemian glass luster vases, the diamond and star cut bowl with crenellated rim on faceted baluster stem, prismatic drops and circular base, 12½in. high.
(Andrew Hartley) $728

A small French ogee shaped glass, probably St. Louis, the body inset with millefiori canes set as flowerheads issuing from engraved foliage, mid 19th century, 3¾in.
(Woolley & Wallis) $1,600

A pair of Murano novelty candlesticks, 24cm. high.
(Bonhams & Brooks) $364

An Edwardian novelty glass claret jug, by Elkington & Co. Ltd., 1904, modelled as a stylized dog, silver buckled collar attached by a chain to a silver-mounted cork stopper, 27.5cm. long.
(Bonhams) $2,100

Unusual pair of glass lovebirds, on a single base with polished pontil, probably Murano, 14in. high.
(Eldred's) $275

'Suzanne', by René Lalique, circa 1925, a frosted and opalescent glass figure of naked female with her robe draped on her outstretched arms, 9in. high.
(Christie's) $6,721

Two lampwork white figures of gondoliers, second half of the 18th century, probably France, Nevers (possibly Haly Workshop), their white jackets edged in and wearing colored ribboned hats, about 3in. high. (Christie's) $1,463

A frosted glass surtout de table, by Baccarat, 1930s, a horse-shoe shaped panel molded with a galleon and mermaids in stormy sea surmounted on rectangular black glass base, 21¼in. high.
(Christie's) $2,856

MUGS

Colorless blown molded glass lemonade, Boston & Sandwich Glass Company, Sandwich, Massachusetts, 1825-35, applied handle, Diamond Diaper pattern, 2³⁄₈in. diameter.(Skinner) $206

A Spanish pale green glass tapering cylindrical mug, with an applied loop handle, a spiralling trail around the upper section and a flared foot, 18th century, 12.5cm.
(Woolley & Wallis) $176

Cobalt blue pressed lacy glass handled tumbler, Val St. Lambert, 1840-45, three bands of scrolling foliate and leaf devices and ribbed handle, 3³⁄₈in. high.
(Skinner) $323

Large dome shaped paperweight, central scrambled rosette, bordered by a yellow circlet, pale blue luminescent ground, 3in. (G.A. Key) $120

A post-war paperweight modelled as a cockerel, incised *Lalique France*, 20.5cm. high. (Christie's) $493

A St. Louis crown weight, mid 19th century, the alternate red and blue and green and red twisted ribbon radiating from a central pink, white and blue setup, 6cm. diameter. (Christie's) $2,726

A St. Louis amber-flash garlanded posy weight, mid 19th century, the posy comprising four florettes in salmon-pink, lime-green, blue and white resting on five green leaves, 2¾in. diameter. (Christie's) $851

'Toby, Éléphant' No. 1192, a clear and frosted elephant paperweight, stencil mark *R.Lalique France*, 8.5cm. high. (Christie's) $1,068

A Clichy blue-ground patterned millefiori weight, mid 19th century, the central pink rose within a circlet of green canes set within a pink and white quatrefoil garland, 3in. diameter. (Christie's) $3,748

A St. Louis fuchsia paperweight, circa 1850, the pink flower with three buds and leaves set on a bed of spiralling white latticinio threads, 8cm. diameter. (Sotheby's) $3,881

Paul Stankard seed pod, flowers and ants paperweight and book, America, 1998, light blue cornflower flanked by yellow flowers among leaves. (Skinner) $2,415

A Baccarat snake weight, mid 19th century, the green reptile with brown mottled spine-markings and black and white eyes, lying coiled on a sand-dune mound, 8cm. diameter. (Christie's) $4,430

A Clichy garlanded posy weight, mid-19th century, the single white, pink and blue florette resting on five green leaves set within a garland of five large pink-centered green canes, 7.5cm. diameter.
(Christie's) $2,726

A New England Glass Co. apple weight, second half of the 19th century, the ripe fruit tinted in pink and orange and resting on a pad of clear glass, 2½in. diameter.
(Christie's) $851

A St. Louis posy weight, formed of six millefiori canes issuing from stems before five leaves, mid 19th century, 8cm. diameter.
(Christie's) $1,036

A St. Louis blue-ground patterned millefiori weight, mid 19th century, the central blue and pink setup with six pendant loops in shades of green and white and lime-green and pink, 3in. diameter.
(Christie's) $2,214

'Grenouille' No. 1146, a clear and frosted paperweight, molded mark *Lalique*, 6.5cm. high.
(Christie's) $7,238

A Baccarat blue and white flower weight, mid 19th century, the flower with five dark-blue petals over five white heart-shaped petals about a pink and white star center, 8cm. diameter.
(Christie's) $1,704

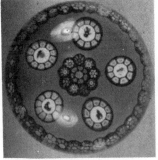

A French blue dahlia weight, mid 19th century, perhaps Pantin, the domed arrangement of overlapping sky-blue petals about a green, pink and yellow center, 7.3cm. diameter.
(Christie's) $2,385

A glass paperweight, set with five canes containing figures or faces around a central millifiori cane, date cane for P.P 1982, 7.5cm.
(Woolley & Wallis) $224

A Baccarat faceted snake paperweight, circa 1850, the coiled green reptile with dark green markings, a red mouth and eyes, 7.8cm.
(Sotheby's) $3,775

'Bouchons Fleurs de Pommiers' No. 493 a clear, frosted, and blue-stained scent bottle and tiara stopper, 13.8cm. high.
(Christie's) $6,580

'La Sirène' a clear, frosted and blue-stained scent bottle and stopper, made for Burmann, molded mark *Lalique*, 10.5cm. high. (Christie's) $2,961

'L'Élégance' a clear, frosted and sepia-stained scent bottle and stopper, made for D'Orsay, molded *D'Orsay* to front, molded mark *R. Lalique*, 9.8cm. high. (Christie's) $3,290

'Cigalia' a clear, frosted and dark green-stained scent bottle and stopper, made for Roger et Gallet, pressed wood presentation box for the next smallest size, bottle unmarked, 12.7cm. high.
(Christie's) $1,645

'Le Succès' a clear, frosted and sepia-stained scent bottle and stopper, made for D'Orsay, molded mark *R. Lalique*, 9.5cm. high. (Christie's) $2,303

'Calendal' a frosted glass scent bottle and stopper, stencil marks *Molinard Paris France*, incised Lalique, 11.5cm. high.
(Christie's) $1,645

'Scarabée' a clear, frosted, and grey-stained scent bottle and stopper, made for Piver, unmarked, 8.5cm. high.
(Christie's) $1,068

'Amphitrite' No. 514, a frosted green glass scent bottle and stopper, engraved *R. Lalique France No.514*, 9.5cm. high.
(Christie's) $4,935

'Pavot' No. 476 a clear, frosted and red-enamelled scent bottle and stopper, engraved *Lalique*, 7cm. high. (Christie's) $5,757

'Paquerettes' a clear and frosted scent bottle and stopper, made for Roger et Gallet, molded mark *R.Lalique*, 8cm. high. (Christie's) $2,632

'Papillons' No. 2650, a frosted and blue-stained perfume burner, molded mark *R. Lalique*, 19cm. high. (Christie's) $658

'Vers le Jour' an amber clear and frosted scent bottle with disc-shaped stopper, made for Worth, molded mark *R. Lalique France*, 10cm. high.(Christie's) $1,151

'Parfum A' (A.K.A. 'Skyscraper') a frosted and black enamelled scent bottle and stopper, made for Lucien Lelong, complete with original metallic presentation box, bottle intaglio molded *R. Lalique France*, bottle 10.3cm. high. (Christie's) $6,580

'La Belle Saison' a clear, frosted, and sepia-stained scent bottle and stopper with original box, made for Houbigant, 10cm. high, box, 11.5cm. high. (Christie's) $2,303

'Styx' a clear, frosted and sepia-stained scent bottle and stopper, made for Coty, complete with original presentation box, intaglio molded *Lalique*, original gold foil paper label, 11.5cm. high. (Christie's) $1,480

'Méplat Deux Figurines' No. 490, a clear, frosted and dark gray-stained scent bottle and stopper, incised *R. Lalique*, 13.5cm. high. (Christie's) $3,619

'No. 7' a butterscotch glass scent bottle and stopper, made for Morabito, stencil mark *Lalique France*, 21.5cm. high. (Christie's) $2,467

'Camille No. 516' a sapphire blue glass scent bottle and stopper, intaglio molded *R. Lalique France*, 6cm. high. (Christie's) $2,796

A glass scent bottle with jewelled gold mounts, Frédéric Philippi, Paris, 1839-1878, overlaid at the shoulders with a gothic gold tracery of quatrefoils and trefoils, height 4¾in. (Sotheby's) $2,520

A ruby flashed glass scent bottle and stopper, decorated with panels of scrolls and flowers, late 19th century, 16cm.
(Woolley & Wallis) $206

A Victorian silver-gilt mounted green glass scent bottle, the tapering oval body with heavy hobnail cuttings, 8½in. overall, probably Birmingham 1884.
(Canterbury) $505

'Paquerettes' Lalique for Roger et Gallet, circa 1919, a clear and frosted scent bottle and stopper of tapering form, the tiara stopper molded as a group of branching daisies, 8cm. high.
(Christie's) $4,470

'Cyclamen' Lalique for Coty, from circa 1909, a clear, frosted and light-green stained scent bottle and stopper, 13.6cm. high.
(Christie's) $3,852

'Le Corail Rouge', Lalique for Forvil, circa 1925, a frosted and red-enamelled scent bottle and stopper, of rectangular form, each molded in low relief with scrolling coral, 10.4cm. high.
(Christie's) $4,376

'Amphitrite' No.514, Lalique for Maison Lalique, circa 1920, a frosted green glass scent bottle and stopper, the bottle molded as a nautilus shell, 9.5cm. high.
(Christie's) $6,126

Samson & Co. porcelain figural perfume bottle, France, late 19th century, as a boy with a vessel seated on a dolphin, the boy's head the stopper, 2⁷/₈in.
(Skinner) $230

'Rosace Figurine' No.488 Lalique for Maison Lalique, circa 1912, molded in relief to front and reverse with four maidens in diaphanous costume, 11cm. high.
(Christie's) $5,401

A glass scent flaçon with enamelled parcel-gilt silver mounts, maker's mark rubbed but possibly *CM* in horizontal lozenge, Paris, circa 1855, the bottle and cap of drop form overlaid en cage with vine leaves and twigs, 5¼in. high. (Sotheby's) $1,596

'Bouquets' a clear, frosted and amber stained scent bottle, made for Jay Thorpe, incised *Lalique,* 7cm. high. (Christie's) $361

A 19th century French gold colored metal mounted blue opaline scent flask of flattened tear shaped form, 5in. high, and green cloth covered case. (Canterbury) $1,041

'Bouchon Eucalyptus' No.507, Lalique for Maison Lalique, circa 1919, a clear, frosted and green-stained bottle, the tiara stopper molded as a crown of eucalyptus berries, with arch of leaves, 13.5cm. high. (Christie's) $15,757

Continental cased set of three perfume bottles, late 19th century, the three square bottles, with gilt-metal rope twist-edged lids set with painted miniatures on ivory under glass, each depicting a European city scene, box 6in. long. (Skinner) $575

Carder Steuben paperweight glass cologne bottle, Corning, New York, circa 1930, faceted stopper in a heavy walled bottle of crystal, internally decorated with white and black cluthra glass and trapped bubbles, 7in. (Skinner) $4,312

Meissen porcelain figural perfume bottle, Germany, late 19th century, formed as a courting couple by an ivy-covered tree trunk, 2½in. long. (Skinner) $633

'Marquila' Lalique for Maison Lalique, circa 1927, a frosted blue glass scent bottle and stopper, molded as an artichoke, 8.5cm. high. (Christie's) $2,275

An early 19th century 'crystallo ceramie' scent bottle, in clear glass, of flattened ovoid shape, containing a sulphide of George III, 6.5cm. high.(Bonhams & Brooks) $500

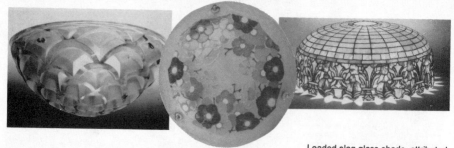

A Lalique 'Ronceaux' clear and frosted plafonnier, after 1926, of circular section molded in high relief with curved motifs, 37.7cm. (Bonhams) $2,900

A glass plafonnier of Art Deco type by Loys Lucha, with relief decoration of blue flowers, signed, 35.5cm. diameter. (Stockholms AV) $716

Leaded slag glass shade, attributed to Duffner and Kimberly, domed shade of light turquoise slag glass segments with an intricately leaded dropped apron of turquoise and amber fleur de lis, 22½in. diameter. (Skinner) $9,775

A gilt bronze mounted plafonnier, 20th century, the domed hobnail cut clear glass shade with berried terminal, issuing from the circlet with ribbon tied laurel border, 8½in. high. (Christie's) $1,692

Pair of Austrian Art glass shades, attributed to Loetz, bell-form lamp shades with ruby red blossom motif above gold papillon flare, 5½in. high. (Skinner) $345

A French oval brass and glass plafonnier, 20th century, the frosted star-cut domed shade issuing from a pierced hinged frame, 21¾ x 16in. (Christie's) $3,270

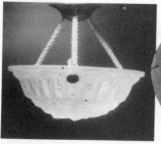

Degue Art Glass ceiling shade, Art Deco style geometric design of etched colorless glass, signed, suspended on four cords with baseplate, 13⁵/₈in. diameter. (Skinner) $575

A Lalique glass plafonnier, the circular bowl molded in relief with acanthus leaves, with ceiling rose and suspension chains, 17½in. wide. (Andrew Hartley) $973

A French frosted glass plafonnier, early 20th century, the ribbon tied reeded circlet suspending a domed faceted shade, re-gilt, 15½in. diameter. (Christie's) $1,453

A Stevens and Williams yellow glass cameo vase, by J. Millward, late 19th century, 32cm.
(Bonhams) $1,519

A Clutha glass vase of waisted form, 9.7cm.
(Christie's) $361

English cameo glass carved vase, olive green baluster body thickly layered in white glass, 8in. high.
(Skinner) $4,312

A Loetz vase, 19.5cm. high.
(Christie's) $447

Carder Steuben gold Aurene 'Peacock Feather' vase, early baluster form with blue peacock feathers pulled through a gold aurene ground, 8in. high.
(Skinner) $4,312

A Bohemian ruby ovoid pedestal vase and domed cover overlaid with a central band of roses and other flowers, circa 1860, 38cm. high.
(Christie's) $1,272

Tiffany iridescent gold glass vase, New York, circa 1907, small flared rim on ovoid vessel of amber glass, 8½in.
(Skinner) $1,955

A Le Verre Français layered glass vase, acid etched with stylized roses, in purple on pink ground, two ring handles, circa 1930. (Galerie Moderne)
          $1,209

A Bohemian flattened oviform blue-tint vase, perhaps Moser, painted with a stag in landscape, on an oval panel, late 19th century, 49cm. high.
(Christie's) $2,245

A Loetz vase, of ovoid form with slender neck and flared rim, with festoons of green and gold iridescence transmuting to cyan and magenta, 19cm.
(Bonhams) $508

Loetz Rusticana Jack-in-the pulpit vase, silvery blue-gold iridescent surface on floriform blossom rim above green vessel, 14in. high.
(Skinner) $402

A Clichy latticinio pink-cased cut baluster vase, mid 19th century, the white spiralling threads encased in pale pink glass, 7½in. high.
(Bonhams) $1,631

A pâte-de-verre glass vase, by Gabriel Argy-Rousseau, 1920s, the frosted glass internally mottled in shades of pink and purple, the body molded in low relief with geometric design, 5¼in. high.
(Christie's) $5,377

Carder Steuben dark blue jade grotesque vase, pillar ribbed abstract rectangular form of deep cobalt jade glass, Steuben fleur-de-lys mark at pontil, 6½in. high.
(Skinner) $3,335

'Languedoc', by René Lalique, circa 1929, a frosted green glass vase, of flattened spherical form with short cylindrical neck, molded in relief with overlapping bands of serrated foliage, 8¾in. high.
(Christie's) $18,483

'Boulouris' No.1094 a clear, frosted and opalescent glass vase, etched stencil mark *R. Lalique France*, 14.4cm. high.
(Christie's) $1,151

René Lalique, vase 'Oran', after 1927, dichroic opalescent/ amber glass, molded in relief with large flowering dahlia blossoms and leaves, 10¼in.
(Sotheby's) $17,400

'Domrémy' No. 979, an opalescent and turquoise-stained vase, engraved *R. Lalique France No. 979*, 21.5cm. high.
(Christie's) $1,397

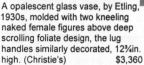

A opalescent glass vase, by Etling, 1930s, molded with two kneeling naked female figures above deep scrolling foliate design, the lug handles similarly decorated, 12¾in. high. (Christie's) $3,360

'Vichy' No. 10-909 a clear, frosted and opalescent vase, stencil mark *R. Lalique France*, 16.5cm. high.
(Christie's) $1,809

An enamelled glass vase, by Leune, probably designed by Auguste-Claude Heligstein, circa 1925, enamelled in circular and angular pattern in blue, turquoise, white and green, with clay red outlining, 7in. high.
(Christie's) $1,847

A Daum and Majorelle glass and wrought iron vase, blown into a wrought iron frame cast with stylized foliate motifs, 18cm. high. (Christie's) $557

'Amiens' No.1023, a topaz clear and frosted glass vase, wheel-engraved *R.Lalique France*, 18cm. high. (Christie's) $2,138

Steuben cluthra vase, wide mouth, on angular body the bubble glass shading from green to white, polished pontil, Steuben fleur-de-lis mark on base, 4¼in. (Skinner) $690

A glass vase, by Édouard Cazaux for David Guéron, 1930s, the clear and frosted glass molded in high relief with four naked females holding fabric sheaths, with geometric lug handles, 9½in. high. (Christie's) $5,377

'Gui' No.948 a green clear, frosted and white-stained vase, etched stencil mark *R. Lalique France*, 17cm. high. (Christie's) $2,303

'Spirales' a glass vase, by René Lalique, circa 1930, in clear, frosted and opalescent glass, molded in high relief with jagged-edged spirals, stencil mark, 6½in. high. (Christie's) $1,512

'Violettes' No. 930 a clear, frosted and opalescent vase, wheel-engraved *R.Lalique France*, 15.5cm. high. (Christie's) $2,467

'Bacchus' No. 10-922 a clear and frosted vase, engraved *R.Lalique*, 17cm. high. (Christie's) $1,480

'Albert' No.958 a topaz clear glass vase, stencil mark *R.Lalique France*, 17cm. high. (Christie's) $1,068

A Jacobite wine-glass, circa 1750, of drawn-trumpet form, the bowl engraved with a rose, bud and half-opened bud, 6¼in. high.
(Christie's) $3,236

A buluster wine glass, circa 1720, the funnel bowl with a tear to the solid cusped lower part, supported on a triple annulated knop, 6in. high.
(Christie's) $1,447

An engraved opaque-twist cordial-glass, circa 1765, the round funnel bowl engraved with a brand of flowering foliage, 6⁷⁄₈in. high.
(Christie's) $1,277

An engraved airtwist wine glass, circa 1750, the pan-topped bowl engraved with a border of flowers and foliage including a daffodil, 6¾in. high.
(Christie's) $851

A deceptive baluster wine glass, circa 1700, the thick straight-sided funnel bowl set on to an angular knop above a base knob and enclosing an elongated tear, 5¼in. high.
(Christie's) $3,748

A baluster wine glass, circa 1715, the generous bell bowl supported on a seven-ringed annulated knopped stem of graduated size, 15.5cm. high.
(Christie's) $8,178

A Beilby enamelled opaque-twist wine glass, circa 1765, the round funnel bowl enamelled in white with flowering swags pendant from the rim, 15cm. high.
(Christie's) $3,408

An engraved opaque-twist wine glass, circa 1765, the ogee bowl engraved with a bust portrait of a Eastern gentleman wearing a feathered turban, 15.5cm. high.
(Christie's) $1,022

An airtwist wine glass, circa 1750, with a bell bowl, the stem with a triple annular collar and filled with spiral threads, on a domed foot, 6½in. high.
(Christie's) $596

A baluster wine glass, circa 1725, the flared bowl with everted lip, the stem with swelling knop section enclosing a tear above a basal knop, 6in. high.
(Christie's) $1,106

A Hanoverian airtwist wine glass, circa 1750, the generous ovoid bowl engraved with the white horse of Hanover, 17cm. high.
(Christie's) $2,726

A Jacobite airtwist wine-glass, mid 18th century, the funnel bowl engraved with a rose and a bud, the stem filled with airtwist spirals 6¼in. high.
(Christie's) $1,363

An engraved airtwist cordial glass, circa 1750, the flared bucket bowl engraved with a border of fruiting-vine, the stem with a central twisted air core, 6¾in. high. (Christie's) $937

An engraved composite-stemmed wine glass, circa 1750, the bowl engraved with a meandering branch of fruiting-vine, 6½in. high. (Christie's) $2,726

A 'Privateer' opaque-twist wine-glass, circa 1760, the slightly flared bucket bowl engraved with a ship in full sail, 6¾in. high. (Christie's) $16,185

A baluster cordial glass, circa 1715, the bell bowl supported on a collar, the stem with swelling waist knop enclosing a large tear, 15.5cm. high. (Christie's) $4,259

An airtwist wine glass, circa 1750, the drawn-trumpet bowl with a solid lower part set on a shoulder-knopped stem filled with spiral threads, 6½in. high. (Christie's) $647

A Beilby opaque-twist wine glass, circa 1765, the generous round funnel bowl enamelled in white in the chinoiserie taste with a statue beneath a pagoda, 15.5cm. high. (Christie's) $14,481

A composite-stemmed wine-glass, circa 1750, of drawn form, the generous ogee bowl with everted rim above a slender stem filled with airtwist spirals, 17.5cm. high. (Christie's) $851

A 'Lynn' opaque-twist wine glass, circa 1765, the generous round funnel bowl with two molded rings, supported on a double-series opaque-twist stem, 6½in. high. (Christie's) $2,385

An engraved quadruple-knop opaque-twist wine glass, circa 1770, the bell bowl engraved with a border of alternate flowerheads, 17.5cm. high. (Christie's) $1,106

A Beilby enamelled opaque-twist wine-glass, circa 1765, the generous ogee bowl enamelled in white with a peacock and a peahen, 6¼in. high. (Christie's) $16,185

A gilt-decorated facet-stemmed wine glass, circa 1770, the funnel bowl gilt in the atelier of James Giles with a loose bouquet, 15.5cm. high. (Christie's) $1,704

An engraved facet-stemmed wine glass, circa 1790, of drawn form, the generous oviform bowl engraved with buchrana and paterae, 5¼in. high.(Christie's) $477

GLOBES

John Russell R.A., London, 1797, an extremely rare 12in. diameter lunar globe, made up of twelve hand-colored stipple-engraved paper gores extending from lunar east to west, 20in. high.
(Christie's) $29,363

A terrestrial pocket globe by John Senex composed of twelve hand colored engraved gores in a black fish skin case with colored celestial map to the interior, globe 2¾in. diameter.
(Andrew Hartley) $5,838

A Husan star globe with glass dome framework and circular scale, makers H. Hughes & Son Ltd, London, 1920, 10½in. square.
(H. C. Chapman) $990

Philip & Son, George, London, circa 1890, a 3in. diameter miniature terrestrial table globe made up of twelve chromolithographed gores and two polar calottes, 6¼in. high.
(Christie's) $604

A pair of Cary's table globes, the terrestrial globe dated 1833, the earlier celestial globe with label dated 1800, on replaced turned oak legs, 19½in. high.
(Woolley & Wallis) $7,040

Edmond Dubail, Paris (c.1905), a 19"/16in. diameter terrestrial globe, mounted on a turned and fluted mahogany style plinth stand, 50in. high.
(Christie's) $4,874

A good Federal terrestrial globe, Josiah Loring, Boston, Massachusetts, dated 1844, of typical form mounted in a circular frame on ring-turned cherrywood legs, 18in. high.
(Sotheby's) $3,162

[(?)] M.P.S.], An [?] early 19th century [?] German 1½in. diameter miniature terrestrial globe made up of twelve hand-colored printed gores, the equatorial and ecliptic ungraduated, text in English.
(Christie's) $345

A Victorian mahogany terrestrial globe, the globe early 20th century and by W & A K Johnston Ltd, made up of two sets of twelve color printed gores, 41in. high overall. (Christie's) $6,108

A gold and enamel snuff box apparently unmarked but probably Geneva, circa 1805, oval, the interior of the lid lined with gold sketched in white enamel with a seascape, 3¼in.
(Sotheby's) $5,364

A George IV two-color gold snuffbox by Alexander James Strachan, (fl.1799 – c. 1850), rectangular with wavy corners an slightly concave sides, 86mm. wide, 161gr. (Bonhams) $7,508

A fine Louis XV-style hardstone and jewelled gold snuffbox, set with panels of circular lapis-lazuli plaques alternating with rectangular plaques, 81mm. wide.
(Bonhams) $36,707

A Continental rococo-style gold and mother of pearl double snuffbox, probably Germany or Austria, the two covers, four sides and base applied with carved mother of pearl decoration, 85mm.
(Bonhams) $10,011

A three color gold lorgnette, the flat oval cover with relief Empire style decoration, part set with small diamonds, possibly French, circa 1800, 12.5cm. long.
(Lempertz) $575

A Louis XVI gold-mounted composition bonbonnière set with miniatures of Gentlemen. 2½in. diameter. (Christie's) $1,382

A Swiss enamelled gold musical snuffbox, by Henri Neisser, marked, Geneva, circa 1800, of curved section, the long lid embellished with an oval reserve containing a ewer filled with flowers, 74mm. wide. (Christie's) $6,674

A Swiss split-pearl set enamelled gold snuffbox, by Guidon, Rémond & Gide, circa 1800, the enamel by Isaac Adam (1768-1841), the cover enamelled with a young peasant couple offering berries to their nude child, 90mm. wide.
(Bonhams) $23,359

A Louis XV enamelled three-color gold snuff box, by Jean-Joseph Barrière, the cover applied with an oval enamel miniature depicting King Louis XIV of France, in armor, 91mm. wide.
(Bonhams) $20,022

An Italian gold piqué composition snuffbox, probably Naples, circa 1740, inlaid overall with gold piqué point, 66mm. wide.
(Bonhams) $5,839

A George III enamelled gold snuffbox set with an enamel miniature, by John Pukhaver (fl.1774-after 1778), oval box, the cover inset with a Maharani in orange dress, 74mm. wide.
(Christie's) $5,006

A rare American gold snuffbox, William Mitchell, Jr., Richmond, VA, circa 1830, the cover mounted later with a rose-diamond set plume of Prince of Wales feathers, 85gm. gross, length 7cm.
(Sotheby's) $5,100

A rare patent rolling head putter, the chromed cylinder with knurled striking area.
(Bonhams) $464

A Jack White 'One-O-One' putter circa 1920, with double-sided 'airship' shaped Rustless Iron head, also stamped *James Braid*.
(Sotheby's) $5,040

A H Philp putter, in thornwood.
(Bonhams) $7,250

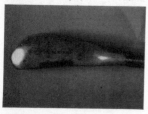

A Wm Park (snr) midspoon with golden beechwood head and later brass sole 39in. overall and 1in. deep face.
(Bonhams & Doyle) $5,750

An F & A Carrick rut nublick with cross mark, 4½in. hosel, the shaft stamped *Chas Davidson Maker Musselburgh*.
(Bonhams & Doyle) $2,875

A Gibson of Kinghorn Jonko putter circa 1928, with original hickory shaft. (Sotheby's) $3,600

A T Morris/ R Kirk playclub, in golden beech with leather face insert, bearing the remains of the Glasgow Exhibition star edge paper label below the grip, 44in.
(Bonhams) $26,100

A rare first-type brass Urquhart's Patent adjustable iron, circa 1895, the smooth faced brass head stamped on back, brass hosel with iron trigger button on front, lancewood shaft.
(Sotheby's) $5.760

An extremely rare 'Whistler' perforated steel shafted mashie, circa 1918, the Wright & Ditson iron head stamped with the patent dates for the shaft,
(Sotheby's) $2,880

A Hendry and Bishop Giant Cardinal Niblick, with 3½in. deep face. (Bonhams) $1,015

An unusual crocquet style putter, the stepped and flattened hemispherical head with horn/ivorine circular face insert.
(Sotheby's) $2,700

A Forgan rut niblick, with greenheart shaft, the head stamped *R Forgan and Sons St Andrews*, with thistle beneath.
(Bonhams) $493

A rare A Knox playclub, in golden beech, with stained shaft.
(Bonhams) $2,610

A Standard Gold Co. Flat Lie Duplex alloy putter, No P1900.
(Bonhams) $319

An unnamed track iron, circa 1860, with hickory shaft.
(Sotheby's) $990

H Philp, a mid spoon, with golden beech head, 1 1/16 face, 39in. (Sotheby's) $6,594

An R Forgan late transitional driver, with golden beech head and Prince of Wales stamp, the shaft also stamped. (Sotheby's) $502

A Tom Morris, St. Andrews, long nosed long spoon, circa 1870, with beech head and hickory shaft. (Sotheby's) $6,624

A mid 19th century lofting iron, with curved face and 4½in. hosel. (Sotheby's) $1,099

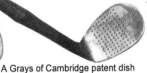

A Grays of Cambridge patent dish faced niblick, by Anderson, with dot punched face the shaft also stamped. (Sotheby's) $173

A R White St Andrews rut niblick, with 4½in. hosel. (Sotheby's) $785

A Robert Forgan, St. Andrews, long nosed brassie, circa 1885, the stained beech head also stamped with Prince of Wales feathers, sheepskin grip. (Sotheby's) $1,242

A fine and rare late 18th century mid spoon, with golden thornwood head, the horn retained by two handmade iron screws with 6in. scare, near mint. (Sotheby's) $37,680

A Hugh Philp, St. Andrews, long nosed short spoon, circa 1840, the golden beech head also stamped _J. Gourlay_, with hickory shaft, stamped _R.T.B._ (Sotheby's) $16,560

A patent spliced head brassie, A.H. Scott, Elie, circa 1908, patent number 21444, persimmon head and original hickory shaft, sheepskin grip. (Sotheby's) $331

An interesting and unusual blacksmith's iron ash shaft and wrought iron head, welded repair at conjunction of hosel and head, 36½in. long. 25oz. (Sotheby's) $8,611

The P.A. Vaile patent center-shafted driver, F.H. Ayres, London, with persimmon head and original hickory shaft, sheepskin grip. (Sotheby's) $662

A Tom Morris, St. Andrews, long spoon, circa 1880, with beech head also stamped _M. Allan._ (Sotheby's) $3,974

A Brown's Patent 'Thistle' rake iron circa 1906, the hickory shaft stamped _CRAIGIE, MONTROSE._ (Sotheby's) $4,968

An R Forgan longnosed grassed driver, in golden beech, 43in. (Sotheby's) $1,413

A fine Allan 27 feather ball circa 1840, by Allan Robertson of St. Andrews, in very good condition, approximately 1¾in.
(Sotheby's) $9,936

A mesh gutty, with owner's stamp *G. Bain*, mint.(Bonhams) $580

A red smooth gutta, with lead core. (Sotheby's) $628

An extremely rare spiral pattern ball, early 20th century, the rubber core ball with cover design of a single continuous spiral ridge and no maker's name.
(Sotheby's) $4,140

A pair of hand hammered gutties, one clearly stamped *Allan* with a triangular owners mark, the other inscribed with a *D* and a cross.
(Sotheby's) $26,243

A highly unusual patterned ball, early 20th century, the rubber core ball with concentric rings to each of the six 'poles', the centers of which are joined by further straight lines, no maker's name.
(Sotheby's) $828

Allan Robertson, a feather ball, with ink written weight *29*, in good condition.
(Sotheby's) $7,850

A Reliable Junior bramble, with red dots to the poles, slight cracks, otherwise near mint.
(Bonhams) $275

A feather ball, of small size now lacking name but in good condition. (Sotheby's) $2,355

Harry B. Wood – Golfing Curios and The Like, 1st Edition, Manchester, 1910; green cloth, gilt; 149pp. (Phillips) $1,155

Charles Crombie, Rules of Golf, the traditional hard back book containing 24 prints; sold together with an accompanying letter, dated 9th August 1918. (Sotheby's) $1,738

A Penfold Man advertising figure, in painted papier mâché, on tapering square plinth, complete with pipe, 19in. (Bonhams) $798

Guy. B. Farrar, The Royal Liverpool Golf Club; A History 1869-1932 (Foreword by Bernard Darwin); 1st Edition, Birkenhead 1933; Bound in full dark green calf. (Phillips) $554

An iron gutty ball press, with arched top rod uprights on shaped base with four handle screw, together with a brass smooth gutta ball mold stamped Allan, with label John Allan, Westward Ho. (Sotheby's) $6,280

A fine and early silver golf medal, the obverse engraved with crossed long nosed clubs and inscribed, gained by Mr. John S. Kemp A.M., November 1832. (Sotheby's) $29,256

An Austrian pottery figure of a gentleman golfer, Turn, Imperial Amphora, circa 1910, the colorfully decorated golfer holding a metal putter and about to address a ball, 12¼in. (Sotheby's) $1,159

David Jackson, Golf Songs and Recitations. Leven, Scotland: Thomas Porter, Second ed. 1895, 64p, illustrated, illustrated wrappers, 16.5cm., ¼ leather. (Bonhams & Doyle) $1,150

A fine silver and enamel salver commemorating the 1933 Ryder Cup, hallmarked Joseph Walton & Co., London, 1928, with a central motif in raised relief of the Ryder Cup trophy between enamelled flags, diameter, 14in. (Sotheby's) $9,936

An undocumented Maestrophone German gramophone, with 86cm. diameter brass horn on lyre support and inlaid wooden case, in working order.
(Auction Team Köln) $4,704

A Cameraphone German miniature gramophone with celluloid horn, wooden case lined with black oil cloth, circa 1925.
(Auction Team Köln) $226

A Polyphon coin operated gramophone in oak case with red painted tin horn, complete with needles, flex and coins.
(Auction Team Köln) $903

An Odeon Paracelsus portable suitcase gramophone, with tooled leather case and brass working parts, in working order.
(Auction Team Köln) $208

An Edison Gem Model A early American gramophone for cylinder discs, in black iron case with aluminum horn and original phonograph reproducer, circa 1910.
(Auction Team Köln) $365

An HMV table wind-up gramophone with automatic turn-off, in walnut case with needle holder and original pick-up, circa 1920.
(Auction Team Köln) $156

An HMV Model 109 table gramophone, the oak case with an HMV No 4 sound box, speed regulator, internal horn enclosed by two cupboard doors.
(Christie's) $181

A Klingsor gramophone, in upright mahogany case with fretted and tinted-glass doors enclosing the strings and horn aperture, sloping flap to the turntable and Klingsor soundbox, 28in. high.
(Christie's) $1,172

A German Nirona tin wind-up gramophone, red with bright transfer decoration, original sound box, circa 1920.
(Auction Team Köln) $391

A Hagenauer brass and stained wood horse head, stamped marks, 32.5cm. high.
(Christie's) $3,948

Hagenauer, reclining figure, 1930s, patinated brass, modelled as a naked female figure lying on her side with one leg bent and supporting herself on her right arm, 53cm. (Sotheby's) $13,920

A brass bowl in the style of Hagenauer, 20cm. diameter.
(Christie's) $361

A Hagenauer brass figure, modelled as a highly stylized female head, stamped factory marks, 49cm. high.
(Christie's) $12,337

Hagenauer, pair of Spanish dancers, 1930s, ebonized wood and brass, the stylized male and female figures in typical garb, with *WHW* monogram, 25cm.
(Sotheby's') $5,880

Franz Hagenauer, lamp, circa 1930, silvered bronze and copper, modelled as a stylized female face, concealing light fitting, with *WHW* monogram, 28.3cm.
(Sotheby's) $5,880

Hagenauer, figure of a Russian musician, circa 1930, ebonised wood and silvered brass, modelled as a highly stylized Russian musician, flat oval base, with *WHW* monogram, 8½in.
(Sotheby's) $4,410

Hagenauer, female head, 1930s, nickel-plated metal, modelled as a highly stylized female three-quarter profile with locks of hair, 12¼in.
(Sotheby's) $9,048

Hagenauer, Borzoi, circa 1930, ebonized wood, modelled as a highly stylized standing dog, on flat oval brass base with traces of silvering, 12in.
(Sotheby's) $4,410

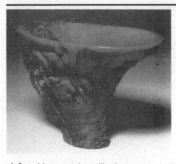

A fine rhinoceros horn libation cup, 17th/18th century, carved to the exterior with The Eight Horses of Muwang and two attendants in a rocky landscape, 7in. wide.
(Christie's) $58,727

A silver mounted rhino horn footed cup, circa 1700, the knopped cylindrical beaker mounted on a turned wood stem and spreading base, 11.7cm. high.
(Christie's) $2,560

A fine and rare rum horn, signed *Michael Byrne*, French and Indian War, dated *1761*, the half-horn meticulously engraved with renderings of military scenes centering the British coat of arms, 13cm. high.
(Sotheby's) $9,600

A turned horn cup, late 17th century, the flared bowl with reeded banding, on a waisted foot, 4¹/₈in. diameter.
(Christie's) $1,463

A George Fouquet hair comb, circa 1900, horn, carved with an openwork decoration of mistletoe branches, inset with small baroque pearls, 9.3cm.
(Sotheby's) $812

A 19th century Scottish silver mounted snuff mull, unmarked, the horn body applied with an initialled cartouche, the hinged silver lid mounted with a cairngorm, 10.5cm. high. (Bonhams) $770

A 19th century Scottish horn snuff mull, having silver mounts, the foliage chased hinged cover with a shaped thumbpiece and inset with a cairngorm, 3in. high.
(Woolley & Wallis) $328

A Continental horn and plated hunting horn table lamp, fitted for electricity, 46cm. high.
(Bonhams & Brooks) $154

Continental gilt-metal-mounted horn mantel ornament, 19th century, mounted with bead and foliate-cast collars, a seated child reading from a page mounted at mid-section, 27in. high.
(Sotheby's) $4,500

An 18th century Russian icon of Christ's descent into Hell and Resurrection, 30 x 25cm. (Arnold) $532

A 19th century Russian icon of St. Nicolas, on board, 31 x 26cm. (Bearne's) $398

A 19th century festival icon, Russian, 35 x 30.5cm. (Arnold) $586

The Dormition of The Mother of God, Russia, in the style of the Strogonov School of the 16th century, painted in strong colors, the Mother of God lies on her bier with the Risen Christ standing holding her soul, 35.2 x 29.2cm. (Christie's) $7,130

A Greek triptych of the Mother of God enthroned with chosen saints, 18th century, the central panel with the Mother of God holding the Christ Child on her left, beneath the Lord Sabaoth within carved arch above, 15¼ x 14¾in. (Christie's) $4,959

Christ Pantocrator, Russia, in the style of the Godunov School, circa 1600, traditionally painted in strong colors, the Savior raises His right hand in blessing while holding the open Gospels in His left, in repoussé, 31.5 x 27cm. (Christie's) $5,347

The Descent from the Cross, Russia, Novgorod School, 15th century, traditionally painted in strong colors, with architectural background, 18½ x 13¾in. (Christie's) $42,251

A Russian icon of six chosen saints, circa 1800, shown full-length including the Guardian Angel, and St. Stefan, Paisii and Anna, with the Vernicle above, 14 x 13cm. (Christie's) $850

Russian icon of the Crucifixion and chosen saints, early 19th century, the brass and enamel cross inlaid into the board, flanked by two seraphim with the Guardian Angel and eighteen saints below. 17¾in. x 15in. (Christie's) $1,150

An 18th century silver octagonal compass sundial, signed *Le Febvre Paris*, the horizontal plate engraved for latitudes 10°,45° and 50°, 6.7cm. long.
(Christie's) $2,502

An unattributed English Culpeper-type microscope with 5 objectives, in original mahogany case, circa 1800, 39cm. high.
(Auction Team Köln) $2,033

A mahogany barograph by Dixon & Hempenstall, Dublin, with eight drums, the case with a base drawer and shaped bracket feet, 38cm. wide. (Thomson Roddick & Medcalf) $783

An 18th century brass German universal equinoctial ring dial, possibly by George F. Brander, the meridian ring with sliding suspension loop, in the original red stained chamois-leather lined etui 11.7cm. diameter.
(Christie's) $4,171

A French mahogany two-day marine chronometer, Breguet Neveu & Cie.; 3rd Series, circa 1840, contained in a two-tier mahogany box, the top with sliding lid to inner viewing port, dial diameter 95mm, box 215 x 180mm.
(Christie's) $17,273

A late 19th century boxwood and lacquered-brass surveyor's sector rule, signed *Winter & Son.21 Grey St. Newcastle on Tyne*, both arms stamped with scales for horizontal distance, angle of dip and thickness on one side, 6½in. long.
(Christie's) $534

A Russian round angle compass, brass with cellulose lacquer finish, on tripod base, circa 1870, 25cm diameter.
(Auction Team Köln) $621

Charles [?] Dien, Paris, a mid-19th century brass planetarium, unsigned, the 1¼in. diameter sunball at the center, with seven ivorine planetballs on separate arms revolving around it, 19¼in. high. (Christie's) $4,600

A brass and cellulose lacquered theodolite, possibly by Süss, Budapest, with compass, circa 1920, 26cm. high.
(Auction Team Köln) $395

Parkes & Handley's patent orrery, 20th century, 3in. diameter terrestrial globe, steel arm with ivorine moonball, 15in. long. (Christie's) **$2,944**

A brass Gunner's sector, French, 18th century, signed *Meunier Md. a la flotte d'Angleterre a paris,* engraved with scales on both sides, 17cm. long when closed. (Bonhams) **$313**

A magnetic detector, by Marconi's Wireless Telegraph Co. Ltd., London No. 47873, with spring motor screw adjustment for tension, and teak case, 18½in. wide, circa 1910. (Christie's) **$16,255**

An 18th century English brass universal equinoctial ring dial, the meridian ring with suspension point, engraved on one side in two quadrants, the other side with declination scale graduated 0°-90°, 6in. diameter. (Christie's) **$2,336**

An early German pocket compass in walnut case with printed copper dial and convex glass, 17/18th century, 60mm. diameter. (Auction Team Köln) **$339**

An early 19th century mining theodolite, signed on the finely engraved compass dial, *Cail Newcastle upon Tyne.,* the telescope with sliding-tube focusing, object glass dust cap, with bubble level, 13¼in. high. (Christie's) **$1,083**

An 18th century Butterfield-Pattern compass-sundial, signed *Sartout Lain Paris,* with liner dials for latitudes 40°, 45° and 50°, the, octagonal plate engraved with names and latitude of twenty-five Continental cities and towns, 7.3cm. long. (Christie's) **$1,501**

A. J. Halden & Co. surveyor's compendium English, early 20th century, signed *J. Halden & Co London,* with compass, level, and printed tables, 16mm. long. (Bonhams) **$297**

Leach's patent projecting microscope no. 227, W.I. Chadwick, Manchester; comprising a lacquered-brass microscope attachment with rack and pinion focusing, lacquered-brass lens barrel, supplementary lenses and slides. (Christie's) **$310**

A set of brass weights, English, mid 20th century, five bell weights from 1lb to 7lbs marked with *GR* cipher, together with an unmarked case of 9 weights from ½ dram to 8oz. in a wooden case, 61cm. wide.
(Bonhams) $294

A pair of blonde tortoiseshell opera glasses, guilloché ground, applied with rose cut diamond initials and date.(Bonhams & Brooks) $560

A Short and Mason barograph, English, mid 20th century, with clockwork recording drum, lacquered brass mechanism, 'concealed' bellows in the plinth base, in glazed mahogany case, 37cm. wide.(Bonhams) $382

A 19th century lacquered-brass Culpeper-type microscope, complete with four objectives, sprung stage, frog plate, tweezers, Lieberkuhn, six ivory sliders and other items, 14in. high.
(Christie's) $1,501

A Victorian brass binocular microscope by Henry Crouch, London, No. 3434, with rack and pinion focusing, circular stage and flamo-concave mirror, 18¼in. high.
(Andrew Hartley) $1,668

A Matthew loft style Culpeper type microscope, English, 1730's-1740s, with octagonal base including a drawer, three slightly bowed brass legs, trefoil stage with 'Key-hole' sprung grip.
(Bonhams) $3,234

A Short and Mason 'Tycos' barograph, English, early 20th century, with clockwork recording drum, laquered brass mechanism, eight aneroid bellows and silvered barometer chapter, 37cm. wide.
(Bonhams & Brooks) $1,294

A Berge brass transit theodolite, English, circa 1800-1810, the 28cm. telescope with rack focus, suspended bubble level, pale blue-green tinted object glass, and lens cap. (Bonhams) $1,029

A set of Edwardian silver plated brass weighing scales, early 20th century, with graduated square platforms and openwork fulcrum, 15in. wide. (Christie's) $544

Cast iron flat bull windmill weight, Fairbury Windmill Weight Company, Fairbury, Nebraska, early 20th century, on original base, 18½in. high. (Skinner) $1,150

Franklin cast iron stove, 19th century with brass ball finials, 31in. wide. (Eldred's) $220

Cast-iron steer head, second quarter 20th century, long horned steer head with features in relief, including stand, 27¼in. long. (Skinner) $1,495

A Victorian cast iron table, circa 1870, the pierced geometric top with scalloped edge, the pierced foliate frame with arched flanges and reeded stretcher, 39in. long. (Christie's) $2,073

Cast metal owl, Swisher & Soules, Decatur, Illinois, second quarter 20th century, two sided with glass eyes and *Swisher Soules Decatur Ill Patpend* embossed on both sides of base.(Sotheby's) $1,955

A wrought-iron fire screen, by Edgar Brandt, circa 1925, the open-frame of fan-shape, composed of outward-bending columns and interlinking scroll motifs, 17¾in. high. (Christie's) $3,197

A cast iron fireback, central panel depicting St George in high relief, 28½in. high, 18th century or possible earlier, and a later fire basket. (Andrew Hartley) $123

A late Victorian cast iron garden seat, the scrolled ends with the Royal coat of arms and portrait roundel, with a wooden slatted back and seat, 74in. wide. (Bonhams) $529

A late Victorian cast iron hall stand, late 19th century, cast in relief with a model of the youthful Hercules wrestling with a snake, bowed to form the retaining rail, 33in. high. (Christie's) $2,171

A pair of inlaid iron abumi (stirrups), signed *MASATOSHI SAKU*, Edo Period (18th century), decorated with cherry blossom scattered on the overall surface in nunome zogan, each 11½in. long.
(Christie's) $4,333

A Regency reeded wrought iron seat with plain slatted seat, reeded triple arcaded back, 73in. wide.
(Andrew Harley) $1,730

Incised iron cleaver with brass and wood handle, probably Northeastern United States, circa 1880, the blade in the form of a woman practising calisthenics, her leg continues to a wood handle, 12¾in. long.
(Skinner) $1,840

A Victorian cast iron conservatory plantstand, comprising six circular trays each pierced with a flower head on a scrolling foliate ground, on an open scrollwork support, 36in. wide.
(Andrew Hartley) $560

Cast-iron firemark, Baltimore Equitable Society, mid 19th century, square plaque with rounded raised edges, clasped hands and *1794* in relief, 10¹/₈in.
(Skinner) $1,380

Cast iron sun face gate weight, Massachusetts, late 18th century, with stand, 9in. diameter.
(Skinner) $10,925

Dog's head cast iron hitching post, America, 19th century, traces of black paint, with stand, 12in. high.
(Skinner) $4,025

A cast iron miniature fire place, English, circa 1850, with raised grate and molded floral decoration, 7¼in. high.
(Bonhams) $252

Cast-iron rooster windmill weight, Elgin Wind Power and Pump Company, Elgin, Illinois, early 20th century, painted taupe with red details, 15¾ x 16½in.
(Skinner) $805

Patinated cast iron head of a cat, America, late 19th century, with stand, 8in. high.
(Skinner) $1,495

One of a pair of 19th century cast iron urns, of shallow semi lobed campana form, with egg and dart rims, on a spreading circular foot and rectangular plinth, 24½ x 41in.
(Bonhams) (Two) $3,381

Cast iron architectural fragment of a lion's head, America, late 19th century, old weathered surface, 15in. high. (Skinner) $1,725

An American painted cast iron hitching post modelled as a jockey, late 19th or early 20th century, shown with one arm outstretched, mounted on a weighted square plinth, 48in. high.
(Christie's) $2,199

A pair of cast iron Labrador retriever andirons, stamped *Liberty Foundry, St. Louis, Missouri*, probably late 19th/early 20th century, each cast in the half-round depicting a profile retriever seated at attention, 13½in. high.
(Christie's) $1,763

A cast iron walking stick stand, late 19th or early 20th century, modelled in relief with the figure of a youthful Hercules wrestling with a snake, 31½in. high.
(Christie's) $2,369

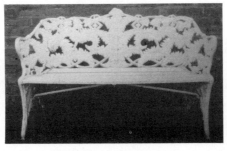

Cast iron 'Squirrel' windmill weight, Elgin Wind Power and Pump Company, Elgin, Illinois, early 20th century, 19½in. high.
(Skinner) $3,737

A Coalbrookdale pattern cast iron fern and blackberry garden seat, circa 1870, with a wooden slatted seat, 57in. wide.
(Bonhams) $1,440

Cast iron horse head hitching post top, America, 19th century, with molded features, old weathered surface, with stand, 11½in. high.
(Skinner) $632

A very early handforged iron, of cast iron with hollow handle, German, circa 1720.
(Auction Team Köln) $261

An early rustic soapstone iron, North European, for heating on open fire, circa 1750, 19cm. long.
(Auction Team Köln) $620

A French cast iron flat iron with pointed sole with cast cherub ornament, cast handle on dolphin posts, circa 1880.
(Auction Team Köln) $85

An early German bell metal forged slug iron, brass cover and closures, handle of forged hoop iron, cool tip, circa 1800, sole plate 20 cm. long.
(Auction Team Köln) $1,863

A large 2-piece flower/leaf iron, iron and cast brass, with wooden handle, French, 19th century.
(Auction Team Köln) $78

A cast iron pointed German flat iron, C-form handle of soft forged iron screwed on to two turned brass pillars, the top of the iron with a decorated brass plate, circa 1880, 16.5cm. long.
(Auction Team Köln) $197

A French brass slug iron with cherry handle and baluster pillars, the plate engraved with floral motifs, circa 1860. (Auction Team Köln) $65

A Tilley kerosene iron by the Tilley Lamp Co., Northern Ireland, silvered case with plastic handle and red kerosene tank, sole plate 19cm. long, circa 1940, in original box. (Auction Team Köln) $93

A French cast iron flat iron, pointed sole with molded sides and decorated with two cherubs holding a vase, cast handle on dolphin-like posts, 12.5cm. long, circa 1880.
(Auction Team Köln) $98

A Swedish charcoal Husqvarna 2 chimney iron, with dragon head chimney, sole 25cm.
(Auction Team Köln) $131

An American combination iron for ironing and pleating, cast iron, for heating on a stove, cast handle, sole plate 15cm. long, after 1871.
(Auction Team Köln) $310

A cast iron French flat iron, pointed sole with foliate decoration, labelled *Fonderies de Sougland Nr. 6*, 17.5cm. long, circa 1880.
(Auction Team Köln) $132

A French wrought iron slug iron of box type, with pointed sole and wooden handle, swing gate with curved decoration, circa 1770, 18cm. long.
(Auction Team Köln) $197

A very heavy Indian charcoal iron of cast brass with curved pillars and wooden handle, circa 1880.
(Auction Team Köln) $115

An East Friesian hammered brass glow iron, with cold tip, with geometric cut ventilation elements, turned walnut handle, circa 1800, 21cm. long.
(Auction Team Köln) $109

A large French cast iron slug iron of box type, ash handle on baluster posts, swing gate, with triangular slug, circa 1750, 18cm. long.
(Auction Team Köln) $131

A rare Gisland Argentinian porcelain electric iron with floral decoration and original box.
(Auction Team Köln) $101

A French brass slug iron, with walnut handle on baluster posts, box type with rounded 17.5cm. sole, circa 1860.
(Auction Team Köln) $119

An unusual Japanese carved and stained ivory group of cormorant fishermen, two children playing with a toy boat nearby, Meiji, 38cm. long. (Bearne's) $2,862

A Chinese ivory libation cup, in the form of an archaic bronze Li, the handle carved as a dragon, Qianlong Yu Zhi mark, 4³/₈in. (Woolley & Wallis) $5,508

18th century Anglo Indian ivory mounted casket shaped box with slightly domed top overlaid with segments of ivory, 11in. wide. (Ewbank) $1,201

A pair of Continental silver and ivory figures, modelled as Beefeaters, one holding a ceremonial spear, London import marks for 1922 and 1923, maker B.H.M., 34cm and 24.5cm. high. (Wintertons) $2,100

Two ivory Okimono, signed Matsuyama, late 19th century, modelled as a pair of hares, the fur incised to resemble the natural texture of the fur, the eyes inlaid in ruby, 6in. long, 8in. high. (Christie's) $8,225

An Art Deco gilded bronze and ivory figure cast and carved after a model by Demetre Chiparus as a partially-clad exotic slave girl dancer poised on one leg, 31cm. high. (Wintertons) $10,472

French Renaissance Revival carved ivory jewelry casket, circa 1870, decorated with panels of frolicking putti, with carved herm stiles, 7½ x 9¾in. (Skinner) $7,475

A patinated bronze and ivory figure cast and carved from a model by A.Kelety, of bare-breasted young girl standing wearing large billowing skirt, on striated onyx base, numbered 43, 29.5cm. high. (Christie's) $23,472

An Anglo Indian ivory veneered travelling writing slope, Vizigapatam, 19th century, decorated overall with penwork banding of entwined foliage, 14½in. wide. (Christie's) $5,076

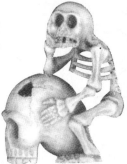

A South German or Austrian carved ivory and wood group, third quarter 19th century, modelled with two cavaliers seated in a tavern playing cards, with attendant figures, 13¾in. wide.
(Christie's) $12,305

An ivory carving of a skeleton, 19th century, carved and pierced with a skeleton standing beside a large skull, 1¾in. high.
(Christie's) $575

A Continental ivory relief, 19th century, set amongst a rural setting with a gentleman and a boy watching a couple rowing with a villa in the background.
(Bonhams) $1,580

A 19th century Mongolian carved ivory group, depicting an old man kneeling and holding a baby before a young warrior seated on a tree stump, 6¼in. high.
(Andrew Hartley) $2,464

A German carved ivory tankard, possibly late 17th or early 18th century, the engine turned cylindrical body with domed cover and later C-scroll handle with pineapple thumbpiece, 5¾in. high.
(Christie's) $15,445

'Contemplation' an ivory figure carved from a model by F.Preiss, 1920s, of a naked young female perched on tree trunk base, on shaped rectangular green onyx base, 11cm. high.
(Christie's) $5,040

A German carved ivory snuff box, early 19th century, in the style of an earlier period, the panels carved in relief, 4¾in. long.
(Christie's) $2,743

A carved ivory figure of St. Sebastian, 19th century, shown standing tied to a tree, with a suit of armor at his feet, loss of right forearm, 7⅞in. high.
(Christie's) $3,291

An Art Deco ivory and marble tazza in the style of Ferdinand Preiss, 24cm., diameter.
(Christie's) $1,400

A carved ivory group of Laocoon, late 19th century, after the Antique, the central figure entwined with a snake, flanked by his two sons, 17.5cm. high.
(Christie's) $1,180

An ivory figure in the style of Ferdinand Preiss, unmarked, 8.2cm. high.
(Christie's) $6,580

A set of five Austrian carved ivory figures of intinerant musicians, early 20th century, each mounted on turned wood barrels, losses and old damages, 15.5cm. high.
(Christie's) $1,354

A pair of Continental carved ivory portrait busts, mid 19th century, in 17th century dress, inscribed *Christina* and *Gustadolf* respectively, 5¼in. high.
(Christie's) $1,817

A wood and ivory group of a street performer, 19th century, holding an implement in one hand and a lead in the other attached to a small monkey, the figure, 8½in. high.
(Christie's) $5,757

A carved ivory triptych bust of a warrior, probably Dieppe, late 19th century, the helmeted figure with hinged cloak, the interior with a battle scene over the three panels, 9½in. overall.
(Christie's) $2,199

A Continental carved ivory figure of a maiden, second half 19th century, in 18th century style rustic dress, feeding birds, on an oval turned socle, 6½in. high.
(Christie's) $3,271

A carved ivory table casket, possibly Swiss, late 19th century, the cover surmounted with a hound, the sides with various trophy heads and game, raised on lion feet, 6in. wide. (Christie's) $2,876

An ivory okimono of Buddha, 19th century, two boy attendants climbing on his shoulders, with their hands on the Buddha's head, 4¾in. high. (Christie's) $329

A pair of teak and brass bound jardinières, late 19th /early 20th century, of elongated size with rounded ends and liners, 65½in. long. (Christie's) $2,715

A Dutch part ebonised jardinière, 19th century, of tapering and ribbed form and veneered with bands of rosewood and sycamore, 15¾in. high. (Christie's) $1,086

A Northern European brass jardinière, late 18th or early 19th century, the tapering oval body with ring handles, repoussé decorated with bands of fruiting foliage, 20½in. wide. (Christie's) $1,810

A 19th century amboyna and ebonised floral marquetry jardinière of oblong form with rounded ends and applied gilt metal mounts, 25½in. wide. (Andrew Hartley) $1,848

An Arts and Crafts copper jardinière, late 19th century, decorated overall with fish and biblical scenes, the cover embossed with a larger fish, 18½in. high over handle. (Christie's) $2,353

One of a pair of Continental stone composite jardinières, first half 20th century, each with square basin, the tapering sides modelled with entwining strapwork in low relief set in reserves, 30in. high. (Christie's) (Two) $790

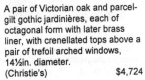

A pair of Victorian oak and parcel-gilt gothic jardinières, each of octagonal form with later brass liner, with crenellated tops above a pair of trefoil arched windows, 14½in. diameter. (Christie's) $4,724

A large brassbound mahogany jardinière, 19th century, of coopered construction, with broad brass bands, the handles later, 30in. high.(Christie's) $8,686

A pair of ormolu mounted mahogany jardinières, 20th century, of rectangular form, with fluted banding to the borders and Greek key to the base, 13½in. high. (Christie's) $11,811

A French Empire mahogany and gilt-metal mounted jardinière, first half of the 19th century, of D-shaped outline, with later brass liner and frieze, 18¾in. wide.
(Christie's) $4,343

A pair of French gilt metal mounted walnut veneered cache pots, last quarter 19th century, with Greek key banding and engine milled foliate borders, 6¼in. high.
(Christie's) $2,362

A 19th century French kingwood and walnut jardinière of molded circular form with stringing, foliate marquetry and gilt metal mounts, pierced gallery, raised on three cabriole supports, 43¾in. high.
(Andrew Hartley) $3,692

A gilt-metal mounted, rosewood jardinière, late 19th/early 20th century, in the Louis XV style, with pierced gallery and metal liner, tapered body with brass mounts and shaped aprons, 25in. wide.
(Christie's) $1,068

A jardinière by C.H. Brannam, Barum, North Devon, the brown ground decorated with blue fish and the tripod feet depicting dolphins, inscribed on base, 17cm. high.
(Thomson Roddick & Medcalf) $174

A brass jardinière, early 19th century, the circular drum bearing three lion mask handles and with Dutch rural scenes and a shield, on three scaly dolphin supports, 32½in. high.(Christie's) $658

A Napoleon III rosewood jardinière, 61cm. wide.
(Bonhams) $2,370

Chinese Guangxu jardinière with a fine European carved giltwood stand, the jardinière decorated in underglaze blue with two dragons amongst flowering branches, diameter 24in.
(David Lay) $4,069

A late 19th century French gilt metal jardinière, 28cm.
(Bonhams) $405

An opal and diamond dress ring set three oval opals intersected by six circular cut diamonds on 18ct. gold shank.
(Anderson & Garland) $748

An antique three-piece cameo suite, of pendant and pair of earrings, each with rectangular carved cameo of lady in flowing robes, openwork three color gold mount. (Brightwells) $2,618

A sapphire and diamond cluster ring, the circular sapphire within a diamond border, each shoulder set single stone on 18ct. gold shank.
(Anderson & Garland) $878

An Art Deco brooch, in the form of a ribbon and bow, pavé set with square cut sapphires and brilliant cut diamonds and with center circular sapphire.
(Wintertons) $2,660

An Edwardian style cluster ring, set with center oval blue sapphire surrounded by brilliant cut diamonds (approximately 1ct total weight), stamped 18ct.
(Wintertons) $840

A 15ct gold brooch of elliptical form set with a center cluster of diamonds and with locket back, hallmarked Birmingham 1904.
(Wintertons) $378

A sapphire and diamond cluster ring, the center cornflower blue sapphire surrounded by old cut brilliants, stamped *18ct.*
(Wintertons) $2,233

An opal and diamond cluster ring, the oval shaped opal cluster set in a surround of small circular cut diamonds on 18ct gold shank.
(Anderson & Garland) $650

A Victorian brooch pendant set with rectangular sapphire surrounded by 24 diamonds.
(Brightwells) $3,339

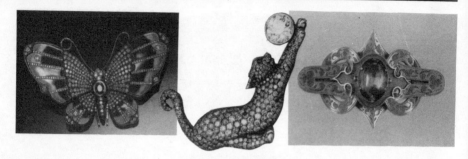

A yellow gold, silver and enamel brooch in the form of a butterfly, set with small diamonds and an oval ruby in the center of the body, diamonds 6ct.
(Finarte) $5,749

Diamond brooch, designed as a cat playing with a ball, the cat pavé-set with brilliant-cut diamonds of various tints.
(Sotheby's) $26,460

A Victorian brooch, with engraved decoration and set with a foliate rose-quartz, (acid tested gold).
(Wintertons) $319

A gold, enamel and rose diamond set pendant watch in the form of a scarab beetle, Swiss, circa 1880, case with naturalistically modelled underside with brooch attachment, 40 x 23mm.
(Christie's) $3,381

A pair of 1940s yellow gold and silver clip brooches as leafy flowers, the domed centers of sapphires of various cuts and brilliants, sapphires circa 80ct.
(Finarte) $10,220

An Art Nouveau gold pendant in the form of a young girl sitting in a hoop of rubies and diamonds, holding a .25ct. diamond, her flowing dress hemmed with diamonds, possibly French, circa 1900, 6.5cm. long.
(Lempertz) $2,355

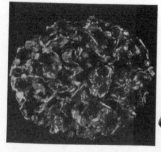

An openwork brooch of modern naturalistic design, weighing approximately 60grms and set with brilliant cut diamonds, hallmarked 14ct gold by J.A.D.
(Wintertons) $566

An antique brooch, in the form of a bull terrier head, pavé set with rose diamonds with ruby eyes and with a gold diamond studded collar, cased.
(Woolley & Wallis) $4,424

A yellow gold Frascarolo clip brooch in the form of a lion, enamelled in red and black, the eyes set with two cabochon chrysoprase, and the muzzle set with diamonds.
(Finarte) $3,834

A gold, enamel and rose diamond set mandolin form watch, Continental, circa 1800, gold body with hinged front cover overlaid with red guilloche enamel, 58 x 25mm. (Christie's) $5,072

Ruby and diamond double clip brooch, 1930s, of stylized knotted ribbon design, set with circular-cut and baguette diamonds and calibré-cut rubies.(Sotheby's) $8,400

A white and yellow gold brooch in the form of a pelican, set with square cut diamonds, sapphires and rubies, the eye set with cabochon ruby. (Finarte) $1,135

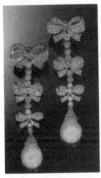
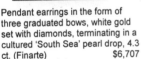
 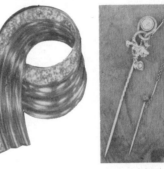

Pendant earrings in the form of three graduated bows, white gold set with diamonds, terminating in a cultured 'South Sea' pearl drop, 4.3 ct. (Finarte) $6,707

1960s Cartier yellow gold and platinum earrings modelled as fluted curlicues, edged with diamonds, 3.60ct. (Finarte) $7,027

A gold cravat pin containing locks of Wellington's & Napoleon's hair, Victor of Waterloo, statesman and politician 1769-1853, military genius, politician, Emperor of France 1804-1814. (Bonhams) $659

Webb yellow gold and black enamel cuff links in the form of a monkey's head, with eyes in red enamel, signed. (Finarte) $1,891

A sapphire and diamond hexagonal cluster dress ring on 18ct. gold shank. (Anderson & Garland) $845

A white gold ring, set with brilliants and navette cut diamonds as stylized petals surrounding an oval cut ruby, ruby 4.85ct., diamonds 3.5ct. (Finarte) $17,248

An Empire style gilt metal bouillotte lamp, 75cm. high.
(Bonhams & Brooks) $634

An opalescent glass table lamp, by Sabino, 1925, modelled as a stylized fish, on a rectangular silvered metal base with light fitting, 24cm. high.
(Christie's) $1,848

Early Edgar Brandt and Daum Art Glass table lamp, France, early 20th century, domed shade reverse-painted on bronze Art Nouveau base, 21in. high.
(Skinner) $14,950

A pair of gilt bronze mounted porcelain table lamps, late 19th or early 20th century, later adapted, the bodies with famille rose decoration of Oriental landscapes and foliage, 15¾in. high.
(Christie's) $1,692

A glass and aluminum table lamp, by Desny, circa 1926, composed of square glass plates positioned on top of one another, with central tapering cylindrical column, 12cm. high. (Christie's) $1,680

A pair of famille verte porcelain vases, 19th century, later gilt bronze mounted and adapted as table lamps, the powder blue grounds with reserves of exotic birds and animals, 18¼in. high.
(Christie's) $7,613

A Chinese porcelain baluster vase, late 19th century, later gilt bronze mounted and adapted as a table lamp, with reserves of figures in landscapes bordered by trailing flowers, foliage and geometric banding, 15in. high.
(Christie's) $3,077

A glass and silvered metal table lamp, attributed to Jacques Adnet, 1930s, the tilting half spherical lamp shade surrounded by circular glass fitted into shaped rectangular metal and later glass base, 12½in. high.
(Christie's) $1,848

A glass and wrought metal table lamp, designed by Louis Majorelle, circa 1900, the glass shade by Daum, the mottled glass shade with applied scarabs, stylized foliate wrought metal base, 19½in. high.
(Christie's) $16,185

Handel reverse-painted roses table lamp, Meriden, Connecticut, circa 1919, number 6688, dome shade reverse-painted with stylized roses, leaves and butterflies on a pastel colored ground.
(Skinner) $16,100

Raoul Larche, Loie fuller lamp, circa 1900, gilt bronze, the dancer with raised arms, wearing a flowing gown extending around her feet to form the base, 17¾in.
(Sotheby's) $22,403

Tiffany Studios, turtleback tile table lamp, 1898-1902, green/brown patinated bronze base, shade composed of geometric glass elements in shades of mottled green, 22in.
(Sotheby's) $29,073

A pair of Victorian onyx and black marble mounted table lamps, late 19th century, the gas fitments above red and green tinted glass reservoirs supported above octagonal onyx platforms, 25¾in. high. overall.
(Christie's) $1,151

Handel, attributed to, waterlily table lamp, circa 1910, the base modelled as a stylized tree trunk, leaded glass shade composed of geometric and shaped glass elements in shades of pink, yellow, blue, green, cream and brown, 57.5cm. (Sotheby's) $8,700

A pair of French porcelain and gilt bronze mounted table lamps, 20th century, the navy blue cylindrical bodies with ropetwist circlets above, rising through waisted socles and scrolling foliate casting to the fitments, 11¾in. high.
(Christie's) $987

A pair of Continental gilt bronze mounted porcelain table lamps, 19th century, decorated with seated Oriental figures amidst foliage, birds and insects with carp in a stream, 23½in. high.
(Christie's) $8,722

A pair of ceramic and gilt metal desk lights, early 20th century, each with Chinese figures of 'dogs of fo', later mounted with an Art Nouveau style openwork frame, 17in. high.(Christie's) $1,810

A pair of gilt bronze bouillotte lamps, 20th century, the adjustable red painted shades with gilt heightening, the three light fittings with female masks to the S-scroll branches, 33¾in. high.
(Christie's) $5,921

LAMPS

Tiffany Studios acorn leaded glass and bronze table lamp, early 20th century, dome shade with geometric segments of striated green and white glass, 20½ - 24½in. (Skinner) $24,150

Tiffany Studios counter balance bronze table lamp, New York, early 20th century, curved arm suspending a dome shade of metal with a geometric border, foliate form arm and counterbalance ball. (Skinner) $5,750

Tiffany Studios pansy table lamp, New York, early 20th century, dome shade with radiating mottled green segments and a central floral border, of multicolored flower blossoms, 22½in. high. (Skinner) $29,900

Handel one-light lily boudoir lamp, Meriden, Connecticut, circa 1903, naturalistic stem form supporting a floriform shade of overlapped green and white slag glass petals and a green slag glass bud, 13in. (Skinner) $460

Obverse-painted mushroom lamp, possibly Pairpoint, 1913, mushroom shade painted with Moorish-style decoration highlighted with clusters of pink and green roses, set in a brass and metal mount with two handles, 14in. high. (Skinner) $690

Bradley & Hubbard table lamp base with mesh shade, circa 1920, nine panelled shade of metal screen mesh with painted and coraline decoration of scallops and flourishes, metal tag *Mutual Sunset Lamp Co.*, 22¼in. high. (Skinner) $632

Tiffany Studios leaded glass and bronze nautilus table lamp, New York, early 20th century, leaded segments of opal white shading to deep green in the form of a nautilus shell, 13½in. high. (Skinner) $10,926

Slag glass lamp shade on a pottery base, American, parasol-form leaded shade of radiating segments of caramel slag glass, sunburst and geometric borders in salmon and orange glass, 29½in. high. (Skinner) $3,450

Tiffany Studios leaded glass geometric shade on a Pittsburgh Lamp Company base, early 20th century, dome shade leaded with horizontal bands of lozenge shapes in pale amber and white, 22½in. (Skinner) $14,950

Handel leaded glass lamp, Meriden, Connecticut, early 20th century, ring accented by a geometric border of blue green glass, parasol shaped shade, diameter 18½in. (Skinner) $1,725

A W.A.S. Benson brass and copper lamp, of hemispherical form on tripod stand with ball and claw feet, and a later shade, 36cm. excluding shade. (Bonhams) $798

Arts & Crafts oak and slag glass table lamp, America, early 20th century, pyramidal shade with scalloped drop apron with round cutouts, 27in. high. (Skinner) $977

Tiffany Studios geometric leaded shade on a pottery base, New York, early 20th century, dome shade of radiating caramel glass segments with a border of striated green square segments near the bottom, 17½in. high.(Skinner) $7,475

Tiffany Studios bronze harp boudoir lamp with pulled feather glass shade, New York, early 20th century, harp suspending a bulbed glass shade with five pulled green and gold feathers on a pale gold luster ground, 13in. high. (Skinner) $5,750

Metal overlay slag glass table lamp, attributed to Riviere Studios, a panelled geometric shade over a shaped base of striated green and white slag glass, pierced leaves on trailing vines overall, 26½in. high. (Skinner) $2,300

A Tiffany bronze counter balance bridge lamp base, with a brown / green patina, the curved double arm with a spherical balance weight, 1920, 56½in. (Woolley & Wallis) $2,720

Pairpoint reverse painted Venetian harbour scene table lamp, H. Fisher, New Bedford, Massachusetts, circa 1915, a Carlisle shade reverse painted with sailing boats in front of a Venetian city in naturalistic colors, 21in. high. (Skinner) $2,645

A Dutch sheet brass lantern, 18th century, of cylindrical form with eight panels, the pierced domed cover with loop handle, 20½in. high. (Christie's) $696

Red painted pine glazed candle lantern, New England, 19th century, the rectangular lantern with pierced top and bentwood handle, old red paint, 16½in. high. (Skinner) $2,415

A gilt-bronze birdcage lantern, in the Rococo style, 20th century, supported from a ring handle, the shaped cylindrical body with a domed upper and lower section, covered all over with acanthus leaves and pierced scrolls, 57in. high. (Christie's) $23,524

A Victorian glazed brass hall lantern, late 19th century, of hexagonal form, the rectangular glazed sides crested with foliage flanked by urns, with waisted conical terminals at the base, 27¾in. high. (Christie's) $1,974

A pair of French gilt bronze mounted frosted glass ceiling lights, early 20th century, the polygonal shades with floral swags and cone terminals, on knopped foliate cast stems, 19¾in. high. (Christie's) $1,692

A Victorian glazed brass hall lantern, last quarter 19th century, the four rectangular glass panes with star-cut centers and bevelled edges, a further star-cut pane beneath as the base, 24¾in. high. (Christie's) $1,151

A gilt bronze mounted frosted glass hall lantern, early 20th century, the shade of baluster form within the naturalistic openwork frame, cast with foliage and C-scrolls, 28in. high. (Christie's) $2,030

A German gilt-metal hall-lantern, 19th century, the rectangular glazed panels headed by acanthus-wrapped rams' heads and with channelled pilasters, 29½in. high. (Christie's) $5,280

A large gilt bronze hexagonal lantern, second quarter 20th century, the panelled frame with tapering underside, the stylized foliate crestings with C-scrolls and berried foliage, 50in. high. (Christie's) $2,030

A Louis Vuitton small zinc trunk, bound in brass, with wooden banding with two leather handles, the interior lined in wood, 23¾ x 18 x 10¾in. (Christie's) $4,333

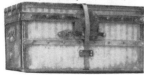

A Louis Vuitton cabin trunk, covered in striped canvas, bound in leather and brass with wooden banding, the interior with purple lattice ribbon on lid, lined in striped fabric, 28 x 16 x 14in. (Christie's) $2,377

A Louis Vuitton hat trunk covered in dark orange material, leather bound with brass lock, catches and leather carrying handles, with two original webbed trays, and Louis Vuitton paper label, 66cm. square. (Onslows) $3,973

A gentleman's crocodile skin travelling case, 20in. wide. (Bonhams) $411

A fine Art Deco crocodile skin lady's travelling vanity case, Asprey of London, circa 1938, in blue stained crocodile skin, the upper section fitted as an overnight case, the lower in beige leather and fitted with four scent bottles etc, 51cm. wide. (Bonhams) $3,973

A case of printed black and brown canvas, bound in leather and brass, the interior labelled *Fendi Roma* – 24 x 16.5 x 8in.; another one similar; and a smaller case, similar 20 x 15 x 7in., circa 1975, some wear. (Christie's) $1,113

A travelling trunk, early 20th century, with a hinged domed lid and door enclosing a fitted interior of six drawers and hanging space, 57½in. wide. (Christie's) $325

A Louis Vuitton motoring trunk, of black Vuittonite, with domed lid, with two levered clasps and two metal handles, 31½ x 13½ x 12in. (Christie's) $1,264

A Louis Vuitton hat box, covered in *LV* monogram canvas and bound in leather and brass with a leather handle, the interior lid with crossed over ribbon, 18 x 18 x 13in. (Christie's) $639

A handbag of beige canvas, bound in tan leather with deep flap and brass fastening, the interior with pockets, stamped *Hermes Paris Made in France*, 14in. base. (Christie's) $2,926

A Louis Vuitton zinc covered brass-bound trunk with brass lock, catches and carrying handles, with original tray and Louis Vuitton paper label, 100 x 50 x 34cm. (Onslows) $2,466

Lampascope Carrée, Lapierre, France; red, yellow and green lacquered-body, with lens and chimney.(Christie's) $469

Carrée lantern, Lapierre, France; stamped-metal body, polychrome-lacquer decoration, with metal lens cap, chimney and internal illuminant.
(Christie's) $87

Biunial lantern, mahogany body, brass fittings, gas regulator, one reflector tray and condenser, chimney, in wooden case.
(Christie's) $1,534

Riche magic lantern, Lapierre, France; pressed-metal decorated body, in red, green, blue and gold polychromed finish, with ventilator and loop handle, lens and condenser, 15in. high.
(Christie's) $89

Biunial lantern, polished mahogany body, lacquered-brass fittings, a pair of 6in. lenses, condensers, gas regulator and a pair of limelight illuminants, with label *A.H. Baird, Scientific Instrument Maker, Edinburgh.*(Christie's) $3,430

Carrée, lantern, Lapierre, France; the black metal body with pierced and impressed decoration, chimney, lens with rack focusing and internally-mounted carbide lamp and glass, 60cm. high.
(Christie's) $397

Cylinder lantern, G. Carette, Nürnberg; the orange-painted body with internal spirit burner, chimney, lens and strips slides in box, in maker's box.(Christie's) $253

Lantern, polished mahogany body, with plaque for W. Banks & Co. Opticians. Bolton, with a safety blow-through jet, leather focusing bellows, condensing lens, projection lens, in a wood box.
(Christie's) $451

Biunial lantern, Newton & Co., London, polished mahogany body, lacquered-brass fittings, illuminant viewing windows, two condensers, with two rack and pinion focusing lenses. (Christie's) $5,055

Primus collapsible lantern, W. Butcher & Sons Ltd., London, metal body, lacquered brass fittings, lens, condenser, with metal plaque stamped *PRIMUS FOLDING LANTERN PATENT 18579.*
(Christie's)　　　　　　$451

A Salon magic lantern by Lapierre, France, with painted tin case, for strips up to 55mm., 1880, 28.5cm. high.
(Auction Team Köln)　　$353

Disc magic lantern, Ernst Plank, Germany; brass body, spirit illuminant, lens, chimney, on wooden base and eight transfer printed disk slides, 5¾in. high.
(Christie's)　　　　　$1,264

Eiffel Tower toy lantern, Aubert, France; red-lacquer and gilt-painted decoration, removable lens and hinged burner tray and spirit burner with retaining clip, 8½in.
(Christie's)　　　　$7,583

Primus gas lantern, Houghton-Butcher Mfg. Co. Ltd., London; mahogany body, brass fittings, metal lamphouse and chimney, square-cut leather focusing bellows. (Christie's)　　　$722

Salon magic lantern, Lapierre, France; metal body, in a red, green, blue and gold polychromed finish, with chimney, lens and condenser, 13in. high. (Christie's)　　$361

Lantern, mahogany body, lacquered-brass fittings, condenser, chimney, panelled lamphouse doors with viewing window, a Wrench-type high power injector jet on stand. (Christie's)　　$867

Megascope lantern, Bing, Nürnberg; red-painted and gilt-lined lamphouse, two projection lenses, two spirit burners with attached reflectors. (Christie's)　　$306

Demonstration lantern, Brady and Martin Ltd., Newcastle; metal lamphouse, mahogany demonstration section, lacquered-brass lens mount and chimney.
(Christie's)　　　　$451

A French sculpted white marble bust of Homer, second half 19th century, after the Antique, 21in. high. (Christie's) $3,552

A large marble figure, carved as a stylized mermaid, unmarked, 65cm. high. (Christie's) $9,047

Carved marble bust of an elegant woman, Kentucky, circa 1870, no stand, 24in. high. (Skinner) $8,625

An Italian carved marble grotesque mask in the 16th century style, with stylized scrolled hair above the furrowed brow, mouth agape, 18¾in. high. (Christie's) $1,175

A pair of French white marble busts of the Venus de Milo and Antinous, second half 19th century, after the Antique, each inscribed to a panel to their bases, 21½in. and 23in. high respectively. (Christie's) $4,674

An Italian sculpted serpentine marble figure of Morgante, after Giambologna, late 19th century, shown naked astride a barrel, holding the barrel's spigot and a wine glass, 16in. high. (Christie's) $2,991

An Italian sculpted white marble of an Emperor, probably 17th century, possibly depicting Nero, shown garlanded and robed, 32¼in. high. (Christie's) $5,609

An Italian Verona marble basin, 18th century, the shallow bowl with lobed underside, on a baluster column and octagonal stepped plinth, 35in. diameter. (Christie's) $7,853

An Italian marble portrait bust in the Roman style, with lapis lazuli and marmo rosso antico embellishments, on a waisted marmo nero marquina socle, 9½in. high. (Christie's) $4,113

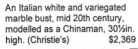

An Italian white and variegated marble bust, mid 20th century, modelled as a Chinaman, 30½in. high. (Christie's) $2,369

A French white marble figure, circa 1866, after a model by Duchoiselle, modelled as a woman fishing in a canoe, 33in. wide. (Christie's) $4,830

A German sculpted white marble bust of a girl, dated 1872, by Robert Cauer the Elder, 1831-1893, shown with garland of lilies to her hair, 26in. high.(Christie's) $8,460

A French white marble group entitled 'L' Amour Désarmé', by Jules-Alfred-Alexandre Dercheu, circa 1880, a scantily clad girl, holding Cupid's arrow in her right hand, holding Cupid away with her left arm, group 31¼in. high. (Christie's) $18,400

A set of four variegated marble urns, 20th century, the waisted necks above baluster bodies with ribbon tied swags, on domed stepped circular bases, 41in. high. (Christie's) $5,429

An Italian marble bust of a Roman, possibly 18th century, modelled looking straight ahead, his togate torso in variegated fawn marble, on a later white marble socle, 13¾in. high overall. (Christie's) $2,533

A sculpted white marble bust of the Duke of Wellington, 19th century, shown with classical drapery, on a waisted circular socle, 28½in. high. (Christie's) $2,199

An Italian marmo giallo Siena tazza, probably the workshops of Benedetto Boschetti, circa 1830, the square flaring dish with central boss, 12in. high, the dish. (Christie's) $10,283

A large white marble bust of an old hag, 19th century, shown with loose drapery about her head and shoulders, 29in. high. (Christie's) $7,106

A Wurlitzer 1050 American jukebox for 50 singles, with plexiglass frame, and internal lighting, 1973. (Auction Team Köln) $6,777

A Black Forest walnut musical chair carved with gentian motifs, the mechanism under the seat, playing six melodies, in working order. (Auction Team Köln) $2,653

Wurlitzer Juke Box, a good 24-selection coin operated music machine, no artists listed, circa 1950s. (Christie's) $9,430

A Wurlitzer juke box, 1950s, with 24-tune record selection, in pointed arch-top case with decorative aluminum mesh front flanked by textured perspex uprights, 76cm. wide. (Bristol) $4,396

An eight air bells in view cylinder musical box, Swiss, late 19th century, with 16cm. cylinder, tune indicator and three saucer shaped bells with colored butterfly strikers and tune sheet in a rosewood case, 46cm. wide.(Bonhams) $529

A Wurlitzer 1015 juke box playing 24 records, with arched top, fully illuminated case and interior mechanism, 60in. high., 32in. wide. (Andrew Hartley) $5,338

Wurlitzer 'Simplex Multi-Selector' juke box, an early wooden cased coin operated music machine combined with 'Strike up the Band' musical automaton by Chicago Coins Band Box. (Christie's) $5,750

A Harmonipan barrel organ, undocumented, possibly by Gavioli, Paris, with pinned wooden cylinder playing eight tunes, 1895. (Auction Team Köln) $3,040

An AMI 'Continental I' jukebox, designed 1961, with curving selection screen above glass dome, revealing turntable mechanism, the speaker with metal grille and star affixed. (Christie's) $3,167

A highly ornamental cast metal dentist's chair, with crank height adjustment, leather upholstery, with iron stand with small cabinet, circa 1900.
(Auction Team Köln) $2,542

A set of dental scaling instruments, a dental elevator and a dentistry related patch box, English, circa 1800, in a plush lined shagreen case. (Bonhams) $362

A J & Wood trepanning set, English, circa 1845, scalpel signed *J.& W. Wood 14 King St Manchester,* 29cm. wide.
(Bonhams) $3,625

An 18th century iron amputation saw, the upper part of the frame indistinctly stamped with a maker's name, with horn pistol-grip handle and decorative tightening screw to the blade, 18½in. long.
(Christie's) $1,011

A lock of Edward IV's hair, King of England 1461-1483, the loop of blondish hair tied with blue silk and mounted on vellum, in an oval ebony frame, old paper label, *Edward IV from his Vault at Windsor 13 March 1789,* 9.7 x 8.7cm. (Bonhams) $735

A rare burnished steel curved [?] bistourie, signed on the shank *GRANGERET COUTr DU ROI A PARIS,* with blade operated by sprung action releasing one guard.
(Christie's) $2,024

An American mahogany dental instrument cabinet, with glass handles, circa 1910, 91cm. wide.
(Auction Team Köln) $1,381

The Owen wooden dentist's chair by C. Ash, London with cast iron height adjustment mechanism, red velvet upholstery and foot-operated drill, circa 1880.
(Auction Team Köln) $8,291

An 'Electric Chair' height adjustable heated seat for home saunas by Heimsauna, Munich, in steelplate with artificial leather seat, 220v, circa 1950.
(Auction Team Köln) $276

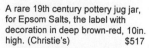

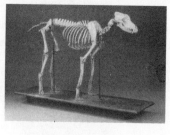

A rare 19th century pottery jug jar, for Epsom Salts, the label with decoration in deep brown-red, 10in. high. (Christie's) $517

'Harry', a fine early 20th century skeleton of a grayhound, with wired joints, on presentation plinth, 45½in. long. (Christie's) $1,036

A 19th century part surgical set, by Weiss London, in red plush-lined brass-bound mahogany case, 39cm. wide. (Christie's) $3,455

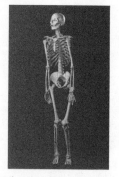

A set of Read artificial teeth, English, second half 19th century, marked *257D* on the metal 'gums', the upper denture with thirteen ivorine teeth held in place with metal pins, the lower with fourteen similar teeth, dentures 5 x 5.5cm. (Bonhams) $191

'Albert', an instructional human skeleton, with articulated skull, sprung ribcage, with wired joints, the pelvis with manufacturer's label for Adam Rouilly& Co. London, 59in. high. (Christie's) $1,036

A 19th century mahogany cabinet, of two short and three long drawers, for medical use, on plinth base, with stand, 37.8cm. wide. (Christie's) $553

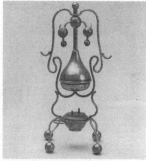

An early 20th-century stainless steel and chrome post-mortem set, by Allen & Hanburys Ltd London, containing three Liston knives, saw, two pairs of scissors, a mallet with chisel etc., original brass-bound mahogany case, 14½in. wide. (Christie's) $276

A gilt metal antiseptic dispenser, French, late 19th century, with naturalistic bark style frame, double burner and pivoting dispenser on four ball feet, 22cm. high. (Bonhams) $191

A 19th century part surgical set, by Mathieu, the brass-mounted walnut case with plaque signed *A Layet*, the lid rising to reveal on the inner surface red chamois leather lining with label of the original contents of the set, 22¾in. wide. (Christie's) $4,491

A bluejohn veneered circular table top, 20th century, 26½in. diameter. (Christie's) $7,728

An amethyst geode, from south Brazil, cut and polished, the outer surface of greenish/blue hue, 32¾in. high. (Christie's) $3,634

A piece of fluorite and rock crystal, the pale lilac fluorite crystals with seam of rock crystal and partial covering of smaller rock crystal, 26 x 17 x 18cm. overall. (Bonhams) $176

An extremely rare fragment of lunar meteorite, Dar al Gani 262, found in the Sahara Desert of Libya on 23 March 1997, 0.7g in weight, ¹¹/₁₆in. long. (Christie's) $14,536

A pair of bluejohn and black and white marble obelisks, late 18th or early 19th century, each on a molded plinth base, restorations, 17in. high. (Christie's) $26,726

A pair of English ormolu-mounted fluorite ewers, in the manner of Matthew Boulton, circa 1890, the overhanging rim above a spirally fluted neck with a satyr mask to the front, 24¼in. high. (Christie's) $21,843

A blue john campana urn, probably early 19th century, on a waisted socle and later stepped black slate plinth, restorations, 20cm. high overall. (Christie's) $4,023

A pair of lapis lazuli candlesticks, second half 19th century, the faceted octagonal bodies with foliate gilt metal mounts to the waisted stems and spreading bases, 10¼in. high. (Christie's) $5,921

Anon, possibly French, Baboon, 1940s, black slate, carved as the figure of a baboon, seated on a base decorated with stylized leaves, 15¼in. (Sotheby's) $3,229

A 19th century mahogany miniature breakfast table, the rectangular canted corner top raised on a baluster turned stem, triform platform base and carved and scrolled feet, 8¾ x 6½in. (Diamond Mills & Co.) $329

A rare Arcade 9 piece bedroom grouping, cast iron, includes two side chairs, rocker, bed, dresser (missing a drawer), and two make-up tables, original paint. (Jacksons) $805

A child's rocking commode wing chair, North Country, 19th century, probably birch, with pierced detail, hinged lid and ogee shaped front frieze. (Christie's) $549

A mid 18th century oak apprentice piece miniature chest, of North Country origin, the top with a heavy molded edge, drawers with walnut banding, 16¾in. wide. (Woolley & Wallis) $1,088

Miniature Empire chest of drawers, two drawers in stepped upper section and three drawers below, brass pulls, 18½in. wide. (Eldreds) $385

Miniature carved and inlaid walnut and burl walnut veneer chest of drawers, early 19th century, New York or New England, the thumb-molded top which overhangs the case includes an inlay with ovolo corners, 14¼in. wide. (Skinner) $3,350

An early 19th century miniature mahogany chest of drawers, two short and three long graduated drawers, oak lined with cockbeading and bone lozenge shaped escutcheons, 11in. wide. (Diamond Mills & Co.) $400

A rare Arcade 5 piece kitchen grouping, cast iron, includes table, two chairs, cabinette, Alaska icebox, original worn paint. (Jacksons) $690

A French gilt metal-mounted mahogany miniature commode, 19th century, the rectangular gray marble top above four long drawers flanked by pilasters, on block feet, 21¾in. wide. (Christie's) $1,320

An Arts and Crafts style overmantel mirror, the shaped plate within a beaten copper surround, decorated with stylized tulips, swallows and animals, 63in. wide.
(Christie's) $1,899

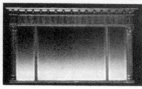

A Victorian carved giltwood and gesso overmantel mirror, with ball decorated cornice and anthemion frieze, inset with triple bevelled plates between half cluster Corinthian columns, 55in. wide.
(Christie's) $2,926

A William IV Irish landscape mirror, the gilt frame with inverted molded cornice above a frieze with a scallop shell suspended on a rope, 27¼ x 4ft.5¾in.
(Woolley & Wallis) $1,727

An early Victorian carved and giltwood triple plate overmantel mirror, with a molded cornice above a leaf and berry frieze, the mirrors divided by reeded ebonized slips, 57in. wide.
(Christie's) $658

A Regency giltwood and gesso overmantel mirror, the rectangular glass plate within a frame applied with classical motifs and columns, surmounted by a ball-studded cornice, 165cm. wide.
(Bearne's) $3,498

An Irish George III lead and mirrored arched interior fan light, in a later mahogany frame, with radiating and swagged divides and four red-glass panels with blue-glass center, 36½in x 69¾in.
(Christie's) $1,280

A 19th century gilt wood overmantel mirror, the cavetto cornice applied with orbs, fluted columns, deep frieze with classical figures in low relief, 55in. long.
(Andrew Hartley) $1,260

An ornate gilt sectional bevelled wall mirror. (Academy) $816

A Regency carved wood and gilded overmantel mirror, of oblong form with cavetto molded cornice, the frieze with trailing oak branch in high relief, 53in. wide.
(Andrew Hartley) $3,550

A gilt mirror, 19th century, with pictorial panels, the dentil molded broken pediment above floral rosette and swag frieze, 46in. wide.
(Christie's) $1,363

A French Empire carved and applied gilt composition frame, with rope-twist and triple bead course recessed between taenias at the outer edge, 28½ x 22¼ x 5⁷⁄₈in.
(Christie's) $1,594

A giltwood overmantel mirror, with mid 18th century oil on canvas, circle of John Thomas Serres (1759-1825), the frame late 19th/early 20th century, 36 x 62in.
(Christie's) $7,728

A giltwood overmantel mirror, 19th century, the rectangular frame within a split column, rope-twist and lotus leaf decorated surround with rosettes to each upper corner, 63in. wide. (Christie's) $2,555

A mahogany and checker-banded cheval mirror, late 19th /early 20th century, with an elongated oval glass flanked by curved uprights with brass swivels and applied bone roundels, 59½in. high. (Christie's) $329

An Art Nouveau oak and marquetry triple plate wall mirror, late 19th century, the bevelled plates within a bevelled surround with stylized foliate and fruiting vines with an ivorine label to the back *JAS.SHOOLBRED & CO.LTD.W.1,* 39½in. wide.(Christie's) $624

Tramp Art Mirror, America, circa 1890-1910, the shaped and laminated sawtooth carved frame with tulip blossom corners enclosing a rectangular bevelled glass mirror, 47in. high. (Skinner) $5,290

A late Victorian gilt composition overmantel mirror, the rounded rectangular plate within a cabochon and rope-twist decorated molded surround, 55in. wide. (Christie's) $987

A giltwood mirror, 20th century, with a central plate and a geometric arrangement of smaller plates with a molded surround and interlaced line and foliate decoration, 47in. wide. (Christie's) $987

A carved and gilt composition overmantel mirror, 20th century, the rectangular plate within an eared waterleaf molded surround with a ribbon-tied, torchère, 53in. high. (Christie's) $1,505

A carved giltwood and ebonized convex mirror, of recent manufacture, the plate within a reeded ebonized slip and surround with ebonized ball ornament, 60in. diameter. (Christie's) $6,334

A Federal giltwood and églomisé looking glass, American, 1815-1825, the rectangular top with molded cornice and outset corners above hanging spherules over an églomisé panel, 54½in. high. (Christie's) $4,465

A George I giltwood and gesso wall mirror, with projecting palmette and lambrequin cresting with dolphins, the later plate within a punched salmon spawn border, 45in. high. (Christie's) $8,686

A Venetian micro-mosaic mirror, circa 1910, of octagonal shape, the top inlaid with a pair of doves carrying a banner inlaid *Venezia*, the side panels each with a Venetian column landmark, 39in. high. (Christie's) $12,925

A carved giltwood and gesso overmantel mirror, 19th century, with ovolo and egg-and-dart border above anthemion foliate scroll frieze, 71in. wide. (Christie's) $5,429

Tiffany Glass & Decorating Company, peacock dressing mirror, 1892-1900, green/brown patinated bronze, the circular mirror in pivoting frame cast with hearts and inlaid with leaded iridescent glass 'eyes', 12¾in. high. (Sotheby's) $17,400

A Chippendale mahogany parcel-gilt looking-glass, American or English, late 18th century, the shaped crest centering a pierced and gilt carved leaf medallion above a rectangular and gilt-carved frame, 24¾in. wide. (Christie's) $9,200

A carved and gilt composition overmantel mirror, 19th century, with a shaped central plate and surrounding marginal mirrors within a frame of foliage, 63in. wide. (Christie's) $3,542

A Victorian gilt composition girandole, the bevelled oval plate within a foliate, berry and beaded surround, with a cabochon centered cresting flanked to either side by winged dragons, 47in. high. (Christie's) $2,138

A William IV gilt composition overmantel mirror, the rectangular plate within an ebonized slip, with foliate headed split projecting columns to either side, 56in. high, 69in. wide. (Christie's) $2,632

A gilt convex mirror, 19th century, the circular plate within an ebonized reeded slip and a ball decorated surround, with a large spread eagle and foliate cresting, 38½in. high. (Christie's) $1,618

Federal gilt gesso mirror, labelled James Todd Portland Looking-Glass Manufactory, 31½in. high. (Skinner) $1,955

Cheval mirror, Edwardian mahogany, satinwood and penwork marquetry with swan neck pediment. (Lots Road) $2,528

A walnut mirror, of William and Mary style, late 19th/early 20th century, 31 x 21in. (Christie's) $5,088

A Chippendale mahogany parcel-gilt looking-glass, American or English, late 18th century, 20¼in. wide. (Christie's) $4,025

Luigi Fontana, wall mirror, 1950, mirrored and pink tinted glass, the reverse with label *Galvanit Fontana, Italy*, 35½in. high. (Sotheby's) $1,288

One of a pair of 19th century gilt framed upright wall mirrors with leafage scroll and cabochon surmount, 4ft.3in. high. (Russell Baldwin & Bright). (Two) $3,863

Classical carved and eglomise looking glass, New York, 1830s, the entablature overhangs a veneered frieze, 38in. high. (Skinner) $460

A Victorian mahogany cheval mirror, the rectangular plate within a cross grained cushion molded surround, 30½in. wide. (Christie's) $1,233

A Chippendale mahogany parcel-gilt looking-glass, American or English, mid to late 18th century, 46in. high. (Christie's) $20,700

An Irish George II gilt-gesso mirror, the shaped rectangular bevelled plate within an acanthus border, 43 x 25¾in. (Christie's) $4,724

A 19th century Biedermeier style mahogany cheval mirror, on column supports with globe finials, 35in. overall. (Skinner) $1,058

Classical mahogany and mahogany veneer looking glass, New York State, probably Utica, 1825-35, 37½in. high. (Skinner) $920

A Venetian glass micro-mosaic table mirror, circa 1870, in the form of a harp, 31¼in. high.
(Christie's) $5,451

A George III satinbirch cheval mirror, the adjustable rectangular later plate, 32in. wide.
(Christie's) $10,902

A 19th century Dutch style octagonal giltwood mirror, 51in. overall.
(Dockrees) $832

Late Federal gilt gesso and wood looking glass, Boston, circa 1820, 57in. high.
(Skinner) $5,175

A Sheraton satinwood framed robing mirror having floral frieze inlay on cheval frame having swan neck surmount, 6ft.5in. high.
(Brightwells) $3,225

A George III mahogany toilet mirror, the shield-shaped plate between shaped supports, 18in. wide.
(Christie's) $838

Continental baroque giltwood mirror framed mirror, second quarter 18th century, 63in. high.
(Skinner) $5,750

Arts and Crafts oak cheval mirror, circa 1912, possibly California, inverted V-shaped crest rail, 75in. high.
(Skinner) $1,725

Impressive Renaissance Revival ebonized and parcel-gilt mirror, circa 1870, 79in. high.
(Skinner) $2,645

Pine boxed giltwood and eglomisé mirror, Continental Northern Europe, 18th century, 21½in.
(Skinner) $2,990

A George III style ormolu mirror, late 19th century, the oval plate in a conforming frame, 50in. high.
(Christie's) $10,350

Federal gilt and églomisé looking glass, Boston or North Shore area, Massachusetts, 1805-15, 33¼in. high.
(Skinner) $1,955

A George III decorated pine oval mirror, in the manner of William Kent, with pierced cartouche shell cresting centered by a gourd shaped pod, inset with an oval plate, 52½in. high. (Christie's) $36,190

A small Regency giltwood convex mirror, 60cm. diameter. (Bonhams & Brooks) $423

A carved giltwood and gesso convex mirror, early 19th century, surmounted by cresting with a deer, on rocky platform flanked by acanthus leaf scrolls, 51in. high. (Christie's) $5,790

A Chippendale carved mahogany looking-glass, labelled by John Elliott, Sr., Philadelphia, 1768-1776, the scrolled pediment above a rectangular molded frame enclosing a conforming glass, 7½in. wide. (Christie's) $6,325

A giltwood overmantel mirror, of George III 'Chinese Chippendale' style, late 19th / early 20th century, the shaped, divided plates within a scrolling foliate border, the bell-hung pagoda cresting with flame finial, 59 x 67in. (Christie's) $23,621

A Chippendale mahogany parcel-gilt looking glass, American or English, mid-18th century, the carved and molded broken swan's-neck pediment centring a spread-winged phoenix, 55in. high. (Christie's) $15,275

A carved giltwood pier mirror, 19th century the rectangular plate with twin arched top within a molded surround carved with acanthus leaves and floral swags, 64in. high. (Christie's) $1,480

A Federal giltwood girandole, Philadelphia, 1790-1810, the spreadwing giltwood eagle perched on a rocky plinth issuing two strands of giltwood spherules, 37in. high. (Christie's) $29,900

An Irish carved giltwood wall mirror, late 18th/early 19th century, with renewal, with later rectangular plate within a pierced foliate and C-scroll surround, 48in. x 28¾in. overall. (Christie's) $5,067

A William and Mary walnut framed mirror, the rectangular bevelled plate within a cushion molded surround lacking a cresting, 35in. high. (Christie's) $5,264

An Edwardian carved mahogany swing frame toilet mirror, 73cm. wide x 82.5cm. high. (Bonhams & Brooks) $339

A Florentine giltwood mirror, circa 1890, with a 'cushion'-shaped pierced foliate frame surmounted by a scrolled cresting piece, 55in. high. (Christie's) $6,440

A Chippendale mahogany parcel-gilt dressing mirror, labelled by John Elliott, Sr. Philadelphia, 1753-1761, rectangular mirror with carved giltwood surround and cusped upper corners within tapering uprights, 17in. wide. (Christie's) $2,760

A late Regency mahogany and ebony strung toilet mirror, with three drawer base, 64cm. wide x 80cm. high. (Bonhams & Brooks) $330

A French ormolu-mounted mahogany cheval mirror, circa 1890, surmounted by ribbon-tied foliage, above a hinged oval bevelled mirror plate, flanked to each side by a scroll support, 69¼in. high. (Christie's) $9,200

A William and Mary walnut and marquetry mirror, the later bevelled rectangular plate within a cushion molded surround decorated with foliate inlaid cartouches, 34in. high. (Christie's) $9,047

An early 19th century mahogany and boxwood strung toilet mirror, 43cm. wide. (Bonhams & Brooks) $693

A Regency gilt composition pier mirror, the rectangular plate between cluster columns, the frieze with anthemion and shell decoration, 21½in. wide. (Christie's) $1,363

Märklin 43cm. clockwork river boat "Havel", painted in lined cream, red and shades of tan, 1924.
(Christie's) $10,845

A rare Bing hand painted steam river boat 'White Star', German, circa 1902, spirit fired live steam model, with gray and orange painted hull, transfer decorated ornate bow, 25¼in.
(Sotheby's) $12,348

Marine shadow box, America, 19th century, depicting a carved model of the three-masted ship 'Big Bonanza', painted black and white, with a tugboat painted black, white, red, and yellow, 25¼ x 48in.
(Skinner) $1,610

A Napoleonic prisoner of war model of a 1st rate ship, late 18th/early 19th century, the wooden hull planked over in bone and baleen with bone planked deck which have been fastened with copper pins, fitted with 128 cannons turned from wood, 29¼ x 13 x 27½in., cased dimensions. (Christie's) $43,700

Cased ship model of the coaster freighter 'Cotolene', hull painted green and black with white upper works, case 36½in. long. (Eldred's) $880

Bassett-Lowke, a 39in. D 36 steam powered destroyer 'Vivacious', 1934, the wooden hull with lead weight, painted red to the water line, gray above with cut out portholes, central section of lower deck detachable, 39in. long. (Bonhams & Brooks) $1,946

An early 19th century prisoner-of-war ship model in bone, three-masted man-o-war, 28-gun, 14in. long including bowsprit, on ivory supports and black japanned base. (Brightwells) $1,175

A Hornby Series Electric E420 'Eton' Locomotive and No. 2 Special Southern Tender No. 900, painted in lined green, 1938. (Christie's) $2,670

SNCF 2-4-1A No. 65, Gauge 1, electric, with full inside motion, Bockholt, 1991, Cat.Ref. 3706, 34½in. long. The driving wheels proved too small, causing track damage. Larger wheels were fitted and the class became 2-4-1C. (Christie's) $18,095

CIWL Pullman 4-axle (twin bogie) passenger coach, prototype, unpainted brass, 53.5cm. (Christie's) $1,266

Bing for Bassett Lowke gauge II Steam Great Central 4-4-0 and Tender, painted in lined black, with twin inside oscillating cylinders, 1902. (Christie's) $4,672

New York Central RR 4-6-4 Commodore Vanderbilt Gauge 1 Electric, Aster, 1985, Cat Ref. 1204/3, 35¾in. long. (Christie's) $6,332

A Märklin style 40cm. four-axleTrain Post Van, Cat. Ref. 19450, lithographed in green, 1937. (Christie's) $1,167

A Hornby Series electric LNER E220 Special 'The Bramham Moor' locomotive and No. 2 Special Tender, painted in light LNER green, 1936. (Christie's) $1,669

DB freight stock: Gauge 1 4-axle (twin bogie) log wagon No. 4336254-7, with load, Bockholt, 1983, Cat.Ref. 3701, 25¾in. (65.5cm.) long. (Christie's) $1,175

An exhibition standard 7mm. finescale two-rail electric model of the LNER class A3 4-6-2 locomotive tender No. 2750 Papyrus, built by J.R. Brierley of nickel silver with external details including fluted motion, cylinder drains, brake and sanding gear. (Christie's) $4,171

A model of a 4-6-0 steam locomotive and tender, live steam spirit fired, the locomotive 21½in. long, the tender 14in. (Lyle) $800

A well engineered 3½in. gauge 0-6-2 side tank locomotive built to the design of Mona, with brazed superhead copper boiler with fittings, 11½ x 27½in., and water tank built as a 7-plank coal wagon with copper tank and flow valve, 14in. long, and a twin bogie driving trolley, 25in. long.
(Christie's) $1,208

A 7mm. finescale two rail electric model of the LMS 0-6-4 side tank locomotive No. 15307, built by Duchess Models with external details including brake gear, tank filler caps, sand boxes, 3½ x 10¾in.
(Christie's) $863

SSB Ce 6/8 II No. 14270, Gauge 1, Electric, "Crocodile", Bockholt, 1978, Cat.Ref. 2581, with detailed driving compartments, 26in. long.
(Christie's) $10,857

A finely engineered 3½in. gauge model of the C.R. 0-6-0 side tank locomotive No. 533, built to the design of Rob Roy by S.W. Blackley with brazed superheated copper boiler, with fittings including water and pressure gauges, 10 x 21½in.
(Christie's) $1,835

A J.N.R. Class C57 4-6-2 No. C575 live steam spirit-fired locomotive and tender, by Aster, with all original fittings and paint, 27in. long.
(Christie's) $1,467

A Hornby Dublo EDP12 passenger train set; comprising Duchess of Montrose locomotive in BR green, RN 46232 and 6 wheel tender, 2 tinplate coaches, in maroon and gray, plus a quantity of track for the set, boxed. (Wallis & Wallis) $120

A 7mm. finescale two rail electric model of the SR March Atlantic 4-4-2 locomotive and tender No. 2424, Beachy Head, built by NW Models with external details including brake gear, fluted connecting and coupling rods, 3¾ x 16¾in. (Christie's) $1,036

A 3½in. gauge model of the 0-6-0 side, tank locomotive No. 349 built to the design of 'Rob Roy' by Geo. S. Stubbs, with brazed superheated copper boiler with water and pressure gauges, safety, blower, whistle, clack and blowdown valves, 10½ x 21¼in.
(Christie's) $1,382

Andy Gump General Thrift Products Bank, cast metal 5¾in. high. (Jacksons) $460

Kyser & Rex lion and monkeys cast iron mechanical bank, missing top monkey, trap and eyes, 8¾in. high. (Jacksons) $316

Baby in egg cast metal bank, missing squeaker and trap, 7in. high. (Jacksons) $69

Green blown-molded glass moneybox, 1835-1845, with one 1841 half-dime and three roosters, ribs twisted to the right, 6¼in. high. (Skinner) $11,750

A fine mechanical cast iron bank, 'Trick Pony' by Shepherd Hardware, most of original paint with nice patina. Trap door missing, 7¾in. long x 8in. high. (Jacksons) $1,495

A J & E Stevens 'Eagles and Eaglets' bank, painted cast-iron nest with eagle feeding two eaglets, on a contemporary wooden counter-top extension, 6¾in., base length. (Christie's) $1,454

Stollwerck's Victoria lithographed tinplate mechanical savings bank and dispenser, for chocolate bars, with Hansel and Gretel motif, 28cm. high, 1894. (Auction Team Köln) $736

J.E. Stevens Co. novelty cast iron bank, missing door and figure, 6½in. high. (Jacksons) $230

A cast iron Tammany mechanical savings bank by J & E Stevens, the figure with gray trousers and dark brown jacket, 1873, 15cm. high. (Auction Team Köln) $508

Circa 1978 Triumph 744cc T140 Bonneville, left-side gearleaver and rear disk brake, finished in metallic brown and yellow. (Bonhams) $4,416

1924 Humber 2 3/4HP 349cc lightweight, with the semi-TT handlebars and footrests, Brooklands fishtail exhaust. (Bonhams & Brooks) $5,382

1926 Chater-Lea 350cc Brooklands Racer, A.C. Woodman's famous 'face cam' engine that used two contoured plates at the top of a vertical gear driven shaft to operate the rocker arms.
(Bonhams & Brooks) $9,936

1977 MZ TS250/1, built in East Germany in the old DKW Works at Zschopau, powered by an inclined single cylinder, air cooled, two stroke engine of 243cc with a four speed gearbox and final drive by chain. (Bonhams & Brooks) $276

Circa 1963 Vespa 150cc Sportique, the link between Bristol and Italy was forged during 1951 with the commencement of licence built production of Vespas, following the withdrawal of Douglas as a motorcycle producer Vespas were shipped into Bristol in 'knocked down' form ready for assembly.
(Bonhams & Brooks) $372

1957 Royal Enfield 350cc Clipper De-Luxe. This example is to original specification in all major respects and is presented in dark green livery, Restored over ten years ago, original registration number, buff logbook and is Swansea registered on a V5 document. (Bonhams & Brooks) $1,518

1912 Triumph 550cc TT Roadster Model sporting machine, with lowered handlebars, girder fork and coil spring front suspension and final drive by belt. (Bonhams & Brooks) $7,866

1934 Triumph 250cc Model L2/1, integrally-forged flywheel and mainshaft set-up with dry sump lubrication, hand gear change, lighting by Lucas Magdyno. (Bonhams & Brooks) $1,932

1962 Zundapp 249cc Trophy, touring model, well equipped with fully valanced mudguards and full width hubs. (Bonhams & Brooks) $621

1985 Sinclair C5 electric tricycle, offered in generally good condition and to original specification in all major respects. (Bonhams & Brooks) $221

1983 Serveta Jet 198cc scooter by Lambretta, 1980s, the jet 200 featuring a central engine for perfectly stability, four speed gears, a single steel tube frame and large 10 inch wheels for comfort and stability, two stroke engine. (Bonhams & Brooks) $863

1970 Norton 750cc Commando, registration no CYA 10J, frame no. 136847, engine no 136847. This black machine is presented in 'fastback' trim with the drum front brake, with a Swansea V5 and an old green log book. (Bonhams & Brooks) $2,070

Circa 1923 Connaught 293cc Popular, frame no. 2637, engine no. WR533. This 293cc example is offered in largely complete condition with the restoration started. The frame is in primer and the rear wheel has been rebuilt. Offered in assembled condition it is not accompanied by any papers. (Bonhams & Brooks) $442

1926 Dunelt 250cc Model K, marketed as 'the supercharged two stroke', the Birmingham-built Dunelt featured a double-diameter piston, this inclined single features hand change lever to a Sturmey Archer gearbox.
(Bonhams & Brooks) $2,208

1974 Velo-Solex 49cc moped, French-built, 49cc engine, developing approximately ·5bhp at 2,000rpm, equipped with horn, lighting, pump and rear carrier. (Bonhams & Brooks) $179

1938 Sun 98cc Autocycle, mounted in a cycle frame, the 98cc autocycle offered 130mpg and direct action spring forks, with a 1½ gallon petrol tank. (Bonhams & Brooks) $442

1928 Sunbeam 347cc Model 2, with a P&H acetylene headlamp, Holdtite rear lamp and leather panniers, black and gold livery.
(Bonhams & Brooks) $5,244

Circa 1976 Montesa 49cc Cota 25 Trials, restored to standard specification in 1995/96, with cycle parts and engine rebuilt 'as new'.
(Bonhams & Brooks) $1,725

Circa 1945 James 125cc military lightweight, powered by a Villiers 9D engine of 122cc with unit construction, three speed gearbox, in military livery with war-time headlamp mask fitted.
(Bonhams & Brooks) $1,242

1956 Triumph 200cc Tiger Cub, registration no. AAS 872, frame no. T25967, engine no. T2063439, restored with old style log book, MoT certificate to 17th July 2002, road fund licence to June 2002 and a V5. (Bonhams & Brooks) $1,794

1954 BSA 497cc A7 Shooting Star, an 'older restoration' this early A7SS is reportedly to original specification and is described as in generally good condition, finished in green, the machine is offered with current MoT and Swansea V5.
(Bonhams & Brooks) $2,760

1930 AJS 498cc S9L, registration no AYM 912 frame no S9L 133631, engine no. S9L 133631, in original condition and is offered with a Swansea V5, an MOT certificate valid until October 2002 and a road fund licence to September 2002.
(Bonhams & Brooks) $2,415

1962 James 150cc, registration no. TSY 843, frame no. DL15A11216, engine no. 15T7654, powered by a 150cc Villiers single cylinder two stroke, in unrestored condition. (Bonhams & Brooks) $276

1926 BSA 350cc registration no. HM 6705, frame no. Z6272, engine no. F 13587, this 349cc side valve single valve single is typical of the firm's output, restored. (Bonhams & Brooks) $3,795

1968 Raleigh 50cc WISP, registration no. 1662 WZ, frame no. 005997, engine no. R154019, gold livery with rear pannier bag, Swansea V5 registration document. (Bonhams & Brooks) $470

1971 Puch 49cc Maxi Model N Moped, registration no. MEF 634J, frame no. 9923399, engine no. 9923399, in red and white livery, with dynamo lighting. (Bonhams & Brooks) $152

1955 BSA 250cc C11G, registration no JCX 828, the C11 evolved during 1954 into the C11G when a Lucas generator replaced the coil and dynamo system previously employed. (Bonhams & Brooks) $414

1966 Triumph 490cc T100SS, finished in the correct green/white, this example is described as in generally good condition and is offered with old-style logbook, MoT to October 2002 and Swansea V5. (Bonhams & Brooks) $2,622

1947 Indian 741-B, registration no. HVU 189, frame no. 25983, engine no. GDA 3471, from one of America's oldest motorcycle manufacturers, with low compression ratio engine of 45 cu. in. (Bonhams & Brooks) $4,416

1912 Scott 3 3/4hp two stroke, water-cooled engine, rigid open frame, foot operated two speed gear and original kick start, 532cc inclined engine, with roller bearings throughout. (Bonhams & Brooks) $9,936

1954 BSA 350cc Gold Star, restored in 1998/99 and in good overall condition, equipped with an alloy fuel tank and 'racing' seat. (Bonhams & Brooks) $4,140

1913 Henderson 1,068cc four cylinder motorcycle, with a Cowey 0-80 speedometer, a P&H acetylene headlamp and generator and a Gloriaphone hand klaxon. (Bonhams & Brooks) $37,260

1968 Honda CB250, restored, in excellent condition, presented in green and white and offered with a fresh MoT certificate and Swansea V5.
(Bonhams & Brooks) $1,065

1960 AJS 500cc Model 18 and Watsonian Monza Sidecar, in good condition in all respects and presented in black, with V5, an MoT certificate valid until the 4th June 2002 and a road fund licence valid until May 2002. (Bonhams & Brooks) $2,201

1914 James 225cc motorcycle, engine: single cylinder, 225cc, ignition by magneto, gearbox: countershaft two speed. (Christie's) $5,673

1938 Sunbeam 250cc Model 14, upswept exhaust pipe, narrower mudguards, chromium plated tank with black top and side panels and a ribbed 3.00 x 21in. front tire. (Bonhams & Brooks) $2,708

An Excelsior motorcycle, 1950s, Reg.No.GUP 749, with Villiers air cooled 2-stroke engine, approximately 150cc), 3-speed gearbox, front and rear drum brakes, flyscreen and original panniers, green finished.
(Bristol) $662

1926 Harley-Davidson 998cc Model F, an export model imported into the UK in 1926, restored to original condition, excellent frame and cycle parts. Finished in green and equipped with acetylene lighting, magneto ignition.
(Bonham & Brooks) $10,500

A rare Simson Schwalbe 50CC motorcycle, 1971, Reg. No. OEU 212J, frame no.486687, finished in mid green, with integral head lamp to the stylish fairings and drum brakes front and rear.
(Bristol) $471

A Symphonium disk musical box, in carved walnut and floral marquetry case, the hinged lid with sepia print inside depicting music making putti, 23in. wide, and a collection of 15½in. disks.
(Andrew Hartley) $2,919

A Polyphon Nr. 6 music box with clock and bells for 56cm. disks, with 118-tone double comb and 12 bells, with 8 disks, circa 1900.
(Auction Team Köln) $4,704

A musical box by George Bendon, playing twelve dance tunes accompanied by nine engraved bells, case veneered in matched figured walnut with tulipwood crossbanding to the lid, 27¼in. wide. (Christie's) $3,109

A bells in view eight-air cylinder musical box, Swiss, late 19th century, with 16cm. cylinder, tune indicator, three-saucer-shaped bells with enamelled butterfly strikers in a rosewood-painted case, 46.5cm. wide. (Bonhams) $735

An automaton musical box playing six airs accompanied by four bells with two painted mandarin strikers, with dancing doll, 36.5cm. wide.
(Christie's) $3,281

A B.H. Abrahams Britannia 11¾in. disk musical box, Swiss, circa 1900, in a veneered and transfer decorated case, with winding handle, 48cm. wide, together with twenty-seven disks.
(Bonhams) $1,029

An Alibert musical snuff box, French, circa 1840-50, with sectional comb in groups of five teeth, in a thermoplastic case with mother-of-pearl buttons, 9.2cm. wide. (Bonhams) $412

A Kalliope Nr. 61 music box with 61-tone double comb for 34cm. disks by Kalliope Musikwerke, Leipzig, the wooden case with engraved name, circa 1900.
(Auction Team Köln) $1,045

A late 19th century musical box with bells, drum and castanets in view, playing 12 airs, on 13in. cylinder, the walnut lid and front inlaid with crossbanding and stringing.
(Brightwells) $1,050

A violin by James Cochrane of Dundee, the two piece back of medium flame with dark brown varnish, dated *1920*.
(Woolley & Wallis) $299

An E-flat Helichon, by Boosey And Co., and engraved Solborn class A, and numbered 9908.
(Christie's) $360

A set of bagpipes of Hutcheon of Edinburgh, circa 1920, with later Kintail pipe chanter and bag.
(Christie's) $750

A Victorian burr maple and parcel-gilt harp, by Sebastian Erard, London, circa 1850, with fluted tapering column upright headed by anthemion and female caryatids and with anthemion-cast base, 67in. high, overall.
(Christie's) $6,900

A symphony 58-note player organ, by Wilcox & White, Meriden, Conn. U.S.A., with twenty-two musical stops, five-octave keyboard and mahogany case, 69in. wide; a stool; and approximately 65 rolls.
(Christie's) $1,714

A silver flute, by Rudall Carte & Co. Ltd, 23 Berners Street London W.1, in its velvet lined case.
(Woolley & Wallis) $420

A late 19th century German Streich zither, trade label for Georg Tiefenbrunner, Pietersplatz, München, in rosewood case, ivory tuning keys and ivory feet, in original fitted case, 19½in.
(Woolley & Wallis) $102

A C. Jeffries 40-button concertina, the ebonized ends with pierced nickel plated floral design mounts and ivory buttons, tooled leather bellows with applied printed paper decoration.
(Lawrences) $695

A brass trumpet, with attachments, inscribed *Solbron,* with documentation and sheet music, in original box.
(Woolley & Wallis) $136

An ivory netsuke of a boy with a large fish, 19th century, carved and pierced with the boy kneeling on the fish holding it down, 4.1cm. wide. (Christie's) $461

A fine stag antler netsuke of a shark, Beisai seal, Edo period, 19th century, the unusually elongated and slender body with the tail slightly curved, 4¾in. long. (Christie's) $8,435

An erotic Japanese ivory netsuke, partly colored, signed *Gyokuei*, circa 1930, 4.5cm. high. (Arnold) $203

An ivory bijin mask netsuke, 19th century, signature to reverse, with a smiling expression, the reverse with tassels tied in a bow, 1¾in. high. (Christie's) $658

An ivory netsuke of a horse, early 19th century, with head turned to one side looking at a small seated monkey on his back, 8.6cm. high. (Christie's) $2,796

An ivory netsuke of a group of masks, early 19th century, incised signature, of oni, a skeleton, a young boy and various other heads with different expressions, 4.1cm. high. (Christie's) $658

A wood netsuke of a demon, 19th century, the horned figure with long hair, carved seated with legs crossed holding an ivory egg in his hands, 4.7cm. wide. (Christie's) $1,068

A large ivory netsuke of a bearded European gentleman, 19th century, signed to reverse, carved standing wearing top hat and coat decorated with beads, holding a small monkey, 16.8cm. high. (Christie's) $4,935

A Kyoto School ivory netsuke of icho seeds, inscribed Mitsuhara. (Bonhams) $440

An early electrical time clock by the Stromberg Electric Co., Chicago, as used in the US Patent Office, circa 1910.
(Auction Team Köln) $121

A Turn Verein Boston early notary seal, finely decorated with original die and counter-die, circa 1890.
(Auction Team Köln) $173

An Ellams Duplicator Diaphragm Model copier, for wax stencils, circa 1910.
(Auction Team Köln) $46

The Calculagraph calculating clock for working out the cost of telephone calls and piece work times, American, 1925.
(Auction Team Köln) $220

An early Abbott Automatic Check perforator, American, 1889.
(Auction Team Köln) $154

American autodial machine with clockwork mechanism, brass casing with viewing window on cast iron base.
(Auction Team Köln) $93

A rare New Era Model 4 check writer, with 'guarantee card' base, dated 1922, American.
(Auction Team Köln) $110

A United States Check Punch check printer, in mahogany case, with automatic forward drive, 1889.
(Auction Team Köln) $469

An early electro-magnetic burglar alarm telegraph by E. Holmes, patented in the USA in 1853, with copy of patent.
(Auction Team Köln) $3,920

The Little Shaver, an early mechanical pencil sharpener, black cast iron with interchangeable razors, 1904.
(Auction Team Köln) $270

A classic Hopkinson & Cope album press, platen size 30 x 45cm. restored, 1884.
(Auction Team Köln) $3,631

A Jupiter 2 mechanical pencil sharpener with hand crank by Guhl & Harbeck, Hamburg, black painted cast metal with gold lettering.
(Auction Team Köln) $237

An American Automatic Pencil Sharpener, with rotating three-blade knife and original metal drawer, 1906.
(Auction Team Köln) $185

A rare Mars check writer, roller restored, in original mahogany case.
(Auction Team Köln) $185

A rare desk-mounted Bayern-Sepp pencil sharpener by KUM, West Germany, on cast metal base with brightly lithographed tinplate case, 9cm. high, circa 1955.
(Auction Team Köln) $176

The Reynolds Envelope Sealer, an early letter sealing machine of amusing design, patented 1910 by the Reynolds Envelope Sealing Co., Chicago, 1910.
(Auction Team Köln) $205

A Roneo pencil sharpener on large plinth base with attractive decoration and rotating blade.
(Auction Team Köln) $423

A small field/portable/morse telegraph by Otto Ganser, Vienna, brass with original lacquer, in original wooden case, 17cm. long,
(Auction Team Köln) $1,159

Kok projector, Pathé, France, 28mm., with hand crank, lens and film spools.(Christie's) $758

Peep egg, English; alabaster body with floral painted decoration, viewing lens, interior revealing printed views of Clifton Downs and mount St Bernard near Coalville, 8in. high.(Christie's) $217

Taxiphote automatic stereoscope, J. Richard, France; 45 x 107mm., polished wood body, nickel-fittings, with automatic slide-changing mechanism. (Christie's) $3,430

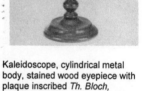

Kaleidoscope, cylindrical metal body, stained wood eyepiece with plaque inscribed *Th. Bloch, Strasbourg*, on a turned wood stand with a fruitwood base, 39cm. (Christie's) $812

Stereo viewer, mahogany body, with a pair of fixed-focus viewing lenses, rear ground-glass screen, double hinged lid revealing twenty-three tissue cards, 32cm. high. (Christie's) $1,625

Phenakistiscope, with two black paper disks, in a replica box and brass holder with rosewood handle. (Christie's) $1,264

A rare erotic Stanhope lens vesta case, German, third quarter of the 19th century, lens showing a photographic erotic scene of a gentleman enjoying the company of two amorous young ladies, 7cm. wide. (Bonhams) $626

Stereo viewer, 10 x 14.5cm., mahogany-veneered body, hinged reflector, in maker's card box, in wood case. (Christie's) $105

Mutoscope-pattern viewer no. 142, floor-standing, blue-painted metal body, electrically coin-operated, top-mounted advertising panel Gamo Bio. Nieuw Programa and one picture reel. (Christie's) $1,625

Cosmos upright cylinder lantern, Jean Schoenner, Nürnberg; polished brass body, slides, and chimney (lacks lens), in maker's fitted box. (Christie's) $246

A French luxury Stéréoscopes L. Legendre stereo viewer for 8.5 x 18cm. slides or cards, in carved walnut case, circa 1890.
(Auction Team Köln) $4,702

Zoetrope, 30cm. diameter painted-metal drum, on a decorated cast metal stand, with seven printed picture strips.
(Christie's) $2,347

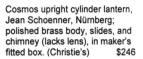

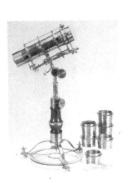

Kaleidoscope, malachite effect finish metal body tube and a stained wood eyepiece, 6¼in. long.
(Christie's) $506

A final kaleidoscope, by W. Leigh, English; the cylindrical body tube with rack and pinion and worm screw geared mechanism, with ivory handle activating two independently periphery geared collar tubes, 16½in. minimum height. (Christie's) $71,435

A pair of black-enamelled and leather-covered prismatic binoculars, signed *Carl Zeiss Jena, No. 7902,* with 3¼in. object lenses, 19¾in. long, in the original wood carrying case.
(Christie's) $6,593

Praxinoscope, E. Reynaud, Paris; 32cm. diameter drum, on a turned-wood stand, with three picture strips. (Christie's) $1,083

Shadow ball, 12cm. diameter ball, with foliate engraved brass decoration and pierced brass work, hinged body, interior with a gimbal mounted illuminant holder.
(Christie's) $234

Planox stereoscope, 6 x 13cm., wood-body. (Christie's) $578

Polyrama Panoptique viewer, 24 x 19cm., paper covered wood body, paper bellows, wood-bound viewing lens, and eight hand colored French lithographed scenes. (Christie's) $1,986

A Victorian papier mâché dressing table case with silver mounted fittings, Jennens & Bettridge, the rectangular case with a painted view, inscribed *Warwick Castle*, with scrolling gilt borders, 11¼in. wide. (Christie's) $1,656

A 19th century papier mâché 'Bulldog Mascot', its head shaking, mouth opening and growling, activated by the lead, 25in. (Boardmans) $301

A painted papier-mâché lacquer box, by the Vishniakov Factoy, Moscow, circa 1881, the detachable slightly domed cover painted with the young Tsar viewing his bride, red interior, 7¼in. diameter. (Christie's) $1,034

A Victorian black papier mâché work table, with gilt and mother of pearl decoration, a fitted interior to the hinged lid, a shaped frieze, 17½in.(Woolley & Wallis) $511

A pair of Victorian pole screen stands with later associated papier mâché screens, the shaped panels, painted with rustic scenes, mounted on lacquered poles, the baluster stems on octagonal bases, 55½in. high. (Christie's) $5,520

A Victorian papier mâché tray, late 19th century, decorated with a colorful parrot amongst flowers, some restoration, 79 x 60cm. (Bonhams) $740

A painted papier-mâché lacquer Easter egg, by the Lukutin Factory, Moscow, 1881-1894, in two halves, one painted with the Resurrection on red ground, the other with a view of the New Palace of the Moscow Kremlin, 6¼in. high. (Christie's) $1,693

A painted papier-mâché lacquer cigarette-box, by the Lukutin Factory, Moscow, 1910-1917?, the hinged cover painted with a boyar maiden in traditional costume presenting a bratina, red interior, 5¼in. long.(Christie's) $1,960

A Victorian papier mâché occasional table, with gilt decoration, the oval scalloped and bevelled snap top centered by a country house, with figures in a landscape, the top 26in. wide. (Christie's) $2,560

Osmia, a pearl and black Progress Extra Luxe pen and pencil set, with Osmia Extra Supra Luxe nib, German, mid-1930s. (Bonhams) $966

Pilot, a white metal 'Chequer', marked *Sterling Silver* with Pilot nib, Japanese, 1970s. (Bonhams) $386

A Parker 41 filigree eyedropper, American, 1905-1918, gold-plated over black hard rubber, Lucky Curve 5 nib. (Bonhams) $3,087

A Parker 51 rolled silver insignia, American, circa 1949, in lined card 51 box, mint. (Bonhams) $1,837

A yellow metal watch pencil, with line decoration marked *14KT* and watch with jewelled Swiss lever movement and silvered arabic numerals signed *GATTLE.* American, 1930s. (Bonhams) $612

Mordan & Riddle, a silver everpointed pencil, with reeded decoration and screw-off terminal set with bloodstone, English, London Hallmark *1827*, together with a white metal Butler pencil, English, 1830s/40s. (Bonhams) $241

A rare Montblanc Toledo-Overlaid 0 Long Safety, German, 1921-1927, Toledo overlaid black hard rubber signed *Mont Blanc* within the lightning bolt and star design, Simplo 14K '0' nib. (Bonhams) $13,120

A Montblanc Rouge et Noir overlaid 00-size safety, Italian circa 1915, two gold-plated oval panels on cap and barrel in a floral and foliate design, cap marked *Rouge Et Noir 18 K.R.,* 14ct. '00' nib. (Bonhams) $3,040

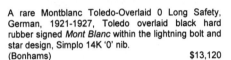

An Omas Colorado, Italian, circa 1945, black celluloid, steel nibs, in unmarked card box. (Bonhams) $2,940

A Montblanc 2EF safety, German for the Spanish market 1920s, mottled red and black hard rubber, 14ct. '2' nib, gold-plated Montblanc accommodation clip. (Bonhams) $2,205

A Montblanc gold-plated 2-size safety, German, 1920s, combined round and octagonal barrel, octagonal cap signed *Mont Blanc*, decorated in a wavy line and foliate design, two floral and foliate bands trimmed in blue enamel with dots, 14ct. '2'nib. (Bonhams) $3,087

A Mabie Todd & Bard hand-engraved yellow metal Swan eyedropper, American, circa 1892, delicately engraved with a floral and abstract design, with over/under fed nib and presentation box with hallmarked silver plaque. (Bonhams) $2,058

A Parker no. 38 Snake, American, 1905-1910, gold-plated overlay of two entwined snakes with glinting green cabochon eyes, Lucky Curve '3' nib, the most famous vintage fountain pen in the world. (Bonhams) $24,000

Namki, a maki-e lacquer pen decorated with traditional musical instruments, a reeded pipe on the barrel, a green instrument on the cap, in iroe-hira-maki-e, with gold nashiji highlights and Namiki 3 nib, Japanese, late 1920s. (Bonhams) $1,127

A gold and enamel Bramah-type pen holder, with foliate decoration, blue and orange flowers, green leaves and cream ground, with bloodstone seal terminal with intaglio swallow and motto *Le Froid Me Chasse*, English or French, mid 19th century. (Bonhams) $773

Security, a black chased hard rubber 3 with Check Protector, and security 3 nib, American, 1920s. The check protector is a series of rolling wheels which could be rolled over the un-used parts of a personal or business check to prevent the recipient changing the details. (Bonhams) $258

A 9 carat gold Waterman's lever-filler, hallmarked London, 1935, barleycorn overlay, large curved Canadian 2 nib. (Bonhams & Brooks) $123

Two Wahl Eversharp lever-fillers, American, circa 1930, comprising a black and pearl Gold Seal Personal Point, 14ct. 'flexible' nib, together with a black and pearl Gold Seal Equipoised, with 14ct. manifold nib. (Bonhams) $162

A silver Waterman's No. 12 'The Golfer', hallmarked London, 1908, repoussé decorated silver sleeve of a golfer in his plus-fours at the end of his swing, over black hard rubber, with original and replacement cap. (Bonhams & Brooks) $5,069

An overlaid Waterman's 42 ½ V Safety, French, 1920s, the white metal overlay marked *Waterman's Argent* and with French control marks, semi-gothic design, 2 nib. (Bonhams & Brooks) $164

A Waterman's 554 Filigree, American, circa 1920, yellow metal over black hard rubber with all parts marked 14ct. curved New York 4 nib. (Bonhams & Brooks) $548

An overlaid Waterman's 42 Safety, Italian, 1930s, gold-plated barley overlay with floral and foliate applique accents, floral cap crown, Reg. U.S. Pat. Off. 2 nib. (Bonhams & Brooks) $548

A Waterman's 0552 ½ L.E.C. Pansy Panel, American, 1920s, gold-plated over black hard rubber, large curved New York 2 nib. (Bonhams & Brooks) $329

A Waterman's 0552½V Sheraton, American, 1920s, gold-plated over black hard rubber, large curved New York 2 nib. (Bonhams & Brooks) $219

Wheeler, a silver musket novelty pencil, marked *G. WHEELER NOVR. 9 1840 No. 454* with finely engraved stock and hinged cover opening for lead reservoir, sliding mechanism, English, 1840s. (Bonhams) $564

A Waterman's basketweave pencil, American, circa 1920, white metal over black hard rubber, barrel and clip marked *Sterling*. (Bonhams & Brooks) $110

An overlaid Waterman's 52½ with Perpetual Calendar, French, circa 1930, plain overlay marked *18K* on clip and with French control marks on cap and barrel, three-color enamelled calendar on cap, 2 nib. (Bonhams & Brooks) $822

A Mabie Todd & Co. Swan silver leverless pen and Fyne Poynt pencil, London, hallmarked 1949 and 1951, fully-covered plain and line design, Swan 3 14ct. nib, propelling pencil, in a velvet-lined red Mabie Todd & Co. box. (Bonhams) $1,397

A rare Montblanc 00-size Safety, German 1920s, mottled red and black hard rubber, 14ct. '00' nib, Montblanc accommodation clip. (Bonhams) $1,440

A Dunhill-Namiki maki-e lacquer balance, Japanese 1930s, in iroe-hira-maki-e, barrel depicting three cranes in flight against a mura-nashiji and oki-birami background. (Bonhams) $1,396

A Waterman's 452 'Gothic', American, 1920s, white metal marked *Sterling* on all parts, Reg. U.S. Pat. Off. 2 nib, together with a red Ripple 52 1/2V. (Bonhams & Brooks) $233

A Montblanc enamelled 0-size baby Safety, German 1920s, black hard rubber, pale green enamel overlay against a wavy line ground, Simplo '0' nib, with a similar pencil. (Bonhams) $3,040

Conklin, a bronze/black Marble Endura, with Endura nib, American, late 1920s. (Bonhams) $153

A Waterman's overlaid 42 Safety, Italian, 1930s, gold-plated over black hard rubber with clip, alternating plain and diamond jacquard panels, upper cap decorated in relief with imps and putti interspersed with trilliums. (Bonhams & Brooks) $822

A Liberty & Co Tudric pewter and enamel box and cover, stamped mark, 13cm. diameter.
(Bonhams) $735

A pewter porridger and ladle, Scottish, late 17th/ early 18th century, the turned bombé shaped porridger flanked by two handles with a lid surmounted by a knopped finial and a ladle, 13½in. wide.
(Christie's) $1,280

A Solklis English pewter inkwell, with glass liner, stamped marks, 0653, 6.5cm. high.
(Bonhams) $441

A Liberty & Co. pewter and enamel mantel clock, designed by Archibald Knox, circa 1902-1905, the shaped rectangular body cast with ivy foliage border, 8¼in. high.
(Christie's) $10,692

A Liberty Tudric pewter and enamel five piece teaset, Archibald Knox, designed 1902-1905, streamlined form cast in relief with stylised honesty sprays on whiplash stems, enamelled in blue and green, hot water 9in. high.
(Christie's) $2,467

A Liberty Tudric pewter ewer with Powell green glass liner, designed by Archibald Knox, circa 1902-1905, compressed ovoid body with swollen cylindrical neck cast with a spray of stylised flowers and foliage, unmarked, 8in. high.
(Christie's) $2,467

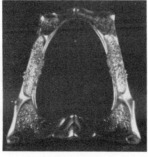

A WMF silvered metal tea and coffee service, stamped factory marks, tray 57cm. diameter.
(Christie's) $2,235

An Art Nouveau silvered metal mirror cast with flowers and leaves, 52cm. high. (Christie's) $596

An Art Nouveau pewter rose bowl, of dished circular form, raised on four shaped reeded legs, stamped Liberty & Co. 067, 35cm. diameter.
(Bonhams) $157

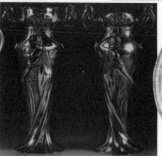

An Orivit pewter two handled wine cooler, of swollen cylinder form with scalloped rim, cast with flora, 23.7cm. (Bonhams) $406

WMF, a pair of figural vases, of twin handled flared cylindrical form with shaped rims, with maidens and flowers in relief, one with clear glass liner, 35.5cm. (Bonhams & Brooks) $2,603

An English pewter plate, late 17th century, with wriggle decoration overall, 22cm. diameter. (Christie's) $755

A Liberty Tudric pewter bowl with James Couper & Sons Clutha glass lining, Archibald Knox, circa 1902-1905, finned tripod support with streamlined bowl pierced and cast with stylized foliage, Clutha glass bowl 7in. high. (Christie's) $4,935

A Liberty pewter, copper and abalone shell mantel clock, attributed to Archibald Knox, circa 1902-1905, rectangular section rising to shaped face, inset with three elliptical abalone shell medallions and, 10in. high. (Christie's) $8,225

A Liberty English pewter three piece teaset, designed by Archibald Knox, circa 1902-1905, cast in relief with stylized honesty on whiplash stems, a similar hot-water and a tobacco jar and cover, teapot 4in. high. (Christie's) $1,233

'For Old Times Sake' a Liberty Tudric twin-handled vase, stamped marks, 010, 20cm. high. (Christie's) $575

A white metal tray, cast with two maidens in profile with stylized flora and foliage; and another with a harpist in relief, 24cm. (Bonhams) $279

A Liberty Tudric jug, stamped marks, 028, 23cm. high. (Bonhams) $515

An Edison Standard Phonograph, in oak case with original cover and black tin horn, with one cylinder, circa 1905.
(Auction Team Köln) $524

A Graphophone phonograph mechanism for a Columbia AT cylinder disk player, with hand crank, circa 1900.
(Auction Team Köln) $198

An Edison fireside phonograph, American, circa 1910, with model 'A' reproducer, bentwood oak cover, crank and painted red horn.
(Bonhams) $494

A Mae Starr phonograph doll with inbuilt phonograph mechanism by the Averill Mfg. Co., New York, for interchangeable wax disks, the doll with mohair wig, circa 1922.
(Auction Team Köln) $836

Edison cylinder phonograph with morning glory-form horn.
(Eldred's) $550

A Prairie du Chien phonolamp, unusual standard lamp with built-in gramophone, three lamps and original shade, circa 1920.
(Auction Team Köln) $2,972

A Moderne Edison disk phonograph, Type A100, No. 98915, with nickel-plated reproducer, gilt-lined bedplate, light oak case, 42in. high.
(Christie's) $589

A Pathé No. 1 early French cylinder disk player, lacking horn and reproducer, circa 1905.
(Auction Team Köln) $261

An Edison A100 ('Moderne') disc phonograph No.100442, with gilt-lined bedplate, disk reproducer, mahogany case with lattice pattern fret, 42in. high, with thirty early disks. (Christie's) $515

Royal Children, a rare photograph of all the children of George V (David, Bertie, Mary, Harry, George and John), signed by each of them, and dated *1916* by Mary, 132 x 89mm., [Sandringham?].
(Bonhams & Brooks) $1,087

Anonymous, Portrait groups of brothers and sisters, 1840s-50s, three sixth-plate daguerreotypes, one lightly hand-tinted, gilt-metal surrounds, in folding cases.
(Christie's) $86,337

Richard M. Nixon (1913-1994) and Golda Meir (1898-1978), signed black and white photograph, 8 x 10in., framed.
(Skinner) $690

Alice Broughton, Frances & Margaret Boughton, gravure on thick tissue, signed in pencil in the lower margin, light creases and a small loss upper right, image 203 x 156mm. (Bonhams) $1,001

Gleb Derujinsky, Carmen, Harper's Bazaar, 1959, silver gelatin print of model Carmen in French bistro La Grenouille, signed on reverse, printed later, image 15 x 15in.
(Skinner) $1,265

Palmieri, photograph of Diana Vreeland, 1960s, framed black and white photograph of Diana Vreeland taken for Women's Wear Daily in the 1960s, printed later, image 10¼ x 13½in.
(Skinner) $633

Ulysses S. Grant, signature *U.S. Grant* on monumental oval portrait photograph, 486 x 381mm., mounted on gold-ruled board with imprint of Bradley & Rulofson, San Francisco.
(Sotheby's) $4,800

Gleb Derujinsky, Harper's Bazaar photograph, 1959, silver gelatin print of a model in a dressing room, signed on reverse, printed later, image 15 x 15in.
(Skinner) $575

Cecil Beaton, mock puppet theatre, vogue, 1936, vintage silver gelatin print of models Angelica Welldon and Nina Matleva, stamped on the reverse, image 10 x 7½in.
(Skinner) $1,265

Cecil Beaton, Vogue, 1936, vintage silver gelatin print of a model in a flowered hat looking in a mirror, stamped *Photographed by Beaton, April 2, 1936*, image 9½ x 7½in.
(Skinner) $748

A mahogany and crossbanded square piano, by John Broadwood & Son, London and dated *1801*, with line inlay, and square tapering legs headed with brass ovals and joined by a shaped undertier, 64½in. wide. (Christie's) $2,302

An early 'square' pianoforte with 5-octave keyboard fitted with two lever stops, the Sheraton mahogany and satinwood case inlaid with marquetry, 5ft.3in. long, by Messrs. A. Bland & Weller, London, circa 1800. (Russell Baldwin & Bright) $814

Steinway grand piano, probably model B. Serial #216138 and also marked *#82840*, manufactured in 1923/24, 6ft.10in. long. (Eldred's) $15,400

A Steinway baby grand piano, early 20th century, rosewood cased, the case stamped *105331* and *A2085*. (Christie's) $11,512

A rare Classical ebonized and stencil decorated mahogany piano-forte, Joseph Hiskey, Baltimore, Maryland, circa 1820, opening to a keyboard, on lyre-form supports, 6ft. 1in. wide.
(Sotheby's) $7,200

A fine satinwood and harewood marquetry piano in the Adam taste, by C. Bechstein, serial no. 78501, the plain shaped lid with simple line inlay above sides decorated with bellflower trophies and swags, with a satinwood piano stool, 201cm. long.
(Bonhams) $19,305

Joseph Csaky, bird, circa 1924, plaster, 19¼in.
(Sotheby's) $16,530

A low relief plaster panel of Leda and the Swan, painted in brown, framed, 96.8cm.
(Bonhams) $368

Cement bear garden ornament, early 20th century, composed of cement over metal armature, weathered black paint, 55in. long.
(Skinner) $17,250

A plaster library bust, of a gentleman in military dress, inscribed to the reverse *D.Maggesi, fecit* and dated *1834*, 29½in. high.
(Christie's) $1,817

A pair of late 19th century Italian plaster figures of a male guitarist and female singer, each in naturalistically painted 18th century costume, 20in. high. (Thomson Roddick & Medcalf) $300

Antoine-Louis Barye, French (1795-1875), Le Général Bonaparte, equestrian statue, plaster, iron, later white paint, 96 x 80 x 40cm.
(Sotheby's) $107,000

A Gandharan plaster head, with serene expression and head-dress, the features naturalistically defined, mounted on a square metal stand, 8¾in. high, 4th century.
(Christie's) $538

Franz von Stuck, serpentine dancers panel, 1895, painted gesso relief, modelled as two female dancers in diaphanous robes, 61.5cm. x 100cm.
(Sotheby's) $14,904

A Gandharan fragmentary stucco head of a Buddha with pendulous earlobes and serene expression, the tightly curled hair worn in topknot, 14in. high, 3rd / 4th century.(Christie's) $2,194

A Polyphon Nr. 43B walnut music box for 39.8cm. disks by Polyphon Musikwerke, Leipzig, 77-tone comb, with one disk, circa 1900. (Auction Team Köln) $1,201

A 19⅝in. upright polyphon with two combs, sprung drive sprocket, coin mechanism with flat-fronted drawer and typical walnut case, replacement pediment, 47½in. high, with approximately 75 discs. (Christie's) $7,222

A Polyphon Nr. 43 music box for 39.8cm. disks, inlaid walnut case with internal illustration, 77-tone comb, with one disk, 1900. (Auction Team Köln) $679

A 15⅝in. upright Polyphon with two combs and coin mechanism, in walnut case with fretwork door, 45½in. high, with 35 discs. (Christie's) $3,793

A 19⅝in. upright Polyphon with two combs, coin mechanism and typical walnut case with pierced spandrels, pediment with clock aperture, 51in. high. (Christie's) $5,740

A Polyphon 15½in. disk musical box, German, circa 1900, No.67454, in a walnut case, 54cm. wide, together with winding handle and thirty-two disks. (Bonhams) $3,388

A 24⅝in. Polyphon with nickel-plated top-wind motor, coin mechanism, balustrade pediment, disk-bin stand with integral drawers, 85in. high, with 27 disks. (Christie's) $10,836

A 19⅝in. table Polyphon, No. 10123, with two combs, in typical panelled and carved case, with inlaid lid, 26½in. wide, with fifteen disks. (Christie's) $3,973

François Dumont, (1751-1831), a lady and gentleman, she, facing left in lace-bordered low-cut cream dress, 71mm. diameter.
(Christie's) $8,887

Robert Mussard, (1713-1777), Stadhouder William IV Charles Henry Friso, Prince of Orange-Nassau, (1711-1751), facing right in gilt-studded armor, 55 x 73mm.
(Christie's) $8,332

Jan Gottlib Jannasch, (d.1804), a young gentleman, facing right in brown coat, spotted yellow waistcoat, signed and dated 1795, 67mm. diameter, silver-gilt frame.
(Christie's) $741

Pierre-Édouard Dagoty, (1775-1871), a boy, facing right in striped blue coat and trousers, 2¼in. diameter, gold mount.
(Christie's) $4,444

Henry Brooke Kirchoffer, circa 1805, an officer of the Royal Staff Corps, wearing scarlet uniform, with silver buttons and epaulettes, gilt-mounted rectangular papier-mâché frame, oval, 78mm. (Bonhams & Brooks) $1,120

Pierre-Édouard Dagoty, (1775-1871), a boy, facing right in striped blue short sleeved jacket and high waisted trousers, signed, 2¼in. diameter, gold mount.
(Christie's) $10,739

Jean-Baptiste Isabey, (1767-1855), a fine miniature of a young lady, facing right in extremely low-cut white dress, signed, oval, 2¾in. high, gilt-metal mount.
(Christie's) $51,842

Antoine Paul Vincent, (fl. circa 1800-1812), a musician, facing right in blue jacket with gold buttons, 110 x 103mm., gilt-metal mount.
(Christie's) $24,070

Antonín Bayer, (1767-), a mother, in profile to the right in white dress, her arms around her daughters, oval, 137mm. high.
(Christie's) $1,481

German School, circa 1810/1815, a young boy, facing right in light blue jacket, oval, 78mm. high, gilt-metal mount. (Christie's) $2,222

Circle of Adélaide Labille-Guiard, circa 1785, the painter Charles-Amédée van Loo, (1718-1795), facing right in red velvet coat and trousers, 3in. diameter, gilt-metal mount. (Christie's) $1,758

Antonín Bayer, (1767-1833), a gentleman believed to be Prince Schwarzenberg, standing with his arms around four young boys, oval, 148mm. high. (Christie's) $2,777

Jean-Baptiste Soyer, (1752-1828), a girl, facing right in claret-colored silk dress, turquoise sash, gold hoop earring, long brown hair, 74mm. diameter, plain gold mount. (Christie's) $2,592

Carl Kronnowetter, (1795-1837), a young officer, facing right in scarlet coat with silver-embroidered blue collar, signed and dated, oval, 74mm. high. (Christie's) $4,629

School of Campana, circa 1780, a mother and her sons, she, facing left in purple and gold striped dress with lace underdress and cuffs, 79mm. diameter, gilt-metal mount. (Christie's) $2,037

Auguste Joseph Carrier, 1800-1875, a lady, facing right in blue dress with fur stole caught under her belt and lace collar, 80mm. high, cast gilt-metal mount. (Christie's) $1,852

David André, (b. 1684), a young lady, facing left in blue silk day-gown with white underslip, enamel on gold, oval, 42mm. high, silver-gilt frame. (Christie's) $2,962

Jeremiah David Alexander Fiorino, (1797-1847), a young lady, facing left in low-cut white silk dress, signed, oval, 92mm. high. (Christie's) $7,036

Franz Lieder, (1780-1859), a young lady, facing right in white dress with high standing pleated collar, signed and dated, *1811*, oval, 3in. (Christie's) $8,887

Pierre-Louis Bouvier, (1765-1836), a young gentleman, facing right in blue coat with gold buttons, 73mm. diameter.(Christie's) $10,183

Anne Mee, (circa 1770/75-1851), a young lady, facing right in white dress, gold brooch pinned at corsage, 100mm. high, silver-gilt frame. (Christie's) $1,666

Adalbert Suchy, (1783-1849), Count Esterházy, Captain of the Hungarian Guard, facing right in fur-bordered scarlet coat, signed, oval, 79mm. high. (Christie's) $10,183

Charles-Pierre Cior, (1769-1840), a young lady, full face in black gauze dress sprigged with flowers, signed, octagonal, 74mm. high. (Christie's) $7,036

Circle of Richard Cosway, R.A., (1742-1821), Sir Wilfred Lawson, Bt., (died 1806), facing right in scarlet coat with blue lapels, 73mm. high. (Christie's) $1,296

Henry Bone, R.A., after Andrew Robertson, (1777-1845), Mrs Robert Hawthorn, facing right in white dress, fringed yellow shawl and blue lined purple cloak, enamel on copper, oval, 3¼in. high. (Christie's) $5,925

Nicolas Claude Vassal, (fl. 1766-1779), a young lady, facing right in lace-bordered purple dress, light green and white ribbon tied at corsage, enamel on copper, 54mm. diameter. (Christie's) $3,148

Richard Cosway, R.A., (1742-1821), a mother and her daughter, the mother facing left in white underdress, scalloped bordered gold striped stole draped on her left shoulder, 45mm. high, gold mount. (Christie's) $4,444

Louis Rodolphe Piccard, (1807-1888), Marie Jomini as a young girl, facing left in lace-bordered white dress, signed and dated, *1832*, oval, 3in. high.
(Christie's) $1,943

Portuguese School, circa 1835, Queen Maria II da Gloria of Portugal, facing left in lace-bordered pale blue dress, 2½in. diameter, gilt-metal mount.
(Christie's) $4,073

Anne Mee, (circa 1770-1851), a young lady, full face in white dress, red and green scarf tied with a green velvet bow in her long curling hair, oval, 68mm. high, gilt-metal frame. (Christie's) $6,480

Louis-Marie Dulieu De Chenevoux, 1752 – after 1795, a young lady as Diana the Huntress, facing left in loose white robe revealing her right breast, signed and dated *Dulieu / 1786*, oval, 98mm. high.
(Christie's) $2,037

Frédéric Dubois, (fl. circa 1780-1819), a young lady, facing right in low-cut white dress and red cashmere stole, signed, 72mm. diameter.
(Christie's) $27,773

Charles Shirreff, (b. circa 1750), Richard Marquis Wellesley, facing left in scarlet coat with loops of chain plait embroidery, oval, 3¼in. high, gilt-metal mount.
(Christie's) $2,037

Louis-Marie Dulieu de Chenevoux, (1752 – after 1795), the miniaturist Rouvier, facing right in purple coat with five alphabetised buttons, frilled cravat, short powdered wig, signed and dated *Dulieu 1790*, enamel on copper, 74mm. high.
(Christie's) $2,222

Carl-Christian Kanz, (1758 – after 1818), a young lady, facing left in white dress, green stole fastened at corsage by a gold brooch suspended from a purple ribbon, signed *Kanz*, enamel on copper, 65mm. diameter, gilt-metal mount.
(Christie's) $3,703

John Barry, (fl. 1784-1827), a young officer, facing left in scarlet coat with buff-colored facings, silver epaulette, frilled cravat and black stock, powdered hair, oval, 81mm. high, gilt-metal frame with twisted rope border.
(Christie's) $7,406

Bal du Moulin Rouge, mounted on linen, 116 x 78cm. (Onslows) $219

John Hassall, Irish Hunting Scene, Stephenson & Co's Biscuits, Londonderry, published by David Allen, mounted on linen, 64 x 51cm. (Onslows) $822

Paul Colin, Tabarin, lithograph in colors, 1928, 24 x 15½in. (Christie's) $3,611

Pirchan, Emil (1884-1957), Emil Pirchan Bühnenentwürfe, lithograph in colors, 1913, printed by München-Eggenfelden, Munich, 48½ x 36in. (Christie's) $920

Choppy, Lino Rosio published by Choppy Paris, mounted on linen, 158 x 118cm. (Onslows) $55

Handschin, Johannes, (1899-1948), Flims, lithograph in colors, circa 1935, printed by Wassermann & Co., Basel, 39½ x 27½in. (Christie's) $796

Brioni, lithograph in colors, printed by Coen & C., Milano, 29½ x 26in. (Christie's) $1,467

Price Daily! Squeeze 'Em and Drink 'Em, The Bitter Sweet Favourites, lemeon caricatures playing the piano, 50 x 38cm. (Onslows) $62

Kola Astier, offset lithograph in colors, backed on linen, 17 x 12in. (Christie's) $604

S Greco, Ireland Fly TWA mounted on linen, 102 x 66cm.. (Onslows) $274

E Mc Knight Kauffer, Germany Fly Pan American, 107 x 70cm. (Onslows) $164

Peter Max, Pan Am 747, published October 1969, 107 x 71cm. (Onslows) $205

Imperial Airways by Air to Anywhere, Quickest Route for Passengers and Goods between Paris-London, Paris-Basle-Zurich, mono photographic, pub Gale & Polden, 76 x 51cm. (Onslows) $1,099

Lucien Cavre, 1re Traversée de l'Atlantique Nord des Français, Costes & Bellonte, lithograph in colors, 1930, printed by La Publicité Sychronisée, Lyon, 15 x 11in. (Christie's) $505

The Greatest Air Service in the World, Hercules & Hannibal, Scylla, Atlanta & Scipio Classes, color lithographic poster catalogue with artwork by V L Danvers, pub December 1933, 75 x 49cm. (Onslows) $220

Raoul Vion, Hélice Normale, lithograph in colors, printed by G. Delattre & Cie., Paris, 63 x 47in. (Christie's) $4,145

Walter Ditz, Süddeutscher Flug 1912, lithograph in colors, 1912 printed by Consée, München, 43½ x 35½in. (Christie's) $1,208

Gwynn, British South American Airways In South America Tomorrow, printed by Vincent Brooks-Day, mounted on linen, 98 x 62cm. (Onslows) $411

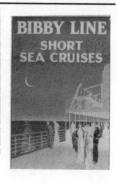

Allan Harker, Batavier Line London-Rotterdam, 101 x 68cm.
(Onslows) $603

Albert Sebille (1874-1953), Compagnie Generale Transatlantique, Havre, New York, lithograph in colors, circa 1910, printed by Ste. Gle. d'Impression, Paris, 31½ x 46in.
(Christie's) $3,000

Anon, Bibby Line Short Sea Cruises, 102 x 65cm.
(Onslows) $548

Poster, Liverpool & Great Western Steam Compy. Ltd., Guion Lion of United States Mail Steamers From Liverpool Every Wednesday and Saturday to New York…printed in red and black with central vignette of steamer (SS Wisconsin), circa 1880, 50 x 38cm.
(Onslows) $411

Leslie Arthur Wilcox, R.I., Three New Ships For The Heysham-Belfast Overnight Service, British Region, London Midland Region, lithograph in colors, 1956, printed by Jordison & Co., Ltd., London, backed on linen, 40 x 50in.
(Christie's) $1,986

William McDowell, "They're Off!" on a White Star Line Holiday to USA & Canada, printed by Charles Birchall no. PW1, mounted on linen, 49 x 33cm. (Onslows) $628

Cie de Navigation Paquet, by Max Ponty, 1929, lithograph in colors, printed by Hachard & Cie, Paris, backed on linen, 41 x 29in.
(Christie's) $1,175

Cunard Line Travellers' Cheques Cashed Here, printed tin hanging notice showing Mauretania, 17 x 24cm., and modern printed tin sign showing Lusitania, 29 x 42cm.
(Onslows) $103

Alick P F Ritchie, Canadian Pacific, Isn't this First Class? to Canada & USA from £38 return, mounted on linen, 101 x 63cm.
(Onslows) $1,884

Vic Welch, Trains Of Our Times, British Railways, London Midland Region, lithograph in colors, 1950 printed by London Lithographers, 40 x 50in. (Christie's) $790

Terence Cuneo, British Railways poster, Forging Ahead – The First British Railways Standard Express Locomotive, circa 1951, printed by Waterlow & Sons Ltd, London and Dunstable, 101 x 126cm. (Bearne's) $966

Anonymous, Isle of Wight, London Brighton and South Coast Railway, lithograph in colors, circa 1905, printed by Partington Advertising Co., backed on japan, 40 x 25in. (Christie's) $1,379

Doris Zinkeisen, Western Highlands, published by LNER, printed by John Waddington, 1936, signed by the artist, mounted on linen, 102 x 127cm. (Onslow's) $822

Modena Express, published by Minarelli, 101 x 71cm. (Onslows) $137

Terence Cuneo, British Railways (Western Region) poster, Clear Road Ahead – 'Monmouth Castle', circa 1949, printed by Waterlow & Sons Ltd, London and Dunstable, 101 x 126cm. (Bearne's) $828

Terence Cuneo, Royal Albert Bridge Saltash Designed And Built by Isambard Kingdom Brunel, published by BRWR, printed by Waterlow, 102 x 127cm. (Onslows) $575

Grun, Relax, Compagnie Maritime des Chargeurs Réunis, published by Bonsch, mounted on linen, 100 x 63cm. (Onslows) $69

Linford, Alan Carr (1926-), Oxford, British Railways, lithograph in colors, circa 1955, printed by Waterlow & Sons Limited, London, 40 x 50in. (Christie's) $1,138

Orient Line Cruises, Norway & Baltic, 20,000 ton Steamers, 101 x 61cm. (Onslows) $283

Picasso, Pablo (1881-1973), Côte d'Azur, lithograph in colors, circa 1962, printed by Mourlot, Paris, 39 x 26in. (Christie's) $1,011

Lee-Hankey, William (1869-1952), Dunoon, LNER, lithograph in colors, circa 1930, printed by McCorquodale & Co., Ltd., London, 40 x 50in. (Christie's) $683

Settala, Lloyd Triestino Africa, published in Italy, mounted on linen, 96 x 63cm. (Onslows) $384

Stanley Pellett, New Zealand Line, Regular Service via Panama Canal, printed by William Brown, 76 x 51cm. (Onslows) $110

Robert Johnston, Devon, British Railways, Western Region, offset lithograph in colors, 1960, printed by The Haycock Press Ltd., London, 40 x 50in. (Christie's) $722

Steinebach Wörthsee, by Wem Engelhardt, circa 1930, lithograph in colors, printed by H. Sonntag & Co., München, on two sheets, 67 x 47in. (Christie's) $858

Paul Ordner, Mont-Revard, PLM, lithograph in colors, circa 1930, printed by M. Décnaux, Paris, backed on linen, 39 x 24½in. (Christie's) $722

B.A. Zelenski, Womens World Ice Skating Championship, lithograph in colors, 1950, printed by Red Proletariat, backed on linen, 28½ x 39in. (Christie's) $1,100

Simon Garnier, Ecole de Ski de la Côte d'Azur, gouache, 1938, 39 x 24in. (Christie's) $1,714

Montana Vermala Sports Simplon Line, sepia photograph by Sadag, 102 x 65cm., and another photographic Schweizer Stadte, 76 x 51cm. (Onslows) $233

Carl Kunst, Bilgeri Ski Ausrustung, published by Reichold & Lang, 51 x 85cm. (Onslows) $123

Alexei Kow (Alexi Kogeynikov 1901-1978), Sports d'Hiver, Air France, lithograph in colors, 1951 printed by Edicta, Paris, backed on linen. 39 x 24in. (Christie's) $992

Suvretta House St Moritz International Favourite, photo/art published by Amstutz mounted on linen, 102 x 65cm. (Onslows) $274

Erich Erler (1870-1946), Winter in Bayern, lithograph in colors, 1905, printed by Klein & Volbert, München, backed on linen, 28½ x 37½in. (Christie's) $4,800

Musati, Cervinia, offset lithograph in colors, 1953, printed by Gros Monti & C., Torino, backed on linen, 27½ x 19½in. (Christie's) $1,534

A pieced cotton quilted coverlet, Lancaster County, Pennsylvania, 1925-1935, worked in variously patterned and colored cotton calico blocks of sample quilting patterns, a mask depicting a face and the names *ELMER, ROLLO* and *ANNIE*, 90 x 68in. (Christie's) $1,528

A pieced and embroidered wool coverlet, American, dated *1899*, worked in sixty-five chenille-embroidered squares centering yellow, red, green, pink, purple, orange, dark blue, turquoise, cream and mint floral bursts, 76 x 66in. (Christie's) $2,760

An Amish pieced wool and cotton quilted coverlet, initialled *J.L.*, Lancaster County, Pennsylvania, early 20th century, worked in the Diamond-in-the-Square pattern centering a red diamond on a square tan ground enclosed by a red inner border and green outer border, 77 x 77in. (Christie's) $1,410

An Amish pieced wool quilted coverlet, Lancaster County, Pennsylvania, late 19th/ early 20th century, worked in red, brown, light blue, cream and green in the Sunshine and Shadow pattern within a red border enclosed by a brown border, 75 x 74½in. (Christie's) $1,410

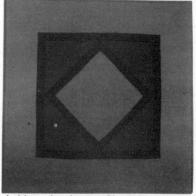

A pieced cotton and wool quilted coverlet, Pennsylvania, circa 1880, worked in red calico and white cotton and wool in the Log Cabin pattern against a green calico ground enclosed by a paisley calico surround, 95 x 90in. (Christie's) $940

An Amish wool and cotton Diamond in the square quilted coverlet, Lancaster County, Pennsylvania, circa 1900, the central pink salmon diamond enclosed by a crimson inner border, 80½in. high, 79½in. wide. (Christie's) $5,640

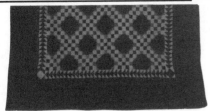

An Amish pieced wool quilted coverlet, Lancaster County, Pennsylvania, circa 1940, worked in purple, salmon, and teal in the Double Irish Chain pattern against a purple ground within a purple and teal Flying Geese inner border, 86½ x 85in. (Christie's) $2,115

An Amish pieced cotton and wool quilted coverlet, Lancaster County, Pennsylvania, circa 1915, worked in red and green in the Bars pattern enclosed within a blue border surrounded by red binding, 82 x 80in. (Christie's) $7,638

An Amish wool and cotton Sunshine and Shadow quilted coverlet, Lancaster County, Pennsylvania, first quarter 20th century, the central square worked in the Sunshine and Shadow pattern in pink, blue, green, salmon, slate, black, purple, sage, cornflower, bone and crimson, 79in. square. (Christie's) $3,055

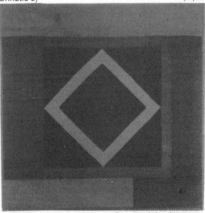

An Amish wool and cotton Diamond in the square quilted coverlet, Lancaster County, Pennsylvania, circa 1900, with plum central diamond framed by sage green surround on a plum ground with orange inner border and blue and blue-gray outer border, 81¼ x 79in. (Christie's) $2,350

An Amish pieced wool, cotton and silk crepe quilted coverlet, Lancaster County, Pennsylvania, circa 1930, worked in the Diamond-in-the-Square pattern centering a cinnamon diamond in a square aqua-marine ground, 76 x 75in. (Christie's) $4,113

A pieced and appliquéd cotton quilted coverlet, American, early 20th century, worked in green and yellow cotton calicoes in four blocks, each centering fern fronds flanked by sawtooth sashing and surround, 86 x 83in. (Christie's) $1,058

A Siemens 31W radio with giant dial, 1930/31.
(Auction Team Köln) $46

An Emerson lacquered mains receiver, No. 414134, with four valves, in wood case with Chinoiserie lacquer on black ground, 10in. wide.
(Christie's) $552

A Sparton Blue Mirror designer radio. (Auction Team Köln) $367

A German Army Type EP 2a direction finding receiver for detecting enemy shortwave transmitters, 70-3,600 KHz range, 1942. (Auction Team Köln) $3,136

A rare German Army Fu.NP.Ea/c close range direction finder for pinpointing enemy transmissions, 1942. (Auction Team Köln) $4,704

A German Army Type Fu.H.E.C. radio receiver to detect and listen to enemy radios, 1944.
(Auction Team Köln) $5,227

A Telefunken Jubilate clock radio for long, medium and short wave reception.
(Auction Team Köln) $52

A Brownie two-stage note magnifier and crystal set in complementary black molded cases, the note magnifier with two valves, 30cm. wide circa 1926.
(Christie's) $1,353

A Lorenz Weekend Junior 4-valve portable radio for mains and battery power, dark red bakelite case, with original carrying case.
(Auction Team Köln) $88

A Siemens Modell 219 radio, 1930/31.
(Auction Team Köln) $130

Dieter Rams, Germany, 'Weltempfanger' World Receiver, model T 1000, for Braun, 1968. Satin finish aluminum body with pierced hole speaker and black leather top.(Bonhams) $1,180

A Siemens Schatulle M47 with 11 valves. (Auction Team Köln) $254

An Elko three valve receiver, the walnut case with black front panel and cupboards below, an oak Amplion horn speaker and a pair of Sterling headphones.
(Christie's) $479

A 5-watt German Army Telefunken Type 5WSc radio transmitter, in original condition, circa 1944.
(Auction Team Köln) $1,724

A Torn.Fu.h German Army radio telephone transmitter, with original valves, 1942.
(Auction Team Köln) $2,613

A German Army Type 15 WSEb radio telephone, 1943.
(Auction Team Köln) $1,306

A Sterling Anodion Four receiver, Type R 1610, No. 2542, with four valves, on hinged walnut base with BBC transfer, 16½in. wide, circa 1924. (Christie's) $3,432

A Bruckner & Stark VE 301G direct current receiver, in wooden casing, 1933. (Auction Team Köln) $99

A tinplate robot Answer Game calculating toy, a rare first model still without cancellation lever, some renovations, circa 1963.
(Auction Team Köln) $792

A 'Robby the Robot' mechanised battery operated robot, Japanese 1955-60, the tinplate Nomura robot finished in black and red, with battery compartments to legs, 13in. tall. (Bonhams) $551

A blue painted tinplate toy Planet Robot by KO-Yoshiya, Japan, clockwork, with rubber hands, and stop lever, after 'Robby the Robot', 22cm. high, circa 1960.
(Auction Team Köln) $394

A Mars King lithographed tinplate battery powered robot, with siren and flashing screen, by S.H. Horikawa, circa 1965, 24cm. high, in original box.
(Auction Team Köln) $459

Masudaya for Linemar 'R-35' Robot, pale metallic silvery-blue lithographed tinplate with red, black and yellow details, battery operated by remote control, 7¼in.
(Christie's) $766

A red lithographed tinplate Cragstan Astronaut robot by Yonezawa, Japan, with flywheel driven by a handle at the back, arms move and it runs about, 24cm. high, circa 1955.
(Auction Team Köln) $493

A blue lithographed tinplate clockwork Super Hero robot, Japanese, with plastic head, 23.5cm. high, circa 1975.
(Auction Team Köln) $158

A Daiya battery operated 'Ranger Robot', Japanese, circa 1955, the plastic and tinplate Robot with clear plastic body showing inner workings, in original box.
(Bonhams & Brooks) $1,237

A lithographed tinplate Super Hero clockwork robot, with plastic head, large golden horns and red wings, 24cm. high, circa 1975, in original box. (Auction Team Köln) $144

Michael Jackson, signed color 8 x 10, half-length standing, singing into microphone.
(Vennett Smith) $96

A Beatles scarf *Beatlemania Sweeps Australia*, 26 x 27in., made in Italy, 1964.
(Collector's Corner) $110

Shania Twain, signed color 8 x 10, half-length wearing exotic corset.
(Vennett Smith) $41

Frank Zappa, signed page, removed from a visitors' book, annotated in his hand Sorry about the Mussels, 1984.
(Vennett Smith) $99

Adam Ant/Stuart Goddard, a cropped military-style black sparkly stage jacket, the front decorated with two rows of silvered metal buttons engraved with floral design.
(Christie's) $727

Paul McCartney, signed and inscribed color 5 x 8, to lower white border, half-length wearing blue T-shirt with one hand raised to mouth. (Vennett Smith) $138

Britney Spears, signed color 8 x 10, half-length in blue dress, first name only.
(Vennett Smith) $73

The Corrs, signed color 8 x 10, by all four members (first names only).
(Vennett Smith) $174

Miles Davis, signed 4 x 6 postcard three quarter length standing holding trumpet, signed *Miles D!*
(Vennett Smith) $206

Simon & Garfunkel, signed color 8 x 10, by both Paul Simon and Art Garfunkel, half-length.
(Vennett Smith) $188

Elvis Presley, signed piece, 3 x 2in., 1960.
(Vennett-Smith) $554

Cher, signed color 8 x 10, full-length kneeling in skimpy top and fishnet tights.
(Vennett Smith) $49

Madonna, signed color 8 x 10, three quarter length standing in revealing pose, wearing exotic jewellery.
(Vennett Smith) $151

A Beatles 'Flip Your Wig' board game, by Milton Bradley, USA, 1964, complete.
(Collector's Corner) $184

Madonna, a two-piece flamenco-style stage outfit, made for Madonna by Jean-Paul Gaultier for her stage performance of Holiday during the 1990 Blonde Ambition Tour, 7 x 5½in.
(Christie's) $21,804

JOHN LEE HOOKER

John Lee Hooker, signed 5.75 x 7.25 magazine photo, head and shoulders with guitar.
(Vennett Smith) $87

INXS, signed 12in. record sleeve to cover, by all six individually, inc. Michael Hutchence, Need You Tonight, record still present.
(Vennett Smith) $165

Stevie Wonder, signed and inscribed 8 x 10, half-length seated by electric organ, scarce.
(Vennett Smith) $87

Elvis Presley, signed postcard, head and shoulders, published by Druck 430, serrated edge. (Vennett Smith) $508

Grease, signed color 10 x 8 by both Olivia Newton John and John Travolta. (Vennett Smith) $131

Meatloaf, signed color 8 x 10, half length with fists clenched. (Vennett Smith) $51

 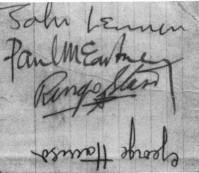 

Grease, signed color 8 x 10, by both John Travolta and Olivia Newton John (partially in dark portion), head and shoulders publicity shot from Grease. (Vennett Smith) $123

The Beatles, a small white feint lined card (3 x 2.5), signed by all four of The Beatles, apparently obtained by the vendor at a concert at Norwich Memorial Hall, Cheshire, in the early 1960s. (Vennett Smith) $1,833

Paul McCartney, signed and inscribed 4 x 6, three quarter length standing with arms folded before microphone, with simple additional doodle of a smiling face beneath signature. (Vennett Smith) $197

Madonna, signed 8 x 10, three quarter length standing in revealing black leather, with another woman kneeling before her in S and M pose. (Vennett Smith) $226

The Spice Girls, signed color 10 x 8 by all five, Melanie Chisholm, Emma Bunton, Victoria Adams, Mel B and Geri Halliwell, each with first names only, three quarter length standing in group pose at open air concert. (Vennett Smith) $151

Elvis Presley, a black and white polka dot cotton long sleeved shirt owned and worn by the King labelled Cutler and Company. (Bonhams) $1,738

A Linda McCartney photograph of Jimi Hendrix, June 1968, printed later, a black and white photograph of Jimi Hendrix playing guitar in the Record Plant, New York, 25.5 x 20cm. (Bonhams) $336

Jimi Hendrix's lucky silver dollar, owned late 1966-early 1970, the 1889 silver one dollar coin with milled edges, carried in Jimi's shoe or hat band, 3.7cm. diameter. (Bonhams) $2,240

A boxing programme autographed by Paul McCartney, Empire Pool, Wembley, March 12th 1974, signed in black ballpoint, on the front of the programme, 25 x 19cm. (Bonhams) $248

An autographed Jimi Hendrix/Walker Brother's Official Tour Programme, signed *Jimi Hendrix, Keep Cool Mitch, Cheers Noel Redding* in blue ballpoint, 26.5 x 20cm. (Bonhams) $1,960

'Four Faces of John Lennon' by Bob Gruen 1974, printed later, taken as part of the photo session for the 'Walls & Bridges' album cover, signed and dated Bob Gruen NYC'90 in silver pen, 72.5 x 69.5cm.(Bonhams) $773

An autographed Jimi Hendrix Experience/The Move Official Tour Programme, November 1967, signed by Roy Wood from The Move and by three members of the Outer Limits, 20.5 x 26.5cm. (Bonhams) $2,800

A guitar autographed by Bo Diddley and Chuck Berry, circa 1997, signed Rock On From Bo Diddley 97 and Chuck Berry in blue marker on the cream body of a Fender Stratocaster. (Bonhams) $469

A Rolling Stones concert poster, Tunlinga, Tennishallen, Stockholm, April 3rd 1966, the black and white poster featuring images of The Rolling Stones, 98 x 69cm. (Bonhams) $1,794

A guitar autographed by The Rolling Stones, signed Mick Jagger, Keith Richards, Charlie B. and Ronnie Wood in black ink on the cream body of a electric Peavey Reactor guitar. (Bonhams) $759

Paul McCartney, signed 4 x 6 postcard, head and shoulders. (Vennett Smith) $123

A pair of gloves owned, worn and autographed by Madonna, the black Givenchy gloves with gold colored studs, signed on one glove Madonna in gold marker, framed. (Bonhams) $828

Gene Vincent, signed concert programme to front cover portrait, The Gene Vincent Show at Belfast. (Vennett Smith) $178

The Beatles, a 2.75 x 5.5 thick card, signed in red by Ringo Starr, Paul McCartney, George Harrison and John Lennon. (Vennett Smith) $1,190

Jimi Hendrix's vintage Epiphone FT79 guitar, owned late 1967-spring 1970, with ivory bound spruce top and ivory bound maple back and sides. (Bonhams) $77,000

Jimi Hendrix's Stars and Stripes stage shirt, 1970, the printed muslin shirt with two button down breast pockets, seven button front, flared collar and sleeves. (Bonhams) $22,400

A rare Track Records promotional poster of Jimi Hendrix, English, late 1967, a black and white portrait of Jimi photographed by Donald Silverstein on October 18th 1967, 74 x 48cm. (Bonhams) $560

An autographed photograph of The Beatles, 1960s, signed John Lennon, Paul McCartney, George Harrison and Ringo Starr in blue ballpoint, on a promotional Dezo Hoffmann photograph. (Bonhams) $5,796

An autographed photograph of Michael Jackson, signed in black marker, on a color promotional photograph, 25 x 20cm. (Bonhams) $152

Bakhshaish Carpet, Northwest Persia, second half 19th century, stepped diamond medallion with rosette pendants, on the camel field, sky blue spandrels, 12ft.2in. by 8ft. (Skinner) $10,350

Hooked rug, probably Amish, Ohio, late 19th /early 20th century, a bold design of multicolored circles, scallops, and sunburst, 39 x 37in. (Skinner) $2,185

Shirvan rug, East Caucasus, last quarter 19th century, three 'Memling' guls in red, royal blue, black, ivory, gold, and tan, 4ft.6in. x 3ft.4in. (Skinner) $431

A Qum carpet, Central Persia, the field with vertical panels containing polychrome flowering, leafy and fruit vines, in shaded brick red border of stylized turtle-palmettes, 344 x 236cm. (Christie's) $3,619

A Caucasian rug from the Karabagh region, the madder ground with two large guls in green, pink and blue, each flanked by a pair of birds, early 20th century, 6ft.6in. x 4ft.3in. (Andrew Hartley) $667

A fine Kashan rug, Central Persia, the shaded medium blue field with palmettes, serrated leaves and floral sprays around a shaded rust medallion with pendants containing rosette centerpiece, 208 x 136cm. (Christie's) $1,397

A Kazak rug, South Caucasus, the blue and red speckled field around two and a half large octagonal panels containing rosettes and hooked panels together with birds and animals, 224 x 140cm. (Christie's) $1,233

A wool and cotton hooked rug, American, 1920-1940, worked in various green-grays, blue, brown, taupe, red, pink, black and orange fibers depicting a Victorian domestic interior with young man proposing to his intended, 46½ x 36in. (Christie's) $11,750

A fine Sarouk rug, West Persia, the shaded indigo field with overall design of delicate floral sprays, in a shaded brick-red border with angular stylized flowering vine, 191 x 127cm. (Christie's) $1,068

A Karachov rug, Central Caucasus, 196 x 142cm.
(Bonhams) $2,499

Soumak carpet, Northeast Caucasus, last quarter 19th century, 8ft. x 6ft.4in.
(Skinner) $7,188

Kuba rug, Northeast Caucasus, mid 19th century, (slight even wear, rewoven ends), 5ft.6in. x 3ft.8in.
(Skinner) $4,887

A fine part silk Qum rug, the ivory field with large polychrome boteh and stylized floral panels on ends and sides, central shaded yellow cusped medallion with pendants containing Mother and Child boteh, 228 x 142cm.
(Christie's) $1,809

One of a pair of Russian silk Qum rugs, woven by Rashti Zadeh, the rust field with central floral medallion in navy blue and ivory, and similar boteh to the corners, 20th century, 60 x 42.
(Andrew Hartley) (Two) $2,712

An antique Kirman Laver rug, South Persia, the indigo field and stylized flowering trees, perching birds, floral sprays together with human figures and plants.
(Christie's) $6,199

Hooked rug, Duchess County, New York, late 19th century, centered with an urn of flowers, chevron border with a leaf at each corner, 92½ x 59½in.
(Skinner) $18,400

A fine antique Kuba-Shirvan rug, the shaded indigo field with two brick-red and ivory stylized, medallions surrounded by hooked lozenges, small rosettes and stepped panels, 147 x 135cm.
(Christie's) $2,055

Tabriz rug, North West Persia, the shaded blue-gray field scattered with animals, palmettes, flowering vine, cloudband and palmette panels, 271 x 178cm.
(Christie's) $1,974

Tekke Main carpet, West Turkestan, mid-19th century, four columns of ten midnight blue, red, ivory, and blue-green main carpet guls on the deep aubergine field, 10ft.4 x 6ft.3in.
(Skinner) $8,625

Figural hooked rug, America, 19th century, the central reserve with eight black and gray chickens surrounded by red and pink flower blossoms, 27½ x 36in.
(Skinner) $690

A semi-antique Paotou rug, dark blue border and pattern on ivory field, 180 x 124cm.
(Stockholms AV) $835

A 'Donnemara' Donegal carpet, designed by C.F.A. Voysey, circa 1902, the field woven in alternate scrolling cartouches of poppies and tulips supported by sinuous foliage, 168 x 123in.
(Christie's) $27,600

A cotton and wool hooked rug, American, dated 1917, worked in red, blue, gray, black, pink, various greens and cream fibres depicting a central abstracted black horse against a cream barn-shaped ground, 41 x 45¼in.
(Christie's) $9,400

A late 19th century Kashan carpet, the center with a series of medallions in ivory pink, blue and yellow on a blue ground, the border with stylized palmettes and flowers on an ivory ground, 415 x 300cm.
(Finarte) $11,499

A Perepedil rug, mid-blue field with typical ram's horn motifs to the center and side divided by a row of archaic animal forms, 5ft.9in. x 4ft.4in.
(Woolley & Wallis) $1,413

Pictorial wool hooked rug, 19th century, naïve depiction of a woman, cow, house, and dog, with a path leading to a pump with trees and flowers, 40 x 44in.
(Skinner) $10,350

Meshed carpet, Northeast Persian, late 19th century, large circular medallion surrounded by floral motifs on the cochineal field, 13ft.8 x 9ft.9in. (Skinner) $4,025

Needlework sampler, *wrought by Elliza H. Emerson aged 12 years*, flanked by two flowering baskets, above two pious verses, 17½ x 16½in. (Skinner) $1,265

Needlework sampler, *Miranda J. Sweet born in Georgetown May 18, 1818*, alphabets and an inspirational verse worked in black thread, 17¼ x 7¾in. (Skinner) $460

Framed Dutch sampler, late 18th/early 19th century, with floral border, central Dutch-style house with windmill above, mermaid below, signed *Elizabet Poth*, frame size 20⅝ x 20⅝in. (Skinner) $575

English cross-stitch sampler, dated *1836*, stitched on muslin with rows of practice motifs including floral vases, peacocks, animals, trees, and human figures, signed *Caroline Brown*, 17 x 16in. (Skinner) $978

Needlework sampler, wrought by Sally Jackson, 1771, Boston Fishing Lady School, row of alphabet above an inspirational verse, the central pictorial panel depicting a hilly landscape with leaping stag, 17½ x 20¾in. (Skinner) $123,500

Needlework sampler, *Charlotte G. Richardson Aged 13yrs. Lancaster 1825*, (Massachusetts), panels of alphabets and numerals with a band of geometric flowers above the identification, 16½ x 16½in. (Skinner) $1,495

Needlework sampler, *Eirene Smith aged 14yrs. East Sudbury June 18th 1816*, alphabet panel above pious verse over a scene with two houses and a pond, 16⅛ x 16⅝in. (Skinner) $2,300

A silk-on-linen needlework sampler, signed by Catherine Congdon (b.1758), Newport, dated *1773*, depicting a shepherdess with crook and male figure in a landscape with animals, 15½in. high, 11½in. wide. (Christie's) $28,750

Knox family needlework register, late 18th/early 19th century, Emily Knox maker, Berwick, Maine, dated *1826*, walnut frame. (Skinner) $2,530

An American No. 1, the head of an American domestic sewing machine, with shuttle and original cover, circa 1875.
(Auction Team Köln) $590

A German Müeller child's chain-stitch sewing machine, circa 1925.
(Auction Team Köln) $141

An early American New England type domestic sewing machine by Nettleton & Raymond, circa 1859, incomplete.
(Auction Team Köln) $214

A Humboldt swing shuttle domestic sewing machine by Haid & Neu, Karlsruhe, with shuttle, circa 1900.
(Auction Team Köln) $235

A Colibri early German child's sewing machine with Bremer & Brückmann name on sewing plate, cover marked *Brunsviga (Grimme Natalis) Braunschweig*, circa 1890.
(Auction Team Köln) $156

An Ideal British chainstitch domestic sewing machine of unusual design, chrome plated and in original box, circa 1920.
(Auction Team Köln) $170

A Colibri child's sewing machine by Bremer & Brückmann, Braunschweig, black cast iron with bright gold decoration, circa 1890.
(Auction Team Köln) $365

A Shaw & Clark Skinny Pillar sewing machine, circa 1864.
(Auction Team Köln) $1,768

A Müller No. 15 child's sewing machine by Müller, Berlin, cast iron with gold decoration, circa 1920.
(Auction Team Köln) $198

A Lead British chain-stitch sewing machine, circa 1930.
(Auction Team Köln) $186

A KK child's sewing machine similar to the Singer 20, circa 1935.
(Auction Team Köln) $85

A Müeller No.0 child's sewing machine with chain-stitch gripper.
(Auction Team Köln) $85

Engraved polychrome decorated whale's tooth, 19th century, obverse depicting a sailor holding an American flag, 4½in. long. (Skinner) $632

Engraved polychrome decorated whale's tooth, 19th century, obverse lettered with *U.S.* above an eagle and American flag, 4¾in. long. (Skinner) $2,300

A fine and rare pair of engraved and scrimshawed walrus tusks, initialled S.L., probably American, dated 1860, engraved as a family record, 16½in. long. (Sotheby's) $6,325

SHELLS

A marine cephalopod mollusc (ammonoidea), of large size, mounted on a marble base, 24½in. high. (Christie's) $1,899

Four late Victorian 'Sailor's Favors', all of octagonal form and mounted on stand with slender cabriole legs, the upper tiers 14in. square, the lower tiers 9in. square. (Canterbury) $4,576

Chinese cameo-carved nautilus shell, 19th century, the shell carved with writhing dragons, birds and animals amidst scrolling floral vines, label reads *U.S. Grant World Tour*. (Sotheby's) $1,440

SILHOUETTES

English School, circa 1780, a young gentleman, profile to the left, with hair en queue, cut-out on card with painted details, oval, 86mm. high. (Bonhams & Brooks) $196

English School, a pair of silhouettes of a lady and gentleman, 19th century, full length portraits, with white heightening, set in glazed rosewood frames with gilt slip 28 x 18cm. (Bonhams) $568

Augustin Edouart, silhouette of the Rev. E Gifford, full length profile to the left, cut out on card, signed and dated *1828*, 9½ x 6¼in. maple frame. (Andrew Hartley) $139

Thomas Wheeler, circa 1767-8, a lady, profile to the right, her hair in a chignon, wearing fichu and dormeuse indoor cap, oval, 90mm. high. (Bonhams) $706

Hubard Gallery, 1832, Peter Cox Esq., full-length, profile to the right, wearing great coat, cut-out on card, rectangular, 8½in. high. (Bonhams & Brooks) $560

John Wass, 1820, a gentleman, profile to the right, wearing coat and stock, painted on card and bronzed, oval, 3in. high. (Bonhams & Brooks) $238

Mrs. Mary Lightfoot, circa 1790, a Gentleman, profile to the right, wearing coat with frilled cravat and bound pigtail wig, painted on plaster, oval, 3½in. high. (Bonhams) $628

August Edouart, 1840, full cut silhouette of Charles Burrall Hoffman, 1837, signed on a lithographed background, 11 x 8in. framed. (Skinner) $1,265

A. Charles, circa 1790, a gentleman, profile to the left, his hair in a Ramillies plait, wearing double-breasted coat with large buttons, oval, 5¼in. high. (Bonhams & Brooks) $490

English School, circa 1790, Frances Couch, as a young Lady, profile to the right, her long hair tied with a ribbon, painted on card, gilded hammered brass frame, oval, 4in. high. (Bonhams) $617

English School, circa 1835, a charming portrait of a girl and a boy; she, profile to the right, wearing low-cut dress, he, profile to the left, wearing Petersham coat, cut-outs on card, 10½in. high. (Bonhams) $580

John Miers, circa 1786-7, a pair of profiles of Henry, 3rd Duke of Buccleuch and his wife Elizabeth, painted on plaster, hammered brass frames, ovals, 88mm. high. (Bonhams) $2,499

George Bruce, circa 1810, Daniel Hay, as a boy, profile to the left, wearing coat, tied stock and frilled cravat, painted on plaster, oval, 3in. high. (Bonhams) $853

English School, circa 1830, a young girl, full-length, profile to the left, wearing dress and pantaloons, she holds a basket, cut-out on card, 7¼in. high. (Bonhams & Brooks) $770

J. ? Watkins, circa 1805, a lady, profile to the left, wearing dress with high collar and white lace ruff. 73mm. high. (Bonhams & Brooks) $252

M. H. Frost, circa 1830, a young gentleman, profile to the left, wearing coat and tied white stock, rectangular, 81mm. high. (Bonhams & Brooks) $392

George Atkinson, 1814, Lieutenant Colonel Henry Le Blanc, profile to the left, with side-whiskers, painted on card and bronzed, dated on reverse and with the sitter's name, oval, 3in. high. (Bonhams) $279

Hubard Gallery, circa 1830, a gentleman, standing, full-length, profile to the left, his hair en queue, wearing long coat, cut-out on card, gilded wood frame, 265mm. high. (Bonhams & Brooks) $224

Mrs. Edward Smyth, 1835, Mrs. Charles Upham Barry (née Emily Matilda Dodd), profile to the left, her hair in an Apollo knot, painted on card and bronzed, oval, 3¾in. high. (Bonhams & Brooks) $630

Augustin Edouart, 1838, William Shorthouse of Moseley, full-length, profile to the left, reading a copy of The Times, cut-out on card on a watercolor background, 304mm. high. (Bonhams) $676

Charles Rosenberg, circa 1808-9, a Lady, profile to the left, wearing edged veil over bonnet decorated with flowers, painted on convex glass backed with card, oval, 72mm. high. (Bonhams) $502

A George II silver basket, Simon Le Sage, London, 1758, shaped oval and on plain rim foot, 31.5cm. long, 24oz. (Christie's) $3,073

An Edwardian silver-gilt basket, William Comyns, 1910, the shaped oval basket with pierced foliate scroll motif sides below a rose and scroll rim, 27.8cm., 53.5oz. (Christie's) $6,251

English silver footed basket, maker's mark *GJ & DF*, London, 1907, oval, the shaped molded rim above reticulated foliate sides with central cartouches, approximately 20 troy oz. 12½in. long. (Skinner) $920

A George II oval swing-handled cake basket, by Samuel Herbert & Co., 1752, the sides pierced with quatrefoils, beads, scrolls and anthemions, the swing handle with cast animal head and fishtail decoration, 36.5cm. long, 63oz. (Bonhams) $7,840

A Russian mounted cut-glass circular swing-handled basket, 1908/17, the rim attractively decorated with continuous pairs of pheasants amidst foliage between floral borders, 26cm. diameter. (Bonhams) $1,400

A George III oval boat-shaped sugar basket by Hester Bateman, 1788, with swing handle, bead borders, oval pedestal foot and engraved squirrel crest, 17.3cm. long, 7oz. (Bonhams) $1,540

Sterling silver cake basket, Tiffany & Co., retailers, America, early 20th century, oblong, the waved pierced rim with molded scrolls and chased foliate decoration, approximately 52 troy oz., 14⅝in. long. (Skinner) $4,025

Napoleon Bonaparte interest:-A Russian bread or fruit basket, 1908/17, the rim applied on either side with a cut-out decoration of Napoleon, during the retreat from Moscow, 22oz. (Bonhams) $1,050

Ball, Black & Company silver sugar basket, New York, 1850s, footed navette form, chase floral and leaf decoration, swing handle, 6¾in. high., approximately 7½ troy oz. (Skinner) $460

Josef Hoffmann, elliptical vase, 1906, silver colored metal, loop handle, the underside stamped *Wiener Werkstätte*, 10¼in. (Sotheby's) $6,960

Sheffield plate reticulated basket, S. Smith & Son, England, second half 19th century, oval, with molded foliate rim, with embossed and reticulated sides and cast foliate handles, length to handles 13¾in. (Skinner) $460

A George III boat shaped sugar basket with a swing handle, engraved body and bead borders by Crispin Fuller, 1793, 17cm. wide, 8oz. (Christie's) $736

A George III silver handled basket, London 1784, John Lambe, the rim and body with two pierced borders with bright-cut decoration, engraved with a foliate swag and pierced with urns, approximate weight 28oz., 37.5cm. long.
(Bonhams & Brooks) $2,590

Continental silver and cut glass basket, probably Austro-Hungarian, mid 19th century, the molded rim above openwork bands with festoons of grape bunches amid portrait busts, approximately 9 troy oz., 9in. high. (Skinner) $575

A George III silver swing-handled basket, Sheffield 1802, Nathaniel Smith, George Smith and James Creswick, gadroon border, wirework body, approximate weight 29oz., 34cm. wide.
(Bonhams & Brooks) $1,820

A Georgian sugar basket, of panelled boat form with swing loop handle, London 1796, marks for Peter and Ann Bateman, 8oz. 1dwt. (Andrew Hartley) $473

A George III Provincial silver swing handled sugar basket, York 1796, reeded borders, reeded swing handle, on a raised spread oval foot, approximate weight 5oz., 12.5cm. wide.
(Bonhams & Brooks) $1,190

Antique American coin silver sugar basket, with swing handle and chased floral decoration, 5¾in. long, 7.2 troy oz.
(Eldred's) $495

A 19th century Chinese silver beaker, marked with pseudo English marks, maker's mark of Sunshing, plain tapering circular form, approximate weight 5oz., 10.3cm. high.
(Bonhams) $441

An early 18th century German parcel-gilt beaker, apparently struck only with two maker's marks, circa 1715, sides embossed with fruit and flowers, 10.7cm. high, 4oz.
(Bonhams) $770

An early 18th century German beaker, by Philipp Stenglin, Augsburg, 1708/10, of tapering shape with a wide band of spiral fluting above a spreading foot, traces of gilding, 12.4cm. high, 5oz.
(Bonhams) $1,260

An Edwardian silver medicine beaker, by Albert Barker, 1907, originally from a travelling dressing table set, the pull-off cover with bark finish, interior with an unmarked gilt funnel and glass liner, 8cm. high.
(Bonhams) $532

A 17th century German beaker, maker's mark rubbed, Cologne, mid 17th century, with engraved strapwork and foliate scroll and fruit motifs, centering figural medallions representing St. John the Baptist and other Religious figures, 8.3cm., 2.25oz. (Christie's) $4,836

An 18th century Continental beaker, probably Scandinavian, tapering circular form, engraved with circular panels of foliate decoration, and inscribed ØP.S, approximate weight 2oz., 7.2cm. high. (Bonhams) $308

BOWLS

A George III Irish sugar bowl, John Lloyd, Dublin, circa 1770, the circular section bowl raised on three shell capped hoof feet, decorated with beaded lobes, 5½in., 6oz.
(Christie's) $596

Frank Whiting lobed bowl, North Attleboro, Massachysetts, early 20th century, circular, the everted rim with openwork edge and molded foliate decoration, approximately 7 troy oz., 7¾in. diameter. (Skinner) $230

An Irish silver bowl and stand, Dublin 1915, George Edward & Son, on four scrolled legs with mythical dolphin feet, with a pierced and engraved Celtic apron, approximately 26oz.
(Bonhams & Brooks) $1,278

Gorham sterling silver and vermeil punch bowl, Providence, 1905, circular, with molded rim, the body with embossed spiral reeding amid chased foliates, approximately 128 troy oz., diameter 15in.
(Skinner) $8,050

An American silver two-handled punch bowl and silver and ivory ladle, Gorham Mfg. Co., Providence, RI, Martelé, .950 standard, 1900-1901, 120oz gross.
(Sotheby's) $43,125

A George III Irish sugar bowl, Matthew West, Dublin, 1784, of circular section, raised on three hoof feet with shell terminals, 5½in., 7oz. (Christie's) $818

An American silver 'Japanese style' ice bowl and liner, Tiffany & Co., New York, 1877-1883, etched with aquatic plants and applied with fish, 606gr., 5in. high.
(Sotheby's) $6,990

An American silver large centerpiece bowl, Gorham Mfg. Co., Providence, RI, 1893, in the form of a large shell, the front with a figure of Venus, 5334gr., 16in. long.
(Sotheby's) $21,850

A George I Scottish covered sugar bowl, raised on a molded spreading foot, the cover with a cut out for a spoon, 3¾in., Harry Beathune, Edinburgh, 1725 , 12oz.
(Woolley & Wallis) $7,938

A late Victorian silver Monteith bowl, London 1898, Joshua Vander, detachable Monteith rim with a scroll border, the bowl with molded borders, approximate weight 50oz., diameter of bowl 26.5cm.
(Bonhams & Brooks) $1,820

Tiffany & Co. presentation bowl, New York, circa 1899, circular, the everted shaped rim with embossed clovers, with presentation inscription to center, approximately 26 troy oz., 12½in. diameter.
(Skinner) $1,150

An Art Nouveau silver bowl, London 1900, Liberty & Co., the exterior of the bowl applied with four stylized scroll legs, approximate weight 6oz., diameter of bowl 10.5cm.
(Bonhams & Brooks) $672

A George IV silver snuff-box, William Eaton, London, 1825, the hinged cover inset with a plaque cast and chased with a hunting scene, with gilt interior, 3¼in. long, 4oz. (Christie's) $3,981

A Continental box, English import marks for William Moering, 1894, each side decorated with genre scenes in the manner of Teniers, 10.7cm. long, 10oz. (Christie's) $564

A silver box and cover by the Guild of Handicrafts, stamped marks, London 1902 (restoration to enamelling), 10.7cm. diameter. (Bonhams) $1,323

An unusual silver biscuit box with cover, Peter L. Krider Co., Philadelphia, circa 1875, the sides repoussé and chased with scenes of ships arriving in a harbor being met by horsemen, a church and a fort, 8in. diameter, 47oz. (Christie's) $4,600

A French enamel box, the sides and hinged lid with French characters. (Bonhams & Brooks) $70

A late Victorian American silver heart shaped box, 1895, maker's mark of Gorham, embossed with floral decoration, inscribed. (Bonhams & Brooks) $210

An early 17th century Spanish parcel-gilt pyx box, pixide, maker's mark Garijo, León, circa 1620, gilt interior, sides and cover chased with band of stylized scrollwork, the cover lacking crucifix, 10.2cm. diameter, 5oz.(Bonhams) $490

A late 19th century Dutch novelty silver box, import marks for London 1892, importer's mark of Thomas Edward Nalty, modelled as a shrew, seated on a textured oval base, weight 2oz., 6cm. long. (Bonhams & Brooks) $350

A Chinese silver tobacco box, apparently unmarked, with various scenes of Chinese figures in landscapes, foliate sides, the hinged cover with a vacant cartouche, approximate weight 5oz., 13cm. long. (Bonhams) $809

German box, .800 fine, late19th/early 20th century, the hinged lid chased and embossed with a military scene, 7½in. long, approximately 13 troy oz. (Skinner) $978

English silver pig-form box, Chester, 1901, with shaped back, the lid engraved, 3 troy oz., 3in. long. (Skinner) $350

Continental silver jewel box, probably Germany, late 19th/ early 20th century, the lid and base with embossed foliate bands, with cast dog mounted to the lid, approximately 17 troy oz., 5¾in. long. (Skinner) $978

A George III silver saucepan, Robert Sharp, London, 1799, of typical form, with open spout and wood baluster handle, 9½in. long over handle, gross 9oz. (Christie's) $1,990

A large Victorian brandy warmer of plain form with turned wood handle, bowl 11.5cm. high, makers mark G.N. over R.H. Chester 1897, 19.6oz. (Bearne's) $409

A George III silver brandy saucepan and cover, Emes & Barnard, London, 1809, tapering body engraved with armorials, domed cover engraved with a crest, 5¼in. high, 662gm. (Sotheby's) $6,437

A George II brandy warming pan, London 1731, maker's mark of Robert Lucas, circular bellied form, turned wooden baluster handle, crested, approximate weight 4oz., 18.5cm. long. (Bonhams) $956

An early George II small brandy saucepan, the squat bellied bowl with a flat base and lip spout, crested and inscribed, by Thomas Cooke (II) & Richard Gurney 1728, 7cm. diameter, of bowl, 3oz. (Christie's) $1,173

A George III silver brandy warming pan and cover, London 1806, John Gwyn Holmes, turned wooden baluster side handle, pull-off cover with reeded border, total weight 17oz., 11cm. high. (Bonhams & Brooks) $1,330

CADDY SPOONS

A George III caddy spoon, pricked with Greek key borders and inset with an oval filigree panel in the bowl, by Samuel Pemberton, Birmingham 1807, 8.25cm. long. (Christie's) $726

Georgian silver caddy spoon in the form of a jockey's cap, limited pricked decoration to bowl, probably Samuel Pemberton of Birmingham, circa 1800. (G.A. Key) $480

A George III caddy spoon, with a canted terminal and an octagonal bowl engraved with a rose flower, by Lawrence & Co, Birmingham 1817, 7cm. long. (Christie's) $472

A George III cast caddy spoon, by George Knight, 1818, the asymmetrical, scalloped rococo bowl with similar handle incorporating a scroll cartouche engraved with an earl's coronet. (Bonhams) $952

A George III silver caddy spoon, Birmingham 1789, Joseph Taylor, modelled as a jockey's cap, with bright cut decoration, the peak engraved with a vacant cartouche, 5cm. long. (Bonhams & Brooks) $1,099

A George III engraved caddy spoon, decorated with cross hatching, Greek key and borderwork, the oval bowl pierced with a border of T-shapes, by Joseph Taylor, Birmingham 1807, 6.5cm. long. (Christie's) $436

A pair of French silver five-light candelabra, Gustav Keller, Paris, circa 1890, the knopped fluted tapering stem issuing from acanthus band and surmounted by a fluted central light, 18½in. high, 235oz. (Bonhams) $8,686

A pair of French cast dwarf candelabra, sponsor's mark of Charles Stuart Harris & Sons, 1914, in the rococo style, each with three scrolling foliate branches, 22cm. high. 71oz.(Bonhams) $1,680

A pair of early 19th century Old Sheffield plated three light candelabra, unmarked, circa 1820, tapering columns, part fluted, foliate scroll borders, reeded scroll branches, fluted urn capitals, 53.5cm. high. (Bonhams) $801

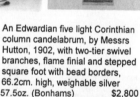

An electroplated five-light candelabrum/centerpiece, the stem and branches modelled as a grape vine with branches of vine leaves and grape tendrils, four scroll branches and a central light with urn capitals, 55.5cm. high. (Bonhams) $864

A pair of George III candelabra, London 1769, probably John Parker and Edward Wakelin, on raised circular bases, fluted decoration, with a laurel border, tapering circular columns with hanging laurel swags, approximate weight 107oz. 37.7cm. high. (Bonhams) $12,320

An Edwardian five light Corinthian column candelabrum, by Messrs Hutton, 1902, with two-tier swivel branches, flame finial and stepped square foot with bead borders, 66.2cm. high, weighable silver 57.5oz. (Bonhams) $2,800

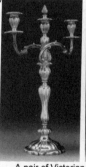

A massive pair of French silver candelabra, A Leroy, Paris, 1st standard export mark, dated *1909*, the stepped circular bases molded with stiff leaves and pendant husk panels below knopped reeded stems, 70¾in. high, 1786oz. (Sotheby's) $51,800

Emmy Roth, candelabrum, circa 1915, silver-colored metal, the elliptical section arms twisting organically around flared central stem, 16½in. (Sotheby's) $10,092

A pair of Victorian silver three-light candelabra, T.J. and N. Creswick, Sheffield, 1847, each on fluted spreading shaped circular base and with baluster stem, 22in. high. (Christie's) $6,521

A rare pair of Old Sheffield plated candlesticks, commemorating four British Admirals and their naval victories over the French, circa 1800, 21.5cm. high.
(Christie's) $1,011

A pair of early 19th century German silver candlesticks, Augsburg 1819, maker's mark probably that of Jeremias Balthasar Heckenauer, of tapering circular form, approximate weight 16oz., 19cm. high.
(Bonhams & Brooks) $1,190

A pair of George II Sheffield plate candlesticks, the loaded square bases with repoussé pelmet molding and vacant cartouches, 10¼in.
(Woolley & Wallis) $353

A pair of late Victorian candlesticks, in mid 18th century style, the loaded shaped square welled bases with leaf corners to knopped silesian stems, 9¾in. high, Hawksworth, Eyre & Co. Ltd., Sheffield 1888.
(Woolley & Wallis) $1,235

Set of four George IV baroque-style silver candlesticks, S.C Younge & Co., Sheffield, 1827, of typical form, the removable bobeches with embossed foliate and shell decoration, weighted, 11¾in.
(Skinner) $5,462

Two George II silver candlesticks, one Bennett Bradshaw and Robert Tyrill, London, 1740; the other London, 1744, maker's mark indistinct, each on shaped square stepped base, 6¾in. high, 29oz.
(Christie's) $4,343

A pair of George III cluster column candlesticks, on rising square bases with ovolo borders and chased with foliate swags, by John Smith, London 1771, 31cm. high, loaded. (Christie's) $4,959

A pair of George V desk-top candlesticks of tapering circular form and hammered finish with beaded edging, 12cm. high, A.E. Jones, Birmingham 1911, weighted.
(Bearne's) $1,887

A pair of late Victorian candlesticks, the columns with ribbon tied festoons, shell and husk candleholders, Mappin & Webb, 10½in. London 1900.
(Woolley & Wallis) $1.680

A calling card case, Birmingham, 1902, approximately 3 troy oz. (Skinner) $350

A Victorian Scottish card case, by James Nasmyth & Co., Edinburgh, 1845, engraved with an oval, scroll-edged cartouche depicting Roslin Castle. (Bonhams) $2,800

A Victorian 'castle-top' card case, by Alfred Taylor, Birmingham, 1856, of shaped rectangular form, the front decorated in high relief with a view of Windsor Castle. (Bonhams) $868

CASKETS

A George V silver mounted tortoise shell casket of sarcophagus shape with guilloche and pendant friezes applied swags, London 1919, 6in. (Russell Baldwin & Bright) $1,176

A William Hutton & Sons silver casket, London, 1906, rectangular form, on four foliate feet, the hinged cover set with strapwork panels mounted with green chrysoprase roundels stamped marks, London 1906, 4in. wide. (Christie's) $3,125

An Edwardian silver rectangular casket, the hinged cover repoussé decorated with an Art Nouveau portrait of a maiden, the interior cedar lined for cigarettes, 6.25in., by Nathan & Hayes, Chester 1906. (Bristol) $488

CASTERS

A fine pair of sugar casters, in George III classical style, the vase shaped bodies with swirling Rococo husk and foliage repoussé decoration 9.25in. high, The Goldsmiths & Silversmiths Co. Ltd., London 1898/1902, 31.5oz. (Woolley & Wallis) $2,156

A rare set of three James II silver casters, Anthony Nelme, London, 1686, of lighthouse form in two sizes, engraved with armorials above crossed plumage and applied girdle, 8in. and 6in. high, 890gr.(Sotheby's) $34,780

A late-Victorian sugar caster, London 1890, Edgar Finley and Hugh Taylor, modelled as a drinking horn, embossed foliate decoration on a matted background, screw off cover, mythical beast scroll handle, approximate weight 6oz. , 13.3cm. high. (Bonhams) $1,047

A silver-plated centerpiece, early 20th century, in the form of a shell mounted with a nude female figure, 22¾in. wide.
(Christie's) $759

Silver plate épergne, England or America, second half 19th century, of typical form, with four branches with cut glass bowls surrounding a central large bowl, 16½in.
(Skinner) $2,070

English silver plate épergne, late 19th/ early 20th century, comprising a central trumpet form vase with banded rim with shell motifs, surrounded by three smaller vases, 21½in.
(Skinner) $748

CHAMBERSTICKS

A George III rounded rectangular chamber candlestick, 15cm. long, Rebecca Emes and Edward Barnard, London 1809, and a plated conical extinguisher, 280gm., 9.0oz. (Bearne's) $377

A George III silver miniature chamberstick, London 1781, beaded borders, the drip pan and extinguisher also with beaded borders, crested with a motto, approximate weight 3oz., diameter of base 9cm.
(Bonhams & Brooks) $392

English chamberstick with snuffer, Lambert, London, 1896, circular with banded rim with pierced pattern on sides, engraved and embossed geometric pattern with foliate swags, 6½in. high, approximately 9 troy oz.
(Skinner) $575

A George II silver chamberstick, Paul de Lamerie, London, 1733, bear's claw crested below a baron's coronet within molded border, 5in. diameter, 252gr.
(Sotheby's) $13,320

A late-Victorian electroplated chamberstick, Hukin and Heath, after a design by Dr. Christopher Dresser, plain cylindrical capital, ebony handle, ribbed conical striker, on four bun feet, 13.5cm. long. (Bonhams) $924

A 19th century Scottish Provincial miniature chamberstick, maker's mark *JL*, possibly Cupar (?), circa 1837, the dished circular base chased with foliate scrolls on a frosted ground, 6cm. diameter, 1.5oz. (Bonhams) $224

A German silver chocolate pot, Johann Mittnacht III, Augsburg, 1751-3, spirally fluted baluster on spreading support molded spout and wood scroll handle, 20cm., 329gm. (Sotheby's) $3,881

A pair of Edward VII chocolate pots of flared cylindrical form with ebony side handles, 7¼in. high, maker's mark *D.F.*, London 1904, 586gm, 18.8oz. (Bearne's) $980

A German silver chocolate pot, Johan Christoph Höning, Augsburg, 1735-1736, fluted pear-shaped and on a plain spreading base, the fluted side hinged domed cover with detachable ball finial, 25cm. high, gross 22oz. (Christie's) $4,710

CIGARETTE CASES

A German cigarette case finely enamelled with two St. Bernard dogs, circa 1900 and applied with three gold monograms, 9cm. long. (Bonhams) $1,120

A late 19th century champlevé-enamelled cigarette case, by Gustav Klingert, Moscow, 1893, decorated with a repetitive geometric design of red, white and blue flowerheads. (Bonhams) $700

An Edwardian silver cigarette case of motoring interest, Birmingham 1907, maker's mark of WJ Myatt & Co. Ltd., the hinged lid embossed with a gentleman's bust seated at the wheel in motoring gear, 8.2cm. high. (Bonhams) $502

CLARET JUGS

French .950 silver and cut glass claret jug, Paris, late 19th/early 20th century, bulbous, the domed lid with cast grape bunch finial and chased beaded spiral reeding, 10¾in. high. (Skinner) $1,610

A pair of Edwardian silver-gilt mounted cut-glass claret jugs, London 1901, Charles Boyton, the silver gilt mounts decorated with bacchanalian masks, grape vine leaves and tendrils, height of jugs 27cm. (Bonhams & Brooks) $10,500

A fine Victorian parcel-gilt mounted glass claret jug, by Frederick Elkington, Birmingham, 1878, the mount chased with mythical beasts flanking urns of bullrushes, 30cm. high. (Bonhams) $4,900

A pair of Victorian silver decanter wagons Edward Barnard & Sons, London, 1844, four vine decorated coasters with turnover rims, turned wood bases, 18½in. long.
(Sotheby's) $29,674

A pair of George IV Sheffield Plate decanter stands, the everted panelled sides with an applied border of grapes on a vine, turned wood bases.
(Woolley & Wallis) $417

A electro-plated double coaster trolley, on four spoked wheels with a turned ivory handle, fruiting vine borders, pierced sides and inset turned wooden bases, 51cm. long.
(Christie's) $699

A set of four George IV wine coasters, on turned wooden bases, the sides chased with vine leaves, bunches of grapes and tendrils, by Younge & Co., Sheffield, 1827, 17cm. high.
(Christie's) $4,710

A matched pair of George III silver wine coasters, London 1771, Robert and David Hennell, and London 1778, William Abdy II, the sides pierced with scroll decoration, diameter 11.5cm.
(Bonhams & Brooks) $3,080

Four William IV silver coasters, Henry Wilkinson & Co, Sheffield, 1833, pierced with bacchanalian masks and urns between fruiting grape vines, turned wood bases, 6in. diameter.
(Sotheby's) $6,749

A late 18th century Irish wine coaster, Dublin, no date letter, circa 1780, maker's mark of Christopher Clarke, pierced and embossed with Bacchanalian putti drinking and sleeping, 12.5cm. diameter.
(Bonhams) $3,542

Two similar George III wine coasters, circular form, with pierced and bright cut decoration, beaded borders, monogrammed, wooden bases, diameters 12cm. and 12.5cm. (Bonhams) $1,848

A set of four early-Victorian silver wine coasters, Henry Wilkinson & Co. Ltd., in the Gothic revival style, stylized acanthus leaf borders, cranberry glass liners, diameter 15cm.
(Bonhams & Brooks) $3,408

A coffee-pot, in early George II style, the tapering body on a molded foot rim, having a cast faceted swan neck spout, 7½in. high, Thomas Bradbury & Son, Sheffield 1928, 20oz. all in. (Woolley & Wallis) $441

Victorian silver plated coffee pot of shaped oval baluster design, chased and embossed with foliate decoration, 9in. tall. (G.A. Key) $77

A George II baluster coffee pot with incised spiral decoration, London 1759, 26oz, makers Thomas Cook and Richard Gurney. (Dee Atkinson & Harrison) $6,270

George III rococo silver coffee pot, W. & J. Priest, London, 1770, pear form, the domed lid with cast wrythen finial and repoussé foliates, the body with repoussé foliate and scroll decoration, 18 troy oz., 9½in. high. (Skinner) $1,610

A George III silver coffee pot, London 1804, George Smith II and Thomas Hayter, canted corners, reeded borders, domed flush hinged lid, with an urn shaped finial, approximate weight 31oz., 26cm. high. (Bonhams & Brooks) $1,680

A George IV coffee pot, London 1824, maker's mark overstruck with that of George Burrows II, embossed with butterflies and foliate scroll decoration, approximate weight 35oz., 28.5cm. high. (Bonhams) $1,543

A Belgian silver coffee-pot, maker's mark *AD*, Mons, 1776, the spirally-fluted pear-shaped body on three scroll feet terminating in shells and scrolls, 14¼in. high, 36oz. gross. (Christie's) $11,178

An early 19th century French silver coffee pot, Paris, circa 1810, maker's mark of L.I., stylized foliate borders, domed hinged lid with leaf capped knop finial, approximate weight 38oz., 33cm. high. (Bonhams & Brooks) $1,400

A Queen Anne silver coffee-pot and stand, Robert Timbrell and Joseph Bell, London, 1709, the body engraved with a coat-of-arms within scrolling foliage, 10½in., gross 27oz. (Christie's) $11,885

A Victorian silver coffee pot, W.M., London, 1848, the footed baluster form with an elongated neck and flaring rim, 2 pieces, 27oz., 10in. high. (Sotheby's) $920

A George II coffee pot by Peter Archambo (I), 1742, with scalloped, leaf-capped spout and knop finial, engraved to one side with a lady's arms, 22cm. high, 23.5oz. (Bonhams) $1,680

Victorian coffee pot, London, 1839, lobed baluster shape with flared scalloped rim, domed and lobed lid with cast flower finial, approximately 31 troy oz, 9¼in. high. (Skinner) $690

A George III silver coffee-pot, Daniel Smith and Robert Sharp, London, 1774, the partly-fluted body chased with drapery swags and applied with three satyr masks, 13in. high, gross 37oz. (Christie's) $4,844

A pair of modern café-au-lait pots, maker's mark and retailer's mark of West & Sons, Dublin 1912, decorated with borders of Celtic strapwork, 18cm. high, 17oz. (Bonhams) $690

A Queen Anne silver coffee-pot, Simon Pantin, London, 1702, with curved faceted spout, the hinged domed cover with baluster finial, 8in. high, gross 18oz. (Christie's) $4,844

George III rococo-style coffee pot, William Shaw, London, 1761, pear-shape with molded rim, the domed repoussé lid with bud finial, approximately 36 troy oz, 12¼in. high. (Skinner) $1,610

An Edwardian silver coffee pot, London 1901, maker's mark of Henry Stratford, tapering circular form, scroll handle, domed hinged cover with a knop finial, approximate weight 23oz. (Bonhams & Brooks) $435

An American silver coffee pot, Gorham Mfg. Co., 1891, baluster form in the Indo-Persian taste, the body with spiral fluting, a band of scrolling and foliate decoration, 9½in. high, gross weight 17oz.. (Christie's) $1,293

Clemens Friedell sterling silver
Martelé fairy compôte, Pasadena,
California, 1914, circular, with
shaped rim, the hammered face
with chased fairies and poppies, on
a circular base, approximately 25
troy oz., 10½in. diameter.
(Skinner) $9,775

CREAM JUGS

A George IV Irish silver cream jug,
Dublin 1825, maker's mark of
Charles Marsh, of circular form,
foliate and shell borders, the body
embossed with floral, foliate and
scroll borders, approximate weight
8oz., 17cm. long.
(Bonhams & Brooks) $232

Pair of Howard & Co. sterling
compôtes, third quarter 19th
century, shell form, on three
dolphin form feet, 8½in. high, 68
troy oz. approximately.
(Skinner) $6,325

An American silver creamer,
Abraham Dubois, Philadelphia circa
1780, of inverted pear form on
pedestal foot with beaded rim,
matched on the top rim, 140gr.,
14.3cm. high.
(Sotheby's) $1,265

Sterling silver rococo-style
compôte, Hamilton & Diesinger,
Philadelphia, circa 1895-1899,
circular, the everted rim with
embossed openwork, 'C' scrolls
and foliates, approximately 15 troy
oz., diameter 9¼in.
(Skinner) $288

A modern Continental cow creamer,
having a hinged cover, decorated
with a bellflower and foliage, 5¾in.
long, London import marks for
1963, 6oz.
(Woolley & Wallis) $735

A mid 18th century silver cream jug,
Dublin, wavy edge borders, leaf
capped scroll handle, the thumb
piece modelled as a lady's head,
weight 6oz. , 11.5cm. high.
(Bonhams & Brooks) $700

An American silver creamer,
maker's mark JF, circa 1770, of
pear form with waved rim and
multiple scroll handle, 131gr., 4¼in.
high. (Sotheby's) $4,025

A rare George II oval cream boat,
on a cast, shaped foot with a
gadroon border, the panelled ogee
body engraved with a monogram,
Peter Taylor, London 1750, 6.75oz.
(Woolley & Wallis) $1,441

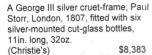

A George III silver cruet-frame, Paul Storr, London, 1807, fitted with six silver-mounted cut-glass bottles, 11in. long, 32oz.
(Christie's) $8,383

A Regency silver egg-cruet with four egg-cups, William Elliott, London, 1817 and 1818, the frame with gadrooned borders and central shell and foliate-clad ring handle, 13cm. square, 628gm.
(Christie's) $2,895

A George III egg cruet, William Elliott, 1818, the stand of oblong gadroon mount form with shell and acanthus decoration to each strut terminating in a shell, rosette, and scroll capped paw foot.
(Christie's) $1,400

A fine Regency cruet, with a central handle, supported by a shell and foliage on a fluted flared stem, to a frame chased with palmettes and fitted with two cut glass oil and vinegar bottles, London, 1810, 17oz.
(Woolley & Wallis) $3,768

A George IV silver six-piece egg cruet, London 1820, Joseph Cradock and William K. Reid, central foliate capped carrying handle, together with a matched set of six George IV silver egg spoons, approximate total 44oz., (Bonhams & Brooks) $1,050

A Hukin & Heath electroplated cruet stand, designed by Dr Christopher Dresser, circa 1880, model 1996, six circular apertures with central bar and D finial stamped marks, 1996, 7½in. high.
(Christie's) $1,400

A five bottle cruet on shell feet, with three silver casters and two molded glass bottles, R. Peaston, London, 1763/4, 25.5cm. high. 1870gr. (Finarte) $4,179

An early 20th century electro-plated cruet frame, of wirework construction modelled as an early flying machine or aeroplane on three wheels, fitted with four egg cups, 26cm. long.
(Christie's) $973

A George III silver eight-bottle cruet stand, London 1818, maker's mark of Solomon Royes and James East Dix, of square form, foliate scroll and shell borders, approximate weighable 35oz., 25cm. wide.
(Bonhams) $1,099

A Queen Anne silver cup, Nathaniel Lock, London, 1708, later engraved with armorials, 5in. high, 12oz 17dwt. (Sotheby's) $2,496

A Queen Anne Britannia standard silver two-handled cup, London 1710, maker's mark over struck with that of Jno. Rand, of plain circular form, approximate weight 12oz. , 9.8cm. high. (Bonhams & Brooks) $1,610

A George III silver gilt cup and cover, London 1809, Solomon Hougham, circular bowl with an acanthus leaf girdle, bifurcated snake handles, weight 122oz., 48cm. high. (Bonhams) $5,082

A George I silver two-handled cup and cover, London 1715, Seth Lofthouse, the body and cover with part fluted decoration and girdles of embossed gadrooned decoration, weight 17.5oz., 18.5cm. high. (Bonhams & Brooks) $980

A Dutch silver windmill cup, Gerrit Valck, Amsterdam, 1635, the bell shaped cup chased with fruit clusters in cartouches on matting, 8in. high, 5oz 12dwt. (Sotheby's) $21,125

A Queen Anne Irish silver two-handled cup, Dublin 1712, David King, two leaf capped flying scroll handles, molded borders and central girdle, approximate weight 23oz., 16.5cm. high. (Bonhams & Brooks) $2,800

A fine George III cup, the pear shaped body engraved with a crest above an armorial, Charles Wright, 12¼in. high, London 1775, 39.5oz. (Woolley & Wallis) $1,216

A Charles II silver tumbler cup, London probably 1682, gilt interior, engraved with plumes, approximate weight 4oz., 5.5cm. height. (Bonhams & Brooks) $1,400

A German parcel-gilt silver cup and cover, Peter Winter, Augsburg, 1680-1685, the body chased with an equestrian battle between Turks and Austrians, 8¾in. high, 18oz. (Christie's) $7,079

An Irish dish ring, pierced and embossed with foliate scrolls, swags and rosettes, maker C.L., Dublin 1898, 9.5oz.
(Wintertons) $2,387

A silver dish, London 1942, Robert Pringle, the edges of the dish pierced with trellis, and stylized floral and foliate decoration, approximate weight 14oz., diameter of bowl 23cm.
(Bonhams) $293

A Victorian entree dish and cover by John Samuel Hunt, with reeded loop handle, and reeded scroll and foliate edging, 11½in. wide, London 1855, 56oz 19dwt.
(Andrew Hartley) $798

An oval mustard dish, Marseilles, third quarter, 18th century, with two pierced containers decorated with volutes, foliage and vines, 8cm. high, 550gm.
(Finarte) $2,120

A George III breakfast dish, of oblong form with turned wood handle and gadrooned borders, the cover engraved with two crests and with a ball finial, 1770, 23.5cm. wide, 30oz gross.
(Christie's) $323

A South American silver basin, unmarked, probably Peruvian, 18th or early 19th century, plain circular on rim foot, with broad everted rim, 16in. diameter, 74oz.
(Christie's) $15,276

An Arts and Crafts silver tazza, London 1925, Artificers' Guild Ltd., the body applied with two medallions depicting galleons, the stem comprising of a cluster of four stylized columns, approximate weight 7oz., height 11.5cm.
(Bonhams & Brooks) $1,050

A pair of George III silver two-handled circular vegetable dishes, William Fountain, London, 1805, mounted with a pair of hinged ring handles, 44oz., length across handles 9in.
(Sotheby's) $1,840

Late Victorian silver plated bacon dish with revolving lid and supported on four bowled curved feet, 10 x 8in., circa 1900.
(G.A. Key) $239

An Austrian dessert-stand, maker's mark *PT*, Vienna, circa 1900, on spreading shaped oval foot, the fluted bowl with shaped rim, 16in. long, 39oz.
(Christie's) $2,795

A George IV silver entrée dish and cover and Old Sheffield Plate stand, Philip Rundell, London, 1821, the stand by Matthew Boulton, the dish engraved twice with crest, 34cm. long, 70oz.(Christie's) $3,353

A late Victorian cake stand, the circular top pierced with scrolling foliage and molded rim with scroll and foliate edging, 11¾in. wide, Birmingham 1900, 22oz.19dwt.
(Andrew Hartley) $667

A late Victorian oval breakfast dish, the engraved cover with ivory thumbpiece, bead edges and a liner, Alfred Browett, Ashbury & Co. (Woolley & Wallis) $235

A novelty parcel-gilt bon-bon dish, in the form of a wheelbarrow with lattice-work sides, by George Fox, 1896, 12.75cm. long, 3oz. (Christie's) $1,083

A German silver-gilt dish, Peter Ra(H)m, Augsburg, circa 1700, the center repoussé and chased with a farmer frightening away two ducks, 16¼in. long, 13oz. (Christie's) $3,353

A modern silver-gilt butter dish and cover, Reid & Sons, Dublin 1916, of oval outline with a cast fruit finial, the sides, cover and foot of openwork scrolls and geometric patterns, 16cm. wide, 12oz. weighable silver. (Bonhams) $872

An early 19th century Spanish silver surgeon barber's dish, Salamanca, reeded and engraved rope work border, with a detachable shaped neck support, with three clips, approximate weight 24oz., 35cm. long. (Bonhams & Brooks) $2,800

A George I Britannia Standard strawberry dish of shallow circular form with a collet foot and scalloped border, by Augustine Courtauld, 1722, 17.5cm. diameter, 10.25oz. (Christie's) $8,066

A mid 18th century Irish silver strawberry dish, Dublin, engraved with scroll, foliate and shell decoration together with a swan and a mythical dolphin, diameter 18.5cm. (Bonhams & Brooks) $2,100

Tiffany & Co. footed serving dish, New York, circa 1891-1902, fan shaped with embossed scroll and foliate rim, the interior reeded with repoussé and engraved foliate decoration, 5½in. high. (Skinner) $2,760

A late 18th century Maltese silver bonbonnière and cover with stand, circa 1775 – 1797, maker's mark of Gio Carlo Cassar, supported on four scroll legs with hoof feet, the dish fitted with a shaped oval stand, width of base 13.5cm. (Bonhams & Brooks) $2,380

A silver presentation scenic ewer of historic interest, Bard & Lamont, Philadelphia, circa 1840, the stem formed as a lotus, 17¾in. high. 48oz.10dwt.
(Christie's) $5,175

English silver and cut glass ewer, London, circa 1904, ovoid with overall cut and pressed decoration, the chased lid with a bud finial, the shoulder with openwork silver mount, 12½in. high.
(Skinner) $4,025

A German parcel-gilt silver ewer, Augsburg, circa 1700, maker's mark indistinct, the body chased with fruits and foliage, 30cm. high, 549gm. (Christie's) $4,099

American silver presentation wine ewer by James Howell, Philadelphia, 1797, turned finial to helmet shaped lid, double scrolled handle, pear shaped body, 14½in. high, 54oz.
(Freeman) $7,560

A pair of silver-mounted glass ewers, marked *Bolin*, St. Petersburg, 1890, amphora-shaped, the glass bodies with twisted fluting, the silver mounts and handles partly engraved as bull-rushes, 27cm. high.
(Christie's) $3,922

Brannam (Barum) small ewer modelled as a penguin and decorated in treacle, shades of green and blue, incised marks and dated *1901*, 9in.
(G.A. Key) $119

A George IV ewer, oviform with a reeded foliate handle, by R. Emes & E. Barnard, 1822, 41.75cm. high, 62.5oz. (Christie's) $2,024

A Chinese silver ewer, maker's mark possibly that of the Tuck Chang, embossed with figural scenes in landscapes, the scroll handle formed as a dragon, approximate weight 23oz., 29cm. high. (Bonhams) $2,352

A Maltese silver ewer, Emido Critien, Malta, 1830, the lower part of the body chased with vertical acanthus leaves, 11½in. high, 21oz.
(Christie's) $2,795

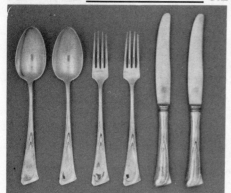

A six piece set of cutlery, the design attributed to Henry van de Velde, circa 1905, manufactured by Koch & Bergfeld, Bremen. (Christie's) $6,815

Set of twelve Gorham Aesthetic movement fish knives, Providence, late 19th century, the blades with ornate monograms, with mixed metal Japanese-style Kozuka handles with molded decoration, 7¾in. long. (Skinner) $2,300

A group of American silver 'Japanese style' flatware, Tiffany & Co., New York late 19th century, comprising: twelve daisy pattern lunch forks, twelve pomegranate pattern dessert knives, twelve poppy pattern butter spreaders, ten blackberry pattern dessert spoons, nine vine pattern teaspoons, and twelve iris pattern demitasse spoons, 67 pieces, 89oz. (Sotheby's) $13,800

A Queen Anne silver basting-spoon, Thomas Sadler, London, 1710, Hanoverian pattern, with deep oval rat-tail bowl, the handle engraved with a crest, 16in. long, 10oz. (Christie's) $5,589

A pair of George III silver gilt grape scissors of finely chased design, London 1819, maker Charles Rawlings and Williams Summers, 18cm. (Thomson Roddick & Medcalf) $638

Hester Bateman, a George III marrow scoop with bright cut engraved shank, the bowl with later presentation initial, marks rubbed, circa 1780. (Woolley & Wallis) $88

A silver canteen for twelve, Sheffield 1931 and 1932, maker's mark of E. Viner, Sandringham Pattern, including 12 table forks, 12 dessert forks, 12 soup spoons, 12 dessert spoons, 12 tea spoons, 12 coffee spoons, 6 table spoons, 2 sauce ladles, 155oz. (Bomhams) $2,772

A George V teaspoon the stem decorated with a golfer in full swing, the reverse with a clubhouse, Birmingham 1922, maker: L & S. (Brightwells) $84

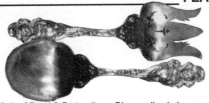

Pair of Reed & Barton 'Love Disarmed' salad servers, Taunton, Massachusetts, 20th century, with molded floral and maiden handles, approximately 16 troy oz., 10¾in. long. (Skinner) $690

A Victorian Scottish Provincial toddy ladle, Robert Robertson, Cupar, circa 1840. (Christie's) $937

An Edwardian serving trowel with molded haft, the triangular blade pierced and chased with Art Nouveau swirling flowers and foliage, 13¾in. wide, Sheffield 1904, 9oz 2dwt.(Andrew Hartley) $348

A George II basting spoon, London 1729, maker's mark possibly that of Lawrence Jones, Hanoverian pattern, oval bowl, the reverse of the terminal engraved with a foliate cartouche and a lozenge, approximate weight 5oz., 33.6cm. long. (Bonhams) $882

A pair of Victorian serving tongs in fiddle and thread pattern with pierced scrolling foliate oblong grips, 10in. wide, London 1865, 6oz 6dwt. (Andrew Hartley) $174

A Chinese silver knife, fork and spoon set, maker's mark possibly that of Sunshing, simulated bamboo handles with thorns, inscribed, length of knife 19.1cm. (Bonhams) $132

A rare James I Scottish trefid spoon, with a slightly different shaped terminal scratched A.H. E.S. on the reverse, repaired, the repairs concealing the town mark and date letter, by Alexander Reid, Edinburgh, circa 1687, assay masters mark of John Borthwick, 19.75cm. long, 1.25oz. (Christie's) $664

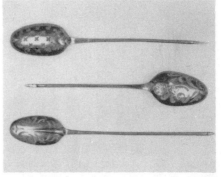

Three mote spoons: including a lace-back example and a rat-tail example, 1oz. (Christie's) $976

A good service, of 'Old English' pattern, with bright cut edges, by Mappin & Webb, 1919, in a mahogany bow fronted cabinet of Sheraton style, 108.5cm., approximate weight without steel items 300oz. (Tennants) $14,444

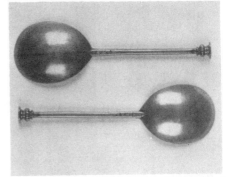

A pair of unascribed Mary I seal-top spoons, the fluted baluster terminals with hexagonal shaped ends, traces of gilding, maker's mark of I.F. in a shield, London, 1556, 16cm. long, 3oz. (Christie's) $10,019

A rare George III mounted coconut goblet, probably by John Laughlin Jnr, circa 1785, on a trumpet foot with a wavy rim, mount and an oval cartouche on one side, 18.25cm. high. (Bonhams) $690

A Bohemian 'alabaster' goblet and a silver cover, mid-19th century, overlaid in pale-green and cut with leaves and broad facets, 8¼in. high overall. (Christie's) $1,152

A Victorian wine goblet, on spreading circular foot with bright-cut decoration with engraved scene of St. Pancras Baths and Wash House, by Daniel & Charles Houle, 1876, 15.5cm. high, 6oz. (Christie's) $796

An Arts and Crafts silver goblet, London 1930, Artificer's Guild Ltd., the rim applied with a band of rose branches, on a raised spread hexagonal base, approximate weight 8oz., 11.75cm. high. (Bonhams & Brooks) $1,050

A Victorian parcel-gilt ewer with a pair of goblets ensuite, by Messrs Barnard, 1875, the ewer of slender ovoid form, all three pieces engraved with spear-head panels of ferns and each bearing a presentation inscription, height of ewer 35cm., 34oz. (Bonhams) $2,030

A George III prize goblet, by Thomas Hayter, 1808, the trumpet foot with reeded band inscribed *The Agricultural Society of the Hundred of West Derby to Mr. James Robinson of Speke for a crop of turnips and for shewing a tup and ewe MDCCCVIII*, 19.7cm., 10oz. (Bonhams) $700

A George III mounted coconut goblet, with reeded borders, a domed circular foot and lined bowl interior, by Thomas Phipps & Edward Robinson (II), 1800, 13cm. high. (Christie's) $796

A silver water pitcher and pair of goblets, Gorham Mfg. Co., Providence, 1874, the lower pitcher body bright-cut engraved with band of scrolls, cornucopiae, and anthemion centering an inscription, the pitcher 12in. high, 42oz. (Christie's) $3,220

A George III thistle shaped goblet with a band of part fluting below a reeded girdle, (gilded interior) by Robert (I) & Samuel Hennell, 1808, 20cm. high, 11.25oz. (Christie's) $807

A silver mounted tortoiseshell inkstand, Birmingham, dated 1946, Mappin and Webb, the rectangular platform on bracket feet and mounted with twin wells, 9½in. wide. (Christie's) $1,725

A late William IV naturalistic parcel-gilt inkstand, modelled as a lily flower and lily pads floating on water, by Walter Jordan, 1836, 17cm. diameter, 10oz. (Christie's) $2,166

An Italian silver inkstand, Lorenzo Petroncelli, Rome, circa 1760, fitted with cylindrical sander and inkpot, candlestick, and bell, 10½in. long, 26oz. (Bonhams) $13,575

A late Victorian oblong inkstand with a pierced gallery and wavy gadrooned rim, by W. Gibbons & J. Langman 1893, 19cm. x 14cm., 12.5oz weighable silver. (Christie's) $1,067

A late Victorian silver inkstand, London 1894, Henry Wilkinson & Co., of shell form, with a stylized beaded border, together with a matching silver mounted glass inkwell, 8oz., width 20.75cm. (Bonhams) $554

A Victorian inkstand of shaped square outline with pierced decoration, floral blades and ball and claw feet, H. Wilkinson & Co, Sheffield 1856, 17cm. wide, 5.75oz weighable silver. (Christie's) $699

A silver and enamel pen tray with chamberstick, Tiffany & Co., New York, 1885-1891, the tray with everted flower and leaf border, one end with small hinged compartment, the other with a curved handle, 8¾in. long; gross weight 9oz. (Christie's) $4,600

A good Edwardian silver and cut glass pocket watch inkwell, the hinged cover containing a giant nickel pocket watch, the face with Roman numerals, by Shepherd & Co., 11cm. (T.R. & M) $609

A rectangular partner's inkstand, raised on claw and ball feet to a rounded corner gadroon edge and a pair of square glass ink pots, 8¾in., J B Chatterley & Sons Ltd, London 1931, 17oz. (Woolley & Wallis) $647

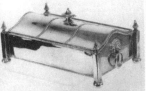

An Edwardian silver inkstand, Sheffield 1904, maker's mark of Lee and Wigfull, of rectangular form, gadroon and ovolo borders, the corners with reeded decoration, on four reeded bracket feet, weighable 21oz., width 23.5cm. (Bonhams & Brooks) $580

An Old Sheffield desk stand, of oblong form with beaded edging and lion mask ring handles, the interior with two square cut glass ink bottles flanking a recessed compartment with hinged lid, early 19th century, 8in. wide. (Andrew Hartley) $389

A late Victorian silver two-handled inkstand, London 1884, F.Wilson, with a pen holder, central box, the lid with surmounted by a stag, with two later matched silver mounted square cut-glass inkwells, length handle to handle 36cm. (Bonhams) $847

A modern copy of George II Guernsey hot milk jug, raised on stepped feet with scroll legs and trefoil appliques to an engraved band, 5in., Makers C J Vander Ltd., London, 1979, 9oz. all in.
(Woolley & Wallis) $470

A late Victorian silver mounted glass lemonade jug, London 1896, William Hutton & Sons Ltd., the mounts with spot hammered decoration, hinged lid with an elephant finial, 25.5cm. high.
(Bonhams & Brooks) $1,680

Attractive late Victorian silver small hotwater jug, well chased and embossed with floral garlands and ribbon ties, on three curved claw feet, 7in. tall, Birmingham 1892.
(G.A. Key) $230

A late 19th century American silver water jug, Tiffany & Co., the body with a large band of embossed decoration depicting nubile ladies playing musical instruments and playful cupids, approximate weight 25oz., 18cm. high.
(Bonhams & Brooks) $1,330

Continental silver toby jug, with English hallmarks for Chester, 1903, of typical form with scroll handle, 3¼in. high, approximately 3 troy oz. (Skinner) $287

An early Victorian Scottish silver hot water jug, Edinburgh 1838, maker's mark of J. McKay, the body with a wide band of scroll and floral decoration against a matted background, 29oz., 23cm. high.
(Bonhams) $1,232

Tiffany & Co. Sterling silver water jug, New York, circa 1879, bulbous, with molded rim and ear handle, approximately 24 troy oz., 7¼in. high. (Skinner) $1,610

An 18th century Continental altar cruet, of urn form on rising pedestal fluted foot, the domed cover similarly fluted, probably Belgian, 18th century, 12.75cm. high.
(Christie's) $2,418

Tiffany & Co. sterling silver floral repoussé jug, New York, 1875-91, bulbous, with molded rim and cast ear handle, approximately 35 troy oz., 7⅝in. (Skinner) $3,738

Victorian silver plated covered bun warmer, Elkington & Co., Birmingham, 1878, oval with hinged dome, with beaded rim, the oval insert with molded rim with embossed beading, 9½in.long. (Skinner) **$402**

Silver overlay hip flask, America, late 19th century, rectangular with engraved foliate overlay with embossed spaniel and reeds to obverse, 5½in.(Skinner) **$977**

A George III Scottish silver lemon strainer, Edinburgh circa 1810, Robert Grey & Son of Glasgow, reeded borders, shaped scroll lug handle, with a clip, approximate weight 3oz., 13.5cm. (Bonhams & Brooks) **$420**

A parcel-gilt silver nef, Pairpoint Brothers, London, 1928, formed in 17th century taste, the elaborately rigged vessel with applied figures and canons, on four wheels, 16in. long,1930.(Sotheby's) **$4,586**

A novelty silver table bell, Chester 1910, GY&Co., retailed by Asprey London, of plain compana form, crested, curved ivory tusk handle, 19cm. high. (Bonhams & Brooks) **$700**

A late Victorian silvered metal spirit barrel dispenser, circa 1870, modelled as a cart, the carriage mounted with three glass spirit barrels, with stopper and taps to the rear suspended with three small buckets, 11½in. (Christie's) **$4,525**

English Victorian coromandel veneered necéssaire, mid 19th century, fitted interior with ten silver lidded glass bottles and boxes, the silver hallmarked for London, 1877, 12¹/₈in. long. (Skinner) **$633**

A novelty cheroot cutter, apparently unmarked, modelled as a young child seated on a potty, hinged at the arms with a base metal cutter fitted at its feet, 3.5cm. high. (Bonhams & Brooks) **$336**

Russian silver kovsh, maker's mark *BC*, probably St. Petersburg, 1854, of typical form, the rim with molded foliates and Cyrillic inscription, with engraved decoration, approximately 13 troy oz., 8in. long.(Skinner) **$805**

A pair of Victorian, with engraved arms, with silver engraved case, perhaps by Charles Corke, Chester, 1913.
(Tennants) $439

A Belgian silver brazier, J.D. Bourgeois, Gent, 1777, on three shell, scroll and foliage supports resting on baluster wood feet, 11.5cm. high, 540gm. gross.
(Christie's) $2,981

A late 18th century child's rattle with engraved decoration, eight attached bells, integral whistle, coral teether and carrying ring, 15cm. long.
(Bearne's) $1,101

A Victorian coromandel toilet case, with brass trim, opening to reveal a fully fitted interior, with silver and glass toilet jars (London 1876), 12¼in. wide.
(Andrew Hartley) $2,780

A 19th century Old Sheffield plated flagon of tapering form with banded body, scrolled handle and flared base, 11¾in.
(Andrew Hartley) $247

A George III flagon, tapering straight sided later embossed and chased with shooting scene, London 1768, Thomas Whipham and Chas Wright, 50oz.
(Brightwells) $2,739

A rare, early George II Provincial lemon strainer with two pierced escutcheon shaped handles, by Johnathan French, Newcastle, 1727, 15.5cm. long, 2oz.
(Christie's) $1,728

A George II orange strainer, Edward Aldridge, circa 1750, of circular section with pierced circle motifs, with two applied leaf and scroll handles, 17.3cm, 3.25oz.
(Christie's) $484

An Austro-Hungarian silver mounted cigar cutter, circa 1900, the body formed from a tusk with a cast and chased silver mount modelled as a boar's head, 18cm. long.
(Bonhams & Brooks) $2,660

A Continental late 19th century model of lady's shoe, in silver colored metal, floral and scroll embossed, 6¼in.
(Woolley & Wallis) $253

A silver and mother of pearl baby's rattle, with pendant loop, two bells, and floral decoration, length 3½in.
(George Kidner) $128

A Victorian gilt posy holder, with engraved decoration and attached chain.
(Woolley & Wallis) $442

A 19th century Chinese silver mug, marked with pseudo English marks, maker's mark of *WE* over *WE* over *WC*, tapering circular form, with an upper and lower band of reeded decoration, approximate weight 8oz., 9.4cm. (Bonhams) $662

American coin silver mug, Eoff & Connor, New York, second quarter 19th century, the molded rim with foliate band, the body with foliate, beaded and embossed reeded bands, approximately 4 troy oz., 3¹/₈in. (Skinner) $287

Tiffany & Co. sterling silver mug, Grosjean & Woodward, New York, 1854-65, circular, the molded rim with beaded band, the body with all-over engine turned decoration, approximately 9 troy oz., 4¹/₈in. high. (Skinner) $431

A George I Britannia standard silver mug, London 1721, William Gamble, of plain tapering form, molded border, scroll handle, approximate weight 12oz., 12.5cm. high.(Bonhams & Brooks) $840

A very large 19th century Chinese Export mug, adapted contemporaneously as a trophy cup, circa 1860, applied with a very large Prussian Imperial Guard eagle badge, the Victorian (English) cover by Robert Hennell, 1861, 32cm. high, 85.5oz. (Bonhams) $3,080

A George II silver mug, London 1748, leaf-capped scroll handle with chased shell terminals, the whole later chased with pheasants and a hunting dog in a wooded landscape, approximately 16oz., 12.5cm. high. (Bonhams & Brooks) $568

A Chinese silver mug, maker's mark of Hung Chong, with sprays of bamboo decoration, on a matted background, approximate weight 7oz., 10.6cm. high. (Bonhams) $441

An Edwardian christening mug, repoussé decorated with a scene of Noah and his wife with the animals and a tree, a gilded interior, William Hutton & Sons Ltd, London 1906, 4oz. (Woolley & Wallis) $343

A George III quart mug, on a skirt foot, a capped with hollow scroll handle engraved initials *W I*I*, with a heart shape terminal, Thomas Wallis 1st, London 1777, 18oz. (Woolley & Wallis) $1,205

Unusual Victorian pail shaped silver mustard with half straight fluted decoration, scrolled handle, plus blue glass liner and plated spoon, London 1893.
(G A Key) $240

Edwardian silver mustard, oval shaped, bright cut decoration and pierced with flower head and scrolled designs, having gadrooned rim, plus blue glass liner, 3½ x 2in. Chester 1901.
(G.A. Key) $165

A mustard pot, with straight sides pierced with scrolls, with engraved slightly domed lid, by John Figg, 1841; also a salt spoon, 4½oz.
(Tennants) $565

A late-Victorian mustard pot, London 1878, Henry Holland, drum form, pierced with scroll decoration, hinged cover with a shell thumbpiece, with blue glass liner, approximate weight 4oz., 7cm. high. (Bonhams) $847

A Liberty & Co. silver mustard pot and salt, hallmarked, Birmingham 1929, hexagonal form, the mustard with domed hinged cover, stamped with geometric bands, on lightly hammered ground, 3in. high. (Christie's) $526

A late Victorian silver mustard pot, London 1895, Daniel Wellby and John Wellby, domed hinged lid, leaf and bud capped scroll handle, approximate weight 6oz., width 11.5cm. (Bonhams) $339

George III silver drum mustard with reeded base and rim, the sides with draped foliate engraving, London 1790, maker *G.G.*
(G A Key) $330

A novelty Victorian silver mustard pot, Robert Hennell, London, 1886, cast in the form of Mr Punch, 4in. high, 242gr.
(Sotheby's) $15,984

Adam style silver mustard on reeded oval foot, the wirework vase shaped body overlaid by swags and ribbon ties, 3in. tall, plus blue glass liner, London 1911 by the Goldsmiths and Silversmiths Co.
(G A Key) $163

A George III silver nutmeg grater, maker's mark only, of CT, pull-off lid and base, domed lid, the base fitted with a steel grater, two molded girdles, 3.5cm. high.
(Bonhams & Brooks) $392

A George III silver nutmeg grater, London 1813, Thomas Phipps & Edward Robinson II, the lid engraved with raying bright-cut and prick-dot decoration.
(Bonhams & Brooks) $1,400

A Continental silver nutmeg grater, circa 1800, apparently unmarked, plain cylindrical form, the hinge lid linked to a hinged side panel, steel grater, ring finial, 4.7cm. high.
(Bonhams & Brooks) $490

An 18th century silver ovoid nutmeg grater, circa 1740, Daniel Field, molded borders, embossed with diagonal bands of floral decoration, screw-off top, circular steel grater, 4.8cm. high.
(Bonhams & Brooks) $980

An early Victorian silver nutmeg grater, Birmingham 1847, Nathaniel Mills, the lid opening to reveal a base metal grater, the whole engraved with bands of engine turned decoration, 4.5cm. wide.
(Bonhams & Brooks) $1,050

A late 18th / early 19th century Continental silver nutmeg grater, circa 1800, plain urn form on a spread rectangular foot, the hinged lid with molded borders, 8.5cm. high.
(Bonhams & Brooks) $2,380

PEPPERS

A pair of mid-Victorian novelty silver pepper pots, London 1860, Charles Thomas Fox & George Fox barrel form, with pierced screw-off lids, approximate weight 97g, 4.8cm. high. (Bonhams) $708

A George III Scottish kitchen pepper pot, Edinburgh 1774, maker's mark of Patrick Robertson, plain cylindrical form, scroll handle, pull off cover with a raised sprinkler, reeded base, approximate weight 2oz., 6.7cm. high.
(Bonhams) $1,078

A pair of Continental novelty silver pepper pots, import marks for Chester 1909, importer's mark of Boaz Moses Landeck, modelled as an 18th century style courting couple, approximate weight 8oz., 11.5cm. high.
(Bonhams & Brooks) $980

A silver photo frame decorated with fairies, stamped marks, 1907, 23cm. high. (Christie's) $329

A silver and oak Art Nouveau mirror, stamped *CC(?)*, Chester 1905, 35cm. high. (Bonhams) $735

A silver and enamel Art Nouveau photo frame, stamped marks, Birmingham 1903 (minor damage), 22.5cm. high. (Bonhams) $882

A Chinese silver photograph frame, maker's mark of Cutshing, embossed with sprigs of bamboo, on a checkered background, 26.8cm. high. (Bonhams) $588

A pair of Edwardian rectangular easel back photograph frames, the silver mounted fronts gadrooned to bead edges, maker's mark overstamped by Marion & Co., Ltd., Birmingham 1903, 8¼ x 6in. inside measurement. (Woolley & Wallis) $911

Boer War interest:- A late Victorian patriotic photograph frame by W.J.Myatt & Co. Ltd., Birmingham, 1900, with easel back, with cartouches of military scenes, 22cm. high. (Bonhams) $1,120

A Victorian silver twin photograph frame, part-marked for 1889, hinged at center, pierced oblong with birds, harpies, putti, animals heads, masks and vacant cartouche, 18.4cm. high, 27.3cm. (Bonhams) $556

Good Edwardian silver mounted photograph frame with heart shaped aperture within a cartouche shaped surround, pierced and embossed, 7½in. x 6in., London 1901. (G.A. Key) $435

Tiffany silver double photograph frame, possibly William Comyns, London, circa 1891, rectangular form with arched top, cast openwork foliate and cupid decoration, 11 troy oz., 11¼in. long. (Skinner) $1,955

An American silver water pitcher, Gorham Mfg. Co., 1887, the baluster body with an applied median band of fan-shaped panels and foliage, 10¼in. high, 36oz. (Christie's) $940

A silver and mixed-metal pitcher, Tiffany & Co., New York, circa 1880, the hand-hammered surface applied with silver and copper carp amid engraved and applied seagrasses, 7¼in. high, 24oz. 10dwt. (Christie's) $18,400

An American silver and other metals 'Japanese style' water pitcher, Tiffany & Co., 1877-1879, the rounded body and cylindrical neck spot-hammered, engraved and applied with aquatic plants, 917gr., 19.4cm. high. (Sotheby's) $20,700

Whiting Harvard University polo trophy pitcher, New York, circa 1892, cylindrical, the waisted body with inscription to front, the circular base with molded scroll decoration, approximately 33 troy oz., 9in. high.(Skinner) $1,380

Pair of Gorham pitchers, third quarter 19th century, the body chased and embossed to lower section with dense floral sprays, 7¾in. high, approximately 35 troy oz. total. (Skinner) $1,610

Gorham water pitcher, Providence, 1895, the rim and base with beaded bands, the handle with cast acanthus decoration, on an octagonal molded base, approximately 26 troy oz., 9¼in. high. (Skinner) $633

An American silver water pitcher, Tiffany & Co., New York, circa 1882, the whole embossed and chased with large-scale water lilies and foliage against a patterned ground, 28oz., 7¾in. high. (Sotheby's) $8,625

Gorham water pitcher, Providence, 1886, plain baluster shape with rolled lip, chased and engraved scroll handle, the body with repoussé foliates on a textured background allover decoration, approximately 21 troy oz., 8in. long. (Skinner) $2,070

An American silver "Japanese style" water pitcher, Tiffany & Co., New York, circa 1880, applied with die-rolled bands, engraved with aquatic plants and applied with swimming fish, 1,135gm., 23.2cm. high. (Sotheby's) $9,000

A late Victorian novelty pin cushion, l.ondon 1895 , James Samuel Bell & Louis Willmott, modelled as a butterfly, the two wings forming the cushions, 13cm. wide.
(Bonhams & Brooks) $770

A late-Victorian silver mounted novelty pin cushion, Chester 1897, John Deakin & William Deakin, modelled as a crown, circular simulated ermine trimmed base, 7cm. wide.
(Bonhams & Brooks) $532

A novelty silver pin cushion, Birmingham, maker's mark of S. Blanckensee and Sons Ltd., modelled as a shoe, wooden base, with later velvet pin cushion and shoelace, 12.5cm. long.
(Bonhams & Brooks) $185

PLATES

A set of twelve silver dinner plates, International Silver Co., Meriden, Connecticut, 20th century, the rim with band of laurel leaves and berries, the border with acanthus leaves amid scrolling foliage,11½in. diameter, 241oz. 10dwt.
(Christie's) $10,350

A set of six chrysanthemum-pattern bread-and-butter plates and a chrysanthemum-pattern bowl, maker's mark of Tiffany & Co., New York, 1907-1947, the plates 6½in. diameter, the bowl 11in. long, 59oz. 10dwt. (Christie's) $4,600

A set of sixteen silver bread and butter plates and a silver bread tray, Gorham Mfg. Co., Providence, 1917, martelé, the bread and butter plates circular, the wavy rim repoussé and chased, the bread tray oval, 7in. diameter, 13¼in. long, 132oz. 10dwt.
(Christie's) $19,550

A set of twelve American silver-gilt plates, William B. Durgin Co., Concord, NH, and Providence, RI, 20th century, the borders chased with shells and sprays of flowers in panels, 265oz.
(Sotheby's) $10,350

Tiffany & Co. cake plate, 1908-1947, circular, the shaped rim with molded foliate edge, the face with reticulated and engraved bands, approximately 47 troy oz., 13¼in. diameter. (Skinner) $1,955

A George III silver oval platter, Paul Storr, London, 1880, the border engraved with an armorial, 35oz., 14¼in. long.
(Sotheby's) $1,840

A Charles II porringer with scrolled handles, embossed with laurel wreaths above acanthus leaves, 7in. wide, London 1680, 5oz. 13dwt.
(Andrew Hartley) $3,360

Gorham baby porringer, 1907, round, the sides embossed with a scene of bears playing and eating, with open scrolled handle, engraved to underside, *Baby 1910*, length to handle 6½in.
(Skinner) $805

Philip Elston, Exeter 1733, an early George II small porringer, the part ribbed and Gothic fluted body to stamped leaf decoration, 6cm. high.
(Woolley & Wallis) $559

A George I silver two-handled porringer, London 1714, Robert Timbrell and Joseph Bell I, the body with part fluted decoration and punched with stylized flowers and leaves, approximate weight 6oz., 8.25cm. high.
(Bonhams & Brooks) $1,960

An American silver porringer, maker's mark *EP* in shaped shield, mid 18th century, of typical form with wide bombé body, keyhole handle engraved with contemporary initials $S^G A$ above the date *1746*, 9oz., 5¼in. diameter.
(Sotheby's) $3,737

A Queen Anne Irish miniature two handled porringer, Dublin 1702, maker's mark of Joseph Walker, circular form, part fluted decoration below a stylized border, with scroll handles, approximate weight 33g., 3.5cm. high.
(Bonhams) $6,160

An Irish Provincial porringer, Robert Goble, Cork, circa 1682, of baluster form with floral and foliate scroll motifs and two applied scroll handles with serrated edge, 9.1cm., 6oz. (Christie's) $8,860

A Queen Anne two handled porringer, London 1703, Timothy Ley, part fluted decoration, ropework girdle, square beaded scroll handles, central scroll mounted oval cartouche, lacquered, approximate weight 12oz., 10.3cm. high. (Bonhams) $1,540

A William and Mary silver porringer, maker's mark of CK, London 1686, two double scroll handles, engraved to the base, *G* over *CA*, *1688*, approximately 8oz., 8.5cm. high. (Bonhams) $1,946

Four Engish silver salts probably London, circa 1760, hallmarks badly worn, chased decoration, 8.8 troy oz. (Eldred's) $330

Three-piece French silver condiment set, Paris, 1819-38, includes a mustard pot with hinged lid and a pair of open salts, shell-form on an oval pedestal foot, 18.0 troy oz. (Eldred's) $1,760

Pair of sterling silver footed salts, with marks for Hester Bateman, London (1781-1782), in shell form. (Eldred's) $935

A set of four George I silver trencher-salts, London, 1723, each plain oblong with cut corners, with molded rims, 8cm. long, 6oz. (Christie's) $2,925

A set of four Victorian parcel-gilt silver figural salts, John Samuel Hunt for Hunt and Roskell, London 1862, modelled as a street urchin and companion, fruit seller and flower girl, 2329gr. (Sotheby's) $36,460

A good set of four Victorian parcel-gilt salts by Charles Favell & Co., Sheffield, 1874, of trefoil form with three projecting points, beaded rims and leaf borders. (Bonhams) $728

One of a pair of George IV salt cellars, London 1824 and 1825, possibly William Eaton, embossed foliate decoration, on three chinaman feet, approximate weight 12oz., 9.5cm. diameter. (Bonhams)   (Two) $462

Pair of Sterling silver oval fenestrated baskets, with London hallmarks for 1903-4, 18.8 troy oz. (Eldred's) $1,100

A George III silver boat-shaped salt, by Hester Bateman, London 1788, with bead borders and turned-over scroll ends, engraved neo-classical armorial to one side, gilt interior, 12.4cm. long, 2.5oz. (Bonhams) $334

German .800 silver fish form sauceboat, late 19th/ early 20th century, in the shape of an open-mouthed fish, with embossed and engraved scales, with glass eyes, approximately 13 troy oz., 10¾in. long. (Skinner) $1,495

George Jensen Inc., USA silver sauceboat, Alphonse Lapaglia, New York, second quarter 20th century, the plain body above applied ball and loop stem, approximately 10 troy oz., 7¼in. long. (Skinner) $460

A pair of silver sauce boats, by C J Vander Ltd., Sheffield 1965, gadroon borders, leaf capped flying scroll handle, each on three shell capped scroll legs with hoof feet, approximately 29oz., 21.5cm. long. (Bonhams) $695

A pair of George III Irish silver sauce-boats, Ambrose Boxwell, Dublin, 1787, each plain oval and on three shell, scroll and hoof feet, 8½in., 22oz.
(Christie's) $5,216

Four unusual George IV silver sauceboats, James Charles Eddington, London, 1829 and 1830, formed as shells on rocaille bases and with leaf capped flying scroll handles, 9½in. long, 2661gr.
(Sotheby's) $33,078

A pair of George II silver sauceboats, Richard Innes, London, 1754, engraved with rococo armorials below shaped rim, 8in. long, 653gm.
(Sotheby's) $4,649

A pair of George II silver sauce-boats, John Pollock, London, 1748, the body with shaped rim and griffin head scroll handle, one side engraved with a crest, 6¾in. long, 21oz. (Christie's) $4,705

Pair of late Victorian silver sauce boats, by James Wakely and Frank Clarke Wheeler, London 1899, gadrooned border, leaf capped scroll handle, shell capped scroll legs with shell feet, approximately 22oz., 21cm. long.
(Bonhams) $862

A mid 18th century Irish silver sauceboat, Dublin, Richard Tudor, the body embossed with floral and scroll decoration, approximate weight 5oz., 14.5cm. long.
(Bonhams & Brooks) $1,190

An early Victorian silver 'Castle Top' snuff box, Birmingham 1844, Nathaniel Mills, the hinged lid decorated in high relief with a civic building possibly in Nottingham, weight 99g., 7cm. wide.
(Bonhams & Brooks) $2,380

A Chinese silver snuff box, marked with Chinese characters, *90* and maker's mark of Wang Hing, rectangular form, the hinged cover and sides embossed with dragons on a matted background, gilt interior approximate weight 2.5oz., 8.8cm. long. (Bonhams) $323

A George III silver-gilt snuff box, London 1813, Thomas Pemberton & Robert Mitchell, sides and base applied with embossed vine leaf borders with vari-gold highlights, approximate weight 114g. 7cm. wide.
(Bonhams & Brooks) $1,120

A French 18th century silver snuff box, Orléans, circa 1768, the hinged lid, embossed with a battle scene on horseback, 8.5cm. wide.
(Bonhams & Brooks) $1,540

A late 19th century French silver snuff box, maker's mark of *S & F* over a star, the hinged lid embossed with a young child drawing the bust of a young lady, signed *Marcus*, approximate weight 131g., 7cm. diameter.
(Bonhams & Brooks) $392

A late 18th century gilt metal snuff box, the hinged lid set with a lapis lazuli panel, overlaid with an embossed and pierced mythological or Biblical scene in rocaille scrolls, 6cm. wide.
(Bonhams & Brooks) $1,092

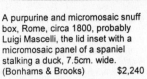

A purpurine and micromosaic snuff box, Rome, circa 1800, probably Luigi Mascelli, the lid inset with a micromosaic panel of a spaniel stalking a duck, 7.5cm. wide.
(Bonhams & Brooks) $2,240

A William IV fox-mask snuff box, by Joseph Willmore, Birmingham, 1835, the oval engine-turned cover with vacant reserve, gilt interior and foliate border, 8cm. long, 2.25oz.
(Bonhams) $3,640

A mid 18th century silver mounted tortoiseshell snuff box, English, apparently unmarked, the mounts with molded borders, stand-away hinge, the lid inlaid with engraved silver and mother of pearl stylized decoration, 7.5cm. wide.
(Bonhams & Brooks) $1,050

A William III silver tankard, London 1695, Samuel Dell, moulded borders, hinged slightly domed lid, weight 24oz., 17.5cm. high. (Bonhams & Brooks) **$4,900**

A late 18th/early 19th century converted, embossed tankard, domed cover, inset with a Danish gilt coin, probably Baltic/Scandinavian, 21cm. high, 23oz. (Christie's) **$1,563**

A George II large tankard of tapered cylindrical form with a domed cover, scroll handle and thumbpiece, by Frances Spilsbury, 1731, 22cm. high, 39.5oz. (Christie's) **$3,542**

A George III silver tankard, Thomas Wallis, London, 1775, with moulded mid-rib, scroll handle, hinged domed cover and openwork scroll thumbpiece, 7½in. high, 29oz. (Christie's) **$2,981**

A mid 17th century Scandinavian silver tankard, Oslo 1641, maker's mark of BP, the hinged lid inscribed *Anders Olvfson Bergete Rasmvs 1650*, approximate weight 30oz., 19cm. high. (Bonhams & Brooks) **$23,800**

A George III tankard, Thomas Whipham & Charles Wright, 1765, of circular section with a central band, the domed lid with an openwork thumbpiece, the handle engraved *A* over *S*l*, 17cm., 12.5oz. (Christie's) **$1,480**

A George III silver tankard, London 1789, Samuel Godbehere and Edward Wigan, domed hinged lid with pierced scroll thumbpiece, scroll handle with a heart shaped terminal, approximate weight 27oz., 20.5cm. high. (Bonhams & Brooks) **$1,610**

A Continental silver-gilt tankard, circa 1600, possibly Hungarian, the body repoussé and chased with three grotesque masks and bunches of fruits within scroll cartouches on matted ground, 7½in. high, 19oz. (Christie's) **$5,962**

A fine German parcel-gilt silver tankard, Hans Lambrecht III, Hamburg, circa 1655, the applied sleeve repoussé and chased with putti emblematic of the Seasons, 26.5cm. high, 2,366gm. (Christie's) **$27,945**

Gorham Aesthetic movement tea and coffee service, Providence, 1880-1881, comprising a teapot, coffee pot, creamer, covered sugar bowl, waste bowl, and kettle on stand, tapered square form, approximately 184 troy oz., 12½in. high. (Skinner) $12,650

Four-piece William Spratling silver and rosewood tea set, Mexico, design created 1958, Provincial pattern, all of silver decorated with six incised curved lines, rosewood handles and finials. (Skinner) $12,000

Repoussé Portuguese tea and coffee set, second quarter 19th century, comprising a teapot, coffee pot, creamer and covered sugar, of baluster form with chased foliates on a textured background, approximately 103 troy oz., coffee pot 11in. high. (Skinner) $1,610

Irish four-piece tea and coffee set, Dublin, 1839-40, comprising a teapot, coffee pot, creamer, and open sugar, all of fluted melon form, the molded rims scalloped with cast melon finials, 75 troy oz., coffee pot 10¼in. high. (Skinner) $5,175

A mid Victorian silver four-piece tea and coffee set, London 1863, Daniel Houle and Charles Houle, bodies engraved with stylized cartouches and stylized and floral decoration, plus a pair of George III silver sugar tongs, approximate weight 75oz., height of coffee pot 26cm. (Bonhams & Brooks) $1,540

Lino Sabattini, a metal como tea and coffee service, designed 1957, for Gallia, comprising a teapot, coffee pot, cream pot and sugar bowl, all of organic streamlined form, and a decanter. (Christie's) $4,098

An American silver four-piece tea and coffee set, Andrew Ellicott Warner, Baltimore, 1817 or 1823, comprising: teapot, coffee pot, waste bowl, and covered sugar urn, the vase-form bodies with foliate bands, 3,592g., 29.2cm. (Sotheby's) $6,600

Gerardus Boyce four-piece tea set, New York, first quarter 19th century, comprising a teapot, creamer, covered sugar and wastebowl, all vasiform with everted lobed rims, foliate engraved and bright-cut bodies, approximately 102 troy oz., teapot 10½in. high. (Skinner) $1,955

Georg Jensen six-piece tea and coffee service, Johan Rohde, Denmark, circa 1915, comprising a teapot, coffee pot, creamer, and covered sugar bowl, all in the 45 C pattern, a 45 C milk jug, and a 45 tea strainer & stand, 96 troy oz., 10½in. high. (Skinner) $13,800

A four-piece William IV tea & coffee service, Charles Reily & George Storer, 1835, each piece of inverted pear form with a central band of robust leaf and flower motifs, raised on an anthemion foot, cream jug and a sugar bowl, each with gilded interiors, height of coffee pot 23.4cm., 74.5oz. (Christie's) $3,290

S. Kirk & Son repoussé silver tea and coffee service, Baltimore, 1880-1890, comprising a teapot, coffee pot, creamer, covered sugar bowl, waste bowl, and kettle on stand, the raised repoussé lids with foliate finials, approximately 163 troy oz. (Skinner) $7,475

A silver and mixed metal tea service, manufactured by Tiffany & Co., circa 1877, comprising: teapot, cream jug, sugar basin, teapot 11.2cm. high. (Christie's) $74,965

Georg Jensen 'No. 736' Art Deco style demitasse set, Harald Nielson, Denmark, first half 20th century, comprising: a coffee pot, creamer, and covered sugar bowl, all cylindrical, oval tray with raised rim and ebony mounted handles, approximately 55 troy oz. (Skinner) $8,050

Bigelow Brothers & Kennard coin silver tea and coffee service, Boston, third quarter 19th century, comprising: a teapot, coffee pot, creamer, and covered sugar bowl, all bulbous, the domed lids with cast flower finials, approximately 92 troy oz., 9½in. high. (Skinner) $1,840

A George II silver tea-caddy, David Willaume, London, 1743, plain oblong with cut corners, molded borders, hinged stepped cover with detachable cylindrical cover, 4¾in. long, 17oz.
(Christie's) $10,805

A good George IV tea caddy by Samuel Dutton, 1825, decorated with panels in high relief after the style of Teniers, depicting tavern scenes under smaller panels depicting dogs searching for or retrieving game, 16.5cm. high, 18.75oz. (Bonhams) $2,940

A George III oval tea caddy, urn shaped finial, bright cut engraved foliate detail, London 1786, oval 14.5cm., 13oz.
(Wintertons) $1,049

A Liberty & Co silver tea caddy and cover, the design attributed to Bernard Cuzner, Birmingham 1912, hammered in low relief with a frieze of fruiting cherries, the domed cover with similar panel, between beaded borders, 5½in. high.
(Christie's) $2,632

A pair of George III silver-gilt tea caddies, London 1790, Michael Starkey, approximate weight 20oz., in a fitted early 19th century lacquered Cantonese box, height of caddies 12cm. high.
(Bonhams & Brooks) $3,640

A George III oval boat shaped tea caddy, with a reeded swing handle, a plain convex molding below the rim, by John Emes, 1806, (the handle a Victorian replacement by Henry Holland), 16.5cm. long, 18.75oz. (Christie's) $3,128

A Tiffany & Co. white metal tea caddy, circa 1880, model 1809, shouldered form hammered with abstract scrolling ground, 7in. high.
(Christie's) $5,757

A pair of George II silver tea-caddies and matching sugar-box, Samuel Taylor, London, 1745, caddies and box 13.5cm. high, 54oz. (Christie's) $11,885

Continental tea caddy, late 19th century, shaped rectangular form, the circular lid with chased spiral reeding and repoussé cherubs, approximately 8 troy oz., 5in. high.
(Skinner) $460

Victorian kettle and stand, Roberts and Slater, Sheffield, 1852, squat baluster form with chased lobing, the lid with repoussé engraved scrolls, 76 troy oz, 14½in. high. (Skinner) $2,530

A George IV Sheffield plate kettle on stand, the circular compressed body with a girdle moulding and engraved with a plumed coronet crest, Matthew Boulton Plate Company.
(Woolley & Wallis) $268

A silver kettle and stand with tray, Gratchev, St. Petersburg, 1896, the kettle of oval section and hinged lid decorated with half-lobing, length of tray 43cm.
(Sotheby's) $4,410

Portuguese .833 silver kettle on stand, second half 19th century, inverted pear form, the domed lid with chased foliates and wood urn finial, approximately 54 troy oz., 14¼in. high. (Skinner) $920

A mid Victorian silver kettle on stand, London 1860, Robert Garrard, of circular panelled form, the stand of panelled circular form, the center with a fitted burner, approximate total weight 87oz., 37cm. high.
(Bonhams & Brooks) $2,660

A Victorian kettle on stand, the compressed globular body engraved with a seahorse pierced with an arrow crest within a garter cartouche, Fordham & Falkener, Sheffield 1876, 36oz. all in. (Woolley & Wallis) $539

Georgian silver chinoiserie kettle on stand, Henry Cowper or Henry Chawner, London, 1790, the domed lid with repoussé fruit and cast flower finial, on a triangular stand 64 troy oz. 16in. high. (Skinner) $1,840

Sheffield Plate tea kettle and stand, Elkington & Co., mid 19th century, the bulbous lobed teapot with domed chased and engraved lid with cast foliate finial, on four foliate feet, 12in. high.
(Skinner) $431

Japanese silver kettle on stand, marked *Arthur & Bond, Yokohama*, late 19th/early 20th century, with finely hammered ground heavily chased and embossed, with burner, approximately 45 troy oz., 13½in. high. (Skinner) $1,840

George III silver teapot, Francis Crump, London, 1764, inverted pear form with gadrooned rim, spirally reeded domed lid with bud finial, approximately 19 troy oz. 7¼in. high.
(Skinner) $920

A George III Irish teapot by Gustavus Byrne, Dublin, 1800, the oblong body with curved sides, fluted corners and bright-engraved bands, 16.75oz.
(Bonhams) $1,008

An American silver teapot, Jacob Hunt, Boston, circa 1750, of apple shape engraved around the cover with foliate strapwork and husks, 631gr. gross, 5¾in. high.
(Sotheby's) $41,400

An 18th century Dutch teapot, Amsterdam circa 1770, maker's mark of Gerrit Brandt, melon form, ivory scroll handle, hinged foliate cover with a melon finial, leaf capped spout, approximate weight 8oz., 12.5cm. high.
(Bonhams) $4,004

A Georgian teapot and stand, of panelled oval form with pineapple finial on domed lid, 11¼in. wide, London 1796, marks for Peter and Ann Bateman, 21oz. 16dwt.
(Andrew Hartley) $973

A George III silver teapot, London 1819, Philip Rundell, the body with a band of stylized foliate decoration against a matted background, approximate weight 32oz., 15.5cm. high.
(Bonhams & Brooks) $1,960

Britannia silver teapot, Crichton Bros., London, 1909, bulbous, with wood mushroom finial, and ear handle, on a molded base, approximately 15 troy oz., 4¾in. high. (Skinner) $403

A mid Victorian silver teapot, Exeter 1853, James and Josiah Williams, domed hinged lid with flower finial, scroll handle, on four bracket feet, approximate weight 23oz., width 28cm. (Bonhams) $559

A Regency teapot, the domed cover with chased pine cone finial, the ogee sides embossed and chased with flowers and foliage, London 1802, 24½oz gross.
(Dreweatt Neate) $588

A George III oval wirework toast rack by Robert Hennell, 1788, the oval base with reeded rim and bracket feet, 17.6cm. long, 6.5oz. (Bonhams) $1,050

A rare James Dixon & Sons electroplated toast rack, designed by Dr. Christopher Dresser, 1880, wirework form, the rectangular base supporting alternate triangular dividers and central T bar handle, 5in. wide.(Christie's) $7,402

George III silver toast rack of seven circular bars to a shaped rectangular base, all supported on four ball feet, London 1814, maker NH. (G.A. Key) $200

TRAYS & SALVERS

A Georgian tray of oval form, the raised fluted rim with reeded edging, 17in. wide, marks for John Crouch and Thomas Hannan, London 1789, 43oz. 19dwt. (Andrew Hartley) $3,058

Hester Bateman Waiter, London, 1787, circular, with molded gadrooned rim, with engraved coat of arms to center, on three pad feet, approximately 8 troy oz., 6³/₈in. (Skinner) $1,035

A late 18th century Russian oval two-handled tray, maker's mark *ED* (cyrillics), Moscow, 1792 with openwork handles and engraved borders, 57.7cm. long, 66oz. (Bonhams) $2,100

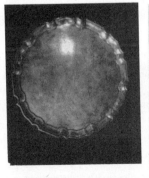

Barbour sterling silver tray, Meriden, Connecticut, early 20th century, rectangular, the waved rim with molded scroll and floral edge, approximately 51 troy oz., 15in. long. (Skinner) $2,070

An Edwardian silver salver, with an engraved crest and signatures, approximately 47oz., 1908, 14in. diameter. (Sworders) $363

Sterling silver dish with repousse foliate and floral border, maker's mark *RC*, untraced, 13in. diameter, 22.0 troy oz. (Eldred's) $770

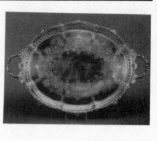

An Edward VII two-handled rectangular tea tray with gadroon, shell and acanthus edging, 74.5cm. over handles, Charles Favell & Co., Sheffield 1905, 166.6oz.
(Bearne's) $1,440

An American silver large tea tray, Gorham Mfg. Co., Providence, RI, 1890, the waved rim deeply embossed and chased with flowers, 6,088gr., 29in. long.
(Sotheby's) $12,650

A modern tea tray, Goldsmiths & Silversmiths Co., 1926, the oval tray with a leaf heightened bead border, with two similar handles, length 70.5cm., 101oz.
(Christie's) $2,996

A modern two-handled oval tea tray, the lobed rim with reeded edging, 66.5cm. over handles, Mappin & Webb, Birmingham 1966, 133.1oz. (Bearne's) $1,440

Pair of large German silver shell form serving trays, scroll bead and leaf handles in textured rays emanating to scalloped border, length: 15¾in., total weight 74oz.
(Freeman) $4,368

A George III two-handled tea tray, of rounded oblong form with a border of gadrooning and foliate shells at the corners, probably by William Stroud, 1809, 60cm. long x 33cm. wide, 72oz.
(Christie's) $4,959

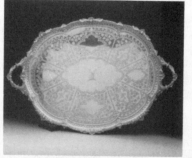

Edwardian Art Nouveau styled silver dressing table tray, well embossed with trailing foliage and similar floral designs, 12 x 9in. Birmingham, 1905.
(G.A. Key) $384

A late Victorian silver two-handled tray, London 1879, Richard Martin and Ebenezer Hall, beaded and foliate borders, foliate scoll handles, approximate weight 132oz., length handle to handle 72.5cm.
(Bonhams & Brooks) $3,920

Tiffany & Co. 'Chrysanthemum' tea tray, New York, 1875-91, rectangular, the everted rim with molded chrysanthemum decoration, approximately 215 troy oz., 27⁷/₈in. long to handles.
(Skinner) $18,400

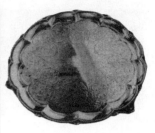

An American silver large well-and-tree platter, Tiffany & Co., New York, 1891-1902, chrysanthemum pattern, on four matching feet, 3,934gr., 24in. long.
(Sotheby's) $6,900

Large halllmarked silver salver of shaped circular design with heavy gadrooned rim, plain center, 15in. diameter, Sheffield 1927, 60oz.
(Aylsham) $825

Good Victorian silver salver of shaped circular design with shell and beaded edge, on three pierced cast feet, 12in. diameter, London 1867, 26½oz.
(Aylsham) $594

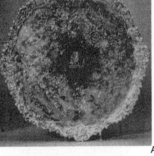

English silver plated salver, Ellis-Barker, Birmingham, late 19th century, circular with shaped rim embossed with foliate and scroll pattern with devil's head medallions. (Skinner) $690

An American silver and other metals 'Japanese style' gourd-shaped tray, Tiffany and Co., New York, circa 1879, with spot-hammered ground, inlaid with an iris plant, 36oz. gross, 16¼in. long.
(Sotheby's) $24,725

Gorham Martelé charger, Providence, circa 1900, the hammered circular charger with shaped and waved rim with chased lobing, approximately 38 troy oz., 13in. diameter.
(Skinner) $5,462

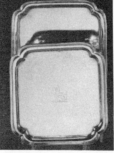

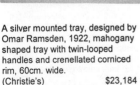

A silver mounted tray, designed by Omar Ramsden, 1922, mahogany shaped tray with twin-looped handles and crenellated corniced rim, 60cm. wide.
(Christie's) $23,184

A pair of George I silver salvers, Edward Cornock, London 1726, square with incurved molded corners, wolf sejant crest and bracket supports, 6in. square, 455gm.
(Sotheby's) $8,940

A Victorian shaped oval two-handled tea tray initialled *H* at the center within a reeded border, 72cm. over handles, Harrison Brothers and Howson, Sheffield 1898, 106oz.
(Bearne's) $1,238

A large Spanish metalware soup tureen and cover of oval bombé form with two handles and four foliate scroll feet, 54cm. long. (Christie's) $2,208

A George III silver soup-tureen and cover, Joseph Angell, London, 1819, the detachable domed cover with rose finial, with flower and foliage border on a matted ground, 16in. wide, 133oz. (Christie's) $8,942

A rare turtle soup tureen, apparently unmarked, the oval body and hinged lid chased and ribbed to imitate turtle shell, applied head and fins, 21½in. long. (Sotheby's) $13,440

Hunt & Roskell, late Storr & Mortimer tureen, London, 1873, urn-shape with everted beaded rim with acanthus leaf band, the domed lid with cast vegetable bunch finial, approximately 212 troy oz, 12¼in. wide. (Skinner) $13,800

A George III two handled sauce tureen and cover, London 1813, maker's mark of Paul Storr, oval bellied form, lion mask mounted shell capped reeded handles, part fluted decoration, gadroon and shell border, approximate weight 41oz., 24cm. long. (Bonhams) $4,620

A fine French Louis XV soup tureen and cover, Valenciennes circa 1768, maker's mark of Philippe Joseph Becquet, oval bellied form, shell capped scroll handles, the domed pull-off cover with line and matted decoration, with an artichoke finial, approximate weight 88oz., overall length 36.5cm. (Bonhams) $12,012

A late 18th/early 19th century French oval soup tureen and stand, by Jacques-Florent-Joseph Beydel, Paris 1798/1809, complete with liner, plain, with stiff leaf borders, length of stand 50.5cm., 159oz. (Bonhams) $5,600

A French silver-gilt soup tureen, cover and stand, Aucoc, Paris, circa 1900, the shaped oval fluted tureen on four foliate pad feet with two ring handles, the stand 18in. long, 191oz. (Christie's) $9,873

Small Edwardian EPBM soup tureen and lid of compressed oval design with cast grapevine rim and standing on four cast curved feet, 13 x 6in. overall, circa 1900. (G.A. Key) $185

Victorian E P B M tea urn of vase shape to a circular base, having lion mask ring handles, baluster finial to lid, 24in. tall.
(Aylsham) $166

Sheffield Plate hot water urn, first half 19th century, with everted repoussé foliate gadrooned rim, the lid with gadrooned edge and reeded foliate finial, 18in. high.
(Skinner) $1,035

A Victorian electroplated tea urn of vase form, with beaded loop handles, a square pedestal foot, and engraved decoration, 61cm. high. (Christie's) $451

English silver plated samovar, mid 19th century, vasiform with beaded scroll handles with ivory mounts, the spout in the form of a goat's head, 23in. high.
(Skinner) $747

A late 18th / early 19th century Old Sheffield plated tea urn, pull-off cover with flower finial and foliate decoration, 36cm. high.
(Bonhams & Brooks) $392

A late Victorian tea urn, the panelled vase shape body engraved with an armorial, reeded moldings, the detachable pinnacle cover with fluted ivory finial, 16in., Richard Martin & Ebenezer Hall, Sheffield, 1893, 59oz. all in.
(Woolley & Wallis) $1,130

VASES

An Edwardian Art Nouveau two handled vase, Birmingham 1901, maker's mark of Liberty and Co. also marked *CYMRIC*, with a textured girdle applied with ten turquoise cabochons, approximate weight 43oz., 34.8cm. high.
(Bonhams) $5,586

A pair of Continental silver filigree and enamel hexagonal vases, late 19th century, the slender baluster bodies with twin handles, on later circular bases, the panels applied with enamel flowers and foliage, 7½in. high. (Christie's) $545

Archibald Knox for Liberty & Co., vase, 1903, the upper broad silver band casing transparent green glass, the upper part inset with turquoise roundels, Birmingham, 1903, 4½in.
(Sotheby's) $15,660

A silver vesta case of rounded rectangular form, one side enamelled with a study of a snarling tiger, American, late 19th century, 6.3cm. (Christie's) $1,852

A brass vesta case in the form of a sleeping piglet, probably English, late 19th century, 5.5cm. (Christie's) $518

An Edwardian vesta case of rectangular form, the front enamelled with a study of a veteran car, Mappin and Webb, London 1905, 5.5cm. (Christie's) $1,388

A silver vesta case of rounded rectangular form, the front enamelled with a shaped oval study of a ballerina, American, Gorham, late 19th century, 6.1cm. (Christie's) $1,666

A Victorian combination vesta case and wick holder, in the form of a horseshoe, the front and reverse engraved with initials and a date, George Unite, Birmingham 1881, 5.4cm. (Christie's) $420

A Victorian vesta case, of rectangular form, the front enamelled with four dominoes and a crown, Saunders and Shepherd, Birmingham 1896, 5cm. (Christie's) $1,316

A Victorian vesta case, of rectangular form, the front enamelled in words and pictures, *A Match For You At Any Time*, the reverse engraved with initials, *L.E.*, Birmingham 1887, 5.5cm. (Christie's) $410

A Victorian vesta case, the front enamelled with a bottle of Bass Pale Ale, a pipe and a glass of beer, George Unite, Birmingham 1897, 4.1cm. (Christie's) $575

A three-color gold vesta case, the body with applied vari-colored gold initials, ferns, foliage, an insect and a turtle and a crane at a waters edge, probably American, late nineteenth century. (Christie's) $2,303

A silver vesta case, double-lidded and engine-turned, one lid with oval vacant cartouche, French, late 19th century, 4.5cm.
(Christie's) $295

A Victorian vesta case, the front enamelled with a standing sentry, Sampson Mordan, London 1886, 6cm. (Christie's) $6,909

An Edwardian vesta case of rectangular form, the front with an enamelled hunting scene, the reverse engraved with initials, Sampson Mordan and Co, London 1901, 5.7cm.
(Christie's) $3,148

A Victorian vesta case, in the form of a bell, the front enamelled with a buoy warning of the presence of asbestos, J.A.&S., Birmingham 1893, 5.2cm.
(Christie's) $1,316

A silver vesta case, in the form of a Napier car radiator grille, the cover engraved *Napier*, the reverse with presentation initials, import marks for London, 1913, 5.4cm.
(Christie's) $822

A plated brass novelty vesta case in the form of a depiction of Ally Sloper, the exterior still bearing much of the original paint, English, late 19th century, 6cm.
(Christie's) $518

A Victorian vesta case, front enamelled with a scene of a figure dressed all in red, George Unite, Birmingham 1886, 4.5cm.
(Christie's) $1,809

A Victorian vesta case, the front enamelled with the phrase, *In Me A Match You'll Always Find*, mark's indistinct, Chester, circa 1885, 4.5cm. (Christie's) $461

A Victorian vesta case, the front enamelled with figures standing in front of a wooden shack, William H. Haseler, Birmingham 1899, 4.5cm.
(Christie's) $904

A George III silver vinaigrette, Birmingham 1811, William Pugh, engraved with a prick-dot circular motif, the cartouche inscribed *Rose* engraved with a single rose. (Bonhams & Brooks) $276

An early Victorian silver 'Castle Top', vinaigrette, Birmingham 1844, Nathaniel Mills the hinged lid applied with an image of Windsor Castle in high relief, 4cm. wide. (Bonhams & Brooks) $4,060

A George III silver gilt vinaigrette, London 1814, William Edwards, applied with embossed vine leaf borders, engine turned decoration, flange thumbpiece, 3.3cm. long. (Bonhams & Brooks) $440

A William IV silver vinaigrette, Birmingham 1834, by Lawrence & Co., of good gauge with engine turned covers and cast floral edge, 3.2cm. (Bonhams) $205

A George III silver vinaigrette, Birmingham 1816, by S. Pemberton, of curved oblong form with canted corners engraved flowers and leafage, gilt interior, 3.8cm. (Bonhams) $269

A late George III scallop shell shape vinaigrette, the hinged cover shell reeded, the gilded interior with a pierced grille, 1⅛in. L Y R, Birmingham 1806. (Woolley & Wallis) $152

An early Victorian silver vinaigrette, Birmingham 1843, Nathaniel Mills, the hinged lid engraved with a scene, possibly Bristol Cathedral, 3.8cm. wide. (Bonhams & Brooks) $1,050

A 19th century gold mounted agate vinaigrette, the hinged lid set with a circular agate panel, engine turned decoration, pierced grille, diameter 2.6cm. (Bonhams & Brooks) $820

An early Victorian silver vinaigrette, Birmingham 1845, Edward Smith, the hinged lid engraved with a river scene on an engine turned radial ground, 3.7cm. wide. (Bonhams & Brooks) $1,050

A George III novelty silver vinaigrette, Birmingham 1790, of Samuel Pemberton, modelled as a purse, bright-cut decoration. (Bonhams & Brooks) $224

A cased early Victorian silver vinaigrette, Birmingham 1839, Nathaniel Mills, the whole engraved with foliate scrolls against a textured ground, 4cm. wide. (Bonhams & Brooks) $570

An early Victorian silver 'Castle Top' vinaigrette, Birmingham 1840, Gervase Wheeler, the hinged lid with a low relief side view of Abbotsford house, 4.2cm. wide. (Bonhams & Brooks) $630

A pair of French silver wine coolers, Fannière Frères, Paris, circa 1870, the lower part of the body with band of broad flutes, the upper part each cast and chased with differing bacchic processions, 9in. high, 275oz. (Christie's) $13,714

A good pair of late period Old Sheffield plated wine coasters with four wide fluted, foliate feet and twin shell and scroll handles, R. Gainsford, Sheffield circa 1815, 34cm. wide.
(Christie's) $4,416

A pair of Transitional period Old Sheffield plated wine coolers on shaped quatrefoil bases with husk matting, circa 1840, 27.5cm. high.
(Christie's) $3,430

A rare silver wine cooler, signed *J.E. Caldwell, Philadelphia*, circa 1835, each handle formed as intertwined vines supporting a fully-modelled horse, 13¼in. high, 172oz, 10dwt.
(Christie's) $31,050

A set of four George III silver wine coolers, S.C. Younge & Co., Sheffield 1817, the campana shaped bodies with two fluted foliage bracket handles, 8½in. high, 206oz. (Christie's) $31,280

Jean Desprès, wine cooler, 1930s, silver-plated metal, slightly tapering cylindrical form, decorated with stylized chain motif and martelé finish, 10in.
(Sotheby's) $3,132

A pair of George III silver wine coolers, Daniel Smith & Robert Sharp, London, 1782-83, armorial engraved between finely cast ram's head handles above fluting, 10¼in., 3950gm.
(Sotheby's) $55,577

A pair of George IV silver wine coolers, William Stroud, London 1825, with two leaf and shell-capped bracket handles with Bacchic mask terminals, 10in. high, 176oz.
(Christie's) $41,492

A pair of German silver wine coolers, Georg Roth, Hanau, circa 1890, after Meissonnier design, baluster with mermaid handles holding serpents, 11in. high, 4969gm.
(Sotheby's) $10,728

A pair of spelter Art Nouveau style female busts, titled 'Cleopatra' and 'Salambo', on flared onyx bases, 13in. (Woolley & Wallis)　$269

Henry Fugère (1872-?), A Racing Skier, a spelter model of a male skier on a base, impressed signature *H Fugère*, 15½in. high. (Christie's)　$2,889

An Art Deco green patinated spelter figural group, of man and jaguar, 48cm. diameter. (Christie's)　$612

A pair of unusual spelter figural candlesticks, third quarter 19th century, modelled as a jockey and a trainer or owner, the hats as nozzles, the bases inscribed *E.Guillemin*, 12¾in. and 12½in. (Christie's)　$2,537

'Diane', a silvered and gilded spelter figure, cast from a model by D.H.Chiparus, of the mythological huntress, poised about to take aim, 64cm. high. (Christie's)　$2,944

'Coquelicot' a patinated spelter bust, cast from a model by E.Villanis, signed in the metal, 41cm. high. (Christie's)　$658

A pair of candlesticks in cold-painted and patinated spelter, unsigned, each 38.8cm. high. (Christie's)　$524

A French polychrome spelter bust of an Arab, late 19th century, on an integral domed square section base cast with stylised foliage, 18in. high. (Christie's)　$1,447

A pair of figural spelter vases, cast from a model by Auguste Moreau, signed in the metal, 29cm. high. (Christie's)　$483

A Gandharan gray stone frieze of three dancing girls and a musician, 11in. wide, 3rd/4th century. (Christie's) $858

A Nepalese gray stone panel, depicting a dancing deity wearing head-dress and jewelry, the left foot raised on a rocky platform metal stand, 24in. high, 12th century. (Christie's) $924

Carved stone wildcat, 20th century, full-bodied form with conforming carved linear design, no stand, 41in. long. (Skinner) $2,990

A Gandharan gray stone head plaque, with elaborate hairstyle, metal stand, 7in. high. (Christie's) $369

Two carved stone corbels, 19th century, each of a satyr mask, 18in. high. (Christie's) $956

Folk Art carved sandstone bust of a man, Michigan, the bust depicting a man wearing a hat and coat, weathered surface, 23¾in. high. (Skinner) $748

A Central Javanese Burobodur style Andesite brick depicting a female bust, holding a flower, metal stand, 10½in. high; and four similar, all 9th century. (Christie's) $2,016

A Continental carved stone urn, first half 20th century, of oval form, with everted rim, the lobed underside above a waisted socle on a square base, 20in. wide. (Christie's) $461

An Eastern Javanese Andesite tile fragment, depicting three figures wearing loose robes, 14in. high, 13th century. (Christie's) $150

A Louis XV Aubusson chinoiserie tapestry, third quarter 18th century, after Jean-Joseph Dumons and from a sketch by François Boucher, possibly by Jean-François Picon, woven in wools and silks, depicting La Danse from the Tenture Chinoise series, 8ft.5½in. x 14ft.11½in. (Christie's) $45,795

A Franco-Flemish pastoral millefleurs tapestry, circa 1500-1520, woven in wools and silks, depicting a noble pastorale and depicting a goat flanked to the left by a lady, to the right by a gentleman pointing to the goat, within a fantasy garden, 4ft.10in. x 7ft.2in. (Christie's) $224,005

A Paris (Atelier du Faubourg Saint-Germain) mythological tapestry, by Raphaël and Sebastien-Francois de la Planche, third quarter 17th century, after designs by Michel I Corneille, woven in wools and silks, depicting Erminia Returns to her Countrymen from the series of Tancred and Clorinda after Torquato Tasso, 10ft.10in. x 10ft.11in. (Christie's) $63,403

A Brussels mythological tapestry, by Jean Baptiste Vermillion, first half 18th century, after designs by Jan Van Orley, woven in wools and silks, from The History of Psyche series, 10ft.8in. x 12ft.2in. (Christie's) $33,005

A Flemish pastoral tapestry, first half 18th century, possibly Audenarde, woven in wools and silks, the rectangular scene depicting country folk eating outside, in a wooded landscape, 102 x 128in. (Christie's) $26,696

A Louis XIV Aubusson pastoral tapestry, woven in wools and silks, depicting an extensive wooden landscape, centered by a couple and a peasant carrying two buckets, 9ft.1in. x 10ft.5in. (Christie's) $9,430

A Chiltern Hugmee musical teddy bear, with blond mohair, black plastic nose, orange and black plastic eyes, keywind musical movement, swivel head and jointed limbs with velvet pads, 17in. high, late 1950s. (Christie's) $534

A Steiff teddy bear, with beige curly mohair, brown and black glass eyes, pronounced snout, brown stitched nose, mouth and claws, swivel head, 19in. tall, 1950s. (Christie's) $1,097

A red Chiltern teddy bear, with amber glass eyes, 17in. tall, 1930s, and an illustrated manuscripted story book of the bear's adventures written by the family's French governess in 1938. (Christie's) $1,255

A Steiff 'Petsy' teddy bear, with remains of brown tipped cream mohair, blue and black glass eyes, remains of pink stitched nose, mouth and claws, swivel head, 16in. tall, circa 1928. (Christie's) $415

A Chad Valley teddy bear, with golden curly mohair, deep amber and black glass eyes, pronounced snout, large black stitched 'button' nose, black stitched mouth, 22in. tall, circa 1938. (Christie's) $822

An early American teddy bear, with dark golden brown mohair, black button eye, ears slotted into head, swivel head, jointed limbs and felt pads, 15in. tall, circa 1908. (Christie's) $251

A Chad Valley teddy bear, with golden mohair, pronounced clipped muzzle, large black stitched nose, mouth and claws, orange and black glass eyes, 25½in. high, 1930s. (Christie's) $667

An early English teddy bear with golden mohair, large clear and black glass eyes painted on reverse, linen pads, card lined feet and hump, 18in. tall, probably William J Terry, circa 1913. (Christie's) $1,090

A Merrythought cheeky teddy bear, with golden artificial silk plush, inset velvet muzzle, ears with bells, swivel head and jointed limbs, 24in. high, circa 1960. (Christie's) $917

A Steiff white teddy bear, German, circa 1935, with brown backed glass eyes, vertically stitched pale brown nose, small hump, 17in. (Sotheby's) $4,586

A blonde mohair Chiltern teddy bear, English, circa 1930, with clear glass eyes, black stitched nose, mouth and claws, swivel head and jointed at arms and legs, 15in. tall. (Bonhams & Brooks) $139

A large Steiff white teddy, German, circa 1950, with long curly mohair fur, brown backed glass eyes, vertically stitched brown nose, jointed limbs, 26in. (Sotheby's) $3,352

A fine Steiff golden bear, German, circa 1906, of long lustrous golden mohair, boot button eyes, pronounced clipped snout with horizontally stitched black nose, 13¾in. (Sotheby's) $3,881

A Merrythought teddy bear, English, circa 1930, the blonde mohair bear with orange glass eye, shaved muzzle and black stitched nose, mouth and webbed claws, 53cm. tall. (Bonhams & Brooks) $792

A Steiff golden teddy bear called 'Hermann', German, circa 1908, with button and remainder of a white label, with boot button eyes, fluffy ears, pronounced snout with vertically stitched nose, 22in. (Sotheby's) $8,467

A large Steiff brown original bear, German, circa 1950, of long reddish brown fur, with large brown backed glass eyes, vertically stitched black nose, 25in. (Sotheby's) $2,293

A golden mohair Farnell teddy bear, English 1930s, with orange glass eyes, embroidered nose and mouth and large ears, fully jointed plump body with tan rexine pads and stitched claws, 20in. tall. (Bonhams & Brooks) $639

A large Steiff golden mohair teddy bear, German, circa 1930, with large brown backed glass eyes, vertically stitched black nose, large round ears, hump, 27½in. (Sotheby's) $7,232

A Steiff Petsy bear, circa 1928, of brown tipped white mohair plush, with blue glass eyes, pointy nose with apricot vertically stitched nose, 16in. (Sotheby's) $12,877

A Farnell teddy bear, English, circa 1940, the golden mohair bear with orange glass eyes, black stitched nose, mouth and claws, 19in. tall. (Bonhams & Brooks) $500

A Steiff golden bear, German, circa 1935, brown backed glass eyes, vertically stitched black nose, hump, tilt growler, 16½in. (Sotheby's) $4,234

A Steiff golden teddy bear, German, circa 1920, button in ear with remainder of white label, with glass eyes, vertically stitched black nose, hump, 24in. (Sotheby's) $5,645

A Chiltern teddy bear, English, circa 1930, the golden mohair teddy with clear glass eyes, black stitched nose, mouth and claws, swivel head and jointed at shoulders and hips, 19in. tall. (Bonhams & Brooks) $389

A black Steiff bear called 'Black Bear', German, circa 1912, of black mohair plush, with black boot button eyes, pronounced clipped snout, one remaining stitch of a black horizontally stitched nose, jointed head and limbs, 13¾in. (Sotheby's) $18,485

A Steiff teddy bear, German, circa 1906, with large black boot button eyes, clipped pronounced snout, vertically stitched black nose, small fluffy ears, hump, 19¾in. (Sotheby's) $5,292

A large teddy bear, possibly by Chad Valley, English, circa 1950, the golden mohair bear with orange glass eyes, black stitched nose and mouth, swivel head and jointed at shoulders and hips, 29in. tall. (Bonhams & Brooks) $153

A Steiff center seam bear, German, circa 1910, of golden mohair with boot button eyes, vertically stitched nose, long clipped snout, round fluffy ears, working growler, 20in. (Sotheby's) $6,174

An SIT French mahogany desk telephone by the Société des Téléphones, Paris, with silvered handset and open mouth-piece, second earpiece and call key.
(Auction Team Köln) $535

A wood-cased Scandinavian line dial machine, with two keys, horn receiver and speech key.
(Auction Team Köln) $736

A field telephone exchange, in portable box with carrying handles, with 26 plugs and one head piece, circa 1938.
(Auction Team Köln) $313

A very rare Ericsson Tunnan local battery desk telephone with semicircular magneto cover, circa 1892.
(Auction Team Köln) $4,698

A Swiss Army Model 1947 telephone, in wooden case with second receiver and folding crank, 1947.
(Auction Team Köln) $94

An L.M. Ericsson skeleton telephone, the handset inscribed *Elektrisk Bureau Kristiania*, with horn mouthpiece and connection rose.
(Auction Team Köln) $1,658

A rare Siemens & Halske percussion ring desk telephone.
(Auction Team Köln) $2,090

An Austrian wooden extension telephone, with press-button, lacking cover.
(Auction Team Köln) $287

An Elektrisk Telefon Kristiania luxury telephone with cast silvered fascia, on cast iron plinth and lion's paw feet, the tin case with gold decoration, circa 1885
(Auction Team Köln) $9,950

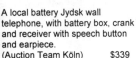

A local battery Jydsk wall telephone, with battery box, crank and receiver with speech button and earpiece.
(Auction Team Köln) $339

A ZBSA 25 'cow's foot' telephone by Friedrich Merk, Munich, with 'Prussian' receiver without mouthpiece horn.
(Auction Team Köln) $491

An undocumented Siemens & Halske Precision telephone in leather mounted walnut and metal case, with double cord, circa 1885.
(Auction Team Köln) $3,869

An L. M. Ericsson Swedish desk telephone in metal case on wooden plinth, with gilt decoration and horn mouthpiece.
(Auction Team Köln) $209

A Bavarian skeleton phone by Friedrich Reiner, Munich, with adjustable microphone and call button, with connection unit, circa 1907. (Auction Team Köln)
                                    $6,795

A National Telephone Company Ltd. local battery desk telephone, British Ericsson model in wooden case, handset with speech button and horn, with connection board, circa 1900.
(Auction Team Köln) $663

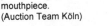
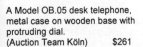

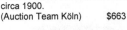

A Model OB.05 desk telephone, metal case on wooden base with protruding dial.
(Auction Team Köln) $261

A special edition Ericsson telephone with round dial, ivory with gold decoration.
(Auction Team Köln) $197

A French desk telephone with frontal dial, earthing button and second earpiece.
(Auction Team Köln) $104

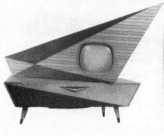

An HMV Model 900 early flat mirror television, in original condition, circa 1937. (Auction Team Köln) $2,113

A rare Kuba de Luxe radio-TV combination set, with Nord-Mende TV and radio, 1962. (Auction Team Köln) $7,318

A Leningrad TV, produced in East Germany for the Soviet market, with 22cm. diameter round picture tubes, 1955. (Auction Team Köln) $557

A Marconi 705 early prewar mirror television, lacking picture tubes and other parts, 1937. (Auction Team Köln) $975

A. G. Marconi vintage television/wireless, model no. VCR52A, serial no. 9532, 20in. wide. x 40in. high. (Sworders) $725

Ekcovision Model TMB 272 early postwar portable television, for mains and car battery-power. (Auction Team Köln) $185

A Pam 405 single standard television, in a walnut case, circa 1961, 61in. screen. (Sworders) $101

General Electric Model 800 bakelite television with 9in. tubes, circa 1948. (Auction Team Köln) $450

A Sobell 107 early postwar alternating current radio/ television, circa 1949. (Auction Team Köln) $435

TENNIS RACKETS

An early tennis racket, circa 1881, with lop-sided head, ash frame, double stringing, convex wedge, engraved *P.T.A.S. Worthing, 1881*, 21¾in. (Sotheby's) $2,153

Fishtail racket, a racket stamped *Army & Navy Co* to throat, 100% strings, with wood loss to one side, slight twist. (Bonhams & Brooks) $229

Fishtail racket, a 'Deamon' fishtail racket, stamped, one string broken, otherwise good. (Bonhams & Brooks) $215

An early F.H. Ayres prize tennis racket, 1881, the flat-top ash frame stamped indistinctly with model name, convex wedge surmounted with a silver shield. (Sotheby's) $2,153

An F.H. Ayres tennis racket, circa 1880, stamped *Superior, 14oz.*, with ash frame, lop-sided head, double stringing, convex wedge and scored regular grip. (Sotheby's) $1,973

The Tournament 2 ball-tail tennis racket, by Geo. G. Bussey & Co. late transitional flat-top head, shoulder wrapping, two-tone strings. (Sotheby's) $1,794

A silver plated novelty clock/barometer, in the form of crossed tennis rackets, the strings of one holding a clock, the other a barometer, 9in. high. (Sotheby's) $2,870

An F.H. Ayres table tennis set, circa 1900, comprising two pairs of vellum drum rackets, 12in. and 13½in. long, and a later F.H. Ayres wooden case with net, fitting and four balls. (Sotheby's) $986

A F.H. Ayres of London tennis racket, circa 1885, with twin-laminated flat top head frame, convex wedge, stamped with manufacturer's and retailer's name to handle. (Sotheby's) $828

A good small head long handled racket with wire collar to handle, inlaid to throat, stamped *C. Rouillard, 4 Rue de Sargents, Amiens.*
(Bonhams & Brooks) $1,359

A Brouaye real tennis prize racket, 1894, with silver mounts to the grip, hallmarked 1893, velvet grip, the convex wedge covered in red morocco.
(Sotheby's) $3,050

Fred Perry, a Slazenger tennis racket impressed with the initials *F.J.P.* and signed in ink by Fred Perry, circa 1935.
(Bearne's) $477

A pair of Victorian terracotta urns, late 19th century, James Stiff and Sons, Lambeth, the circular bodies with waisted necks with lion masks suspending bell-flower swags to the sides, 23in. high.
(Christie's) $2,199

A terracotta bust of a bishop, 19th century, 14½in. high.
(Christie's) $556

'Belle Histoire', a terracotta figure group, cast from a model by Ch.Raphael Peyre, of three small girls seated huddled together, 53cm. diameter.
(Christie's) $920

A terracotta group of bacchic revellers, probably 18th century, circle of Clodion, a female figure, her hair entwined with vines shown seated on the back of a faun, 14in. high. (Christie's) $8,722

A pair of Continental simulated terracotta busts on plinths, 20th century, one modelled as Pan, the other as a classical style female, above rectangular section breakfronted plinths, 56in. high.
(Christie's) $1,068

A pair of Austrian terracotta figures of a North African man and woman, late 19th or early 20th century, Goldscheider, Vienna, each shown in typical dress, 18¼in. high.
(Christie's) $4,738

Two Austrian polychrome painted terracotta figures of Negro youths, early 20th century, both wearing a fez, 29in. high and 25½in. high.
(Christie's) $2,907

A terracotta bust in the style of Hagenauer, molded mark *Mod.35* to base, 15.5cm. high.
(Christie's) $289

An Austrian polychrome painted terracotta figure of a Negro youth, early 20th century, wearing a fez and shorts, 59½in. high.
(Christie's) $6,904

An embroidered panel, by Lily Yeats, circa 1900, embroidered in silk with an orchard of apple trees in blossom, 10 x 14in.
(Christie's) $2,512

A post classic Rio Grande blanket, circa 1890, woven as a single panel, in handspun wool, in rich red, purple, green, white, dark brown and orange, 90 x 48½in.
(Sotheby's) $3,162

The 37-star 'American Bunting' National flag presented to President Abraham Lincoln by General B.F. Butler, Lowell, Massachusetts, April 11, 1865, approximate length 12ft. by 6ft. wide.
(Sotheby's) $58,250

A fine canvaswork picture, initialled *S.I.*, Connecticut, mid-18th century, brightly colored, crewel-embroidered wool on a canvas ground, 19in. x 14¼in.
(Sotheby's) $203,750

A fine silk embroidered picture, Elizabeth Gray, circa 1820, Lady Elizabeth Gray Petitioning King Edward IV for the Restoration of her Husband's Lands, 28ft. x 30in.
(Sotheby's) $21,450

A fine silk-embroidered mourning picture, The Emblem of America, H. Pearson, probably Byfield Academy, Newburyport, Massachusetts, early 19th century, with George Washington and Liberty, 12¾in. high x 11in. wide.
(Sotheby's) $28,350

A fine, important and rare silk embroidered sconce, Ann Marsh, Philadelphia, 1727-1730, in silk stitches on a silk ground with a double-handled footed urn filled with luxurious blossoms, 17 x 9¾in.
(Sotheby's) $170,750

A fine Imperial yellow silk throne cover, embroidered with bats and cloud bands with silks and metallic threads, 84 x 84cm, Qing Dynasty.
(Bonhams) $801

An English silk embroidered picture, 17th century, depicting a scene from the life of Abraham, set within a garden landscape with animals 10 x 14in., 18th century.
(Christie's) $10,120

A Regency tôle peinte oval tray, early 19th century, the red ground with central reserve painted with Napoleonic soldiers resting in a landscape, 30½in. wide.
(Christie's) $2,944

A French zinc bath, 19th century, with raised ends and twin ring handles to the sides, 26½in. high, 63in. long. (Christie's) $1,472

Painted tin document box, America, late 18th/early 19th century, attributed to Mercy North, Flycreek, New York, the front decorated with two birds and leafy branches of fruit, 6½in. wide.
(Skinner) $1,150

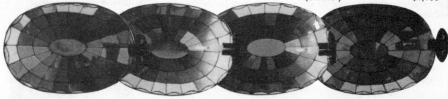

A set of four mirrored tôleware wall sconces, mid 19th century, 12¾in. high x 8½in. (Sotheby's) $9,600

A George III japanned metal tray, circa 1800, the black ground painted with a figure of a sailor holding a Union Jack flag and a figure of Athena standing either side of a medallion portraying the head of George III, 30½in. long.
(Christie's) $1,840

A French tôle peinte jardinière, first half 19th century, of navette outline with wavy border and twin swan neck handles, the brown ground with gilt heightened borders and oval foliate reserves, 11¼in. wide.
(Christie's) $1,120

A Victorian Birmingham tin coal purdonium, painted black and gilt, the hinged cover with a picture of 'The Monarch of the Glen', cast handles and feet, with shovel.
(Woolley & Wallis) $356

Painted tin rowing scull, America, circa 1920, with painted wood and composition articulated rowers, scull 40in. long. (Skinner) $2,300

A Dutch beech skew mouth blockschaaf with Goodman type C mouth, scroll carving surrounding the date *1760* and roundel to wedge, struck *ADH*.
(David Stanley) $385

A 17/18th century French claw hammer head with attractive decoration to both cheeks.
(David Stanley) $133

An exceptionally high quality boxwood chamfer plane, with two wedges and two cutters for cutting a double chamfer, three boxwood and one removable brass spacer, unique 19th century cabinetmaker's tool.
(Tool Shop Auctions) $1,920

A pair of 17½in. wheelright's or coachbuilder's calipers, typical brass arm engraved with the owner's name.
(Tool Shop Auctions) $176

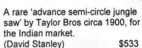

A rare 'advance semi-circle jungle saw' by Taylor Bros circa 1900, for the Indian market.
(David Stanley) $533

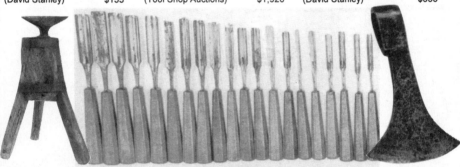

An anvil for banding irons on a three legged nailed and bound elm base, 12in. long, 28in. tall.
(Tool Shop Auctions) $434

A magnificent set of 26 carving gouges by W. Stanley, 1833, with the traditional original beech handles, in virtually unused condition.
(Tony Murland) $1,129

An 18th century French carpenter's axe head with elaborate 'B' touch mark surrounded by stars.
(David Stanley) $207

A rare 7⅞in. d/t steel parallel smoother by Mathieson with rosewood infill, screw construction with early brass lever cap.
(David Stanley) $562

A little used early German cock auger with two Crown shaped adjusting screws and turned grip.
(David Stanley) $296

A rare moving fillister by King & Peach with two brass thumbscrew side adjustments to fence, graduated on heel and toe.
(David Stanley) $207

A fascinating 18th century tool with carved handle, probably a form of barking spud.
(Tool Shop Auctions) $42

A pair of decorative French 23in. steel dividers, typical well formed foliate styled hinge typical of these 18th century tools.
(Tool Shop Auctions) $560

A nicely made burr maple and brass circle cutter, 15in. long, used mainly for cutting holes in pine washstands, circa 1850.
(Charles Tomlinson) $150

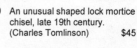

An attractive mahogany straight edge with brass plumb bob, circa 1850.
(Charles Tomlinson) $90

A handled boxwood stair rail shave with adjustable fence, circa 1870.
(Charles Tomlinson) $90

An unusual shaped lock mortice chisel, late 19th century.
(Charles Tomlinson) $45

A small barking iron or 'wrong iron' used to remove bark from smaller branches or 'wrongs'. Barking irons were used for removing bark, which was sold for tanning leather.
(Tool Shop Auctions) $56

A brass fronted beech bullnose plane with Cupid's bow decoration, approximately 4in. long, circa 1860.
(Charles Tomlinson) $60

An extremely sought after, complete, example of Branan's combined dipping and calculating rule, unsigned, fitted together end to end the two sections form a typical 4ft. diagonal gauging rod.
(Tool Shop Auctions) $5,600

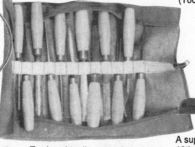

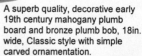

A good pair of 16½in., 18th century wrought iron English wheelwright's calipers.
(Tool Shop Auctions) $56

Twelve virtually unused carving gouges by Henry Taylor in a canvas roll.
(Tool Shop Auctions) $200

A superb quality, decorative early 19th century mahogany plumb board and bronze plumb bob, 18in. wide, Classic style with simple carved ornamentation.
(Tool Shop Auctions) $658

A very 19th century fine herb chopper with rosewood and ivory handle.
(Tool Shop Auctions) $168

A mahogany triptych cabinet containing 75 hand tools by Holtzapffel in beech, ebony and other hardwood handles, 31in. high.
(Christie's) $2,760

A stone carving ax head from Bordeaux, 15in. edge.
(Tool Shop Auctions) $119

TOOLS

A steel and rosewood Irish Pattern chariout plane with heart decoration, 8in. long, circa 1880.
(Charles Tomlinson) $90

A brass and boxwood twofold 18th century rule with handcut numbering, 18in.
(Tool Shop Auctions) $176

A rare timber stamping hammer, No.3 HT Co.
(Tool Shop Auctions) $72

An ornate brass inlaid ebony spirit level by Buist of Edinburgh 9in. long, late 19th century.
(Charles Tomlinson) $105

A 17th century hammer head with nicely flared claws and decoration.
(Tool Shop Auctions) $152

An early hand forged English long mortising ax, 12½in. head and 3¾in. edge.
(Tool Shop Auctions) $70

A large pair of 23in. iron dividers, early 18th century, pitted.
(Tony Murland) $116

An ebony stocked Tri Square with unusually decorative brasswork by Marples, Sheffield, circa 1890.
(Charles Tomlinson) $120

An early quadrant balance, Sylvester Patentee, by Geo. Salter and Co., to weigh 110lbs.
(Tool Shop Auctions) $63

A rare French cooper's bung hole rasp.(Tool Shop Auctions) $67

Circa 1920s toolkit and airpump.
(Christie's) $207

A beautifully carved boxwood spice grinder, provenance unknown, 19th century.
(Tool Shop Auctions) $70

A steel soled gunmetal Norris 50 G smoothing plane with walnut infill, early 20th century.
(Charles Tomlinson) $600

A steel Lancashire pattern shoulder plane with brass lever and mahogany handle, 9in. long, late 19th century.
(Charles Tomlinson) $120

A 10in. diameter copper oil filler.
(Tool Shop Auctions) $192

The General, extremely rare general riding hobbyhorse, parasol and moving sword arm on three wheels, in original box, 5½in. high.
(Christie's) $7,254

A Schuco Elektro-Construction battery powered tinplate fire engine, with adjustable ladder and handbrake on right rear wheel, post 1956.
(Auction Team Köln) $1,473

An early German polar bear, with white wool plush, black boot button eyes, cream felt pads and tail operating head movement, 15in. long, circa 1910, possibly Strunz.
(Christie's) $359

A Mighty Mike weightlifter tinplate and plastic toy by K & Co., Japan, the bear lifts the weights up and down, battery powered, circa 1958.
(Auction Team Köln) $132

Set 26 Boer Infantry, at the slope, fixed bayonets, 1902.
(Christie's) $553

An original Knickerbocker Mickey Mouse by the Knickerbocker Toy Co., New York, fabric, with plaster feet for stability, 38cm. high, circa 1932.
(Auction Team Köln) $870

An American doll's pram, metal frame with turned wood handle, basketwork body with wooden base, adjustable backrest and hood, 94cm. long, circa 1930.
(Auction Team Köln) $131

The mechanical foot race, extremely rare clockwork toy comprising two men with cast-metal heads, hands and lower legs, dressed in silk costumes, running around a painted and paper covered tented viewing area with flag. (Christie's) $12,954

A German pull-along toy, the composition-headed trainer with cloth clothing, the stick and the plush bear's head nodding when pulled along, circa 1900, 31cm.
(Bristol) $951

A Picard-style clockwork tinplate Hispano Suiza'Alfonso XIII' toy car, hand painted in turquoise with gold lines, rubber tires, 1912, 40.5cm.
(Auction Team Köln) $14,528

A Tipp & Co. No. 59 lithographed tinplate clockwork motorcycle, circa 1950, 18cm. long.
(Auction Team Köln) $198

A German Induphon 138 tin toy gramophone with integral horn, wind-up mechanism, with Argentinian retailer's stamp.
(Auction Team Köln) $310

A bear on a scooter, red painted tinplate clockwork toy, the bear with gold mohair with glass eyes and stitched nose, Gebr. FEWO, Made In US Zone, Germany, 16cm. high, circa 1950.
(Auction Team Köln) $214

A very unusual 1960s Matchbox Yesteryear wall mounted plastic display case as a gilt picture frame, approximately 18 x 15in., 4 white plastic shelves containing 16 Yesteryear vehicles.
(Wallis & Wallis) $141

A rare Schuco Fox and Goose clockwork tinplate toy, with lithographed case, the fox with plush head and glass eyes, post 1956.
(Auction Team Köln) $468

A Wells-Brimtoy Mickey Mouse handcar, English, 1930s, tinplate clockwork with painted celluloid Mickey and Minnie figures, in original box.
(Sotheby's) $1,171

Carved oak and wrought iron sled, probably Pennsylvania, 19th century, with carved horse head, traces of polychrome decoration, 37in. long. (Skinner) $3,105

Child's puzzle board, possibly New York, circa 1890-1900, old black paint, 18½ x 12in.
(Skinner) $1,495

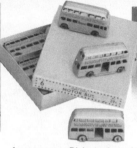

'Knorr', a Steiff pig on wheels, with pale cream mohair, black boot button eyes and button in ear, standing on metal spoked wheels joined by metal frame, 20in. long, circa 1910.
(Christie's) $1,097

A rare pre war Dinky trade pack of 6 29a Motor buses, in yellow and silver, 'Marmite' adverts to sides, small solid metal wheels, boxed, with dividers.
(Wallis & Wallis) $2,862

A Lines Brothers Vauxhall sports coupé, English, circa 1930, with flutted bonnet and windshield, finished in maroon with tax disk, driving licence, tool box with tools, Shell oil and petrol cans, 56½in. long. (Sotheby's) $1,411

A scarce tinplate Mickey Mouse Drummer, Nifty Toys, German, 1930, the flat tinplate figure of Mickey with closed smiling mouth, pie eyes wearing red shorts and orange shoes, arms jointed at the elbows, 7in. high.
(Bonhams) $2,070

Mickey and Minnie by Deans Rag Book Soft Toys, English, 1930s, the velvet figures having white faces with printed features, Mickey wearing blue shorts, Minnie a pink skirt, both 7½in. tall.
(Bonhams) $331

Corgi gift set 22 James Bond, 1980-82, the set containing a Space Shuttle, Lotus Esprit, Aston Martin rockets and bandits, together with a Spears James Bond 007 game.
(Bonhams & Brooks) $1,112

GI Joe with painted blue eyes and painted black hair dressed as a Combat Soldier with M1 rifle, belt, helmet, back pack, boots, canteen and cover. (Christie's) $471

Three cold painted lead models of seated cats, with nodding heads, wearing bonnets and dresses taking tea at an oval table, 3in. high. (Woolley & Wallis) $290

A Hermann Panda, with black and white mohair, deep amber and black glass eyes, clipped plush cut muzzle, black stitched nose, cream felt open mouth, 9in. tall, 1950s.
(Christie's) $237

A large Doll & Cie tinplate clockwork convertible motor car, German, 1920s, hand painted in maroon with cream lining, tin radiator surround with replaced cap to top, hinged doors with metal handles, 20in. long.
(Bonhams) **$2,346**

A rare pre war Dinky Trade pack of 6 caravans, 5 color variations, 2 cream/red, yellow/cream, beige/dark brown, beige/blue and light green and dark green.
(Wallis & Wallis) **$1,431**

A pre war Dinky No 62t Armstrong Whitworth Whitley bomber with shadow shading, in dark brown and green camouflage, with black underside, boxed, with paperwork.
(Wallis & Wallis) **$278**

A Scalextric 007 James Bond Set, including white Aston Martin DB4 with ejecting man and detachable roof section, black Mercedes-Benz 190SL with driver and armed passenger, Gunman, Revolving Rock, 1967-1968.
(Bonhams & Brooks) **$2,167**

A Japanese clockwork Popeye, painted celluloid with head raising mechanism, loose swinging arms, smoking pipe, in original illustrated box, 8¼in. high, early 1930s.
(Christie's) **$903**

A Victorian glass bead work house, English, circa 1890, the red, yellow, green and white exotic beaded house with pillared front door, bay windows, and domed roof, 16in. wide.
(Bonhams & Brooks) **$1,195**

A Lehmann EPL686 'Berolina' tinplate convertible, German, circa 1920, the clockwork car finished in dark blue and red, with spoked wheels, running boards, folding seats to rear compartment, 6¾in. long. (Bonhams) **$897**

A Steiff Kangaroo, with cream and beige mohair with airbrushed features, brown and black glass eyes, gray felt inner ears, 19in. tall, 1950s, and a Joey, velvet covered with brown, 3½in. tall, 1950s.
(Christie's) **$273**

A Lehmann EPL679 'ITO' Sedan, German, 1920s, the clockwork Sedan finished in red and black with cream lining, red and cream wheels, running boards and blue uniformed driver, 7in. long.
(Bonhams) **$828**

 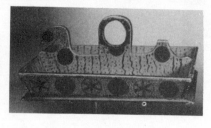 

An Edwardian mahogany and inlaid wood tray, early 20th century, of oval form with wavy raised outer edge, inset with boxwood and fruitwoods with musical instruments in the center, 26¼in. wide. (Christie's) $312

Carved and painted pine cutlery tray, American, mid-19th century, shaped divider with cut-out handle and whimsically painted molded base, 12¾ x 11¼in. (Skinner) $8,625

A George III mahogany and inlaid oval tray, circa 1790, the tray centred by an inlaid fan paterae, with tulipwood banding and enclosed by a waved gallery rim, 26in. wide. (Bonhams) $1,737

An Omega Workshops marquetry two-handled tray, Omega Workshops, circa 1913-1914, the tray inlaid with holly, ebony and fruitwood with a stylized mahout riding an elephant, 29in. wide including handles. (Christie's) $5,216

French Empire tôle tray, first half 19th century, oval, with handled gallery, gilt decorated at perimeter with scrolling flat leaves, cornucopia, and eagles, 26in. long. (Skinner) $920

A George III mahogany tray on a later stand, the oval tray with waved gallery inlaid with boxwood lines, the later stand with plain frieze, 28½in. wide. (Christie's) $2,377

An early 19th century papier mâché tray on stand, 80cm. wide. (Bonhams) $786

A Victorian mahogany butler's tray, the stand later, the rectangular top with arched hinged sides pierced with carrying handles, on four chamfered and reeded legs, 31in. wide. (Christie's) $1,999

Boris Lacroix, two-handled tray, circa 1930, varnished vellum surface on oak within nickel plated metal band, 50cm. wide over handles. (Sotheby's) $4,865

An Edwardian satinwood tea tray of hexagonal form with string inlay, waved edge with brass loop handles, the centre painted with fruit within a leaf surround, 20½in. wide. (Andrew Hartley) **$832**

A 19th century mahogany and marquetry tray on a later table base, 80cm. wide. (Bonhams) **$810**

An Italian gilt-varnished silvered ('Mecca') and Lacca Povera tray, mid 18th century, Venice, central field with scrolling foliage and trelliswork panels, centered by a stylized sunflower motif, 31 x 19in. (Christie's) **$6,674**

A black lacquer and decorated papier mâché tray, 19th century, with later base, the serpentine shaped dished tray with central floral bouquet and heightening to the borders, 32½in. wide. (Christie's) **$410**

A Victorian papier mâché tray, third quarter 19th century, of serpentine outline, the black ground painted with a foliate spray to the center, the raised rim gilt heightened with bell-flowers and further foliage, 31½in. wide. (Christie's) **$575**

A black lacquered and chinoiserie decorated oval shaped table, 20th century, the top with raised sides decorated with butterflies and foliage with an inset landscape scene, on ring-turned simulated bamboo legs, 33¾in. wide. (Christie's) **$790**

A 19th century mahogany butler's tray and stand, the rectangular tray with a three quarter gallery and pierced handles, 75 x 59cm. (Tennants) **$1,962**

A Victorian papier mâché tray, third quarter 19th century, with inset mother of pearl and gilt heightened foliate decoration to the center, 29¼in. wide. (Christie's) **$904**

A George III mahogany butler's tray, the oval tray with hinged sides fitted with brass carrying handles, 40in. wide. (Christie's) **$2,062**

A Spirit mask, Coastal Region, Lower Sepik, Papua New Guinea, of pointed oval form, the middle part carved with slanted eyes within a heart-shaped face, tapering to a pointed nose with flared nostrils, 50cm. high. (Bonhams) $706

A Eastern Pende Giphogo mask, D.R. Congo, the domed cap with forehead ridge and topknot, protruding nose and ears, stepped flaring beard, large slit-pierced eyes, 33cm. high. (Bonhams) $882

A Senufo kpelie mask, Ivory Coast, the slender heart-shaped face pierced with slits, surmounted by a pair of arched horns, 28cm. (Bonhams) $1,088

A Nayarit seated female figure, Ixtlan de Rio style, West Mexico, Protoclassic, circa 100BC-AD250, wearing nose ring, multiple ear ornaments, headband and a zigzag patterned skirt, 36cm. (Bonhams) $1,305

A Punu mask, Gabon, the pointed oval face painted with creamy white pigment, the temples and forehead with square and lozenge cicatrised scars, 31.5cm. (Bonhams) $3,770

A Nayarit seated female figure, San Sebastian style, West Mexico, Protoclassic circa 100BC-AD250, with legs to one side, holding a cup on her right knee, 32cm. (Bonhams) $1,450

A Punu mask, Gabon, the oval face carved in shallow relief with arched brows and horizontal line across both cheeks and nose, 26cm. (Bonhams) $1,160

A Dan mask, Liberia, wit pierced almond eyes rimmed with aluminum, nose with flared nostrils, 23cm. tall. (Bonhams) $1,176

An Athabascan Octopus bag, North America, each side panel embroidered with trees or shrubs, issuing exotic flowers in multicolored glass seed beads, 54cm. (Bonhams) $2,320

A Yoruba kneeling figure, Nigeria, showing filed teeth, pointed breasts, with the hands held to the pronounced pubic region, 26cm.
(Bonhams) $588

A Malangan mask, tatanua, New Ireland, the face carved with pierced demi-lune eyes set with operculum pupils, 41cm.
(Bonhams) $2,175

Maternity figure and children, West Africa, hardwood with cloth decoration, 19½in.
(G.A. Key) $64

A Salampasu mask, D.R. Congo, the large, domed forehead bulging above broad slit eyes and a short, wedge nose, the pointed chin with later rope beard and rattan ball, 29cm. (Bonhams) $1,450

A fine Southern African headrest, probably Tsonga, Mozambique, the gently bowed, rectangular platform with diagonal carved bands at each end, and suspending rectangular lugs, 14cm.
(Bonhams) $13,050

A fine Baule heddle pulley, on Inagaki base, Ivory Coast, the U-shaped frame with incised herringbone decoration and forming shoulders rising to a cylindrical neck, 17cm. high.
(Bonhams) $2,669

A Huari/Nazca coca bag, Peru, tapestry-woven on both sides with two distinct panels, in mustard, dark green, red and purple, 31cm.
(Bonhams) $870

A Chontal green schist mask, Mexico, carved with square ears, pierced oval eyes beneath straight brows, 17.5cm.
(Bonhams) $252

A fine Idoma figure, Nigeria, the female seated on a circular stool, arms carved free of the body and resting on bent knees, 80cm. high.
(Bonhams) $10,990

An Imperial Model B British typebar machine with Ideal keyboard and double shift key, 1908.
(Auction Team Köln) $395

A Mignon Model 4 Deluxe bronze and gold colored German pointer typewriter, 1923.
(Auction Team Köln) $1,358

A German Rofa Model 4 machine with straight 3-row keyboard and upright type bars, 1923.
(Auction Team Köln) $331

A Sholes Visible No. 4 (Meiselbach) typewriter, an extreme result of the search for a visible type process, 1901.
(Auction Team Köln) $7,318

A Germania No. 5 German understrike typewriter by H. & A. Scheffer under licence from the Jewett company, circa 1900.
(Auction Team Köln) $731

A rare Commercial Visible No. 6 typebar machine with backward hammer action, with elegant 'wasp waist', 1898.
(Auction Team Köln) $2,487

A German Venus front strike typebar machine by Müller & Zentsch, Saxony, 1923.
(Auction Team Köln) $1,105

A Reliance Visible (Pittsburg 12) American typebar machine, with visible type, lacking ribbons and matrices, 1908.
(Auction Team Köln) $365

An (Armstrong No. 8) Herald typewriter, French model of the American typebar machine, 1903.
(Auction Team Köln) $365

An Edelmann German typewheel pointer machine with enamel dial, 1897.
(Auction Team Köln) $731

A New American Typewriter No. 5 index typewriter with carriage at right angles to the type direction, 1890.
(Auction Team Köln) $888

An early Typo model of the French version of the decorative British Imperial Model B typebar machine, with round Ideal keyboard, 1914.
(Auction Team Köln) $365

An American Jewett No. 3 understrike machine with full keyboard, the forerunner of the German Germania machine, by the Duplex Typewriter Co, 1898.
(Auction Team Köln) $1,547

The Correspondent, an export version of the Rofa Model IV German typebar machine with three row keyboard and upright typebars, 1923.
(Auction Team Köln) $607

The world's first typewriter, a Malling Hansen Writing Ball, with 54 spring-driven hemispherical type balls; one of only 180 produced, 1867. (Auction Team Köln)
$84,000

An Imperial Model B 3-row British typebar machine with round Ideal keyboard and double shift keys, 1914.
(Auction Team Köln) $386

A Hammond Model 1 typewriter with round Ideal keyboard and thick 'piano' keys, with wooden case, restored, circa 1880.
(Auction Team Köln) $1,326

An Edison Mimeograph Typewriter No. 1 by A.B. Dick & Co., Chicago for preparing wax matrices for copying, 1894.
(Auction Team Köln) $12,161

The Chicago cylinder typewriter with unique color ribbon design and backward hammer action, swivel platen for easier legibility, American, 1898.
(Auction Team Köln) $1,045

'The Morris Type-Writer', 1885, extremely rare American index typewriter by The Hoggson & Pettis Mfg. Co., New Haven, Conn./USA. With original wooden box, *only six molds known world-wide!* (Auction Team Köln) $22,340

A Mignon Model 2, the British version of the German pointer typewriter, restored, 1905.
(Auction Team Köln) $442

A Pittsburgh Visible No. 10 American typebar machine which solved the problem of visible type, 1902.
(Auction Team Köln) $391

A Sholes & Glidden typewriter, the first really successful typewriter, with gold decoration and adjustable manuscript holder, 1873.
(AuctionTeamKöln) $33,167

A copper colored Remington Sholes No. 7 typewriter, American understrike machine, 1901.
(Auction Team Köln) $2,090

A Hebrew script Hermes 3000 Swiss four-row portable typewriter by E. Paillard & Cie, Yverdon, in original case, circa 1960.
(Auction Team Köln) $62

A Kanzler No. 4 German typebar machine with 8 characters on each lever, double shift key, 1912.
(Auction Team Köln) $888

A Pittsburgh Visible No. 10 American typebar machine, the keyboard and all typebars can be replaced by means of two levers, 1902.
(Auction Team Köln) $718

A Columbia Index No. 1 type wheel machine by the New York watchmaker Charles Spiro, the first index typewriter with proportional script, 1883.
(Auction Team Köln) $5,749

A portable Blickensderfer No. 5 type wheel machine, in original wooden case, American, 1893.
(Auction Team Köln) $276

A Graphic early Berlin pointer typewriter, with original rubber type platen, works by pressing lever on left hand pillar, circa 1895.
(Auction Team Köln) $3,835

An Odell No.1b, the first mass produced model of the decorative American pointer typewriter, with 'Indian' motif on base, early model by Levi Judson Odellin, 1888.
(Auction Team Köln) $1,547

A round Rofa typewriter with Ideal keyboard, 1921.
(Auction Team Köln) $367

A rare Cardinal German typebar machine from the clock factory of D. Fürtwangler, with revolutionary technical improvements, 1923.
(Auction Team Köln) $828

An American Flyer Model 1 tinplate toy typewriter, with two-row type wheel, 1933.
(Auction Team Köln) $240

A Densmore No. 1, the first model of the classic American understrike machine, 1891.
(Auction Team Köln) $1,105

An Odell No. 4 decorative American pointer typewriter by Farquhar & Albrecht, Chicago, lacking ribbons, 1889.
(Auction Team Köln) $679

A cast copper dove weathervane, American, late 19th/early 20th century, the full-bodied profile form of a spreadwing dove with olive branch grasped in its beak, 24¾in. high. (Christie's) $8,225

A fine molded and gilded copper fish weathervane, American, third quarter 19th century, the full bodied pike with molded sheet metal fins, 27½in. long.
(Sotheby's) $9,200

A molded and gilded copper weathervane, American, late 19th century, the flat, full-bodied figure in profile depicting the angel Gabriel in flight, 29in. wide.
(Christie's) $6,900

Cast and sheet iron rooster weathervane, attributed to Rochester Iron Works, New England, mid 19th century, painted and gold-leafed surface, approximately 71½in.
(Skinner) $31,050

A molded copper Indian weathervane, American, late 19th century, standing in profile holding an arrow in one hand and bow in the other, 37in. high.
(Christie's) $12,650

A paint decorated sheet iron flag weathervane, American, 20th century, in the form of a waving American flag, mounted on a cylindrical support, 18½in. high.
(Christie's) $1,175

A gilded copper weather vane, late 18th century, pierced with a griffin within a shield, losses, 17in. high, and a later stand.
(Christie's) $1,043

Gilt molded copper flying horse weathervane, late 19th century, verdigris and partial gilt surface, 19 x 24½in. (Skinner) $1,840

Painted sheet metal rooster weathervane, circa 1900, yellow over gilt, with stand, 15in. high x 11¾in. wide.
(Skinner) $1,840

Gilt copper and zinc hackney horse weathervane, America, late 19th century, zinc head on full body horse, gilt over yellow paint with traces of verdigris, with stand, 32in. long. (Skinner) **$4,888**

A molded copper elephant weathervane, American, 20th century, the full-bodied elephant with articulated ears, tusks, trunk, legs and tail, 22in. high, 35½in. wide. (Christie's) **$8,225**

Copper full-bodied trotting horse weathervane, America, late 19th century, verdigris surface, with black metal stand, 16½in. high, 26½in. long. (Skinner) **$4,312**

Molded copper pig weather vane, late 19th century, weathered dark verdigris surface with traces of gilt, including stand, 32in. wide. (Skinner) **$32,200**

A molded copper setter weathervane, American, late 19th/early 20th century, the profile dog with rounded eyes, pressed mouth, articulated fur and serrated pointing tail depicted walking on a cylindrical base, 35in . wide. (Christie's) **$6,463**

A copper and zinc molded horse and sulky weathervane, attributed to J.W. Fiske, New York, circa 1880, molded in the round with articulated galloping horse straining at the reins of a two-wheel buggy with seated and costumed jockey, 39½in. long. (Christie's) **$18,800**

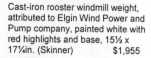

Cast-iron rooster windmill weight, attributed to Elgin Wind Power and Pump company, painted white with red highlights and base, 15½ x 17¼in. (Skinner) $1,955

Flat cast iron bull windmill weight, probably Fairbury Windmill Company, Fairbury, Nebraska, early 20th century, 24½in. wide. (Skinner) $862

Cast iron rooster windmill weight, Elgin Wind Power and Pump Company, Elgin, Illinois, early 20th century, identified with raised numbers on the tail, 16½in. high. (Skinner) $1,495

Cast-iron 'Mogul' rooster windmill weight, attributed to Elgin Wind Power and Pump Company, late 19th century, painted white with red and yellow details, 18¾ x 20in. (Skinner) $3,105

Cast-iron squirrel windmill weight, attributed to Elgin Wind Power and Pump Company, Elgin, Illinois, early 20th century, light brown paint on original base, 17¼ x 13½in. (Skinner) $3,220

Cast-iron rooster windmill weight, attributed to Elgin Wind Power and Pump Company, early 20th century, painted white with red and black highlights, 19 x 18in. (Skinner) $805

Cast-iron full-body bull windmill weight, attributed to Simpson Windmill and Machine Company, Fairbury, Nebraska, early 20th century, traces of red and white paint. (Skinner) $1,092

Cast-iron rooster windmill weight, attributed to Elgin Wind Power and Pump Company, Elgin, Illinois, early 20th century, painted silver and white with red highlights, 18¾ x 15½in. (Skinner) $1,150

Cast-iron flat bull windmill weight, Fairbury Windmill Weight Company, Fairbury, Nebraska, early 20th century, raised letters, painted silver, 19½ x 24½in. (Skinner) $633

Shaker blue painted butter churn, made of pine, the rectangular shaped receptacle with square sides, with turned handle at side, fitted lid with slotted bar seal, 19in. long. (Skinner) $402

A relief-carved and painted pine and lithographed George Washington on horseback, American, 19th century, with lithographed face and relief-carved arm and hand, 20½in. high. (Sotheby's) $6,600

A carved and paint-decorated snowy owl, American, 20th century, carved in the full round with articulated feathers, eyes, beak, wings, and claws, 25in. high. (Christie's) $10,575

A carved pine figure of a boy playing a flute, probably South German or Austrian, late 19th or early 20th century, shown seated on a tree stump, 35in. high. (Christie's) $1,607

A pair of carved giltwood eagles 19th/20th century, perched on a stylised stump and gazing to the side, 32½in. high. (Sotheby's) $4,200

A Japanese gold lacquered wood model of an actor, decorated in hiramakie, iroe-hiramakie, kirigane and nashiji, 2¼in. high, 19th century. (Christie's) $585

A carved wood decanter stand, probably south German or Austrian, late 19th century, modelled as a cart with twin platforms, the center with three bacchic cherubs, the wheels as entwined snakes, 18½in. long. (Christie's) $2,369

Large wooden banded firkin, 19th century, dark mustard buttermilk paint, 15½in. diameter. (Sotheby's) $1,725

A pair of stained wood waste paper bins, of recent manufacture, the sides as book spines decorated in gilt with titles, 14in. high. (Christie's) $3,271

A French brass mounted mahogany roulette wheel, circa 1920, the circular dished bowl on a tapering base, 32in. wide.
(Christie's) $3,619

A yew or fruitwood master salt, late 18th century, the bowl with everted lip, on a circular stepped foot, 5½in. diameter. (Christie's) $801

18th century mahogany cheese coaster, molded at either end with roundels, 15in.
(G.A. Key) $377

A carved and painted ship's figurehead, American, 19th century, fully carved in the round in the form of a young woman with black ringleted hair, partially unclad in a blue dress, 35½in. high.
(Christie's) $7,638

Group of eight carved and painted wooden puppets and related materials, Ortana, Pennsylvania, early 20th century, a black man, a skull, the devil, a burglar, three male characters, the mouth of an alligator.
(Skinner) $7,475

A carved and giltwood eagle, American, late 19th century, the full-bodied form facing right with spreadwings and articulated feathers, beak and talons, 34½in. high. (Christie's) $16,100

Carved and polychrome painted figure, 19th century, possibly a Quaker lady with a turquoise jewel at her neck, wearing a full-length red dress and white apron, 20¼in. high with stand.
(Skinner) $17,250

A burr-maple covered pot, probably 17th century, later embellished in sheet brass, 5in. diameter, 5¼in. high. (Christie's) $2,495

Carved and painted wood and gesso urn with flame architectural ornament, 19th century, flattened back on urn painted in shades of tan, putty, and white, 29½in. high.
(Skinner) $2,185

A brass decorated gourd nut, 19th century, modelled as an inkwell, with foliate ornament overall and circular banding to the cover and base, 2½in. high. (Christie's) $456

A Regency mahogany cheese sledge, fitted with an adjustable divider, with scrolled ends and set on brass and leather castors, 42cm. wide. (Bonhams) $1,355

A burr-yew bottle-coaster, mid 18th century, of typical form, with simple molded upright rim, 6½in. diameter. (Christie's) $1,070

A rare English sycamore wassail bowl, circa 1600, decorated overall with incised pyrographic roundels and intersected segments, the tapering bowl supported on a baluster knopped stem and circular spreading foot, height overall 16in. (Christie's) $33,120

A carved wood eagle, stamped on base, *S. Jansen Miller, Dryden, New York, No. 8, A.D. 1933.*, the spread-wing form on a rocky plinth and facing left, 25in. high. (Christie's) $3,760

A carved mahogany eagle, American, 20th century, with articulated eyes, beak and feathers above spread wings over a swelled breast, the taloned feet perched on a scrolled base, 31in. high. (Christie's) $3,760

A carved and painted figure of a boxer, America, late 19th century, carved in the round, the standing male figure with articulated hair, facial features and costume, 83in. high. (Christie's) $28,200

A lignum vitae wassail bowl, second half 17th century, the bowl with two reeded bands, on a waisted socle and spreading circular foot, 9in. high, 9in. diameter. (Christie's) $5,520

A Black Forest carved and stained wood model of an owl, early 20th century, possibly an inkstand, with hinged head and interior recess, 12¼in. high. (Christie's) $2,180

A Victorian carved and stained wood eagle lectern, late 19th century, the bird carved and shown standing on an orb, with wings displayed supporting the hinged platform above, 28½in. high.
(Christie's) $1,448

Polychrome carved pine doll's head, America, early 19th century, original paint with blue eyes and brown hair, with stand, 8¼in. high.
(Skinner) $34,500

Polychrome carved wood head of a man, America, 19th century, early white, black, and red painted surface, no stand, 6in. high.
(Skinner) $1,840

Carved pine head of a lady, New England, 19th century, with prominent features and flower hair ornament, wearing a zinc-brimmed hat tied with bow, 18in. high.
(Skinner) $4,600

Polychrome carved pine fan-tail rooster, Pennsylvania, circa 1800-20, yellow, brown, and red paint, no stand, 9¼in. high.
(Skinner) $5,175

Carved burl head of a man, attributed to Moses Ogden, (1844-1919), Angelica, New York, with applied eyes and moustache over open mouth and torso with arched hollowed opening, 21in. high.
(Skinner) $690

Polychrome carved pine and tin policeman whirligig, American, late 19th century, the figure with moustache and beard, his arms constructed with tin at the elbows, 18⅛in. high.
(Skinner) $11,500

Painted round ring-toss board, early 20th century, black numerals on white disks, sage green ground, iron hooks, 17in. diameter.
(Skinner) $1,495

Birch tree-branch leg, early 20th century, the natural shape of a leg joined by a branch retaining bark terminating in a sculpted foot with a pointed shoe on tall heel, with stand, 23in. high.
(Skinner) $23,000

Polychrome carved speckled rooster, Pennsylvania, circa 1840, red, mustard yellow, and brown paint, 9½in. long.
(Skinner) $4,312

Carved branch sculpture of a leaping lady's legs, John Wacher, Iowa, mid 20th century, the lower torso with plaid wrap, with stand, 23in. wide.
(Skinner) $24,150

Burl and twig sculpture of a man with extended arms, Moses Ogden (1844-1919), Angelica, New York, with carved facial features, hand, and playful hair, 13¾in. high.
(Skinner) $690

Pair of carved pine figures of a man and woman, America, 19th century, old natural surface, with stands, height of man 19¼in., height of woman 14½in.
(Skinner) $12,650

Carved polychrome sun face, America, early 19th century, with molded edge, with stand, 14in. diameter.(Skinner) $16,100

Polychrome carved portrait bust of a young man, America, circa 1910, with black, brown, white, and red paint, with stand, 11¼in. high, 9in. wide, 3½in. deep.
(Skinner) $17,250

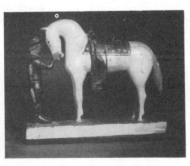

Carved maple head of a man, probably America, early 20th century, signed *EIW*, with weathered surface, 16in. high.
(Skinner) $2,070

Polychrome carved figure of a horse and groom, America, early 20th century, with leather Western saddle, with stand, 13in. long.
(Skinner) $5,175

A Victorian dog's head tobacco box, late 19th century, the hinged head with inset glass eyes and with later leather studded collar, 8¾in. high.
(Christie's) $8,324

Painted wooden parcheesi game board, circa 1880, broadboard ends on square game board painted in shades of red, black, mustard, and cream, 18 x 18in.
(Skinner) $862

Great horned owl with dead crow, The Herters Decoy Factory, Waseca, Minnesota, second quarter 20th century, crow of balsa, owl also of balsa with wooden horns, bear claw bill, and wooden legs and perch.
(Sotheby's) $2,300

An oak plate bucket, iron bound with a division, iron plate carrying handles, 18in.
(Woolley & Wallis) $109

A carved polychrome group of the Pieta, North Italian, early 16th century, her left hand replaced and his right hand broken, 32¼in. high.
(Bonhams) $3,588

A pair of Burmese giltwood and lacquer figures of angels, both with loosely curled hair, wings issuing from the back and fins from the backs of the legs, 13in. high, 18/19th century.
(Christie's) $588

A pair of large lacquered vases, mid 20th century, the red ground with gilt heightening overall, with reserves of Oriental landscapes, on conforming stands, 52in. high overall. (Christie's) $3,046

Ethnic stool of Ashaaiti Tribe, bowed formed seat, pierced heavy supports to rectangular base.
(G.A. Key) $157

An early 19th century cylindrical tea caddy, mahogany veneered with satinwood banded and inlaid stringing, 4¼in. high.
(Woolley & Wallis) $82

A William III elm Royal coat-of-arms, the central cartouche carved with the Duke of Nassau's escutcheon, and with surrounding mottos, 57in. wide.
(Christie's) $8,636

INDEX

INDEX

INDEX